Promoting Community Change

Making It Happen in the Real World

FIFTH EDITION

MARK S. HOMAN

BROOKS/COLE
CENGAGE Learning

Australia • Brazil • Japan • Korea • Mexico • Singapore • Spain • United Kingdom • United States

BROOKS/COLE
CENGAGE Learning

Promoting Community Change: Making It Happen in the Real World, **Fifth Edition**
Mark S. Homan

Publisher: Linda Schreiber-Ganster

Acquisitions Editor: Seth Dobrin

Developmental Editor: Liana Monari

Assistant Editor: Arwen Petty

Editorial Assistant: Rachel McDonald

Media Editor: Dennis Fitzgerald

Marketing Manager: Trent Whatcott

Marketing Assistant: Darlene Macanan

Marketing Communications Manager:
  Tami Strang

Content Project Manager: Michelle Cole

Creative Director: Rob Hugel

Art Director: Caryl Gorska

Print Buyer: Karen Hunt

Rights Acquisitions Account Manager, Text:
  Roberta Broyer

Rights Acquisitions Account Manager, Image:
  Leitha Etheridge-Sims

Production Service: Integra

Text Designer: Lisa Henry

Photo Researcher: Bill Smith Group

Copy Editor: Kay Mikel

Cover Image: Jerry Silverberg / Getty Images

Compositor: Integra

For product information and technology assistance, contact us at **Cengage Learning Customer & Sales Support, 1-800-354-9706.**

For permission to use material from this text or product, submit all requests online at **www.cengage.com/permissions**.

Further permissions questions can be e-mailed to **permissionrequest@cengage.com**.

Library of Congress Control Number: 2009943179

ISBN-13: 978-0-8400-3195-2
ISBN-10: 0-8400-3195-5

Brooks/Cole
20 Davis Drive
Belmont, CA 94002-3098
USA

Cengage Learning is a leading provider of customized learning solutions with office locations around the globe, including Singapore, the United Kingdom, Australia, Mexico, Brazil, and Japan. Locate your local office at **www.cengage.com/international**.

Cengage Learning products are represented in Canada by Nelson Education, Ltd.

To learn more about Brooks/Cole, visit **www.cengage.com/brookscole**
Purchase any of our products at your local college store or at our preferred online store **www.CengageBrain.com**.

Printed in the United States of America
1 2 3 4 5 6 7 14 13 12 11 10

Contents

About the Author

Tom Veneklasen

Mark S. Homan recently retired from the Social Services Department at Pima Community College, where he served as Department Chair and taught for more than 30 years. In addition to these duties, Mark has served as adjunct faculty and guest lecturer for numerous other colleges, universities, and training consortia in the United States, Russia, and Sweden. He received his MSW from Arizona State University in 1975 and is a Licensed Clinical Social Worker.

Mark is a strong advocate of community empowerment. He uses his own very active involvement in the community to contribute to its improvement and to increase his own learning. For more than 35 years he has worked with diverse populations in urban, rural, and reservation communities on a broad range of issues, including neighborhood stabilization and empowerment, hunger, reproductive rights, children with special health care needs, community mental health, family planning, community health work, capital punishment, public schools and community development, political campaign organizing, foster care, and adoption. In addition to his roles as organizer, lobbyist, consultant, and teacher, Mark has developed and directed several human services programs. He also is a founding member of many community organizations and agencies and has served on numerous community boards and councils.

Mark is the author of *Rules of the Game: Lessons from the Field of Community Change*, which is used both as a textbook and as a practical guide for community change agents. It is based on his many years of experience in community organization and development work. He has conducted many workshops and delivered numerous keynote speeches and presentations dealing with various aspects of community building and community power. He is frequently asked by public and private organizations to assist them in increasing their effectiveness. Mark has been the recipient of numerous awards for teaching excellence and for work with communities.

At this stage in his career, Mark has come to accept the fact that he will not be playing shortstop for the San Francisco Giants, but he is getting reacquainted with his guitar.

✳

Preface

A pleasing voice singing softly to the background music playing through the store's sound system comfortably encouraged customers like me to stay a while and spend some money. I looked around to see what angel was so beautifully supplying the lyrics to the sanitized melody drifting down from overhead. She was somewhere between 45 and 65. Cut too often by the hard edges of life, her hair was disheveled, and the deep lines etched in her face spoke of too much sun and probably too many other trials. Her layered clothes draped loosely, with frayed sleeves and missing buttons.

In mid-verse she stopped singing and started arguing with someone only she could see. The argument lapsed, and with an awkward gait she pushed her shopping cart up to the pharmacy counter. Now you can usually ring up a few items from the store along with the purchase of your prescriptions, but an almost full cart? No, you were to go to the cashiers at the front of the store with a cart. I watched to see how the young clerk at the counter would treat her customer with the shuffle, tattered clothes, and cart full of merchandise. She did so with respect, not pity, not good-humored tolerance, but respect. Her own sort of song perhaps.

I came to think of this woman as Betty, as she reminded me of a friend from years ago. Another customer, a young woman, approached the counter. She looked at Betty and asked, "How are you getting home?" "I ride the bus," came the reply. "That looks like a lot to carry to the bus stop. Can I give you a ride home?" Complete strangers, at least until now. Another pleasant surprise. "Sure, Honey." "Okay, let me go tell my friend." "Thanks, I want to go get some beer if you are going to give me a ride." Okay, I thought, end of pleasant surprise. But no. "Don't take too long, okay?," her chauffeur asked, and walked away to tell her friend about their passenger.

The line at the pharmacy counter was growing. What was taking so long? Now the pharmacist had joined the clerk at the counter, both trying to talk with another customer, who was growing more agitated. The talking wasn't going so well. The customer spoke only Spanish, and the pharmacist and the clerk could speak only English, slowly and, it seemed, a bit loudly. I thought I might try to help, but before I made it to the trio, Betty leaned in and started talking, in Spanish. I could tell that Spanish wasn't her first language, but she was doing a pretty good job helping the conversation along. She listened to the pharmacist and explained things to the lady. She listened to the lady and explained things to the pharmacist. Lots of talking and heads nodding.

Returning to my seat, a woman in line stopped me. Her tailored clothes had only seen this season and every hair on her head was in its designated place. "Why doesn't that old woman leave the pharmacist alone? We're standing in line, and she is just butting in causing problems." "Well," I said, "actually she is solving problems. The other lady had a problem with her prescription and she is translating so that the pharmacist and the lady can understand each other." She looked back at me, paused a moment, then smiled and said, "Well, God bless her." The pharmacist smiled. The counter clerk smiled. The lady smiled. Then she gave Betty a hug. Betty's ride came up, and she and Betty started walking to the door at the front of the store. I don't know if Betty ever got her beer.

The overriding theme of this book is that there is strength in each of us individually and power together. Each of us has something to contribute, but we may not recognize the opportunity or feel confident. As an agent of change, you will see opportunities to make a difference. As an organizer, you will be connecting people to the issue, to each other, and to the organization that you will build together. The "organization" may be small and temporary, just a few people coming together to get something done that they couldn't do alone. It may start small, working to make one thing better, and grow into an organization with a name and a structure that involves the talents and passion of many people to make a lot of things better.

Betty's story is much like our own, filled with the unplanned intersection of the lives of complete strangers and new friends. Each of us has some talent, yet we become stronger by accepting the talents of others as well. Strengthened by our resolve and faith in one another, we can create tremendous change.

Workers in health and human services are in a unique position to help write more of these stories. Each day we see people who want things to be different. Some are enthusiastic and confident. Some have been humiliated, frightened, scorned, and disregarded. We see in these same people the flicker of faith and the glow of hope. We see their abilities and uncommon gifts. We see that most have some connections with others and the potential to make more connections. We also see the dedication, skill, and determination of our colleagues. We know that the only reason we are with these people is to work with them to make a change in their circumstances. We might ask ourselves: What kind of change do we think is possible? Or even, what kind of change do we even think about?

Although most students are still trained to deal with individual cases and most professionals replay that training in their work, more and more students and professionals are committed to helping people lead more full and satisfying lives by recognizing that people share many things in common. These students and practitioners are helping to expand our vision of what needs to be done. They have realized that we can never truly help free all those individuals and families from their hardships until we change the harmful conditions they face.

Further, we are extending what we know from our work with individuals and families to improving community conditions. We certainly know that people are affected by their environment. We know also that most good work with individuals and families places ultimate authority for decisions and actions in the hands of those individuals and families. We know that most good work builds on the strengths that individuals and families bring to the situation. We can't just change the game when our work is intended to benefit a larger number of people who have something in common. We can't just look at their problems. We can't take power and authority away from the people we are trying to help, keeping it for ourselves or those who give us funding. We can no longer keep people disconnected from each other and from the larger issues that affect their lives. We can't design programs *for* people giving them little say in how programs should be designed and run. It may be routine, but it would not be good work. Students, practitioners, and professors are questioning and changing this routine.

We can create new routines, ones that commonly bring people together to improve their shared circumstance. New routines that develop the leadership and power of the people affected by a condition, regularly drawing on their perspectives, information, and abilities as the ordinary way we do our work. New routines that bring us as practitioners together to collaborate and learn from each other to further build our knowledge and skills for community level intervention.

This new edition of *Promoting Community Change* will give you a solid foundation to do this work. You will find here basic principles to guide your efforts. You will find tips and some tricks to make things easier. You will see that this enterprise is not only meaningful, but exciting, and not always just work, but a joy.

I recognize that many of you do not see yourselves as community activists, nor do you see yourself working for community change as your primary professional role. I have taken that into active consideration in writing this edition. Throughout their careers all social workers, human services workers, public health workers, and other dedicated helping people realize well-being will be confronted by the challenge to promote change. Even if it is not your primary professional role, I want you to know that it is an important role, recognize the part you can play, and believe that you can work for change. For those of you who envision a larger role for yourself in promoting community development and building community organizations, you will find information here to deepen your commitment, increase your confidence, and strengthen your effectiveness.

Promoting community change is not something you should only study and discuss in theory. It is something you should learn how to do, which is what this book emphasizes. Part 1 looks at the need for community change, considers how community change activities relate to the change agent's professional and personal life, and provides a theoretical framework to deepen your understanding and give you direction.

Part 2 gives clear, practical guidance on how to go about the business of promoting change. Each of these chapters concentrates on a specific issue with which a successful change agent needs to be familiar.

Part 3 offers more detailed insights into three common arenas of change. These chapters help you understand typical settings where change can occur. Building on principles and techniques described in earlier chapters, you are introduced to particular knowledge and skills that apply to these circumstances.

Key Changes for the Fifth Edition

The moment you believe you are powerless you will indeed be powerless. Sometimes we fail to recognize that we are giving away our power. Sometimes the potential for increasing our influence by partnering with the power of others remains hidden. It helps to stop and think about these things. In this edition there is a stronger emphasis on inquiry and reflection. You will find an examination of *appreciative inquiry*, an orientation that acknowledges and builds on the understanding that in any situation some things have worked well and are working well. The spirit of this perspective flows throughout the book. I have introduced the concept of *reflective practice* to invite you to mine your experiences for new insights and confidence.

I have learned quite a bit from reading what others have written about the practice of community change, but I have learned much with and from people in the community as well. Residents of neighborhoods, students in the classroom, professionals working in agencies, and mentors all have informed my views. I also have learned by reflecting on my experiences, drawing many new discoveries from them. I have applied this new learning to this fifth edition.

The more I take part in efforts to make community change, the more profoundly I realize the wealth of human talent and other assets all around me. This new edition places an even greater emphasis on the recognition of strengths and links a *strengths-based approach* to issues of social justice and community development. I have more clearly presented the complementary, but sometimes different approaches to action for social justice and efforts to develop community capital and capacity.

The *community development model* can be a little difficult to get your hands around. So I have extended the consideration of community development, adding a review of essential criteria, more illustration of the concept of community capital, and an exploration of the notion of capacity building, along with the link between of levels of capacity and levels of development.

Fundamental principles give you a foundation on which you will continue to build your knowledge and understanding. To strengthen this foundation I am advancing the idea of the *four cornerstones of community practice*, showing how they relate to and reinforce each other.

More and more people are using new methods of communication, and if we want to communicate with them, we had better learn these methods. Information technology has introduced a box full of tools that an organizer can use to raise money, map community characteristics, communicate with and mobilize supporters, and inform the general public. An era of what might be called *cyber-organizing* is upon us. This edition offers a number of new approaches to help you expand your repertoire of organizing tools.

The nature of your workplace will greatly affect what you will do as a professional and how you will do it. As professionals if we are not intentionally engaged in improving the system in which we work, we support the maintenance of the problems we face in trying to do our jobs. This edition brings more attention to the responsibility you will have in *helping your workplace become healthier and more productive* while giving you some means for acting on that responsibility.

Bank failures, housing foreclosure, rising unemployment and a host of other woes have become numbingly common stories in the daily news. Though some see a faint light of recovery on the horizon, the anguish caused by economic stress continues to be felt by more families and communities in every region of the country and indeed throughout the world. Health and humans services workers scramble to meet growing demand while they watch financial support to meet that demand dwindle or get rerouted. This edition takes notice of this situation, highlighting consequences and challenges in a troubled economy, inviting you to reconsider the very approaches we use in the work that we do along with giving you some ideas for *fund-raising in difficult times*.

Although much of what we do as change agents is to spark new change, we also influence the nature of change that is occurring around us, sometimes accelerating its pace or altering its direction. The fact is that change is always taking place. This edition includes a snapshot of current conditions that have a bearing on community work. *Updated data, information on new regulations, introduction of innovative methods*, and other features keep information relevant to the real world where you will be promoting community change.

You will find a *group activity* at the end of each chapter that will provide you and your colleagues with an opportunity to test out some ideas and expand your learning by putting some of your ideas into play.

As you make your way through the chapters, picture yourself in your own neighborhood, your college, or possibly the agency where you work. Maybe you will be waiting for a prescription to be filled and see a story unfold around you. Maybe you will find that you are scripting your own story, creating a change in a community that will be better off because you are playing a part.

Tried and True Features

I have had the benefit of working in both an academic environment and many different community contexts. The voice I bring to each chapter's discussion is informed by these experiences and by the writings of other change agents and scholars. The examination of issues should not be too distant from the place where learning needs to be applied. I want you to easily make that connection.

I recognize that many of you are juggling your understanding of concepts of community change with ideas and information from other courses that jostle for your attention. I also recognize that fairly soon you will become practitioners who want to succeed in the work you are doing. You will work alongside practitioners who are also readers of this book.

While writing this book, I frequently asked myself two questions: "What do I wish I had known when I was starting out?" and "How do I keep discovery fresh after years of experience?" The answers to these questions have guided my selection of topics and the depth of my descriptions. In my work I have found that many seemingly little adjustments in how you look at things or act on things can lead to big differences in how things turn out. These continue to find their way into the pages of this book.

Community change is an interesting, exciting, and, at times, humorous activity. I hope you get a flavor of this in my description of the subject. I approach you, the reader, as a potential change agent and a partner in discovery. Several features of the book support this approach.

Chapter Highlights orient you to key theoretical principles and other important points contained in the chapter. From time to time I ask you to Take a Moment to Discover, inviting you to consider how the material relates to your personal experiences, or I suggest some simple activity that can help you solidify your understanding of the topic. Change Agent Tips offer specific tricks of the trade that deal with typical situations or problems, and cartoons lighten the discussion and illustrate concepts. Fundamental ideas are clarified or defined in brief Capturing Concepts sections, and Did You Know? features provide additional information on topics under discussion. The Global Perspectives boxes provide an expansive international look at specific chapter topics. To help you see and think further about how material connects with the world outside the classroom, each chapter ends with a brief story that brings chapter concepts into focus.

This book is written for all those students and professionals who truly want to make a difference. I hope you find inspiration, direction, and confidence in the following pages.

You will certainly find challenges in the real world. With your sense of purpose and the knowledge you gain from this book, you will be better prepared to face those challenges.

I learn quite a bit from my students and from the members of communities with whom I work. I'd like to learn from you as well. So this is an invitation for you to send me stories—discoveries you have made or challenges you have faced. You can send them to Brooks/Cole, Cengage Learning, 20 Davis Drive, Belmont CA 94002, Attn: Mark S. Homan/Helping Professions Team. I'll read them and draw insights from your perspectives. Thanks.

Acknowledgments

Writing a book is somewhat similar to building a community organization. Each is the manifestation of the contributions of work and talent from a diverse group of people. An organizer attuned to members of a community will make necessary adjustments to keep things moving forward and more or less on track, while not getting in the way of people doing their jobs. An author needs to listen, make adjustments, draw on offered support, and rely on the skills of partners whose particular jobs improve the final product. As an author, though, I have the final responsibility to see that the information is accurate and useful. Any errors are the result of my mistakes or inattention.

Many people have helped to strengthen this new edition. Jo Namsik, Pima Community College library services specialist, has helped me make my way to library resources throughout the world and to find treasures of the written word. No challenge was too big or too small. She helped me get the material I needed and improved my own skills by knowing where to look and how.

Lou Albert, Pima Community College West Campus President, went to bat to help make college resources available. His dedication to social justice and the scholarship of practice continues to set an example.

Karen Koevary, Reference Librarian and Supervisor of the Grants and Non-profit Information Center of the Tucson Pima Public Library, has kept me current with the rich variety of information available through the Foundation Center and its Cooperating Collections. Helping me mine the treasures of the Grants and Nonprofit Information Center and linking me with other collections brought a wealth of information on fund-raising and resource development into this new edition.

Attorney Abby Levine and her colleagues Christina Peltier and Nayantara Mehta from the Alliance for Justice responded graciously to my request to strengthen my understanding of relevant laws and regulations governing lobbying by nonprofits. Their careful scrutiny of what I had written on the topic significantly improved that section. As attorneys they wanted to make sure I put in a disclaimer that the passage provides a general overview of information and does not constitute legal advice. There, Abby, I did it. The commitment to social justice of these women and the Alliance give important allies to all who do this work.

Chris McNamara and Stephanie Pendrys from United Way of Tucson Southern Arizona did their best to see that I understood how mapping and communication technology could be used in the real world. I have valued the time they spent giving me demonstrations and information, and I have particularly appreciated their patience.

Karina Pedroza so many times went above and beyond the call of duty. In fact, she really didn't have any duty, just a real desire to help. Her expertise got me through some unexpected computer glitches, and her assistance getting many little things done has made a big difference.

The Community Development Circle of Friends—Bill Lofquist, Dan Duncan, Nan Carle, Jaimie Leopold, and Neil Vance—never cease to amaze me with how much they have experienced and learned and how ready they are to share and test that learning.

The ready, irreverent wit and keen insight of cartoonist David Fitzsimmons brightens each chapter. In the face of all the silliness and surliness he sees as the syndicated editorial page cartoonist of the *Arizona Daily Star*, he holds true to his belief in human dignity.

The added light of reviewers' thoughtful questions and suggestions have helped me see some things I might have overlooked and bring complex concepts into sharper focus: Jessica Cabness, University of South Florida, School of Social Work; Salene Cowher, Edinboro University; Amanda Marie Gengler, Barton College; Krishna L. Guadalupe, Division of Social Work, Sacramento State University; Christie Bernklau Halvor, Concordia University–Portland; Ronald Maurer, Trevecca Nazarene University; Kelly Mills-Dick, Skidmore College; Carmen Negron, New York City College of Technology; and Deborah M. Wilson, Troy University–Augusta.

The reader sees the words as they appear on the printed page. What is not seen is the delicate and demanding work that goes into refining expression that is aided by the hand of a skillful copyeditor. I have the highest respect for Kay Mikel, whose ability and judgment I trust. She has helped my sometimes lumbering prose step a bit more lightly.

The responsiveness and expertise of the Brooks/Cole, Cengage Learning team has been so valuable to this project. Liana Monari, Seth Dobrin, Trent Whatcott, Arwen Petty, Michelle Cole, and Rachel McDonald certainly know their business. What is equally important is that they know how to go about their business in a professional and friendly manner.

My wonderful family. I sit back, trying to think of what to say. I start to mention your gifts—patience, encouragement, permitting me my distraction, smiles at my enthusiasm, ideas I hadn't thought of—and I realize the list will grow too long and just become a list. For a man who lives so easily with words, I find that whatever ones I try to string together can't quite hold what I want you to hear. For now, simply this: The gift of your love sustains and emboldens me. I am a much better man because of you.

✳

PART I

Responding to the Need for Community Change

Norman Karpenfussen didn't know how much longer he could put up with this insubordination. He could remember, word for word, the warnings issued to staff in his last two memos. If anyone were to question his memory, he could pull the memos from the file and show them. Every memo, in fact everything that issued forth from his office, was copied and placed in a file. Norman liked everything in its place. Norman liked order and orders. The sounds coming from the agency conference room (right next door to his office) flouted these very notions, and Norman could feel the anger rising up in him.

Norman allowed himself a shrewd little smile as he recalled the words of his last memo: "No member of the Health Clinic staff, including volunteers, is authorized to speak to private citizens regarding the alleged matter of contamination of groundwater in the vicinity. Such action is not under the purview [he particularly liked that word] of this agency and is an unwarranted exacerbation [he liked that one too] of an increasingly volatile situation. Any staff member ignoring this admonition will be dealt with in accordance with the full measure of the administrator's authority [he loved that one]."

His smile quickly faded as the scraping of chairs in the adjoining room brought him once again to the realization that preparations for a community meeting were under way—a meeting organized by the clinic's staff. How could this have happened? The staff used to be so docile, so afraid of his authority, so afraid of him, that they almost apologized when suggesting any new direction for the agency. He knew that the people in the surrounding community were poor, uneducated immigrants, if, indeed, they were legal at all, and they needed to be treated like children lest their fears get the better of them. His staff had seemed to think so too. Now this! His staff, stirring up trouble, organizing the community to protest the City's supposed cover-up of groundwater contamination, raising fears of dangers to community health. This was not their job. Didn't they know that? The Neighborhood Health Clinic's purpose was to treat sick people, refer people to other programs in the community, and maybe do a little counseling. They were certainly not supposed to be agitators. Norman realized he would have to go next door and put a stop to all this nonsense.

As Norman opened the door, he was greeted by Grace Marquez, the director of volunteers, who seemed to be running the show. "Welcome, Mr. Karpenfussen," she said with a smile. "Ladies and gentlemen," she continued, "this is Mr. Karpenfussen, our Executive Director, who has come to join us. He will explain the clinic's role in helping you get your groundwater cleaned up." And then Mrs. Gaxiola, a longtime Clinic volunteer, chimed in…"Senõras y senõres, les presento al Senõr Karpenfussen…" Now what am I going to do? Norman wondered.

Part 1 introduces you to the idea of promoting community change—the idea that you do not have to contribute to the presence of problems by inattention and inaction. I believe you should look at, not look away from, problems that go beyond the individual and be willing to confront those problems with the knowledge and skills at your disposal. You cannot take sole responsibility for the problems you see, nor can you tackle them all, but you can make a conscious decision to help change policies and improve conditions that affect the lives of people in your community. Further, you have the opportunity to bring people together to discover the personal gifts and other community assets that may lie hidden from view. With community members you can figure out how to use these resources to strengthen the community and improve the lives of its individual members. It is important to acknowledge this as a legitimate, if not fundamental, part of your role as a social worker, public health worker, or human services professional.

As in any significant aspect of your life, being a community change agent requires a sense of con-

viction and balance. This is not to be confused with being devoid of passion—far from it! Your strong feelings that the rights of the people you serve be acknowledged and fully granted provide a necessary fuel to your involvement. A spirit of principle should infuse your actions, but your passion should not substitute for purpose.

Four chapters make up Part 1. In Chapter 1, Understanding the Challenge to Change, I provide an overview of the enterprise of community change. You will glimpse the range of community conditions you may confront as a professional working in the human services field. Together we will reflect on the pursuit of social justice as a vital calling for those who enter this field of work and explore some of the fundamental issues involved in working to promote change, including the critical importance of recognizing the diversity of cultures. This discussion will help you see the community itself, not just its individual members, as a client, and I describe a number of ways your work can help improve your community. We will even examine the word "client" to help you understand that your relationship with people is one of partnership, not dependency. Finally, I discuss the value of idealism as a source of strength and clarity for your work.

In Chapter 2, Theoretical Frameworks for Community Change, I present the theoretical principles that provide a structure for understanding how you can promote action to change conditions that affect people. Having a strong theoretical base for your actions will help you to interpret what is occurring and gauge what is likely to occur from the actions you take. Six foundation theoretical frameworks, along with the cornerstones of community building, will guide your understanding. We examine the elements that contribute to a healthy community and the circumstances that must be present for change to occur. It is the wealth

RESPONDING TO THE NEED FOR COMMUNITY CHANGE

of communities that we use to promote change and build community strength. We will go beyond an understanding of wealth as only money, recognizing nine different forms of community wealth or capital. We will consider how forms of oppression contribute to many of the problems we need to face. We will come to value people as beings who transform our world, not just adapt to it. We will recognize that in every situation something is going well or has gone well, and so we will use the spirit and insight of appreciative inquiry to give us a powerful perspective. Several models of community change are described, which will acquaint you with a variety of different approaches. I introduce the factors necessary for you to achieve success, including the orientation toward this work that will strengthen and direct your efforts. As an agent of community change, your ability to recognize and develop the assets available in the community and your belief that the members of the community are the most important contributors to actions and decisions will influence everything you do.

Chapter 3, Relating Community Change to Professional Practice, focuses on the role community change plays in the provision of service. Perhaps you aren't sure how community change fits with your picture of what people in the human services professions do. This is a common and legitimate reservation. Many workers are not striving very visibly for community change, so it is hard to recognize its function. To help explore this issue, we examine the basic purposes of social welfare, surveying traditional approaches used by human services professionals and relating community change activities to professional values. I encourage you to look at the difference between a more common service approach and one that builds on and develops combined strengths to make a sustained difference in community functioning. I invite you to question professional tolerance for conditions that not only harm clients but also restrict the extent and quality of professional services themselves. I also ask you to think about the connection you will make as a professional between what you think and what you do. Your professional preparation gives you the theoretical framework and practical skills you can put to use in the context of community change. You start off well equipped for this kind of work.

In Chapter 4, Putting Yourself in the Picture, the focus is on you as a change agent. Much of the writing in the field of community change talks about community change agents, almost as if we were talking about a group of people it would be nice to know about…but not become. I take a different approach and speak directly to you as an individual who will be involved in the business of promoting community change. I encourage you to develop the habit of reflective practice to promote your self-awareness and elevate your effectiveness. Everyday matters with which you must contend as a worker engaged in community change are examined: How do you get your boss to go along with your change efforts? How do you fit activism in with other aspects of your job? How do you avoid becoming burned out? Finally, I discuss the value of some simple, down-to-earth tips that will increase your effectiveness.

Working to promote community change is an exciting endeavor that will energize you and make your decision to become a professional in the field of human services more meaningful. Many of the changes you make may seem small or relatively minor, but they represent a new direction that over time will account for meaningful improvement of a situation. Some of your efforts may start small, but you will see them grow to secure significant changes. Perhaps you will even initiate actions that substantially alter the balance of power in your community, producing significant, permanent change. All these opportunities are open to you as a worker in the health and human services field. All of them result in a situation that is better for your having acted. All give you the chance to help eliminate problems rather than contribute to their maintenance by helping you to recognize strengths, your own and others', and using them to build a better future.

I invite you to consider these opportunities more fully in the following pages.

Chapter 1

Understanding the
Challenge to Change

CHAPTER HIGHLIGHTS

- Acknowledge systemic problems
- Confront the challenge to promote change
- Recognize clients as community members
- Acknowledge human concern and helpful action
- Discover how you can have an impact in your professional role
- Learn that you cannot and should not do everything yourself
- Understand the terms *community, community problems,* and *community change*
- Face the fact of oppression and privilege

- Learn the lesson of empowerment
- Understand and deal with resistance to change
- Recognize the differences in superficial versus fundamental change
- Acquire cultural competence
- Value diversity in our increasingly diverse society
- Understand that the community is the client
- Identify the range of community change opportunities
- Retain your idealism

WHAT'S GOING ON OUT THERE?

Beginning in the 1930s through his death in 1972, Saul Alinsky upset the comfortable status quo of the "haves" in many communities through his social action organizing of the "have-nots." He was the founder of the Industrial Areas Foundation (IAF), which trains organizers and builds organizations whose primary purpose is power and whose chief product is social change (IAF, 2009). Some time back he made these observations on social workers:

They come to the people of the slums not to help them rebel and fight their way out of the muck...most social work does not even reach the submerged masses. Social work is largely a middle class activity and guided by a middle class psychology. In the rare instances where it reaches the slum dwellers it seeks to get them adjusted to their environment so they will live in hell and like it. A higher form of social treason would be difficult to conceive. (as quoted in Meyer, 1945)

Strong words aren't they? How do they apply to the way you will provide human services? Will you address only the singular problems of individuals, or will you stand back from time to time and bring into focus the larger picture these individual images combine to form? Will you look beyond the immediate situation to understand the fundamental barriers your clients face? Will you shake your head and wring your hands, or will you do something about it? What kind of a human services worker do you intend to be?

You will come to realize that a variety of forces outside your office contribute to the problems people bring to your office. Paying attention to those outside forces may improve the lives of the people you see every day in your agencies more than the individual service you offer there. Maybe some of these people wouldn't have to come to you at all had you addressed these outside forces directly.

What You Will See If You Look

You may find it hard to ignore the call to social justice and action if you are willing to open your eyes and your ears. The Children's Defense Fund (2009a, 2009b) reports that every day in America, eight children or teens are killed by firearms—one child every 3 hours; 155 children are arrested for violent crimes—one child every 9 minutes; 2,145 babies are born without health insurance—one baby every 41 seconds; 2,421 children are confirmed as abused or neglected—one child every 35 seconds; 2,483 babies are born into poverty—one baby every 35 seconds; 3,477 children are arrested—one child every 25 seconds; 1,511 public school children are corporally punished—one student every 17 seconds of a school day; 2,467 high school students drop out—one student every 10 seconds; 18,221 public school students are suspended—one student every second of every school day. Every day this occurs—every day. Is this a condition that you find acceptable?

The U.S. Census Bureau (2008b) reports that 37.3 million people lived in poverty in 2007. Children are particularly hard hit. More than 13 million children are poor, and almost half of them—about 5.8 million children—live in deep poverty, in homes whose incomes fall below 50% of the poverty line (DeNavas-Walt, Proctor, & Smith, 2008). More than 45% of households headed by women with no husband present and with children under age five are poor (U.S. Census Bureau, 2008b). Don't get sick. With no health insurance, almost 46 million Americans have to gamble that they will get through each day without illness or injury (DeNavas-Walt et al., 2008). Is this a condition you find acceptable?

Income inequality keeps us a nation apart. Forty percent of Americans receive only 12% of the nation's income, while the top 20% receive almost half of all the income, as much as all the "lower" 80% combined (DeNavas-Walt et al., 2008). A few Americans, just 5%, take in more than one fifth of all the income. The Economic Policy Institute and the Center on Budget and Policy Priorities report concludes that in the last 2 decades, the incomes of the richest families climbed substantially, while the incomes of middle- and low-income families saw only modest increases (Bernstein, McNichol, & Lyons, 2006). In fact, in the last 2 decades the average income of the richest 20% of families increased more than *17 times* that of the poorest 20%. Is this a condition you find acceptable?

When the U.S. Department of Health and Human Services (2005) examined the health and well-being of children, it found that social and economic factors have a noticeable affect on children's health. Not only are the children directly affected, but the physical and mental health of children can affect the family as a whole. Low-income children are more likely to be in poorer health and are twice as likely to have socioemotional difficulties. They are more likely to live in neighborhoods that do not feel safe or supportive, and they miss more days of school. Moreover, the physical and emotional health of a child's mother affects how she can care for her children, and it has an impact on the health and well-being of the entire family. Mothers in low-income families are much less likely than mothers in higher-income families to be in excellent or very good physical and mental health themselves. Furthermore, higher levels of parenting aggravation are more likely in lower-income families. The report notes that "these circumstances may combine to put children in low-income families at a health, developmental, and educational disadvantage" (p. 5). Is this a condition you find acceptable?

What happens to children when a parent loses a job? In early 2009, more than 13 million workers were out of a job, 5.3 million more than just over a year before (Bureau of Labor Statistics, 2009c). A father's involuntary job loss increases the likelihood that children will repeat a grade or be suspended or expelled from school (Kalil & Ziol-Guest, 2008). With parental job loss, middle-class children are less likely to obtain any postsecondary education, and the effect for Black children is four times as strong (Kalil & Wightman, 2009). One event can set in motion a host of other long-term consequences. Is this a condition you find acceptable?

What's it like to be hungry? After completing more than 52,000 in-person interviews and reviewing responses to more than 31,000 questionnaires from member agencies, researchers for Second Harvest (now called Feeding America), the nation's largest organization of emergency food providers, discovered these compelling facts: 42% of clients choose between paying for food, utilities, or heating fuel; 35% must decide between paying for food or rent or a mortgage; and 32% face a choice between paying for food and medicine or medical care (Cohen, Kim, & Ohls, 2006). These are daily decisions that many Americans know nothing about. But this is not news to more than 36 million Americans, including over 12 million children who, according to the U.S. Department of Agriculture, suffered from "food insecurity" during 2007, even before the recession reached its deepest level (Nord, Andrews, & Carlson, 2008). Food insecurity means that "they were uncertain of having, or unable to acquire, enough food to meet the basic needs for all household members because they had insufficient money and other resources for food" (p. 4). More than 30% of households with children headed by a single woman were food insecure in 2007. More attention is being directed to hunger among older per-

sons as well. An analysis of senior hunger between 2001 and 2005 found that over 11% of all seniors—more than 5 million older adults—were at least marginally food insecure (Ziliak, Gunderson, & Haist, 2008), and in 2007 the number of food insecure older adults continues to grow (Nord et al., 2008). Is this a condition that you find acceptable?

In almost all states the price of child care for two children is greater than half the median income for single parents, and the cost of infant care alone is higher than a year's tuition at a 4-year public college (Totah, 2008). What effect might this have? In Los Angeles a hospital van dropped off a homeless paraplegic man and left him crawling in the street with a broken colostomy bag, an incident of what police called "homeless dumping." City officials have accused more than a dozen area hospitals of this practice (Associated Press, 2007). What does that say about our level of care and caring? According to Staudt, Huddleston, and Kraucunas (2008) at the National Academy of Sciences, carbon dioxide is at the highest level in at least 650,000 years and continues to rise. Does this get you a little hot under the collar? Are all these conditions acceptable to you?

Of course, many people in other parts of the world struggle even more. The World Bank (2009) tells us that more than 1.4 billion people eke out a living on less than $1.25 a day. How about this? Is this acceptable to you as well?

Maybe the state will authorize only a few days of treatment for a young client of yours who needs much more than that to cope with years of being the victim of molestation. You might wonder how the administrators of the school district you work for can go jetting from this conference to the next, yet deny the use of a school bus for fifth graders to go on an educational outing because of a "lack of funding for travel." How frustrated will you be when you realize that the young man sitting across from you, disheveled and insolent, has had four different doctors in the last year "directing" his treatment, and that his case is not a whole lot different from others you have seen this week? Continued patterns of violence bring women to emergency rooms and the response is…maybe some counseling. Perhaps in your community neighbors are disconnected from each other, disillusioned, and shrink in fear behind locked doors. You watch community members rich in insight and skill being ignored while professional colleagues busy themselves creating yet another service

CAPTURING CONCEPTS
The Client

I have struggled to find the best term to identify the people with whom we work to change conditions that affect their lives. There is no one good term to describe this relationship. Some writers prefer the term *consumer,* but this implies a greater sense of choice than many people really have. It also implies that people are only users, not contributors. The term *recipient* conveys a rather passive role. *Patient* implies an illness.

Some have suggested that the term *citizen* conveys a sense of dignity and equality. This is useful, although it falls short of the implication of a professional relationship, and others have questioned whether *noncitizens* would consider themselves included. Though *partner* is

often a good term, it is so broad that it doesn't recognize any particular sort of partnership.

Client is the most common, and it is likely that it is the designation with which you are most familiar. Although it comes as close as any to connoting a relationship characterized by respect and professionalism, it may unintentionally convey notions of dependency rather than partnership. I will use this term only when describing a relationship or circumstance where the use of "client" reveals a particular meaning. Throughout this text I more commonly use **member** or **participant** to refer to those with whom you have a professional helping relationship, including those with whom you will be working to promote community change.

program. These are actual situations workers face. Are these conditions you find acceptable?

Other problems are less sweeping or poignant; you will see some evidence of them almost daily as you work in human services. Taken together, they imply that the people you work with have little dignity. Clients have to wait too long for an appointment, wait too long to be seen on the day of their appointment, and have too little time with you or other professionals when they are finally seen. All they are given are appointments; rarely are they given the opportunity to come together in an organized way to change the conditions that seem to call for all these appointments. But they are given forms, lots forms, often lengthy and confusing.

Some agency staff are insensitive, unhelpful, or downright rude. Are these conditions you find acceptable? Will you grow to accept a system that employs denial and defensiveness as primary responses? Will you care if workers and agencies are isolated from the day-to-day lives of the people they are supposed to assist? Will you too ignore those who are chronically unrecognized and unreached? Will you tolerate mediocrity as the standard of your profession and keep silent about a "service" system that lives in fear of being found out?

Many of us don't like to be confronted with these questions. We get fidgety and hope they will just go away…but they don't. Can't somebody else just do something?

These challenges are yours. These are situations you will face. "Oh great," you may be thinking, "here I am planning to help make the lives of individuals or families happier and more fulfilling, and now I'm expected to save the whole world."

Relax. Unless your presence here on earth is some fantastic historical event, you are not going to save the world (though some of you may well have a pretty significant impact on it). Many of you are not going to work for community change as your primary professional role. Many of you will be case managers, therapists, or generalist human services practitioners. But all of you will be confronted from time to time with the challenge to promote change. All of you will face barriers to your practice. All of you will have your professional ethics tested. Will you respond or look away?

Beyond a Consideration of Problems

An honest reflection on the many national, community, and personal problems that exist can be intimidating, even discouraging. You may look at our provision of human services in the face of so many difficulties and conclude that people just don't care about each other. Plain and simple, we—including you—just don't care. That could be, but, frankly, I don't think so. Take another look.

CAPTURING CONCEPTS
Community, Community Problems, and Community Change

Throughout this book you will be encouraged to consider concerns that affect a community of people and that can be addressed through the actions of a community of people working together. But what exactly is a community? For our purposes, a **community** consists of a number of people with something in common that connects them in some way and that distinguishes them from others. This common connection could be a place where members live—a city or a neighborhood. It may be an activity, like a job, or perhaps their ethnic identification provides the connection. When I use the term *community,* I do not presuppose any particular size or number of people.

Some communities are fully developed, recognizing certain common interests and working to provide mutual benefits. Members of other communities may barely even notice any common bond or characteristic among themselves. Communities are usually made up of sets of smaller communities. For example, cities have different neighborhoods, universities have different colleges and departments, softball leagues have different teams, and so on. When I refer to "your" community, I mean any of those sets of people with whom you are connected in some way and whose interests or actions are important enough for you to be concerned about.

Communities have ongoing needs that require attention. These needs are quite different from symptoms or conditions of weakness, or what some might label as "needy." These needs can include things such as the health of members, economic vitality, or effective policy making. Communities also have extensive assets to meet those needs and to flourish in the process. Some

of these assets will be recognized and well applied; others will be undiscovered, undervalued, and unused.

When these needs are not adequately met and discomfort to members results, **community problems** exist. If things stay the same, the problems and the discomfort will persist. The word "problem" has been used in many ways. Some use it to convey neediness, a seemingly intractable condition, or even a temporary irritant; I use the term here simply to mean a condition that blocks human and community development. You can view a problem as an invitation to change or action, seeing the problem as the distance between where you are and where you want to be. It is a state of tension that recognizes both current unwanted conditions and better, future conditions. The only way to noticeably build strength or to get rid of the problems or to reduce them is for people to do things differently. This means **community change** must occur.

Community change also occurs through **community development** when members recognize their assets and discover how to use them in more productive ways. Because communities function as systems, community change can be seen as system change. Community change is the process of producing modification or innovation in attitudes, policies, or practices in the community for the purpose of reducing (or eliminating) problems, providing for general improvement in the way needs are met, or developing assets for the benefit of its members. This process enhances the quality of life of individual members and the relationships among members. Community change means community improvement. The terms can be used interchangeably. In Chapter 5 you will learn more about communities.

People are burdened by their fears, held back by their prejudices, and confused by their myths. This is undeniable. These factors exist, and they play a part in shaping what is available to enhance the quality of life. But just as these limitations are facts of life, so too is the genuine concern we feel for those in distress. People are moved by suffering, emboldened in the face of injustice, and strengthened by their desire to contribute. People are touched by the recognition of their common humanity.

If you believe people have an interest in and the capacity for good, you will act to capitalize on it. If you don't, you will quickly be burned out in your cynicism. Surely, your belief in good will be tested, sometimes to the point where you fail to see its signs right around you, but you will pass these tests. You will find strength and energy when you convert the power of caring and common decency into an active force to counter those influences that flaw the system in which you work as a professional. You will also find examples of effective practices in your community and tremendous wealth beyond dollars that you can use to change conditions that you find unacceptable.

Thousands of public school students are suspended each day, but millions are not. Every day many families do not have enough to eat, but many more are well fed. Ignoring or rationalizing pain and suffering will callous our souls and bring threats even closer. Recognizing these conditions can spur us to action, and realizing that we can learn by looking at what is working well can give us confidence and direction.

You care enough to think about your own involvement in human services. Don't you think it highly unlikely that you are the *only one* who feels this way?

CAN YOU REALLY DO ANYTHING TO MAKE A DIFFERENCE?

Perhaps a better question is this: Can you do anything about *any* of the challenges you encounter? You will have to leave many matters for other people, but you can tackle a fair share of your own quite well. Some thought, some planning, some common sense, some interest, a sense of purpose, and a touch of luck are the basic ingredients. You can do quite a lot with just these. Add some understanding of human behavior, some recognition of resources available to you, some skill in determining tactics, and some creativity and you have a potent combination that will definitely produce results. All these components are available to any human services worker.

You can provide significant leadership in bringing people together to make needed changes although you may not be the only leader or even the most "important" one. You can make a difference in your community even if you have other primary professional responsibilities, especially as you develop the leadership of others. But remember this fundamental principle: Any problem that involves more than one person requires the involvement of more people than just you to resolve it. In other words, don't try to do everything by yourself. I often use the word "you," but generally I mean not only you as an individual but those with whom you are working as well.

Community problems, like personal problems, provide opportunities for growth or decline. Persistent patterns of denial or withdrawal harm the community or service agency just as they harm the individual. Halfhearted or poorly managed attempts at solving problems and building capacity can prove discouraging. However, purposeful, organized efforts—even less than perfect ones—yield results that can improve present conditions and set the stage for creating new opportunities and effectively meeting future challenges. Recognizing and confronting problems and looking to what you already have that you can use creates the possibility that things will be different, most likely better.

When problems are accepted as permanent, these opportunities for change are missed. As you work in this field, you will go beyond fixing problems. Problem fixing tends toward temporary solutions, often isolating a problem from the very conditions that spawn it. Using the tension that exists in the naming of a problem as a starting point for action and gaining confidence from knowing that in any situation something works, you can use action to address the immediate situation in a way that leaves the community more capable of improving basic conditions.

SOME BASIC ISSUES THAT DESERVE YOUR ATTENTION

As you begin to think about confronting some of the problems you will routinely encounter as a worker in the helping professions, consider the following themes: oppression, empowerment, resistance to working for change, and fundamental or superficial responses to hardship.

Confronting Oppression

You will tangle with a host of problems throughout your career. A common connection between many, if not most, of the persistent social problems you will encounter is oppression. You may not see oppression when you intervene in a problem situation. You may see intimate partner violence or child abuse or poverty. If you look deeper into any particular incident, you are likely to recognize oppression and understand that what you are dealing with at the moment is one of its expressions. This can be a sobering realization, and you may be tempted to turn away from it. Recognizing oppression requires us to examine our professional role. Is it our professional responsibility to attend to the by-products of oppression, or is it our job to steadily chip away at the political, social, and economic structures that support it? Do we act to transform those structures, or do we acquiesce to them? What forms of oppression affect you? How? Where can you begin to make a dent? With whom?

I believe it is fundamental that we recognize the presence of oppression as a force affecting the work that we do. If we are silent on the subject of oppression, we become its partner. I encourage you to continue learning about this complex process that ensnarls many of our interactions. Teasing apart its many strands requires a lot of inquiry. A good starting place can be found in the works of Paulo Friere, the Brazilian educator and author whose writings have influenced millions throughout the world. A strong advocate of popular education, which builds on the experiences and abilities of participants with an intent to build both knowledge and political consciousness, Friere's books, particularly *Pedagogy of the Oppressed* (2000), *Pedagogy of Hope* (1995), and *Education for Critical Consciousness* (1973), are rich with an examination of oppression and steps toward liberation. A number of his ideas are included in the following discussion.

Just what is oppression? Oppression is the systematic subjugation of people, their rights, opportunities, hopes, and beliefs to benefit the interests of others who have the power to maintain the current state of affairs. Oppression removes the power of free decision making from those affected by decisions and places it in the hands of others who use that power to keep control. It occurs both as a process of suppression and as a structure of patterned relationships in a system that supports and validates the process (Lum, 2004).

There are many forms of oppression. Systems that use racism to hold people down and in conflict with one another are oppressive. So are economic systems that exploit people and their labor and social welfare systems that stigmatize participants. On a smaller scale, the dictatorial teacher who humiliates a student who dares to question, the abusive husband who demands complete allegiance to the "rights" of his position, and the boss who trots out the policy manual to end any discussion of workplace injustice act out of an oppressive tradition.

Oppression is sustained when people are separated from one another and the recognition of their shared conditions and interests. Splintering a pervasive condition into a million disconnected dots or faces of anguish may keep us from seeing the condition clearly and acting powerfully to change it. When we keep individuals and families locked apart as separate cases, we may be contributing to keeping oppressive structures in place.

Oppression commonly comes with some justification, a rationale for characterizing current practices as good and proper. As a result, oppression censors examination and punishes those who question. Oppression quells exploring any alternative. By manipulating and limiting discussion itself, those who oppress can block any other alternative from clear view. With few options presented, and those not well understood, most people don't even think that something different is possible. They see what is before them—how things are—as the only way things can be. As a result, those who experience oppression may not recognize it themselves.

Still, many people do feel that things aren't right, even if they cannot name the source of their dissatisfaction. They do not have true commitment to the current situation, only acquiescence to it. Others may see the actual situation as so impossible to change that they withdraw from even thinking about doing so. In retreat, they may come to justify the current situation as a form of accommodation to it, even taking hold of myths that validate current conditions. They commit to an imagined situation that masks the real one.

Those who are oppressed will sometimes resist those who challenge prevailing conditions because the challenge requires a new accommodation, one that they believe cannot succeed. They may have bought into the notion that they are "less than"— less worthy, less able, less deserving. This can create guilt and self-hatred, leading to even greater submission and obedience to the oppressor (Deutsch, 2005). Their beliefs about themselves may be a reflection of the beliefs held about them by the oppressor. Freedom from oppression requires a kind of responsibility that the oppressed may not believe they are capable to fulfill, so they hand over their power to others. When this happens, people become co-conspirators to their own oppression.

It is not uncommon for those who experience oppression to act as oppressors themselves. They have "learned" how to behave when in positions of authority or power. As oppressed people act to oppress one another, they keep themselves weak in the face of larger oppression.

Some who are oppressed may derive a feeling of power by identifying with those who oppress or currying their favor. They may want to look the same, act the same, and espouse the same political beliefs and slogans. They vicariously participate in the power of the other. Becoming more like those who hold power may be a way of reducing the fear of the powerful, or the fear of their own lack of power. You may have seen a form of this early on in the group of children who hang around the playground bully.

When prevailing structures that govern social, economic, and political relationships are assumed to be valid, those who don't succeed or don't fit in are seen as the only failures. It is the pathology of the individual, not the structure itself, that attracts our attention.

Confronting oppression requires us to confront privilege, including our own. We need to acknowledge a sometimes almost invisible system of unearned advantages and exemptions that provides a straighter, smoother path for some, while making the journey much more difficult for others. There is nothing wrong with a straight, smooth path. What is wrong is to reserve this road for some and deny it to others. Privilege often comes at the expense of others. You may be waiting in line to get into a club when someone considered more special is ushered to the front, as if it is his right, but not yours. He gets in; you get to stay outside. I visited a very old, very beautiful church in Mexico, built in the days when the Spaniards were colonizing the area. The labor of indigenous people built the mar-

velous structure. However, once it was completed, they were not allowed inside. That privilege was reserved for those who ordered the work, not the ones who did the work. Where else do you notice that some are inside where things are nicer and easier, and others are left outside? Those inside may not even notice that there are others in a different place. Privilege is often unquestioned by those who share its benefits; they just assume this is how things are. Well, this is how things are for some people. They are quite different for other people. Are you willing to recognize this? Should you do anything about it?

Oppression affects both the oppressor and the oppressed. The conditions that prevail affect all of us. Being fully human goes beyond being rich or politically powerful; we do not gain freedom from oppression by becoming new oppressors. Freedom is not just trading places. If our moving forward is purchased at the price of keeping others from achieving their potential, we have been made poorer by the transaction. All oppressors justify their oppression, even ones who had once been its victims. We gain freedom by setting forth new patterns of relationships that dignify all parties.

If you are going to address conditions of oppression, you will need to do this alongside those who are most keenly affected. Their acting on their own behalf is what makes the action legitimate. Oppression continues as we do things *for* people rather than *with* them. The presence of oppression and its consequences are better revealed through "reflection and action upon the world in order to transform it" (Friere, 2000, p. 51).

This is lifelong work. Whether you care for those who suffer from oppression or care enough to work to end oppression, you will choose the work you will do. Because even small acts of oppression are connected to larger patterns, whenever you act to confront oppression, you will have achieved something beyond the immediate circumstance.

Empowerment

Working with others to promote change requires more than you being a leader and collecting a bunch of followers. To be successful, you will be working with others who are acting powerfully and in concert. People can come to feel more capable through the skills they acquire, but it is through their connections with others that they become more powerful. You will assist your partners in developing stronger beliefs in their own personal power and in the power of your organized group. When people feel a greater sense of worth and personal competence and control, they recognize that they can participate with others to influence conditions that affect them. This process and its outcome are known as *empowerment* (Bishop, 2002; DuBois & Krogsrud-Miley, 2005; Gutierrez, 1995; Gutierrez, Parsons & Cox 2003; Mancoske & Hunzeker, 1994; Segal, Gerdes, & Steiner, 2010). You cannot make people feel and act more powerfully, but you can increase the likelihood that they will act with power.

Empowerment of those participating in a change effort depends on five factors:

- Personal interest or investment in the project—a feeling of being an important part of things
- Belief in the possibility of a successful outcome
- Development and recognition of individual and group resources
- Opportunities to take action and to make meaningful contributions
- Recognition of common interests and common risk taking

By keeping these five simple points in mind, you can further the process of empowerment considerably. First, provide members with opportunities for making decisions and for performing tasks. Group leaders need to spread these opportunities around. Second, offer encouragement to one another. This should be done in a way that communicates a belief in each member's capabilities. Third, recognize members' contributions and their results, as well as the overall progress that is taking place. This will keep the focus on productivity and accomplishment. It will also build members' beliefs in their capabilities. Fourth, act as a group whenever possible. Finally, together reflect on your actions and what you have learned from them. This will give members an experience of united power and reinforce an awareness of common commitment and shared risk taking.

Some specific techniques for helping members discover their own power are discussed in Chapter 6. However, if you remember only these basic

---

▶ Take a Moment to Discover ◀

Why don't people, especially human services professionals, take up the banner for change more readily and more often? The best answer is probably found by questioning yourself: "When I see something that needs to be changed, why don't I act?" How do any of these responses fit your reactions?

- I'm afraid of what might happen.
- I really don't know enough about the situation.
- I'm afraid that people won't like me, especially my friends or colleagues or people I think are more important than I am.
- I don't think anyone really sees the situation in the same way that I do.
- I really don't have the right to make changes.
- I really don't deserve for things to be better.
- I really don't know what to do.
- I'm too busy...with more important matters.
- It's too big, and I'm only one person.
- It's not my job.

Choose any one of these responses and think about it for a minute. What ways could you devise to challenge the statement?

---

elements of empowerment and the strategies promoting them, you will find that you are not doing things all by yourself.

Resistance to Working for Change

A good insight into resistance is provided by Filley, House, and Kerr (1976), who describe the phenomenon of "sunk costs" to explain a source of opposition to change. It may be hard to leave something as simple as a poker hand or something as dramatic as a war if a lot of money, time, or justification have been sunk into it. We can talk ourselves into continuing to do things even if there is little good reason for doing so. Many people, or at least enough people in a position to make a difference, have made a significant investment in either shaping the current situation or learning how to function within it. Change suggests that the time, energy, skill, or experience these people have invested is no longer relevant or needed. Change implies that these investments were either poorly spent or are no longer of value. Considered from this standpoint, the introduction of a new invention or a new procedure may threaten individuals' investments in their own experiences and may even jeopardize their careers. Further, people who have invested an extraordinary amount of time and effort to master the game as it is currently played may well be unreceptive to playing it differently.

Perhaps the most profound source of resistance to change is simply what we tell ourselves. People who hold onto problems frequently send themselves messages that rob them of their power by stating and confirming current limitations—both real and imagined—in a way that implies that constraints are forever fixed. People who act to improve problem conditions acknowledge current limitations but acknowledge current assets as well. They are willing to use assets to test limitations and to break them down.

If you take assertive action, you may receive some direct benefits. You will also feel better about yourself and be more highly regarded by others who have taken part in the experience, including opponents.

Change can cause discomfort and provoke fear. Even little changes, like gaining or losing weight, can cause discomfort. Your clothes don't feel right, and people look at you differently. Major changes are often accompanied by more significant discomforts. Parents must let go of their accustomed control over their children as they grow; children chafe at parental direction that no longer seems reasonable. These are times of anxiety and anger. The mayor and the city council don't want to share their power with those who used to be so docile, so apathetic. Those who have always been favored in community decisions don't like others receiving attention. Those who want change don't even act until their discomfort with present conditions provokes them to act. Someone will feel uncomfortable in some way when change is under way. Attempts to prevent or quiet this discomfort are powerful sources of resistance.

Change means things aren't predictable anymore. This can be scary. Uncertainty produces tension. A child caught alone in a candy store when the lights suddenly go out knows there are goodies all around, but the darkness may hide monsters as well. Danger may lurk behind what we do not see or do not know.

There is nothing wrong with feeling some trepidation about promoting change. It is fairly natural. Here are some steps you can take to overcome your hesitancy.

- *Confront the source of your concerns.* If time is a concern, see how you can better organize the things you have to do. If uncertainty about the outcome or the success of the effort bothers you, take stock of your assets, including the things you know how to do, the support you currently have, and other factors working in your favor. Knowing that you can improve the odds in your favor may help you accept a lack of certainty as a condition of working for change.

- *Develop support.* Act in concert with others so you can share the work, receive encouragement, and benefit from group problem-solving efforts. Purposefully cultivate support and increase communication with others who have promoted change. This will go a long way toward building your confidence and overcoming resistance.

- *Look at what you have that you can use.* In any situation you will be able to find a variety of things that can help. This could be some special skills or talents, helpful connections, even passion or energy. Maybe public dissatisfaction can work in your favor, maybe there are helpful policies in place, or maybe there are some helpful habits that you can put to use. You might find a meeting place, a copy machine, a website, a newsletter, some special event that is taking place, tools from shovels to listservs, and on and on. Once you start seeing all the things around you that you can use, it is pretty encouraging to realize that you already have a lot going for you.

- *Remind yourself of why the change is important.* If you keep in touch with the feelings that provoked your interest in the first place, you will have a strong source of motivation. Consider what the consequences of inattention will be.

- *Take advantage of training opportunities.* Participate in workshops, classes, or in-service training programs to increase your knowledge and skills in program development or community change. This will strengthen your sense of personal capability.

- *Identify a simple starting point.* Feelings of being overwhelmed can undermine your willingness to take action. Look for easy ways to get started.

- *Decide to act.* "Sort of" doing things will lead to mediocre results and discontent. Make a clear decision to act.

- *Reflect on your actions.* Think about how you and others acted and reacted in the situation and draw on this learning to strengthen your future actions. Doing this with others who act along with you will deepen your discoveries and strengthen your learning.

Weeds and Roots, Bandages and Balms

I remember mowing the lawn when I was a kid. (I remember mowing the lawn last week, too, but that's a different story.) One section of the yard produced a fair number of weeds. As is the nature and duty of weeds, they grew faster than the grass. I was supposed to pull them, but pulling weeds was not how I envisioned spending a summer's day, not when there was baseball to be played. To save time, I just mowed the whole yard—grass and weeds and all. Heck, the weeds were green; who would know? It worked, too, for a week.

I won't go into the details, but the subsequent conversation on the matter with my mother (Supervisor of Grounds) went something like this: "You didn't do an adequate job. Forget baseball today. I want all the weeds pulled out. Now!"

"Shucks, Mom, what's the big deal? Nobody can tell the difference anyway…. Well, okay" (the last sentence having been offered in response to a look that conveyed that further argument would not benefit my cause).

The yard did look better when I was done. Yes, the grass did eventually replace the weeds, which, by the way, needed more than one afternoon's attention. But looking around, it's pretty easy to see that I'm not the only one who tries to skip grabbing a problem by its roots.

▶ Take a Moment to Discover ◀

Why do we put so much energy into developing shelters for people who are homeless instead of getting rid of homelessness? Why do we feel so good about food banks providing emergency food instead of taking steps to eliminate hunger and the widespread need for emergency food? Are these problems too big for a nation like ours to solve? Hardly, though we can con ourselves into thinking so.

There are probably a hundred reasons why we mow over the weeds rather than pull them out by the roots. Let's look at some of the reasons community problems remain despite the fact that we are well aware of them.

- We believe that we don't have the time to do the job right.

- The problems are hopelessly complex. Where do we start?

- It is too much work.

- It is better to smooth things over than to cause disruption.

- The people who would be disturbed by changing things are more important than the people who are hurting now.

- The people who are feeling the problem aren't worth the trouble.

- Significant intervention costs too much.

- Major surgery might kill the patient.

- We would rather cover up things we don't want to look at.

- We fear the possibility that things are out of control, or will be.

- It is just a bad habit.

- It is easier to shut up those who feel the problem than it is to challenge those in authority because those in need are less threatening and are appreciative of any help we can give them.

- We need to feel that we are at least doing something.

- When we are up to our behinds in alligators, we forget that our original intention was to drain the swamp.

Consider this list. Is this the way a nation or a community responds? How might this guide your actions as an agent of community change?

Operation and Regeneration

Not every change requires a change in national priorities. Something as simple as involving participants in program planning, developing a food buying club, or replacing dollars for massive new road projects with dollars for bike paths may constitute a significant new direction. By tugging at the "weeds" that detract from the beauty of your community, you make room for new, more positive growth.

As you might guess, not all weeds are easy to pull. So, too, some of the problems you face will have long histories and deeply entrenched interests. Getting rid of them requires sustained and powerful action. If your work is not primarily in the area of community change, playing a prominent organizing or leadership role may seem a bit daunting. However, even in these cases you have ample opportunity to play a supporting role.

Finally, weeds may never disappear altogether. Maybe signs of racial discrimination have disappeared from your school. Perhaps procedures that undermine dignity have been removed from your agency. Even in areas that look pretty clear, weeds will crop up from time to time. Just keep an eye out to prevent them from taking over again.

THE NEED FOR CULTURAL AWARENESS, RESPECT, AND COMPETENCE

"Nobody is showing up at the meetings," I said. "Oh, yes they are," came the response. "We just meet a little differently than you do. We all get together at Marta's house and talk. By the time we leave, everyone has had a chance to say what they want." One lesson.

"We can't seem to get anyone interested in getting something going around here. What's the matter?" His smile told me that he had taken for granted that I knew some things that I didn't. "Well, for one thing, everybody has a family member who just maybe hasn't completed all the legal paperwork to be here. Maybe even the whole family. Staying a little less visible might strike them as a good idea." Another lesson.

"I have never had such a hard time trying to figure out where we should hold a first meeting," I said, probably with a little exasperation. "These things have to be done carefully," my guide reminded me. "It's a big reservation. Just where we meet for the first time matters. We can't look like we are making one leader or one family seem more important." Yet one more lesson.

One of the themes that runs through the work of community change is that everything happens through relationships that generate and use the investment of time as well as the varied perspectives and skills of many people. The three most fundamental elements of any relationship are communication, trust, and mutual interest.

Cultural differences provide a unique broadening of perspectives and a variety of skills. They also provide challenges to communication, trust, and the recognition of mutual interest. Ignorance of different ways of experiencing the world and expressing that experience can lead to mistakes in understanding and limiting access to ability. What is different is less predictable. Uncertainty can produce excitement and inquiry, but it can also produce fear and anxiety, which are barriers to trust.

Effective change agents understand that issues of trust and possibilities for miscommunication and blurred common interest are present in any relationship, and that these are more likely when people from various backgrounds are working together. Effective change agents develop linguistic competence, the capacity to communicate effectively with diverse groups in a language that is easily understood by all parties in communication (Goode & Jones, 2008). Difficulty in understanding one another is heightened when conflict and power imbalances have characterized the history of the groups' interactions. When individuals of different cultures engage each other, each may misjudge the other's actions based on learned expectations. Individuals are bringing their own unique history with the other group, along with the influence of political relationships. They bring stereotypes, prescribed patterns of communication, etiquette, and problem-solving approaches as well (Potts, 2005). They also may well bring an intent to work with and learn from each other and to accomplish something of importance. Thus, being culturally competent is imperative for change agents.

DID YOU KNOW?   Standards for Cultural Competence in Social Work Practice

1. **Ethics and Values.** Social workers shall function in accordance with the values, ethics, and standards of the profession, recognizing how personal and professional values may conflict with or accommodate the needs of diverse clients.

2. **Self-Awareness.** Social workers shall seek to develop an understanding of their own personal cultural values and beliefs as one way of appreciating the importance of multicultural identities in the lives of people.

3. **Cross-Cultural Knowledge.** Social workers have and continue to develop specialized knowledge and understanding about the history, traditions, values, family systems, and artistic expressions of major client groups that they serve.

4. **Cross-Cultural Skills.** Social workers shall use appropriate methodological approaches, skills, and techniques that reflect the workers' understanding of the role of culture in the helping process.

5. **Service Delivery.** Social workers shall be knowledgeable about and skillful in terms of services available in the community and broader society and be able to make appropriate referrals for their diverse clients.

6. **Empowerment and Advocacy.** Social workers shall be aware of the effect of social policies and programs on diverse client populations, advocating for and with clients whenever appropriate.

7. **Diverse Workforce.** Social workers shall support and advocate for recruitment, admissions, and hiring and retention efforts in social work programs and agencies that ensure the diversity within the profession.

8. **Professional Education.** Social workers shall advocate for and participate in educational and training programs that help advance cultural competence within the profession.

9. **Language Diversity.** Social workers shall seek to provide or advocate for the provision of information, referrals, and services in the language appropriate to the client, which may include use of interpreters.

10. **Cross-Cultural Leadership.** Social workers shall be able to communicate information about diverse client groups to other professionals.

SOURCE: Copyright 2001, National Association of Social Workers, Inc., *NASW Standards for Cultural Competence in Social Work Practice.*

What Is Cultural Competence?

Cultural competence is the capacity to respond appropriately to the various cultural environments in which we may participate, enabling us to strengthen our relationships and accomplish our mutual purposes. Cultural competence is both a value and an essential set of skills in our mobile, fluid society.

The National Association of Social Worker's (NASW, 2001) 10 standards of cultural competence in social work practice describe an array of knowledge, skills, and expected behaviors that demonstrate the ability to function effectively with diverse groups. They challenge professionals to increase awareness of their own attitudes and practices as well as awareness of conditions that harm or promote cultural respect. Further, they require social workers to take a leadership role in promoting the cultural awareness of other professionals. The National Organization for Human Services is considering weaving standards of cultural competence into their Code of Ethics to underscore the central role this plays in all human services work (Gates, 2009). Many other professions have developed standards for cultural competence. Check to see how the profession with which you most closely identify has addressed cultural competence.

Social workers and other human service professionals have a responsibility to improve their own capability, but they also need to foster competence in the organizations they develop or work for. Just as we reflect on our own practice, we must take leadership in assisting organizations to examine how prevailing policies and practices affect diverse groups.

The Technical Assistance Partnership for Child and Family Mental Health (TA Partnership) has put together a comprehensive implementation guide for cultural and linguistic competence (Martinez & Van Buren, 2008). This superb resource covers six different domains of an organization: governance and organizational infrastructure; services and supports; planning and continuous quality improvement; collaboration; communication; and workforce. Each domain addresses a number of distinct focus areas. The report provides implementation strategies, community examples/best practices, resources/tools, and performance indicators/measures for each domain with links to supporting material and real community examples.

The National Center for Cultural Competence (NCCP) underscores the importance of self-assessment as a tool to help health and human service organizations increase their capacity for relevant and effective cultural practices at the organizational level (Goode, Jones, & Mason, 2002). This self-assessment should help organizations do the following:

- Gauge the degree to which organizations are effectively addressing the needs and preferences of culturally and linguistically diverse groups;

- Establish partnerships that will meaningfully involve consumers and key community stakeholders;

- Improve consumer access to and utilization of services and enabling supports;

- Increase consumer satisfaction with services received;

- Strategically plan for the systematic incorporation of culturally and linguistically competent policies, structures, and practices;

- Allocate personnel and fiscal resources to enhance the delivery of services and enabling supports that are culturally and linguistically competent; and

- Determine individual and collective strengths and areas for growth.

The NASW Standards, the TA Partnership, and the NCCP self-assessment embrace the framework for achieving cultural competence developed by Cross, Bazron, Dennis, and Isaacs (1989). This framework involves the capacity to (1) value diversity, (2) conduct self-assessment, (3) recognize and relate effectively to the dynamics of difference, (4) acquire and institutionalize cultural knowledge, and (5) develop adaptations to programs and services to resonate with the cultural contexts of the individuals and communities served.

The first step in working with any group of people is to assume that you have much to learn about them, and they about you. Further, you need to learn about factors that influence your relationship. This is always true, but special attention and reflection is especially important in situations in which you are working with people whose culture and life experiences are different from your own.

To successfully work with anyone or any community, you must have some idea about how people see and relate to the world. You can only approach people within their frame of reference—their ability to recognize, pay attention to, and make sense of what is happening. Fundamental to this notion is the understanding that other people perceive the world in a different way than you do and that sometimes their perceptions are quite different. Respecting those differences shows that you value that other person. If you remain culturally insensitive or ignorant, you increase the risk that you will act in a way that is irrelevant or even offensive. This is hardly a promising style. Awareness of and respect for cultural differences recognizes the legitimacy of another's experience and its significance to your common enterprise (Gutierrez, 1995; Lum, 2004).

A few training workshops won't be enough. We all know that, but we don't seem to put that knowledge into practice very well. Delivering culturally appropriate direct services is more rare than common (Fong & Gibbs, 1995). It requires an honest commitment. The challenge to appreciate another's perspective, shaped by different experiences and cultural standards, has always been upon us. But today in the United States this challenge grows stronger.

Our Increasingly Diverse Society

The faces of this nation are changing. One of the
more fascinating developments is that in the 2000
census for the first time the U.S. Census Bureau
asked Americans to reflect on their multiracial and
multiethnic heritage. By allowing individuals to
select more than one racial or ethnic group with
whom they identify, the Census Bureau now has
more than 60 different categories of identification.
Almost 7 million Americans identified with more
than one group in the 2000 census (U.S. Census
Bureau, 2001), and the number of people who
identify themselves as being of two or more races
is projected to grow to more than 16 million by
2050. This provides a richer picture of the nation
and makes projections based on older groupings less
comparable. Though we cannot yet fully benefit
from looking at trends over time for a much
more diverse understanding of the U.S. population,
using projections based on earlier groupings, the
U.S. Census Bureau (1991, 2004, 2005, 2008a)
provides some useful insights on the palette that
paints the picture of America.

The population categorized as minority, now
about one third of the U.S. population, will
become the majority in 2042 and represent 54%
of the nation in 2050. The Hispanic or Latino population (Mexican, Central and South American,
Puerto Rican, Cuban, and other Spanish-speaking
peoples) is growing rapidly and is now the country's
second largest racial or ethnic group. This group of

Americans will nearly triple from almost 47 million
in 2008 to almost 133 million by 2050, growing
from 9% of the U.S. population in 1990 to over
30% in 2050. The Asian population is growing at
just about the same rate, from about 16 million in
2008 to more than 41 million in 2050, from 3% to
more than 9%. The African American population is
also experiencing a steady increase, from just over
41 million in 2008 to almost 68 million by 2050,
becoming 15% of the U.S. population at that time.
The number of American Indian and Alaska Native
Americans will approach 9 million in 2050, increasing from almost 5 million in 2008, accounting for
2% of the nation's population. The Native Hawi-
ian and Other Pacific Islander population is
expected to more than double from a little more
than 1 million to well over 2 million. The White
population will grow from 200 million to 203 million; this is the slowest growing population group
in the United States today. As a percentage of the
total U.S. population, the White population will
drop 20% between 2008 and 2050, from 66% of
the total to 46%.

Our population is growing older as well. In
2030 when all of the baby boomers have reached
the age of 65, nearly 1 in 5 residents will be 65 or
older. This age group will increase to almost 89
million by 2050, more than doubling the number
of almost 38 million older Americans in 2008. The
percentage of even older Americans, those 85 years
or older, will more than triple, from over 5 million
in 2008 to 19 million in 2050.

These population shifts bring into sharp focus
the need for people to learn more about one
another and more about cultural diversity itself.
We can less and less afford to live in ignorance.

Respect for cultural diversity requires that you
confront the fact of racism. Rooted in ignorance
and fear, racism pits different groups of people
against each other by viewing those who are different as a threat that must be contained, if not
defeated. Differences between groups are identified,
seen as evidence of some sort of defect in the other
group, and exaggerated. The other group then
comes to be explained or even defined in terms of
these exaggerated imperfections. These demeaning
attitudes are directed at different ethnic groups as
well as at different so-called racial groups.

CAPTURING CONCEPTS
Developing Cultural Sensitivity

The term **culture** gets tossed around pretty freely and has been defined broadly. In my view, culture represents the beliefs, norms, customs, and practices that groups use to affirm and convey their shared identity and to understand the world and guide their engagement of it.

Rivera and Erlich (1998) describe culture as "a collection of behaviors and beliefs that constitute standards for deciding what is, standards for deciding what can be, standards for deciding how one feels about it, standards for deciding what to do about it, and standards for deciding how to go about doing it" (p. 8). Barker (1999) defines culture as "the customs, habits, skills, technology, arts, values, ideology, science, and religious and political behavior of a group of people in a specific time period" (p. 114).

Notions of culture are not limited to identified ethnic groups. Many groups have developed standards or customs for interpreting the world and acting in it (Longres, 2000). Members of fraternities and sororities have their own culture. Employees of large public welfare agencies experience the culture of their organizations. Police officers have a special language and established codes of behavior that reflect their perception of their uniqueness. Regardless of the cultural group you may be addressing, cultural knowledge, cultural awareness, and cultural sensitivity are necessary to smooth your way.

When you take the time to familiarize yourself with selected cultural characteristics, such as the history, values, belief systems, and behaviors of the members of another group, you are acquiring **cultural knowledge** (Adams, 1995). You can use this knowledge to develop sensitivity and understanding of another ethnic group.

Cultural awareness usually involves internal changes in attitudes and values that emphasize the qualities of openness and flexibility that people

develop in relation to others. Cultural awareness must be supplemented with cultural knowledge (Adams, 1995).

Knowing that cultural differences as well as similarities exist, without assigning values (better or worse, right or wrong) to those cultural differences, is a sign of **cultural sensitivity** (Texas Department of Health, 1997).

"**Cultural competence** is a set of congruent behaviors, attitudes, and policies that come together in a system, agency, or among professionals and enables that system, agency, or those professionals to work effectively in cross-cultural situations" (Cross et al., 1989, p. 13). The Center for Effective Collaboration and Practice views competency in cross-cultural functioning as "learning new patterns of behavior and effectively applying them in the appropriate settings" (King, Simms, & Osher, 2000, p. 3). It includes an understanding of "the effect of culture on the person in environment—what an individual's culture means to him or her in all of his or her systems" (Segal et al., 2010, p. 157). Martin and Vaughn (2007) identify four components of cultural competence: awareness of one's own cultural worldview; attitude toward cultural differences; knowledge of different cultural practices and worldviews; and cross-cultural skills to understand, communicate with, and effectively interact with people across cultures.

Cultural competency emphasizes the idea of *effectively* operating in different cultural contexts using your knowledge, sensitivity, and awareness. "'This is beyond awareness or sensitivity,' says Marva Benjamin of the Georgetown Technical Assistance Center for Children's Mental Health" (Center for Effective Collaboration and Practice, 2006, p. 1). Lorraine Marais (2008, p. 5) asks, "Can we walk between worlds?"

The entire notion of race is ambiguous; Marger (2009) calls it "one of the most misunderstood, misused, and often dangerous concepts in the modern world" (p. 13). Racism has categorized people of different skin color, different religions, or different nationalities. Although the concept of race has

dubious scientific validity, the ideas of "different from" and "less than" can be very powerful.

Racism allows the fear and consequent dislike of others simply because they are members of different groups to have more potency than the belief in the potential for gain that could occur by working

together. It breaks down the ability of members of one group to work effectively with members of another. This is further aggravated by the perception that there is a limited rather than an expanding (or potentially expanding) set of resources over which groups must fight. One group's gain must therefore be seen as another's loss. Any attempt by one group to better its position must be done at the expense of the other. The group in the most advantaged position must protect the system that grants them their edge and to "rationalize and legitimate these patterns of dominance and subordination, and racism has usually served this function" (Marger, 2009, p. 19). These built-in advantages are so commonly accepted as normal by the privileged group that they don't even notice they are there. When those well-entrenched arrangements are challenged—when equal accommodations are sought by a less advantaged group or when one group seems to be thwarted in its efforts to improve its lot—conflict heightens the fears and divisions.

What is good or bad about a system in our society is measured against how it is seen as helping one group at the expense of another. That fear, recognized or not, acknowledged or not, colors almost all our perceptions. Competing groups hold one another responsible for what is going wrong (Marger, 2009; Shepard, 1991).

The expected way for members of diverse ethnic or racial groups to be successful is to deny their own culture in favor of adopting attributes of the dominant group. The dominant group, in many overt or subtle ways, demands allegiance to its own culture in exchange for social and economic benefits. By eroding the strength of diverse groups, the dominant group reduces the potential of diverse groups to threaten the status quo. Some members of diverse groups may try to resist this control by undermining or attacking the interests of the dominant group. Others, succumbing to hopelessness and despair, may exploit one another or simply refuse to participate at all. Still others may sacrifice their cultural identity to make economic gains while harboring a deep-seated resentment for the exchange they have made. Actions such as these result in a loss for all groups (Devore & Schlesinger, 2000).

Even the informal racism rooted in our institutions, norms, and traditions divides people and leads to differences in opportunity. These more subtle forms of racism perpetuate patterns of discrimination and their consequences. For example, Alesina and Glaeser (2004) examined a host of factors to better understand why European countries provide much more extensive welfare supports than the United States. They found that a fundamental reason for this difference is the range of diversity in the United States, along with an exploitation of that diversity to keep groups in conflict with each other. Richardson and London (2007) found that structural racism is the key factor contributing to persistent rural poverty and that efforts to reduce poverty could not be effective until barriers caused by historic racism were intentionally addressed. Many problems you will see as a worker are expressions of these fears and divisions. And as a worker your own relationship with the community you are trying to help may be colored by racism. Devaluing those who are different or the need to keep somebody different from getting ahead means that opportunities for mutual gain are squandered and a lot of people will be left behind. Further, efforts to help those suffering the effects from all this must be marginal, keeping the semblance of peace while preventing groups from stepping out of their place.

Racism has consequences for everyone involved in a community change effort. A group that has directly suffered from racism may need to confront not only the immediate issue at hand but the racist conditions that led to it and continue to support it. A group whose practices have limited another group's freedom and choice may need to examine whether their desired course of action in a particular circumstance perpetuates these practices. A multiethnic group may need to face the strain of a history of divisiveness.

Difficulties can arise when members of different cultural groups interact with one another. Some misunderstandings can be expected when groups have different cultural norms, rituals, and belief systems. However, when one group historically has politically, economically, and culturally subjugated another, limiting that group's opportunities and expressions, the undercurrents of tension and anxiety are profound. The burden becomes even heavier when members of the offending group are ignorant of this history or deny it altogether.

Certainly a possibility of such tension exists when White workers attempt to organize people of color or when groups that are predominately White attempt to collaborate with other people of color. This tension has affected, for example, the collaboration of White feminists and feminists of color. Women of color have harbored and have expressed deep dissatisfaction with an agenda focused too exclusively on gender, not giving sufficient attention to matters of White racism in which White women have participated (Gutierrez & Lewis, 1995; Lum, 2004). The failure of White feminists to acknowledge the role that racism plays in the lives of women of color has been a hindrance to more powerful action.

Marger (2009) reminds us that dominance of one group over another is an enduring fact of human life. In the United States this takes the form of Anglo conformity. Despite pluralistic rhetoric, "the preeminence of Anglo cultural values has consistently underlain public policies in education, language, law, welfare, and religion.... From the beginning, the expectation held sway that entering groups—immigrant, conquered, or enslaved—would conform to this core culture" (p. 115). Marger suggests that the following hierarchy can be identified in the United States today:

1. *Top tier:* White Protestants of various national origins, for whom ethnicity has no real significance except to distinguish them from the remainder of the ethnic hierarchy.

2. *Intermediate tier:* White ethnics of specific national origins (mostly Catholic and Jewish) and many Asians, for whom ethnicity continues to play a role in the distribution of society's rewards and continues to influence social life, but in both instances, decreasingly so.

3. *Bottom tier:* Racial/ethnic groups, including Blacks, Hispanics, American Indians, and some Asians, for whom ethnicity today has the greatest consequences and for whom it continues to shape the basic aspects of social life. (p. 135).

This hierarchy has remained amazingly resilient for a century and a half, and though distance among groups has been reduced, their rank order hasn't. Further, the gap between the bottom group and the other two is much greater than between the top two.

As an agent of community change, you cannot ignore the fact that these conditions affect you, the people with whom you work, and your relationships. Is it hopeless? Should we live only in fear and guilt? No, of course not. We should live in acknowledgment of this reality and in reflection on what our actions do to maintain or challenge disabling social conditions like racism. We should be challenged, not dispirited. Though these conditions are an aspect of our relationship, other aspects have meaning as well; among these is a belief in our abilities to contend with our impediments.

People of goodwill can build on their common interests and employ their unique strengths to break down barriers. We can learn.

Valuing Diversity

Diversity is a source for strengthening the effectiveness of groups who can learn how to draw forth its potential. In any situation in which you find yourself—school, neighborhood, job—you will be among people who are different from you in some ways and different from one another. This provides different perspectives, interpretations, tools, and predictive models for making sense of the world (Page, 2007). When used effectively, these differences can unlock creativity and dramatically improve quality and performance. When ignored, misunderstood, or mishandled, they can lead to discord and breakdown.

Understanding differences between groups is central to an appreciation of human diversity. Johnson (2001) points out, "though there are common human needs, people fulfill those needs in different ways" (p. 9). In fact, behavior cannot be understood apart from the cultural context in which it occurs. For example, going out in public with one side of your face painted blue and the other side painted white, further adorned by pictures of the devil, could raise a few eyebrows. If you compound that by yelling and wildly waving your arms, you could get arrested—unless you happen to be in Cameron Indoor Stadium, the University of Duke's basketball arena, cheering for the Duke Blue Devils. In this situation, your behavior is not only perfectly understandable but is encouraged. As Johnson

explains, affirming human diversity means understanding that "normal" behavior is situational. Behavior is "appropriate or inappropriate relative to the social situation in which a person is operating. What may be appropriate in one situation may be inappropriate in another" (p. 9).

Although it is important to appreciate differences, it is a mistake to regard all individuals solely in terms of the general traits of their culture. Shulman (1991) warns of the dangers of "teaching culturally specific techniques that are then implemented without regard to within-group heterogeneity" (p. 227). This results in new stereotypes that reduce members of the group to simple categories of behavior and response. Cormier and Hackney (1993) caution that knowing something about a culture does not mean that you know its individual members. Shulman (1991) also emphasizes a crucial skill that involves "the use of cultural knowledge to prepare for and to understand clients' lives and helping encounters while avoiding the trap of using generalizations to substitute for the here and now" (p. 228). He further points out that not differentiating in the "application of culturally sensitive principles can itself be an inadvertent form of racism" (p. 228). Members of any group vary in the extent of their identification with specific cultural characteristics. Acknowledging the potential for differences helps you to avoid replacing one stereotype with another.

What should you know to work with culturally diverse client groups? A general understanding of the cultures involved is a necessary first step (Nelson-Jones, 1992). Important cultural factors include values; ways of relating to other persons, the physical world, and the spiritual world; family structure and the nature of family relationships; history, including the meaning attached to change and development; communication patterns, including nonverbal aspects; community life and structure; and coping mechanisms (Johnson & Yanca, 2007). It is also important to understand the experience of the diverse group with the dominant culture (Corey & Corey, 2011; Devore & Schlesinger, 2000; Gutierrez & Lewis, 1995; Johnson & Yanca, 2007; Lum, 2004; Marger, 2009; Rivera & Erlich, 1998). For example, what is the history of this group? How much and what type of interaction has there been between the groups? What similarities and differences exist between the groups? How have group members reacted to efforts by the dominant group to control them? What impact have these experiences had on each group? By answering questions like these, you begin to develop an awareness of the sources of harmony and tension that are likely to affect the way members of different groups work together.

Rivera and Erlich (1998, pp. 13–17) list a number of important considerations when working with diverse communities of color:

- Become familiar with customs, traditions, social networks, and values.
- Learn the language and subgroup slang.
- Understand leadership styles and development.
- Know who has power, and recognize sources of mediating influences between ethnic communities and wider communities.
- Review past organizing strategies, and analyze their strengths and limitations.
- Acquire skills in conscientization (developing a critical consciousness) and empowerment.
- Acquire skills in assessing community psychology.
- Be aware of your personal strengths and limitations.

Rivera and Erlich wisely point out that these are a set of ideals, adding that "those few who have already attained the lofty heights described can probably also walk on water" (pp. 12–13).

Of all the things to know, perhaps the most important is to know yourself. Question the biases you hold, your fears, assumptions, expectations, intentions, desire and capability to learn, and the limitations of your own experiences. An honest appraisal will increase your self-awareness and give you confidence in gaining a better awareness of others. You will never master it all, not because it is hopeless but because it is a lifelong process of learning. Accept the simple fact that you can never fully understand another's experience and perspective. You can, however, move to greater and greater levels of understanding.

If you don't know something you need to know, ask. An important aspect of working with any client is your ability to gather information to increase your understanding. This is true whether the client is an individual or a community.

Here are a few more ideas that can increase your cultural competence:

- Find resource people, particularly from the community, who can help you understand the group with whom you will be working (Fong & Gibbs, 1995; Lum, 2004).
- Recognize that you are coming to the community not to do things for them but with them.
- Avoid romantically stereotyping any group. It's dishonest.
- Refuse to define any group solely in terms of its oppression. That is a demeaning and limiting view.
- Teach what you are learning. Do not support by your silence those words and behaviors that diminish members of other groups.
- Encourage other voices to speak, and listen to them.
- Acknowledge that your life experiences influence your perceptions and that other people's life experiences shape their perceptions as well. Acknowledge that these can be very different.

I cannot provide the key factors for each different group with whom you might be working. You will have to find out these things for yourself. Do be skeptical about anyone who purports to tell you all about any group. There are more than 500 Native American tribal groups; although there may be some common perspectives, there are some significant differences as well (Edwards & Edwards, 1995). Be wary of those who know what you should do when "working with Latinos." Which Latinos? Cubans? Salvadorans? Those living in the Southwest or those living in New York? I think you get the point. Members of groups with a common identity share many cultural beliefs, but there are distinct and important differences as well. Read, participate in community events, reflect on what does and does not work, talk to people, and, yes, do go to some of those workshops (Gutierrez & Lewis, 1995).

GLOBAL PERSPECTIVES

ROMANIA—In many Romanian families, violence against women is still seen as "normal."

A study conducted last year in spring by the Centre for Urban and Regional Sociology (CURS), in Bucharest, revealed that over 21 percent of women have faced assault, either in their current relationships or in the past.

A staggering 63 percent of women abused at home said the violence took place regularly and in multiple forms, from physical abuse and even sexual violence, to denigration and verbal humiliation....

Campaigners in Romania have very effectively used the media to break the public silence around the issue of domestic violence against women, and lobby for changes in laws.

Over many weeks, public interest ads featuring celebrities, both male and female, from the world of music and the electronic media, with artificial bruises and scars, have been telecast on many TV channels and discussed in the press and on blogs (Claudia Ciobanu, 2009).

SWEDEN/UNITED STATES—We live in a "global village," with a steadily increasing interdependence between "villagers." Our village has many problems and conflicts that require a great deal of goodwill and creativity to solve. There is one professional group in the village that has the specific qualifications needed to tackle the problems: professional social workers. But in order to be able to handle the rapidly changing situation, with all of the complicated problems, the whole

profession must be imbued with a broadened and enlightened vision, one that incorporates both a global consciousness and new types of knowledge and skills. As we move into the 21st century, the minimum requirement is that social workers should be prepared to work locally in an increasingly multicultural society. This requires an international consciousness so that we are aware of the ways in which global events and forces affect the world's peoples and how people find the strength to endure and grow (Geza Nagy & Diane Falk, 2000, p. 57).

ETHIOPIA—The development work being carried out by the indigenous Oromo NGO Hundee [resonates with Oromo culture]. Significantly, the word hundee designates "root(s)" and stands for the social and cultural origins of the Oromo. In particular, it refers to the primary or principal root, which the Oromo trace back to Horo, their apical ancestor. The term evokes the blood ties and the kinship affiliations that link the Oromo communities to one another in time and space. It stands, in short, for the people, their land and their culture.... Hundee's philosophy of development is based on the view that culture represents a fundamental force for social and economic change. This approach is founded on the premise that if meaningful development is to take place, it must build on the roots that have given the Oromo society its unique cultural identity (Aneesa Kassam, 2002, pp. 72–73).

CANADA—The growing diversity of society and organizations means that we need to make greater efforts to include those with different backgrounds, interests and perspectives in the processes of leadership and governance, if we want those processes to be legitimate and effective.... Greater inclusion of diverse people and perspectives is most likely to occur when the value of that inclusion can be connected to the achievement of broader organizational and societal goals. An understanding of that connection is far more likely to motivate sustainable positive action and real results than are externally imposed standards and accountability measures (Steven Rosell, 2000, p. 14).

TANZANIA—[The late Julius Nyerere, president of Tanzania for 20 years, was asked by World Bank experts "Why have you failed?"] Nyerere answered: "The British Empire left us a country with 85 percent illiterates, two engineers, and 12 doctors. When I left office [in 1985], we had 9 percent illiterates and thousands of engineers and doctors. I left office 13 years ago. Then our income per capita was twice what it is today; now we have one-third less children in our schools and public health and social services are in ruins. During these 13 years, Tanzania has done everything that the World Bank and the International Monetary fund have demanded."

And Julius Nyerere passed the question back to the World Bank experts: "Why have you failed?" (as cited in Poley, 2001, p. 164).

With all this emphasis on differences, do not lose sight of the many similarities among people. By exaggerating differences or focusing on them to the exclusion of our similarities, we run the risk of overemphasizing our separateness (Corey & Corey, 2011). This can make it very difficult for people of different cultures to acknowledge their ability to work together.

Working for social justice is clearly linked with working to end practices supported by and contributing to cultural ignorance and intolerance. Your ability to effectively promote change requires that you continually learn how to make your own work meaningful and effective with diverse populations. Further, you have a responsibility to reflect on how your own cultural beliefs and practices affect your relationships with the people you serve.

Cultural diversity is a powerful fact of everyday life. While this may be somewhat new in our awareness, it has, of course, existed as long as there have been different cultures. Because culture so strongly influences how we see and make sense of the world in order to act in it, I have given it special attention. There are, of course, many different forms of diversity. Each characteristic that we have may be shared with others and may differentiate us from others. Within any population you will find similarities and differences. Those who share the similarities may well share some common perspectives and rituals that can assume a cultural dimension. Although some of these cultural attributes may be just slight, some may be significant. Forms of diversity can be related to gender, age, class, sexual orientation, urban/rural, physical or mental abilities, belief (such as religious faith), education, and on and on. Differences can provide a rich set of perspectives to strengthen understanding and action. They can spawn fear and prejudice as well. It is important to understand that although you share many things in common with the community you are helping to organize, there are differences as well.

THE COMMUNITY AS CLIENT

When we hear the word *client,* most of us think of an individual who needs some assistance to solve a personal problem. But you can have a professional relationship with a community of people as well (Figure 1.1). Just like an individual or a family, a community has resources and limitations. Communities have established coping mechanisms to deal with problems. To promote change in a community, the community must believe in its own ability to change and must take

responsibility for its actions or inactions. Communities warrant professional partnership.

Some problems are community problems. They directly or indirectly touch most if not every member of the community. Gang violence, AIDS, and inadequate health care will persist if we work on them only at the individual level. Community problems must be addressed by the community that feels the problem. When you are able to see the community as a distinct entity capable of taking action, you understand that you can relate to the community as a partner in an effort to promote well-being (Kettner, Daley, & Nichols, 1985).

Jim Jackson came into class Monday morning, late, and he was fuming. "Mr. Jackson," the professor commented, "it looks like your week is getting off to a bad start." "Damn bookstore," Jim snapped.

Once again the campus bookstore had unlocked its doors 10 minutes later than the posted 8:30 a.m. opening time. Even if it did open on time, many students almost certainly would be late because their classes begin at 8:40 a.m. Students often schedule classes back-to-back and dash off to jobs as soon as class is over. There just is not a lot of time to buy books once the semester starts. Class cancellations and other schedule changes over the first couple of weeks of the semester can also make for trying times for many students.

The professor and the rest of the class could offer a little group support by letting Jim blow off steam and by showing him that they understand it has been a frustrating morning for him. A couple of students might comment that they too have experienced similar exasperation. Maybe group members will share books until Jim can get his own. It is also possible that someone can sit down with Jim to help him plan his schedule differently so he can get to the bookstore when it is open and still make it to class on time. All these approaches have some benefit, but the problem remains. They put a bandage on the situation, providing some attention to the discomfort and a little temporary relief while covering the real sore from view. The fact is that Jim is not the only person affected by the bookstore's insensitivity and poor planning. The entire class has been involved—some have had the same experience as Jim, others have had class disrupted by an

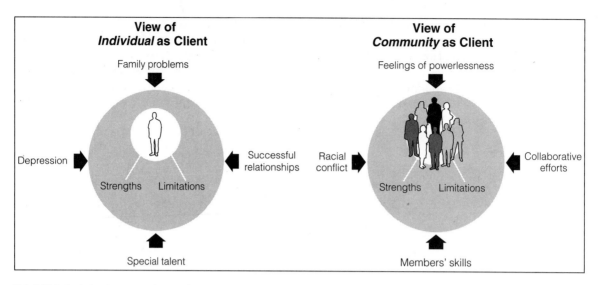

FIGURE 1.1 Conceptualizing the Client

angry latecomer. The bookstore's policies and practices affect the student community, not just Jim.

Once this is realized, the focus can shift from helping Jim to improving the community. It doesn't take long for the class to work out a strategy for involving other students in confronting the bookstore about its hours of operation, especially during the first month of the semester. By looking at the student community as the "client" in need of attention, the perception provides a strategy for change that does more than temporarily relieve one person's discomfort.

There are many examples of the community as client. Perhaps a major employer pulls out of town, throwing the whole community into crisis. Those who have lost their jobs are in a daze. So, too, are the shopkeepers whose businesses will suffer. So are the educators who see a major part of the tax base disappear. How will the community come together to deal with this disruption of so many lives? How will it attend to immediate needs as well as long-term ones? Or will this crisis further weaken an endangered community?

The suicide of a popular high school student shocks a small rural town. His parents and friends are distraught, and the entire student body is stunned. Is a community response to the tragedy possible?

Recognizing that people share common interests allows you to approach the community in a way that unifies individual concerns and capabilities. This is a much more powerful approach than separating each individual problem, one from the other. Certainly, individuals experience common problems in unique ways. Yet by acting on the commonness of experience rather than the uniqueness, you open the door to the possibility of shared action. This orientation allows for the combination of energy and resources to create fundamental community change.

TARGETS FOR COMMUNITY CHANGE

Where can you start? How can you begin to make an impact on your community? Your desire to improve conditions you and the people you assist face can take you into five basic arenas of action. In addition to being active in the community itself, you can have a considerable effect by making efforts to improve the service delivery system, directing attention to your own agency, working in the political field, or taking action through the courts. A variety of different settings or organizational sponsors can be home to community change efforts. Some may be the focus of your efforts, some may support the work you do elsewhere, and some can be both. Most commonly you will find this work done in and through neighborhoods, schools, faith communities, health and human service organizations, professional associations (including labor), interest group organizations (such as child welfare), and political organizations.

Community Development and Organization

Of the many forms of community activities, six are fairly typical for change agents.

1. *Community development* links people with one another and with different types of wealth in the community to change conditions leading to improvement in the quality of life. These activities start with currently available assets to put into place new community resources, attitudes, and practices that continue to expand the community's potential to provide for full and meaningful lives for its members. Development can occur within a neighborhood or beyond a neighborhood to include a broader community of people with shared interests. The community development approach is discussed in more detail in Chapter 2.

2. *Neighborhood empowerment* helps people within a particular geographic area develop their resources and lay claim to their right to control their own destiny. After the family, the neighborhood is the first building block of the community. Helping people in a neighborhood band together to determine their own living conditions is a primary strategy for improving the quality of a community. Approaches to strengthening neighborhoods are discussed in depth in Chapter 13.

3. *Community problem solving* is another approach for bringing people together. Using this method, you bring together various, even apparently competing interests within a community to creatively resolve a particular problem that affects them all. Crime, transportation, education, or environmental concerns could be the focus of such an effort. Though no per-

manent organization for redistributing community power is likely to be put in place, this approach is liable to stimulate a discovery of underlying community issues that may be the focus of future problem-solving efforts. Further, members of the community gain experience working with one another, which may have benefits beyond the resolution of the particular problem being tackled at the moment.

4. *Developing community support systems* is another way to promote community change efforts. This approach counters the painful aspect of living in a community of strangers. People who do not feel they are part of the community live in numbing isolation, struggling alone against problems that can overwhelm them. A community is a rich source of sustenance that can offer practical assistance and psychological support, but people need to find each other amid all the noise and confusion. Developing community support systems provides the means for community members to be in routine contact with one another in a climate of giving and receiving. They go beyond complaining and consoling to development methods of mutual assistance. Parents grappling with the challenges of caring for children with mental illnesses, teens struggling with the consequences of pregnancy, human services workers feeling separated from the ideals that originally brought them to their profession—all could gain strength from a system of mutual assistance and support. This set of activities reflects a development orientation.

5. *Community education* is a basic means for assisting the community by bringing matters to the community's attention and preparing it for knowledgeable action. Keeping the community from ignoring the interests of its citizens or from relying on myths to guide its direction is a steady challenge.

6. *Developing a broad-based community organization* that wields real power and works to redistribute community resources and access to community decision making is a meaningful approach for producing far-reaching change.

The presence of such an organization establishes a new force within the community to recognize and take sustained action on issues that affect people other than the rich and powerful. These organizations activate many members of the community to press for a clearly articulated issue agenda. They often use the strength (including the financial support) of significant community institutions, such as religious congregations, as critical building blocks. In larger communities these organizations mobilize thousands of people. Unless you intend to specialize in the practice of community organization and development, you will probably not serve as the lead organizer of such a group. However, there will be many important leadership roles within this type of organization that you can fill.

Improving the Service Delivery System

An emphasis on services as the main method of improving conditions that affect people is limited and may well serve to maintain an unjust status quo. Some services are useful, however, and a change agent can help improve their effectiveness and even alter their orientation. Also, given the sheer number of services, there are many occasions to have an impact. At least five opportunities await you if you want to make improvements in the service arena:

- Change program regulations.
- Improve program orientation and delivery.
- Encourage collaboration between agencies.
- Develop a new program.
- Empower clients.

Public program regulations, believe it or not, are not always developed with a keen eye for discerning the most effective manner of benefiting program participants. Sometimes those who establish the rules are looking out for other interests (Fabricant, 1985; Lipsky, 1984). You will face regulations that frustrate at least as much as they help. You can join the chorus of souls who would rather complain than act, or you can start your own choir, giving voice to the need for

change. Confronting regulations that hinder your work will make life easier for you and for the people you work with. Many workers simply conclude that "those are the rules and we can't change them." They are wrong. Yes, regulations established by the federal government are more difficult to change than regulations generated by local authorities, but any and all are subject to scrutiny and modification. A well-organized group, perhaps working in alliance with other groups, can make great improvements in services simply by changing regulations, thereby helping a program work better.

Similarly, remaining attentive to opportunities for program improvement can lead you to helpful changes in the way services are provided. Experimenting with program design and service methods can result in significant benefits for both the sponsoring agency and the participant. By capitalizing on a desire by both line staff and management to do a better job more easily, you can accomplish some significant gains. Old habits and other barriers to innovation exist, but forces for program improvement also exist in most situations. Service improvement includes reexamining the very orientation of the program. Does the service keep participants isolated from each other, dependent on the agency, and divorced from acknowledging community conditions that affect them? Are participants defined only in terms of a need and treated as needy? Does the service replace forms of community responsibility and potential for community strengthening? If any part of any of these questions is true, you will find some openings for productive engagement.

Collaboration between human services agencies is not a common state of affairs in many communities. Not only do agencies not work with each other, they sometimes undermine one another's efforts. This can be baffling and discouraging to new human services workers, and it certainly can interfere with participants' opportunities to receive the best services. Helping agencies overcome their individualistic ways and their jealousies and fears of working together, even on a very limited project, can provide for the creative and efficient use of limited resources and set the stage for future collaborative efforts. Developing a new human services program or agency to add to the community's arsenal of resources is an exciting and productive endeavor. This kind of activity sparks the creative interest of people who not only like the prospect of providing a needed service but who also enjoy the process of bringing an idea to life.

Organizing clients is an underused approach to upgrading community services. Actively assisting client populations to act powerfully to hold the service delivery system accountable is not a common human services activity. Neither do human services workers routinely and systematically involve participants in planning, developing, and refining services in a way that vests them with real authority. Given what we profess about the right of the client to self-determination and the need for clients to recognize and assume responsibility for important aspects of their lives, client involvement would seem to be almost automatic. It is not. A counseling approach that so routinely denies clients' input and responsible decision making would be roundly criticized in professional circles. Yet paternalistic attitudes regarding what is best for the client remain fairly unchallenged in the arena of service delivery. This state of affairs offers a wonderful opportunity to human services workers who seek fundamental changes in the way services are provided. Certainly, such an approach must include an awareness of the risks. Altering the perception of clients as powerless and dependent is a challenge in itself. Regarding those who make use of public programs as relatively powerless and dependent sustains the interests of many individuals both inside and outside the human services system. You must understand that those interests will feel threatened when you work to increase client participation in decision making.

Making Improvements Within Your Own Agency

You will not often need to look beyond your own agency to recognize situations that call for change. Much of what you can do to improve the human services system in your community applies just as well to the organization for which you work. Needed changes in agency regulations, policies, or procedures may demand your attention. You will have the opportunity to create new programs or to improve existing ones to respond to local conditions. Seeing your own agency as a community of people engaged in a shared enterprise will give you opportunity and direction for using worker talents and other assets to promote conditions within the agency that foster an environment of personal development and effective, common purpose. Developing more cooperative working relationships among members of the staff and volunteers may well be a necessity. Finally, helping participants have a legitimate say over the way services are developed and enacted will undoubtedly be both a challenge and an opportunity.

Few systems, in fact none that I can think of, are created perfectly. It is always possible to make things better. This is as true for your own agency as it is for any other system we humans have fashioned. Chapter 14 is dedicated to helping you be effective in promoting change in your agency.

Policy Change and Political Involvement

Public policies profoundly affect many situations you face as a human services worker. Policies can maintain unjust practices or remove them. Policies can provide what is available to benefit people or to severely restrict them. Your participation in the political process can lead to profound changes in people's lives. It occurs in two fundamental areas. The first and most obvious is electing people to office in the first place. In this instance you will be working in a political campaign. The second involves dealing with the people who have been elected, working to influence them as they perform the duties of their office. This work is generally referred to as lobbying. (Although lobbying is most often directed at elected officials, it is not limited to them. Other policymakers, such as regulators, can be the focus of lobbying activities.) Lobbying involves your use of argument and political power to help shape the development of public policy, usually by refining and promoting the passage of "good" policies, or by blocking the advancement of "bad" ones. Lobbying is the focus of Chapter 15.

Working to elect or to influence government officials at local, state, or national levels is a powerful means of affecting policies that regulate behavior as well as those that shape how existing resources are distributed and who has access to policies that are being developed. The efforts of an organized, dedicated group of people can have a tremendous impact here, even if these people do not have much money. Don't accept the myth that nonprofits are not permitted to lobby. They can. (This is discussed further in Chapter 15.)

Using the Courts

Shaping laws through the political process may contribute to improving conditions in your community, but using those laws currently in place may have far-reaching consequences as well. The courts do not solve all our problems for us, but they can "mediate interpretations of our own indecisiveness" (Pollack, 2003, p. 1). Essentially, this is what you are doing when you work through the courts.

You may well find that the rights of the people you serve are being ignored and, in practice, denied. Litigation can secure the action the people you work with require. Getting powerful interests in the community to apply rights and protections equally to all its citizens may take more than good intentions. The courts may have to step in and hold individuals or even the public at large accountable. Legal action is examined in Chapter 12.

Opportunities for taking part in the process of strengthening your community are plentiful. Through your participation, you may gain experience in a wide variety of change venues. Much like different games, each arena will hold its special appeal and unique challenges. You will come to appreciate the impact you can have regardless of where you perform.

A MODEST RECOGNITION OF IDEALISM

Most real progress occurs when individuals take hold of the idea that there is a better, more humane, or more just way. They assert that our capacity for excellence, in ourselves and in our affairs with one another, matters and that acting on that capacity is as much a choice as is rejecting it. These people are just not willing to settle for mediocrity or meanness; they are idealists.

Idealism is the belief that things could be better, that they should be better, and that an individual can play a part in making them so. This is not easy. Idealism requires faith, commitment, and courage. There is certainly an imposing array of forces to push back against a belief in a higher purpose. Greed, corruption, selfishness, deceit, and their kin are real, and they easily discourage the faint of heart.

It requires no challenge to be seduced into cynicism. Cynicism is a cowardly condition. It is resignation, a retreat from the test of principle. It is easy. In an attempt to justify an unwillingness to contend, cynicism argues for impotence. Cynicism turns away because it cannot face up to the demands of character.

Idealism is not to be confused with naiveté. Idealism is a purposeful, powerful belief. A real idealist is willing to take a hard, uncompromising look at the world and reckon with it, trusting in his or her own power, the strength of decency, and others who share those convictions. An idealist simply refuses to capitulate to a plodding dullness of spirit. Francisco Sagasti (1990) said, "at least we have the capacity to imagine a better situation than the one we are in at present.... The basis of our optimism is being able to link imagination, visions of what can be better, what can work...to existing situations... and work out from them."

Someone may say to you, "You are an idealist." Take it as a compliment.

CONCLUSION

No matter what role you play in providing human services, you will recognize opportunities to determine a new direction in furthering human growth.

Sometimes it will not be enough to tackle problems one at a time or to tolerate inefficiencies or abuses that are an affront to human dignity. You will not allow ignorance to keep problems alive, and you will no longer accept community problems as inevitable or unsolvable.

You will acknowledge that there are a number of sources of community problems, but there is also a huge reservoir of concern and resources to deal with them. You will recognize that others share your capacity to care and to act.

You will come to believe you can make a contribution in a fundamental way. You will learn how to overcome your own and others' resistance to change. You will combine your talents and actions with others in ways that increase your belief in your abilities and your potential to make a difference.

You will come to see that problems are not isolated phenomena touching individuals only. You will see how they affect a community of people, and you will work with that community to solve them. You will recognize and respect the different cultural perspectives on the issues all of you face. You will learn how the unique strengths of different cultures add vitality to your overall effort. You will become competent in building respectful relationships with people whose culture is different from yours.

You will learn different ways to express your interest in making things better. You may work to help a neighborhood develop or utilize its resources. You may start a new program in response to a recognized community issue. You may help elect an ally to office. Or you may work to determine a greater role for community members in changing conditions or shaping the services that can improve the quality of their lives.

You will hold to your ideals, and you will act on them. You will have understood well the challenge to change.

ENOUGH OF NOT ENOUGH

Aleisha didn't show up today. She got evicted. Well, she and her kids got evicted, and now she's disappeared. He could see Aleisha for all the authorized sessions. He could see her sister too, and maybe even her neighbor, and the neighbor's cousin and friend. Maybe, if he lasts a few more years, he could see Aleisha's children, if anyone ever finds them.

It's just not enough. Alvin knew that. Five years now, 5 years of long days and the statistics keep getting worse. Behind each of those numbers, each one of the hundreds or thousands or even millions of numbers—depending on which set of numbers you're looking at and how far your gaze takes you—behind each one there is a face and a story. There are more faces than 5 years ago it seems. More poverty, more meth, more border crossers dying in the desert. There just doesn't seem to be more outrage though, just more acceptance of all this, and maybe that's the worst more of all. What's one man, one woman to do, Alvin wonders. Find out if there are other men and other women who are thinking the same thing, I guess, he answers himself. Surely, I can't be the only person in this profession, even the only person in this office, who feels the same way. I've heard the grumbling, the complaints. So why are we content with just nodding our heads to each other in understanding? Don't we think that it's our job to do something about those numbers, those faces? Or is our job simply to wait until they become numbers before we get involved? It's not like we're not working; maybe we're not doing the right work. What could we here in our office do? What's a starting point for us? What do we have that we can use? Who could we get to join us or whom do we join? How can we get that feeling again that what we do matters? That all of us working together feel and really are powerful? What *could* we do? What do I have to learn? Maybe the real question is—what do I have to decide?

So many questions, but Alvin finds himself leaning forward, not settling back. The questions are more intriguing than daunting. We're connected to lots of different people, he thinks. Clients, for starters. Is that the only way to think about them? Of course, my colleagues here, and there are people from other agencies and organizations. The local government officials and staff we work with might be interested, even the police. There are also the businesspeople who feel good about giving us money from time to time, the high school kids, and the people from different faith communities, who have done things for us. Lots of people who look at things so differently, who don't even speak the same language.

I'm starting to get a little carried away. I've got lots of clients to see, he sighs. But he does some-thing curious. He doesn't reach for a case file. He reaches for his pen, makes a few notes and picks up the phone. Shay answers. "Shay, it's Alvin. Want to get an early lunch? I'm buying. I've been thinking of some things that I want to talk about with you."

REFLECTION QUESTIONS

1. Can Alvin really do anything to change those numbers?

2. How is it that we have come to accept serious social problems as "that's the way things are"?

3. How can people come to feel powerful in challenging conditions?

4. What is needed to get a diverse group of people working together effectively?

5. What might be available in Alvin's situation that he could use?

6. How long will Alvin keep going in what seems to be a new direction? What will determine the answer?

7. What does Alvin need to decide?

8. Who will be included in Alvin's work? Who might get left out?

9. What notes did Alvin scribble? What will Alvin say to Shay? How will she respond?

GROUP ACTIVITY: OVERCOMING RETICENCE TO CHANGE

There are many reasons we and others don't act to promote needed change. The more we recognize what gets in our way, and the more we recognize what we have to help us move past those barriers, the more likely we will be to do some of the things that need to be done.

Divide into teams of four members. You and your team will examine the Moment to Discover on page 12 or page 14.

1. As a team, decide which Moment to Discover will be the focus of your discussion. (2 minutes)

2. Review the material individually and select the three statements that resonate most with you. (2 minutes)

3. Select one that you would like to change, and develop one strategy for changing that response. (2 minutes)

4. Discuss the Moment to Discover as a team, identifying one of each person's statements and strategies. (10 minutes)

5. As a team, prepare a report regarding the three most important things you learned that you could teach to the larger group. (5 minutes)

6. Teach your lesson to the larger group. (2 minutes)

HELPFUL WEBSITES

Links to the organizations briefly described here are on the companion website at www.cengage.com/humansvcs/homan.

U.S. Department of Health and Human Services. The department has developed National Standards for Culturally and Linguistically Appropriate Services in Health Care. The final report was issued in March 2001 and includes a glossary that has a definition of cultural competence.

Spirit of 1848. The Spirit of 1848 is a network of people concerned about social inequalities in health. Their purpose is to spur new connections among those involved in different areas of public health who are working on diverse public health issues (whether as researchers, practitioners, teachers, activists, or all of the above) and live scattered across diverse regions of the United States and other countries. The focus is to understand and change how social divisions based on social class, race/ethnicity, gender, sexual identity, and age affect the public's health.

Industrial Areas Foundation (IAF). Founded by legendary organizer and author Saul Alinsky, the IAF trains organizers and builds organizations whose primary purpose is power—the ability to act—and whose chief product is social change. The site offers case examples of social action organizations, information on IAF affiliates throughout the nation, contacts with IAF staff, and a few books related to social action organizing.

Georgetown University. The university provides direction to individuals and organizations that intend to increase their cultural competence. This site has links to other organizations and publications and provides direct responses to your questions.

Center on Budget and Policy Priorities. The center offers excellent analyses on budget issues and has up-to-date information, numerous publications, and a very helpful staff. This a great place to begin exploring budget issues that affect everyday Americans.

U.S. Census Bureau. Tasked with tracking population trends in the United States, the Census Bureau is your starting point to a treasure-trove of information.

Massive Change. All economies and ecologies are becoming global, relational, and interconnected. To understand and harness these emerging forces, there is an urgent need to articulate precisely what we are doing to ourselves and to our world. This is the ambition of Massive Change, which asks the question, "Now that we can do anything, what will we do?"

Chapter 2

Theoretical Frameworks for Community Change

CHAPTER HIGHLIGHTS

- Systems theory offers insight to community functioning
- Chaos theory suggests small changes can have big consequences
- Healthy communities produce healthy people
- Nine domains of community capital
- Key role of social capital
- Theories of power, organizing, action, and culture affect change
- Close communities provide a context for action

- Conflicts, crises, and relationships can promote action
- Organizing models for community change
- Change can transform as well as fix
- Theory and philosophy of praxiology
- Appreciative inquiry
- Community development model can strengthen the community
- Social action can initiate community development

Principles can direct action for change, but they are like so many puzzle pieces scattered over the kitchen table. To begin to make some sense out of the emerging picture, it is often helpful to find those pieces with a straight side—the frame that holds the picture together. Fundamental principles provide such a frame for understanding how you can promote action to change conditions that affect people. This framework does not reveal the whole picture, just its outlines, and maybe a few central ideas you can build around. Other concepts will be provided throughout this book. Fitting those concepts together will help you bring your own picture to life.

Through organized action, you can indeed make a difference. Deciding to do the best you can is all that is required to start. Understanding some basic notions about how all this works will make it a lot easier for you. A commitment to continue learning doesn't guarantee success, but it certainly increases the chance of a successful outcome.

The framework for action presented in this chapter provides the foundation theories and organizing models you will need to shape your efforts to promote change. Why should you even care about theory when it is the action that makes the difference? Isn't discussion of theory a way to keep from having to deal with the demands of change that the real world thrusts on us, ready for action or not? After all, don't we live in a real world instead of a theoretical one?

Good questions. I've asked them myself. In fact, asking questions will lead you toward becoming a more grounded promoter of change. Asking questions will help you become a good theorist as well. You see, a good promoter of change is well grounded in theory (Martinez-Brawley, 2000).

Action does make the difference, but if you do not transfer your learning from one situation to another, you are always making it up as you go along. That means that your strategies and tactics are based on guesswork or maybe faith in inspiration—pretty inefficient. Frankly, most of us act in accordance with some theory, some notion that if I take some particular action I predict that some particular result will occur. Or for me to take a particular action, I first need to have a particular set of things in place. Whether that has to do with buying a car, asking someone for a date, or changing harmful conditions in a community, we usually are guided by some type of theory. Sometimes we know what it is; sometimes it is murkier.

This chapter brings theoretical principles and conceptual models into the light, so you are clearly aware of the ideas that guide your actions, making them more purposeful, and probably more effective. Good theory will help you know what to expect and what you can do about it. Also, like any other tool, good theory should be easy to understand and use.

The fundamental theory of change is that good theory will produce good action, and good action will produce good results. A related theory is that purposefully learning from your experience will provide better theory, which in turn leads to better action. Theory devoid of action may be irrelevant. Action devoid of theory may be irrelevant as well.

Although no manageable set of theories can hope to describe every dimension of human interaction, a number of foundation theoretical frameworks and propositions inform work for community change. *Systems theory* is the fundamental operating theory, offering an overview of how things work; that is, explaining what each living thing needs to do to survive and take care of itself. Systems theory demonstrates the dynamics of connections within entities as well among entities within a broader system. It will help you make sense of what is happening around you, why people and institutions are acting and reacting the way they do, and what might be needed to get them to act differently. *Chaos theory* will help you see that small changes can have large, often unpredictable consequences.

Healthy communities focus on increasing the health of communities, helping them to function better to meet the needs and promote the development of their individual members. As this is the intended outcome of your work, it's a good idea to consider just what makes a healthy community.

The idea of close communities provides the most relevant context for change activities because it is here we most clearly feel the need to act and believe we can make the most difference. Change agents who can connect their work in close communities with others can create a force for broader change.

The *theory of community change* will help you see what agents of change must take into account as they act to promote purposeful change. *Appreciative inquiry theory,* when applied to *transformation, praxis,* and *community development,* will bring the four *cornerstone principles of community building* to life. A review of *organizing models for community change* will help you see how theory is connected to various approaches for producing change.

You will recognize elements described in this framework for action in the chapters that follow—sometimes in the forefront, sometimes singing harmony in the chorus. Other basic concepts of change will inform your understanding of how you can act to increase the health of your community.

SYSTEMS THEORY AND COMMUNITIES

Each organism—a city, a neighborhood, an individual—is a system that requires ongoing input in the form of nutrients and other energy. The system takes in energy to grow, produce, and sustain life and to maintain its equilibrium. Maintaining equilibrium or balance is one of the core concerns of any system. A system acts when it feels out of balance. Though a system may act to regain balance, it may do so without adequately addressing the need or discomfort that created the imbalance to begin with. It can be a temporary adjustment or fix, leading the system to respond with temporary fixes to chronic conditions that the system doesn't recognize or feel able to deal with. A system will more likely take radical action when it is more aware of conditions that affect it and when the imbalance has achieved the level of crisis.

A number of authors have helped inform my view of systems, among them Anderson, Carter, and Lowe (1999); Cowan and Egan (1979); Brill and Levine (2005); Senge, Kleiner, Roberts, Ross, and Smith (1994); Dubois and Krogsrud-Miley (2005); Johnson and Schwartz (1997); Kirst-Ashman and Hull (2009); Lumsden, Lumsden, and Wiethoff (2010); Napier and Gershenfeld (2004); Nicholas (2003); and Schmolling, Youkeles, and Burger (1997). The notion of systems theory is consistent with the ecological perspective of human interaction. All systems sit within a broader environment in which a variety of forces are acting. A reciprocal relationship exists between the system and the environment in which it operates. That is, when a system acts, it creates a number of reactions in the broader environment. What occurs in the broader environment also produces responses within the system. Sometimes what occurs in the relationship is intentional; there is a mutual exchange. Often actions and reactions are not planned or purposeful. Yet even in these cases there is an effect on both the system and the larger environment. This broader environment may be a source of nourishment or toxins. Managing this relationship effectively is a vital matter for the health of the system.

Those outside the system may recognize or point out needs, but only when those within the system adopt this belief will genuine action take place. Although actions may be taken in response to another's intervention, these actions may be superficial, designed to meet the need of pleasing the other party (system) or offsetting the use of resources that resistance would require.

For example, when you were younger, your mom may have often pointed out that you needed to clean up your room. You didn't feel this need, but you halfheartedly cleaned up the room to avoid some other discomfort. Perhaps a neighborhood engages in discriminatory housing practices. If the people in the neighborhood do not feel the need for open access, they will make only halfhearted attempts to avoid lawsuits, attorney's fees, and other consequences. If these same neighbors begin to value all potential members, they will act on their own to ensure openness.

As the system processes the input it receives, this energy is converted to productive output, which is expressed in activity (such as work), in seeking new input, or in discarding used input as waste. Further, each system interprets the reactions it receives from the broader environment and makes adjustments, operating as a thermostat to regulate itself and maintain social balance.

All systems act to meet needs for survival, if not growth. When a need is felt, the system experiences a kind of imbalance, which leads to action to meet the need. The cycle of a system is to effectively take in energy, deliver that energy to parts that need it, use the energy, and express its use in the form of productivity or waste and use the responses to its actions as feedback for new input. Anything that impairs its ability to do any of these things will harm the system. Anything that promotes its ability will strengthen the system. If subsystems act inefficiently or ineffectively, using methods that are harmful to the system, the system as a whole suffers. If the system uses methods that harm other systems, the relationships between systems suffer, and what the system would otherwise receive from the relationship is diminished or tainted. If the system does not recognize or misinterprets the responses to its actions, its future choices may be misguided.

For example, a person who abuses alcohol to numb emotional pain can experience illness and emotional distress. The part of that individual system that craves alcohol will harm other parts of the system that don't hold such a powerful influence over the system's behavior. Or consider a community agency that exploits its workers, demanding high caseloads and paying low salaries. It is likely to suffer from high turnover, low morale, and poor productivity. If that same agency is uncooperative with other agencies and misrepresents how it uses its money, it may suffer a loss of its reputation in the community, lose opportunities for collaborative partnerships, and even see its funding terminated.

Another important aspect of systems theory is the notion that a system operates in some degree of relationship to other systems. Further, each particular system is part of a larger set of systems and is itself made up of smaller sets of systems. For example, a neighborhood is part of a city, which is part of a county, which is part of a state, and so on. Within the neighborhood itself are several streets, and on each street are a number of households, and within each household are individuals. Even individuals are made up of various smaller systems, such as a respiratory system, a skeletal system, and so on.

No matter which system you look at, it must be able to meet its needs and nourish its internal parts while at the same time managing its relationships with the series of larger systems within which it lives.

As a result of the interconnectedness of systems, what happens in any part of the system affects the entire system, and what occurs outside the system can also affect the system. To take a closer look at how this works, imagine that the system we are talking about is you. If you have too much harmful food or drink in your stomach, your well-being is affected. You feel pain in a part of your body, you don't feel like moving around or going to work, and even your outlook on life suffers. One of your subsystems—your digestive system—has affected how your whole body functions today. Now let's say that you are feeling fine until you learn that the plant where you work is being closed and you are going to be out of a job. In this case something that has occurred outside yourself—in another system—affects your well-being.

Whether the system is an individual or a family or a community, transactions that occur within and between systems can affect a number of people. The closer you are to the transaction, the more strongly you will feel its effect. You feel your stomachache or your loss of a job more keenly than other members of your household do, but they are likely to be affected as well. Your immediate neighbors, the places where you shop, and other people whom your life touches may also be affected, but the more distant their connection with you, the less likely they are to notice.

Systems theory helps us understand that the actions of a group of people within the community can positively or negatively affect the health of the community and its members, resulting in an opportunity or a risk. It can also help us to see that actions that occur outside the community itself also affect community health. Here, too, are conditions of opportunity or risk.

A healthy community takes care of its component parts while conducting transactions with larger systems so that it gets what it needs. A change agent can use this understanding to help a community take care of itself, perhaps by encouraging a group within the community to assert its rights to get the attention it needs or by helping a number of groups within the community work together for mutual benefit. A change agent might also assist a community by helping it relate more effectively to a wider community in which it sits. At an even broader level, a change agent can help provoke a response from the wider community (including government) to fulfill its responsibilities to smaller communities. This may take the form of providing direct resources (such as money), technical assistance, legal protection, or other support a smaller community needs so that it can flourish. (Systems theory is explained in more detail in Chapter 3.)

Chaos Theory

Understanding how a system functions does not necessarily enable us to precisely predict how it will function. Although some things are more likely, they are not certain. The complexity of the system makes it difficult to know where all these patterns might be heading and the consequent effects they might produce. Chaos theory shows us that a small change can have a large consequence, particularly when a system is interacting with other systems (Nicholas, 2003). A system is always in some state of change.

In 1961 a meteorologist from MIT, Edward Lorenz, wanted to run some weather simulations. Now remember, in 1961 computers did not have lots of memory and storage. So to save time, he rounded off some numbers in a way that shouldn't have made a difference and started the program again. He was surprised when this small, seemingly inconsequential change led to very different predictions of weather. The pattern that emerged from his computer looked like a butterfly, which led to the term "Butterfly Effect," meaning that even tiny changes in a system may lead to very large changes in the overall system. For example, the flapping of a butterfly's wings may be just enough of a nudge to set in motion a sequence of reactions that can change a weather pattern, preventing a tornado from dropping down some place across the world, or leading it there (Lorenz, 2001).

In any system in which many forces are acting at the same time, one small action can lead to monumental differences. The change you are working to create might do this.

HEALTHY COMMUNITIES PRODUCE HEALTHY PEOPLE

Healthy communities tend to produce healthy people. Distressed and depressed communities tend to produce distressed and depressed people. What is health? The World Health Organization (1948) has defined health as "the state of complete physical, mental, and social well being, and not merely the absence of disease and infirmity." Fostering healthy communities is the fundamental purpose of community change. Workers in human services are directly concerned with the well-being of people; strengthening communities promotes individual as well as group health. The consequences of health or distress are experienced by all members of the community; therefore, promoting healthy communities serves both our self-interest and our interest in others.

It is naive to assume that people can be divorced from their surroundings (Lynch, 1996). Consistently significant for all but the tiniest handful of people is participation in the human community. We do not live apart from it, and the communities we create affect each and every one of us. We derive physical, intellectual, emotional, and spiritual sustenance from our membership in the human community. We cannot pursue our interests or correct our maladies without regard to the presence and actions of others. Even acts of exploitation or withdrawal require a community to give them meaning.

Healthy communities can more readily fend off harmful forces from outside while finding and using productive forces that can benefit members. Unhealthy communities are vulnerable to external destructive influences and are unable to draw in adequate levels of vitalizing energy. We thrive in a healthy environment; we wither in an unhealthy one.

Healthy communities meet the needs and utilize the abilities of their members. Larger, more comprehensive communities can provide for a full range of members' physical, social, emotional, intellectual, and spiritual requirements. Smaller or more narrowly defined communities may be organized around a particular set of interests; for example, faith communities primarily attend to spiritual necessities. Whether the community is comprehensive or narrow, it can be considered healthy if the expectations of its members regarding what it should provide are met.

In healthy communities, members are able to meet their needs sufficiently well that energy can be directed beyond matters of basic survival to those of personal and community development (Kesler, 2000). Healthy communities provide ways for members not only to survive but to grow; not only to receive but to contribute. Four contributors to community health that change agents should acknowledge are (1) functioning to meet system requirements, (2) recognizing and valuing resources, (3) acting to include all members, and (4) promoting the interaction of community capital.

Functioning to Meet System Requirements

A healthy community sustains healthy connections among its members as well as with other sources of strength within the community, such as safe housing, natural resources, and social institutions like schools. A healthy community also maintains connections outside itself to access what the community needs: raw materials for manufacturing, capital for economic development, or new forms of art to engage the human spirit. Sustainable community development requires attention to system requirements and the interaction of the system elements to meet those requirements (Scherch, 2000).

Faulty connections can weaken the community. Anything that restricts access to a needed resource represents a faulty connection. For example, inadequate public transportation systems can block members' access to employment. Racism or hetero-sexism can interfere with relationships among people (Berkman & Zinberg, 1997; DiAngelo, 1997; Dubois & Krogsrud-Miley, 2005). Connections to unsafe substances also weaken. A tainted water supply or using harmful drugs are two examples of these types of faulty connections.

The ability of the community to meet its needs and manage its relationships with other communities and broader systems will affect the health and development of its individual members, which, in turn, will affect the overall health of the community (Netting, Kettner, & McMurtry, 1998).

Recognizing and Valuing Resources

A healthy community acknowledges its resources and uses them to foster growth of the community and its members. These resources include natural elements (such as rivers or minerals), elements shaped by human intervention (such as bridges and public libraries), and talents and skills available throughout the population (such as music and storytelling). A healthy community demonstrates an appreciation of the value of these resources, particularly valuing its members.

Unhealthy communities see only the limitations imposed by their problems and faulty connections. These define the community. Change efforts that promote a deficit orientation reinforce this belief.

Healthy communities believe in their abilities and assets. Change efforts that promote this notion accelerate the discovery and use of community strengths (Kretzmann & McKnight, 1993; Lofquist, 1996; McKnight, 1995; Ronnby, 1995; Scheie, Williams, Mayer, Kroll, & Dewar, 1997a; Suchman, 1994).

Including All Members

Healthy communities are inclusive communities. They purposefully seek methods for including members in community benefits and community decision making. Flowing from the notion of recognizing resources, healthy communities believe that every person has something to contribute, and they accept the challenge of accepting all their members.

Unhealthy communities turn to exclusivity as a response to difficulties. They find formal and informal

---

◄ Take a Moment to Discover ►

As you drive around, ride the bus, or walk through town today, notice the people who are more or less pushed to the fringes of the community, those people who certainly aren't invited into the life of the community. Who are they? The scruffy guy with the "Will Work for Food" sign? That teenager with the baggy pants, or the one carrying her soon-to-be-born baby? How about that woman who is cursing at the cars, the trees, and the street signs as she pushes a shopping cart crammed with her life's possessions? What do you think about these people? How do you invite them in? How do you help keep them away from the rest of us? Do you have any gated or walled neighborhoods in your community? What's that all about? Are there people in your workplace or where you go to school that you wish you could get rid of? You can probably justify your feelings, can't you? Inclusivity is not easy.

---

ways for excluding those whose behaviors or appearance are different. Different becomes bad. Children with developmental disabilities are excluded from schools, people of color are discouraged from home buying, and the encampments of "homeless" people are bulldozed. The rationalizations of exclusivity seek to protect privilege and keep the community from facing the very real challenges of inclusivity and power sharing.

Healthy communities provide mechanisms for affiliation, shared problem solving, and mutual growth. They appreciate and celebrate differences. They recognize that although diversity can be challenging, it is a resource, a richness, and a benefit.

Promoting Community Capital

The concept of community capital is one of the most important orientations for understanding communities and acting to promote their health. It flows from a strength perspective, giving the organizer an array of things to work with rather than work away from. We commonly think of capital only in terms of money, but that can be a pretty narrow and limiting view. A community may not have a lot of money, but it can still be rich with other forms of capital. If wealth only means money, we would treat that community as if it were poor, and we would miss

seeing and making use of the many forms of wealth that can be grown and linked to further enrich a community. Each community relies on different forms of capital to maintain itself and grow stronger. It is important to recognize these various forms of capital as real wealth. Community capital is linked more with power than money.

Daniels (2002) defines capital as "the stock of capacity to do something." Sampson and Bean (2006) add that capital is something that can be converted into status, actual resources, or access. A healthy community needs a sufficient supply of various forms of capital. Further, these forms of wealth must continue to grow and be easily linked to bring new community features to life. Pretty (2000) has identified a number of sources of capital, including natural or environmental, physical, financial or economic, human, and social. Daniels (2002) adds political capital. The development and exchange of information adds another source of capital. Spiritual capital and cultural capital are important sources of community wealth as well. Looking at a community with a focus on all its problems and deficiencies will give you and its members a particular attitude and perspective. Looking at a community through the lens of its wealth creates a very different view.

Environmental capital includes the natural features and resources of the area. For example, forests, open spaces, mountains, rivers, desert arroyos, lakes, weather, sun, snow, unique flora, and fauna. These qualities help to define a sense of place and provide important aspects of identity. A community garden may be lurking under a weed-strewn lot. A mountain trail can be a walk through history, reconnecting young people with a disappearing culture. Environmental factors can provide economic assets, health, recreation, energy production, places for solitude or gathering, and a host of other benefits.

Physical capital refers to things that have been added to the natural environment by human hands. This includes roads, buildings, architecture, landscaping, parks, lighting, sidewalks, and other forms of infrastructure. These elements can further define a place and reinforce identity. Physical capital also includes other important durable goods such as backhoes, busses, windmills, and other devices. Water harvesting can bring color and shade to an arid landscape. A library can be a place where people not only find books but meet neighbors. Constructed features can be sources of pride, places to meet or play, protection against the elements, conveniences that make life easier, or pathways for connecting people. Machines can make human strength more efficient, enabling us to do more in less time.

Economic capital comes in the form of financial wealth, as well as mechanisms for producing and exchanging things of monetary value. This includes jobs, businesses, particularly locally owned businesses, products made for export outside the community, credit, purchasing power, and bartering. Residents in a low-income neighborhood have found it easy to exchange the bounty from their fruit trees and small gardens. In another community neighbors have pooled their money to create a loan fund for housing improvement. Money can be used to provide needed goods and services, items that go beyond basic need to add to the quality of life, and social and political status and influence. Systems of trade can connect people with what they want without any money changing hands.

Political capital involves access to the system of policy setting and enforcement in the community. It includes having personal relationships with policymakers and having the ability to exchange something—for example, votes, campaign support, or public attention—for political favors. A large, organized corps of campaign volunteers from local business owners and employees find that their concerns are not pushed to the side when political decisions are made. The rabbi introduces his good friend, the City Council Member, to members of the congregation who want to speak to her. Public policies affect almost every aspect of our lives. They can protect or harm, limit or expand basic rights, and create opportunities or favor a special few. The ability to influence the development and adherence to polices has far-reaching consequences.

Human capital is the central source of wealth for the community. It involves having access to the stored skills, talents, passion, energy, and health of the members of the community and members' willingness to contribute them. Carpentry, storytelling, cooking, haircutting, guitar playing, car repair, almost an endless set of skills can be found in any medium-sized group. Many groups have gathered the gifts of the head (what we know, who we know, and intellectual abilities), the hands (what we can do and our physical abilities), and the heart (our passions and our emotional resources) to build a storehouse of assets and ways to connect people to each other and efforts to strengthen the community. Using the neighborhood listserv, residents are asked to identify the talents they would be willing to offer to their neighbors for free, exchange, or

below normal market fees. This talent bank is posted to the neighborhood website, helping neighbors get help or get work during difficult economic times. At a meeting, parents of children with special health care needs write down all their gifts of head, hands, and hearts, each one on an index card. They announce them and post them on the wall. The group studies the asset wall to start to identify projects the group could work on. A community is, most of all, its people. This is the fundamental wealth of a community. Efforts to make the community better must start with them.

Information capital is the generation, accumulation, storage, retrieval, and exchange of data, information, and knowledge. This includes access to databases, newspapers, stories, schools, libraries, public records, and people with a long history. Research and educational activities help contribute to information capital. An environmental health agency tracks the number of employees in all of the auto body repair and paint shops in an area who have received training on handling toxic substances, using the information to identify potential leaders and continue cleaning the community. A group of high school students uses the school district budget documents and education department regulations to keep valuable programs from being cut. Information is a fundamental form of power to protect or create. It can shape public perception of an issue and move people to action.

Spiritual capital is found in members' belief in something larger than themselves and their subsequent search for meaning and commitment to a life that calls forth their best. This includes organized expressions such as meditation groups, religious centers, sweat lodges, and ecumenical practices. It also includes a personal sense of wonder and awe, contemplation of larger mysteries, meditation, and reflection. Though spirituality may be formed into faith and practiced as religion, it extends beyond these. An office worker talking to a colleague about the hardships of so many in the community who have lost their jobs asks, "What can we do?" and soon an office food drive is under way. Responding to a call for social justice, a group raises their voices in song, affirming their shared connection and enlivening the collective spirit. Members of a faith community gather to examine their teachings on social justice and decide on a project to put their beliefs into action. Admittedly, this form of wealth is hard to get your hands around, and it often goes unrecognized and unutilized by organizers. Yet this wealth exists in any community. It is a power that moves us beyond self-interest, even beyond a sense of right and wrong. When members support one another in exploring and acting on a deeper meaning, they create a powerful form of wealth that infuses the community with a purpose beyond simply satisfying the immediate concerns of daily existence.

Cultural capital is the wealth that exists in communities from the habits, artistic expressions, understood norms, and shared traditions, rituals, and beliefs, which provide reference points, identity, and meaning to its members. These can be seen in seasonal rituals, recognized norms and customs, local art and music, historical artifacts, and other forms of cultural expression. Cultural capital includes knowing how to act and interact within a particular context, so it includes notions of cultural competence as well. Tohono O'Odham parents and teens discuss *himdag,* the values and path to cultural identity that incorporates everything in life that makes us unique as individuals and as a people, and ask each other how that is manifested in their village. Elsewhere another group gathers. It has been a while since any of them have served, but today they still feel the honor and still respond to *semper fi.* Drawing from a recognized culture strengthens personal and group identity and signifies shared experiences and a common purpose. This form of wealth is a powerful source of cohesion, helping a community create structures for mutual learning, deal with adversity as a member of a group rather than alone, and providing a unified force for action and celebration.

Healthy communities need all these forms of capital, but just as important, they need community attitudes and practices that promote the *interaction* of these forms of capital. Essentially, this is what community organization and development is all about, the ability to recognize capital, help it to grow, and combine it with other forms of capital so that communities become stronger and healthier, improving the well-being of all its members. A key element in promoting the necessary interaction of community capital is *social capital.* Because of its fundamental value to a community, this form of community wealth receives special attention.

The Functions of Social Capital.   Social capital is the system of community norms and interrelationships that produce trust, collaborative action, and community consciousness. A community rich in social capital will likely undertake efforts to develop other forms of capital that may be in short supply in the community. However, building social capital itself is rarely the main goal of a community change effort. It doesn't really work that way. Social capital is built and used in the process to create change on other specific issues, and then, if maintained, it becomes a source of wealth that makes other efforts easier and more effective (Putnam, Feldstein, & Cohen, 2003).

First introduced in 1916 by the social reformer L. J. Hanifan, the concept of social capital has received increased attention in recent years. Pierre Bourdieu (1986), a French theorist, helped to bring the concept into more current discussion. He looked at an individual's access to resources contained in a network of relationships. Subsequently, both Robert Putnam (1993, 1995, 1996, 2000, 2004) and James Coleman (1988, 1993) have examined social capital from a community perspective.

In the last few years there has been an explosion of debate about the concept of social capital. Some claim that the concept has grown fuzzy and that there is an inattention to matters of power and power imbalances between disenfranchised communities and the larger community or society (DeFilippis, 2001; Minkler & Wallerstein, 2005). Others describe how economic determinants affect the type of social capital accumulated (Owen & Videras, 2006), and some argue about whether social capital resides in individuals or in the community (Kawachi, Kim, Coutts, & Subramanian, 2004). Certainly, the idea has provoked lots of attention, passion, and maybe "more heat than light" (p. 682).

Much of the criticism of social capital seems to stem from too narrow an understanding of what it is, how it works, and how it can be used. Social capital refers to individual and community wealth derived from active engagement of individuals with other members of the community and with what might be called "community life." These engagements provide opportunities for affiliation among members and benefits to the community. Social capital is developed through a network of trusting connections that members of communities have with each other, as well as with those outside the community. These connections not only create access to other resources (including other networks) but make it easier to bring people together to mobilize their power.

Social capital strengthens both individuals and communities through networks of connections, and this notion has tremendous merit for community change agents. Community capacity, the ability for members to act effectively to improve community functioning, and social capital are mutually reinforcing. Building community capacity leads to a growth in social capital, and building social capital can lead to increased community capacity (McDonald & Denning, 2008). Like any other form of wealth, it must be recognized, valued, and used if it is going to mean much. It is a resource that grows as it is used and becomes depleted when it is not used.

Trustworthiness, the readiness to offer and receive assistance, or to respond helpfully when expected to do so, is a critical component of social capital (Putnam, 2004). Schneider (2006) has emphasized that "social capital involves much more than connections; it depends on context-specific trust over time" (p. 359). Without trust, people will not offer their own resources, nor as readily recognize or be willing to use those of others. In an atmosphere of trust, people are more willing to commit to both specific relationships, such as neighbor to neighbor or worker to worker, and more general ones, such as the neighborhood itself. Features of social organization include civic enterprises such as voter turnout, newspaper readership, and membership in groups such as the League of Women Voters, PTA, Elks Club, labor unions, or even choral societies (Putnam 1993, 1995, 1996). In other words, we create social capital whenever we become involved with the affairs of our community and with one another in routine, often organized ways.

Social capital is a source of fundamental strength for the community. Individuals directly benefit from their own connections, but they also benefit from living in a healthy community. If crime is low, for example, all members of the community benefit. Communities with strong social bonding that are rich in social capital experience lower school dropout rates, less juvenile delinquency, and less drug use (Case & Katz, 1991; Coleman, 1988; Green, 2001; Zunz, 1997). Strong bonding with school can reduce teen pregnancy (Hawkins, Lonczak, Abbott, Kosterman, & Catalano, 2002). Coleman's (1988) studies on school performance suggest that social capital available in the outside community can substitute for that missing from the family. Kawachi and colleagues (2004) have identified 31 studies both in the United States and abroad where the presence or absence of social capital affected the health of community members on topics ranging from binge drinking, to violent crime, to children's behavioral health, to tuberculosis, AIDS, suicide, and overall mortality. Schneider (2006) has found that recognizing and using social capital improves the effectiveness of social welfare programs. In communities with strong social capital, members pitch in to solve common problems (Herbert, 1996) and increase the moral quality of community life (Papworth, 1995). Governance structures and other social institutions function better, and life is simply easier (Putnam, 1995).

In contrast, communities in which the stock of social capital is low are trapped in mistrust and a belief that dealing with community affairs is somebody else's problem. People feel powerless and exploited, and even representative government works less well (Putnam, 1993). People tend not to cooperate because they can't count on others to cooperate (Organization for Economic Co-operation and Development, 2001).

Thomas Sander (2005a), executive director of Harvard's Saguaro Civic Engagement in America Project, points out that the economic class gap is held in place by a social capital class gap. Poorer communities often have lower levels of social capital; people participate in fewer networks and know fewer influential people, placing them at a disadvantage for access to jobs, education, and resources during times of emergencies. This situation is likely to continue as young people from lower-income families and who have less formal education are far less likely than their more affluent peers to participate in politics or church or to volunteer for an organization (Spring, Dietz, & Grimm, 2007). Though the opportunities are improving, schools in low-income areas are still much less likely to offer service learning (Corporation for National and

Community Service, 2008a). This situation not only increases economic class distinctions but civic haves and have-nots as well.

The presence of social capital can help sustain a community's norms. Unfortunately, these norms may include intolerance and authoritarian rigidity (Coleman, 1993; Portes & Landolt, 1996; Putnam, 1996). In a closed community, these attitudes are difficult to change. Putnam (2000) identifies two kinds of social capital: "bonding" social capital occurs within groups of people who are pretty much similar to each other, and "bridging" social capital occurs between disparate groups. Bonding capital deepens the sense of affiliation among members of a particular network, whereas bridging capital helps different groups recognize shared interests and make connections. As healthy communities open up to new information and ideas, intolerance is challenged. Simon Szreter and Michael Woolcock (2004) have added the idea of "linking" social capital, which includes developing norms of respect and networks of trusting relationships among groups across the power spectrum of the community. If there is no linkage among groups with different levels of power, the gains for groups with less power will be limited. If bridging or linking does not occur, groups with high degrees of social capital can exclude others from access to political, economic, and other assets, so development of bridging and linking social capital becomes particularly important. Of course, groups with strong bonding capital can more readily mobilize their power and assert their right to access.

According to Putnam (1995, 2000) and Harvard's Saguaro Seminar (2006), the United States has experienced a remarkable decline in civic engagement and social capital since 1960. Nowadays, people vote less often, visit neighbors less often, attend fewer public meetings, are much less likely to be members of clubs and organizations, and so on. One striking piece of information is representative of the nation's movement toward individual pursuits: More Americans are bowling today than ever before, but participation in bowling leagues has plummeted, leading Putnam (1995) to capture the nation's declining social capital with the phrase, "bowling alone." Not only are we bowling alone, but we don't seem to be talking with each other as deeply either. In the past 2 decades, the number of people saying there is no one with whom they discuss impor-

tant matters has almost tripled (McPherson, Smith-Lovin, & Brashears, 2006), and the number of confidents has declined by a third. The average American now trusts only two people with important conversations, down from three people 20 years ago. The percentage of people who talk to at least one person who is not connected to them by kinship has dropped dramatically as well, from just over 80.1% to 57.2%. This sharp decline in core social networks has occurred with a shift away from ties formed in neighborhood and community contexts. Other researchers have found that Americans have a much larger group with whom they have what they term "close relationships"; half have 15 or more. They also found that Americans see almost half of these close relations once a week (Boase, Horrigan, Wellman, & Rainie, 2006). Although it seems that we keep more or less frequent contact with our friends and family, the intensity, and maybe even the duration, of these contacts has changed.

What has caused this decrease in connection among us? Putnam (2000) believed some of the decline was caused by urban sprawl, with people commuting longer distances, women leaving unpaid community networks for the workplace, younger generations not valuing civic connections, and, of course, television, which has planted us on the couch and away from conversations with our neighbors. In fact, one key distinction between people who volunteer and those who don't is that nonvolunteers spend 463 more hours watching TV: that is more than ten 40-hour workweeks in front of the tube (Corporation for National and Community Service, 2008b). Others blame the helping professions for easing out citizenship and creating fractured client communities (Kretzmann & McKnight, 1993; McKnight, 1995). Of course, the bogeyman "Big Government" also has been indicted (Olasky, 1996). Maybe we move around so much that we don't really get to know one another well. According to the U.S. Postal Service (2008b), more than 42 million Americans move every year, generating more than 46 million address changes.

Is technology keeping us apart? Our social engagement began to diminish well before most people had heard of e-mail and before cell phones and smartphones became required communication and fashion accessories. Cell phones and communication through the Internet may have expanded our reach but decreased the deeper connections found in face-to-face contacts (McPherson et al., 2006). Boase and his colleagues (2006) disagree, claiming that use of technology increases rather than decreases contact. However, other than using e-mail features to contact a number of people at once, this research didn't address a group of people coming together at the same time and place to collaborate or just spend time together. In fact, it stressed the notion of asynchronous communication to celebrate "networked individualism."

Are we doomed to blog postings, e-mail exchanges, texting, 140-character tweets, or talk that fits into halftime or commercial breaks? Will we give up those fancy shirts with our name stitched above the pocket and go bowling alone? Maybe. Is this inevitable? I think not.

There are some signs of a reemergence of civic engagement and a civil society. Michael McDonald (2008), with the U.S. Election Project at George Mason University, reports that voter turnout of eligible voters in the 2008 presidential election was the highest in 40 years, following a trend of higher turnout from the previous election. Community groups are being formed to solve local problems and to shape community decisions (Herbert, 1996; Putnam et al., 2003; Rimsza, 2000). Local governments are actively seeking community members to help set local budget priorities (Ibanez, 1997). Whether these developments represent a new direction is an open question. The Saguaro Seminar (2001) provided a detailed benchmark assessment of 40 communities nationwide across 29 states, identifying a range of challenges and opportunities for building social capital. Future assessments can measure growth or decline from this benchmark. The Metro Chicago Information Center (2008) has constructed a Community Vitality Index to score aspects of community health in Chicago's neighborhoods as well as in the surrounding area. A key element of this index is tracking social capital. The Current Population Survey, a joint project between the Bureau of Labor Statistics and the Census Bureau, surveys more than 50,000 households monthly and began measuring civic engagement, a key aspect of social capital, in 2008. Clearly, there is a mounting interest in all this.

Other recent trends are mixed, but most appear to be promising. Participation in service learning, an approach to education from kindergarten through graduate school that emphasizes civic responsibility and uses the community as the context for learning, has continued to grow in colleges but has declined in elementary schools (Campus Compact, 2008; Corporation for National and Community Service, 2008a). The Pew Charitable Trust, the Stuart Mott Foundation, and others have redirected support to strengthening neighborhoods. The Kettering Foundation is engaged in promoting citizen participation and effective community dialogue to strengthen the foundations of democracy, and the University of New Hampshire, the University of Oregon, and Stanford University, among other institutions of higher learning, are actively engaged in research and support for "Deliberative Democracy." The Corporation for National and Community Services estimates that 55% of teenagers volunteer in a year, contributing more than 1.3 billion hours of their time. Only 5% of those teens did so as part of a school requirement (Grimm, Dietz, Spring, Arey, & Foster-Bey, 2005). The annual report on incoming college freshman conducted by the Higher Education Research Institute found noteworthy increases in categories relating to social capital, such as an increase in willingness to help others, intent to participate in community service, a belief in the importance of becoming a community leader, and becoming more politically engaged (Pryor, Hurtado, Saenz, Santos, & Korn, 2007; Pryor, Hurtado, DeAngelo, Sharkness, Romero, Korn, & Tran, 2009). The Corporation for National and Community Service (2008c) reported that nearly 61 Americans volunteered in 2007, more than a million more than the previous year, but more than 4 million fewer than volunteered in 2005 (Bureau of Labor Statistics, 2009d). This doesn't even account for the many ways people assist one another through informal helping networks, which are common forms of helping in some communities.

How might technology affect our future relationships? Is it only a threat? Might technology promote meaningful interaction? Boase and his colleagues (2006) found that different types of community conversations are occurring, and people are gaining access to different forms of networks that increase their access to resources and provide assistance with critical life decisions. Neighborhood listservs and blogs have not only become mechanisms for exchanging ideas and information but for bringing people together for group activities such as neighborhood tree planting, social

Most of us are less engaged in our communities than our parents were. Yet some of us are beginning to value a life more connected to a community of people outside our work. What do you notice about your own contributions to social capital? How many civic organizations do you participate in? When was the last time you went to a community meeting that wasn't required by your work? How often do you vote?

Do you shop at stores that are locally owned, or do you spend your time and dollars at one of those huge merchandise warehouses owned by a national chain? Is public affairs somebody else's business, maybe just the politicians'?

gatherings, helping neighbors find jobs, and political action. Meetup.com, one of the Internet's "convening technologies," shows promise for bringing people together and deepening social capital (Sander, 2005b; Fairbanks, 2008).

Communities marked by a lack of social connectedness fail to meet the needs of their members, who end up living in fear and pessimism. If we are to live in healthy communities, opportunities for increasing social capital need to be developed. However, Putnam (1993) cautions, "social capital is not a substitute for effective public policy but rather a prerequisite for it and, in part, a consequence of it" (p. 42). Agents of community change must be willing to use social capital to promote a synergy between private organizations and government (Fosler, 2002).

Why spend so much time on social capital? Though there are many good reasons, two stand out. First, if used well, it is the type of community wealth that makes everything else work. Bringing people together, recognizing shared identity, affiliation, and interests, while increasing the willingness and ability to offer and receive things of value, is at the core of what we do. Further, it promotes the ability of people to deal with conditions outside the community that affect its health while gaining access to important, additional resources by creating connections beyond the immediate community. Second, a service first or service only orientation that characterizes most professional human service activity rarely brings people together. As Schneider's (2006) thoughtful research discovered,

the absence or presence of social capital within communities, among communities, and even among agencies can critically shape the effectiveness of the work we do. If you are not acting to build social capital in the work you are doing, you need to rethink the work you are doing.

CLOSE COMMUNITIES PROVIDE A CONTEXT FOR ACTION

Close communities are collections of people, larger than our family and immediate circle of friends, to whom we generally relate and from whom we draw identity and meaning. The problems and benefits of these communities most noticeably affect us, and we and our immediate associates can have at least some degree of influence in regard to these factors. These communities are close to us, hence the term, and may be our small town or the part of a large city in which we live. We all belong to several close communities; they include our place of work, the school we attend, our local professional association, or our faith community, among others. Close communities provide the most likely arena for community change activities.

The larger community may seem distant from us, but close communities offer a context in which our actions are meaningful. Two benefits accrue from a focus on close communities. First, it is easier to mobilize for action. Precisely because we can have an impact on these communities, we are more likely to engage in purposeful action to improve conditions there. We already have relationships with a number of other community members; action within this community close at hand is simply more relevant. Second, transforming our close communities holds the promise for transforming the society of which they are a part. The whole is benefited when people are encouraged to strengthen its parts. Papworth (1995) expressed this point well: "Realize that the future belongs not to the mass and the giant but to the small and the local, if only because nobody can be healthier than the cells of which it is comprised" (p. 214).

Two significant dangers exist with this focus on close communities. First, we may divorce ourselves from the struggles and the hopes of other communities or fail to recognize that a number of issues cross community lines. Second, while working to strengthen the close community, we may engage in perceived gain that is only temporary if we do not link our work to larger forces that shape the conditions within which we are acting (Forrest & Kearns, 2001; Wiborg, 1998). Changing close communities, particularly when they become connected with the efforts of other close communities, begins to assemble a critical mass for larger change—much more than just focusing on one individual apart from others who share a similar circumstance.

Capital punishment, air quality, and welfare reform transcend distinct communities. Addressing these issues requires an alliance of communities. Even though the focus of our action on broader issues may more effectively take place in the context of our close community, the power of our action increases when we ally our efforts with those of other communities.

For smaller local communities such as neighborhoods to assist one another, governing structures that promote a healthy interconnectedness among communities are necessary. Change agents must overcome attitudes that local communities can ignore one another without consequence or that local benefits only result from a competition of local interests. These attitudes are ultimately destructive, reducing the flow of resources and increasing the possibility of surrender of local control through manipulation.

The notion of community change may seem so big and intimidating that potential change agents do not consider its value or its possibility. However, by initiating community change in our close communities, we begin to see its benefits.

THEORETICAL PERSPECTIVES ON COMMUNITY CHANGE

Theories related to community change are neither isolated nor independent; rather, they are an amalgam of theoretical propositions drawn from a wide range of writers and augmented by practical experience. These include theories of power, organizing, action, culture, and change. Each proposition is brought to life by a number of principles, which are derived from theory and informed by experience. An organizer mindful of how these strains play out in a particular situation can compose a series of actions that will provoke the desired response.

Power

Sufficient power focused on a sufficiently narrow point will produce a reaction that will lead to change. In the field of community change, power is the capacity to move people in a desired direction to accomplish some desired end. You can accomplish nothing without power.

Animating Principles.   Power is not to be confused with dominance. Power is based on the ability to provoke a response. Power can be used to dominate, to collaborate, or to educate. Normative or moral power drives actions for a perceived good. This can become a reservoir of strength and commitment.

Everything happens through relationships. Where there is no relating, there is no reaction, no power. Once a relationship has been established, actions, particularly planned actions, are as much about the relationship—affirming, preserving, or changing it— as they are about a particular benefit to any particular actor. The more established the relationship, the more predictable it becomes.

Power comes through connections and the ability to mobilize the resources, assets, and forces available through those connections (here, *force* means a supply of energy, not the assertion of one's will over another). Resources include relationships with other actors, money, information, skills, and influence. An actor who has more connections is able to mobilize more resources and has more potential power than an actor with fewer connections.

Power is most efficiently and effectively used when it is organized in the performance of planned tasks while at the same time being open to the creative opportunities of the moment. There must be a clear goal in mind, which can change as learning from experience provides new information.

The notion of social exchange holds that the dependency of one actor on the resources of another actor leads the holder of the resources to be more powerful in the relationship. Dependency is sometimes assumed, not real, and sometimes unrecognized. The perception of the dependency will affect behavior more than the actual state of dependency.

Perceived self-interest is the greatest source of influence. This includes the self-interest involved in the structure of relationships. When those who are to benefit from the change have the power to decide its direction, the change becomes more relevant and sustainable.

The base of power of the actor must be larger than the issue the actor is working on. If it is smaller, the actor must break the issue into smaller parts, build the base of power, or both. An actor can build or lose power by acting.

Organizing and Organizations

Change efforts that are planned, organized, and sustained will produce more than those that are random and sporadic. Power increases when needed elements are brought into the change effort; the elements are aligned with other elements; the alignment uses the capacity of each element and stimulates the further growth of capacity; and alignment and use are directed toward a specific goal. The amount of organizing required depends on the size and nature of the change being sought and the number of elements present in the situation.

Animating Principles.   One person can start an organized effort, but any change that affects more than one person requires the involvement of more than one person. One person does not produce significant change by acting alone. People acting together over time to produce a desired result create a relationship called an organization.

Organizations are put together to amass and use power to accomplish a purpose. With the use of purposeful planning, task accomplishment, and evaluation, organizations are able to focus available resources, accomplish goals, and learn from experiences to draw in even more resources and use them more effectively. Organizations are built around issues that clarify the

desire for change, motivate participants, and serve as a focus for action. Organizations can have varying degrees of structure. Inattention to the basic aspects of organizational sustainability will cause an organization to flounder.

In any change effort enough people need to be involved to cause the external environment to take necessary notice and to respond, as well as to provide support and empowerment to the members of the community or group taking action. Sufficient numbers provide diversity of talent and other important resources, such as time.

Organizers must understand the context in which they are acting. The perception of a shared threat can overcome differences and bring people together.

Organizing around stopping something is easier than organizing around starting something. To continue to develop, however, organizations need to move past resistance and develop and promote an agenda of their own.

Change agents must be particularly attuned to community conditions, cultural norms, an array of assets and unmet needs, relationships among members, and the relationship of the community to the broader environment. Ignorance of these factors will create barriers and inefficiency.

Organizations that are committed to learning which elements are needed, how to bring them into the organization, and how to align and use them will be more efficient and effective than those not committed to learning.

Organizations need to nurture and strengthen the relationships among their members as well as take actions to achieve their goals. Every member of the organization has information or a skill that can be used by the organization. Organizations need to match levels of involvement with the current level of interest, knowledge, confidence, and skill of participants. Healthy organizations act to increase levels of involvement of participants.

The longer the intended life of the organization, the more important matters of relationship become. The organizer of a change effort must have sanction from those being organized to perform that role and must have credibility among those being organized.

Organizations depend on the vision, work, and risk-taking abilities of "leading lights" (Ronnby,

1998), whose presence instills confidence in other participants. Organizations require a range of leadership abilities and must continually seek out and develop new leadership. Relationships that members of the organization have with people outside the organization must be used to bring new members to the organization.

Organizations are built around the work of well-functioning small groups, who can reach out and mobilize other people and assets. Organizations can start very, very small and be developed through action. Actions must be within the abilities of the organization. Actions are used to advance the organization's agenda, draw in new resources, confidence, learning, community attention, people, and leadership, which enable the organization to take subsequent, more significant actions. Each organization goes through discernable phases of development including introduction; initial action; emergence of leadership and structure; letdown, loss of members, and floundering; recommitment, new tasks, and new members; sustained action; and continued growth, decline, or termination.

Participants in an organization change through action and experience. So does their world. They change as their world changes and as their experience changes. That is, they need to react differently to conditions that have become different through the change effort. Also, their experiences have given them a different view of the world and themselves in relation to it, and it has provided practical learning.

Action

Community change only occurs through action, and actions can only occur when a certain number of preconditions exist. Much as certain conditions are required before a thunderstorm can crack the heavens and drench the earth, a number of factors need to exist before community action will take place. Actions in promoting community change are intended to provoke a response from other people. It is the response that actually sets in motion the process of change.

Animating Principles.   There must be a tension between current discomfort with the present situation and attraction to a new situation. People will act for change only if they are uncomfortable enough with

the current circumstances or excited enough by a new possibility. Otherwise, they will maintain the status quo—even if they spend a lot of time complaining about it. Complaining releases pressure for change and affirms feelings of impotence.

Over time a community can grow accustomed to its discomfort, even growing to tolerate incrementally increasing levels of frustration. A change agent may well act to stoke irritations so that members can break out of their passive acceptance of harmful circumstances.

Taking action requires a belief in the possibility that action will produce a successful outcome. Only in extreme circumstances of duress will people act with little hope that they can be successful. More commonly, we only do things if we think we have some chance of accomplishing what we intend. Whether it's giving up smoking, learning to play the guitar, or fighting city hall, we won't choose to do anything we really don't think will work out. There has to be some reasonable chance for success.

Recognition of a course of action must be present before action can take place. People may be prepared to act, and willing to act, but not know how to act. One of the most frustrating experiences is wanting to do something but not knowing what to do. In an emergency situation, people can feel helpless even though they are highly motivated to act. For an action to occur, it has to exist in the awareness of the people who must act. Unless you can see what to do, you can't do it. Further, appropriate strategies and tactics for acting must be available and recognized.

The credibility of the organizers of the effort, validity of the issue, and sustainability of the organization must be strong for action to continue. People only commit to and respond to things they believe are real. A sufficient degree of credibility will always be a precursor to the next level of action. The organization must continually meet spoken and unspoken tests of credibility prior to any action being taken.

Action requires a sufficient degree of emotion. Intellectual understanding is insufficient for action. There has to be some level of feeling—joy, anger, excitement, frustration. Change agents must do more than provide information. They must arouse feelings, particularly an enthusiasm for action. Negative residue will be a disincentive for action. If a history of failed attempts precedes the current change effort, the organizers will have an added, invisible barrier to overcome.

Perception of a threat is a strong motivator for action. This is a particular form of discomfort with the present situation. The belief that a loss will occur if no action is taken will provoke action. The more imminent the threat, the more readily people will be moved to action.

Each new level of an organization's action requires renewed commitment and conviction. Though past success can bring confidence, each new level presents a new condition and the uncertainty and other forms of resistance that new conditions bring. Successful action can motivate for new action—or it can lead to complacency.

Culture

Actions involved in promoting community change must take into account the perceptions, experiences, values, norms, and rituals of the people affected by the change. Cultural values determine what is of importance to care about, what has meaning, and what has worth. Cultural norms describe which behaviors are permissible and which are not permissible. Cultural rituals are specific practices that adhere to important events and elevate their meaning.

The perception of reality is culturally bound and socially constructed by experiences, interactions, and the meanings attached to those experiences. Culture both defines and sustains relationships. People act within a cultural framework, not outside it. Cultures, for example, organizational cultures, may be a good focus for change, but one must understand the power of the culture when one is operating within it. The stronger one's identity with a group, the more powerful that group will be in molding perception. The way we perceive our world affects how we relate to it and how we interpret the responses we get from our actions, influencing the future actions we will take.

Animating Principles.   Any person participates within a number of different subcommunities—ethnic, religious, professional, geographic, and so on—and each of these cultural groups will influence the person to varying degrees. People often do not realize that they are using their own cultural framework as the starting point for analysis and action. This includes organizers.

Interpretation of events is a product of group influence, including the group's historical interpretations. More continued and intense exposure to a group's belief system will more firmly shape the individual's perception as will exposure to the artifacts and rituals that support the belief system and reinforce group membership and identity. Decisions, behaviors, and group actions that fit within the cultural framework will be relevant and motivating. Those that are inconsistent will produce conflict or be irrelevant.

Change

Change is inevitable and ongoing. Change occurs when a sufficient number of forces heading in a similar direction coalesce to alter the behavior of the system on which they are operating. This not only provides energy for change, but it attracts and develops new energy as well. Skillful and purposeful action can accelerate the pace of change and influence its nature and direction.

Animating Principles.   Change requires a sufficiently receptive environment. Most any system will accept minor, incremental change as long as adaptations to the change do not require a troubling expense, including allocation of time or money or new behaviors. These changes occur almost without notice. Over time these adaptations will lead to a changed system.

However, if the desired change attracts or requires more attention of the system, it must receive active support from enough of the system for change to occur. This means that a sufficient number of system elements care enough to support the change to overcome opposition or the inertia of the status quo. The entire system need not be supportive. It only needs to allow the change.

If the system is hostile, the change will not take root under current conditions. Trying to force the change will provoke insurmountable resistance. The conditions must first be altered to make change more palatable.

There will always be resistance to change. Resistance comes from many sources. These can be internal, such as doubt, ingrained habits, rationalization of the benefit of the status quo, or even a lack of belief in one's own rights. They can also be external when the

GLOBAL PERSPECTIVES

MEXICO—In about 1955, a teenage Mexican boy named Juan Quezada found a cave near the village of Mata Ortiz, Chihuahua, containing some ceramic pots created by the ancient Paquime.

He started to experiment with locally available materials to try to re-create the pottery. In 1971, after about 16 years of work, he figured out how to do it. He later taught the skill to his extended family members.

Gradually, more and more people learned, and today there are hundreds of artists in Mata Ortiz who make exquisite handmade pottery appreciated by collectors worldwide.

Quezada, now 68, said he decided to share his skills with other people in Mata Ortiz, including family and friends, because he thought it was the right thing to do.

"I was eating well and I was dressed well," he said. "I didn't want to be living well while others were not."

Now, many families in Mata Ortiz and the surrounding area benefit greatly as a result of Quezada's ingenuity and generosity (Jonathan Shacat, 2008).

Note: In a village of about 2,000 people there are now more than 400 working potters.

INDIA—Activities are structured… with a strong conviction that, however "poor" people are in material assets, they have skills, experience, and social networks that are the building blocks of improving their livelihood…. The Self Employed Women's Association's (SEWA) organizing has always been member centered and participatory. The local communities, under emerging women's leadership, identify opportunities and address issues of priority to them…. This is not easy or uniform

but gradually more and more people get involved and take ownership (Coady International Institute, 2006, p. 7).

NEW ZEALAND—[The European concept of social capital separates family from community.] In contrast, the Maori concept of family (*whanau*) moves seamlessly from the immediate family to the wider family network (*hapu*) and the tribe (*iwi*), where the (extended) family becomes the community and the community is made up of the (extended) family. Social capital is created through networks and relationships that are within all of these expressions of "family" (or community). Thus, in the Maori context, the distinction between cultural and social capital disappears. Cultural capital is an important aspect of social capital, and social capital is an expression of cultural capital in practice. Social capital is based on and grows from the norms, values, networks and ways of operating that are the core of cultural capital….

Membership in customary Maori associations is based on an exchange of obligations and acceptance by the group…. The concept of obligation-driven membership includes obligations based on a common ancestry and the cultural dimension that obliges one to act in certain ways…. This sense of obligation underpins a Maori concept of voluntary activity. Key concepts of Maori society that relate to social capital include *manaaki* (cultural obligation to welcome and care for visitors) and *hapai* (the requirement to apply the concept of uplifting/enhancement) and *tautoko* (providing support within the community) (David Robinson & Tuwhakairiora Williams, 2001, pp. 55–56).

GREAT BRITAIN—So what makes us happy? Almost half of the people (surveyed)—48%—say that relationships are the biggest factor in making them happy. Second is health (at) 24%. When we asked people to choose the two most important sources of happiness in their lives, out of 1001 people only 77 said work fulfillment (M. Easton, 2006).

IRELAND—The Taoiseach has announced a task force to promote citizen participation in communities and in society, acknowledging that the pressures of modern working life threaten Ireland's traditional family and social ties. The task force will have six months to report on how to encourage people to volunteer to work in everything from parish activities, credit unions, sporting and scouting activities. (Prime Minister) Bertie Ahern implied that the "more demanding" society we had now militated against Ireland's traditional social cohesion…. Mr. Ahern said a society's health was determined not only by economic growth and higher living standards but by "mutual support and solidarity based on shared values" (M. Brennock, 2005).

SERBIA—Women at Work['s] aim is to facilitate women strengthening and defining their own economic networks. We do this by:

- Creating a Directory listing the many skills and business by women in a specific area.
- Broadening the income generating capacities and funding base of local women's groups.

(continued)

● **GLOBAL PERSPECTIVES** *(continued)*

- Coordinating the means of communicating women's economic initiatives in a Newsletter.

- Increasing information exchange by organizing the first comprehensive mailing list for women's initiatives....

- Organizing non-traditional skills training; the first home repair workshops for women (Women at Work, 2002, p. 1).

change requires that others behave differently. External actors also are plagued with doubts, habits, rationalizations, and lack of belief in the rights of those seeking the change. External resistance is heightened when these others feel that a change transgresses prior agreements or results in a loss of power, control, or access to other valued resources. The degree of resistance relates to the number of adaptations that need to be made and who has to make them. These adaptations can require building new relationships, acquiring new competencies, assuming new attitudes and beliefs, or rejecting conditions that the actor has helped to create.

Temporary change is more readily accepted. Over time, change that continues to make demands on the system may come to be resisted. For change to persist, it must be institutionalized. Change requires agreement to new structures and allocation of new resources or reallocation of existing ones. Until these agreements are in place and routine, the reality of change is suspect. As Julian (1973) observed, change comes about when a "significant number of people-or a number of significant people"-agree that a problem exists (p. 9).

SUPPORTING THEORETICAL PROPOSITIONS

In addition to the broad foundation theories just examined, through experience you will discover numerous supporting notions that will inform your understanding of how things work. Three of these deal with conflict, crisis, and relationships—matters all change agents encounter. Let's take a closer look.

Conflict Affects Commitment to Organizing for Change

Before a group can begin to work together, it really must be able to work together. Standing disagreements, jealousies, and rivalries cannot coexist with a commitment to work for change. How many times have you seen this in a family, a group working on a class assignment, a congregation in a faith community, or an office staff?

The presence of a climate of conflict will erode commitment and eat away at the foundation for building a better future. The only exception to this is when the competing groups face a common enemy. That shared interest in an opponent will move antagonisms to the background, but it won't get rid of them. Though the parties may temporarily set differences aside, they are there, lurking beneath the surface. The fear and mistrust are never too far from the work. Resources are warily shared, and the awareness of a temporary truce weakens the relationships on which success depends. If the common enemy appears to be getting the upper hand, competing groups may turn on each other in frustration and blame, becoming unwitting accomplices with their opponent.

For development to occur, internal conflict must be relatively low. Although development activities can help bring people together, if conflict levels are too high, the development or community change work can exacerbate conflicts. Some conflict is inevitable; we don't erase it. We need to develop skills to handle it in a way that resolves the matter and leaves the group more capable of dealing with additional challenges.

If development activities are to be a form of conflict reduction, even resolution, the parties involved must recognize and agree to this strategy. Otherwise, they will undermine the effort to confirm their perceptions and positions. That initial agreement itself requires some reduction in conflict.

Crisis Can Contribute to Community Action

A crisis, a sudden and overwhelming onset of threats, shocks the system. The system is out of balance. The world has suddenly changed, and the system must change as well. A system in disequilibrium is most open to change. Old patterns and perceptions seem irrelevant or inadequate. Something different must be put in place.

Crises wrench a community from its inattention and ignorance, and they explode denial. Because a feeling of crisis cannot exist without the agreement of the threatened system, the system must respond to the demands that the crisis makes. That is, it is the system itself that defines the crisis. It is the system's recognition of impending danger. Crisis is the partnership of threatening conditions and the perception of the system to them. Ignorance of these conditions, no matter how threatening, will lead to no change activity. Imagine the occupants of a boat singing merrily as they head down the river toward the waterfall just around the bend.

A popular high school teacher dies a violent death. Arsenic is discovered in the town's only water supply. Widespread abuse of children by trusted clergy is uncovered. The world as we believed it to be or pretended it to be no longer exists. Crisis can stir us to action.

Crisis can produce retreat as well as engagement, as if running away from the threat can make it go away. If crisis conditions upset but don't overwhelm the system, engagement is the more likely response. If the crisis passes quickly, old patterns may well reassert themselves.

Working Relationships Require Communication, Trust, and Mutual Interest

In community change everything happens through relationships. As people act and react with one another, they create a new organism called a relationship. Among other things, this organism gives meaning to words and actions, defines roles, and sets boundaries of anticipated or acceptable behavior.

Each person comes to the relationship with ideas, information, energy, talents, money, power, or other resources. Not only does each person bring these, but each also brings a network of other relationships as well as all the resources and networks available there. The matter of influence, acting and reacting, requires the participation of another.

An exchange of resources flows more easily through healthy relationships than through those blocked by hurt or fear. Greater openness increases the flow of resources; restraint restricts them. Relationships depend on three necessary ingredients: communication, trust, and mutual interests. Relationships take time to mature into full openness, and they need frequent maintenance attention to keep harmful elements from blocking easy access.

An organization characterized by the ability to develop and maintain healthy relationships will have more available resources, will be better able to weather unexpected storms and challenge setbacks, and will be able to use more of its energy for focused action. It will be more powerful as a result.

ORGANIZING MODELS FOR COMMUNITY CHANGE

Communities vary by culture, interest, geography, and a host of other factors, which render models for organizing community change somewhat imprecise. Furthermore, there is no one prototypical or standard "community" in which we can see various models in operation. Still, it is helpful to consider some different general approaches to the business of change.

Given this understanding, what are some of the directions change efforts may take? Jack Rothman (1968) described three models of community change: locality development, social planning, and social action. *Locality development* involves "broad participation of a wide spectrum of people at the local community level in goal determination and action" (p. 23). This process emphasizes economic and social progress. It is intended that a "wide range of community people [are] involved in determining their 'felt' needs and solving their own problems" (p. 30). Thus this model has a kind of self-help orientation to it.

The *social planning* approach "emphasizes a technical process of problem solving with regard to substantive social problems, such as delinquency, housing, and mental health" (p. 24). This model envisions that change occurring in a complex world calls for deliberate, rational steps. Such efforts require expert planners to guide changes through a maze of bureaucratic barriers with the intention of "establishing, arranging, and delivering goods and services to people who need them" (p. 24). Often this approach leads to an orientation of providing services as the way to respond to recognized problems.

Social action methods seek more fundamental changes. They presuppose "a disadvantaged segment of the population that needs to be organized…to make adequate demands on the larger community… making basic changes in major institutions or community practices" (p. 24). The types of changes sought through social action are a redistribution of power, the reallocation of resources, or changes in community decision making. Fisher (2005) observes that because this approach engages in oppositional politics, it tends to be the least practiced in social agencies. He goes on to make the point that "it is this type of community intervention that most lives up to the social justice and social change mission of social work" (p. 51).

Rothman and Tropman (1987) suggested policy practice and administrative practice as additional approaches for enacting or managing change at a broader level. Further, they suggest that we often need to blend models as we are acting in the real world. *Policy practice* involves identifying, analyzing, refining or developing, and implementing policies that guide the operations of government and non-governmental organizations that have an impact on individuals, groups, and communities. *Administrative practice* involves organizational development and manipulation, including some of the following abilities and activities: assessing community needs and assets, designing programs, maintaining community relationships, and facilitating consensus among organizational constituencies. The administrator guides the processes by which service organizations order and arrange their activities and resources to accomplish their missions. This is more clearly present in a service orientation.

Kramer and Specht (1983) described two basic approaches to community organizing: community development and social planning. *Community development* methods work directly with the people who are feeling the problem to mobilize them to take action. Social action activities are included under community development in this model. Emphasizing participation of the previously unaffiliated or those who may be considered "victims," they note that "a typical feature of such efforts is their concern with building new organizations among people who have not been previously organized to take social action on a problem" (pp. 15–16). Kramer and Specht's description of *social planning* activities is similar to Rothman's, characterized by actions designed to coordinate or change the practices of community agencies. "[A] major feature of this model is that the action system is composed of people who are legally and structurally tied to community agencies and organizations, and their behavior is regulated and guided by these commitments" (p. 16).

Rubin and Rubin (2008) described four types of community organizations: social action, economic and social development, network, and national advocacy and support organizations. *Social action* directly pressures government and businesses, using confrontation to make changes, redirecting resources to communities in need, and enhancing human rights. *Economic and social development* provides goods and services that are generally unavailable to the poor. These organizations help workers have a say in how companies are run or provide social services with a focus on empowerment. *Network* organizations bring other social change organizations together, coordinating their efforts. *National advocacy coalitions* and *support organizations* gain information about a problem, share information among organizations, and lobby politicians and regulators.

Each of these approaches organizes people in one of three ways. In the first case, people come together to solve a particular problem or make a particular improvement. Although the use of power is necessary for success, it is seen as the means for achieving the goal rather than being the goal itself. Much of the community change work you will be involved with as a human services worker will be problem focused. Even though these efforts may be short in duration and have a limited scope, it is important to leave the community in a more empowered condition upon completion of the change episode.

In the second case, people come together for the purpose of developing and asserting their own power or capacity, often attempting to change the way the larger community functions to address the concerns of the group being organized. These groups generally have a broader agenda of issues, and they use the issues to build the group while using the group to tackle the issue. This approach seeks to establish a permanent organization able to take on a variety of issues, some not even recognized by early participants. If working for community change becomes the focus of your professional work, you may devote a lot of your time to operations like these.

The third case involves the development approach. Community development is intended to increase the capabilities of a group of people in order for them to increase their efficacy. The goals are to achieve their intended purposes and to provide for more full and satisfying lives for all members of the group or community. Development is really about three things: increasing the capability of a community to act effectively; increasing the number and usefulness of community assets to benefit its members; and ensuring that members of the community own the process and the results. This includes the notion of member access to assets. Community development is described in more detail in the last section of this chapter.

Communities can benefit from any method that addresses community issues in a way that recognizes the capabilities and rights of its members. There is no one "best" approach for all circumstances. Having said that, I believe strategies that draw from community building philosophy and practices generally hold a greater likelihood of promoting the health of communities.

FOUR CORNERSTONES OF COMMUNITY BUILDING

Four cornerstone principles support the practice and philosophy of community building. These cornerstones draw together a foundation of animating themes that run through this work. The first prin-

ciple is movement beyond problem solving toward changing conditions, bringing a new order of things to life. The second is the belief that the people who are affected by conditions should play a fundamental role in improving conditions. The third is that an active spirit of inquiry and learning nourishes the endeavor. The final principle is that efforts are directed by the recognition and use of available strengths, including forms of community capital and the building of new strengths.

Over the years I have worked in this field, I have come to learn that it is our strengths, not our problems, our best experiences, not our worst, and our wealth, not our poverty that we must pay most attention to. These are the sources of our power to change the things that need to be changed and create new patterns and practices that lead to the health of communities and the people who live or work within them.

The following perspectives and practices—transformation, praxis, appreciative inquiry, and community development—bring these principles to life.

Change and Transformation

We can engage the process of change at many levels. Many of the changes you will help to make will affect a narrow set of interests and not be noticed by the larger community or society. Still, even within the confines of these interests, you can help alter patterns of relationships and elevate the awareness of how our acting with each other has consequences beyond the immediate situation.

Human life finds interests and draws meaning beyond our engagement with immediate demands. We transform our world as we experience it. "It is as transforming and creating beings that humans, in their permanent relations with reality, produce not only material goods—tangible objects—but also social institutions, ideas, and concepts" (Friere, 2000, p. 101). We not only act in the world but think about it as well, and we shape the world as we both act and reflect. We can look not only at what is but ask what it means. What action is implied—and what is our part in all of this, particularly in relation to others? Transformation goes beyond merely creating things or adding new features to a landscape, or even creating new efficiencies. Transformation generates new products created with a sense of purpose and meaning that affirm human dignity and elevate the human spirit. Transformation is not satisfied with just taking care of a particular problem; it goes beneath the problem to alter the condition that produced it in the first place. When we deeply engage the process of change, we provide more lasting benefit and call attention to the power of human potential. Moving beyond action to reflection, which informs our future action and reflection, can lead to transformative change.

Theory and Philosophy of Praxiology

Praxiology is a cumbersome word and a complex theory, yet a useful one for promoters of community change. Praxiology (from the Greek word *praxis,* which means action) provides a consideration of human action that has both personal and social consequences. The foundations of this theory are linked with social learning theory (that we learn through our interaction with others and our perceptions of the consequences of our actions) and social construction theory (that we perceive and attach meaning to objects, events, and processes with which we interact and that our daily interactions with others shape our reality; Meenaghan, Gibbons, & McNutt, 2005; Wismer, 2007). They are further drawn from a diverse array of philosophers, economists, and educators, including Martin Buber, Paulo Freire, Karel Kosik, Karl Marx, and Ludvig von Mises.

The central theme of praxiology is that people act purposefully to satisfy their needs and to improve their future, and that change most effectively proceeds from an interactive process of reflection and action. Our actions are determined by a number of factors, including our perception of the world, what we want from it, what we think we are capable of doing, and what we expect will happen as a result of our actions. These perceptions merge into an immediate theory of action at the moment of acting. We develop our thoughts while we are acting, and we develop our actions from our thoughts. Both using our knowledge and increasing our knowledge are occurring while we are acting.

So you can see that our actions start with our perception of the world, and according to this theory,

we get our knowledge of the world by acting in it and reflecting on our actions, even if those reflections last but a moment. More purposeful analysis, clarity of action, and active reflection can accelerate the acquisition of knowledge, which in turn will affect future analysis, action, and reflection.

This provides an important perspective for change agents. People not only learn about the world from acting in it, but they change it as well. We come to see people with whom we are working as active co-creators of the world, not just passive objects who are manipulated. This can be a dramatic shift in thinking, not only for organizers but for individuals themselves.

Community change is all about the process of people coming together to a place where they are willing and capable of taking effective action. The factors that influence how people come to know and act, how they come to believe in their dignity, and how they come to trust themselves and others who struggle alongside them become important matters of inquiry for change agents.

Praxiology leads us to consider what action is possible given what people believe about themselves as individuals and as a group, what they believe about how their world operates, and what they, as individuals and as a group, believe they want at this time and can do. Engaging in critical reflection can run the risk that community members will be overwhelmed and fall into what Stephen Brookfield (2000, p. 145) calls an "energy-sapping, radical pessimism," which will demoralize rather than energize. To counter this, Peters, Gregoire, and Hittleman (2004) encourage change agents to first focus on what is going good, strong, and right in the situation. It is essential that we act to build understanding in a context of hope.

Guided by this philosophy, we promote the notion of people believing in themselves, their own learning, and the value of their own ideas. We move past the belief that only others' ideas have merit, a framework that reinforces dependency and compliance, not creativity and leadership. Locally generated knowledge has tremendous value. People are not only more committed to their actions when these are connected to their own thoughts, assumptions, and desires, but the actions themselves become more relevant. People will grow and develop through their own insights and actions.

Knowledge that is gained through experience and is shared is more firmly rooted than knowledge received from other sources. Both using our knowledge and increasing our knowledge are occurring while we are acting. Thus our knowledge and capacity for effective action grows as does our group unity and our willingness to take action. Learning isn't only about adding knowledge or learning a particular skill. It is about learning for action—action that will change the world.

The process of praxis connects personal conditions with collective ones and private actions with public ones. As members of an action-oriented group engage in praxis, participants become more competent, confident, united, and powerful. Shared understanding brings recognition of community and of cohesion—and the end of disabling isolation.

Sometimes we bring people together to plan; sometimes to act. We also need to come together to learn. Organizers use an understanding of praxis to bring people together to reflect on their experience and the learning they are deriving from that experience to strengthen their relationships and embolden their purpose. Effective praxis requires an effective group. Open and critical discussion must take place in an encouraging, supportive, and respectful atmosphere. Otherwise old patterns of dominance and denial can persist under the guise of dialogue, and the prevailing wisdom might turn out not to be so wise after all.

A critical aspect of this philosophy is the belief in human dignity and the acceptance of one's personal dignity. Praxis wrests people from the prison and the comfort of victimhood and draws them to freedom and the challenges of believing in dignity. The belief in dignity raises the question of responsibility—that knowing and acting may be moral choices as well as practical ones.

Mutual learning is stressed rather than the expert acting on the uninformed. Organizers are partners in learning and acting. They help create the process that leads to collective understanding and participate along with others in using the products of that shared understanding. Though organizers and others with particular knowledge and experience contribute their perspectives, a basic and necessary assumption is that everyone has knowledge and insights. Change agents need to resist the temptation to sneak in their own ideas while appearing to be partners. Even well-intentioned change agents can be manipulators. When faced with this temptation, be open both about your beliefs and about listening to the beliefs of others, knowing that it is the beliefs of the people who must act and accept the consequences of acting that count most.

Acting in tune with this empowering orientation develops conscientization, a powerful, transformative, critical consciousness of the workings of one's world and one's workings in relation to it. People are liberated from modes of thinking taught and learned that succumb to current conditions as inevitable. They are challenged to go beyond what they had thought possible, creating a new awareness of what is possible.

Engaging in praxis requires reflection on personal dignity and public responsibility, an analysis of current conditions (why things are the way they are), an assessment of opportunities for action, theories about what will produce successful intervention and action, and further reflection and dialogue. The process creates a discovery of personal and collective efficacy and a willingness to change the world by acting and learning.

Appreciative Inquiry

In every community situation there are some things that are going well: things that give life to the community and keep it going. Without these things the community would collapse. When times are difficult, we may only notice the problems, but in every present difficulty there are past successes.

Much of what we get out of life is what we choose to pay attention to and give meaning to. If we choose to look at problems, that is what we will find, and the problems will assume an even greater power to define our experience. If, however, we choose to recognize, value, and validate real-life examples of relationships and practices that contribute to community health, these will embolden us to shape a promising future. In both our history and our present we have sources of strength that we can draw on to shape our future. When we are stuck in mediocrity or decline, we may have only a blurry belief that there exist, somewhere, things that have worked or do work. We may have to purposefully search them out and recognize their benefits. We may need to engage in appreciative inquiry.

Growing out of work at Case Western Reserve University in the 70s, appreciative inquiry (often referred to as AI) has become the subject of a growing body of research and is steadily gaining adherents. At its core is the belief that there are positive influences in any organization or community that give it life and activate members' competencies and energies (Cooperrider & Srivastva, 1987).

Appreciative inquiry is based on the idea that what you pay attention to you produce. Paying attention to what you want is probably much better than paying attention to what you don't want (Bushe, 2001). We tend to create what we are studying. How we study affects what we create. If your change efforts focus only on problems, that is about all you will ever find. The discovery of one problem leads to the discovery of another and another, and on and on. If you look through another lens for positive elements instead of problems, and discover what brings these elements about and keeps them going, you will find more and more of these. The very act of inquiry itself liberates the spirit and sets positive energy in motion and leads to change. Collaborative inquiry is a highlight of this approach. A cross section of the community participates in examination, reflection, and the development of shared understanding and the creation of new models for action.

Appreciative inquiry does not ignore the existence of problems. Common problems or issues are an impetus to change (Bushe, 2007). Comfort does not lead to a desire for change, discomfort or tension does, including the tension created by the excitement of new possibilities and the recognition of new opportunities. What may prompt change does not have to limit how efforts to produce change can proceed. The direction we take when we are moved to change will profoundly influence where we end up and what we use to get us there.

Appreciate inquiry unabashedly directs us to focus on the positive: "Instead of focusing on the negatives…and trying to change them, it looks at what works well and uses that as a foundation for future development" (Seel, 2008, p. 1). As long as we are moving to the future, we should bring along the best of the past and present (Hammond, 1998).

An emphasis on the positive has powerful, productive consequences. Connection with positive experiences provides a kind of armor to self-doubt. Further, these positive images provide the energy that lead to awareness of new, and perhaps very different, ideas and actions (Cooperrider, 1990). It widens the scope of attention and promotes the ability to consider a range of options. A positive orientation opens us to more creativity and a willingness to appreciate and learn from others (Fredrickson, 2006; Fredrickson & Branigan, 2005; Isen, 2000; Waugh & Fredrickson, 2006).

This process of inquiry is generative. Past successes provide a springboard for new ideas, new ways of understanding conditions, and new ways of doing things. Bushe (2007) stated that this quest will "make available decisions and actions that weren't available or didn't occur to us before" (p. 30). Past experience carried into future actions makes the future less scary (Hammond, 1998). With the spirit and enthusiasm generated by an intentional discovery of our very best and pondering how these extraordinary moments can become our common ones, something transformative begins to take place. Prevailing assumptions are challenged, giving way to new realities. Appreciative inquiry calls forth our dreams, our competence, and our creativity. It seeks "people's best intentions and noblest aspirations, attempting a collective envisioning of what the group could be at its very best" (Bushe, 2001, p. 118). Because appreciative inquiry is grounded in actual experience, it is not pie in the sky (Seel, 2008).

Underlying Principles and Assumptions. Appreciative inquiry may be as much a philosophy as a practical approach, informed with thoughtful theory (Watkins & Mohr, 2001). Five key principles guide its application (Cooperrider et al., 2008):

1. *Constructionist principle.* Social construction theory undergirds the appreciative inquiry approach, fitting well with the orientation discussed in praxiology. This theory holds that we don't just experience reality, we create it. Our sense of "what is" and "what will be" is shaped by myriad forces, including language, cultural values, our learning from previous experiences, perceptions of others whose opinions affect us, and so on. These affect what we see and how

we understand what we see. This becomes our reality. What we focus on matters.

2. *Simultaneity principle.* Inquiry leads to change, which fosters more inquiry and change. More traditional approaches start with a problem analysis stage, defining and diagnosing what the problem is before any action takes place. The idea is that we can't do anything before we complete a diagnosis. Sometimes this can stall a desire to act, asking people to wait until we have a thorough understanding of what's wrong. It can lead to paralysis by analysis and be a discouraging, rather than energizing, experience. Some groups stay stuck in this phase or never go beyond it. After all, it is easier to analyze and critique than to act. Appreciative inquiry certainly believes in inquiry, promoting an understanding of important elements in the situation. However, similar to notions of praxis, we learn by inquiring and doing. The very act of appreciative, collaborative inquiry leads to a new construction of reality and change. Simply asking good questions sets change in motion. "Inquiry is intervention" (Cooperrider et al., 2008, p. 9).

3. *Poetic principle.* Think about what happens when people get together, maybe sharing a ride home or just having coffee. What are they doing? They are telling stories. Stories are powerful forms of communication. We use them to relive and make sense of our experiences. They are powerful tools for promoting organizational change (Denning, 2004). A community or an organization is not frozen in time; it is a story continuing to unfold with a yesterday, today, and tomorrow. Each of us feels the story and helps to shape it each day. Appreciative inquiry makes use of stories to connect people more intimately with their experiences, finding and feeling elements that the daily grind may have shoved into the corner like the stack of old pictures you meant to put in an album. Looking at them anew reminds you that you are still connected to that time. As people are engaged in sharing their positive stories with one another, both listener and storyteller recognize a mutual connection

and are changed by the experience. Both listener and storyteller see themselves in the story.

4. *Anticipatory principle.* The way we look at the future, what we think will happen, affects how we behave today. "If we have a particularly desirable image of the future, we are likely to behave in ways to bring it about" (Seel, 2008, p. 5).

5. *Positive principle.* If we focus on problems, that will be all that we see. In fact, we will see one problem after another after another, perhaps to the point that we create problems where none exist. A positive orientation, looking to what has worked or what does work, not only validates the reality and value of these experiences but appreciates the people involved in the inquiry in the first place. As a collaborative enterprise, appreciative inquiry demonstrates support and encouragement to those involved in the inquiry and the positive reality that emerges from this process.

Characteristics of Inquiry. Organizational change flows in the direction of its inquiries (Seel, 2008). If you want to keep finding problems, keep asking about them. If you want to find more and more of what is good that can open up possibilities and be put to use, ask about that. Here are four positive characteristics to guide the process of inquiry (Cooperrider et al., 2008; Seel, 2008):

Appreciative: Look for what gives life to the organization. Every organization has things that work. What are the "exceptional moments" and the positive core that animate the organization and its members?

Applicable: Look for what is going on during the best of times for clues to discover practical things that can be put to use. What factors are at play? Understanding what has led to the good things that have happened can lead to creating an even better future.

Provocative: Look for imagination, passion, and boldness. A community or organization is always in some sort of change, capable of being more than it is, and able to discover

CAPTURING CONCEPTS

Sue Hammond (1998) draws eight assumptions from fundamental principles of appreciative inquiry:

1. In every society, organization, or group, something works.
2. What we focus on becomes our reality.
3. Reality is created in the moment, and there are multiple realities.
4. The act of asking questions of an organization or group influences the group in some way.
5. People have more confidence and comfort to journey to the future (the unknown) when they carry forward parts of the past (the known).
6. If we carry parts of the past forward, they should be what is best about the past.
7. It is important to value differences.
8. The language we use creates our reality.

how to direct its own transformation. The seeds of what might be can be found in looking at the best of what is. Finding out what provokes people to go beyond the ordinary will lead to extraordinary results.

Collaborative: Look together. Shared inquiry from all parts of the community or organization brings varied perspectives, investment in creating the future, and a sense of power to make the provocative possible. Knowledge and relationships are created simultaneously. Members become co-creators of their destiny.

The 4/D Process. Appreciative inquiry begins with the selection of an affirmative topic, a bold description of what the community desires and wants to learn more about. (Some refer to this as the "Define" phase, noting a "5/D" process [Chupp, n.d.].) Selecting a topic that energizes people, that gets them to let go of the assumed "givens" of the current situation, sets the process of inquiry in motion (Stevenson, 2006). Appreciative inquiry approaches often use the following four phases, which flow from this selection (Bushe, 2007, Cooperrider et al., 2008; Seel, 2008; Stevenson, 2006).

Discovery. Discovering what works begins the process of inquiry. The idea is to do more of what works. In this phase individuals share their values of excellence, generally through structured interviews. How ques-tions are asked is important. A cross section of the community or organization is involved in this step, and stories emerge that reveal the positive core that gives life to the community. The conversations lead to trust and bonding.

Dream. Based on the discovery of what has been the best in the life of the community, members, working initially in small groups, begin to envision what might be. Key themes from stories exchanged in the discovery phase stimulate more innovative images of what members can produce. Common values and aspirations come to the surface. Members come to recognize that they are not alone in wanting something better. The shared recognition leads to a belief that better is also possible.

Design. Moving from vision to decision, members determine how the exceptional can become the routine. What we will do is drawn from what has actually been done. Grounding innovation in reality promotes confidence. Members will become so excited about what can be done that they intend to do it. They not only identify what new beliefs and practices will be put into place but which key relationships will influence how and how well these innovations will work. Organizers avoid dragging down the process with

THEORETICAL FRAMEWORKS FOR COMMUNITY CHANGE 61

forced consensus in endless meetings. Rather, the spirit of innovation enlivens this stage. Decision leads to implementation.

Destiny. Realization that we live together with what we create together moves the group to act on its discoveries, dreams, and designs. From the beginning, members have to believe that they can act on what they have created together. They don't have to wait around for some authority or committee to give them permission. The process of inquiry has already set change in motion. Improvisations, learning, and refinement become common characteristics of community life, which leads to a new community culture.

Appreciative inquiry was developed for use in improving the effectiveness of organizations, but it has become a valuable tool beyond organizational development. Business organizations, human service organizations, religious organizations, and community organizations can use this approach to transform their work, and it has proved valuable in neighborhoods and other community settings as well (Alban Institute, 2007; Cooperrider, 2008a; Hall & Hammond, 1998; Trevino, 2008). For example, Houston's Neighborhood Centers Inc. is applying appreciative inquiry to their work in neighborhoods as well as to the way the agency itself functions (Higgs, 2008; Neighborhood Centers Inc., 2009).

Sounds a little naive, doesn't it? Just focus on the good things and good things will follow? One criticism of appreciative inquiry is that it ignores problems that can haunt an organization's effectiveness. In fact, appreciative inquiry accepts that problems exist and that they can be the motivation for change (Bushe, 2007). You can't get rid of problems, though, until you change the conditions under which they grow. Old problems do not survive in healthy new conditions. The question is how do you best get to that new condition? A central belief of appreciative inquiry is that you can better choose what steps to take by using what works rather than using what doesn't work. It is harder to see what does works if you don't start by looking at that first.

A more difficult challenge is having truthful communications among people with different power and interests. Acknowledging this challenge to begin with helps, along with agreeing on some basic procedures or ground rules for making communication safe and equal. Careful attention needs to be given to making sure true stakeholders are part of the process: for example, those in authority should not just sit on the sidelines. Interviews need to be conducted thoughtfully, including matching who converses with whom. Participants may need to accept that "professional malcontents" may undermine the process. Even so, these individuals will be given their say, encouraged to reframe their perspective, and given the chance to become committed. For appreciative inquiry to work, participants need to understand and trust the process and each other (Elliott, 1999).

The Community Development Model

Selection of any organizing model should be geared to the immediate situation and the goals and organizational needs and abilities of the group intending to take action. A community development orientation provides for the continued strengthening of the community, promoting conditions for greater health and reduced vulnerability. For that reason, we will take a closer look at this model.

Community development puts into place new, additional, or improved community resources, behaviors, attitudes, and practices that strengthen community health, capital, and relationships. It is essentially a strengths-based approach to community change. Community development occurs when members recognize their assets and discover how to use them in more productive ways.

Community development *recognizes sources of wealth* (or community capital) that exist in the community, *helps those sources to grow*, and *links them with one another* to form a stronger, more capable community. Fundamental to this approach is the belief that *members of the community itself have the primary responsibility for decision making and action.* Community development produces self-reliant, self-sustaining communities that mobilize resources for the benefit of their members.

These activities start with using currently available assets to put into place new community resources, attitudes, and practices that continue to expand the community's potential to provide for full and meaningful lives for its members. Development can occur within a neighborhood or beyond a neighborhood to include a broader community of people with shared interests. Community development is intended to increase the capabilities of a group of people in order for them to increase their efficacy: to achieve their intended purposes and to provide for more full and satisfying lives for all members of the group or community.

Community development is really about three things: capacity building, asset building, and ownership. For an activity to be considered community development, all three of these elements must be present.

Crucial to the notion of community development is building *community capacity*. Community capacity is the ability of a community to effectively and confidently act on its own behalf to provide for the well-being and draw forth the contribution of its members. That is, community members know how to work with each other to take care of the community and to help it grow stronger. Community capacity is both a sense of *shared responsibility* of residents and others for the welfare of its members and the *competence* of the community to act on that responsibility (Kirst-Ashman & Hull, 2009). Capacity is derived from a community's ability to store and make use of forms of power or wealth, particularly knowledge and skill (Delgado, 2000). A community (or an individual) with increased capacity knows more things, can do more things, can do them better, and is able to retain all this for easy access while expanding its potential for continued growth. Increased capacity leads to increased efficacy, which is the ability to produce a desired result or accomplish what you intend to accomplish. It also increases the motivation to set and achieve goals.

Communities that have increased capacity and efficacy are under less stress and are less likely to act inefficiently, ineffectively, or in ways that harm relationships. The abilities of communities to discover, create, and mobilize resources—both internal and external—to meet their requirements prevents or reduces the likelihood that they will engage in harmful or destructive activities. If communities can get what they need through healthy methods, they are less likely to try to do so in unhealthy ways. And if they continue to increase their abilities, even more of their interests will be met. This increased confidence encourages communities to continue to take care of themselves and to further develop their capacities, reducing harmful stress on the system.

Community development engages in *asset building*, increasing the number and usefulness of community assets that are available for members to use to improve their own lives as well as to build a sense of community and identity. This could include assets such as jobs, parks, new activities that bring people together and use their talents, and even new organizations. If you are doing some cooking, wouldn't it be nice to have a well-stocked pantry and a good spice rack to give you a selection of things you can use to put together a really good meal? If you are raising a family, wouldn't it be nice to live in a community that has a lot to offer?

A community functions around certain activities to fulfill its requirements for health. Among these basic requirements are environmental, physical, economic, political, educational and informational, cultural, spiritual, and social and emotional requirements. (These are described more fully in Chapter 5.) Community development brings forth new resources or new ways to meet these requirements. Although each of these aspects of community functioning can be the focus of development efforts, community development usually takes one of three broad forms: economic development, physical development, or social infrastructure development.

Economic development is concerned with the production of goods and services for generating and distributing financial wealth. This includes increasing the diversity and number of jobs or other income-producing activities. *Physical development* addresses the quality and number of the more tangible elements of a community, such as roads, housing, parks, sewers, sidewalks, or even landscape features. *Social infrastructure development* involves expanding its network of relationships, improving interaction among its members, bringing people together to prevent or solve community problems, enlarging the pool of talent and knowledge, and promoting member contributions to the common good. Taken together they all advance the health of the community by promoting its capacity to mobilize and connect other forms of capital to provide for its members and create conditions that enhance the quality of life.

The *ownership* of the enterprise is the final necessary ingredient of community development. We need to answer the question, "Who does this belong to?" If an outside organization or unit of government provides something to the community with little or no community involvement, particularly involvement in decision making, this is not true community development. Ownership includes having the final say on matters affecting the project, doing much of the work to bring the project to life and implement it, and playing an important role in taking care of what the project produces. You need to believe that a community is capable of assuming the responsibility of ownership before you can engage in community development.

Elements of Community Development. Let's take a closer look at the elements of community development. Some of these elements can be found in the work of Brueggemann (2006), Burkey (1993), Kretzmann and McKnight (1993), Lofquist (1996), McKnight (1995), and Ronnby (1995, 1996, 1998).

Build on Community Assets. Resources are what a community has going for it. Problems or unmet needs can be springboards to action, but action occurs through the use of resources. The simple act of recognizing assets gives a community a sense of confidence and a willingness and some energy to take action. When the community believes that assets exist, it finds them and uses them. This principle affects the entire way you as a change agent look at a community and decide what to do.

Increase Skills of Individuals. Engaging in the experience, particularly coupled with reflection and dialogue, teaches skills, be they fund-raising, media relations, conducting meetings, planning, or dealing with member conflicts. Potency and competency are related concepts. Also important are the mem-

bers' beliefs in their ability to teach new skills to other community members.

Connect People with One Another. The community development process builds relationships and shares talents, information, work, and energy—everything happens through relationships. Connecting people with one another in a purposeful manner produces clear, intended benefits. However, unintended, serendipitous benefits can also be most intriguing. The fundamental question for building an organization is, "Whom else should we be talking to?" Once this question becomes a habit, members will expect to build new relationships and will look forward to doing so.

In the early stages of organization, community members tend to funnel communication through the person who has initiated the organizing action or through a few other visible leaders. This is natural and understandable. These individuals are common points of contact, and they generally convey some degree of confidence. It is easy to reinforce this process in many subtle ways. It is also very limiting to the organization if this pattern persists. Patterns that increase interaction among members and promote less hierarchical or centralizing relationships increase strength.

Connect Existing Resources. Any project requires the assembly of resources, and it is rare to find them all in one place. The notion that "we can't do it because we don't have ..." commonly stalls development of good ideas. Assume two things. First, the group attempting to bring something to life does not have everything it needs. Second, most of what is needed can be found in the community. Any enterprise in your community, public or private, profit or volunteer, is a resource. Special interests or hobbies are resources. So are trees or water or a parcel of land.

Whenever you connect resources you create investors. You extend ownership and participation in the project, broadening its base of support. By connecting resources, you get the things you need, but perhaps more important, you connect more people to what you are doing and why.

Community Building Questions

Promoting community change goes beyond simply solving a problem or changing a circumstance. It extends to developing the capacity of the community to recognize conditions that need to be changed as well as the willingness and the ability to act. As change agents and community members, consider how the answers to these questions can inform your decisions and actions as you move toward change.

1. Is there an identified community? If so, who has defined it? How is it defined? If not, is one identifiable?

2. Does the project build skills of community members? Can these be identified?

3. Does the project produce new leaders and new teachers? What processes are intended to produce new leaders and new teachers? That is, what intentional steps will be taken?

4. Who owns the project? How is this seen? Who holds decision-making authority? If ownership is external, what processes are in place to transfer ownership to the members of the community? Which members?

5. Does the project produce new community resources that can exist apart from the project or after the intended life of the project? How will this occur?

6. Do the benefits or resources created by the project in turn create new benefits or resources?

7. Which community capacities or assets will the project build upon? How will these be expanded by the project?

8. Which community conditions does the project intend to change?

9. How does the project promote inclusivity?

10. How does the project build social capital?

11. How does the project acknowledge and meet system requirements?

Create or Increase Community Resources. Community development adds to the community's stock of routinely available assets. Look beyond solving an immediate problem with an eye to bringing something new into existence that will continue to benefit the community. A child care cooperative, a water well, a basketball court, a social club, an art class, a choir, a new business, a tree-lined street—all enrich the community.

Assume Ownership of Direction, Action, and Resources. Community members do not just approve plans, they create them. Community members do not just provide input, they make decisions. The community decides what to do and how to do it. What they produce is theirs.

Promote the Expectation that Community Members Will Do All Work Possible. We more fully value the things we create, and we learn much better the things we do for ourselves. Here is an example from very basic community development to illustrate this point.

Imagine a community that could really use a park. "Build us a park," they say. "Nope," I say, "but I will help you build a park." The community needs some technical guidance to figure out all the things that need

to be done to build a park. Next, the community must decide what they can do right now. And, if they want that park, community members must do the work. (If the size of the project outstrips the available resources, community members may choose to work alongside others who can provide help.) Next the community must look at things they can't do now but that they can learn how to do in a reasonable amount of time, maybe something like installing lighting fixtures. Teaching is a nurturing process and must address issues of confidence and belief in ability. Just because you know somebody can learn something doesn't mean that they know it too. Finally, only those things that still remain on the list will be done by people outside the community. The community has its park, more skilled members, and a sense of its ability.

Too often we train people for dependency, helplessness, and hopelessness. We train them to believe that they can't do things themselves. We usually do this in unthinking kindness—in the name of helping. Ask yourself: Whose park do we want it to be?

Create Beneficial External Relationships. Each community has a tremendous number of yet undiscovered assets, but it is likely that it will still need to draw in more resources from outside its boundaries.

It may need to ally with other communities to increase power. It may need to draw support from public sources. It may need to create economic enterprises that attract new dollars into its economy. Some specialized talents or particular materials may need to be imported.

Constructive relationships help promote an exchange of resources between the community and others, and it provides for collaborative partnerships among different communities for mutual benefit. Maintaining wider relationships also creates opportunities to influence external forces that affect the community.

Foster Community Self-Reliance and Confidence. All these actions help a community to believe in itself and its abilities. It forgets how to back down and back away. When confronted with a challenge, members of the community assume that they can figure out what to do and do it. Also, they believe that they will be able to meet other challenges that come their way.

Build Self-Sustaining Organizations. For a community to continue to grow in strength, a mechanism for community decision making and action must be maintained. A community must continue to develop new leadership, extend connections to new members, and maintain existing ones. It is more likely to do this by remaining active, taking on new challenges from time to time. The organization takes care of itself as it takes care of community issues.

Enhance the Quality of Life. Community development strives to move past problems to believe that better is possible, it is even likely, it is certainly deserved, and it can be expected.

Social Action and Community Development. The work of community change often needs to pursue two different, but related paths. The first is that of social justice, asserting the inherent worth and dignity of each person and ensuring that the rights and opportunities of all members are secured and acted upon. This includes eliminating the many forms of inequality in access to housing, health care, income, education, political voice, and other benefits of a society (Jansson, 2009). The second is

the development of the community's wealth or assets so that members are able to take full measure of the opportunities they have to lead full and satisfying lives and to contribute to the healthy functioning of their community. A fully developed community is much less vulnerable. It becomes self-reliant, manages its relationships with forces outside the community, and is able to assert its interests. Both inequality and inattention to a community's strengths sap the ability of a community to develop.

Development activities enable a community to move forward on community building activities. Yet on some occasions, community groups need to first secure rights or opportunities that are being denied to them. Further, movement to a new condition is often preceded by heightened irritation and coming to grips with what is causing the discomfort. Anger and frustration associated with problems spur people to action. Social action can get a community moving. Groups frequently need to go through a period of social action to assert the case for communities whose members have been exploited or ignored by powerful interests from outside the immediate community. In these situations the conflict-oriented strategies typical of social action may be needed to initiate a new order in the wider community that recognizes and responds to the rights of the close community. In fact, a community group may need to engage in an extended period of social action before it can direct significant attention to development efforts. The conflict period can be followed by transition stages during which the group moves into more collaborative or developmental approaches (see Figure 2.1).

Social action can bring issues to light and an organization to life, but the community may become stuck there—developing its conflict skills but little else. To become truly empowered, a community must move beyond reaction and assert its own agenda, cultivating the internal assets that can provide its members with a high quality of life. It needs to become self-directing, self-evaluating, and self-renewing. Some aspect of community development work must take place very early in the organization's life for three reasons. First, many members of the community will shy away from a conflict agenda. However, these individuals still care about the community and want to contribute in some

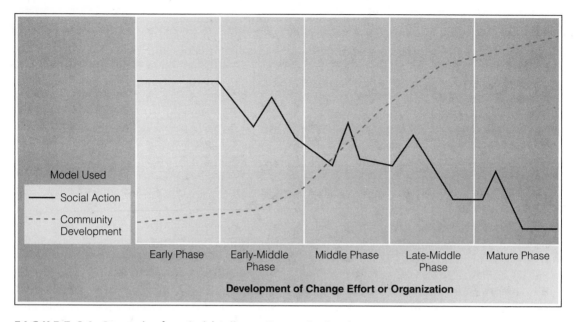

FIGURE 2.1 Progression from Social Action to Community Development

way. Development activities provide an opportunity to help. Second, development activities provide visible signs that the community intends to thrive and is doing so. These indicators become sources of encouragement and pride. Third, development activities create new resources and promote investment. These solidify the community's foundation and strengthen its ability to engage in conflict while discouraging the opposition.

Even though a community may move from confrontation to development, it may need to invoke conflict strategies from time to time to prevent exploitation, to gain access to resources to which it has a rightful claim, or to bring a sense of drama to boost interest. The more a community is developed, the stronger it becomes and the less vulnerable it is to external threats. Well-organized neighborhoods, for example, that have constructively developed their internal assets usually get their fair share of resources and are rarely targeted as dumping grounds.

Conflict may be necessary because you cannot pursue opportunities if you cannot exercise your rights. Being concerned with people's rights is the starting point, but we must also pay attention to people's abilities and responsibilities. Many change advocates—often those

from outside the community—miss this point. Treating people as needy rather than as able and responsible is demeaning, disrespectful, and patronizing.

Social action can be seen as liberating a community from oppressive conditions and altering power relationships. Community development extends liberation by increasing community capacity to build the power of self-reliance and collaborative relationships. Social action efforts tend to bring people together with an outward focus to change or get the most of what is out there. It somewhat depends on what is out there to help the community function. Development efforts tend to bring people together with more of an inward focus to change or get the most from what is in there. It somewhat depends on what is in there to help the community function. Obviously both are necessary. If external conditions and pressures are so harmful or stifling, the community cannot achieve its potential and will likely decline. If internal strengths and asset development do not occur, the community will function poorly and become dependent on others for its survival.

Social action is often needed to achieve social justice. Community development is often needed to affirm and fulfill the promise of social justice.

CONCLUSION

Effective action is grounded in good theory. Several different theoretical perspectives inform the work of community change. Commitment to building a strong theory base involves consideration of the clarifying ideas of scholars, activists, and especially partners in the community who are working to promote change. A practitioner's use of theory guides action, and reflection on that action strengthens theory.

A change agent must be able to recognize and build on the resources available in the community. This requires both a belief in the presence of resources and an ability to note opportunities for their use. A change agent who sees only threats and weaknesses will invite the community to stay stuck in the belief of dependency and powerlessness.

One significant set of resources can be found in the people themselves. Believing in these resources means that you believe in the ability of the people to define their own issues and to rely on themselves to make their own decisions.

Look for signs of strength whenever you can, and draw attention to them. What you look at affects what you produce. Act on belief in power, abilities, and rights, not victimhood. People, as individuals or as a community, move forward

> ### ▶ Take a Moment to Discover ◀
>
> Take a closer look at your community, either one of your close communities or the wider community. What do you see? What resources can you name that might be underutilized? What treasures might be hidden from view? See if today you can identify something of value that you didn't really recognize before.

only through the use of their abilities. Perhaps the most important contributor to a community's success is a belief in its abilities rather than a belief in its problems. Help foster that belief.

You will become a more effective change agent as you deepen your understanding of theoretical principles that give guidance to action. As you put theories to the test and refine them, you will discover principles of your own.

Understanding these concepts is important, but understanding is demonstrated and becomes meaningful only through action. Change comes by acting. Learn to apply these principles in practical ways that encourage community action.

WE'RE JUST DONE FIGHTING

Camiliano stood there in the middle of the street in the middle of the day in the hot month of June. He wanted to see as much as he could see of the neighborhood. Not many cars now, this time of day, this time of year, so he felt safe. It was the first time he had felt something like safety in the past 10 years. The view wasn't very impressive. The old homes looked faded, maybe it was just the harsh light. And thirsty, maybe it was the dusty dirt that had slowly replaced the green grass that was there when all this started. Parched weeds were the predominant landscape feature. But Camy, as his friends called him, felt good. They'd won.

What used to be a vibrant neighborhood seemed condemned by a planner's pen. The state university, the most powerful institution in the city, had decided they would tear down much of the neighborhood to make

room for, well, anything the university wanted. They told Camy and his neighbors that there was nothing they could do about it. They had the right to tear it down. Camy didn't have the right to live there anymore. You sell your house to the university when they want it at the price they want, or they'd just condemn the property and take it. Of course, the university wouldn't tell you when they were going to do this—maybe next year, maybe 10 years from now. You just wait till it happens and don't fix things up because you won't get your money back from any improvements. Things started to fall apart, houses and families. So most people just left, selling their homes for as much as they could get to a new set of owners, absentee landlords who could get the rent from students no matter what the place looked like.

But Camy did not leave, and some others stayed as well. They had never organized around anything, but when they found out that they were to lose their homes, they came together. The group trusted Camy and a couple of the others who got things started. They felt they might have a chance to win, but they didn't feel that they had much to lose. The small organization continued to grow over the years. They had just enough power to keep delaying things—"the inevitable" the university called it. But their tactics worked to buy them time while the organization grew. They learned how and where to apply pressure and how to take action. Each thing they did, each conversation they had with each other, taught them something valuable. They formed alliances with other neighborhood organizations. They made the best use of their connections to draw political leaders into the fray, including those from other parts of the state that sat on the legislative committee that oversaw the university's budget. They drew attention to the university's arrogance in carefully planned media events. Neighbors became bold. They kept things up—and they all kept together, the renters, the students, those whose families had lived there for generations, and the newly arrived. They discovered that this was more than about

houses; it was about their own dignity and their right to assert it. The university was no longer dealing with one little, scared neighborhood.

The university decided it needed a new plan. It decided it didn't need all that land after all. It took 10 long years. It took a toll on the once proud neighborhood. It took organizing. It took power and action. It took neighbors from different backgrounds learning to trust each other and work together. Now, things had changed. A new agreement was in place, one that could only be altered with the neighborhood's consent, one that had other built-in protections just in case the university was tempted to change its mind.

Camy looked across the street to his grandmother's home and remembered the parties they'd had there. He saw the empty lots where other grandmothers' homes once stood, torn down by university machines, no longer of use to the institution. He saw Melody's front yard, full of vibrant plants, a splash of color made brighter by the surrounding drabness. Then again, Melody was an artist. Montserrat, Camy's wife, came out to meet him, put her arms around his waist and said, "we're finally done." "No," he replied smiling, "we're just done fighting."

REFLECTION QUESTIONS

1. How does understanding how systems operate help you make sense of what happened?

2. Which theoretical principles were at play?

3. What did the neighborhood have that could make the university respond?

4. What do you think helped to sustain this organization for so long?

5. What might the experiences and conversations have taught the neighbors?

6. How might social action lead to community development?

7. What components for community development are in place?

GROUP ACTIVITY: BUILDING ON YOUR EXPERIENCE

Each time a community of people works together, something works well. Often, a lot of things work well. When faced with the inevitable problems, though, we may overlook the helpful things that

are present in the situation. The problems can end up defining our experience. A more powerful approach involves recognizing what is working and building on those real events and practices to become stronger and prevent a lot of problems. This allows us to build and use energy for progress instead of using a lot of energy to keep fixing things, which could stall your efforts.

Divide into teams of four members. Select a close community that those in your group are members of such as the class community, a neighborhood, or a community agency.

1. Identify an experience doing something together that members of this community have shared. (2 minutes)

2. Working in pairs, list some things that went well in that experience that you could build on for future efforts. (5 minutes)

3. Meet with the other pair. Each pair describes the positive elements they have identified. (5–10 minutes)

4. Together design a symbol that represents one element the team does not want to forget. (5–10 minutes)

5. Each team explains its symbol to the larger group. (2 minutes)

HELPFUL WEBSITES

Links to the organizations briefly described here are on the companion website at www.cengage.com/humansvcs/homan.

Paulo Freire Institute. UCLA brings together scholars and critics who intend to show how Freire's ideas can work in the real world. In addition to links to other Freireian resources, you will find an online journal with contributions from academics and activists alike.

The Saguaro Seminar: Civic Engagement in America. This ongoing project, sponsored by Professor Robert D. Putnam at the John F. Kennedy School of Government at Harvard University, focuses on expanding what we know about our levels of trust and community engagement and on developing strategies and efforts to increase this engagement. Multiple links provide access to social capital research, emerging news regarding social capital and community engagement, and valuable measurement data of social capital and community engagement.

Appreciative Inquiry Commons. Case Western Reserve University hosts this site, which is a worldwide portal devoted to the fullest sharing of academic resources and practical tools on appreciative inquiry and the rapidly growing discipline of positive change. The site is rich with case study information, research, and many other tools to help you understand and apply appreciative inquiry. Many consider Case Western Reserve as the birthplace and home of appreciative inquiry.

Center for Community Change. The center works with low-income people to build power and reshape their communities. Along with news and project updates, practical information on a host of topics is available including advocacy, community development tools, community organization, leadership training, coalition building, and economic development.

Communication Initiative. Providing descriptions of many theories of change from an international perspective, this is a rich site with access to publications, development news, planning and evaluation methods, and much more.

PART II

✳

Putting the Pieces Together

It will be cold again tonight, maybe more snow. Things look so pretty all covered over with clean, fresh snow. Sarah gazes out her office window at the few remaining patches left over from the storm three nights ago. Most of the snow has turned to slush—dirty, wet, looking colder. Maybe it will all turn to ice by this evening. The drive home could be dangerous.

What must it be like not to have a home? Where do those people go when the weather is like this? Is the ice better for them or the slush? Sarah shivers, glad the heater in her Chevy will take her warm to her apartment. She knows some apartments have no heat. The bills are unpaid. Service is shut off. In some homes family budgets will require the heat to be kept so low that people wear their coats indoors.

Yes, some people will spend the night in cardboard bedrooms, some will be hungry, some will be sick, some will get drunk, and some will get hit tonight by a "loved" one. Sarah knows what's out there. Sometimes it seems too much.

She thinks about "her" old people. She has been a case manager for more than a year now. Almost all her clients are elderly, and almost all of them are alone. All of them used to be children. They used to be teenagers. Back then did they ever think of growing old, of living alone, of being afraid of teenagers? Sarah wishes she could do more for them and for all those problems she can see out her window even with her eyes closed. Some things out there are working, she knows, and people have lots of gifts. Maybe they are hidden behind closed doors or blank stares, or maybe they are in plain sight if you just know how to look.

How else could a worker spend her time dealing with any one of these things that trouble her, she wonders. If she tried, could she squeeze more work into the same number of hours? Could she find a way to make adjustments in her work assignments? Would it all be a burden, or would it be exciting? For a moment she imagines herself working to change things. The picture isn't quite clear, but she can tell she is doing something new. She envisions the faces of some of her old people, and she can see them smiling. Why? What's different? Sarah notices that she too is actually smiling just thinking about it. Why?

Picking up the ringing phone, Sarah dismisses these thoughts. It's time to get back to work. The response to her hello comes from Greg Danory, another case manager.

"What's up, Greg?"

"I've been talking with Jo Ann Handford, a counselor at Davis Junior High. She wants to work with us on a program to have some of the junior high kids visit some of the elderly people in the neighborhoods around the school. They might do a little yard work and some shopping from time to time. Or they might just visit. She would like to meet next week to talk about it some more. What do you think?"

"Well, Greg, I think that's a start. Oh, and remember to bring along a few of the kids."

After a few more minutes of conversation, Sarah puts the phone down and once again looks outside. Even though the scene appears bleak, Sarah is glad she has an office with a window.

Maybe Sarah will work to bring junior high school students and elderly citizens together in a way that benefits both groups. Maybe she will work to change utility company policies to keep families warm on cold winter nights. Maybe she will develop socialization activities with people who otherwise would have almost no human contact. She wonders what her role would look like and what she could expect from others. In undertaking any of these efforts, what would Sarah need to know to bring about change?

Part 2 provides a number of answers to that question and gives you a strong foundation to build on. As a worker involved in promoting community change, you will learn quite a lot simply by experience. However, having a foundation to build on will make learning easier and success more likely.

Chapter 5, Knowing Your Community, contains a number of perspectives on communities and key community characteristics. You will increase your awareness of how communities function to meet their needs and the assets they can draw upon. Methods for discovering unmet community needs and unrecognized talents and resources will be offered, and you will understand the importance of recognizing a community's capacity and readiness to change. You will learn how to involve community members in researching and acting on the issues they see, including using tools like mapping technology to give you a good picture.

Change is produced by the use of power, and Chapter 6, Power, describes the concept of power and its use in promoting community change. You will learn how to recognize who has power in a community, and you will be introduced to techniques for building your own power. One essential aspect of community change, empowering others, will be examined as well.

Chapter 7, Powerful Planning, explores the importance of planning and shows you how to prevent planning from being a colossal waste of time. Each step in the planning process is described with an emphasis on making planning activities useful in the real world. You will learn to identify and deal with potential pitfalls to effective planning. Recognizing that problems can be either simple, complicated, or complex will help you understand how to deal with them. You will discover different ways for community members to shape the planning process, using their unique knowledge and abilities. You will see how the values that people hold dear can drive planning and understand how to evaluate your work.

Chapter 8, People—The Most Valuable Resource, examines ways to attract people to your change effort and ways to maintain their participation. "Everything happens through relationships" is a fundamental principle in organizing. You will find ways to build and strengthen relationships, and especially develop leadership. Because most people involved in community change efforts volunteer their time, working with volunteers is discussed. Our communities are increasingly diverse, and understanding the importance of recognizing and valuing cultural differences while acknowledging similarities among people of all cultures is vital to success. You will be presented with some reflections on how people respond to various challenges inherent in working for change, which will help you anticipate problems and strengthen commitment.

Chapter 9, Raising Other Resources, looks at how you can obtain needed items or services for little or no money and how you can raise the money you do need. You will increase your understanding of methods for generating support from individuals and organizations. Particular fund-raising techniques will be explained, including using information technology and writing and submitting grant proposals.

Chapter 10, Getting the Word Out, details various methods of communication with the members of your own organization and with the public at large, and it helps you to figure out which approaches you should take with various target groups. You will learn how to use low-cost publicity techniques, and you will be provided with guidelines for working with both print and electronic media to get in and on the news. You will appreciate that people are using different forms of communication, such as social networking, and you will see how to use a variety of tools to reach many more people.

Chapter 11, Building the Organized Effort, takes you through the steps of developing an organization. You will learn the importance of issues and how to use them to provoke and maintain action. You will understand how much structure your organization needs and how you and others you work with can modify or replace unproductive procedures. You will see that building an organizational identity bonds people together, and you will know that you need to be building the organization as you do the work of the organization. Again, you will value the crucial importance of developing leadership and learn the four most important things that an organizer needs to do.

Much of the work of organizations is really the work of small groups, so significant attention is given to matters of group process. As a change agent, you will conduct many meetings, and guidelines for running effective meetings are offered. You will examine different types of organizations and their purposes and learn the process for formally incorporating an organization. Of course, you want to keep your organization going and growing, and we explore the factors that are necessary for sustainability, recognizing that money, though important, is the least significant factor.

Chapter 12, Taking Action—Strategies and Tactics, is the final chapter in Part 2. Basic strategies and tactics for implementing action are described along with a discussion of the strengths and limitations of various approaches. You will consider some fundamental ethical issues involved in your decisions to take action or to refrain from action. You will gain some insights into the strategies and tactics that may be used against you by an opponent. A final list of "commandments" is presented to keep you on the right track.

In almost every chapter you will see how using information technology can make your work more productive and extend its reach. You will understand how the power of basic technology tools will increase the power of your organization.

In actual practice many things occur almost simultaneously to build and strengthen an organized change effort. Involving people, acquiring other resources, and developing issues are all part of the process of putting together an organization that can make its presence known and take action. You really won't be working on one aspect of the effort in isolation from another. All these elements relate to one another. By artificially separating these elements, we can give each element closer inspection; this tends to be how things work in textbooks. Understand that this is not how things work in the world in which we live.

What may have started out as a vague dissatisfaction, or even outrage, will, as a result of your commitment, turn into something more important and more potent. As you move toward accomplishment, you will notice that you will have brought something into existence, given something life. You will cultivate a group of people who will be involved in doing things on purpose, recognizing that they have a lot to bring to the table. The way that they relate to one another, and the way the things they do relate to each other, will produce change.

Chapter 3

Relating Community Change to Professional Practice

CHAPTER HIGHLIGHTS

- Remediation, accommodation, and community change
- Working for change is a fundamental professional role
- Purposes of social welfare
- Residual, institutional, and development views of social welfare
- Levels of capacity and development
- Fundamental difference between development and service
- Workers as change agents

- Considerations of the term *client*
- Five stages of partnership
- Relationship between change efforts and professional values
- Limits of superficial caring and its consequences
- Pick your causes
- Applications of systems theory
- You already have many skills for community change

In this chapter we take a closer look at how change activities fit with social work and human services. As you work to alleviate human distress and develop community strength, how can you respond to conditions that directly confront the profession itself? For example, Child Protective Services workers often labor under unreasonable demands that hamper their effectiveness. This is unfair to the children served by the worker, it is unfair to the worker, and it is unfair to the profession as a whole. All workers bear the criticism of a skeptical public all too willing to see the profession as the culprit in a situation in which meager resources produce meager results.

You may not be satisfied working only with individual cases. You may want to work on community conditions that promote or hamper well-being, but can you really do this as a professional? Let us hope that private citizens take action on these issues, but let us also hope that actions to shape our communities and our public policies are well informed by professional social work and human services leadership. If not us, whom do we expect to do this work?

You may have questions regarding the relationship of community and policy change to professional practice. Many students and practitioners in social work, human services, public health, recreation work, or other disciplines envision a very limited role for themselves in community change, yet they have a rich body of knowledge, powerful values, and a variety of skills to contribute. Dinitto and McNeece (1989) pointed out that social work's multilevel perspective makes the profession particularly well equipped to develop social welfare policies. Schmolling and colleagues (1997) emphasized the importance of social policy development for human services workers. They believe "human services workers can be, and often are, instrumental in determining unmet needs and in influencing policy" (pp. 283–284).

There should be a connection between our theories, perceptions, and analyses and our strategies for dealing with things. For example, are the struggles people encounter primarily caused by individual behaviors alone? If so, remediation strategies should be our primary focus. If we believe individuals and social and community institutions, processes, and conditions cannot or should not be changed, then accommodation is our primary orientation. If we believe these struggles are caused by social, political, or economic forces, then community and social change strategies are our primary course.

We cannot believe one set of factors is the primary cause of a condition and then use a response that is geared to different circumstances. That is, we cannot believe community conditions lead to the challenges we face and then primarily engage in remediation efforts. There has to be a link between what we believe and what we do. Frankly, there is a connection. What we do reflects what we believe. Maybe our work to accommodate or take care of people says that we are good at this and we hope others are good at doing other things. Maybe it says that we believe this is the best that we can do. Maybe our work to improve conditions says that we believe we can do better.

Creating healthy communities calls our attention to social justice. Commenting on the work to promote community health, Lawrence Wallack

(2005) poignantly observed, "successful health promotion relies less on our ability to disseminate health information, and more on our efforts to establish a fairer and just society" (p. 428). Too often our work gets confused with charity, where the key elements are neediness and giving, not partnership with those who are in need and challenge to prevailing conditions that produce that need. A national radio report on growing economic hardship and hunger uses the term "charities" and "nonprofits" interchangeably, as if that is all nonprofits do (Fessler, 2008).

Community change efforts clearly are critical to our professional practice. We need to see this as part of our job. This is something we should do within our professional role, not outside of it. Here's why. First, taking action on problems at the community level and building community strength responds to the basic purposes of social welfare. Second, it is one of the principal methods of traditional practice. Third, it is consistent with our ethics and our values. Fourth, it is needed to assert and protect our sanction for effective professional practice. Fifth, we have a strong theoretical base that aids our analysis of the situation and provides the direction for action. Finally, our training clearly provides us with a base of skills to be effective in this endeavor. Let's take a close look at each of these points.

BASIC PURPOSES OF SOCIAL WELFARE

Social welfare can be considered both as a condition and as the processes intended to produce the condition. James Midgely (2009) notes that the term derived from the greeting "farewell," meaning go and be well, has been reduced to a series of services provided for the poor. He defines social welfare as "a condition or state of human well-being that exists when people's needs are met, problems are managed, and opportunities are maximized" (p. 6). This is a condition that affects individuals, families, communities, and societies (Midgely, 1995).

The *Encyclopedia of Social Work* defines social welfare more as the process or set of activities intended to produce this condition, considering it "the full range of organized activities of voluntary and governmental agencies that seek to prevent, alleviate, or contribute to the solution to recognized social problems, or to improve the well-being of individuals, groups, or communities" (Pumphrey, 1971, p. 1446). The International Federation of Social Workers and the International Association of Schools of Social Work (IFSW/IASSW, 2001) take an even stronger stand, defining social work this way: "The social work profession promotes social change, problem solving in human relationships, and the empowerment and liberation of people to enhance well-being.... Principles of human rights and social justice are fundamental to social work" (p. 5). Many professions in health and human services voice a similar call. To provide for the welfare of both the individual and the society, social welfare institutions act to prevent social problems; treat or resolve social problems; educate ourselves, our clients, our policymakers, and our communities about rights, responsibilities, problems, and possibilities; explore how to use what we have to create what we want; enhance the quality of people's lives; and (though we are sometimes reluctant to acknowledge this) enforce measures of social control to preserve social stability. To an important degree, each of these ends depends on community change efforts for its accomplishment.

We cannot prevent high school students from dropping out unless we are willing to make changes in our schools. We cannot assist a cocaine-abusing father of three kids if no treatment programs are available when he is willing to confront his condition. We cannot expect a community to be well informed about child abuse if we do not speak out to the people who most need to know. We cannot help people reach their full potential if the best we can offer is support for their labor to survive the daily struggle of their lives. We cannot promote social stability if we fragment our nation's social problems into 10 million isolated sorrows. Clearly, we are called to go beyond the routine if we intend to meet social welfare goals. And we are called to do this with skill and purpose.

Three Views of Social Welfare

Three approaches to achieving the purpose of social welfare are the residual, institutional, and develop-

ment approaches. Community and institutional change figure prominently in two of them. Let's take a closer look.

The *residual approach* characterizes much of the social welfare system in the United States (Wilensky & Lebeaux, 1965). This approach assumes that the family and the market economy are the proper sources for meeting people's needs. Social welfare provides a safety net of supplementary services to catch those individuals who fall through the cracks (Burt & Pittman, 1985). Of course, they must fall first.

Certain basic assumptions go hand in hand with the residual approach. Individuals and families receive the main attention of residual efforts. The problems confronted are seen as being caused by those being helped rather than by the structural ineffectiveness of the systems in which these people participate. For example, families need help because they don't work hard enough, not because the prevailing wage rates are too low to feed a family. The first order of business is to encourage the recipient to change, to become more adequate. Services are provided on a temporary basis to get the recipient back in the game. The game itself is not much changed.

Often individuals must prove that they need the assistance and that they are worthy of it. Because individuals are seen as inadequate, there is usually some stigma attached to receiving services, and a dependency relationship is likely to develop. Typical residual programs include Temporary Assistance to Needy Families (TANF), counseling programs, and job training programs.

The *institutional approach* is based on a different set of assumptions (Wilensky & Lebeaux, 1965). This approach sees welfare efforts as responses to shared social conditions. These problems affect a large number of people in common, not one at a time. Services are the right of the client, regardless of the degree of the problem. There is no requirement to prove need or worthiness; that is assumed.

Institutional programs are routinely available and accessible, and those using them are not expected to undergo changes themselves because there is no assumption that something is wrong with them in the first place. Institutional programs are seen as appropriate primary sources for meeting needs, and there is little or no stigma attached to participation (Moroney, 1991).

Our public education system is an example of an institutional response to a common problem—ignorance. Students do not need to prove that they are ignorant before being admitted to first grade, nor that they have failed in learning sufficiently at home. Other examples include social insurance programs such as retirement benefits under Social Security or a full national health insurance program.

Change efforts are directed at our societal institutions, improving the availability as well as the appropriateness of resources rather than improving the person making use of them. Here the emphasis is on narrowing the cracks in the system, not catching the people who fall through them.

This story about a young woman who was walking along the bank of a river will help you see the difference between residual and institutional approaches to social welfare. It was a lovely spring day, and as is required on such days, butterflies flitted about and birds sang in the trees. Suddenly the young woman's pleasant daydreaming was broken by cries from the river: "Help me! Save me!" She dashed to the river and, seeing a person in desperate need of help, jumped in and pulled the struggling soul from the water.

Barely had she caught her breath when once again she heard cries of "Help me! Save me!" In a flash she was in the river again, rescuing another victim from peril.

By this time a small crowd had gathered. When she jumped in yet a third time (a little slower now, she was not in that great of shape) to save another drowning individual, they all marveled at her courage and ability. But as she sat gasping for breath at the river's edge, more cries could be heard from the water. Instead of plunging back into the river, she struggled to her feet and began walking—away, up the river.

The crowd couldn't believe it, and they shouted, "You can't leave. Don't you see that people need your help here?"

"Yes," she sighed, "I can see that."

"Where are you going?" they demanded.

"I'm going up the river to see who's kicking all these people into the water to begin with, and I'm going to put a stop to it there!"

The residual approach is the downstream form of helping. The institutional approach is the upstream form.

A third major view of social welfare is the *development approach* (Dolgoff & Feldstein, 2007;

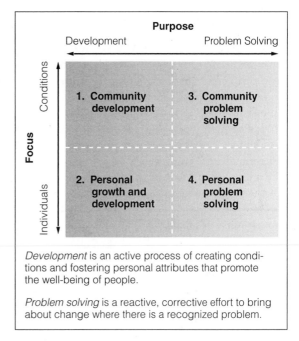

FIGURE 3.1 The Arenas of Action
SOURCE: Lofquist, 1996

Lofquist, 1996). Using this approach, delivery of services moves beyond a problem orientation. According to this view, "it is possible for society to set up a social welfare institution simply to make living better, to improve the quality of life, and to fulfill human development, not necessarily to solve a problem or aid those in distress" (Dolgoff & Feldstein, 2007, p. 138).

Figure 3.1 compares problem solving with development. Instead of correcting one individual problem after another and another, community development can prevent problems by improving conditions that affect people.

Community development, which grows, connects, and mobilizes forms of community capital to increase the store of community assets and promote community capacity and ownership of the process, was discussed in detail in Chapter 2. Development approaches, though, can operate at different levels.

Five Levels of Capacity and Development

Social workers and other human service professionals work with people at a number of different levels in a host of settings. At each level you are helping people develop their ability to effectively use their talents and grow in new directions. The people you work with will be able to accomplish what they intend to accomplish and increase their motivation to set and achieve goals. In the process you will help them use what they know, recognize undiscovered strengths, and cultivate new capabilities. They will relate more effectively to their environment and form productive relationships and manage more difficult ones. Through your partnership they will face and meet challenges, learning from the experience to become more capable in engaging future ones. They will not only see that the glass is half full of valuable assets, but has room to grow, and they may come to see that they can get a bigger glass. You will have helped them to develop their capacity.

It may be useful to think about five different levels of capacity, each with a corresponding level of development. You may decide to help develop *individual capacity*. If so, you will promote *personal* development. You may decide to help develop *group capacity*. If so, you will promote *group or family development*. You may decide to help develop *organizational capacity*. If so, you will promote *organizational development*. You may decide to help develop *community capacity*. If so, you will promote *community development*. You may decide to help develop *political capacity*. If so, you will promote *policy development*.

The choices you make regarding how you best take part in the helping process will guide your focus, the type of work you do, and the level of development you will help promote. Each of these levels of development work has a number of corresponding professional roles. Your role as a counselor, family therapist, organizational consultant, community organizer, or lobbyist will relate to the level of impact you want to achieve. Three of these capacity building levels—organizational capacity, community capacity, and political capacity—involve some form of community work, demanding skills in bringing numbers of people together to change conditions.

Your work can lead from one system level to another as conditions indicate larger levels of involvement.

Development versus Service

A development approach is very different from the service approach that more commonly typifies profes-

sional activity. Development approaches build on strengths, identifying resources within the individual, the group, or the community that can be more fully cultivated and utilized. The emphasis is on potential, not problem. The strengths perspective in working with families incorporates many development features (Early & GlenMaye, 2000).

A service orientation, which often shapes professional activity, starts with the identification of a problem or an unmet need. This approach looks at what's not there: What of value is missing? It then delivers services to provide what is missing or to take care of people who are missing what they need.

A service approach looks for holes to fill. A development approach looks around for things or potential to cultivate or resources to build with. Because services rarely change conditions, but rather supply accommodations to them, they tend to perpetuate need. Development actions help to improve a condition by augmenting the strengths to create something new.

How workers look at a situation and think about what to do affects the nature of the professional relationship that is developed. Service is more characterized by a differential in power between the professional worker, who is a more powerful expert, and the recipient, who is dependent on what the worker can deliver. Here it is easy to fall into roles of giver and receiver or of expert authority and needy complier. The development approach is characterized more by equality in power between professional workers and those who benefit from the improved conditions by partnering with the worker to improve conditions. Here the roles are of partners.

Service is often given in an attitude of caring, with a desire to alleviate pain or discomfort. Sometimes it is provided with the intent of social control to manage the behavior of individuals or whole classes of people through the periodic distribution of a needed resource.

Think about how you see your job and the people who benefit from your work. Do you intend to help them feel better by giving them something they don't have? Or do you intend to find out what they have and see how they want to use these things to enhance their lives?

Here is a snapshot of the key differences between service and development approaches.

Service	Development
Focuses on problems	Focuses on assets and capacities
Is episodic	Is ongoing
Reinforces power imbalances	Equalizes power relationships
Promotes passivity	Promotes capability and power
Relies on experts	Relies on partnerships
Recipient owns the problem	Mutual ownership of possibilities
Recipient is isolated and dependent	Links people with shared interests
Gives gifts to meet needs	Recognizes gifts and fuels abilities
Focuses on what is missing	Focuses on what is available
Wants to give	Wants to build
Believes "this is the best we can do"	Asks "what can we be?"
Maintains conditions	Changes conditions
Fixes	Prevents
Expects no contributions by others	Requires contribution

An additional limitation of a service orientation is that it is heavily dependent on public funding (Gronbjerg, 2004). This is a narrow base of support. Even in prosperous economic times, it is a struggle for programs and services to garner the funding they seek. During times of economic stress, these programs are among the first to be cut. The recent economic downturn has resulted in many sharp, painful cuts. A system that is built primarily around programs of service faces additional strain when more and more people look to these programs to get help. Demand increases while funding decreases. When services are most sought, they become less available. An approach that is heavily service oriented has little to fall back on.

A development orientation prevents many problems from happening in the first place, and it responds differently when problems do occur. Assistance is provided within a development framework that may engage professional workers, but this is more fully integrated into the community, using a much broader network of community relationships. For example, as

a way of promoting both employment of neighborhood residents and lower costs for work, one neighborhood has developed a talent bank, linking residents who have special skills with residents who need and are willing to pay for them (Veneklasen, 2009). During times of economic hardship, mutual helping and community interdependence provide a much broader base of support. Development approaches are not so dependent on program funding by political bodies tasked with figuring out what to cut in the face of dwindling tax revenues.

TRADITIONAL APPROACHES TO PROFESSIONAL PRACTICE

Does community change really have a place in the delivery of social work and human services? Aren't most workers busy working directly with people in need? And, frankly, are there any jobs out there for change agents? Good questions. The answer to them all is yes. But maybe you want more than a simple yes. Here is the "why" to the yes.

Working as a Change Agent

Let's start with the first question: Is promotion of community change really a fundamental professional activity for social workers and other human service professionals? These professionals have historically been involved in activities to reform community policies and practices, particularly ones that affected low-income and working-class people (Jacobs, 2001; Reisch & Gorin, 2001). We acted not only to serve the disenfranchised, but to enfranchise as well. It has been part of our very identity. Is that still true today? Many would answer no; we leave that up to others.

Well, where have all the workers gone? To therapy? To private practice? Jacobs (2001) describes social work's drift from its mission of social justice toward the practice of individual therapy. She asserts that the "leadership role in innovative systems reform and social change work has virtually disappeared" (p. 51). The National Association of Social Workers ([NASW], 2009) has developed practice sections for social work affiliation. The largest is private practice.

Lots of workers are engaged in activities that have little to do with altering community forces that harm rather than help. But that does not describe "all the workers." The simple fact that there is discussion in the professional ranks regarding the possibility of our losing our mission indicates that the mission has some value.

Workers in human services are change agents, at least the good ones are. True, too many end up being problem processors rather than problem solvers or problem preventers. You know the type. They are the plague of all professions or occupations. They lose sleep wondering where or to whom they can pass problems along. Clients are shifted from one person, department, agency, and, if possible, state to the next until they and their problems get lost. This is called making problems go away. Of course, the real problem in the eyes of workers such as these is that they may be forced to actually grapple with things, some of which may be out of the ordinary.

To work in human services requires a willingness to take part in changing a condition. If that only means helping someone qualify for a public assistance program, rest assured that this is a pretty significant "only" in the life of that individual. Because of the nature of their work or perhaps because of the depth of their commitment, many workers go beyond making these individual but very real changes. Some assist community members in changing how they respond emotionally and behaviorally to their circumstances. Others assist in making changes in those circumstances. The differences are really only in scope, focus, and intensity. All workers must accept the simple fact that improvement means that something has to change—and they will play a part in promoting that change. Moving toward community change occurs when workers can link private anguish with public conditions and act on that understanding.

Both NASW (2002) and the National Organization for Human Services ([NOHS], 2002) identify community organization practice as a fundamental role. Perhaps we need to recommit to the things we say we are about—and actually be about them. The fact that recent political circumstances have led many workers to rekindle their activist fires shows that we can still draw on our roots (O'Neill, 2002). Ezell (2001) offered a clear, poignant observation: "everyone is an advocate, but the problem is that

most people advocate for the status quo" (p. 10). What sort of professional advocate do you intend to be?

All jobs in human services require skill in changing conditions, but most workers are not full-time community change agents. However, all workers will be confronted by the challenge to seek changes in the way things are—*all workers*. Although few individuals are hired specifically for their ability to promote community change, most workers are expected not only to provide social services but also to improve delivery of those services. However, this may reflect both training and the interests of workers in human services.

There are many positions in community organization and development throughout the country. Demand is growing, and you will see opportunities if you cast your eye in that direction. In fact, as interest in using community organization and development methods increases, public and private agencies are having a difficult time finding enough people with these skills (Jacobs, 2006). The following chapters not only introduce you to some of the possible roles in community change but to some organizations involved in the work as well. Your ability to take an active part in community leadership will be a definite asset, especially for positions requiring more professional responsibility. The jobs out there—the ones that mean anything—require more than just filling out forms.

Direct Work with Individuals

Most human service workers work directly with people; unfortunately, we are not short of people who seek our help. A worker who is too busy to assist a client in learning how to contend more powerfully with the situations causing discomfort is much like a teacher who insists that students passively receive information and ask no questions because there is so much material to cover. Perhaps a worker with an individual client focus will not play a major role in changing the conditions that affect the people he works with, but even that worker can do three specific things to make a larger impact:

1. Assist the individual to understand the forces in the environment that are causing distress, and

DID YOU KNOW?   Continuum of Family Involvement

In Arizona workers and community members who are parents of children with special health care needs have built a process for more fully involving families in shaping the conditions that affect families and children. To help both workers and families see that their partnership can go far beyond providing services to one family at a time, they look at family involvement as a continuum and describe different levels of involvement.

1. **Parenting.** This is family involvement at the most basic, most important level: caring for the child, nurturing the child's development, establishing a routine, modeling problem solving, and attending to the child's activities.

2. **Personal development.** Taking advantage of and creating opportunities for self-growth: reading a newsletter, requesting and using parent-to-parent match, going to a support group, attending a workshop or other training.

3. **Participation.** Providing input to agency personnel by participating in planning and policy development activities: providing a family perspective on what is needed and what works. (This is what many agencies see as family involvement.)

4. **Planning and implementing family support activities.** Moving beyond personal needs to organize and plan activities for and with other families: facilitating a support group or meeting, contributing to a newsletter, being a parent mentor, and providing training to other families, organizations, agency personnel, and professionals.

5. **Policy making and community development.** Partnering with professionals and other parents with decision-making authority to take action within the community and the state; recognizing, mobilizing, and increasing community assets to enhance opportunities for children with special needs; working with legislators on policies that affect families; and working on systems change.

Family involvement is most productive when parents, professionals, and other community members come together in true partnership and collaboration to take action on specific issues within the community or the state that will enhance the quality of life there.

SOURCE: Developed by Parent-Led Community Action Teams, supported by the Arizona Department of Health Services, Office for Children with Special Health Care Needs.

---

help that person to develop skills to confront these forces.

2. Identify those who can play a major role in fostering change, which could include bringing similarly affected clients together or referring them to other programs or other professionals.

3. Bring the existence of harmful conditions to the attention of those who are in a position to act on that awareness.

These steps don't require that you master difficult new skills; they simply require that you adopt an attitude that these activities are a necessary consideration in responding effectively.

One perspective holds that the role of social work really is to provide enough services to the less powerful so they will not make larger demands that would threaten the prevailing balance of power (Richan & Mendelsohn, 1973). Although the idea of a gap between the politically powerful and those with little political power isn't much of a surprise, perhaps applying it to social work is. According to this notion, social work collaborates with the powerful, acting as a buffer to keep the gap in place. By focusing on individuals and promoting the belief that individual inadequacy or failure are at the root of individual and societal problems, social workers provide some modest help while diverting attention from fundamental injustices. *Nothing fundamental changes.* In fact, it is only when the flaws in social institutions threaten the interests of the powerful that broader changes are tolerated.

Perhaps you think this is so. Perhaps you think it is not. I hope you are at least thinking about it.

Five Stages of Partnership Development

The notion of partnership is central to working with people to promote community change. Five levels of development characterize the partnership relationship between health and human service professionals in service delivery roles and members of the community.

- At the *first level,* by far the most predominant, professionals talk to professionals about clients and the problems they are having.
- In some instances things go a little further—to the *second level.* Here professionals talk to clients. This is usually one-way communication directed "downward" from those with more power to those with less power.
- At the *third level,* community members who have something in common begin talking with one another about shared concerns.
- And at *level four,* organized groups of community members talk to professionals. Here it is the community members who initiate the conversation and the professionals who are expected to respond. (This level is rarely reached.)
- The *fifth level* of partnership (the most developed) is characterized by organized members of the community and professionals working together. They don't just talk to each other; they use their respective resources to collaborate on issues of common concern—concerns selected by the community members.

As an agent of change, at what level do you think your relationship with clients has "gone far enough"?

A Place for Community Change

Let's examine how this business of community change fits into the basic methods used by professionals providing human services. Imagine you are looking at a five-pointed star (Figure 3.2). At each tip is one of the five basic activities or methods:

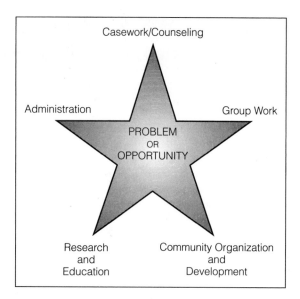

FIGURE 3.2 Basic Methods

Casework/counseling, which involves face-to-face contact with individuals and families to help them resolve problems

Group work, which uses the resources and support available among members of a group to assist the members in achieving individual or shared goals

Community organization and development, which brings people together to get, maintain, and use power to improve the conditions they face

Research and education, which involves developing and testing theories, discovering information, and communicating theories and information to people who can put them to use

Administration, which involves managing or operating social welfare programs or agencies

Each tip of the star indicates a valid approach to human services. In the middle of the star is the problem or opportunity faced by community members. Improving conditions may involve using one approach or several sequential approaches to intervention.

As a worker in the health or human services field, you will function mainly as a caseworker or

GLOBAL PERSPECTIVES

INTERNATIONAL FEDERA-
TION OF SOCIAL WORKERS—
Social workers in all settings engage
every day with children, men and
women struggling to realise…basic
rights to health. For example, social
workers support families whose poverty makes securing the conditions for
health and the purchase of health care
unattainable, including households
headed by children whose parents have
died from AIDS; homeless people,
migrants and other excluded groups
facing barriers to securing shelter, employment or education, including indigenous peoples whose social and
emotional difficulties are rooted in the
violation of their cultural integrity and
land rights; women and children suffering from the physical and emotional
health consequences of violence and
trauma, often linked to substance misuse. In every case people's lives are
compromised and impaired because of
global and local inequity. The inequitable distribution of health reflects the
inequitable distribution of the resources
human beings require for sustainable,
continuous development and growth
(International Policy on Health
approved by the IFSW General
Meeting, Salvador de Bahia, Brazil
August 14, 2008).

AUSTRALIA—Some social
workers—probably a minority—see
community development as a key
practice skill that should be utilized
in most social work interventions.
Others—probably a majority—view
community development as a specialist skill only to be utilized by
those working specifically as community development workers. The
latter position tends to lead to the
marginalization of community
development within social work

practice and education….Most of
my practice had been limited to
individual-based casework in areas such
as child protection, income security,
and crisis counseling. However, I had
worked as a Social Policy Officer at the
AASW (Australian Association for
Social Work) for one year. This
experience confirmed my belief
that social policy and community
development interventions were an
integral part of social work practice, and
that individual or group work needed
to be complemented by collective
activism to be effective (Philip Mendes,
2009, pp. 250–251).

BARBADOS—Most experts on
development agree that economic
growth does not in itself ensure a
better distribution of income and
services, but that social development,
which incorporates principles such as
cooperation, social justice and the
transformation of social and
economic structures, is necessary….
[Detractors warn that] most social
service workers have difficulty making
the connection between the broad
definitions of social development and
their day-to-day activities….
The social work curriculum is
heavily influence by the case work
approach….Barbados has been
undergoing a process of economic
development supported mainly by
tourism, resulting in cultural pene-
tration, the breaking down of traditional values, erosion of the extended
family, pockets of poverty and a host
of attendant problems. To date, the
profession's response has been reactive, with minimal impact….
[There is arguably an expanded
role for field education to] act as a
force for organizational change and
as a catalyst for social development….

[T]here is also room for further collaboration between field education
and the profession to help it develop a
voice in social policy-making which it
lacks to date (Tucker Rambally, 1999,
pp. 486–494).

ZIMBABWE—Since the 1970s a
clarion call has continuously sounded
for the social work profession in Africa
to shed its remedial outlook and assume
greater relevance, in order for the profession to more meaningfully address
the needs of the continent's masses….
… [F]or social work on the continent to become relevant, the profession must assume a developmental
orientation, and this has to start at the
level of education….
The developmental approach has
been recommended to the social work
profession in Africa for a variety of
reasons. Most compelling of these is
the fact that because of a general lack of
resources the continent of Africa can
hardly afford the luxury of continuing
to employ the remedial strategy, an
approach which over the years has
proved particularly costly….[I]t is clear
that the developmental strategy is not
simply suitable for social work institutions in Africa alone; the approach can
also be effectively utilized in other
regions of the world, particularly the
third world, where resources are
scarce (Rodreck Mupedziswa, 2001,
pp. 285–297).

EL SALVADOR—El Salvador
endured a violent civil war from 1979
to 1992 that took the lives of some
70,000 to 75,000 people, most of them
poor. Early this year the country was
devastated twice in one month by
earthquakes that took the lives of about
1,250 people, and injured another
8,000, and left many more homeless.

(continued)

● **GLOBAL PERSPECTIVES** *(continued)*

Most of the country's wealth continues to be concentrated in the hands of a few families and right-wing forces still prominent politically. Poor communities continue to struggle to overcome these hardships and to cope with the failure of the peace accords to measurably improve their lives.

As the primary caretakers of their families, women carry additional burdens. They experience discrimination in the labor market, and are sometimes the victims of family violence fueled by the frustrations of poverty and a deep-seated tradition of machismo. AMUSAMECO has designed a project of ongoing weekly meetings with groups of women in several poor and marginalized communities around San Salvador. Trained mental health workers will facilitate the meetings where women will learn relaxation techniques and discuss their experience of loss. Meetings also address their basic rights to health care, education, employment, and housing, and women's issues such as gender equality, self-esteem, and the right to protection against violence....The program aims to empower participants to become protagonists acting to improve their lives (Allen et al., 2002, p. 63).

SOUTH AFRICA—In the past, social work training was skewed towards the maintenance of the status quo of colonial apartheid and did not provide practitioners with the relevant skills to deal with the problems of the majority African population which was mainly disempowered and disenfranchised.... In the pursuit of relevant social work practice in the new order, social work education must therefore be transformed. Indeed, we should like to see the reorientation of all human service practitioners to the demands of a new democratic environment....

Social work is a Western concept and at times has found itself conflicting with the social terrains of Africa....Rather, in clinging to the traditional model, the profession appears to avoid issues inherent to development such as productivity, changing gender roles, people's participation, resource sufficiency, and rural development....

In order for the educators to become relevant in the new socio-economic and political environment, they have first and foremost to unlearn past teaching methods and be conversant with developmental trends....[A]cademics are not grounded in theories of development and are also very averse to developmental social work or social development because they have never practised nor bothered to become acquainted with them (Dovhani Mamphiswana & Ndangwa Noyoo, 2000, pp. 21–29).

counselor; a group worker or group therapist; a community organizer, developer, or planner; an educator or researcher; or an administrator. However, rarely will you function exclusively in your primary role. At each level of practice, you will come face to face with situations that call out for action to improve the conditions of a group of people.

For a caseworker who routinely assists pregnant teens, it may not be enough that young women understand the importance of prenatal care if such care is not available. A group worker running men's groups may find that many divorced men long for a closer relationship with their children but that certain forms of legal bias consistently interfere with that desire. Of course, workers with neighborhood or other community groups can easily identify common problems shared by the people they serve. Educators cannot be oblivious to the institutional shortcomings that can block students' abilities to learn effectively. All of us working in social service agencies benefit when the community is informed about what we are doing and why. Administrators can acknowledge program limitations imposed by policies and regulations and can develop new program responses to community conditions.

IMPLICATIONS OF PROFESSIONAL VALUES

Your values guide you to determine what is important, what you should do or refrain from doing. Social work professionals feel a strong call to work for social justice. "Most of the issues social workers confront are directly or indirectly related to injustice" (Segal et al., 2010, p. 67). Social work's strong value base fosters an expectation for action and provides the rationale for these efforts. Other professional groups also require their members to do

more than sit by and watch. For example, the National Association of Social Workers *Code of Ethics* (2008), the *Ethical Standards of Human Service Professionals* (NOHS, 2000), and the *Principles of the Ethical Practice of Public Health* (Public Health Leadership Society, 2002) clearly call for workers to acknowledge their ethical responsibility to promote the general welfare of society through action and advocacy. This is not a casual recommendation to be pursued as a matter of convenience—it is a fundamental ethical responsibility equal to any other matter contained in the codes.

Using categories established by Levy (1973) and drawing on the work of a number of other authors, Morales and Sheafor (1986) describe the critical values that should direct professional practice:

- *Values as preferred conceptions of people.* This orientation focuses on people and their relationship to the environment. Five key statements characterize this category. First, professional human services workers believe in the inherent worth and dignity of all people (Klein, 1972). Second, each person has an inherent capacity and drive toward change that provides her with the potential for development throughout a lifetime (Gordon, 1965). Third, people have responsibility for themselves as individuals and for their fellow human beings, including society. Fourth, people need to belong. Fifth, although people have needs in common, each person is unique and different from all others (Bartlett, 1958).

- *Values as preferred outcomes for people.* This orientation focuses on quality of life issues and the way society should be organized so people can achieve fulfillment. Three value statements appear in this category. First, society must provide opportunities for growth and development that enable each person to realize his fullest potential (Smalley, 1967). Second, society must provide resources and services to help people meet their needs and to avoid such problems as hunger, inadequate education, discrimination, illness without care, and inadequate housing. Third, people must have equal opportunity to participate in molding society (Pumphrey, 1959).

- *Values as preferred instruments for dealing with people.* This orientation focuses on how people should be treated. Morales and Sheafor (1986) describe this as a belief that "all people should be treated with respect and dignity, should have maximum opportunity to determine the direction of their lives, should be urged and helped to interact with other people to build a society responsive to the needs of everyone, and should be recognized as unique individuals rather than put into stereotypes, because of some particular characteristic or life experience" (p. 207).

The call to action echoes throughout these statements of professional values. Can you hear it? There will be times when our values conflict with our experience. This can be a motivating force for change. The actions you take as a professional are an acknowledgment of your commitment to these fundamental beliefs. Author after author writing on social work identifies either case advocacy or cause advocacy as necessary professional skills (Brueggemann, 2006; Dinitto & McNeece, 1989; Dubois & Krogsrud-Miley, 2005; Ezell, 2001; Federico, 1984; Jansson, 2008; Johnson & Yanca, 2007; Kirst-Ashman & Hull, 2009; Meenaghan & Washington, 1980; Morales & Sheafor, 2010; Pincus & Minahan, 1973; Schmolling et al., 1997; Segal et al., 2010). You will probably struggle to live up to these ideals throughout your career (Piccard, 1988). Still, it is not enough to simply agree to the importance of these values. You must act on them.

UNDER THE GUISE OF CARING

What level of response is needed to effectively confront the suffering that often brings people to the attention of human service professionals? Imagine that you are working in a school and a third-grade teacher brings Amanda to your attention.

Her family calls its 1993 Impala station wagon home. She is dirty, her hair a haven for lice, the soles on her only pair of shoes threaten to abandon her at any time. She's not doing well in school, can barely read even the simplest of words, and seems unable to get along with other members of the class. What do you think is needed here?

- A new pair of shoes?
- A bath?
- A trip to the nurse's office to deal with the lice?
- A note sent home to the parents of all the other kids warning them of the possible lice infestation at the school?

- A referral to the school psychologist?
- A call to Child Protective Services alerting them to the possibility of neglect?
- A visit to the classroom to see how her classmates treat her?
- Arrange temporary shelter facilities for her, her siblings, and her mom, with the hope that her father can find space in the men's shelter program?
- Establish a shelter care program for families?
- Establish a transitional housing program that would help families like Amanda's get back on their feet?
- Establish an organization with people who are homeless to advocate for decent housing and the provision of development-oriented support?
- Take action against the very forces within your community that lead to homelessness?

There is a lot that you can do, isn't there? How much will you actually do? Where will you stop? Who carries on from there? What determines your answers to these questions?

Perhaps all you think you can do is help Amanda in her struggle with the problems brought about because she has no real home. Are you actually going to go one step beyond responding to the immediate situation? Are you really going to do anything to reduce homelessness?

While you are mulling all this over, there is a knock at the door. The fourth-grade teacher wants to talk with you about Sam. He has a black eye. His dad got drunk last night and hit him. One more child. One more set of problems. What will you do?

The Painful Limits of Limited Action

If we respond to the presence of disturbing social conditions within our midst by working primarily to soften the pain they cause, does this imply a tolerance for their existence? We appear to be so caring in our efforts to respond to problems, scurrying about helping this Amanda and that one, never confronting the evils that caused Amanda to need our aid. We are so busy with all this caring that we have little time or inclination to do anything else. Does the shallowness of our attention and our action

⊟ Take a Moment to Discover ⊟

The following statements urging active involvement in improving social agencies and social conditions appear in the *Code of Ethics of the National Association of Social Workers* (NASW, 2008). Consider each statement carefully and imagine a situation in which you would put each principle into practice.

- Social workers should work to improve employing agencies' policies and procedures, and the efficiency and effectiveness of their services.

- Social workers should not allow an employing organization's policies, procedures, regulations, or administrative orders to interfere with their ethical practice of social work.

- Social workers should promote the general welfare of society, from local to global levels, and the development of people, their communities, and their environments.

- Social workers should advocate for living conditions conducive to the fulfillment of basic human needs and promote social, economic, political, and cultural values and institutions that are compatible with the realization of social justice.

- Social workers should facilitate informed participation by the public in shaping social policies and institutions.

- Social workers should engage in social and political action that seeks to ensure that all persons have equal access to the resources, employment, services, and opportunities that they require in order to meet their basic human needs and to develop fully.

- Social workers should be aware of the impact of the political arena on practice, and should advocate for changes in policy and legislation to improve social conditions in order to meet basic human needs and promote social justice.

- Social workers should act to prevent and eliminate domination, exploitation, and discrimination against any person, group, or class on the basis of race, ethnicity, national origin, color, sex, sexual orientation, gender identity or expression, age, marital status, political belief, religion, immigration status, or mental or physical disability.

The National Organization for Human Services (2000, pp. 61–68) also requires a firm commitment from human service workers to social justice and to strengthening service delivery.

- Where laws are harmful to individuals, groups or communities, human service professionals consider the conflict between the values of obeying the law and the values of serving people and may decide to initiate social action.

- Human service professionals keep informed about current social issues as they affect the client and the community. They share that information with clients, groups, and community as part of their work.

- Human service professionals advocate for the rights of all members of society, particularly those who are members of minorities and groups at which discriminatory practices have historically been directed.

- Human service professionals participate in efforts to establish and maintain employment conditions conducive to high-quality client services.

The Public Health Leadership Society (2002) *Principles of the Ethical Practices of Public Health* (endorsed by the American Public Health Association) strongly asserts public health workers' commitment to building healthy communities and promoting the power of disenfranchised community members. A powerful set of beliefs and values underlie their ethical principles:

> Identifying and promoting the fundamental requirements for health in a community are of primary concern to public health.
>
> The way in which a society is structured is reflected in the health of a community. The primary concern of public health is with these underlying structural aspects. While some important public health programs are curative in nature, the field as a whole must never lose sight of underlying causes and prevention. Because fundamental social structures affect many aspects of health, addressing the fundamental causes rather than more proximal causes is more truly preventive. (p. 3)

Ethical principles for public health workers include the following:

- Public health policies, programs, and priorities should be developed and evaluated through processes that ensure an opportunity for input from community members.

- Public health should advocate and work for the empowerment of disenfranchised community members, aiming to ensure that the basic resources and conditions necessary for health are accessible to all.

- Public health should seek the information needed to implement effective policies and programs that protect and promote health.

Take a Moment to Discover *(continued)*

- Public health institutions should provide communities with the information they have that is needed for decisions on policies or programs and should obtain the community's consent for their implementation.
- Public health programs and policies should incorporate a variety of approaches that anticipate and respect diverse values, beliefs, and cultures in the community.

- Public health programs and policies should be implemented in a manner that most enhances the physical and social environment.
- Public health institutions and their employees should engage in collaborations and affiliations in ways that build the public's trust and the institution's effectiveness. (pp. 1–16)

guarantee that there will be many an Amanda in need? What is the real effect of all our busyness?

Make no mistake about it, the actions we take do lessen the discomfort and bring some relief to those who are affected. However, we may be insensitive to the fact that our limited actions indicate endorsement of, or at least acquiescence to, these conditions that call for all our hurry and scramble. Under the guise of caring, we have reached a point of acceptance of conditions that produce the pain we try to ease.

Imagine that you are a worker for Child Protective Services with a caseload of 29 clients. The Child Welfare League of America (2006; Pace, 2006) recommends an optimal maximum caseload of no more than 15 clients. Your supervisor walks into your office with another case. You handle 20 cases competently and professionally. You handle 25 with some degree of effectiveness. How much real, constructive service do you provide to a caseload of 30?

You cannot say no to number 30. Why did you say yes? Are you truly caring for having done so? Would you have been reprimanded for refusing? How did you and your colleagues end up in such a situation? Does your acceptance of this unreasonable burden demonstrate your dedication and service to those who need you? How much benefit do they really receive? Under the guise of caring, you just can't say no. You stay busy doing your best to keep patching things up. You feel so overwhelmed. Do you really have no other choice?

If you believe your efforts matter—that they do in fact improve people's lives—should you accept limitations on your effectiveness and the consequent reduction in the benefit people will experi-

ence? Will you just be thankful for whatever kind of support you get? How will you participate in making decisions on how effectively you can provide service? Or is that none of your business? To whom do you want to leave these decisions?

You have learned how to juggle; in fact, you are pretty good at it. You are able to juggle five balls at once. All of them are safe as you toss them into the air—but five is the limit. What happens if someone tosses you number six? What is the effect on the first five? What happens to all your other cases when you say yes to number 30?

Social work and human services are hemmed in by suspicion and lack of community support. We do not practice in a vacuum. Jansson (2005) stated that social workers are "more subject to social policies that control, restrict, and regulate their practice" than are most other professions (p. 9). Meenaghan and Washington (1980) recognized that our careers are continually shaped by changes in the social welfare institution. They pointed out that it simultaneously helps, limits, and shapes the ways we deal with people in trouble. Should we as social workers and human services professionals attempt to shape this institution that shapes our practice?

I believe you do have options for challenging the circumstances that lead to the problems you confront. And I believe you have options for creating conditions that permit you to do effective work. These options include recognizing both our right and our responsibility to improve the conditions under which we work, which is the focus of Chapter 14. Our work environments affect what we do, how we do it, and how we relate to one another in this human service enterprise. Our work environment can foster energy, purpose, and enthusiasm or quite the opposite. We are participants in this process; our actions or inactions play a part in giving us what we get in the places we work.

In my experience, workers who have acted thoughtfully and purposefully to confront and resolve systemic problems have produced many positive results. It isn't simple. It isn't impossible. Like any worthwhile professional activity, it is challenging, engaging, periodically frustrating, yet often satisfying, and potentially exhilarating. Simply putting up with problems is hardly ever gratifying, and although it seems safer, it is not easy. You will receive a fuller measure of professional satisfaction by promoting changes that both you and your clients deserve.

Picking the Hills You Are Going to Fight On

No matter what your primary area of professional practice may be, you will encounter situations that will challenge you to extend your change efforts beyond the immediate problem situation to produce fundamental change. The examples just discussed illustrate two types of challenges you are likely to face. The first involves pursuing a problem to broader levels to address factors external to the people with whom you are working that contribute to the discomfort they are experiencing. This is similar to what a therapist commonly does when pursuing or exploring intrapersonal issues and establishing a therapeutic relationship. Knowing that the "presenting" problem may well not be the "real" problem, the therapist must probe deeper to discover the actual source of a client's dissatisfaction, just as you must explore a broad range of external issues that ensnare the people you work with and contribute to dissatisfaction. The second example calls for you to challenge the limitations placed on your ability to perform at the optimum level. If the demands of your job far outweigh the resources you have to do your job (including such intangible things as time and authority), both you and those you intend to help have little hope of success. The ongoing frustrations of this situation will eat away at whatever effectiveness you may have—and at you as well.

With every single person or group you encounter, and in any practice environment in which you work, you will face problems that need to be addressed through organized action for systemic change. This is a sobering and somewhat intimidating thought. Once you recognize the effects that larger forces have on the people you work with and the effectiveness of your practice, you will discover many opportunities to participate in meaningful change activities. But guess what? You can't do them all, not even most of them. As a wise professor once told me, "You have to pick the hills you're going to fight on." You do have to fight some battles. At least, I believe you have to. But be selective about the battles you choose to fight— the decision to fight must be followed by the decision to fight effectively. Taking on all challenges will leave you more exhausted than successful. To say a bona fide yes to something means you have to say no to something else.

So, how do you choose? Here are some guidelines. Choose an issue you are genuinely interested in (both intellectually and emotionally). Choose a situation you commonly confront. Evaluate whether you can make a meaningful contribution of time, talent, or wisdom. Structure your effort so it has some likelihood of success. Address the matter in an effective way.

Remember that changing one regulation or one agency policy can have far-reaching consequences. You are not responsible for solving all the world's problems or bringing forth all its potential, but you can contribute to improving things quite a bit. There are a lot of hills out there. Pick yours.

YOU HAVE THE THEORETICAL BASE

Biologist Ludwig von Bertalanffy is credited with being among the first to describe the importance of understanding the interactions among the parts of an organism and between the organism and its environment as keys to understanding the organism itself (Napier & Gershenfeld, 2004). This body of thought has come to be known as systems theory, a way of understanding an organism through the "reciprocal relationships between the elements which constitute a whole" (Barker, 1999, p. 477).

Systems theory has had a tremendous impact on our understanding of human behavior and social development. Prior to this, a "mechanistic" approach, rooted in simplistic cause and effect explanations, was often employed. Brill and Levine (2005) pointed out that human services workers have recognized the usefulness of the concept of the individual in the situation. However, a fascination with psychoanalytic theory drew attention away from this approach to practice. Brill (1998) noted that current perspectives have moved away from these static diagnosis and cure concepts to a greater awareness and understanding of the usefulness of the people in systems model.

As described in Chapter 2, a systems orientation is fundamental to understanding communities. The framework for action outlines a clear way to analyze situations and make decisions about what you must do as a professional practitioner.

Major Features of a Systems Perspective

A system is a whole made up of interrelated parts (Brill & Levine, 2005). These parts exist in a state of balance or equilibrium. When a change occurs in one part of a system, compensatory changes take place throughout the system to establish a new balance. As a result, systems are characterized by dynamic tension—a constant adjustment between the status quo and change.

Each system has a measure of independence but is also linked to larger and smaller systems in a variety of ways. When a change occurs in one system, it will also affect other related systems. When a system fails to receive sufficient inputs, it will go into a state of decline. Conversely, if a system receives too much input, it may be overwhelmed. Both occurrences result in breakdown of the system. Maintaining healthy systems requires constant feedback and adjustment.

Think about some of the systems in which you operate. In addition to your primary system—yourself—you also routinely participate in four broader levels of systems described by Cowan and Egan (1979). *Microsystems,* or personal settings, are the small immediate systems of our everyday lives. These include our family, friendship groups, work settings, and classrooms. The *mesosystem,* or network of personal settings, involves interaction of our immediate

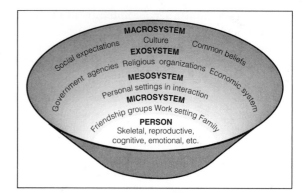

F I G U R E 3.3 Extending Systems Model

systems with one another. What happens in one personal system has an impact on other systems. For example, what happens in your family can affect your participation in the classroom. The *exosystem,* or the larger institutions of our society, does not directly and immediately envelop us but does influence our personal systems and our network of personal systems. The exosystem includes government agencies, religious organizations, and the economic system. These systems also interact with one another while they influence our more immediate systems. The *macrosystem,* or culture, influences all the other systems of our lives and includes our common beliefs, acceptable forms of behavior and social relationships, and our expectations (see Figure 3.3 for a graphic depiction of this model).

A systems orientation is so much a part of social work that it has become part of the definition of that profession: "The practice of social work requires knowledge of human development and behavior; of social, economic, and cultural institutions; and of the *interaction* of all these factors" [emphasis added] (NASW, 1973, pp. 4–5). "Utilizing theories of human behavior and social systems, social work intervenes at points where people interact with their environments" (IFSW/IASSW, 2001, p. 5).

When you approach a situation, ask these questions (Brill & Levine, 2005):

1. What are the boundaries of the system or systems with which you are dealing?

2. What are the patterns and channels of communication both within the individual system under consideration and among the related external systems?

3. What are the explicit and implicit rules that govern the relationship among the parts, both internally and externally, particularly with respect to input (openness to new ideas or materials), processing (working with all the materials), and outgo (feedback or results of this work)?

Recognizing that individual and community issues are parts of a whole will increase your understanding of circumstances that people face and your ability to provide help. The basic point to all this is that as systems are affecting people, people are also affecting systems (Cowan & Egan, 1979).

Applications of a Systems Perspective

All this may sound a little mind-boggling. Here are some ways these basic concepts could apply to situations you might well encounter.

- It may help you to understand that individuals' difficulties can stem from their interactions with other people or other systems and the ways they internally process or handle these interactions.
- It may aid you in working with individuals to process or make use of their interactions with the world around them in a new or different way to help them regain a better balance and achieve growth.
- It may show that people not only can process differently but also can behave differently toward their environment.
- It also shows that individuals can affect their environment, not just be affected by it.
- It explains that the situations people face are dynamic, not static, and can help you identify opportunities to capitalize on forces working for change to assist them in using these forces to move the flow of events in the desired direction.
- It may help you in analyzing the interrelationships community members have with their world and in discovering areas in which these interrelationships can be improved; you can then identify various points and various methods of intervention.

- It will enable you to see that a larger, apparently more powerful system can be changed if feedback from subsystems demands it.
- It will remind you that this larger, more powerful system interacts with other systems, equal or even more powerful, and that this also affects the system's balance.
- It will help you to understand that you are part of a system too, a helping (and at times not so helping) system that provides you with both resources and obstacles—a system that those looking for help have engaged.
- It can help keep you from being overwhelmed by providing a practical framework for making sense out of what is going on.

When you understand the forces at play, you will uncover many opportunities for beneficial change, including assisting people to change conditions around them. Your awareness of systems will guide you in selecting the proper context for your action or the points at which you may intervene to help resolve the situation in a way that best meets the interests of the community members with whom you work. This may call for you to work toward community or policy change.

YOU HAVE THE SKILLS
YOU NEED

The notion of promoting community change may sound pretty intimidating, even if you do understand the need for it and its place in professional practice. This may be particularly true if you see yourself as primarily working with individuals or families and you are more comfortable doing that type of work. You may not be confident that you can pull off change in a larger system. You may think you need to develop a whole new set of skills, quite different from those you use in working with individual problems.

This is a legitimate concern. Which skills, if any, do health and human services workers commonly have that can be useful in promoting community change? A review of basic skills drawn from a number of social work and human services texts should shed some light on this question. While reading through these lists, consider how each skill could be useful to you as you work for community change.

Schmolling, Youkeles, and Burger (1997, pp. 214–219) identified several characteristics of effective helpers:

Empathy—the ability to see things from another's point of view

Genuineness—the expression of true feelings

Objective/subjective balance—the ability to stand back and view a situation accurately but without becoming detached from personal feelings

Self-awareness—the quality of knowing oneself, including the knowledge of one's values, feelings, attitudes and beliefs, fears and desires, and strengths and weaknesses

Acceptance—the ability to view the client's feelings, attitudes, and opinions as worthy of consideration without necessarily approving of the client's behavior

Desire to help—enthusiasm in promoting the growth and development of others without creating unnecessary dependency; includes a basic belief that those being served do have the fundamental ability to change

Patience—the ability to wait and be steadfast, understanding that different people do things at different times, in different ways, and for different reasons according to individual capacities

Brill and Levine (2005, pp. 176–179) identified six basic skills for effectiveness:

Differential diagnosis—the capacity to understand the uniqueness of the client and the situation and to adapt techniques to this uniqueness

Timing—the ability to establish the proper tempo in working with the client, matching the pace of activities with the client's ability to use them, and selecting the crucial point in time to apply intervention techniques

Partialization—the ability to assess the whole situation and break it down into manageable units and help the client think about and decide where to begin

Focus—concentrating both the worker's and the client's efforts on the significant aspect of the situation that requires work and retaining focus until some conclusion has been reached

Establishing partnership—clarifying the association between the worker and the client so that each understands the role and tasks of the other

Structure—establishing the setting and the boundaries that are most conducive to the work that needs to be done and using an orderly, yet flexible process of problem solving

NASW (1982, pp. 17–18) has offered the following inventory of skills essential to the practice of social work:

- Skill in listening to others with understanding and purpose

- Skill in eliciting information and in assembling relevant facts to prepare a social history, assessment, and report

- Skill in creating and maintaining professional helping relationships and in using oneself in relationships

- Skill in observing and interpreting verbal and nonverbal behavior and in using knowledge of personality theory and diagnostic methods

- Skill in engaging clients (including individuals, families, groups, and communities) in efforts to resolve their own problems and in gaining trust

- Skill in discussing sensitive emotional subjects in a nonthreatening and supportive manner

- Skill in creating innovative solutions to clients' needs

- Skill in determining the need to end therapeutic relationships and how to do so

- Skill in conducting research or in interpreting findings of research studies and professional literature

- Skill in mediating and negotiating between conflicting parties

- Skill in providing interorganizational liaison services

- Skill in interpreting or communicating social needs to funding sources, the public, or legislators

NOHS's (2002) inventory of human service competencies includes the following:

- Understanding the nature of human systems: individual, group, organization, community and society, and their major interactions

- Understanding the conditions that promote or limit optimal functioning

- Skill in identifying and selecting interventions that promote growth and goal attainment

- Skill in planning, implementing, and evaluating interventions

These skills and competencies define your talents as a social worker or human services professional, but they do not define the context of your work. They do not imply limitations on what you can do. Just the opposite.

You may easily see yourself applying these skills in helping individuals and families. You may view this activity with some degree of confidence but look with uncertainty on applying these skills to work for community change. Take heart. You don't suddenly lose your abilities when you address problems that have larger implications. In fact, the fundamental skills you need to work at the individual level are the same skills you use when you work for community change.

Your ability to use systems analysis will help you make sense of this larger arena of practice. The larger system behaves in much the same way smaller systems do. Your understanding of the principles underlying systems will clarify what you need to do no matter what the size of the practice arena. The way you use your capabilities may vary according to the change effort you are pursuing, but the same fundamental competencies will guide you in your work. Just like any area of practice, your increased experience will help you discover more and more about what you are doing. You will accumulate your own bundle of tricks, and you will borrow some from other change agents.

As you enter the arena of community change, you will find that the fundamental skills you possess as a professional in health and human services will help you get the job done. You just need to make the decision to enter, even if only every now and then.

CONCLUSION

As a professional in the health and human services arena, you will assist people in their efforts to lead full and satisfying lives. You will encounter many obstacles that interfere with that purpose. But, if you take the time to look, you will discover many opportunities and assets that can aid you as well. Efforts directed to community or policy change can remove obstacles; you can use those opportunities to make a difference. You may use a development approach, moving past the provision of services to the mobilization of resources to change conditions. These efforts help to further important social welfare goals.

Engaging in change efforts is consistent with basic professional practice methods. Your professional values not only support such activity, they call for it. You have the theoretical knowledge to make sense out of the situations you face and to determine effective avenues for intervention. Your training provides you with the skills to initiate and even to pursue action.

You will be challenged to take action. That much is certain. You may not know how you will respond to those challenges, or even if you will allow yourself to recognize them. But if you do so with a sense of purpose and an intention to be effective, you will offer a challenge to conditions that limit human potential.

MORE THAN VICTIMS

Lorena's husband beat her up last night. Again. Before he passed out. Again. Of course, she didn't report it. Who is she going to call? The police? And then what, get shipped back to Mexico? You think

Rey is not going to find her there? "Soy atrapando. Soy muriendo." Yes, she is trapped in a many stranded web. Yes, she is dying, body and soul. And Lorena is just one woman in the intimate partner violence support group whose stories are all beginning to sound the same.

Few of the women speak English. None has yet been able to get legal status to be in this country, much less this room. All are in abusive relationships. Some of the men are Latino; some are Anglos who brought women to the United States with promises of a wonderful life. Some life. Most have little formal education, and each of them hears how stupid she is. How they need to just stay home, nobody would hire them. The men's pay, if they get it, brings a few things from the market that become dinner and is part of what keeps the landlord happy. Each has children who try to hide from the violence.

Each has something more. They have each other. They have some things that they can do. Cook, add numbers quickly, take care of kids, sew, sing, make a garden grow. Lots of things. Lorena was a schoolteacher back home. Some have family here. Some know people at church. They all know you.

The support group helps get them through another day, though, maybe soon, someone will not get through the night. They know you care. You say it with your eyes as well as your words, but right now you don't know what to say. What are you going to do about this?

REFLECTION QUESTIONS

1. What issues do you see?
2. If you were operating from a service orientation, what would you do?
3. If you were operating from a development orientation, what would you do?
4. What might the women be able to do with what they have?
5. What partnership opportunities exist here?
6. What matters of social justice or confronting oppression do you recognize?
7. What skills do you have that you could use in this situation?
8. What skills would you want to learn?
9. Which values direct your actions?
10. Do you find yourself affirming or challenging stereotypes? What might these be?
11. How does using systems theory help you understand what is going on and what to do?
12. What role do you see Lorena and the other women playing?

GROUP ACTIVITY: DEVELOPING YOUR CODE OF ETHICS

Your ethics represent your professional code of conduct founded on and required by a set of moral principles. They are more than matters of effectiveness; they are a set of moral obligations. Because of your deeply held personal and professional values, you will engage in or refrain from engaging in certain actions. What you choose to do is a practical application of your ethics. It all starts with your ethical base. What values call you to work to promote change, and what principles guide that work?

1. Divide into teams of five members. Working individually in your group, prepare two

ethics statements that will guide your work as a community organizer or developer. Write your statements on a 3 × 5 note card. (5 minutes)
2. Place all five note cards in a pile in the middle of the group, and shuffle the cards. (1 minute)
3. One member reads each card to the rest of the team. Afterward the cards are arranged so that all members can see them. (5 minutes)
4. Using the ethics statements that your team members have provided, develop a Code of

Ethics for your team containing at least seven statements. (15 minutes)

5. Display your team's Code of Ethics on a poster. (5 minutes)

6. Present your team's Code of Ethics to the larger group. (5 minutes)

HELPFUL WEBSITES

Links to the organizations briefly described here are on the companion website at www.cengage.com/humansvcc/homan.

National Association of Social Workers (NASW). This is the largest national social work organization. Information on the profession, news about policy and advocacy issues, and links to various operations within the organization are available here.

National Organization for Human Services (NOHS). This organization promotes the development of the human services profession through collaborative efforts of faculty, professionals, and students. The organization assists in curriculum development, research, education, and advocacy on issues affecting human services professionals and the people they serve. NOHS is a student-, practitioner- and faculty-friendly organization.

The National Organizers Alliance. This is an organization for organizers. In addition to a job bank and a retirement pension program, the organization's newsletter, *NOA's Ark,* keeps organizers thinking and connected.

The Midwest Academy. Probably the best-known school for community organization, good information is available here regarding direct action organizing.

The New Social Worker. This organization is geared to those considering social work careers, students, or recent graduates. Discussion groups, a jobs page, and an online magazine highlight job opportunities.

Applied Research Center. A public policy, educational, and research institute that focuses on issues of race and social change, the center takes a global viewpoint and links organizers and activists around the world to advance thinking on these issues and to share knowledge. Their online magazine, *Color-Lines,* and links to other organizations are also available here.

Rural Development Leadership Network. This is a national multicultural social change organization that supports community-based development in poor rural areas through hands-on projects, education and skills building, leadership development, and networking. The organization supports emerging leaders from poor rural areas to spearhead development projects and designs related study through which they may earn a certificate or academic credential (bachelor's or master's degree, or a PhD).

Chapter 4

Putting Yourself
in the Picture

CHAPTER HIGHLIGHTS

- Five conditions for taking action
- Four responses to unacceptable conditions
- Giving yourself permission to act
- Your current strengths and abilities
- Sanction or approval for your work
- Standing, the right to take action
- Fitting change activities to your job
- Sometimes you will work without approval

- Reflective practice
- Community change and a healthy personal life
- Self-awareness
- Burnout, an avoidable disease
- Keys to personal effectiveness
- Five ways to establish and maintain credibility

Some of the primary elements for understanding the subject of community change were presented in Chapter 1. Chapter 2 provided a framework for making use of the underlying principles for promoting change. In Chapter 3 we looked at how this business of promoting community change relates to the profession, its theoretical base, its skills, and its values. Where do you fit into the picture? Can you see yourself working on small or large community change efforts? What do you need to take into account as you take on this challenge? What do you see getting in your way?

You will confront a host of questions as you consider initiating change. Your ability to answer these questions will determine whether or not you move past "considering" and on to action. And the way you answer will govern how satisfying your efforts are when you decide to act. You will have to choose between accepting conditions as they are or putting yourself into the action. Either choice has consequences—for your clients, your family, your community, and yourself, professionally and personally.

In this chapter we explore issues you will routinely address as you engage in the process of change, with each new situation ready to rob or to increase your power to meet the next challenge. Handling these issues well will increase your sense of accomplishment and add to your effectiveness. Handling them poorly can discourage you from continuing the game.

The simple fact is that when I talk about promoting change, I am talking to you, not about somebody else. You are not just out to understand what this process is about. You are out to understand how you can take part in it. So you need to answer some questions for yourself, questions you will keep answering as long as you actively pursue or avoid pursuing change. All this boils down to your ability to act effectively and to gain a measure of satisfaction from your actions that will enhance, or at the very least not detract from, your personal and professional life.

TAKING ACTION

You are a social worker, a human services worker, a public health worker, a change agent. How does it all fit? What does this process require of you? To enable you to take action and to sustain your effort, five conditions must be met.

1. You have to know that an action is needed.
2. You have to know what action can be taken.
3. You have to feel competent to perform the action.
4. You have to feel relatively safe to do so.
5. You have to receive sufficient encouragement or fulfillment to continue to take needed actions.

Meeting these conditions involves a set of beliefs, values, and abilities, but it also requires thoughtful management of a number of personal matters that can motivate or interfere with your desire to take action. To begin with, you must recognize the need for action; then you must give yourself permission to act.

Recognizing the Need for Action

It is hard to act on something unless you see the need to do so. This is a pretty simple concept, but a fundamental one. Some workers plod along with some vague notion that things just aren't right, but that is as far as they go. They do not see possibilities, nor do they grasp the politics involved in shaping community conditions or even the types of services provided, how much is provided, or how services are provided. They don't think about whether we should just rely on services to improve the quality of people's lives or ask if there are better options. If you do not consciously stop to think about these things, it is unlikely that you will recognize challenges and opportunities with a degree of clarity sufficient to move you to action.

Although it is hard to imagine, some workers just do not perceive that there is a problem to be solved. Others learn to avoid looking or to avoid thinking about what they see. This ability to keep recognition outside conscious awareness requires a degree of work at first. After a while, however, you can become quite good at it, and it will become second nature. Sad, perhaps, but common. Recognizing issues means that you will have to identify the current situation as unacceptable, and then you will have to respond.

Responding to Unacceptable Circumstances

Once a problem situation has been identified, you have four options for action (see Figure 4.1). First, you can change your perception by identifying the situation as acceptable. Then you can accept it. Your second option is to leave the situation. This can be done by emotionally withdrawing or by actually leaving. Your third choice is to identify the situation as unacceptable and then try to accept it. This is a common approach—one that leads to a lot of complaining, demoralized workers. Finally, you can identify the situation as unacceptable and act to change it. Each option has very real consequences, both for you and for your community. If you allow yourself to see possibilities, there is an implied challenge to do something. Not everyone is comfortable with challenges like that.

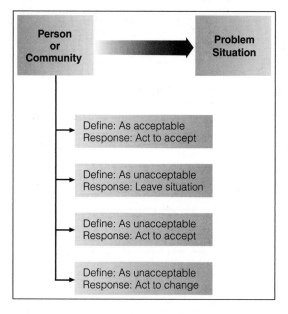

FIGURE 4.1 Choices for Dealing with Problem Situations

You cannot become equally involved in rectifying all the problems you see. Remember, you have to pick the hills you are going to fight on. As you acknowledge the efforts you do make, you will learn what you can work on and what you should let go. Your ability to manage your responses to the situations you encounter is an important skill you will continue to refine. This goes hand in hand with your ability to recognize problem situations in the first place.

Giving Yourself Permission to Act

Few halfhearted attempts will be more than halfway successful. If you are going to act on a situation, you have to decide to do so. Allow yourself to believe that you can be successful, and behave according to that belief. You will then make the commitment to do the things you think you need to do to accomplish your goal.

Remember that you can have several levels of goals, from bringing the matter to the attention of someone in a better position to act to building an organization that will empower people to promote change. Once you decide to act, you will not just try to do things—you will do them.

RECOGNIZE YOUR ABILITY TO PROMOTE CHANGE

It is common to think you need to do more than you really have to do. You may feel that you are not up to the task. You may even feel overwhelmed.

In fact, a common mistake in both perception and strategy is to think you need to do it all yourself. Sitting here reading this you know that isn't true, yet somewhere down the road you may trick yourself into believing it. For those times ahead, let me offer this reminder: You do not own the problem by yourself, nor should you take sole responsibility for solving it.

Most challenging situations have a number of contributing factors as well as a certain history, including things that are working or have worked well. You need other perspectives and other resources. That means you need other people. Keeping that in mind, let's consider what you can offer. You have basic helping skills. Build on your strengths, and you will quickly add additional skills that fit this particular circumstance. You really don't need to know everything to get started. You will learn.

The most difficult things to master are the subtleties of empowering others, developing strategies and tactics, and negotiating and maintaining agreements. Perhaps you can think of these as the artistic side of being a change agent; everything else is pretty much a matter of information. You will gain what you need through experience as long as you adhere to three principles. First, cultivate and unlock your creativity. Second, actively seek to discover your ignorance so you can replace it with knowledge. Third, pay attention to what seems to be working well and build on that.

Leadership skills are particularly valuable. You may feel confident about your leadership abilities, or you may not yet be able to clearly see your leadership potential. In either case, your leadership abilities will grow with experience and will be important contributors to your success. However, it is also important to recognize that these skills are available in most groups of people. An essential skill you will continue to develop is the ability to draw these leadership qualities from those involved with

◄ Take a Moment to Discover ►

Think about how you commonly handle problems, even routine problems. The tires on the old Chevy may have little tread left. The landlord promised, for the third time, that he would fix the roof. The people working at the college financial aid office seem to be having a good time joking with each other while you sit, and sit, and sit a while longer. You look at the coins in the palm of your hand and realize that the cashier didn't give you the right change; you are 50 cents short. How do you handle situations like these? How do your various responses leave you feeling?

you in the effort to promote change. As long as you remember that your abilities complement the talents other people bring to the production, you will recognize that you have a multitude of skills at your group's disposal.

DEVELOPING SANCTION

A critical issue you will face as a change agent is that of gaining sanction for your efforts. This involves both the perception that your efforts are legitimate and credible and receiving the approval necessary for you to proceed. Without sanction, your efforts will be met with disinterest or with opposition. First, sanction must come from the people you are organizing. Next, it must come from those who have some say over your actions, especially if your activities deviate from what you routinely do or are expected to do. This usually means your employer, if you are doing the work on company or agency time, or your family, if you are doing it on family time.

Gaining Consent from Those Who
Must Move to Action

Frequently you will not have sanction when you begin working for change. Two elements are key in gaining sanction. The first has to do with your *standing* and how you project yourself and your intentions. The second involves gaining a measure

of *endorsement* from those whose opinion matters to those who will be drawn into the change episode.

What right do you have to take up the issue in the first place? If you are a member of the affected group, you have standing almost automatically. However, if you are not a member, you may need to answer some questions regarding your credentials.

If you take the issue seriously and demonstrate a sense of purpose, you are much more likely to get a favorable response than if you approach your concerns apologetically or doubtfully. You don't have to—and shouldn't—communicate that you know all the answers, but you should communicate that you think answers can be found and that you are willing to help find them. Further, you need to show that this pursuit is not simply intended to resolve your own personal discomfort. You need to frankly demonstrate your genuine attention to the issue at hand and to the interests of the others involved.

The second step is to find people receptive to your idea and work with them. Obviously, you must start with whomever is available and interested, but the more credible these people are within the group whose sanction you need the better off you will be. These supporters can guide you in establishing a working relationship with others whose backing will be important to the effort. The display of endorsement by opinion leaders can help ease the concerns of the skeptical.

Don't worry about convincing everyone of your sound moral character and the seriousness of your intent. Focus on the people you will be working with or who otherwise are aware of your efforts. In some change efforts this may well involve only a handful of people.

Integrating Your Change Efforts with
Your Job Responsibilities

Gaining support from your supervisors and coworkers will make life a lot easier for you (Russo, 1993). If you believe your efforts are a legitimate fulfillment of your professional agency responsibilities, treat it as part of your job. I realize that this may be more easily said than done.

There are different ways to gain acceptance. One way is to get explicit permission for your

---

⏩ Take a Moment to Discover ⏪

You can sabotage your own efforts with the things you tell yourself—or you can embolden them. Do you really believe you have the right to act powerfully? Do you think you have the ability to do so? What do you tell yourself about this? The way you answer these questions will dictate what you do. Your actions are a direct response to the messages you send yourself. What are they?

Think of a difficult situation you are currently facing. Identify all the things you tell yourself that could undermine your resolve. Now, identify all the things you can tell yourself that will strengthen your resolve.

Which set of messages do you hear?

---

involvement. Another option is to do some work related to the change and then seek permission for what you have already started. You may become engaged in implementing change without ever getting permission—your role just evolves and becomes accepted. There are potential gains and losses from each approach. You will have to figure out what would work best for you and your situation.

When I can choose equally from these three options, my personal preference is really behind door number two—I like to be able to show something real rather than seek support for an idea. It is easy for supervisors to say no if they don't really know what you are talking about and if no real interest has had time to develop. Once some work is under way and the idea has gained some momentum, it is more difficult for a supervisor to turn down a proposal. So I like to get something started. I also like to get support when I can. It is helpful to have support for your activities if for no other reason than it is less stressful, but it also puts more resources at your disposal.

Gaining support from your supervisor is a four-step process. The best place to start is with what your supervisor is likely to hear.

1. Outline the issue as you see it. Use statistics, specific incidents, and case examples to clarify and dramatize the situation. You want to provoke attention and show that you have done your homework. This is a critical step. If your supervisor doesn't share some of your perception that a problem that needs correcting exists, it is unlikely that you will receive support for your efforts to correct it.

2. Describe the response you see as appropriate to address the issue, and include a description of your role in the process. Briefly identify a few of the obstacles you will encounter, and show how your approach addresses them. You do not need to have the exact answer to every conceivable problem, but you do need to demonstrate a willingness to acknowledge and deal with legitimate concerns. In fact, it is usually wise to invite your supervisor to be part of the problem resolution process.

3. Emphasize the philosophy behind your intent to tackle the issue, and demonstrate the benefits of your involvement. You may want to show how your proposal relates to the agency mission and to your and perhaps your supervisor's professional values. You certainly want to point out how the effort benefits the agency and the people the agency serves. The more specific and down-to-earth your description is the better.

4. Enroll your supervisor in the effort, if only intellectually. You may want to ask for ideas about making the change effort more effective. (Hint: Don't ask what's wrong with your ideas, or your supervisor just may tell you. Your purpose is to get everyone thinking about how *to do* things, not how *not* to do them.) If there is a role for your supervisor to play in the change effort, you may want to identify it.

Anticipate questions, and be prepared to respond to them. Throughout your presentation, consciously avoid falling into the possibly very attractive trap of showing how your supervisor is ignorant and wrong whereas you are knowledgeable and right.

Be careful about being so committed to a particular course of action that you cannot entertain any different way of doing things. Your supervisor will probably offer some ideas. Remain flexible. This may be a way for your supervisor to put his or her mark on the project, giving your supervisor an investment in its success. Often, suggestions do

GLOBAL PERSPECTIVES

SCOTLAND

At the end of the day, capacity builders, the rarest of beasts, need to build their own capacity as capacity builders, to question their reality.... The reflective capacity building practitioner is an ideal to cultivate and aim for in the world of community learning and development (Andrew McDonald & Phil Denning, 2008, p. 2).

ZIMBABWE—A Movement

It awakens our soul
  our inner courage
  our reason for being
It commands us to discipline
calling us to attention
  to be at our stations alert,
tapping our energy and creativity,
  while we willingly give
  our suffering and defeat
  our joy and our laughter
to the Unknown.

We are called to
  dance at the sea,
  dream in the desert and
  sing on the mountains,
So that we can discover
  ourselves
  in a New World
  which crumbles old realities
  and refuses to be named.

SOURCE: Sally J. Timmel (as cited in Hope & Timmel, 1992, p. 80)

not pose an either-or dilemma. You can usually incorporate new ideas along with those you had planned to act on. Don't discount the possibility that you can learn something—that a different perspective can improve on your approach. If you are not open to this possibility, you run the risk of diluting if not rejecting the support you need.

If you really believe the project is a good idea and you need the consent of your supervisor to pursue it, don't take no for an answer. Over time you will develop a variety of skills to keep the process going until you get the answer you want. You will acquire phrases such as "It looks like I've got a few more things to work on before I come back to you again," or perhaps, "I'll do some more thinking on this over the next week or two before we talk about it again." You may have to get another person or two to repeat the request at another time. You may even need to force the issue through the use of pressure. If it is important, you will learn how to be persistent.

Given that it is helpful to garner support if you can get it, remember that it may be appropriate to pursue your change effort without receiving formal approval. It may be unnecessary for you to seek approval, or the effort to gain approval may be such a major hassle that you end up creating another considerable obstacle that saps your energy and stands in the way of your success.

There may be circumstances in which you not only engage in change-producing activities without permission but do so in a covert or "underground"

manner. The fact is that unobtrusive means are often used in promoting change, particularly within organizations. As Brager and Holloway (1978) pointed out, it is considered acceptable for an administrator to use more indirect means to introduce change, but it is no less ethical for a worker to do so simply because her place in the hierarchy may be lower. Here are some guidelines from Brager and Holloway to help you weigh the appropriateness of your use of covert influence to promote change, particularly within your own agency:

- Unobtrusive means should be used only when the problem the worker has identified compromises the needs and rights of clients or potential clients.

- The actions undertaken by the worker must adhere to the values of social work and other human services professions.

- Workers should employ unobtrusive measures only when the formal organizational mechanisms have already been exhausted or when, on the basis of past experience, it can be inferred that these formal mechanisms will result in failure.

- Workers must be aware as they begin the change effort that they carry responsibility for any negative consequences that flow from it. The only risks permissible are risks to themselves or risks that clients and colleagues understand and have agreed to share.

Whatever approach you take, it should be a conscious choice based on an honest appraisal of your work situation. Just don't con yourself.

Juggling Your Immediate Duties on the Job

You have decided that your change efforts are a legitimate part of your job, and you have gained agency support. Now you have to fit this in with your other assignments. This usually involves fitting more work into the same amount of time as well as some degree of job restructuring. You may ask colleagues if they are willing to take on some of your duties, but remember you may want them involved in the change effort too. You may decide that certain other aspects of your job will have to wait or not get done at all, otherwise work on the change effort won't get done. You will have to become more efficient at managing your time, but you have to recognize that your involvement requires an investment of time. If you don't acknowledge this and deal with it, you are going to end up feeling frazzled, and you may become unpleasant to be around instead of being the charming person you are now.

REFLECTIVE PRACTICE

The meeting just ended and you are sitting there wondering what the heck just happened. Very good. Maybe the outcome was better than expected, maybe not, but your thinking about what led to the result means that you are committed to learning. You may be moving toward reflective practice.

Reflective practice involves setting aside some time to learn from our experiences. We not only look at what happened, we also think about what it means. Reflection not only involves pondering, but active inquiry as well. You not only observe, but you ask yourself questions.

You don't always do what you are told. Most of the time, you do what you tell yourself to do. Where does this come from? Knowledge is embedded in the experiences of your work (Amulya,

2004). Experience alone can contribute to your learning, but experience can teach you much, much more when you actively reflect on it. When you engage in reflective practice, you mine your experiences to reveal knowledge that could go undiscovered if you did not purposefully look for it.

Donald Schön (1983) introduced the idea of reflective practice in the 1980s, but it springs from roots that draw from the past. The roots of reflective practice reach back as far as Buddha and Socrates, and wind through the work of educators like John Dewey (York-Barr, Sommers, Ghere, & Montie, 2006). It has found a particular home in the literature on teacher education, though as a practice it can apply to any profession.

Reflective practice moves you past looking back at a situation to rationalize or justify your actions, a routine that is pretty easy to fall into. It encourages you to confront those actions, that is, to take an honest look at them. It becomes conscious thought coupled with a commitment to change (York-Barr et al., 2006). For reflection to genuinely be a lens into the world of practice, it must question taken-for-granted assumptions and encourage you to see your actions through others' eyes (Loughran, 2002).

Our work environment, the hectic pace of our lives, and even the expectations of a broader culture often discourages us from peeking beneath the surface of things. We can get very busy with all our work, but feel dissatisfied with what we are doing. Maybe we are stuck in a rut, knowing we are only marginally effective, or maybe we don't really feel good about what we are doing. Reflective practice helps you to see where there is a fit between what you believe, value, and do, and where there is some incongruence. You recognize both what you can build on and discover sources of tension that can lead you to make some changes in what you believe, what you value, or what you do.

Everything is in the process of change; we need to be as well. There is much that we can carry over from past experience to meet new situations, but we need to open ourselves to new ways of thinking and acting as well if we are going to be effective in the new world we meet every day. The more we are tuned in to what is going on, the more easily we can make adjustments to become even more effective. We become good at reflection in action, reflection on action, and reflection for action (Killion & Todnem, 1991; Schön, 1987).

When engaged in reflection, you not only look for signs of effectiveness or tension but identify and examine the underlying assumptions that led you to take this action rather than that one. You find yourself asking What do I know? and How have I come to know it? In addition to reflecting on my experience, how else can I come to know? What might be some other sources of knowledge or insight? You move to a recognition and refinement of your theories of action, what predictions you are making and why you are making those predictions. Your actions reveal your theories. Are you aware of those theories of action?

Reflective practice is a form of experiential learning that encourages you to seek out other perspectives as well. You will learn from conversations with others engaged in your work, particularly those who have had more experience than you do, and you will think about how you can use the guidance you are receiving. To this you will add some reading, which can introduce you to new ideas and practices that you and your colleagues hadn't considered.

You can engage in reflection in a formal way with a specific design for examination, or you can simply determine some particular elements you want to reflect on and make this routine. Reflective practice is as much your general approach as it is the particular activities you take to do it. It becomes a good habit to get into.

Reflective practice certainly connects with the notion of praxis (see Chapter 2). While it can be used to promote small group effectiveness as well, here the starting point is with your own, personal experience. You will have an eagerness to think about and learn from what you are doing, what others see you doing, and what you can learn from what others have thought about as well. Along the way you will find out more about the process of change, about others who are acting and reacting in the situation, and, most important, about yourself.

You must decide: do you act out of habit or do you reflect out of habit and then act?

KEEPING YOUR PERSONAL LIFE HAPPY AND HEALTHY

Promoting change is a fascinating and at times seductive process that can distort your sense of your own importance and the importance (or lesser importance) of other people and other aspects of your life. One of the sad yet common images in this business of promoting change is the portrait of a person gung ho to save the world while losing his family in the process. Relationships can suffer through inattention or irritation with conflicting demands, but they don't have to. Relationships may be strengthened, but this requires attention to their importance in both word and deed. Most of the change agents I have known are vital, interesting, and curiously self-centered people. Their vitality and enthusiasm for accepting and meeting challenges make them enjoyable to be around. However, they seem to lose perspective on the importance of commonplace concerns as much of their world revolves around their community activities. This can become tiresome.

Some change efforts, particularly more complex ones, are an imaginative and challenging break from the ordinary. They can take on a life of their own and make the dull, routine matters of everyday job and life a little, well, dull and routine.

Organizing a change effort means that you are bringing something new to life. It requires attention and nurturing, involving a new set of relationships, or perhaps old ones experienced in a new way. You are already affiliated with a number of groups, each of which demands something of you. Negotiating your way through these competing and sometimes directly conflicting demands is tricky business, especially while you are absorbed with a new set of tasks and relationships. You need to have a sense of which relationships or affiliations are most important to you and which most need your attention. It also means that you need to think about the type of attention each needs.

Situations are dynamic. You can't pull out some magical calculator and precisely assign each group its proper share of your emotional energy and time. Nonetheless, from time to time you should reflect on these various memberships and determine whether your response to them reflects what you believe about their relative importance.

Common Pitfalls

Handling multiple memberships is certainly not an impossible task; you do it all the time. But it may be helpful to consider some of the familiar hazards to integrating your change efforts with your personal life.

- *Taking yourself for granted.* You may be used to taking on anything that comes your way, so you decide to take on a little bit more, maybe a lot more. You may find yourself always thinking of things that need to be done. You are too busy to eat lunch. You don't just sit and visit with people because you feel that you can't afford to spend time not accomplishing anything. You don't learn and retell any new jokes. You stop singing in the shower. And you worry—a lot—about wasting your time.

  Maybe you worry about what other people are thinking, and you wonder how you could do more to please them. You stifle your own thoughts lest you be thought of as disagreeable. You respond to others' requests for help but rarely ask for any yourself.

  Or maybe you sell yourself short, measuring your own standards for excellence against those of others who have grown stagnant. You may end up bringing your own standards down a notch or two, conceding to the prevailing mediocrity. You may fall into an attitude that says: "As long as we are doing something, well, that's all right; there is so much to do." Perhaps, then, it is not only your standards you sell short but your capabilities as well.

- *Taking other people for granted.* This can cut two ways. The first is that you expect others to be as interested and committed to the change effort as you are. They should just naturally understand what you need and provide it, probably immediately, whenever you ask. You project a kind of "drop everything you are doing and take care of me" attitude. Although this is undeniably rude, those around you are usually pretty good at helping you see what you are doing so you have a chance to make some changes.

  The other perhaps more common way of taking people for granted is insidious and may be more destructive. This is the practice of

---

◨ Take a Moment to Discover ◨

You have a job, you go to school, you spend time with your friends, and maybe you even volunteer a few hours a month. How do you do all this and keep a smile on your face? Well, sometimes you aren't smiling.

Think back over the last year at how many times you had to juggle various responsibilities to do what was important to you. Pick a time when things were going smoothly. During this time, what were you doing or not doing that helped? Now consider a situation when all these activities seemed to be more trouble than they were worth. What were you doing or not doing that was different? What would you like to change about how you act in these situations?

Nobody is going to hear your answer to these next questions but you, so you can be simple, clear, and direct. What do you like to blame other people for that is really your responsibility? What do you blame yourself for that is really someone else's responsibility? What would you like to change about how you act in these situations? You might want to write down your answers.

---

ignoring people and not asking them for assistance and input, really not expecting much of them. In the personal realm, this involves not including them in your enthusiasms or fears as well as keeping yourself apart from their world.

- *Spreading yourself too thin.* Once you have gotten a taste of involvement in community change, you see and respond to opportunities everywhere. Your work leads you to other active people who invite you to take part in this or that project. They all seem interesting and important. It doesn't take long before you are up to your hip pockets in commitments. You do a lot of a little bit, scrambling to hold up your end of the deal, without really grabbing hold of anything. You find that you are distracted a lot of the time, and your effectiveness suffers even though you can probably continue to put on a good show for a while.

- *Being impatient with routine duties.* If you are not careful, you get to thinking you are pretty doggone important—if not you personally, at least your work certainly is. You become irritated at heretofore common responsibilities, and even at the people who expect you to perform them.

- *Losing track of your commitments.* You forget that you scheduled an important meeting at the same time you promised your spouse that the two of you would finally take the time for dinner and a movie, with the promise of something more exciting to follow. So much is going on, sometimes so quickly, that your attention becomes focused on the demands immediately before you. Other matters fade into fuzzy afterthought.

Avoiding the Traps and Benefiting from the Experience

Being involved in efforts to promote community change is invigorating. Blending these activities with other important aspects of your life should mean more than just keeping yourself out of trouble. The following hints are basic reminders of things you probably already know. Just remember that they are easily forgotten.

- *Self-awareness is a prerequisite.* The most valuable thing you have to offer is yourself. The more you are in tune with yourself, the more you can refine and improve your ability to contribute to and benefit from participation. Pay attention to how you act in and react to various situations. How do you feel about things? What do you think is important? Daily you have many chances to discover a little more about yourself than you now know. Decide to take advantage of this. Engaging in reflective practice will help. You will know yourself better next month than you do now, and less well now than you will next year. Be willing to learn and relearn. You will need to do both.

- *Take what you do seriously, but don't take yourself too seriously.* Make no mistake about it, you are important to the success of the enterprise. Things probably won't go "just as well without you." Thinking otherwise may well be an excuse for wishy-washy commitments. Your participation does mean something, but it's not the only thing. So take what you do seriously—but don't take yourself too seriously.

You are going to foul up a time or two, or maybe more. When this occurs, accept it. Don't waste a lot of energy pretending you have everything under control and that you always know exactly what you are doing. You don't. Act fully on what you believe in and what you value, according to the best of your ability.

At the same time, be able to laugh at yourself. Learn from other people, and keep your contributions in perspective.

- *Remind yourself of what is important in your life and act on it.* Family, friends, mobile home racing, or whatever is important to you still deserves an active place in your life. You need to spend time on these things. Depending on the particular challenge of the moment, one thing or another will receive more of your attention, but overall the balance of your time should be spent in accordance with what you believe to be important. The way you budget your money is a clear indication of what you value. The way you budget your time is as well.

- *Understand the demands each membership requires of you.* Each group holds expectations of what membership means. Make sure you know what these expectations are and that they are the same ones you hold for yourself. If not, you may need to negotiate a new set of expectations. Before you take on new responsibilities, consider how new demands on your time fit with your current affiliations.

A couple of reminders could be helpful here. People tend to forget things that they really don't want to believe in the first place. Be prepared to remind others what the extent of your involvement can be. Don't just talk about what you can't do, but do clarify the limits of what you can do.

You may have to clearly decrease your participation in some of your memberships, or end them altogether, at least temporarily. If you are adding a new, significant activity, something has to give. What will it be?

- *Develop the ability to be in more than one place at a time.* Figure out what a group needs from you, and see how they can get it, even if that means they don't get it directly from you. This includes seeing who else can do the things you assume that only you can or should do. (This is an assumption that should be routinely challenged.) Give some thought to what you, and you alone, really need to do and where opportunities exist to involve others. Some tasks really are routine; they don't require any special expertise to be handled adequately. Sure, no one can do quite as conscientious a job as you (I hope you don't seriously believe this), but somehow the group will muddle through. When you take on something that someone else can do, particularly someone with fewer responsibilities in the organization, you not only unnecessarily burden yourself but you close off openings for others to contribute, thereby losing the chance to expand the organization's base. Picture how things that are important to you and to the success of your effort can get done, either by design or happenstance, if you just aren't able to do them.

- *Write things down.* When you agree to do something, jot it down or put it in your BlackBerry, Treo, iPhone, iPodtouch, or wherever you keep your reminders. Do it then and there. You will swear at the time that you won't forget, but let a day or two go by and you may well notice this queasy feeling that you are supposed to be doing something but you just can't remember what it is. Keep your tasks and commitments before you in a way that you will remember them, and pay attention to them in a timely manner. The easiest way to do this is to write things down.

A brief note here about priorities. You write down or schedule those things that are *not* routine. If you are scheduling things that should be routine—for example, time with your kids—take a second look at what has become routine in your life and what you are trying to fit in.

TEN PONDERING QUESTIONS

Often we go through life just being busy and trying to get things done. We may only accidentally pick up the learning awaiting us unless we take time to reflect on our experiences and mine them for discovery. I've used these 10 questions in my own

work and with groups engaged in promoting change. They have helped members gain a better understanding of themselves and their relationship to their work, its meaning, to one another, and to the world in which we live. If you recall the matter of praxis discussed in Chapter 2, you can see how these questions can be helpful. I use these questions routinely to learn from my own experience. Take time to ponder these questions to see if they help you understand how you fit into the picture.

1. What have I learned about myself as a result of my involvement? How do I think differently about myself now?

2. What have I learned about my community? How do I think differently about my community?

3. What have I learned about how change takes place? What theories have I developed?

4. How have my reflections and my dialogue with others brought new understanding or knowledge?

5. What do I better understand about how collective action both maintains conditions as well as changes them?

6. What have I learned about how people can organize themselves and shape their existence?

7. How does the interplay between group members allow everyone to express and develop their capacity?

8. What are some of the "big" questions I have been asking myself?

9. How have I connected my beliefs, my experiences, and my actions?

10. How have I become more aware of myself and my world? What do I see now that I didn't see before? How have I become better at looking?

AVOID BURNOUT

Effectively integrating your change activities with your personal life will go a long way toward preventing the dreaded disease of burnout. Going through the

SUDDENLY, BILL, WHO TYPICALLY TRIES TO DO EVERYTHING HIMSELF, STOPS SMOLDERING AND SPONTANEOUSLY COMBUSTS AT HIS DESK... LEAVING THREE MORE PROJECTS UNFINISHED.

motions after you have lost a sense of appreciation or worth for those motions and what they are to produce is burnout. It is the loss of the will to challenge or find valued meaning in a situation. Edelwich and Brodsky (1980) described the phenomenon of burnout as "a progressive loss of idealism, energy, and purpose" (p. 14). Bryan (1980) said that burnout "kills the motivating spirit" that causes people to get involved in social change work in the first place. Burnout may lead professionals to leave the field altogether (Arrington, 2008).

Compassion fatigue is a phenomenon related to burnout. Particularly affecting people in the caregiving professions, compassion fatigue is a condition related the stress of working with people who have been traumatized. Workers can experience vicarious trauma and end up losing feeling grounded in the world around them (Bush, 2009; Hoffman, Palladino, & Barnett, 2007; Joinson, 1992).

Pretty chilly thoughts, aren't they? Is burnout a natural consequence of working in health and human services? I don't believe so. Avoiding burnout involves managing factors that are within your control and recognizing those that are outside your control. In fact, accepting ambiguity and the need for flexibility may be healthier than expecting clarity and control in

all parts of your job (Meyerson, 1994). Knowing this is one thing; practicing it is another.

Arches (1997) pointed out that responses to burnout in human services have too often focused on the individual, leading to the perception that the phenomenon is private trouble. Because it affects more than just the individual worker, burnout has public consequences and may well be caused by conditions in the workplace and public policies that workers have not effectively challenged. Arches argued that alleviating burnout requires commitment to social change, a change that invites workers to help one another understand the political nature of their frustration. Working together, in collaboration with the people they serve, human services professionals can create vehicles for instituting change. "Burnout is a call for action" (p. 60).

There are many useful strategies to help you maintain your sense of purpose and renew your spirit. Here are some ideas to consider:

- Develop, recognize, and be able to rely on a strong value base from which you can draw strength. Find meaning and importance in what you do.

- Develop the skills to address the situations you routinely face.

- Develop some "perspective-taking" abilities. Don't overvalue your disappointments or undervalue your gains and victories.

- Take care of the things that are important to you personally. Confront what is bothering you.

- Get a life apart from your job or a particular change effort and attend to it.

- Do what you need to do to experience success. Get your work done. You will probably be more intolerant and frustrated with other people when you don't feel good about your own efforts.

- Make mistakes.

- Don't own others' mistakes.

- Have fun. Enjoy the challenge and the people. Capitalize on the energy the tasks and relationships bring. Every now and again take the focus off the "things that need to be done." Take advantage of opportunities to laugh, to be a little silly, or just to play.

- Look forward to dessert. Put things in your life that you can look forward to. If you can't see anything really enjoyable in your very near future, a stressful present can be more troubling. But if you know that at the end of the day you are going to a basketball game with your buddy, or going out to dinner with a friend, it will be easier to make it through the green beans the day might pile on your plate.

Corey and Corey (2011, pp. 323–324) provided some additional thoughts:

- Look at your behavior to determine if it is working for you. Ask yourself if you are really doing what you want to be doing.

- Look at your expectations to determine whether they are realistic.

- Focus on aspects of your work that you have the power to change.

- Colleagues can provide you with new information, insights, and perspectives. In the helping professions, the companionship of colleagues can be a great asset.

- Create a support group. You can take the initiative to organize your colleagues to listen to one another and provide help. You can gain strength and hope by forming meaningful alliances with colleagues.

A final tip comes from Blumenfeld and Alpern (1986):

- Purposefully develop the skill to discover humor in the situations you face.

SOME KEYS TO PERSONAL EFFECTIVENESS

You may well be surprised at how much you are able to accomplish once you decide to take on the challenge of change. You will also discover, no doubt, that many people don't play this game very well. They just can't seem to use themselves effectively. You will be surprised at how quickly you can be taken seriously. Some practical pointers can direct you to more productive involvement. You might call these the elemental do's and don'ts for personal effectiveness. These notions refer only to you—to your attitudes and conduct. They are uniquely within your control. They tell you how to use yourself.

- *Don't set arbitrary limits on yourself.* Plenty of people will tell you what you can't do; there is no need to add to the list. You may give yourself messages that keep you from acting powerfully. These are self-imposed shackles, and they may not be easy to change. (It is likely that you have repeated them to yourself so often that you believe they are true.) Acknowledge disempowering messages ("I don't know anything about this." "I can't do anything about this.") and repeatedly give yourself new, more powerful messages ("I know some pretty useful things." "There are a number of things I can do about this."). Just remember, the moment you believe you are powerless, you will indeed be powerless—emblazon this on your heart.

- *Don't make excuses.* Aside from the fact that excuses are irritating, they seduce you into a "can't do" mentality. You can easily get used to looking for reasons to explain why you aren't doing what you need to do. This places the control on forces outside yourself, robbing you of the ability to direct your own actions. If you look hard enough, you can always find a reason you can't accomplish something. Be honest with yourself. "I can't" often means "I won't." Take responsibility for things, and get on with it. You will take yourself more seriously and others will too.

- *Acknowledge the presence of problems.* Accept the fact of certain conditions, but not the inevitability of them. You can acknowledge the presence of problems or obstacles without giving in to them. "That's just the way things are" can be a self-defeating statement, implying a kind of permanence about particular circumstances. "That's just the way things are right now" provides a much different orientation. Alinsky (1972) reminded us to be realistic radicals—to take the world as it is, not as it should be. Your job is to help move it to where it should be.

- *Don't contract the disease of being right.* Undoubtedly, you will make a strong stand for your beliefs from time to time. You may use the appearance of intransigence as a negotiating ploy. You may secure the high moral ground in an effort to distinguish yourself from an opponent. These are purposeful actions that may well lead to success, but they are different from the disease of "being right." Those so afflicted are unable to consider a perspective different from their own. Their actions are not purposeful so much as they are reflexive. So invested are they in "being right" that adopting a different idea or behavior equals "being wrong," a possibility that is truly frightening and must be avoided at all costs. A lot of energy is wasted in an effort to be right. You usually have to make other people "wrong" in the process. Not only does this limit your learning, but it also cuts off the possibility of generating potentially useful agreements. And it definitely makes your company an unwelcome event. Get in the habit of listening as aggressively as you speak, and identify areas of potential agreement. You can then decide how you want to proceed, and you can act on purpose.

- *Remember why you are doing this.* Understand that your purpose is to be effective: not cautious, though this may be important; not loud, though

Take a Moment to Discover

Your ordinary ways of looking at, thinking about, and responding to situations provide patterns that can severely restrict your actions. This is a pretty common human condition. You eliminate a host of possibilities simply because you never allow yourself to consider them. And nobody but you did this to you. Furthermore, don't be surprised if you routinely make up rules for yourself about how things work or what you aren't allowed to do. Check to see if barriers are of your own creation.

Get in the habit of asking yourself, "Who says so?" To help you get beyond the confines of too rigid thinking, use some creative thinking to solve the puzzle of the nine dots. Can you connect the nine dots below with four straight lines without removing your pencil from the page or retracing any line?

Did you solve the puzzle? If not, the answer appears on the next page.

SOURCE: Based on Napier & Gershenfeld, 2004.

this may be necessary; not fired, though this may be fruitful. Your purpose is to be effective.

THE FINAL FIVE

Aside from all the (possibly) bright ideas this book may offer, you can do five simple things to quickly establish yourself and maintain your credibility: adopt a success attitude, be prepared, follow through, acknowledge people, and say thank-you. When you do this, you will be far and away more influential than most people you encounter in this business of change. You will notice this quickly.

- *Adopt a success attitude.* You do this all the time in other areas of your life. Maybe you are shopping for that particular birthday present that will bring a look of joy to your child's face. You don't know exactly what it looks like, but you know you will find it. So you keep shopping until you do. Maybe the darn car won't start. You are not sure what is wrong, but you know that if you tinker with this or fiddle with that you will eventually get the thing going again. You expect to accomplish these things, and things just sort of naturally work out. Assuming you will prevail provides a potent orientation for approaching the challenge before you. It creates a forceful self-fulfilling prophecy that helps you take setbacks in stride and keep going. This is true whether you are shopping, fixing your car, or making things better in your community.

- *Be prepared.* Have a clear picture of the outcome you intend to achieve from each activity in your change effort—a rally, a meeting, or even just a telephone call. Think through what you need to do to achieve that outcome, and get ready to do it. If you need to communicate with someone, don't hesitate to practice what you need to say. You will be much more confident when your message feels right. Often you will need to get information or mull over some facts. Do your homework. When you sit down at a meeting, you will be far ahead of those who are thinking about these things for the first time.

- *Follow through on your commitments, thoroughly and on time.* You will hear the refrain "it's in process" more often than you will ever care to recall. Roughly translated, this usually means: "Shoot, I forgot I was supposed to get that done until you just now reminded me. I'll get working on that pretty soon, I think." Don't learn that phrase.

- *Acknowledge people and what they say.* This is one of the most eloquent things you can do. By providing people with individual recognition, you meet an important human need. Your ability to acknowledge others enhances you both. As you take others more seriously, you in turn are taken more seriously yourself. It is almost unavoidable. You don't have to agree with someone to acknowledge her point. It is helpful to repeat the message and your understanding of its importance. If you are asked a question, it is a good idea to check with the asker to be sure you answered the question. Learn people's names, and use them.

- *Say thank-you.* Not very complicated, is it? But surprisingly, not often consistently done. A "thank-you" allows you to respectfully complete an exchange, and it is noticed and appreciated. It will set you apart.

True, there is more to the business of change than these five simple points, but more than anything else I can think of, paying attention to these points or ignoring them seem to set apart those who accomplish a lot from those who accomplish little. If you remember and put into practice these elementary precepts, you will develop a significant amount of influence and encounter at least a fair amount of success.

CONCLUSION

Congratulations, you are no longer shouting from the safety of the sidelines. You are in the game. Your commitment reflects your recognition that you have some of the necessary skills and an understanding that new opportunities will help you to learn more. You have decided whose endorsement of your actions is needed, and you are getting that support.

This whole business of promoting change is about doing. It isn't about wishing, though you will have a few wishes. It isn't about hoping, though your hopes will guide your actions. It is about doing, about acting positively to produce a desired result.

You are a change agent. That is a noble thing to be. It truly and unapologetically is. But you are more—an employee, a parent, a partner, a person who likes to sit in the sun with a good book or play

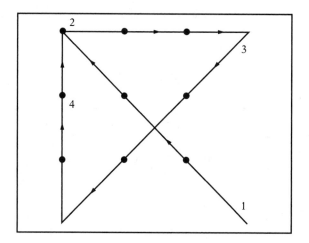

Answer to the nine-dot puzzle on page 109.

yourself into exhaustion on the basketball court. All these personas are important, and you must balance your involvement to nurture them all.

What you offer to any change effort is you—your information, beliefs, insight, values, intelligence, emotions, and actions. Regardless of the manner or

level of your participation, you should reflect on the principles that will guide your involvement in the most powerful and effective way. After all, investing your own time and talent is the most meaningful contribution you can make; you will want to be sure it is well spent.

A CALL FROM HOME

It took a while, but you stopped complaining about conditions and started to act on them. You recognized that you had some choices in this matter, and you recognized that you have professional competence to act effectively.

This is exciting. You can feel the energy. Much different than sitting behind the desk dispensing understanding nods to the occupant of the visitor's chair. Much more interesting than filling out forms and documenting your day. Here you get to be with people who are making a difference, intent on changing the way things work, making things better for the people who come into that office. Even better, people have come to see you as an important part of the process. You are even getting a bit of a reputation, and other groups wanting to get something done are asking you for help. You feel that you can go into any community situation and have people respond to your direction.

You are acting on your ethics, not sacrificing them to "the way things are." Your cell phone rings—it is

the best way for people to reach you now as you always seem to be on your way to someplace else. You check your caller ID; a call from home. Well, that's not quite as exciting as a call from the mayor's office, but you'll take it. No, you didn't call your son's teacher. Yes, you said you would. Yes, you will get to it. You are just real busy right now.

It's hard for other people to get a picture of what it is that you are doing. They just can't see how important your work is, and that doesn't even count your regular job. You wish you could get some support there, but that doesn't seem likely. Your boss and your colleagues are still stuck in that service mentality. You'd think that the people you are trying to help would pitch in and do more things, but they don't seem to care much about what you are doing either. Enough of this feeling sorry for yourself. Pretty soon you will be with Jan and Brian and the rest, and then things will shift into high gear again. Your cell phone rings…

REFLECTION QUESTIONS

1. What benefits do you receive from your work that keeps you motivated?

2. How do you see other people who are affected by the work that you do? Whom don't you see?

3. What do you think you will be feeling a year from now? Why?

4. What do you need to take care of that you may be overlooking? What will happen if you do?

5. What will happen if you do not address this need now?

6. What is contributing to your effectiveness? What's getting in the way of your effectiveness?

7. What changes might you want to make? What steps do you need to take to make them?

8. What do you want to keep doing?

GROUP ACTIVITY: BUILDING THE CHANGE AGENT
FROM THE GROUND UP

Okay, here's your chance. Since Dr. Frankenstein is out of town (something about a mob), you have been assigned to create the ideal community change agent. Your "picture" of your change agent should include what *you* would need to have to put *yourself* fully into the picture.

1. Divide the larger group into teams of four members, and begin by drawing a life-sized person using newsprint or several flip chart sheets taped together.

2. Using words, drawings, and pictures from magazines, create your ideal change agent. Consider putting some of these things into your picture: (20–30 minutes)

    • What you know

    • What values you have

• What tools you use to be effective
• How you recognize the need for action
• How you recognize your ability to promote change and give yourself permission to act
• How you develop sanction
• How you keep your personal life happy and healthy
• How you ponder or reflect
• How you avoid burnout
• How you establish personal effectiveness

3. Use your portrait to teach the larger group about "putting yourself into the picture." (5 minutes)

HELPFUL WEBSITES

Links to the organizations briefly described here are on the companion website at www.cengage.com/humansvcs/homan.

Neighborhood Funder's Group. A national network of foundations and philanthropic organizations that support community efforts to improve economic and social conditions in low-income neighborhoods, this organization has many publications, including the very useful *Community Organizing Toolbox.* This is not a grant-making organization. You can also obtain their newsletter, *NFG Reports,* along with information on job opportunities, NFG projects, and links to some valuable progressive organization websites. This is a very rich site.

Low Income Networking and Communications Project. Promoting discussion, information exchange, and coalition building among low-income groups, the LINC project is part of the Welfare Law Center. It focuses on welfare issues and has links to many grassroots organizations. The emphasis is on how information technology can aid in organizing for change.

National Housing Institute. The focus of this organization is on housing, and their work brings together activists, journalists, and others interested in promoting social justice. Their Rooflines blog and *Shelterforce* magazine provide excellent forums for learning.

The Simpson's Archive. Keep up to date on developments in Springfield while keeping up with Bart and the gang. Here you will find a synopsis of every Simpson's episode, sneak previews for upcoming shows, and a reminder of the importance of irreverence and not taking yourself too seriously.

Chapter 5

✳

Knowing Your Community

CHAPTER HIGHLIGHTS

- Perspectives on "community"
- Geographic and interest communities
- Community subsystems
- Benefit, action, and target communities
- Peripheral community
- Basic community characteristics
- Community functioning
- Sources of community capital: environmental, physical, economic, human, political, informational, spiritual, cultural, and social
- Participatory action research
- Unmet community needs
- Dangers of needs assessments
- Identifying and valuing community assets

- Community readiness for change
- Five stages of community life
- The many resources of the library
- Organizations as sources of information
- Individuals as sources of information: guided key informant discussions, focus groups, surveys, and questionnaires
- Mapping technology
- Internet sources
- Windshield surveys
- The value of lists
- Newspapers are more than just news
- Using your eyes and ears as research tools

A good idea doesn't live apart from the community in which it is to be implemented. There is much more you need to find out to know whether your idea is really practical and useful or whether there are other, better ideas out there. You need to know what response to anticipate from various parts of the community and where you might get opposition or support. The community is where all this will happen, so you had better find out more about it.

How you approach your community will be based on what you want to know about it. It is that basic. The community is a contributor of resources and allies and a provider of pitfalls and opponents. You want to know where these are—where to go to get what you need and whom or what to avoid. You want to understand its rhythms and culture, how it makes sense of things, what it knows, what it values, and how it responds to the idea of change. The community is, after all, where the need for change, the effort to make that change, and the resistance to change coexist. In fact, it is the community itself that will be slightly or significantly changed by your efforts. This is where the game is played. You need to know the size and shape of the field and what the other players can do.

PERSPECTIVES ON COMMUNITY

Just how much you need to know will depend on the nature of the problem, the size or extent of the change being pursued, and the kind of organization you want to put together. Three ways of looking at your community are important to your understanding. The first involves perceiving your community as a community. The second examines the component parts of the community, acknowledging that it is made up of several smaller "subcommunities." The third focuses on those individuals and groups drawn into your arena of action.

Your Community as a Community

There are a number of ways to think about what a community is. The first, most obvious way is to think about it as a geographic area, a place with defined physical boundaries. If you were flying over the area in a small plane, you could actually see these boundaries. Certain streets mark a neighborhood's borders. The limits of a mobile home park or an apartment complex can be clearly determined. The most fundamental characteristic of these geographic communities is that they are places of residence. People are familiar with them because they live there.

Some communities are defined by individuals' shared interests, activities, affection, or common identity. These characteristics differentiate them from others. These interest or identificational communities might be called food stamp recipients, single parents,

laryngectomy patients, or members of the Simon Cowell fan club (Longres, 2000). Where these people live does not determine their membership in the community. Meenaghan and Gibbons (2000) describe solidarity and ontological communities of people who have a common heritage, such as religion, language, ethnicity, or culture. These communities assert their own strong identity within the context of larger, more complex modern communities.

People are usually members of geographic as well as interest communities. Perhaps you live in an apartment complex in a certain city and you attend college. You have some common interests with people who live in the same place you do. But you also share some things in common with other students at your college. At lunch, after the exam has been rehashed, you and some other students may talk about good or not so good landlords or apartment managers. Some of your classmates also rent. So here you are. You reside in a particular city. You live in a particular apartment complex. You are a renter. You are a student. Already you are a member of four distinct communities, two geographic and two interest or identificational.

The notions of geographic, solidarity, and interest or identificational can be seen in these definitions for the word *community*.

- "Community: a group of individuals or families that share certain values, services, institutions, interests, or geographic proximity" (Barker, 1999, p. 89).

- "Community, or a 'sense of community,' exists when two or more people work together toward the accomplishment of mutually desirable goals (conditions)" (Lofquist, 1993, p. 8).

- "A community is a territorially bounded social system or set of interlocking or integrated functional subsystems (economic, political, religious, ethical, educational, legal, socializing, reproductive, etc.) serving a resident population, plus the material culture or physical plant through which the subsystems operate" (Bernard, 1972, p. 163).

Some observers describe community as a state of being that provides its members with a context for empowered development. In this sense, community is both a process and a desired outcome. Palmer

(1993) suggested that community is found at the intersection of the inward and outward life:

> Community is a place where the connections felt in our hearts make themselves known in the bonds between people, and where the tuggings and pullings of those bonds keep opening our hearts. (p. 88)

Peck (1987) described the difficulty of establishing a community, but made it clear that the attempt is well worth the effort:

> Community [is] a group of individuals who have learned how to communicate honestly with each other, whose relationships go deeper than their masks of composure, and who have developed some significant commitment to "rejoice together, mourn together," and to "delight in each other, make others' conditions our own." … Genuine community is not easily achieved or easily maintained; its avowed goal is to seek ways in which to live with ourselves and others in love and peace…. Once a group has achieved community, the single most common thing members express is, "I feel safe here." (pp. 59, 163, 67)

Lloyd-Jones (1989) pointed out the benefits that accrue from coming together to form a community:

> Individuals both enlarge and restrict their own freedoms by joining such a community. But whatever restriction results is far surpassed by the individual's and the group's ability to achieve established goals while at the same time creating mutual support and pride. (pp. 2–3)

And Brueggemann (2006) called attention to community as a necessary condition for human development:

> Communities are natural human associations based on ties of intimate personal relationships and shared experiences in which each of us mutually provide meaning in our lives, meet our needs for affiliation, and accomplish interpersonal goals…. Your individual self cannot, in fact, reach its full realization in

isolation but only as you are nurtured, guided, and suffused with the life of the communal social relationships in which you exist. Our predisposition to community insures that we become the persons we were meant to become, discover who we are as people, and construct a culture that would be impossible for single, isolated individuals to accomplish alone. (p. 116)

You may view community through a variety of lenses. It may be considered a place, a set of interests, an identity, a purposeful grouping of individuals into a common whole, a fundamental capacity of our humanness, a state of being, a manner of people relating to one another, or a provider of benefits that result from effective interaction. To work with a community, it is important to picture it in terms of distinctness—the clear common characteristics that connect its members. These connections provide the potential for a variety of benefits, particularly if members can recognize them and act on them.

For our purposes then:

> *A community is a number of people who share a distinct location, belief, interest, activity, or other characteristic that clearly identifies their commonality and differentiates them from those not sharing it. This common distinction is sufficiently evident that members of the community are able to recognize it, even though they may not currently have this recognition. Effectively acting on their recognition may lead members to more complete personal and mutual development.*

Communities and Subcommunities

Communities operate on a variety of levels. Recall the discussion of systems theory from Chapters 2 and 3. A systems perspective is helpful in understanding various component parts and levels of communities, from the broad to the very immediate. Using a geographic community as an example, the broad community has a name such as Seattle, Des Moines, or Flagstaff. If you look on a map, you see the name printed next to a circle or maybe just a small dot. You may live near the town, but not really in it. Perhaps your kids go to school in Oakwood, but you actually live on a farm several miles away. Still, you see yourself as residing in the Oakwood area, or at least in Vermillion County.

A second level of your community consists of smaller divisions that describe sets of people within the broad community. Neighborhoods, the business community, the farming community, gangs, and the medical community are all types of second-level communities that may exist within this broader community. Some of these smaller communities are clearly defined. Their members frequently associate with one another, and they clearly understand their affiliation with other community members.

Various rituals, boundary lines, or other cues remind people of their membership. If you go to school in Pocatello, you know you are a member of the university community because you go to the Idaho State University campus several times a week. You see other students or other faculty and talk to them as part of your day-to-day life. You easily identify yourself with the university community.

Other second-level communities are not so readily identifiable. Perhaps you are a single parent. There may be quite a few single parents in Pocatello, but you don't know who they are. You don't routinely get together as single parents. No one issues you an identification card that certifies you as a member of this community. Yet you most certainly do share many things in common with other single parents in Pocatello. This second-level community is real, but the relationships among its members are much less clearly defined.

The more members of a community relate to one another or to an identified place, institution, or activity, the more likely they will be to recognize their membership in the community. The relationship among members is likely to be more patterned as well.

These subcommunities can be divided into even more specific levels. Back in Pocatello (first level) you have the religious community (second level), and within that community you have the Mormon community, the Catholic community, the Jewish community, or the Muslim community (third level). If you need to, you can break these communities down even further (fourth level) into wards, parishes, and congregations (Figure 5.1). The more you break things down, the more likely you are to come to affiliations that are directly meaningful to individuals. People usually find their immediate group to be

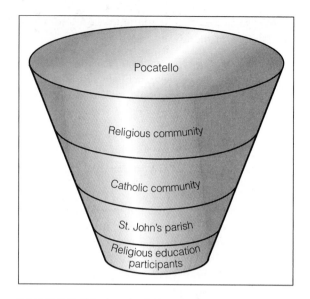

FIGURE 5.1   Levels of Community

significant in influencing what they do and how they think about what they do. Think about yourself as a student. Your college and the particular department you are affiliated with in that college influence how you spend your time. However, the particular class you take really influences how you spend your time. Your class is a much more immediate group than your college.

You will probably want to work at some particular level of community with which you identify, whose functioning affects your interests enough that you notice it, and where you believe your actions can have some degree of impact. This set of people and institutions close at hand is called your *close community,* described more fully in Chapter 2.

Do you need to keep dividing things down until you personally know everyone in the whole city? No, you don't. But you do need to understand that these various subdivisions exist. These close communities may be interlocking (fitting together so that action is coordinated), overlapping (sharing some common feature), or fairly independent from one another. Each of these configurations has some degree of power and is a potential source of support or opposition. Knowing how your community breaks down and what sets of relationships exist within it provide some insights regarding whom you may want to involve and how. It will also alert you to potential forces of resistance and guide you in ways to reduce that resistance.

Communities in Your Arena of Action

Most of the changes you work on will provoke the interest of only a small segment of the broad community. The more important a group or segment of the community is to your effort, the more you should know about it. The less important it is, the less you need to know.

The immediate community or communities you need to know about are those involved in your particular arena of action (Kettner et al., 1985): the benefit community, the action community, and the target or response community. In some cases these component parts will be actual communities of people. In other instances you might more easily think of them as systems.

The *benefit community* includes those people who currently experience the problem or condition that needs improving and could benefit from its resolution. Their endorsement of the change effort is a precondition for action. There are few exceptions to this general rule. Only in emergency situations or when members of a benefit community are simply unable to give their consent (for example, infants) would this rule not apply. Further, members of the benefit community should be involved as key participants in the change process itself. They become active leaders, not passive recipients.

The *action community* consists of those who recognize or could easily recognize that a problem or opportunity exists and may be willing to take action. This includes the principal change agents as well as all those others who could contribute to making the change.

The *target* or *response community* encompasses those whose policies, actions, or inactions somehow perpetuate the current condition. This community controls the resources the benefit community needs. For worthwhile change to occur, members of this community must change their practices. Sometimes they are very willing to do so; sometimes they are not. The more carefully you pinpoint this group, the more effectively you can focus your strategy.

You may not find three distinct community groups in your arena of action. For example, if you are working with a neighborhood to develop a program to visit elderly residents who live alone, the neighborhood itself is the community that is mobilized, that benefits, and that must respond for change.

A COMMUNITY OF PARADERS COMMUNES WITH THE LARGER COMMUNITY.

If you are working with that same neighborhood to pressure banks to provide more loans to residents, then the target of your effort is the banks. The neighborhood is both the action community you mobilize as well as the benefit community. If you mobilize schoolteachers on behalf of (or better, alongside) teens who are homeless to put pressure on the city government to provide shelter facilities, three distinct benefit, action, and target communities can be identified.

Although your main focus is on your arena of action, information on *peripheral communities*— communities whose interests your actions may affect but do not now affect directly—is also important. Peripheral communities are not currently in the game: They are standing around on the sidelines, some watching what is going on, some not paying the slightest attention. Even if you can't take time to find out much about them, you should identify who they are so you can stimulate support or quiet or counter opposition. In the example of teachers working with teens who are homeless, peripheral communities could include social service providers, neighborhoods adjacent to the proposed shelter facilities, and the police department.

The complexity of the issue, its size, its potential for controversy, and the range of communities it will probably affect will tell you how much community knowledge you need to have. As you come to know more about your community, you will become more confident about what you can do to make it better.

WHAT TO LOOK FOR IN YOUR COMMUNITY

There's a knock on the door. "Dadgummit!" you hiss, then quickly look around to see if anyone caught you uttering such an uncharacteristic obscenity. It seems like every time you sit back to watch Vanna light up those letters, you get interrupted. It's never during the commercial, never. Oh, well, better see who it is. No one else ever gets the door.

"Hi, Vern Kadukey. Glad to meet you," comes the greeting.

"Vern Kadukey?" you ask.

"That's right. Just moved in across the street. Thought I'd come by and get to know you, find out what sort of family lives here, and check out the house. You mind?"

"Uh, well, no, I guess not. Come on in." Stepping across the threshold, Vern trips on the curled up edge of the rug. "Sorry, Vern, I guess we're used to that. Let me move the laundry off the couch so you can sit down."

"No, that's okay. I'll just stroll around a bit. Hey, your faucet's dripping. Don't you know how to fix a leak?"

"Uh, well, I was going to get around to it." Geez, if I knew this guy was coming over, I would have cleaned the bathroom. Maybe I'd better steer him to the garden. At least that's been weeded.

"Want to go see the garden, Vern?"

"Sure, why not. Say, what's this on the fridge?"

"That's the list of who's supposed to do the dishes and take out the garbage. You can see it's not my week." Why the heck am I explaining to this guy?

"No, I mean the little pig magnet. The one eating the ice cream. It says 'Do you really need this?' It's not holdin' up nuthin'. What's it here for?"

"Look, Vern, maybe you should come back another time. I was just in the middle of something pretty important. Okay?"

"Sure. Hey, look! The Wheel's on the tube. Mind if I stay and watch?"

Oh, God....

What did Vern see? What did he begin to know about you and your family? About the place you live? What would he be likely to notice that you wouldn't see? What conclusions would he reach? How accurate would these be? What could he do to make them more accurate?

If Vern spent a little more time in the place you live, keeping his eyes and ears open, asking questions, and doing a little outside investigating, he'd have a pretty good working understanding of your household. He'd figure out how big your living space is, how things are structured to accomplish than a researcher: you are a change agent, maybe even an activist. Just be an informed one. To begin with, you need to understand the basic characteristics of your community and how the community functions to meet its needs.

Remember that your community could be your school, the agency for which you work, the congregation of your synagogue, mosque, meeting house, or church, or your city. Although these are distinct categories, they sometimes overlap. Think of them as lenses through which you look at your community. These categories represent general things to look for; you will have to determine the specific information you need based on the situation you are confronting.

Basic Community Characteristics

This information is chiefly objective; that is, it consists of facts. You could get much of this information by riding around in a helicopter (great fun) or by reading (moderate fun). You may not have to set foot in town. A sampling of questions is provided to give you some guidance in understanding your community's characteristics and the way it functions.

One of the first things you'll want to know are the physical features of your community.

- How big is it? What are the dimensions of this community?

- Where do people gather? Are there common places where people meet, either coincidentally or on purpose? This could be the train station, the synagogue, or the office bathroom.

- Are there key landmarks or points of reference? In Cuernavaca everyone knows the Zócalo. In Washington, D.C. the Washington Monument is hard to miss, and in Atlanta most people can find their way to Turner Field. This could, however, just as easily mean the park, the junior high school, or Mr. Smedly's office.

- What does this community look like? Is it dirty or clean, old or new, well maintained or in need of repair?

- What are the natural features of the community? Perhaps there is a flood every spring. Maybe there is an abundance of water, trees, and mosquitoes. Water might be a scarce

certain goals, how people feel about certain things, and a host of other household factors. To some extent that's what you are doing when you walk into a community and start looking around. Looking at a community is not a whole lot different from looking at a house and a household unprepared for visitors. Thinking about your community as a household will give you some clues for understanding it better.

Let me stress that you can and should get moving on your change effort before you have each and every piece of information available on your community. You can spend a lifetime studying and still not know everything you would like to know. You have to balance your need for action with your need for information.

Some of you will want to use lack of information as an excuse for inaction. Others will want to dive in headfirst without checking to see how deep the water is. In actual practice, you gather some information (you need to determine how much), and then act. And you keep gathering information while you are taking action.

The better informed you are, the more efficiently and effectively you can use your time. This increases your chances for success and reduces the role of luck, especially bad luck. But you are more resource, and cacti may dot the landscape. The fact that your community is hot or cold, rainy, dry, or mountainous could have an effect on what people do.

Of course, a community isn't a community without people. What do you know about these folks?

- What is the population of this community? Does this number fluctuate? In some communities there are 10,000 people in the summer and 40,000 in the winter. There may be 100 people during the day and none at night. Perhaps the members of the community (for example, most students at a college) only stay for a certain period of time and then move on.

- What is the demographic breakdown? You may want to know how old or young the people are. Whether or not they are married may be important. Income, educational background, ethnic diversity, and cultural traditions could be significant.

- How long have these people been a part of this community? Someone who arrived a month ago will have a different perspective than someone who has been around for 23 years.

- How often do members interact and in what ways do people interact? Some of these are routine, such as going to lunch with coworkers or shopping at the grocery store. Some occur on special occasions, such as block parties or community festivals.

- What do the families look like? A community in which there is a predominance of two-parent, one-marriage families with an average of five children is likely to be different from one in which the typical family consists of two unmarried adults living together without children.

- What is the population density? Are there a lot of people in a small space, or a lot of space with few people?

Looking at the characteristics of a community gives you a picture of the significant aspects or component parts of the community. This is like a snapshot. You see the parts, but you don't see them doing anything. If you were capturing the community with a video camera, you would be gathering information in the second category—you'd see how the community functions.

How the Community Functions

How a community functions is in a way its very essence. One way to look at functioning is to examine how the community endeavors to meet its needs. There is a difference between needs, wants, and problems, and for our purposes needs are those things a community requires to meet its goals and to sustain itself. Need in this sense is necessity, not a lack of something. These are routine, ongoing challenges the community must address. As such they are different from problems, which are needs that have not been properly addressed.

As the community functions to take care of itself, it draws on and further develops the domains of capital that contribute to its health. So, community capital is both used to meet the community's requirements to sustain itself and grow stronger, and it is produced by attempts to meet those requirements. Community capital is wealth; need is what the community has to take care of. As you recall from Chapter 2, those domains of community capital are environmental, physical, economic, human, political, informational, cultural, spiritual, and social (Daniels, 2002; Pretty, 2000). Just like anything you may pay attention to and recognize as important, communities tend to generate needed capital the more they recognize its importance and purposefully attend to its growth. These nine domains become focal points for community development.

As you examine how current requirements are being met and capital generated, ask yourself, "How did things get to be this way?" Understanding history can be an important key to deciphering the present.

Environmental Requirements and Capital.   The natural environment provides us with a place to be and the elements we need for our very survival. A community needs to protect and maintain this foundation of life.

- Is the air clean to breathe and the water pure to drink?

- Are open spaces available for recreation and visual appreciation? How much trash litters the community?

- Is there an adequate number and variety of healthy plant and animal life? Which parcels of land can be used for a different purpose?

- Which landscape features can be resource attractors? Do community members recognize natural elements as defining characteristics? How do environmental conditions affect human interaction?

Physical Requirements and Capital.   This set of requirements includes those that help us take care of our bodies as well as those that deal with the things we make or build.

- Do people have consistent access to adequate food, shelter, and clothing?

- Is adequate medical care available on a timely and affordable basis?

- Are roads and other transportation systems adequate for getting people to and from their destinations in a timely and safe manner?

- Are there community projects built by volunteers whose completion symbolizes concrete achievements? Murals, gardens, playgrounds, and sculptures are good examples of these (Delgado, 2000).

- Are the waste and drainage systems adequate to protect health and maintain visual attractiveness?

- What is the condition of buildings?

- Are all the systems routinely maintained to prevent problems?

Economic Requirements and Capital.   The community's economic system provides a way for its members to develop the means to acquire things that are important to them. Usually, this means money. Each community has some economic needs.

- How do people get access to goods and services?

- What are the income and occupation levels of specialized populations; for example, women, people of color, older people, and so on? What barriers to equal opportunity exist for these groups?

- Are opportunities plentiful or limited?

- What untapped economic resources exist?

- Do methods of exchange that don't depend on money exist, such as bartering?

- How is money earned and produced in this community? What are its major industries and services? Is it in growth or decline?

- Does money stay and circulate within the community, or does it leave the community?

- Do members make their money outside or within the community?

- What forces outside the community influence its economic health?

Human Development Requirements and Capital. The community relies on the abilities of its members to produce goods and services, solve problems, affirm identity, and manage relationships. Where do they get these abilities, and how do they enhance them? Which are seen as important?

- How are talents recognized and skills developed?

- Are contributions by some members overlooked; for example, community members who are young, old, or homeless?

- Do members willingly offer their abilities for community efforts?

- Are members eager for action or passive and pessimistic?

- How does the skill and knowledge of members affect economic conditions?

- How are nonmarket talents valued?

- Which new capabilities do current conditions require?

- What talents and skills exist among community members?

Political Requirements and Capital.   Community life requires a continuous series of decisions on matters that affect its members. This process involves forming policies that manage resources and relationships. Each community faces a set of political requirements, and it will develop a governance or decision-making structure if it intends to respond to those requirements. Governance structures usually have clearly spelled out procedures for gathering information, making decisions, developing rules or laws, describing those rules or laws, and enforcing them. These procedures describe who is allowed to participate in the process and how (Fellin, 2001). Policies generated by political bodies outside of the immediate community (city councils, legislatures, and Congress) have a significant impact on the community. Each community needs to be able to develop its own policies and to influence the policies developed elsewhere that affect its health.

- What connections do members have to sources of political power both within and outside the community?

- Do members believe they have a right to participate in policy making?

- What is the formal process for making community decisions? What are the limits and the extent of this process? That is, over what matters is it empowered to decide, and what matters are seen as none of its business? Which services or functions does local government or the local administration see as its responsibility?

- What are the formal governmental structures? What are the formal positions of leadership and decision making, and who holds them? These are the people authorized or acknowledged by the community to provide direction. Community members often recognize them by their titles: mayor, principal, supervisor, and board member are a few of these titles.

- What are the informal processes for making community decisions? Each formal process has an informal one that operates within it or outside of it. The formal process often relies on this informal process or is made irrelevant by it. A description of the informal process is the answer to the question: How do things really work? You'll need to dig a little deeper to discover this process. Be on your guard against cynical paranoia as you do your digging. Informal processes usually depend on relationships or convenience and inconvenience. Frankly, few decisions, though admittedly

some, are important enough to warrant development of grand conspiracies.

- What are the informal positions of leadership and decision making, and who holds them? These positions usually don't have titles or the power is greater than the title. The people to whom formal leaders commonly look in fear or for support and ideas are likely candidates.

- How do people recognize problems? Some communities rely on official reports. Others acknowledge problems when somebody throws a temper tantrum. Some communities have structures for discovering problems, whereas others have patterned ways to avoid looking.

- Who is expected to be quiet, and who is allowed to speak up?

- What are the likely bases of power? In each community some things give people a better chance at getting what they want. Find out what these are. (Power is explored in more detail in Chapter 6.)

- How are community decisions carried out in practice?

- What does the community have that it can use to influence political decisions or exchange for political favors?

Information and Communication Requirements and Capital. "Cogito, ergo sum," said René Descartes: "I think, therefore I am." People think and ponder. They want and need to know more. A community needs to know about itself and the world in which it operates. The community has to have information and methods for developing, transmitting, and receiving that information. This set of requirements can be called the community's information and communication requirements.

- How do members of the community learn what is going on in the community? In the world?

- How skilled are members in the use of information technology? What values support or limit its use? Where do members have access to information technology?

- How do people decide what is true?

- To whom do people listen (bishop, radio talk show host, shop steward)? Who has acknowledged credibility?

- What mechanisms exist for identificational communities to exchange ideas and information? How does the presence or absence of mechanisms affect their ability to even identify as a community?

- What schools and training programs exist for community members? How good are they? What is the degree of community control over these? How is access to them determined? How much financial support do they receive?

- How is new knowledge generated, tested, and communicated?

- What is the philosophical and editorial bias of the major formal providers of news? This could include newspapers, radio, television, employee newsletters, staff meetings, and other mechanisms set up to provide news. How reliable are they?

- What are the informal methods of providing news? What philosophical and editorial bias exists there? This could include the grapevine or rumor mill, the underground or alternative press, unofficial memoranda, and other methods people use to communicate their perceptions of "what is really going on." How reliable are they?

- What important information doesn't get communicated to community members? How do you know this?

- How interested are community members in communicating with one another?

Cultural Requirements and Capital. A community's culture binds people together and affirms their identity. The values of the community are found in its culture; its beauty and emotion are expressed in art and music. Culture helps us to know who we are and how to be with one another and with the world around us. If there is little identifiable culture, or if traditional behavior is not routinely practiced, the community is likely to have problems with its very identity, and members may

feel lost. Through rituals and traditions culture provides a set of accepted frameworks for behavior and meaning making. This can be as simple as shaking hands or as elaborate as Yaqui Holy Week practices. Community members may be part of smaller cultural communities; it is important to recognize these subcommunities in your assessment.

- What do forms of art and music reveal about the community's perception of itself, its members, and its place in the world?

- How is culture seen? What cultural artifacts exist?

- What roles are different members of the community expected to play; women, men, young, old, and others?

- What influence does culture play in the lives of community members? To what extent are stated cultural values practiced in everyday life?

- To what extent do traditional cultural beliefs and practices remain? Which have been replaced by a broader, more commercial culture?

- Which cultural traditions and values support and which inhibit the social, political, and economic aspirations of community members? How is support utilized? How are tensions handled?

- Which cultural norms and values might operate out of sight of a casual observer?

- Are differences among cultures valued beyond curiosity or quaintness?

- What forms of cultural conflict exist between groups?

- How is language used to affirm culture?

- Which other gifts preserve community traditions and identity and keep members connected to their culture? How are they passed on to younger or newer community members?

Spiritual Requirements and Capital. As human beings we have a need to feel connected to something beyond our relationship to the physical world. Spirituality invites us to think about our place in a larger order. Inherent in spirituality are notions of the meaning of life and our responsibility to ourselves, to other people, and to other elements of our environment. Spirituality generally involves a call to a set of beliefs and practices that develop and affirm our inherent value, the value of other people and things that we experience, and the value of our relationships to them. Spirituality is marked by reflection and a quest for a deepening of understanding and growth in integrity. The pull toward matters that can be called spiritual is one of the things that make us human. An individual or a community disconnected from its spiritual interests will attend to a more narrow set of interests and may well be adrift. Participation in organized religion is one highly visible way that people act to meet their spiritual needs, but it is by no means the only way.

- How is spirituality valued by community members? Is it openly discussed?

- In what ways do members attend to their spiritual interests?

- What different forms of spirituality are you aware of in your community?

- Is the distinction between spirituality and religiosity recognized?

- Do the community's religious groups collaborate and recognize that different religions have value for different community members? Or is there marked intolerance by religious groups toward other religions and nonbelievers?

- How are the spiritual capacities of community members called forth into action to improve the community?

Social and Emotional Requirements and Capital. Just like individuals, communities have social and emotional requirements. Forming and maintaining relationships is an integral function of the community. People like to get together and feel they are part of something, or they need to get together to accomplish something. It's hard to play baseball by yourself, so Little Leagues are formed. Rotary clubs give businesspeople an opportunity to see each other every week. Myriad associations, clubs, and organizations exist within your community. Feelings of well-being and confidence in the future are necessary if a community is to achieve its potential.

- Do members of the community have the desire and the ability to work together?

- Do members of the community feel safe and secure?

- Do members trust one another?

- Do members have a strong sense of community identity? Do they take pride in the community and their membership in it?

- What are the sources of pride (Go Tigers!), embarrassment (It will be fixed soon.), fear (I hope it doesn't blow up.), joy (I knew we could do it!), and other feelings?

- Are members confident of their own and others' abilities, including the ability to maintain relationships and recognize and resolve problems?

- Do members feel a part of the community and cared for by other members?

- Do members feel free to contribute to the community and to achieve personal goals?

- What groupings and networks of relationships occur within the community? Many of these have names and rules of membership. Knowing about these linkages can help you understand how your community works and provide you with better access to people.

- How and where do people have fun?

- How does the community handle its deviants?

- How do members spend their time and money? Looking at what people do and how they commit their resources will tell you what people value.

The more interested you become in your community, the more you will want to understand it and what it requires. This is not a major project. You will simply begin to look at and think about your community in a different way.

One sage observer of baseball noted that a team needs to do five things well: hit, hit with power, run, catch, and throw. The average baseball fan knows this. When, as they often do, fans consider the fortunes of their favorite team, they think about these requirements and how they are being met. How solid is the pitching staff? Do we need a good late reliever? They worry that the fancy fielding shortstop can't hit a lick. Would we be better off if we traded that good base stealer for a power hitter? You are like a baseball fan, but instead of a team you have a community. Start thinking about which forms of community capital require more development. As you proceed, you will ask more questions, and you will gain a deeper understanding of the community's assets and what it needs and the extent to which these assets are recognized and the needs are or are not being met.

PARTICIPATORY ACTION RESEARCH

Participatory action research (PAR) is one approach for involving members in understanding community conditions and taking action to make them better. Other terms used to describe similar approaches include *action research,* which was the early form of this approach, *community-based participatory research,* and *collaborative research.* The notion is that those who most experience the events and rhythms of the community are the most qualified to investigate it and direct how information is used (DePoy, Hartman, & Haslett, 1999). Appreciative inquiry, which was discussed in Chapter 2, is a type of participatory research. PAR is a form of inquiry that is intended to yield discoveries to promote action, refine understanding for future action, and continue to develop members' capacities. This is an orientation that is fundamental for community change work.

Effective change agents recognize that those who are most affected by plans and decisions should play a critical role in shaping those plans and decisions. Helping to generate the information on which plans and decisions are made is a crucial role. Community members are active in all phases of the research process from identifying the issue to be addressed, designing research questions and developing the methodology, collecting and analyzing the data, and disseminating the findings. Participatory action research invites participants to dig dee-

per to understand conditions that affect them, but you can use PAR on matters great and small.

Traditional research is directed toward finding out about something or finding out if something worked. Assessment is designed and carried out by "experts," who are not members of the community. Sometimes they give the information back to the community for it to use, but very often they give the information to someone else—a community planning body, a funding source, or colleagues, who listen at a conference or read about it in a professional journal. This type of research is extractive; it takes information out of the community and uses it elsewhere.

Participatory action research flows from the notion of praxis—reflection and action in dialogue with others (see Chapter 2)—and focuses on understanding in order to promote action and change (Stoecker, 2005). This approach to research is grounded in the belief that participating in discovery and action based on that discovery is liberating. People who are affected by conditions are seen and see themselves as capable. They are not dependent on others to define their experience for them and take action on their behalf. By better understanding forces that affect what is happening in the community, members are more capable of acting with intention and effectiveness, and then learning from their experience to refine future actions.

You have probably been faced with a troublesome situation in which you don't really understand what is happening. You don't know what to do, much less where to start. That's a frustrating and powerless feeling. You may end up doing nothing. You may try to push away those feelings, or you may dwell on them. Either way, it can sap your energy. In some communities people face things that they don't understand and that they feel are out of their control. They have the same feelings of frustration and powerlessness. Maybe these are students in a school, or even their teachers. Maybe they are members of a neighborhood where violence, drug abuse, and unemployment are daily companions. Maybe they are parents caught in a system that is supposed to offer help to their children but seems to offer little more than roadblocks.

A community assessment process that brings people together to use their shared experience and insight to direct their own inquiry to make sense of things so that they can do something about them goes a long way toward changing feelings of frustration and powerlessness to capability and purpose. Such a process builds on the elements of community development, people doing for themselves, rather than service, people doing for other people. People are not subjects to be studied or statistics to be recorded; they are researchers and actors who understand and create change, both in themselves and in their communities.

Principles of Participatory Action Research

Participatory action research can be used in a host of situations. Here are the basic principles of PAR:

- Research is intended to deepen understanding, produce theories of action, and result in action.
- Actions lead to new and transformed relationships, both within the community and outside of it.
- People who are affected by conditions play central roles in determining what is to be studied, how it is to be studied, and how to use the information gathered.
- Information becomes a source of wealth that is owned by the community.
- The process is intended to build the power of the community.
- The process is collaborative; members work with and learn from one another.
- The process requires critical self-examination.
- The process involves cycles of reflection, planning, and action, observation, theory generation, new planning, action, and so on.
- The process is based on hypothesis generation, hypothesis testing with valid and reliable techniques, critical analysis of findings, and distribution of information.

Certainly, change efforts addressing neighborhood conditions or rural community development are very likely candidates for using PAR. It is also effective in working to change organizations: for example, helping special education teachers to examine their work, develop strategies for improving effectiveness, and gain a sense of efficacy and professional self-reliance (Bryan & Sullivan-Burstein, 1998). Those who are involved in health and human services can use PAR to change the way the system operates and to change the power relationships among providers and participants. Working in partnership with community members to examine conditions and determine needed action can provoke a deeper awareness on the part of community institutions to circumstances in the community and their responsibility to partner with residents (Brown et al., 2008). Burstein, Bryan, and Chao (2005) engaged young people with special health needs to clarify and test assumptions about their ability to handle situations they faced. This led to young people and their family members recognizing greater options for meaningful independent living. They found that "PAR's emphasis on the scientific process as a means of problem solving is empowering. It helps participants focus on solutions rather than personal frailties" (p. 200). In each case, participants' ownership of the research process from the very beginning led them to value the information and to engage in actions to change the condition. Feelings of frustration were replaced with feelings of empowerment.

Participatory action research can be a helpful approach to evaluation (Coombe, 2005; Stoecker, 2005), to getting young people more connected with their power to change communities (Lynn, 2005), and to examine and act on conditions that affect whole classes of people and broader social relationships (PARfem, 2003). Whenever you are working with people who share a common condition, PAR has tremendous potential for increasing understanding for effective change. Sounds useful. So how do you go about doing it?

Implementing the PAR Process

A number of authors have described various elements of the PAR process (Alvarez & Gutiérrez, 2001; Bessette, 2004; Bryan, 2005; Seymour-Rolls & Hughes, 2000; Stoecker, 2005). For participant research to work effectively, it must fit the style of all the stakeholders, teamwork and collaboration skills need to be strong, and a core group from the community must maintain consistent involvement. This means that the purposes for the research as well the various roles and duties must be clear and meaningful for all participants. In most cases of true participatory action research, community members and professionals work together to create intervention strategies with no preconceived notions. In some cases, though, they can work together to improve the relevance and effectiveness of planned interventions (Gallagher, Truglio-Londrigan, & Levin, 2009).

PAR is commonly used at two different levels. The first is the assessment level, engaging in research to better understand conditions and identifying issues for possible action. The second is the action level: focusing on a selected issue or condition to be changed, engaging in research to better understand the issue, guiding action, and testing chosen approaches. These two levels have been called the proactive process (issue discovery) and the reactive process (issue action) (Craig, 2009).

The overall process involves a number of phases that repeat over time. Some key steps in the process are described next.

Initial Preparation. Bring the group together—you first need to have a group willing to engage in the process and build their working relationships—this step includes the identification of who needs to be involved in the process. Provide group training on the process where all participants can teach and learn from each other. Groups need to have confidence in what they are doing and need to understand elements of the scientific process, examine the philosophy that supports the approach, develop methods for communication, including critical dialogue, and learn how to skillfully use the tools the group decides it will use. Training should be straightforward without overcomplicating the process.

Build some energy around embarking on a new way of doing things. The way you introduce the idea to people can make it an exciting new approach or make the whole thing seem like just a lot of work. Excitement, creativity, and confidence need to go together.

The PAR approach is generally used for making a change in the general conditions of things—changing things that have been in place for a while rather than those that are crying for immediate action—but it can become a general way of doing things. We begin by asking these questions:

- What are we looking at?
- What do we know or need to know about it?
- What hypothesis will guide our action?
- What do we have that we can use?
- What specific things will we do?
- How will we see if our actions produced the result we predicted?
- How will we use our analysis to refine our future action?

Action Steps. Remember, this is a research project, one that is intended to produce not just information but action and change. Again, think of taking these steps in two stages. You do them first in the assessment stage to give you the information you need to determine what specific change you will seek and to prepare yourself for action. Then you repeat the same steps in the action stage once you have narrowed things down to the particular goal that will be your focus.

Determine the focus of the effort. What is it that you are working on at this point? Initially in the assessment stage this is likely to involve an overall assessment of the community or situation, or an aspect of the community, such as health; in the action stage this step is used to identify the particular problem or condition to be improved.

Determine what is known and what is unknown about the focus of the effort. As appreciative inquiry reminds us, it is helpful to learn about what works and what practices and relationships produce helpful results.

Select a goal. In the assessment phase you decide what you want to know about the broader situation; in the action phase you select the specific change or outcome you want to achieve.

Construct your hypothesis. This is your statement about what action will produce what outcome: if we do *X,* then *Y* will happen. In the assessment stage, specify what primary action you predict will produce what you want to know. In the action stage, specify what primary action will produce the change you want.

Identify your resources. List the resources you will use to do what you want to do. Start by asking, "What do we have that we can use?"

Determine how you will implement your strategy. What do you need to do to use your resources to perform the action?

Develop a plan to test the effectiveness of your chosen strategy. Identify data that needs to be collected, a method for doing so, and how you will analyze the outcome of your effort. Use these data to test whether your strategy will work.

Implement your strategy and collect the data. Put into motion what you have decided to do, and gather all the information that you have decided to gather.

Analyze the results to see what happened. What do the data that you collected tell you? Did you produce what you wanted? Did *Y* occur or not? Did something else occur? What have you learned from this? What theories have emerged?

Share the results with key constituencies. Ask yourself if there is anyone else who needs to have this information. How will they use it?

Use what you have learned to guide future action.

No method of research is perfect. Participatory action research has some inherent limitations, but if you are aware of them, you can deal with them. The first is a lack of objectivity. Traditional research emphasizes dispassionate observation and analysis. Participatory methods are hardly dispassionate. It is the passion that fuels involvement in the first place.

However, with a clear intention to use information that promotes effectiveness, with good training and understanding about how to view information, and with collaborative critical analysis, the lack of objectivity need not be a barrier. All research is interpreted through the often unseen filter or cultural framework of its viewers, whether this is research viewed by other professors or by other neighbors. Being mindful of this and remaining committed to open, critical dialogue will lead to good information. Those involved in participatory methods really want to get it right because what happens as a result directly affects them.

It is often helpful to get assistance from those who have research and assessment expertise, particularly those who know how to use participatory methods. They can provide guidance on important aspects regarding research design and tools. Those from outside the community who are involved in the assessment and research (this might be you) need to be particularly mindful of the empowering intent of PAR (Coombe, 2005). A lack of sensitivity to this purpose can create unnecessary conflict and undermine the effort. Professionals must be good teachers, not just good technicians.

Depending on the focus of the research project, PAR can require quite an investment of time (Coombe, 2005). Like any good organizing effort, there are multiple roles for participants to play and opportunities for increasing community capacity. Like any effort, if a few people end up having to do all the work, they will get burned out and frustrated with other members. Be clear about how narrow or broad your focus will be, and firm up the commitments necessary to undertake a research project.

Finally, make sure that some members of the community, perhaps those with more recognized power or more formal education, do not take over the process. Like any other tool, PAR can lead to manipulation, unwitting or intentional. Again, preparation regarding the nature of PAR, including the use of supportive critical inquiry and attention to evolving trends within the group, will help you deal with this potential problem.

CHANGE AGENT TIP

One particularly effective technique both for helping community members take a close look at their community and to get members' views on what they see as important may not be a survey but a camera. This approach, called *photovoice,* was developed by Caroline Wang and Mary Ann Burris. It invites members to photograph their everyday realities. Here, those who have traditionally been the subject of such work become its creators, while simultaneously learning a new skill that can enhance their lives (Photo-Voice, 2009). Many people are uncomfortable with writing or public speaking. Photography adds another form of communication members can use to capture and reveal their world. Participants come together to look at the pictures and examine what they depict about the community and members' experiences. A five-step process known as SHOWED is sometimes used to guide this examination (Shaffer, 1983):

- What do you *see* here?
- What is really *happening* here?
- How does this relate to *our* lives?
- *Why* does this problem, concern, or strength *exist*?
- What can we *do* about it?

This method has been used with many different groups: youth, recent immigrants, parents of children with developmental disabilities, people who are homeless, people with intellectual disabilities, and neighborhood residents. It generates enthusiasm and unlocks creativity in ways that more traditional approaches may miss. It also puts community members at the center of the discovery process.

SOURCE: Jurkowski (2008), McDonald, Sarche, and Wang (2005), Carle (2006), and Wang (2003).

All of the methods for discovery described in the following pages can incorporate participatory approaches.

ASSESSING THE COMMUNITY'S NEEDS AND RESOURCES

Ideally, a community meets the needs of all its members. Of course, this ideal functioning hardly ever occurs. A community's needs are often undiscovered, undeclared, or considered unimportant by those who could do something about them. Part of your job as a change agent is to reverse that situation. You will work to help the community effectively declare what it needs, so these needs will be considered important enough to be met, and discover and build its resources, so the community can act to strengthen itself.

All communities have resources, starting with the information, abilities, and relationships among its members. However, few communities have all the resources they need to flourish. A community, like any other system, needs adequate input, and it needs to effectively use the resources it has. If input to a community is cut off because of the inattention

or the disregard of the larger community, or if the community is unable to draw in necessary external resources, it is likely to wither, and it may even turn on itself. If the community has many of the resources it needs but does not use these effectively, it may flounder as well.

To provide your community with the information it needs, it is helpful to conduct a community assessment. An assessment should be congruent with a strengths perspective, producing both needed change and increased empowerment (Hancock & Minkler, 2005). As with any other aspect of community change, it is important that members of the community play a significant role in researching the community. (The PAR model discussed previously explains one way to do this.) The generation of information heightens awareness and can provide an impetus to change. If members of the community are not involved in the discovery process, you may miss an important opportunity to develop the necessary investment of community members in the change process.

Needs Assessments

Conducting a needs assessment is a tricky business. Do not define the community according to its unmet needs or its problems, or even worse, its symptoms of deeper problems. This will do little more

GLOBAL PERSPECTIVES

NICARAGUA—Grupo Tierra has used community mapping precisely because it is oriented towards empowering local communities. By helping local communities to visualise their territory, using geo-referencing techniques, Grupo Tierra contributes to their participation in a horizontal dialogue with governments and economic powers, where they can put forward their concerns and demands.

A community map is the representation a community has of its territory. Community members decide what they want to represent on the map, in most cases, community boundaries, land use, infrastructure and water supplies.

It is important that groups from the different sectors of the community (men and women, youngsters and elders) participate in order to have a diversity of viewpoints (Stefano Di Gessa, Peter Poole, & Timothy Bending, 2008, pp. 30–31).

INDONESIA—YLK Sulsel [the South Sulawesi Consumer Organization] has been mapping its assets in two ways, as tangible and intangible assets. Tangible assets are real assets

that can be accounted for. It is technology or equipment that applies in empowering groups. Intangible assets could be a skill, expertise, and knowledge. The life cycle of an organization is determined by the manner in which both assets are managed….

Logically, each kind of asset, both tangible and intangible, can be maximized. The use of communications media in a democratic political system, for example, can reform the awareness of a community about its political rights. The use of knowledge of political democracy can create an inspiration and provide moral support to the community to keep it struggling to build an egalitarian community, just, and equitable. Good management and maintenance of assets will extend the life of a community. If, for example, good asset management can maintain a highway, phone, water, hospital, and other health services, then the life cycle of city communities will be longer…. This is what YLK Sulsel aspires to (Zohra Andi Baso, 2000, pp. 1–4).

SWEDEN—If we agree that the development of communities should have its point of departure in the local community, then we must have knowledge of and insight into the essence of social life there: traditions, culture, social harmony and antagonism, etc….

It is essential to include the areas' interaction and value systems in the analysis and the strategy discussion. A comprehensive perspective is required for an understanding of how human beings develop both life and survival strategies….

[These become relevant in the development of social economy, which] is concerned with people's conditions of living and how they make use of resources: human, cultural, social, material, economic (in its narrowest sense) and ecological resources. These are all used to keep and increase the quality of life for the members and for the local community.

Social economy means having the central point based on human capability and human resources (Alf Ronnby, 1998, pp. 67–72).

than produce a catalog of maladies that everyone knows about anyway. It reduces the community to a repository of problems and confirms desperation. Hopelessness, apathy, and dependency thrive under those conditions. If a needs assessment is the only method of understanding a community, it will likely do more harm than good. It is such a commonly used approach in social service agencies that it is important for us to consider it. However, it may well reflect a deficit-oriented, service only approach that will produce few, if any, meaningful changes. If you have not worked at least equally as hard to discover the many layers of community assets and potential, you have not done your job. You will end up with an inaccurate understanding

of the community, and you will not know how to engage it properly.

So, should you bother to conduct a needs assessment? If all you intend to do is to count the community's problems, then, no. Don't do one. If your intent is to discover issues for action, using and developing the community's capabilities, then your assessment may lead to valuable information about community issues. A needs assessment measures unmet needs. Some look at service needs or services not currently provided, often reinforcing a service approach. You can understand, though, that there are a variety of forms of assistance. Some of these are formal services; many others are informal practices of mutual support. In most cases a needs assessment looks at community needs that are not being met or necessary resources or activities that are not being provided in the community.

At the beginning your main concern is to clarify your focus. You want to start off on the right track. You also want to know that what you are doing matters. A needs or issue assessment will tell you this. It helps to identify barriers to community health, uncover possible issues, and raise community consciousness and commitment to action.

When a community cannot meet its goals or sustain itself, the community has unmet needs or problems. Goals don't have to be clearly written down. They can be commonly understood. For example, teen parents don't get together and write down the goal: "To have healthy children." Common sense will tell you such a goal exists. If medical care is required to meet this goal, and if members of the community don't receive medical care, then adequate medical care becomes an unmet need, a community issue. You will be attempting to discover such unmet needs, those sources of frustration or barriers to a community's ability to flourish.

An unmet need is not the same thing as a malady. Simply saying that a community has this problem or that problem doesn't do much for understanding unmet needs. You may ask, "What's not here that should be here?" or "What's not happening that should be happening?" That is quite different from asking, "What are all the bad things here?" Juvenile delinquency or low-birth-weight babies are maladies or a symptom. Unmet needs may have something to do with recreation, adult involvement, jobs, or the availability of medical care.

A needs assessment is a process for identifying the range of a community's inadequately addressed requirements or for more clearly understanding a particular unmet need. In either event, it is intended to result in a "reduction of uncertainty" (McKillip, 1987, p. 19). In addition to an examination of the extent and intensity of a need, the assessment should examine how often the need is felt, for how long, and by whom.

The assessment can include a large population group; for example, a city, a six-county area, or even a state. Or it can look at the unmet needs of a smaller population; for example, a neighborhood, a church congregation, or workers in an agency.

Further, it can be designed to uncover any unmet needs or only those in a certain area, say, mental health or recreation (Lewis, Packard, & Lewis, 2007). Needs assessments are typically performed for one of three reasons:

- To see if there is any need for action
- To help design or direct some already contemplated action
- To confirm what we already know and to justify an already decided action

The first case forces us to look at a situation we might have been ignoring or simply are oblivious to. In the second case, problems have come to our attention, but we don't have a solid grip on their dimensions. Because we want to increase the odds that our actions will be effective, we take some time to consider what actions are most required. In the third case, we don't really intend to learn anything, so we usually don't. The purpose is to justify a desired course of action, so we really only pay attention to information that supports that claim. This approach is geared more to public relations than to discovery and sometimes convinces decision makers or funders that action should be taken (Zastrow, 2007).

To design your assessment, you need to determine seven things:

- The community whose unmet needs you intend to clarify
- The range of needs you intend to examine
- The process for getting the information you need
- The method you will use to interpret the information
- The time and money you have to do this
- Who will own this information
- How this information will be used

Gathering information about your community and its issues is an essential step in community change, and much has been written about the various methods for accomplishing that task. The following approaches to obtaining information about your community's needs (as well as some of the more general steps for gaining a better insight into your community described later in the chapter) are drawn from the work of Brueggemann (2006), Hancock and Minkler (2005), Kahn (1994), Lewis, Packard, and Lewis (2007), Lotspeich and Kleymeyer (1976), Martí-Costa and Serrano-Garciá (1995), Neuber, Atkins, Jacobson, and Reuterman (1980), Warren and Warren (1984), Warheit, Bell, and Schwab (1984), Berkowitz (1982), McKillip (1987), and Zastrow (2007).

A beginning step in the process is to look at the kinds of needs you want to examine. Again, if you are only looking at service needs, you are starting with the assumption that services are the primary approach to community health and sustainability. Do question that assumption. Brueggemann (2006) described needs in normative or demand terms. Normative definitions involve comparing one group's experiences with what others in the community expect as normal conditions. If a particular group of people does not have access to medical care—or education or transportation or any other community resource that is commonly available to others—you can identify an unmet need that places the group in an unhealthy or disadvantaged situation. Demand definitions relate to those sets of needs that a particular group express as necessary. Demand data also can describe the number of people requiring this resource who would make use of it. For example, only those who are terminally ill and their families may understand the importance of hospice. The number of those who fit this category and who would intend to use the resource would help clarify the unmet need. Those who do not experience the condition or otherwise understand it may not be included in the determination of need. They may not support a community's response to it.

It is sometimes helpful to combine both normative and demand data to help the community at large better understand an issue. Once you have determined the type of data you want to collect, a good start is to look at information that already exists. Existent or extant data are contained in statistics that have already been collected and analyzed and in reports that have been written. At the beginning you may be unsure about just what information you need. That's all right. Most projects start out that way. Get some of the information you

think you need, and then review it. This will help you focus future inquiry.

To augment this extant data, get the views of members of the community. Your issue or needs assessment will have little value if the voices of community members do not shape the results. This step involves deciding how many members you need to hear from and who those members are. Thinking this through will help you determine how to approach them. Do you talk with people individually or in a group? Do you extend an open invitation to anyone who is interested (for example, hold a public hearing), or do you select participants? Do you mail out a questionnaire or meet with people face to face? These are some of the questions you need to answer.

A couple of additional points should be made regarding this aspect of your data collection process. First, get the perspectives of people who feel the need as well as those who could potentially feel the need. Second, have an eye to the future. Gather information from people whose support you will need down the road as you respond to the issues you identify. Collect the information in a way that strengthens the likelihood of their future involvement. Two sets of people are important for future contacts. One set includes the people who will decide on the course of action in response to the recognition of these community conditions, including those who have influence on these decision makers. The second set includes those people who will implement the action.

Once you have gathered opinions and information from community members, you need to address the second problem area; that is, you need to figure out what it all means. Think about the credibility of your sources, the intensity with which the information is offered, and how frequently it is mentioned. Decide whose facts and opinions carry the most weight with you. Statistics and reports give factual information but are often devoid of feeling, that special human quality that rounds out our understanding of an issue. Conversely, those who feel a problem or who feel intensely about it often lack objectivity. You need to determine which sources give you valid and meaningful information.

Next, decide how to gauge the intensity of the information. There are opinions and there are strongly held opinions; there are feelings and there are strongly held feelings. It is important to weigh the depth or intensity of the opinions and feelings you receive. Some problems will be felt mildly by many people. Some will be felt intensely, though by fewer people. Acknowledge this intensity and decide how you will account for it in your response. The frequency with which an unmet need is mentioned by multiple sources is a good indication that you need to pay attention to it. If today on the train, at work, at the store, and at home different people have told you that you have your shirt on backward, there might just be something to it.

Assessing a community's unmet needs opens the possibility for discovery and declaration. You may help the community become more acutely aware of conditions that block its healthy growth. Your investigation may help the community realize that its unmet needs are a result of its not using its resources effectively. You may help it demand its fair allocation of resources from the broader community within which it sets. Your assessment should yield issues around which you can mobilize for action, which may start with attention to matters you can act on quickly.

A key question is whose assets do you intend to mobilize to respond to the conditions you uncover? If you use the issues you discover to energize the community to recognize and use its strengths for self-improvement, or if issues call members to action leading to the reallocation of power and resources within the broader community, you have used the information well. If, however, you don't first look to the community that is the focus of your attention, you are likely to create a response that is out of context with the experience of community members. You will have reinforced the notion that community members are unable or unneeded. Further, you are likely to promote dependency by describing the community as "needy" and dependent on the kindness of strangers for its improvement.

Resource or Asset Assessments

As you answer questions about community conditions, recognize that the community has many resources available to fashion effective responses. Just because needs are not adequately being met does not necessarily mean that resources don't exist to do the job. Part of the problem has to do with decisions on how resources are allocated. Another part of the problem involves our ability to recognize and develop resources. Though some additional help from outside the community may be required, you will discover that you have a lot more going for you than you thought.

No matter how poor or frightened or lacking in immediate power, each community has resources it can use to make significant improvement, including the most important resource, people. In fact, a crucial element for success is your ability to recognize and build on actual and potential capabilities that exist in your community. This, not concern over limitations, will be the foundation of your work. An overemphasis on liabilities is a serious error that colors problem solving in shades of inadequacy and dependence, undermining any attempt at empowerment.

If you remember from the discussion in Chapter 2, the entire process of developing communities depends on your ability to recognize and build on community assets. A needs or issue assessment provides valuable information but yields only a limited view of the community. To complete your work and pinpoint the location of your community's sometimes hidden wealth, you need to do a resource assessment or asset map (Brueggemann, 2006; Delgado, 2000; Kretzmann & McKnight 1997; Lewis et al., 2007; Zastrow, 2007). A needs assessment can help give you an issue focus; a resource or asset assessment gives you the energy. In fact, resource assessments can give you a focus as well. You can just as well start with a resource assessment to guide your action as a needs assessment. Instead of asking what blockage do we need to get rid of, or what access do we need to open, you can ask what can we do or create with all of the things we have.

You are able to use the same approaches for a resource assessment as you do for a needs assessment: gather extant data, get information directly from community members, and make and record observations. The methods for community data gathering described later in this chapter can be applied to discovering resources.

CHANGE AGENT TIP

Here are two simple guides to help you recognize important factors in your community. The first relates to a particular focus, in this case health. By first identifying your vision you can better focus your assessment.

Community Assessment Tool

Vision

All residents have sufficient information and knowledge to make healthy decisions regarding their and others'

physical health. Readily accessible products and services exist to support healthy decision making. Public policies, community practices, and programs of education, service, and action foster these conditions. There are a sufficient number of current and emerging leaders to sustain healthy conditions.

Current Assets	Assets Yet to Be Developed	Current Barriers	Possible New Barriers	What We Have to Further Develop Assets or Overcome Barriers
Currently held knowledge (Note, for example, the types of information you may want to gather for this asset. You would gather similar information for each of the following assets.)	Important knowledge not currently held (or incorrect information believed to be true)	Policies and practices that prevent knowledge to be developed or shared	Emergence of organized efforts to prevent knowledge development and dissemination	Media support; current community concern; network of supporters and communicators
Current readily available products				
Current readily available services				
Current supporting public policies				
Current supporting community practices				
Currently supportive community associations				
Current supporting programs of education				
Current supporting programs of service				
Current supporting programs of action				
Current and emerging leaders				
Currently available forms of community capital				
Current readiness for change (time, interest, capability, awareness, etc.)				

Using the Wealth of Our Community

This second tool helps you to discover your community's wealth through the various forms of community capital.

Community Capital	Where Do We Find It?	How Can We Use It?
Environmental: land, water, trees, natural features, etc.		
Physical: roads, buildings, other infrastructure, health and vigor of the people, etc.		
Economic: money, systems of exchange, activities for producing income, etc.		
Human: leadership, skills and abilities of people, their interests, passions, energy, etc.		
Political: access to policymakers, ability to set own policies, political clout, etc.		
Informational: generation, accumulation, ability to retrieve data, information, knowledge, etc.		
Cultural: artistic expressions, traditions, rituals, shared norms and beliefs, etc.		
Spiritual: members' belief in something larger than themselves, search for meaning, commitment to calling forth their best, etc.		
Social: system of community norms, practices and interrelationships that produce trust, collaborative action, community consciousness, etc.		

Almost anything is a potential resource. Part of the trick is to start seeing things as potential resources. In one sense, resources can be classified according to the needs they meet. For example, if people need to eat, food is the corresponding resource. If people need access to community decisions, the courts could be a corresponding resource. But confining resources to distinct need categories is a tricky and mistaken business. Most things can be used in many ways. The last thing you want to do is limit the use of a resource or limit your thinking about it.

Books, for example, are great resources. You can read them and acquire knowledge. You can also use them to adjust the height of your Power-Point projection system. They are great for putting on a stack of papers to keep them from blowing away. You can drop a big book on the floor and wake up half the class. Books are a great resource.

A complete catalog of your community's resources would be a lifetime's work. Focus your attention on what you want to accomplish, then think of all the resources that could apply. The process of discovering community resources never ends. Each time you take an action, you use resources. If you track these assets, you will have an updated inventory of available community capital (Kretzmann & McKnight, 1993).

To discover your community resources, ask members of the community some of these questions:

- What natural resources exist in your community? Examples are land, water, and trees.

- What tangible human-made things exist in your community? Examples are cars, bridges, and libraries.

- What forms of currency are available in your community? Examples include money, barter, and favors.

- What skills and talents exist in your community? Examples include artistic talents, carpentry skills, and computer programming abilities.

- What human qualities and values exist in your community? Examples are honesty, determination, and passion.

- What systems have developed to serve members? Examples are democracy, employee grievance procedures, and games.

- What are the major institutions in your community? Faith communities, schools, and government centers are examples of important institutions.

- What information and knowledge is available in your community? Examples include scientific knowledge, historical knowledge, and inside information.

- What cultural traditions enliven the community and give it identity? Music, festivals, and healing practices are likely to exist in your community.

- How are members supported in the search for meaning? Examples include spiritual and religious study groups, meditation instruction, and retreat centers.

- What relationships have members of this community developed? Examples include family, friends, natural helping networks, or business associates.

- What resource, asset, or potential contribution do you possess?

- What resources could serve more purposes? For example, a house can also be a meeting place; a church can also be a shelter; an office softball team can also be a mutual support group.

- What resources do you have a personal connection with?

- What resources can be combined to produce new resources? For example, what could be produced with a storage room and a dozen employees who each own 100 books?

Stressing the asset-based community development (ABCD) approach, Kretzmann and McKnight (1993, 1997) provided another useful framework for looking at community resources. Their capacity inventory examined four areas of assets: skills information, community skills, enterprising interests and experience, and personal information. Here are some sources of community assets:

Capacities of individuals: The talents of individuals in the community provide the fundamental bank of assets for the community.

Gifts of "strangers": When the contributions of marginalized citizens in our midst—the young, the old, those with developmental disabilities—become habitually recognized and integrated, the process of community building becomes inclusive.

Associations of citizens: Associations such as faith communities, ethnic organizations, Boy Scouts and Girl Scouts, and groups of citizens working together empower individuals and amplify gifts.

Local private, public, and nonprofit institutions: These institutions represent significant concentrations of resources, including facilities, materials and equipment, purchasing power, and technical skills.

Physical assets: Land, buildings, and streets, for example, are assets that enhance the community and, if underused, might be more fully developed.

Capacity finders and developers: These are the community leaders who are clearly oriented to finding and mobilizing assets, particularly encouraging ways for resources to be linked to each other.

Susan Blood (2001) added *cultural knowledge* as an important component to asset mapping. Cultural knowledge includes the knowledge held by indigenous people, whose ancestors have long inhabited a region, or people who are new to a region, who bring their own traditions to a new community. Other forms of community strength might be found in its stores of resistance, the ability of individuals to struggle against oppressive circumstances, and in its resilience, the positive, adaptive abilities of people in the face of adversity (Longres, 2000).

Many resources go unacknowledged because people don't think they are important. When you begin to see the potential value of things, you will discover resources you never knew existed. Over time, instead of wondering, "What can we do about (some problem)?" you may find yourself asking, "What can we do with all these things we have?" This is a very different question.

Readiness and Disposition to Change

All communities have some capacity to change, though some have more constraints than others. Some of the constraints are real. For example, the law may limit the political involvement of certain public employees. Some are practical; for example, single parents may spend most of their time and energy taking care of day-to-day job and family challenges. Many are attitudinal; people believe that nobody else cares or that things simply can't be changed. They may have little experience or understanding of organizing, or maybe even the mood of the community does not ready it for struggle (Olney, 2001). Even though communities may want things to change, it may be hard for them to confront pervasive values

---

◄► Take a Moment to Discover ◄►

See if you can find someone in your office, class, or neighborhood who can provide, for free or below normal cost, one of these skills or resources either themselves or through someone they know:

Gourmet cooking

Advanced computer skills

Grant writing expertise

Political lobbying

Fund-raising experience

Musician

Juggler

Plumber

News reporter

Mechanic

---

that sustain the status quo. Change requires that we give up a set of beliefs and practices. This is a hard thing for many people to do (Nelson, 2000).

Each community also differs in its disposition to change. Some communities are happy with things just the way they are. Others have grown used to things, tolerating what they don't like. Still others are ready to do something—anything—that might make a difference, now. The desire for change often involves correcting injustices, but it is not limited to this. It can also involve providing new opportunities or challenges, escaping the boredom of the routine, or just doing something fun.

Researchers at the Tri-Ethnic Center for Prevention Research at Colorado State University have identified six dimensions of readiness: community efforts (programs, activities, policies, and so forth), community knowledge of the efforts (the extent to which members know about efforts), leadership support (includes appointed leaders and influential community members), community climate (prevailing attitudes about the issue), community knowledge about the issue (what members know about causes and consequences), and resources related to the issue (people, money, time, space, and so forth) (Plested, Edwards, & Jumper-Thurman, 2006). The community may be strong in one area, but weak in another. If weaker areas are not strengthened, the entire effort may drag or even

CAPTURING CONCEPTS
Five Stages of Community Life

In the **Waiting Place** people in the community hold a deep sense that things are not working right, but they cannot quite put their finger on exactly what it is or what to do about it. It is a kind of "felt unknown." They may be locked into old patterns, such as finger-pointing and looking to place blame.

In the **Impasse** stage a community hits rock bottom. You hear people saying such things as "enough is enough!" There is a noticeable sense of urgency in people's voices. Though people may feel isolated from others and mistrust may run deep, things have crystallized enough that the need for action is clear. Often people are afraid that they are losing their future; they are tired of "waiting."

During the **Catalytic** stage, a small group of people and organizations emerge to take risks and experiment in ways that challenge existing norms of how the community works. People begin to discover that they share common aspirations for their community and that they can, in small ways, start to make a difference.

Over the course of the **Growth** stage, groups of catalysts expand, networks grow and expand, and a

sense of common purpose and direction take root. People see clear signs that the community is moving forward and can feel and experience much greater leadership. People's confidence in themselves and their community grows. As this stage is moving toward its end, people will start to tire, and networks may begin to fray a bit. New groups asserting a particular view may arise, possibly leading to fragmentation.

A community in the **Sustain and Renew** stage must find ways to bring along new leaders and a new set of spark plugs. Without them the community will stagnate and possibly begin to decline. To make a successful transformation to sustain and renew, the community will take on especially deeply rooted issues that were beyond the community's ability in the first four stages. Purposeful attention is required to reach out and include those who may still have been left behind. The community shares gains with all its members, and not just the economic gains. Here the community is tending to its soul.

SOURCE: Harwood Group (1999).

fail. Examining each dimension of readiness will help you understand what is occurring and help you decide where you need to put some effort toward helping the community move forward. In keeping with a development orientation, the highest level of readiness is strong community ownership of the effort.

Understanding your community's ability to challenge constraints that are real, practical, or imagined, and its desire to do something different, are crucial in directing your activities as a change agent. Capacity and desire for change can be evaluated by asking these questions:

- Are there legal limits on activities that apply specifically to your community?
- How strong is the community on each dimension of readiness?
- How much discretionary time do people really have?

- What really rankles people in your community?
- Do people have a history of working together?
- Is there a sense of community or shared experience?
- Do people complain about things? Do they complain publicly or in private?
- Do people talk about how they wish things would be? To whom do they talk?
- Are people who voice a desire for change criticized and put down or encouraged and supported?
- Are people intimidated by those in positions of authority?
- Do people recognize when they are not doing what they want to do or when they are doing what they don't want to do?
- Have change attempts failed or succeeded in the past?

- Do people go outside official channels to solve problems?
- Is anyone exploring change in any way right now?

As you answer these questions, and the ones you will surely add, you will build a storehouse of information that will make things a lot smoother for you now and help your change efforts.

HOW TO FIND OUT WHAT YOU NEED TO KNOW

You should now have a better idea of what you need to know about your community. In this section, a number of specific sources of information are described together with some ideas on how you can use those sources. Remember, "you" includes all those with whom you are working. Involving other people in all aspects of the discovery process will increase the likelihood that you are gathering helpful information, developing ownership of the project, creating opportunities for leadership, and elevating the value of the information to the group.

Valuing the Library

Welcome to the library. Step inside. It is comfortable, peaceful (unless it's the college library the week before papers are due), and packed with information. Take a break from whatever you are doing and spend an afternoon at the library. Your public library has a treasure trove of information about your community, and so does your college or university library.

While spending some time in the library can be enjoyable, you can gain a wealth of information online through your library. You may well find community health and social service resources, community and civic groups, and information on local history. Your library is likely to subscribe to databases, which the library needs to pay for, but which you can use for free. Databases will have information that is not on the Web, and the information has been reviewed for accuracy. Databases are especially useful for newspaper and magazine articles, biographical information, business statistics, grants research, and access to many other directories. Your database search will likely yield more reliable results than what you would get exploring the Internet. It's also nice to know that you can ask a librarian for help (Pima County Public Library, 2009).

If you do plan to visit the library, prepare some questions in advance. This will give the librarian a better idea of how to help you. It will also help you focus your inquiry. Most librarians are very helpful. Not only do they know books and where to find them, but most enjoy helping people uncover information and discover the other wonders of their library, such as audiovisual resources, access to databases, maps, and much more.

You should be able to accomplish several things during your visit to the library, especially if you come prepared with questions. Certainly, you want some specific information about your community. Particular facts, figures, names, and background information will help you answer some of the questions you have. It is also important to become familiar with the sources themselves. You will never be able to write down or remember everything that is potentially valuable. That's why we have libraries—so you can go back when you need the information.

In addition to a wealth of online sources, a typical library will have many publications describing aspects of your community. Some of these will be national publications, some state, and some local. Some will be put together by the government, including special reports, such as a report by a special task force on homelessness. Others are put together by private groups, perhaps banks or special interest organizations. Most libraries can borrow from other libraries through interlibrary loan. They also purchase or accept material from organizations if there appears to be sufficient demand for it. Check to see if one of your local libraries is a depository for the Government Printing Office or for the Census Bureau. If not, see if you can find out where one is. A depository houses some or all of the publications of these two government agencies.

If you can't find something, don't be shy about asking the librarian for help.

Special Libraries

Special libraries may exist in your community. Not all areas have these, so check with your local public library to discover special libraries in your area.

Law libraries. These special libraries exist for the purposes of legal research and are usually part of a university law school.

Specialized government libraries. Local and state planning departments often have their own libraries. Various community plans can be found here along with valuable background data on community makeup and growth patterns. Most state capitols have state government libraries and archives that provide library services to state legislators and other government decision makers. They routinely provide background information on issues to state politicians and agency people. Although you can go in person, it is usually helpful to go through your state legislator with a request for information. Local governments often have their own reference libraries serving city or county staff and elected officials.

Check to see how accessible these library services are to the general public. You can usually have someone, a staff member or public official, make the request for you (especially if they know you) if you can't make it easily on your own. Special libraries have wide access to information and are a potentially valuable resource.

Leaving the Library and Looking for More

You have this sneaking suspicion that there may be more to finding out about your community than sitting in the library. Suspicion confirmed. You will need multiple sources of information to increase the reliability of your information. Actually, you could go crazy with all this and never get any other work done.

So, where else? Your next stop would include various agencies, organizations, and interest groups that know something about your community. These include government agencies and private groups, both profit and nonprofit. Some of these (for example, government agencies) might not actually be physically in your community. However, most state and federal agencies collect information about groups of people such as elementary school children or geographic communities such as Durham, North Carolina.

What kinds of organizations could provide useful information? Look for organizations that do at least one of the following things.

Sell your community. Economic development corporations, visitors' bureaus, tourism organizations, chambers of commerce, convention bureaus, and travel organizations know about your community.

Sell in or from your community. Franchise organizations (for example, McDonald's), radio stations, homebuilders associations, real estate associations, banks, and newly arrived major employers are examples of organizations that need to understand the retail or labor markets of your community.

Serve your community. Councils on aging, the United Way, social service providers, religious organizations, and schools become aware of your community's needs through their day-to-day service activities.

State a particular concern about your community. Public interest organizations such as environmental organizations, anticrime organizations, minority affairs organizations, and business organizations all have particular issues they advocate and around which they generate information.

Study your community. Associations of counties, leagues of cities and towns, state and federal agencies, universities, planning and marketing companies, and consulting companies may collect or generate information about your community.

Once you have established a good general understanding of your community, you will probably want more specific information on some particular aspect of it. Perhaps you want to know more about subcommunities within your broad community (for example, manufactured housing). Or maybe you want to know more about specific conditions within your community (for example, childhood illness). In fact, you will probably move very rapidly to this level of inquiry.

Unless you intend to mobilize your entire broad community about something, you will study the broad level only to understand the setting or context in which your close community operates. Though you continue to improve your understanding of the broad community, you will acquire more information about your close community and the situation it faces. Review the five sets of organizations that have some particular knowledge about the broad community, and select those most likely to have the kind of specific information you need.

What are you likely to get from these sources? First, personal perspectives—talk to people. Most people are happy to tell you just what they think. Ask them. These added viewpoints of people who work in an area that is of interest to you can fill in the blanks you find in written material. A further advantage is that this gives you the chance to start building a personal relationship with this source, which could be helpful in the future.

Next, get statistics and other data. Some of this will be descriptive, and some will be numbers, charts, and graphs. All are pieces of the puzzle. Taken together they will help provide you with a picture of your community. Prepared reports may also be available. Somebody has taken the time to sit down and write about what is going on in your community. They have collected and analyzed information for you. You might as well make use of this effort. Will any of these sources just give you information if you ask? Can you waltz into McDonald's, order a Big Mac and fries, and say: "By the way, may I also have an analysis of projected population growth to go?" No, you will need to work with your contacts within the organization for that, but you can get the burger and fries.

It is generally pretty easy to get information from government, educational, and social service agencies. Information from those that sell the community and from public interest groups is also generally available. Private for-profit firms are less willing to offer what they know, especially if information is something they sell or if it is accumulated to give them a competitive advantage. However, just because a firm is private, don't automatically assume that it only collects information for its own purposes. Many do publish reports to the community.

Because it is so easy to get information from available sources, you may not want to waste your time trying to get something from a reluctant source. It should take no more than a day's worth of work to get all the beginning information you need from these sources. Spend about half an hour figuring out what you need to know, half an hour figuring out who might know it, and half an hour looking up phone numbers and getting Web addresses and databases. After an hour and a half of phone calls, and an hour in front of your computer screen, you will probably have all the initial information you need on its way to you. Unless you came to work late, it is about time to break for lunch now.

You will more than likely spend a few more hours in the next couple of days following new leads, following up on messages, talking to people on the phone, and following a trail of Internet clues. After a total of eight hours' work, you will have quite a lot in your file. (Remember, you do have to read this stuff.) As time goes on, you will refine your questions and get more precise information.

You have spent some time in the library and you have received information from organizations, but you are still not satisfied. All right, what now? "What about regular people?" you ask. "Shouldn't I get some information directly from individuals?" Yes, you should, but which ones? You don't want to spend the rest of your life doing background. Whether you are talking about your broad community or your close community, there are three groups of people whose ideas you can solicit.

People from the *leadership group* could provide you with important insights. These are opinion leaders (people whose point of view helps shape other people's points of view), action leaders (people who can get other people to follow or do things), and representative leaders (people who represent the community to people outside the community). It is a good idea to ask leaders whose help you may need down the road.

The next group is the *knowledgeable group*, people who are likely to have either general or specific knowledge about the community. These people have a particular area of expertise (for example, traffic engineer), are particularly involved in the community (for example, community activist), hold a particular belief about the community (for example, a political columnist), or hold a position that gives them a somewhat unique perspective (for example, police officer).

The final group is the *at large group*. This consists of members of the community in general with no particular regard to who they are, what they do, or what they may know.

You have a range of folks from which to choose. Here are some basic ways to get the information, ideas, and opinions people have to offer. Each of these techniques can become part of your participatory action research approach.

Guided Key Informant Discussions.   Ideally this is a face-to-face discussion, although it can take place over the phone. These conversations are generally pretty easy to set up if you know the person, and still quite possible even if you don't. Simply call and ask if you can have 10 to 15 minutes of their time to discuss the topic. It is hard for people to legitimately deny a 10- or 15-minute request. Most will end up giving you much more time. Even if they don't, you can get quite a bit done in 15 minutes. Prepare in advance six basic questions you would like to cover. You can allow the discussion to flow; just make sure your points get covered.

It is particularly important to include members of the group affected by conditions as key informants. If your work involves an area like a neighborhood, you will want to organize a simple door-to-door cam-

paign, talking with a designated number of people in your target area.

Active participation in the life of your community is valuable because this involvement puts you in a position to know and to be known. Two benefits flow from this: You learn more about the things you come in contact with, and you increase your network of personal contacts. Each person you meet also has a network of personal contacts. At the conclusion of *every* conversation you should ask the question: "Who else should we be talking to?" This provides you with access to each person's networks of contacts and the information and resources available there. By asking this question at the conclusion of every conversation, you have an almost endless source of contacts and alliances that you continue to build. It is also helpful to ask if you can use the person's name when you make your contact. If you are generally known in the community or recommended by someone who is known, things will be a lot easier for you. People are more willing to go out of the routine to help a friend, or the friend of a friend, than they are to help a stranger.

Focus Groups.   This creative atmosphere for gathering information and building interest in a topic is comprised of people who bring particular perspectives to discussion of an issue. The group explores the topic with guidance from a moderator. It is usually a good idea to get a mix of people from all three groups previously mentioned: leadership, knowledge, and at large. You don't necessarily want only people who already agree with each other.

A well-run focus group can help members gain confidence in speaking about difficult topics and dig deeper into an issue. They can be a particularly effective way for change agents to tap into the shared values and cultural norms that can affect how the community at large responds to complicated issues (Lewis, West, Bautista, Greenberg, & Done-Perez, 2005).

A focus group provides a lively exchange of ideas and opinions. Although the group may arrive at a generally agreed-on point of view, this is not required. Key questions around a certain topic (focus) are prepared in advance. The questions are structured to allow the conversation to flow yet remain on track. Some questions are simple and straightforward; others require more thoughtful consideration. A moderator or facilitator asks the questions and directs the discussion, making sure all participants have an opportunity to add their 2 cents worth. Acting as facilitator for a focus group can be a good role for a nonprofessional community member (Krueger & King, 1997). The facilitator will see to it that an atmosphere of open discussion prevails. For example, although disagreement is appropriate, intimidation is not. A policy of nonattribution is sometimes followed to encourage frankness. This policy means that although the overall results of the discussion may be used, no particular remark or opinion will be attributed to any participant.

Surveys and Questionnaires. Surveys can be administered in person, over the phone, online, or through electronic or post mail. The more personal the approach is, the more success you will have in getting the survey completed. This is a good way to get detailed, specific, and consistent information.

A survey can be used to collect information, such as a catalog of the skills of individuals or the nature of the contributions they would like to make. You can also use a survey to identify interests or concerns or to gather opinions. These types of surveys require a little more care. You can design a scientific survey process that is highly reliable (it can be repeated over and over with the same degree of accuracy) and valid (the information you receive is a correct and meaningful reflection of the group represented in the survey). You are the judge of how scientific you need to be, but six important factors should be considered.

1. *Population to be surveyed.* Are you asking the right people? If you want to know which

school activities high school students like best, don't ask the teachers, ask the students.

2. *Sampling.* How many from the general population do you intend to ask, and how will they be selected? If you know the people you want to talk to and their number is small enough, you can ask each one. However, you may want to know what a lot of people think. In this case, your survey group should accurately reflect the general population. If you ask only three high school students about their favorite activity, you might hear things that most other students aren't interested in at all. So sample size is important. You also need a good cross-section of the population. If you surveyed 100 male freshmen, junior varsity, and varsity football players, you might have a good sample size, but their opinions might not accurately reflect those of the entire student body. Some method of picking people at random is needed. This means that selection of a person to be surveyed is left entirely to chance.

3. *Design the survey instrument.* Figure out what you really need to know, and devise questions that will give you that information. Most often you are better off if you can ask closed-ended instead of open-ended questions. Closed-ended questions are those in which respondents pick from choices you already offer. All they have to do is circle a letter or a number, or write down a letter, number, or single word. They don't have to write down their own ideas. They merely react to the choices offered.

    At times it is a good idea to ask one or two open-ended questions to give respondents a chance to add their own ideas. A more personal method of administration gives greater opportunities for open-ended questions. Generally, though, the fewer questions of this type the better. Open-ended questions often put people off. They may not want to take the time and energy to respond. Further, the more you ask people to write, the more time you will spend trying to read the handwriting and guessing what the respondent really means.

    Be careful not to let bias creep into your questions. For example, asking, "Do you encourage keeping our children ignorant and unprepared for the future?" may not yield accurate information on how a person will vote on a school bond election.

The length of the survey is also an important matter. A survey that is too long will discourage people from responding. If people don't complete the survey, it doesn't do you any good. During your pretest (described next), record how long it takes people to complete the survey. You can then let future respondents know how long it will take them to complete it. On the top of the survey itself you can write: "This survey takes only 5 minutes to complete."

4. *Accuracy and clarity.* One of the great fallacies in communication is that people know what we mean. After all, we are always so clear—aren't we? Did you ever get frustrated trying to figure out just what a professor was asking on an objective test? You know, if you look at it one way, the answer is "A"; if you look at it another way, the answer is "C." Believe me, you will run into the same problems with your survey. So after you have written it, do a pretest—administer your survey to a handful of people who are not in your survey sample. See if they clearly understand what you are asking. Did these questions, even if clearly understood, provide you with the information you wanted? You will find that most of the time you have to revise some survey questions.

5. *Administering the instrument.* The way you conduct the survey is important. Several problems can sneak in. For example, a survey administered by an interviewer, someone who verbally asks the prepared questions, is open to bias. Interviewers should practice beforehand and be critiqued to make sure that none of their mannerisms, including tone of voice, tend to promote certain responses. E-mail and other online surveys and those conducted by traditional post mail have problems as well. Respondents to these surveys are likely to be those most interested in the topic. Their ideas may not represent the entire population. The more the survey is sent to a group not expecting to

receive it, the more likely this will occur. You have put a lot of work into preparation of the survey; make sure it is conducted properly. Try to anticipate problems and prevent them.

Finally, respondents need to feel safe to answer honestly. You may need to explain how the results will and will not be used. You also may need to guarantee that the survey will be answered anonymously.

6. *Compiling and analyzing the results.* How you look at the pieces of information and how they relate to each other will help you get a more complete picture. Ask questions that give you clear data so you don't have to guess what the respondent means.

In summary, for your survey to be helpful you need to ask enough of the right people the right questions in a way that makes it likely they will accurately respond to the survey, giving you information you can interpret and use.

Using Mapping Technology. Sometimes you may find yourself wondering where in the world you are with this work. Mapping technology might help you find out. A map can create a picture of the place and the information you are working with.

Maps can provide at least four basic benefits. First, of course, they can show you what's between where you are and where you want to go. They can give you direction to help keep you from getting lost, making your travel more efficient. That's a pretty common purpose, whether you are working for community change or just trying to get to Aunt Irsle's place for Thanksgiving dinner. Second, a map provides you a bird's eye view to help you place things in context, noting spatial relationships, boundaries of action and identity, and unique elements of geography that help to define a place. Third, maps become a source of information that you can draw upon to add to your understanding of your arena of action. Fourth, maps can be a place for you to record the information you collect to display it in a visual field.

Most people are familiar with the first two functions. The increasing availability of mapping technology, however, brings the last two into greater prominence for change agents. A storehouse of data has been gathered, usually by some official sources, and digitally coded into maps. So much is already there, you just need to use a mapping application to pull it out and put it on a map you create of whatever area you are working in. Here is just a sample of information readily available that you can retrieve, much of which you can place on your own map or series of maps:

- Street addresses for each parcel of land
- Ownership of each parcel
- Crime data for a specific area
- Number of people living on each block
- Stress indicators for a specific area
- Development plans for a specific area
- Aerial views of a specific area, using ortho-photography (an aerial photograph that has been geometrically corrected to represent actual distances)
- Neighborhood association names and boundaries
- Voting districts
- Poverty data
- Schools, libraries, police stations, fire stations, and other facilities in the area

Remember, this is just a sample. There is much more. You can imagine how helpful this information can be as you begin organizing a place, like a neighborhood. But what about the information you gather? In some mapping applications, not only can you transfer information embedded in maps to the one you create, but you can also add information of your own. One good example for this use is the Barrio Sustainability Project in Tucson, Arizona.

In this project organizers are bringing the community together to increase community health by promoting healthy diets, locally produced food, indigenous leadership, particularly among young people, and self-reliance. They are farming, in a neighborhood in the middle of the city, in the middle of the Sonoran desert. They can track and represent on a map each food-producing plant already growing in neighbors' yards. The can show each plot of open space, both those that have been planted and those that are potential planting sites. As they begin to clean

up the area, they can identify places that are the best spots for the City to drop off large refuse collection containers to be filled in a weekend clean up effort. They can show sources of pollution that need attention, water harvesting sites, the distribution of neighborhood leaders, and those who learned farming skills generations ago. They are just getting started. Gathering their own information and creating their own picture on a map helps to bring the project and the neighborhood alive.

Once you have created your map you can use it in a number of ways. By representing information in an understandable format, especially for visual learners, it becomes an important tool in decision making. It helps you to see information, current conditions, and decide what this means and what you want to do about it, including how you will use the assets that are no longer hidden. Maps tell a story, often more powerfully than a written report. You are able to illustrate your community's circumstances and dreams to community members, media, and policymakers. Map making can quickly become an act of community building. Members of the community learn more deeply as they work together to gather available information or generate new information and turn that into a portrait of their community, a portrait that can continue to be refined by more knowledge. Like any work of communal art, this endeavor offers a number of interesting roles that people can easily fill.

What do you need to get started? Three things: a mapping application, some expertise, and data. The mapping application is the interactive technology that enables you to build your own map and record information on it. These may be available for you to use through a community agency such as the United Way, a local governmental agency, particularly a planning department or library, or an area college or university. Don't be surprised if you find a willingness to share this resource and help you learn how to use it.

A little bit of expertise is helpful. You may well find people in your community who already know how to use mapping applications or students who are willing to partner with you on a project. If not, it is pretty easy to learn. This technology can be very sophisticated, but you can readily learn most of what you will need to know and use. Most applications have tutorials, and some agencies and colleges offer hands-on training.

Finally, of course, you need the data to bring the map alive. As I mentioned earlier, data can easily be imported to your site from data sets that already exist, and some applications let you create your own data as well. Geocoding allows you to take a tabular data set, say addresses from an Excel file, and match the information from your table to the geography of the map. This is easier to use than it sounds. Your words and numbers can become symbols on a map, depending on how you would like them displayed. A number of mapping resources are currently available:

Google Earth lets you can fly around the world and zoom in on your particular neck of the woods with satellite imagery, giving you some amazing pictures, including 3D images of buildings and terrain. The basic package is free.

Policy Map has a rich set of data available to record into your own map, and you can add your own information as well. Some of their services are free, but others can be a bit pricey.

DataPlace Beta is a free service of *DataPlace* that, among other things, offers Neighborhood Metrics to help you create custom maps revealing important trends: for example, home foreclosure risk.

Environmental Systems Research Institute (ESRI), through the *ESRI Conservation Program*, offers nonprofits and libraries a year's worth of software and training in collaboration with *TechSoup* for less than $200.

The *Center for Applied Research and Environmental Systems (CARES)* and the *Rural Policy Research Institute (RUPRI)* have merged. Working through the University of Missouri they offer *U.S. Interactive Maps*, which will help you to make a map of your area using the wealth of data they have available. They also have developed the *Community Issues Management (CIM)* project. Working in five partner communities, Charleston, South Carolina; Columbia, Missouri; Lehigh Valley, Pennsylvania; Detroit, Michigan;

and Tucson, Arizona, CIM is developing a process for actively engaging community members in contributing to a community-wide database and assisting them in learning how to create maps for their own uses. In some communities CIM is collaborating with United Way affiliates, who hope to eventually expand this resource throughout their network.

Other local and regional mapping resources, like Central Indiana's *SAVI Interactive,* are available to help you create your own map.

Preparing and updating a map of your area rich with information will help you learn, make decisions, and tell your story well.

Other Online Sources.   Local governments typically have websites with a home page that describes government functions as well as how to directly contact the particular service you might need. Budget information, city services, and even agendas of upcoming meetings are routinely provided. Some communities have detailed and very useful information; others provide only a general overview. However, each will lead you to other sources of more specific information. You can locate businesses, schools, or places of worship. History, community events, and key environmental features are typically available. Some cities provide detailed descriptions of neighborhoods along with the names of neighborhood leaders and ways to contact them. You can find out about various community organizations and associations, major employers, and current community issues. You can easily get maps of neighborhoods or of the entire community.

You can obtain valuable data on the makeup of your community or neighborhood through the U.S. Census Bureau, including maps and information down to the census block level. A census block corresponds to individual city blocks bounded by streets, though in rural areas this may be square miles and have some boundaries that are not streets. There are more than 8 million census blocks in the United States, so you can get information for a very targeted area. The Census Bureau also provides information on other factors, such as poverty, as well as a list of facts about your city.

Some newspapers in larger communities have broken the community into much smaller neighborhood sections and provide online news targeted to each area. They may even provide weekly e-mail newsletters for ZIP code areas in the community. Other useful websites with valuable links include the local Chamber of Commerce and colleges and universities that serve the area.

What if you want to find out what people are thinking? Online survey discussion and survey tools can help an organization identify issues, discuss them, and rank issues by importance. Dozens of companies can help you set up your survey, get people to your survey, collect responses, and even analyze the results. SurveyMonkey is one resource that provides its service free for a survey of 100 people with 10 or fewer questions.

Informal Methods

If you intend to find out about your community, it is almost impossible not to. All sorts of tidbits of information on your community are out there all the time. Anything from the way streets are named and the number of locks people have on their doors to good and bad gossip will tell you something. Once you have decided to notice things, you will. Here are a few ways of keeping your eyes and ears open that will be particularly helpful to you.

Windshield Surveys. A windshield survey is an easy, even enjoyable way to deepen your understanding of an area through direct observation. You will want to follow some simple steps to make sure that the time you put into driving around gives you some useful information.

First, determine what you are looking for. You may want to consider a range of things such as the type and conditions of homes or other structures, open spaces, the number, age, and ethnicity of the people you see, specific indicators of economic wealth or poverty, expressions of culture, the type and condition of businesses, meeting places, and so on. Ask yourself, what might we see that will help us to learn what we want to know? Next, prepare a simple form for gathering the information. You might have a checklist or categories for things you are looking at. You want to get more than just general impressions, so your form

should help you record specific numbers, or give you some sort of ranking scale for what you see. You can record descriptions of each address or each block. You decide how detailed you want the information to be.

Once you know what you are looking for and how to keep track of your observations, decide where you will go. It is helpful to map out your route and keep a map with you on your tour. Thinking about when you should go is the next step. The information that you gather will vary by time of day and day of the week. You may want to go at different times to give yourself a better feel for the place. The last stage of preparation is to resolve to leave your biases at home. The more you can look with eyes open to discovery rather than ready to see only what you expect to see, the more you will learn.

Now you are ready to go. It is a good idea to go with a partner or two. You may focus on the road a bit more, making for a less exciting trip, but having more than one perspective can help moderate any bias that might have come along for the ride. Further, it gives more of your members a way to be involved in gathering information and provides some other eyes to see what you might have missed. Having two teams recording the same area allows you to compare notes and further moderate bias (Centers for Disease Control, 2007).

One member of your team can bring along a digital camera to help prepare a visual record. These pictures can be a striking complement to the information found in your forms and help dramatize future presentations.

You want to make sure that you remember what you see, so it is very important to record your information as you go along, documenting details. You can put a lot of this information on the map you may be creating, using mapping technology.

Although you can cover more ground by driving around, you might see more if you get out and walk, or even hop on your bike and take a ride through the area. However you approach it, doing a windshield survey can be a good exercise in getting a close-up view of the area where you are working.

Collect Lists. You can start building a kind of who's who in your community from lists. Who is on the board of directors of the theater company or the art museum? Who are major donors to the ballet or symphony? Either because they need to look good, have the time and money to do so, or because they genuinely want to influence the culture of the community, supporters of the arts are often important people. Other lists are important as well; in fact, almost all lists of names can be useful. If you get a list, keep it. Here are some types of lists you may find useful:

- *Membership lists.* Members of neighborhood associations, homeowner associations, country clubs or other private clubs, the chamber of commerce, or professional organizations such as the bar association are potentially useful. Any organization that has members will probably have a membership list.

- *Donor lists.* Programs for special events such as a dinner, groundbreaking ceremony, or special recognition ceremony often list major contributors who made the event possible.

- *Political contributors.* Political candidates have to file statements identifying their contributors. These are available through the Secretary of State's office. These lists can come in handy.

- *Lists of officers or boards of directors.* Business, civic, and social service organizations often seek strong people to serve as board members or officers. Many organizations list their officers, board members, and other supporters on their letterhead. Save these. Usually these people are at least moderately important and have some interest in the issue their organization addresses.

- *Officers of political parties.* These lists include people who have clearly decided to become involved in community affairs. They want to be around power and perhaps be seen as powerful. To some extent they shape the direction of their parties and influence the behavior of officeholders. Precinct committee people and district officers are particularly useful. The local party headquarters or someone active in party politics will have this list of names.

Create your own lists. One of the best ways to do this is by keeping track of announcements for things such as recent hirings and promotions and recipients of awards or other honors. These can

◄ Take a Moment to Discover ►

If you work at a social service agency or another type of organization that sees itself as serving the community, are you able to name the leaders of the neighborhood where your agency sits? That is, the people who actually live there. How many people working at the agency can name these leaders? How many actually know them? What do your answers tell you about whom the agency sees as its valuable partners?

If you don't work at an organization of this type, go interview someone who does, and see what they have to say.

usually be found in the local paper. Take advantage of any opportunity you have to get a list. Keep them all in a file for easy reference.

Newspapers Provide More Than the News. News is important, of course. Read the local news section of the paper to keep abreast of what is going on in your community. The newspaper website will have options for exploration of archived material as well. You can track the progress of particular issues or particular groups this way. In addition to the general news, pay attention to other sections as well. The editorial point of view of the leading paper usually reflects the prevailing political philosophy of the general community. Pay attention to the editorial position on issues as well as the paper's selection of syndicated columnists.

The section related to business or money often features articles or brief announcements on current or up-and-coming community business leaders. Stories on the community's economic health or particular sectors of the economy are found here too. The community events calendar can introduce you to various groups within the community. The society pages may help you learn about key movers and shakers who waltz across your community, and the obituary column may help you trace kinship lines (Kahn, 1994).

Letters to the editor can cue you to issues ready to boil, as well as what people think about them. And the classified section provides clues about the types and number of jobs available, as well as wage rates. You can also get a good indication of the cost and availability of certain goods and services, such as housing and child care.

When you look at the newspaper, read more than the news. Clip and save those articles you find valuable. Your files on these will serve as good future references.

Strike Up Conversations.   Be willing to ask people about their perspective on the community. People waiting around for something, like a bus or for the machine to finish the rinse cycle at the laundromat, are often willing to pass the time in conversation. People who hear other people talk—barbers, hairdressers, and bartenders, for example—often don't mind sharing a perception or two. The letter carrier often has good insights on the area she serves; so does the person working the cash register in the cafeteria. These are not interviews, just conversations, perhaps a sadly forgotten art. By just shooting the breeze, you might get a good idea of how the wind blows.

Observe. Walk around. Ride the bus. Get on your bike. Heck, drive your car if you have to. Even if you don't go out of your way to consider your agency, neighborhood, or city from a different perspective, see if you can learn just one new thing a week. That is not a lot to ask. After a year you will have learned at least 50 things you wouldn't have otherwise, and probably many more than that.

CONCLUSION

As you move from "I" to "we," you will involve people in a way that results in all of you working together to accomplish the goals you share. Depending on the situation you face and how you intend to approach it, you may be working with a handful of people or thousands. These people may come together to work on a specific issue, having little sense that they are a community, or these people may already be involved in a well-established community, strengthened with traditions and recognized by a name. Whoever these people are, you should know about them.

Your community extends from broad to specific groups. It includes geographic and interest groups, some of which are highly structured, whereas others may never actually get together as a community. Based on your general understanding of your community's dynamics, and directed by the issue at hand, you need a better awareness of the communities you will mobilize for action, those that will benefit from that action, and those from which you will demand a response.

Get to know the basic characteristics of the people in your community. Grasp how the community functions to meet its needs. Identify unmet community needs, and understand what improvements may be needed as you go about making a difference in your community. Most important, evaluate the resources your community has on hand as well as ones it could develop. This information will help you to better gauge its capacity to work toward change.

Rely on a variety of sources and techniques to increase your understanding—but don't get stuck in the information gathering phase and forget about taking action. By discovering the wealth of information in the library, gathering reports from community groups, or just talking to people, you will see your community as alive and fascinating. Of course, the best way to learn about your community is to be involved with it.

You can get to know basketball by reading up on it and watching it on TV, but you really learn basketball by playing it. The more you play, the more what you read and watch will make sense and be enjoyable. The way to understand your community is to participate in it—take part in its life.

MORE THAN A WALK IN THE PARK

There was dust everywhere. Caught in the cracks in the sidewalks, in the cracks of the worn park benches, in the cracks crinkling the face of the old guy crumpled beneath the cardboard he used for shade this time of year, still numbed from whatever got him to sleep last night or early this morning. Grit covered everything; even the park grass seemed dirty.

The vacant lot, hemmed in by drooping strands of wire warning off anyone who might want to wander there, seemed to have grown a good crop of broken liquor bottles, old tires, and white plastic bags marked with the grocery chain logo. The wires must not work very well.

It was Sunday morning, and the strains of the Grace Emmanuel choir floated over the scene. Six women from the neighborhood walking club strode by with their early morning resolve to exercise their muscles and their right to be out from behind locked doors. On they walked, past the "Elect Matos" signs Sylvia had placed every 100 yards or so to mark their progress around the perimeter of the park and to call attention to progress of another sort. Carmen Matos wasn't with them this morning; she was getting ready for the radio talk show at 10 o'clock. They talked about Carmen and the questions they had thought up to call in to the show about the new program the community college was developing along with the neighborhood and the hospital so that health careers and the money that went with them could be real options for local people. As they approached the north end of the park, talk turned to the school, whose walls rose up from the park's border. What should be done about that? How are our children going to be prepared for any jobs, much less well-paying ones?

A seventh partner joined the discussion as the group moved to the park's west side, past the banner announcing next week's Dia De San Juan fiesta. Now plans for the fiesta took hold of the conversation. Who's helping out with the dancers? Who is bringing the food? Who will be making the music? Where will the local artists display their works? They already knew most of the answers, but it was fun to talk about. They probably didn't notice that they were walking faster as their voices rose, bringing harmony to Grace Emmanuel. Maybe, they hoped, it would finally rain.

REFLECTION QUESTIONS

1. What did you notice most of all in this story?
2. What forms of community capital did you recognize?
3. What steps would you take to begin working with this community? Why would you take those steps?
4. What do you think the residents notice? What might they not see?
5. What kind of assessment process might they undertake to discover more about their neighborhood?
6. What sources of information would they draw upon? How might that come about? As a change agent what would be your role?
7. If an assessment were done, then what?

GROUP ACTIVITY: GETTING TO KNOW YOUR COMMUNITY EXERCISE

Learning about your community is important and rewarding, and it can be a lot of fun as well. Of course, the more you know about something, the better you can relate to it. In our work the ability to relate effectively to your community is fundamental.

1. Divide the larger group into teams of five members. Each team has 20 minutes to find out as much as it can about your college community. Though you should find out as much as you can in this time, here are some things that you *must* discover:

   - The number of students at your college

   - The number of students attending your college from countries outside the United States

   - The annual budget for the college

   - Three things that students who are not from your major wish to see changed at the college

   - The name of a carpenter who is not from your major

   - The name of someone, again from a different major, who plays a musical instrument

   - A different skill that a college staff member has

   - The office location and three services provided by the Academic Support Office (or similar office that provides tutoring, support for students with disabilities, and so forth)

   - Two resources that would be helpful in organizing members of the college community

   - One other piece of interesting information.

2. In addition, each team selects one of the items below to add to its list:

   - Identify one issue that the student government is working on.

   - Provide the names of five different student organizations.

   - Provide the name of the person who decides the number of handicap parking spaces.

   - Gather two cultural artifacts.

   - Explain at least two ways that librarians can help you with research for your assignments.

3. Think of your answers to the following questions while you are completing this exercise, and be prepared to discuss them.

   - How did your team organize to gather the information in the time allotted?

   - What personal limitations did you have to challenge in order to gather this information?

   - What are you learning from this experience that you can use in gathering information about communities?

   - What is one other key discovery about organizing that you have you made?

   - What skills you are using?

4. Discuss your team's experience and prepare a brief report to the larger group. (5–10 minutes)

5. Provide your team's report to the larger group on your experience and the information you gathered. (5 minutes)

6. Use the chart below to score your team's effort.

Information Needed	Information Obtained	Points Possible	Team Score
Number of students		10	
Number of students from outside the country		5	
Annual budget		5	
Three things that need changing		20	
Carpenter		10	
Musician		10	
Additional skill of staff		5	
Academic Support Office		15	
Organizing resources		10	
One other thing		5	
Assigned item		5	
Team Total Score			

HELPFUL WEBSITES

Links to the organizations briefly described here are on the companion website at www.cengage.com/humansvcs/homan.

U.S. Census Bureau Subject Index. Here you can find census data from A to Z.

Institute for Community Research. Here you will find a wealth of information about collaborative research, such as participatory action research, as well as links to a number of helpful publications in the field. The organization makes a particular effort to include the voices of youth.

Sanborn Maps. Digital, large-scale plans of more than 12,000 U.S. cities and towns, from 1867 to 1970, drawn at a scale of 50 feet to an inch are available here. Developed to help fire insurance companies assess the risk of particular properties, they have amazing detail about buildings and the surrounding areas. Many libraries subscribe to this service, which requires a username and password.

Scorecard. Sponsored by the Environmental Defense Fund, a wealth of data on pollution affecting neighborhoods is amassed here. Enter your ZIP code to find out what pollutants are being released in your community and who is responsible for this pollution.

Chapter 6

✳

Power

CHAPTER HIGHLIGHTS

- Power, fundamental to change
- Political and relationship power
- Definitions, attitudes, and elements of power
- Fear of power
- Bases of power in a community
- Bases of power in a group
- Who holds power
- Power–issue relationship
- Your own bases of power
- Strategies for building power
- Personal credibility and power
- Become part of power circles
- Information and power
- Act powerfully
- Rights, responsibilities, and consequences of using power
- Develop the power of others

Power—the word itself provokes reaction. We need it. We use it. It often slips unsolicited into our daydreams, at times with pleasure, at others with vexation. Whether or not we are willing to acknowledge the role power plays in our actions, it will affect what we are doing at any given moment.

In an escape from proper etiquette, I will speak frankly of power, for nothing is more central to promoting change than your ability to generate and use power. You cannot promote change without using power. Acting responsibly, you cannot simultaneously want things to be different and not want to be powerful. It is as simple, and as difficult, as that.

In Chapter 5 you were introduced to the importance of knowing your community, and you were given some steps to help you in that endeavor. You need to understand the circumstances in which you are building and applying power for its generation and use to have focus and be effective. You will come up against the fact that you need power to provoke a response. You will need to figure out how you can increase your ability to take part in community decisions and to influence those decisions. You will recognize that having a good idea is only a start, and your base of power needs to be larger than the issue you face.

What is power? Why do you need it? Who has it? How can you get it and use it? And how can you empower others? In the following pages I will offer some basic answers to these questions and examine other issues pertaining to power that merit your attention.

There are many notions of power, ranging from abstract formulations of power as a force that produces a change, to practical notions of power by which machines make available energy more efficient, to personal notions of power over one's self. Of all these various types of power, I will be concerned primarily with two types: political power, which is used to make or shape policies that have an impact on people, and what might be called relationship power, which is the power to influence how people relate to one another.

You must be conscious of how power is understood and used within your group. Even the word "power" may conjure up notions of exploitation or abuse. Under those circumstances, it is natural for people to want to distance themselves from notions of power. Strengthening communities requires the use of power, so your awareness of different cultural interpretations and applications of power is a necessary aspect of your ability to build the power necessary to change conditions.

WHAT IS POWER?

In the field of community change, power is the capacity to move people in a desired direction to accomplish some end. Domhoff (2005b) described power as "being able to realize wishes, to produce the effects you want to produce. It is one of the basic dimensions of all human experience, whether at the interpersonal, group, or societal level" (p. 1). Robinson and Hannah (1994) described power as "the ability to realize one's values in the world" (p. 77). Rubin and Rubin (2008) have described power as "the ability to affect decisions that shape social outcomes" (p. 13). Building on Bertrand Russell's perception of power, Dennis Wrong (2004) added a social dimension by implying that power necessarily involves relationships between people. He defined power as "the capacity of some persons to produce intended and foreseen effects on others" (p. 2). Dugan (2003) says power is the "capacity to bring about change" (p. 1), and it can come from within, from without, or from a combination of the two. Kirst-Ashman

and Hull (2009) added that power includes the "ability to prevent someone from doing something they want to do" (p. 294).

These definitions all suggest that power is something a person or organization possesses and is willing to use. Power involves some sense of purpose or intention. We expect to meet some need or receive some benefit through the use of power. So, having power means that you can get what you want, or what you think you want, by having people behave or respond the way you want them to. They may very well want to respond this way, but for some reason have not yet done so.

Sounds pretty devious and self-serving, doesn't it? Perhaps it is more devious to be coy about power and more dishonest to deny the fact that we have intentions we act upon. Much like the youth with a flashlight and magazines, we have hidden our notions of power under the covers for far too long. It's time for an open assessment of power.

Power is not dominance. Dominance is the way some people use power. Collaboration is the way other people use power. You can powerfully participate with other parties to create mutually acceptable solutions, even parties whose interests are different or in apparent conflict with yours. You may combine your power with that of another group to bring something new to life. You can use your power to force an opponent to end exploitive or destructive practices. You can use your power to work with others to improve a condition. You can use your power to create. Power is both energy and influence.

Domhoff (2005b) distinguished two types of power. The first is *collective* power, which is the capacity of a group to realize its common goals, which flows from its organization, cooperation, morale, and technology. The second, the one most people think of when the subject of power comes up, is *distributive* power. That is concerned with who has power over whom and what.

The use of power does not have to be manipulative, but it can be. It does not have to be noble, but it can be. It may be used for evil just as well as for good (Wartenberg, 1990). If you notice the use of power and like what was accomplished, you will probably think that use of power is fine. If you disagree with the purpose and the application, not only will you be upset about the use of power but you will probably notice it more as well.

Power does not imply stiff resistance. Nor does it require a struggle or a fight. Yet this is how we often conceive of power: people being forced to do something they don't want to do by someone who can make them do it. This is neither a healthy nor an accurate picture of power, but those images haunt the corners of our understanding of this basic concept. The greater the opposition, the more the use of power will be seen, simply because there is a clash of power. If a win–lose brawl ensues, things could get ugly. Here, it is both the clash and the manner chosen to resolve the differences that call attention to power and shape our reactions to it. It is not simply the presence of power.

Power can be used in a spirit of cooperation as easily as it can occur in a climate of conflict. If you and your friends are trying to decide where to go for pizza, you may rely on the recommendations of one or two members of your group. Hearing their strong endorsement of Juan O'Grady's as the best place in town to get pizza, you willingly go along, even though you have reservations about the name. The pizza turns out to be as good as promised. Power was used— someone moved a group of people, quite literally, in a desired direction. The fact that there was no difficult conflict does not mean no power was used.

In and of itself, power is neither good nor bad. It is simply, and importantly, the necessary element that provides the impetus in the process of making things different. Elizabeth Power (2001) noted, "in the face of change, power counts" (p. 176). That it may be used to dignify or demean depends on the user, not the tool.

Does power derive from the person? Are some people simply more powerful than others? Or is there more to it than that? Power, like many other things in life, depends on the situation, although particular people can have power in many situations. The basic question is this: Can you get these particular people to behave in this particular way at this particular time? The relative degree and location of power in a situation is determined by the interplay among the individuals and groups involved. By changing who the respondents are, what they are supposed to do, or the context in which the behavior is supposed to occur, the power of a particular individual will necessarily increase or decrease.

A classroom teacher may tell students to complete a number of math problems in the next half hour. The students are expected to comply or face some sort of sanction. An hour later, the same teacher is in the middle of a faculty meeting on budget cuts and makes the same request of fellow faculty members. The teacher's colleagues might not respond so readily. In fact, they might well think this teacher needs a little time off and a little help … and not with math problems. The same request produced different results in different situations. In the first instance, the teacher is considered powerful. In the second, the teacher is considered disturbed.

Borrowing from social exchange theory, one view of power involves interactions in relationships between people. For example, if someone were to influence you, the power flows from your perception that someone has control over resources (for example, time, money, information, freedom, affection) that are important to you and that that individual is willing to exercise control to your benefit or detriment. Thus, you behave in a way to achieve the gain or avoid the loss you believe will be caused by being provided with or denied these resources. The more you are dependent on an individual for those resources, and the more important the consequences of their use or withholding are to you, the more that individual is likely to influence you.

If you need food stamps, you may do what the food stamp worker tells you to do, even if this means you have to do things you ordinarily wouldn't do. You may answer questions about your private circumstances or gather documentation that proves your need for assistance. You do all this to make sure the worker provides the food stamps that keep you and your family from going hungry. If you are working in collaboration with a group from an adjoining neighborhood to clean up graffiti in the area, the time and location of your first project may be influenced by your need to use one another's tools, paint, and volunteers, along with your desire to establish a cooperative relationship that may benefit you on other matters. Each group working by itself might have made a choice different from the one required by the relationship. The key here is the perception that someone has control over resources you believe to be important. Whether or not they actually do have control and whether or not those resources are really

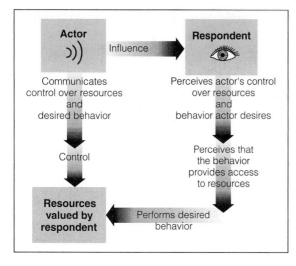

FIGURE 6.1 Pathways of Intentional Influence Attempt

important is not significant. If you believe this to be the case, you will act; if not, you won't.

What occurs in relationships between individuals also holds true in relationships between groups. An individual or group who desires influence must somehow communicate the potential for controlling resources. Further, to be effective, this must be done in a way that provides an opportunity for those being influenced to perform the desired behavior. These pathways to power are shown in Figure 6.1.

As an example of how this could work, imagine the plight of Earl Blern. Earl is an agency director being urged by members of the community to change certain agency procedures community members believe restrict access to service. A program designed to benefit women who work outside the home operates from 9:00 a.m. to 4:00 p.m. Monday through Friday. These hours are convenient for the agency but make it impossible for most women who are to benefit from the program to participate. After all, many are at work during those hours.

Earl is fearful that this well-organized community group will go directly to his board of directors and pressure them to fire him if he does not make the changes they want. So Earl complies with the group's demands and changes the hours. Earl perceived that through their contacts with the board and the pressure they can bring to bear, the community can control a resource that is very important to

him: namely, the board's favor and, ultimately, his job. The group has power. It was able to accomplish its purpose by changing Earl's behavior from refusal to modify the program's hours of operation to acceptance.

What if this group wasn't really organized? What if they not only didn't know anyone on Earl's board but didn't even think about talking to the board at all? It doesn't matter. Earl's perception of the situation governed his response.

What if the situation were completely different? What if Earl perceived the group as being poorly organized with no plans to talk to his board or that no one would listen if they did? He would probably continue to resist. Even if Earl's perceptions were way off base, the group would have no power with him until he got a different message, one that changed his perception.

Finally, what if the group immediately put pressure on the board, and Earl was fired? The group would have been powerful over Earl, but they would not have accomplished their goal. By denying Earl the opportunity to change his behavior in the desired direction, by giving him the message too late, the group would not have been effective with Earl. Maybe the next director will comply, but it is a little late for old Earl to remedy the situation.

DO YOU NEED POWER?

If you want people to move in a particular direction, you have to use some form of power to get them there. It is as basic as the laws of physics. To change the direction of something or to overcome the inertia of the status quo, some force (power) must be applied to accelerate motion in the desired direction.

You will learn over and over and over again that simply because an idea "makes sense" has little bearing on what happens. You have probably learned this a time or two already. Do you ever have trouble getting around to paying your bills, or doing your studying, or maybe even losing a recalcitrant pound or 20? Did you find that the discovery or introduction of good ideas, ones that were reasonable and "made sense," just wasn't enough to change what was happening? It is not that we lack good ideas. It is not that we don't know how to do things more effectively. It is that

G. William Domhoff (2005c), who has spent a lifetime studying power, pointed out that social change agents don't pay enough attention to what can be learned from social science research. He provided these important lessons.

1. Social-psychological studies of small groups show that "moral exemplars"—those who stand outside the general consensus—are likely to first be labeled "extremists," but they can be very effective, with one important qualification. They can't be too extreme or they will just be ignored. The trick is to be just extreme enough to be an "effective extremist."

2. Historical case studies show that a very small number of highly organized and disciplined people, drawing great energy from their strong moral beliefs and confidence in their shared theoretical analysis, can have great impact.

3. Change agents need to understand the differences between themselves and other people. Most people are focused on the joys and necessities of everyday life. They won't leave their routines unless those routines are disrupted. Change agents, on the other hand, may be willing to sacrifice their everyday lives, including family, schooling, and career, to work on social change every waking minute. This means that they need to be patient. They need to be patient with other people and either wait for or help create disruption that can lead people to action. If they create disruption, they must do so without alienating those they wish to become supporters.

4. Change agents must take the social structure of their own society seriously. They have to pay attention to the country's history, culture, and form of government. They can't just copy methods of change agents from other countries and expect them to work the same here.

5. It's not philosophy or "Grand Theory" that will be helpful, but social structure, history, group dynamics, and strategy that matter. Change agents should take the findings of the social sciences seriously.

we don't often move past talking about ideas to acting on them, to implementing them, powerfully. Old habits, old beliefs, and old fears get in the way. These must be overcome to bring something new into existence.

The purpose you intend to achieve will require that people do things differently from the way they do them now. Some of these people won't mind—in fact, they may want to change—but other people will resist. Some force must be applied to awaken support, to get supporters acting in concert, or to overcome opponents.

Understand that somebody's interests are being met by the way things are at the moment. The bigger your issue, the more somebodies we are talking about. They are used to things the way they are. They may not want them to be different. Further, some of these people are much more used to getting their way than to giving way. They are used to telling other people what to do. They don't like being told. These people aren't going to like what you are doing. They may not even like you. They are going to try to stop you. Big surprise. These people will use their power to protect and to further what they see as their interests. How do you intend to deal with that challenge? How are you going to use your power?

FEAR OF POWER

Your boss just dropped the grant application on your desk. It's an inch thick. There are lots of guidelines, rules, and requirements in that inch. You've never really applied for a grant before. The thing looks a foot tall by the time you leave your office and head for home. You are on a lonely stretch of highway, and the car sounds like it's going to conk out. Do you get sweaty palms, do you get irritable, or are you pretty confident that you can figure out the problem? You are driving into San Francisco for the first time, and it is rush hour. Between you and your downtown hotel is a maze of one-way streets up and down those maddening hills. Not quite like your home in Santa Fe. Feel alittle uncomfortable, a little testy?

When we are not accustomed to something, especially if that something makes demands on us, we tend to fear it some—Where will it lead me? What if I get it all wrong?—so we get our defenses up. When was the last time you had a serious conversation about power? Have you ever? Is it any wonder then that many of us feel so uncomfortable, so inept, when it comes to dealing with power?

You can learn to write a grant proposal. You can discover how to fix your car. Maps can guide you through a city. But power? Who ever instructed you on that? Is there anything else so fundamental about which we receive so little training? Yet we are expected to use power daily. Parents are helped with their concerns about children's obedience. Teachers are instructed on classroom management. Supervisors are trained to get the most from their staffs. Where in any of this is there an honest discussion of power? Yet issues of power are central to all of these situations.

Power makes many demands on those who hold and use it (Bermant & Warwick, 1985). Handling power in an appropriate manner must be done with respect for the rights and legitimate interests of others. This requires that you be aware of others and pay attention to their rights. It means that you must wrestle with the perplexities of what constitutes "legitimate interests." Using power, you have to accept the risk that you will make mistakes and that these mistakes will have consequences. You must be responsible for your actions and accept accountability for them.

Significant change is often attended by significant conflict. In fact, there will always be some degree of conflict in a situation of community change, even those largely cooperative in nature. Some of this conflict can be handled creatively and amicably. Some of it will bring anger and the vexations that accompany hostility. At times, people may not only resent what you are doing but resent *you* personally. People may not like you, and you may not like them. Using power will expose the conflict and bring it more clearly into focus.

If you intend to develop power and put it to use, you must let go of convenient old excuses that explain away the presence of intolerable conditions. You must cast off the rhetoric and habits of power-lessness. When you act powerfully, you must learn not to horde power but to invest it in others as a means of producing more.

If you fear power, you may actually wish to avoid the responsibility, work, conflict, or other demands it brings. However, if you deal realistically and honestly with power, if you continue to learn more about it, you will become more at ease with its use. Whether your efforts involve an office, a classroom, a city, or beyond, you will feel more alive, and you will discover a profound sense of personal fulfillment simply from knowing that you are willing to take part in making a difference.

WHO HAS POWER?

In a community, a fundamental source of power involves control over resources considered important to the members of the community. Getting a fix on how power is rooted in your community can give you a sense of how and why things happen. Your actions will cause repercussions that may help some and frustrate others. Understanding the bases of power that may be affected by your actions will help you spot potential opponents and allies. Finally, your awareness of sources of community power will help you figure out where you and your associates may lay claim to some.

Several bases of power exist within a community. Although the bases I will describe relate to a common city or town, these bases exist to some extent in the subcommunities and interest communities within the city or town as well, such as a neighborhood, a school, or a professional group. If you are promoting change in this type of community, keep its characteristics in mind, and you will see how the bases of power apply to it as well.

The more bases of power you have, the more you are perceived as being willing to exercise power, and the greater your personal credibility, the more likely it is that you will be powerful. In addition to formal bases, a passionate commitment to a moral cause can generate power. Here the power comes both from

CAPTURING CONCEPTS
Bases of Power in a Community

Information. Those who control the symbols of information and the interpretation of those symbols are likely to be among the most influential individuals.

Money. People with money can get their way in exchange for their money.

Laws. Determining and applying the rules can determine who wins the game.

Constituencies. Power over people in a group as well as the power to mobilize a large group can have a significant influence on the community.

Energy and natural resources. The more concentrated the energy source or the more limited and locally valued the natural resource, the more powerful those who control these resources will be.

Goods and services. The more important products or services are to the local economy, the more powerful those who control these products will be.

Network participation. Having a lot of connections in the community provides access to resources and an increased ability to mobilize people.

Family. Special favors and inside information are often offered to family members, and the community may defer to members of well-known families.

History. Knowing a community's history, how it has approached similar issues, and where the skeletons are buried can be used to powerful advantage.

Status occupations. Occupations that draw prominence and deference give power to the individual or group of individuals currently holding that position.

Illegal actions. Illegal activity expands the scope of the game, giving power to those who go beyond the accepted limits or rules of play.

Personality. A personable or intimidating style can extend an individual's power by charging the atmosphere.

within and from its ability to attract other passionate participants. Don't forget that "you" can refer to your group or an institution such as a church, not just to you as an individual.

Common Bases of Power in a Community

There are a dozen bases of power common to most communities. The larger the community, the less likely control over a particular power base will be concentrated in a few hands. In these communities, power may be more fragmented and shifting as competition and the dynamic complexities of the community result in an ongoing ascendancy and descendancy of various individuals and groups. With so much going on at the same time, one particular individual's power in a particular sphere of community activity may be great, but relative to other individuals and other spheres, it may be much less overall. Although more and varied forces are at play keeping larger communities in motion, remember that all communities are in some state of change.

Some power relationships are based on perception and dependency. De Jouvenel (1958) described power as having three dimensions: It is extensive if the respondents are many; it is comprehensive if the actor can move the respondents to a variety of actions; and it is intensive if the actor's bidding can be pushed far without the loss of compliance (p. 160).

In your consideration of power bases, keep in mind that a person must be willing (or be perceived as willing) to use power for the power base to be meaningful. Bases provide the opportunity for power; they don't guarantee it. Let's look more closely at some of these bases of power.

1. *Information.* Possession of knowledge and the ability to control what other people know gives tremendous advantages. Information is the currency of tactical action. People who have a lot more information than others certainly have a clearer perception of what they need to do. In an information age, those who control the symbols of information and

the interpretation of those symbols are likely to be among the most influential (Luke, 1989). Power is rooted in perception, so this is a very strong base indeed.

Examples of people with this base of power include newspaper editors, talk show hosts, educators, gossips, gatekeepers (those who control the flow of information to decision makers), preachers, computer wizards, and political confidants.

2. *Money.* If it is not true that anything and anyone has a price, then it is darn close to being true. Money provides the single easiest access to other things. Those with a lot of money can buy much of what they want, or they can tie things up so that other people can't use them. Moneyed people can buy land or products, contribute to candidates or the United Way, hire attorneys or public relations consultants, and still have enough left over for a cup of coffee and a doughnut.

Most people want money. To get money, they have to go to the people who have it. This creates quite a dependency on those who have money or can provide access to it. (Recall that dependency is the other basic component of power relationships.) In a culture obsessed with money, it is worthwhile to acknowledge that people are fascinated by the rich as kind of cultural superstars. They defer to the affluent simply because of the status wealth confers.

Examples of people with this base of power include rich people, bankers, investment coordinators and deal makers, employers, and community foundations.

3. *Laws.* The ability to make, interpret, and enforce the policies governing a community confers a great measure of authority. Determining and applying the rules can determine who wins the game. Rule making within a community includes formal law, agency, or business regulation, as well as company policy. More often than not, laws are designed to maintain the prevailing orthodoxy rather than to challenge beliefs or redistribute power or other resources. To the extent that those in

power willingly participate in redistribution, it is often a stratagem to raise the stakes against more radical protest. The ability to exercise a degree of influence over who fills rule-making positions is a formidable function. Of course, those who influence the rule makers themselves have power. To a large extent, this is what community power is all about.

Examples of people with this base of power include key players in legislative bodies (mayors, city council members, county commissioners, state legislators, members of Congress), campaign strategists, workers, contributors, members of selection committees, chiefs of police, county sheriffs, attorneys, judges, members of regulatory bodies, lobbyists, and community executives (city manager, school principal, or chief executive officer of a company).

4. *Constituencies.* The ability to influence the lives or behavior of large groups of people provides significant power in a community. This also includes the power inherent in the ability through organization to mobilize a constituency of those with shared values and interests. This includes power over people in the group as well as power of the group. It may also refer to the power that occurs because the interests of many people in an identifiable group are involved. If the people in the group are dependent on someone for something (for example, a job or a degree), that individual has influence over those people. The power of the group is demonstrated when others are dependent on the approval of the group itself for something (for example, votes or purchases). Community members may act on behalf of the interests of a large group if there is a perception that harming the group's interests harms the community as a whole.

Examples of people and groups with this base of power include major employers, labor leaders, community organizations, business and professional associations, community activists, religious leaders, local political party leaders, and college presidents.

5. *Energy and natural resources.* This refers to the ability to control the use of or regulate access to energy produced by means such as natural gas, coal, nuclear sources, rivers, oil, and maybe someday the sun and wind. This may include the power company or the gas station (particularly if it is the only one in town). Control over specific natural resources such as land, water, timber, and the like are included in this category as well. The more concentrated the energy source or the more limited and locally valued the natural resource, the more powerful this base will be.

Examples of people with this base of power include utility company executives, environmental activists, real estate developers, members of resource regulatory bodies, gasoline distributors, farmers, and water users' associations.

6. *Goods and services.* The more important the product or service is to the local economy, the more noteworthy this base of power will be. Also, those dealing with high-priced yet common products (cars and houses) tend to be more powerful. Again, the more limited the access to the good or service, the more powerful those who control it are likely to be.

Examples of people with this base of power include department store owners and executives, new car dealers, grain elevator owners, construction company owners, hospital executives, mental health executives, cable television executives, and economic developers.

7. *Network participation.* The good ol' boy network does exist, and the good ol' girl network is emerging. Having a lot of connections in the community provides ready access to resources and the ability to mobilize select groups of people quickly. It plainly helps to know a lot of people. In addition, each member of a particular network participates in other networks. Through this process, a person's name, reputation, and influence can begin to grow. There is an assumption that if everybody knows so-and-so or hears the name pop up frequently, this must be an important person (or group). Networks include formal organizations such as the Chamber of Commerce as well as informal affiliations such as business associates. Members of certain groups with select admission criteria are often accorded more influence within the community. Their members may look out for one another a little more to affirm group identity.

Examples of people with this base of power include those who have taken part in numerous community activities, members of civic and service organizations (for example, Rotary, Lions, Soroptimist), active members of churches, synagogues, or mosques, members of agency or organization boards of directors, owners of businesses, members of country clubs and other private clubs, and members of local leadership groups (for example, 2010 Committee, Phoenix Forty).

8. *Family.* Blood usually does run thicker than water. Family members have a sort of "preferred customer" status with one another. Special favors, inside information, and similar advantages are offered to members of a family in ways they are not routinely offered to those outside the family. Family membership generally grants immediate access to relatives who play important roles in the community. Family members are part of a fundamental network. The longer standing, the larger, and the more influential a family is, the more opportunities it provides. This includes deference by others in the community to those who are simply members of important families as well as the relationships prominent families often develop among themselves.

Examples of those with this base of power include…how about members of influential families?

9. *History.* Knowing the traditions of a place, what has gone on before, and where the skeletons are buried can provide insightful advantage for understanding current philosophies and actions. Though history doesn't exactly repeat itself, certain trends do cycle. A clear understanding of a community's history can increase credibility. By directly or

indirectly relating proposed actions to past patterns, common spoken and unspoken beliefs and fears can be used to great advantage.

Examples of people with this base of power include media reporters, local historians, and long-time active community residents (especially school, religious, business, and political leaders).

10. *Status occupations*. Certain occupations draw prominence and deference. Some provide a kind of community celebrity that attracts interest and even fawning attention. More weight is attached to the words and actions of these people either because their occupation endows them with a degree of expertise or morality believed to be the province of a select few or because the recipient feels favored by the attention.

Examples of people with this base of power include rabbis, imams, bishops, physicians, head coaches, attorneys, and professional athletes.

11. *Illegal actions*. Some people just don't play by the rules, or perhaps they play by a different set of rules. The standard limits on action just don't apply to the game they are playing. If the consequences of resisting are acceptable to the resister, resistance is likely to continue. However, assessing the likely consequences usually involves a circumscribed set of possibilities based on assumptions of legitimate behavior. When those assumptions no longer apply, the consequences become difficult to determine or are unmanageable. Resistance begins to break down. The whole idea of overcoming resistance is to make the consequences for resisting less attractive than accepting the proposed action. Removing the limitations of legality or morality can provide an individual with a vast array of options to develop strategies and overcome resistance.

If someone says, "Do this, or we'll see you in court," you face a difficult but understandable dilemma for which you can prepare. However, if you are told, "Do this, or we'll have someone break your legs"—and you believe them—you have a different feeling about the situation entirely. Illegal activity provides an expanded game. The potential use of violence is just one form it may take. If one person is willing to use rational argument, whereas another is willing to use argument, bribery, and threats of violence, the latter simply has more weapons. Dealing with this situation is not always as easy as going to the police. Sometimes the illegal participants are the police.

Examples of people with this base of power include gang members, members of traditional organized crime families, drug dealers, neighborhood bullies, and back room deal makers.

12. *Personality*. Some people have developed a personal manner that attracts enthusiasm, support, and respect like a magnet. They project a sense of purpose and confidence in their own and others' ability to accomplish goals. They spark in others a belief that problems can and will be addressed. Others have developed an intimidating presence. They act like they should be taken seriously and use confrontational techniques to discourage opposition. Still others are just so likable and persistent that it is hard to say no to them.

Regardless of the particular approach used, individuals with this base accomplish what they want through dint of their personality and a single-minded belief in what they are doing. They have an air of assurance and are not intimidated by others. The best of these can use a variety of styles and match them to the situation. They have made getting their own way into a kind of performance art.

Though this base of power is different from the preceding ones in that the only resource is one's self, it is nonetheless an important one. Ultimately, the atmosphere created determines success, and personality can be an instrumental force in establishing the right atmosphere.

Common Bases of Power in a Group

Much of the real action of community change occurs within small groups. It is here that most of the work and most of the decisions take place. The basic aspects of power—perception of dependency within relationships—certainly apply to small groups, especially since it is the relationship among members that is the essence of a group. Johnson and Johnson (2009, pp. 232–235) discuss six useful categories of power within groups.

Reward power occurs when an individual responds to the behavior of other group members by dispensing valued positive consequences or by removing negative ones. This results in group members wanting to gain this person's favor and strengthen the relationship between them.

Coercive power is just the reverse. This exists when an individual can respond by punishing other members. Members feel forced to go along to avoid discomfort.

Legitimate power is based on the group's belief that the individual has influence over them due to that member's position. For example, the treasurer may have some authority over dispensing group funds, or the chairperson may manage group discussion.

Referent power is established when others want to identify with or be like a particular individual—or even want to be liked by that person. Sometimes group members comply out of respect; sometimes they do so to seek approval from a popular person. Remember how people sought the approval of the most popular person in high school? That is one example of referent power.

Expert power flows from those who have unique knowledge or abilities that are honestly offered to the group for its benefit. However, if people begin to feel inadequate around such an individual, her power can diminish.

Informational power is similar to expert power. In this case, the group is influenced by the individual's particular access to information and his ability to think and communicate clearly.

These bases of power address the dynamics of what is occurring within a group and how its members relate not only to one another but also as members of a group. They also apply to how the members relate to the objectives of the group. Further, how you look at things and the attitude you convey also affects how people respond. Not only does an appreciative mind-set increase influence, but having a positive attitude gives people more informal influence within organizations than more common sources such as control over resources or information (Baker, Cross, & Wooten, 2003; Bushe, 2007).

Determining Who Holds Power

Power fluctuates within a community as new actors and new issues present themselves for consideration. This occurs even in fairly small communities, such as a hospital or a school. New problems, new opportunities, and new personnel create shifts in power. Domhoff (2008) identified four indicators of power: who benefits from having things that are valued; who governs; who wins when there are arguments over issues; and who has a reputation for power.

A good way to determine who has power is by talking to people, especially the more active members of your interest community. Ask these people who influences them. Who do they respond to and why? Then ask them who their most difficult opponents and most effective (not just nice, but effective) supporters are. Get some idea of what makes someone difficult or effective. Next, get a picture of whom they see influencing other people and how this influence occurs. Finally, ask whom they think others would say are powerful and why, and then find out who would be on their list and why. This process will lead to many an interesting conversation, a number of good insights on community power, and a beginning assessment of the power present in your arena of action.

GLOBAL PERSPECTIVES

ETHIOPIA—When the spider webs unite, they can tie up a lion. (Ethiopian proverb)

SRI LANKA—Using life-centered power is not the same as power sharing. The concept of sharing power is a familiar one. However, we do not always recognize the reality that power sharing also contains elements of arrogance and dominance. Who is it that decides how the "cake" of power is to be cut and how it is to be shared? Or when it is to be cut or not cut? Inequalities can be incorporated into power sharing. But when we are able to experience power with each other, we become interdependent and the transformation of one leads to the transformation of all. Similarly, the oppression of one leads to the oppression of all. In experiencing power *with each other* we are interconnected. We are drawn to work together while respecting each one's identity and affirming our mutual need for each other.... Life-centered power is the pivot for instituting life-giving change. It becomes the catalyst for the kind of change that makes transformation of the personal, the organizational, the communal and the global achievable (Ranjini Wickramaratne-Rebera, 1998).

ASIA—I appeal to you—do not do anything, even with the best of intentions that will destroy the little power and strength we possess. If you want to empower the poor, please first trust the poor. Have confidence in the people's knowledge and wisdom. The people can teach you—and not the other way round. Do not come to teach the poor and impose your values and strategies because of a false notion that the poor are ignorant, lethargic and need to be shaken up (Karunawathie Menike, as cited in Liamzon, 1997, p. 3).

TAIWAN—[W]omen in Taiwan have not passively accepted their position, but rather, they have tried with their limited resources to resist their subordination.... Women chairs [of community development associations] have sought to change traditional relationships in the community through competing for leadership positions which take them out of the domestic realm. These women's efforts can convince residents that women should get actively involved in community politics when they want to carry out their ideas....

The female chairs have also challenged the definition of mothering as constructed by the government in its Community Development Project.... They have actively claimed what is necessary for a definition of good mothering, and have redefined it through their own actions (Yen-Yi Huang, 2001, pp. 369–371).

ITALY—Empowerment is a word that conjures varying connotations, reactions and images. On one hand, examples come to mind of massive demonstrations of people power in the streets clamouring for change. On the other hand, there is widespread outgrowth of awakening of individuals actively taking decisions and actions, taking responsibilities and control over their lives, moving from resignation and subservience to active involvement....

People's organizations [POs] or grassroots organizations define empowerment with a sharp political focus. Empowerment for POs often means social transformation, changing structures that are barriers to change. Even when people's organizations work for economic empowerment, they seek to transform, rather than merely accept, the structures and systems which act as barriers to their obtaining economic and political power (Christina Liamzon, 1997, pp. 3–4).

Recall the value of lists. Get lists of every group, organization, or event that involves community power. See whose names appear frequently and where. If you can, note who seems to associate with whom or how tentacles of power reach out into the community and come together again (Male, 1993). Obviously, you can put a lot of time into this, but once you have a base of information, you will pick up lists as a matter of habit. Be sure to review them to keep up to date. While you are gathering lists, make up a few of your own with your perception

of who is well stationed in the various power bases in your community.

Remember that local newspapers and magazines commonly prepare community power analyses and feature stories on prominent community leaders as well as rising stars. Special reports on sectors of the community (for example, a review of major employers) can come in handy. Keep on the lookout for these.

Those with power are often more comfortable directing the action from behind the scenes than being on center stage. Watch what is going on in your community in general, and with regard to your issue in particular. Is more attention than normal being given to a particular area of town, a particular industry, a particular ethnic group, or a particular issue? Why? Has the normally outspoken critic of this or that grown uncharacteristically quiet? Is there a new road being built to a vacant piece of land? Hmmm…

Pay attention to where and how limited resources are allocated. Which schools get additional space? Which programs get expanded? Notice how undesirable issues are handled. Whose budget gets cut? Where does the hazardous waste get dumped?

Look also to see who responds to whom. Who is asking the questions? To whom do people turn for answers? Who seems to take direction; who seems to give it? Who asks permission? Who provides it? Who can call people to a meeting for tomorrow at 10:00 a.m. and be sure that everyone will show up?

Finally, analyze all this good information. What tentative conclusions can you reach about who is benefiting by plans, decisions, and actions? Who is losing? Who is gaining? Who is paying? People may tell you that they are afraid to do things "because of the risks involved." What is seen as a risk? Who controls the negative consequences if things don't work out? What are they? Asking questions such as these will help you determine who controls the limits of the action and who establishes new boundaries. By gathering information, keeping your eyes and ears open, and calculating who seems to be getting their way and under what circumstances, you will have a good gauge for which actors hold the power in your community.

Powerful Elites

While there may well be a somewhat cohesive set of powerful elites in any community and in the nation itself, this is not a machine that works with perfect efficiency. Not only are there cracks, conflict, and inattention within these elites, others in the community or nation have some measure of power as well. This power, however, may well be fragmented. These various centers of fragmented power may have influence at certain times and within certain spheres, but by themselves they do not measure up to the power that elite groups have. Infighting among those with less power reduces their field of influence and helps to preserve the status quo. Should these groups find a way to coalesce their power, matters would be different. As Domhoff (2008) said, "figuring out how these disparate oppositional forces might become united enough to take advantage of the divisions within the power elite would be a worthy challenge" (p. 26).

As we begin to discover the process of power building, we continue to move forward, even if piece by piece, interest group by interest group, neighborhood by neighborhood, and neighborhoods with neighborhoods. By finding our common interest and acting with common purpose, we shift the expression of power in the community.

Understanding the Power–Issue Relationship

Your base of power must be larger than this issue you are working on. A base smaller than the issue is a formula for failure. Yet this is a common construction for most organizations, especially when they are starting out. Essentially there are two responses to remedy this situation (Figure 6.2).

The first step is to partialize the issue. This approach involves separating the goal into distinct aspects and pursuing each aspect, one at a time. (This can also refer to separating a community into component subgroups and organizing one group at a time.) Frequently this is done by breaking the goal down into its sequential steps. You then concentrate on phases of the change, taking the less risky or controversial ones first. For example, you may not be able to make all the changes you want in the operation of the local Food Stamp office. Problems exist in the way the program is operated, the hours of operation don't meet the needs of the community, the application form is too long, and the staff is rude to the clients. By partializing the change episode, you may first concentrate on implementing a series of in-service training workshops designed to sensitize the staff to the needs and anxieties of the clients. From this

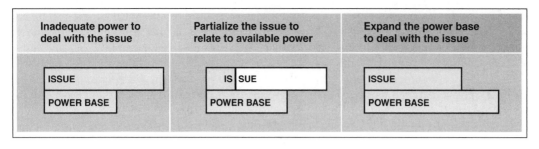

Inadequate power to deal with the issue	Partialize the issue to relate to available power	Expand the power base to deal with the issue
ISSUE	IS|SUE	ISSUE
POWER BASE	POWER BASE	POWER BASE

FIGURE 6.2   Relationship Between Your Issue and Power

may come a greater awareness of the validity of other concerns, and the staff may become allies for agency change rather than opponents of it.

Partializing helps you set the stage for future efforts. It provides your organization with the motivation of a victory while giving you a stepping-stone to additional challenges. The danger is that you may settle for this initial victory and never move on to more meaningful changes. Bear in mind that the target might grant you a small gain as a type of concession to buy you off or distract you from more sweeping changes. It is necessary to keep the goal you have partialized in clear perspective.

The second procedure is to expand your base of power. Generally you do this by acting on a more limited aspect of the overall goal—the partialized portion. You act not only to accomplish that immediate goal but to intentionally draw in additional resources (greater numbers, community attention, money, expertise, and so on) as you are acting. As your base of power grows, you are able to take on greater and greater parts of the issue, and then you can move further to deal with other issues. With more successes, more power, including strengthened alliances with like-minded groups, you can "move these victories to a larger scale" (Mirazo, Hicks, Taylor, & Ferlazzo, 2001, p. 41).

ASSESSING AND BUILDING YOUR OWN BASES OF POWER

Never forget that the moment you believe you are powerless, you are indeed powerless. Action itself implies the use of power. How will you respond to the opportunities before you? Maybe you don't have all the power you need. But you want to accomplish something, and you recognize that you do have some tools to start with. What could they be? Let's take a look.

One thing you probably have is a good perspective on the problem situation. You know that people are unhappy or hurting and that the condition is unacceptable. A certain power comes from being on the right side of an issue. It may not be enough by itself to win, but it can get you and others going, help sustain you through the tough times, and put your opponents on the defensive. Knowing all you can about a problem, its harmful consequences, and the moral issues involved can be real assets.

Review the bases of power within your community. Which of these are available to you at least to some degree? Do you have any expertise or information not commonly held in your community? Can you speak with professional authority or on the basis of a sound grasp of the particular subject with which you are dealing? Do you hold any position of authority or leadership? Here is a tough one: Does anybody like or respect you?

Take a look at the resources at your disposal. Can you mobilize a constituency, or at least begin to? Can you talk to a community group to help shape their thinking, or can you get a favorable story on the 6 o'clock news? Does anyone from whom you need a response depend on you for anything, or perhaps depend on you not to do something? Can you deliver votes? Are laws or regulations in place that can serve your interests? Can you embarrass any important person or group? See Kahn (1970, 1994) and Amidei (1987) for more on these topics.

One of the fundamental resources at your disposal is cooperation or compliance. To go along or to "do what you are told" involves a series of actions you can take or withhold. The possibility of many people acting together in organized noncompliance offers a potentially potent advantage (Sharp, 1973b).

You probably have some claim on at least one base of community power if not more. Take a good look at the possible power capital you possess. Be sure to include your own personal assets. You probably routinely overlook or undervalue a few of the things you have going for you. Now look at those who are or will be working with you as you build an organized effort to promote change in your community. What emerges when each person takes stock of her own power inventory? This evaluation should provide you with a more encouraging picture of the means you and your group can use to assert your interests.

Establishing your own ability to influence the flow of events involves three basic strategies: making use of existing power, building power through organization, and developing personal power.

Making Use of Existing Power

The purpose of this strategy is to provide you with well-positioned allies. Two avenues are available for using existing power. First, you can purposefully recruit powerful community members who may be willing to support your aims. (I will refer to those individuals who hold power as influential community members, or ICMs.) Second, you can form alliances with existing power blocs, particularly organizations sympathetic to your cause or those that share a common enemy with you.

The first step in involving those who already have power in the community is to take stock of the connections you and your supporters have. Next, get in touch with those ICMs whose help you think you will need. Obviously, this is easier if a relationship already exists. You may need to spend some time reaffirming your relationship, even while you are asking for assistance. Don't hesitate to approach ICMs you don't know if you believe they may be interested in your cause. Working together could be the start of a valuable relationship.

When recruiting the support of ICMs, invite them to understand your problems. Once they have a good grasp of the situation, ask them how—not if—they would be able to help out. Be prepared to ask for a specific type of involvement. Generally, ICMs can serve your effort in one of three ways:

⏏ Take a Moment to Discover ⏏

When you are faced with a situation that really bothers you, one you would like to change, what are some of the first things that go through your mind? How do these thoughts lead you toward or away from purposeful action? How do they help or hinder your effectiveness?

---

1. Influential community members can serve as window dressing to provide a certain credibility to your endeavor by signing a letter supporting your position, appearing with you in public, or allowing their names to appear on your letterhead. In this case, ICMs do little more than lend their names and stature to your cause.

2. ICMs may go to bat for you on specific problems, using their personal relationships or their position in the community to intervene on your behalf. This may provide immediate benefit while helping you to be taken more seriously in the future.

3. You may recruit ICMs as ongoing participants in your work. You benefit from their direct involvement and get plugged into the current of community power.

While considering which powerful individuals to call on for support, also see which groups or organizations can lend you some of their strength. You may be overmatched as a single neighborhood contending with an insensitive city hall, but if the powerful neighborhood coalition from across town endorses your operation, the scope of the conflict becomes much different. Look to groups outside your immediate conflict, especially those who will regard your struggle as a reflection of their own. Figure out which organizations have issues, interests, or people similar to yours. Are any of your members also members of one of these groups? Forming alliances with other organizations is an important, ongoing component of the development of power. Supporting organizations can provide you with the same type of help you can get from individuals, although because of policies and internal issues they usually cannot respond as quickly.

Whether your added support comes from powerful individuals or organizations, receiving the backing of those who already have power can get you right into the game. A caution should be sounded, however. Using the power of ICMs and other organizations may not help you build your organization. The more you rely on them for success, the less you rely on yourselves.

Building Power through Organization

The most significant and enduring strategy for effective community change is to create a base of power for yourselves. By mobilizing the interest, action, and power of others, you can develop an organized constituency, an authentic base of power. Organizing is a fundamental approach open to any community change agent.

When individuals concentrate their power by acting together in planned, purposeful ways, much can be achieved. Chapter 11 contains a detailed examination of the process of developing an organization.

In most situations you will quickly confront the limitations of your own power and the limits of your own time and energy. You simply need other people, and they need you. This is not only a matter of effectiveness but also one of ethics. It is unlikely that you alone have such a command of the issues that you can speak for all concerned. It is hard to know what really is best for everyone. People are not commonly so anointed, though some may act like it. If you are doing all the talking and all the work, you leave no room for anyone else. You deny them the prerogative and responsibility to act on their own behalf. Frankly, what gives you the right?

DEVELOPING PERSONAL POWER IN THE BROAD COMMUNITY

Each person in your action community has the potential for increasing his power. Personal power flows from three sources of credibility:

Credibility as a person: Do you do what you say you are going to do? Can people rely on

CHANGE AGENT TIP

Give each member of your action group an index card. Ask each person to list the three most powerful members of the community they would be willing to ask for a favor. Though few of the names you get may be among the very most powerful, you will begin to discover your organization's access to higher levels of community clout. These connections will help you establish a bank of power from which you may draw, and it may also provide you with names of potential new members of your action group.

you? Do you make excuses? Do you take control of your actions? Can you be trusted?

Credibility of your information: Is your information accurate? Is it timely? Does it consider a different point of view? Is it comprehensive, or is something left out, perhaps purposefully?

Credibility of your power base: Will others actively support you? Do you have any resources to withhold or deliver?

Increasing your power requires strengthening these various sources. How do you do this? Let's look at these issues in reverse order.

Putting Yourself in the Power Loop

Extensive personal networks are a form of social capital (see Chapter 2). Good change agents intentionally and regularly add to their network of connections. Building your own personal network gives you a variety of contacts in the community and access to a broader range of community power and resources. The simple fact that a lot of people know you builds your reputation and credibility.

Insinuating yourself into powerful circles involves placing yourself in position to be known and positively regarded by people with community influence so that you may affect community decisions and use the new relationships you develop to assist your continued efforts to improve the community. You do this by building your credibility in a situation in which people with power relate to you as a person who is capable and at least equal to others they value in a situation that they take seriously. Now I don't want to give the impression that you can waltz in and become fully accepted in any group, nor that there aren't some very exclusive

groups that may never include you as a member. Still, you can be integrated into some pretty vital groups without too much difficulty.

It can be a little flattering to be given attention and welcome by those who have power and prominence. In some subtle ways you may be asked or you may choose to relax your beliefs or sense of purpose in order to keep in good favor. Softening your commitment to social justice and to those in the community who are commonly left outside the circles of community power is not worth the exchange. Know that keeping your identity and allegiance can be a challenge, one that met well will enhance your standing, not reduce it.

Where do you start? You may have more opportunities than you think. Influential community members gather in a variety of groups to work on community issues. Certainly these gatherings serve other purposes for ICMs, such as relationship building and exchanging gossip. They can serve the same purposes for you too. The community issue focus, however, provides working contact with people who possess more power in the community than you do. Keep in mind that if you act like you belong, people will tend to treat you that way. Here are some groups that can be found in most communities:

• *Local agency boards of directors* generally include a number of ICMs. Because you are not joining a board just to meet people, focus on those agencies whose mission reflects your own interests. From the work you have done so far, you may have established contacts in the community or in the agency itself who can recommend you as a candidate for the board. If so, you have already started the process of becoming included in community decision making. If you don't know someone who could "sponsor" you, contact the agency director, board chair, or head of the board's nominating committee and let them know of your interest. Spots on agency boards come up routinely, and you stand a decent chance of being selected if you show a genuine interest and can communicate what you can offer to the organization.

- *Community action, problem-solving,* or *issue groups* often attract community leaders and provide opportunities for "unknowns" to shine. The major requirements are to show up, start talking, and start working.

- *Political campaigns* are always looking for responsible workers. With your willingness to take on tasks and your competence in performing them well, you will find a steady increase in responsibility and recognition. The more campaigns you work, the more campaign expertise you will develop, and the more your assistance and input will be sought. The relationship you develop with the candidate can be beneficial when she takes office. Working closely with the candidate's staff, advisers, and active supporters is also helpful, as they themselves may be or may become important community figures.

- *Public boards and commissions* can provide you with a position of influence. Some state and local governments are fairly littered with such bodies; a number of them even do important work. The clerk of each governmental jurisdiction (for example, state, county, city, or town) should be able to provide you with a list of the various boards and commissions and their vacancies, along with information on the appointment process.

Other possibilities include groups that plan and coordinate special events such as an annual parade or fair, various task forces on topics of immediate community interest, and United Way committees. Don't be shy about inviting yourself into something that attracts your interest and the interest of other key members of the community.

Because much of the work in these situations takes place in face-to-face group activity, you have a good chance to make a favorable impression. This is especially true when working in newly formed groups where leadership vacuums exist and rela-

tionship boundaries haven't yet been established. Prepare yourself to perform capably, speak up, and take the time to get to know people. You will soon find that you will have accomplished something important simply by demystifying your perception of people who hold power. Those with measurable clout are not markedly different from anyone else. Some are friendly, some obnoxious; some are dynamic, some dull; some are easily open to new relationships, and some are reticent.

You are not alone when you walk into a room to address community affairs. You bring along a measure of power through your affiliation with an organization that can act powerfully to assert its interests. Your network of other relationships and your reputation come along as well. Whether it is how you introduce yourself, references you make, or in some other low key manner, you will make known your tie to your organization. Recognizing your assets will help you act with confidence, which further extends your influence.

Unknown commodities are a little suspect. You are, too, if you are an unknown, so get known. You don't need to be accompanied by a brass band. If you are noticeably competent and even likable, you will be recognized, and you will find yourself included in more discussions of greater importance.

Using Information

Having solid information will assure you of a measure of credibility. People give more weight to the words of someone who knows what she is talking about. Don't you? Doing your homework involves not only collecting pertinent information but also organizing it in a way that speaks to what is on the mind of your listener. Of course, this means you had better get a good idea of what actually is on that listener's mind.

Know your topic well enough that you can cite a few specific references or note specific facts. Then check to see what is missing. See if you are uncomfortable discussing any particular aspect. This might indicate that you don't really know something you think you should know. Or look at your argument from the opposite point of view. Can you identify where it is vulnerable, where you cannot really use data to justify what you believe to be true? Once you have done this honestly, you will have a good grasp of the subject and be able to communicate it clearly.

You can undermine your credibility by misrepresenting the particulars of the matter. If certain details don't support your position, you are better off acknowledging them and comparing them against the prevailing strength of the information that does support your claims.

Having a good feel for your topic and for the situation in which you are discussing it will give you confidence. You will also give confidence to those who need to determine a course of action by supplying them with a good foundation of information on which they can support a decision. When people depend on you because of the reliability of your information, you have a lot of influence.

Inspiring Confidence

Act powerfully. How you set the stage for action and how you act can influence the immediate progress of events. It is far better to be the driver than to be taken for a ride. Quite a few books have been written on the subject of building personal power. Some promote the use of intimidation; others stress cooperation. Regardless of the strategy you choose, certain fundamentals should be observed to use and maintain your personal power. These apply particularly to situations in which your organization's efforts are being resisted.

Act on purpose. Be in charge of your own behavior. Make sure your actions relate directly to the effect you want to produce. If you do not have an intentional outcome for what you are doing, you will probably end up responding to someone or something else.

Act unapologetically. You believe you have a right to your position and that you deserve the benefits you seek. Communicate this. If you aren't convinced of the legitimacy of your interests, why should anyone else be? If you are convinced of this, why would you communicate that you aren't?

Set the agenda. You determine what will and will not be discussed as issues. Don't get sidetracked; stick to the essential points. If other items are brought up, acknowledge them.

If these are genuinely important to the other party, you will need to attend to them in the course of your efforts to reach a productive resolution. However, don't allow these other matters to substitute for your concerns.

Don't impose arbitrary limits on your own behavior. Your choice of actions should be measured against ethics and effectiveness. Ask yourself if you are keeping your possibilities for action open and creative. Be willing to be outrageous and unpredictable. You have enough rules to live by. Don't waste your time making up new ones.

Don't get locked into one pattern of behavior. Be willing to change your approach while holding firm to your goal. You limit your effectiveness by becoming too predictable.

Consider your short- and long-term gains and losses. The way you handle the situation today will have consequences for tomorrow. Remain attentive, and be honest about what you are doing. You can easily rationalize compliant behavior, thinking you are making things easier to handle at some indiscernible point in the future, when you really just want to avoid a fight. Of course, the reverse could also be true. You may just want to fight now and ignore the consequences. There is no simple answer here. Consider how you can produce an immediate gain in such a way that long-term gains become more likely.

Be on the lookout for areas of agreement. If the emphasis is on disagreement, that will be the only result. The whole point is to forge an agreement, one that serves your interests. Be aware of common interpretations, beliefs, and values. Observe when the other party is willing to move in a direction acceptable to you. Though the agreement may not be so much a formal declaration as a change in behavior, you had better be able to detect signs that can guide you to a satisfactory outcome.

Acknowledge others' need for influence. Each person needs to feel some measure of influence in a relationship. Know that this exists. If you do not intend to allow an opponent any influence, realize that this will increase resistance. Providing room for another party's influence in a way that does not detract from your interests increases the chances for a satisfactory conclusion.

Hold' em accountable. Whenever you reach an agreement in word with another party, make sure you have a way to see if it is being honored in deed. Then pay attention to see that it continues to be. If you allow the other party to ignore an agreement, it doesn't really exist, and you send the message that you are not serious about the agreements you reach. Don't accept excuses for breaches that could have been controlled.

Remember that all behavior is purposeful. What is the other party telling you by its response? How do you use this information? How are you responding? How do you use this information?

Ask forgiveness, not permission. How often have you seen people give up their own authority to act by first asking for someone else's approval? You may have done this yourself. Don't lightly give away your authority to act. If you determine that something needs to be done, do it, understanding that there may be some consequences you will have to deal with later. Frankly, most of the time this involves an apology for not consenting to someone else's control.

Don't make excuses. Accept responsibility. Blaming others is not only irritating but communicates that others determine your fate, not you.

USING YOUR POWER

Does pursuing your interests faithfully mean that you have to stop being friendly? Of course not. You can be friendly while firmly holding people to their agreements. You can be thoughtful of others while not being dissuaded from what your

---

▶ Take a Moment to Discover ◀

Think back on a time when someone was able to silence you, someone who acted like you did not have the right to raise an issue or voice disagreement. How did this happen? How did you feel about your response? How could you now handle a situation like this differently?

---

organization needs to accomplish. Acting powerfully does not imply that you become a less pleasant person, just a more intentional one.

Every change effort involves a "statement about why particular people at a particular time may be ready to challenge power, how they can, and why they should" (Cox, 1987b, p. 241). When you use power, you are respecting your rights and the legitimate rights of others. Many of the opponents you will encounter want to maintain policies and continue behaviors demeaning to whole classes of citizens. They do not have a right to do this. Although you must acknowledge their interests, you need not accept them as legitimate. It is too bad that change may be painful for those who have grown used to having things their way at the expense of others. However, it is not your responsibility to ease their discomfort by pursuing your goals with a diminished sense of purpose. You are not called upon to protect the illegitimate interests of others, no matter how entrenched or long-held they are. The interests of those who struggle with you deserve far more respect.

When you battle *powerful ignorance*, you are likely to meet resistance from those who want to hold onto their practiced ways of understanding things or from those who do not have enough concern to listen to what you have to say. This can be frustrating. It is almost like you are trying to get people who are standing still to start moving, and moving in the right direction. When you take on *powerful interests*, your struggle is more difficult. In this case, you are trying to turn or move past people who are pushing you backward.

Whenever your pursuits challenge the advantages of powerful others and the routines that support those advantages, your own legitimacy to act will be criticized. Whether parents or teachers or bosses or mayors, people with power often believe they have a right to do exactly what they are doing. When you come along to challenge this notion, you are almost automatically seen as acting improperly. A common tactic is to attack your very right to question (Staples, 2004).

Somewhere along the line someone may well call you naive or misguided or even pigheaded. Maybe you will be called troublemaker or rebel or even radical. Some of you are not used to being treated this way and may find these charges upsetting. That is understandable. Those of you who intend to make a career out of promoting change will get used to this. As long as your picture of yourself comes from you and from the people working alongside you, this won't be much of a problem. If, however, your perception of yourself and your organization's legitimacy comes from those you are confronting, you may begin second-guessing yourself.

In fact, the community at large may assume that those who traditionally control the directions of the community simply have the right to do so (Rubin & Rubin, 2008). Challenging this notion not only requires effective organization but ultimately a change in community attitudes regarding who has the right to hold power. In a community conflict, you often need to promote your group's right to challenge accepted practice. You may have to inoculate the community (and your supporters as well) against the tactic of discrediting your efforts by predicting that it will occur and by clearly articulating your message.

When you use your power to get a response from those who do not share your goals, information, or values, you are likely to meet some opposition. This is a predictable part of the process, one you must address with a clear sense of purpose and a secure belief in the validity of your interests. Your use of personal power to influence elements in a situation should be directed toward advancing the interests of your group. Effective use of personal power aids in developing the power of your organization.

EMPOWERING OTHERS

A fundamental task in promoting community change is fostering conditions and beliefs that help develop the power of others. The success of your

effort requires it. More than anything else, your limits are defined by a lack of power. The more people your organization has who are capable of acting powerfully, the more you are able to erase limitations. An organized effort with many people acting powerfully and confidently in concert is far more effective than one with a strong leader and a lot of hopeful followers.

Empowerment involves overcoming sets of beliefs, oppressive structures, and stifling routines that keep people and their concerns isolated from one another (Friere, 1973; Gutiérrez, 1995). This includes challenging norms governing worker–client relationships that ignore political issues, keeping these outside the helping process. Some agencies are hesitant to invite clients into the political process. Some question whether it is ethical to do so. Is it ethical not to? Wenocur (1992) argued that an emphasis on helping ordinary people gain sufficient knowledge and skill to make systems respond to their needs is the highest priority in fields such as social work as it is essentially related to the fundamental value of self-determination.

If a mother with whom you were working did not have enough food to feed her family, would you do anything? If this same mother did not have enough power to challenge legislative budget decisions that affected her family, maybe crucial programs such as child care support, would you do anything? Recognizing interests held in common with others in similar circumstances and the ability to connect with one another in purposeful action builds a foundation for strength (Crowfoot, Chesler, & Boulet, 1983; Parsons, 1989). Intentionally promoting the development of knowledge and skills through reflective action builds on that foundation (Gutiérrez, Parsons, & Cox, 1998). Erwin (2008) has put it very well, "This kind of empowerment is not the paternalistic giving of power, but rather an unveiling of the power that is there" (p. 1571).

"Oh, great," you're thinking, "I not only have to become more powerful myself, but now I have to worry about how to make everybody else more powerful too. How the heck am I supposed to do that?" Well, rest easy. It is not your job to make everybody powerful; you probably couldn't even if you tried. It is your job to encourage the process. It begins with

Economic constraints have led to reductions in
many state and local budgets. It is often programs
assisting the most vulnerable that are among the
first to feel the budget axe. Gutiérrez and Lewis
(1994) have emphasized the importance of helping
people make the "connection between personal
problems and political issues" (p. 31). What do you
think about helping your clients to become
involved in the political process? Do you think you
should advocate on behalf of the people you
serve? Do you think you should purposefully assist
them to advocate for themselves?

the idea that people will work together to overcome
obstacles, and it is first expressed in the way you work
with others. Empowerment also means overcoming
relationships where the provider of help holds the
power and the receiver of the help does not. We
need to examine the nature of our relationships
with those with whom we partner to promote
change. Rose (2000) challenged us "to create relationships in which meaning (is) being produced not
received, where participants (are) equally valid contributors to defining and shaping the process, product,
and purpose of their interaction" (p. 411). This does
not require a lot of effort, and it will save you some.

Empowering others requires that you look for
guidance to some of the basic notions of power.
Recall that power involves possessing resources,
influencing others, and determining direction.
Many opportunities exist for those involved in
your effort to discover and use resources they
have and to develop new ones. Members can influence one another as well as those outside the organization. Each member will determine what steps
he will take to further the cause, and each will have
occasion to shape the direction of the overall effort.
All these opportunities exist. You just have to recognize them and take advantage of them while promoting the notion that others do the same. The
catch is that you have to value these opportunities
to even see them in the first place.

You reverse the process of empowerment when
you deny opportunities to other participants or when
you accept or even encourage them to give opportunities away. Don't kid yourself, this will happen. As

soon as you get in the habit of thinking "I can do it
better myself," you are closing off chances for others
to do as well as you, or to learn to do as well. (By the
way, just because things are done differently from the
way you would do them does not mean they aren't
done as well.) And, yes, people do routinely give
away the power they have. How many times have
you heard "Oh, I'm not really good at anything" or
"I don't know; it's up to you"?

Once people begin to believe in their own
power, they value and make more available their
contributions. The result is a richer and stronger
organization. Clearly, you alone are not responsible
for increasing the power of other participants,
although the greater the role you play in the change
effort, the more attention you need to give this
concern. Let's look at a number of simple steps
that can help you create and take advantage of
openings for others to step forward:

- *Ask questions and ask for input.* By seeking
  information you don't have and by valuing
  another's ideas, you reinforce something very
  fundamental. You counteract a common
  powerful fear people have of being thought of
  as stupid, as somehow less. You can always
  acknowledge what someone says, if only by
  restating the comment to demonstrate that you
  have clearly heard it. Accepting every part of
  every viewpoint is phony, though you can
  generally find something of value in a response.
  Learn to disagree without putting down an
  idea or the person who offered it. Recognize
  good ideas and their originator, and allow other
  people to have better ideas than yours.

- *Reroute questions.* Feel free to pass on questions
  asked of you to other people. An occasional,
  "I don't know, what do you think, Hank?" can
  draw in more people.

- *Promote access to decision making.* Decisions reflect
  the will of those who have power. If decisions
  rest on the ideas of a few, only a few will be
  powerful. If they rest on the input of many,
  many will be powerful (Brown, 1991).

- *Give recognition and credit whenever you can.* A
  simple "Good idea, Gladys" or "Thanks for
  helping out at the meeting yesterday, Zach" can

be valuable. Commenting on contributions in the presence of others provides a nice acknowledgment. Formal recognition, such as including names in a newsletter story, awarding certificates, and even humorous awards, can be useful too. Let people take credit for the work they have done, but don't tolerate members fighting over credit. If this occurs, it can be devastating. Such squabbling is usually a symptom of too little credit being given out, not too much.

- *Rarely accept statements of inability.* "I can't" or "I don't know" will probably be declared more often than you care to hear. Don't buy it, at least not easily. Be willing to ask questions like "If you can't do this, what can you do instead?" or "Can you think of just one thing?" When you stop believing in people's *in*abilities, you will learn a number of techniques to encourage their abilities.

- *Promote the distribution of responsibility and authority.* There is plenty to do in a change effort. Help spread the tasks around. Ask for help yourself. If someone takes on a project, let that person handle it without you hovering, and certainly don't redo it all after they think they are done. Although coordination of effort is important, there are many things people can be in charge of, especially if they have a clear understanding of expectations and a chance to shape them.

- *Develop a strong group or organizational identity.* People draw strength from feeling that they are part of something. Their affiliation with others in something that is named and recognized is affirming and enlarges their sense of self.

- *Promote the acceptance of mistakes and acknowledge your own.* Few things are as debilitating as the fear of making a mistake that is going to be made into a big deal. People learn from their mistakes. Sometimes they learn not to try again. They can also learn how to improve by building on what they have done. Look first to compliment, and question the need to criticize. Include yourself in this too. Acknowledge and learn from your own mistakes without making a big deal about them.

- *Encourage the development and awareness of resources.* Recalling the relationship of resource use to power, your group needs to do more than increase members' sense of their own personal competence as they shape the nature and direction of the change effort. The organization must cultivate resources that may be used to increase its power. As part owners of these resources, members of the organization experience an expansion of power.

- *Promote the relevance of actions.* Actions members are expected to take in the name of the organization, especially those that challenge authority, must fit their picture of how the world works. It must make sense to them (Cox, 1987b).

- *Promote the recognition of success.* Your organization will win victories, some minor, some major. Pay attention to them. Empowerment occurs through success and the confirmation of effectiveness success implies. This is true for the successes individuals achieve on their own as well as for those they achieve as members of a group. Just by pulling together you are all going to feel and be more powerful. Yet you will have done even more if the process you use in bringing people together helps them discover and believe in their own personal potency. The most powerful organizations are made up of powerful people. When people feel empowered, they see themselves differently, as more capable, more responsible, and more willing to shape forces rather than be shaped by them. This has consequences far beyond the immediate events.

CONCLUSION

Every relationship embraces power. It is the very root of all our relationships. Every relationship involves people responding to one another. With no response there is no relating, no relationship. Relationships, between lovers, between students and teachers, between competing interests in the community, are all marked by the interchange of expectation and reply. To be in a relationship is to influence and to be influenced.

Power affects everything we do: it is not only useful; it is essential. Power can be used to enhance the parties in a relationship or to exploit them. If one or more of the parties are dissatisfied with what they are receiving from the relationship, they must use their power to change things for the better. But they can only do this if they believe they have the ability and the right to do so.

If you are going to promote change, you need power. If you are going to be powerful, you need to decide whether you are going to be purposefully powerful or accidentally powerful. If you are going to use power, you must do so knowing that others may not like it. If you intend to be successful, not merely self-important, you will cultivate the power of your partners. Both power and impotence impose choices and consequences. When you make the choice to act with power, you help set the direction. No longer will you just be told where to go.

HIDDEN TREASURES

Lots of big plans. Not too many people to make them happen yet. It doesn't take much looking around to see that lots of things could be better. You cross the street so you don't have to encounter the group of young men with sullen looks who only seem to come to life when they see someone to taunt. Glad that it's only a short distance to Millie's small store, café, meeting place where you and Al and Tina are getting together to sit and talk, still you pick up your pace a bit. You walk by more boarded up businesses than busy ones. Each empty space is a hollow sign that a few more jobs have left. Oh, well, nobody seems to have money to spend anyway.

You are early, so you sit by the window and look across the street to the playground wedged in between the blackened red brick buildings that guard the perimeter, or maybe trap it. Lots of babies and little kids live around here, but none are in the playground, of course. The backboards haven't felt the press of a ball for a long, long time. Something about there being no baskets probably accounts for the stillness. The swing sets have lost their chains, but at least the concrete picnic tables are in place, decorated by a confusion of scrawled notes and half-hearted images. Even the graffiti seems tired. You had forgotten there was even a playground there. You are probably not the only one who no longer notices.

The scuffling from overhead lets you know that the dance class is beginning. This is the new one for the kids. Later on the old guys will be tuning up. You hope they will open the windows so the notes will bring a little cool into the hot evening.

Good to see that the community college is opening up some space next to the payday loan place. You wonder which door people will walk through. The local community newspaper, which your old high school friend publishes, sits on the table with a picture of the children from the track club. Medals and smiles—they must train at the school. The investigation into the conditions of that rat trap of an apartment building on Elm has gone nowhere, just like the investigations of other properties in the past. Seems that the City Lights development group is turning some apartments down by the river into condos. How did they get the sidewalks fixed and the old park put back into shape? What happened to the people who lived in the apartments? You see that the new city council member will be speaking at the church tomorrow night; no doubt the pastor will make sure there is a good turnout. And the garden club has new officers. Garden club?

Al sits down, pulling you from your reading, just as Tina comes through the door. With her booming personality, you can feel Tina coming into the room before you even see her. Okay, there are three of us. We all live and work here. Tina runs the beauty shop, and Al works the reference desk at the library. Al could probably have any job he wants because of his family, but the library suits him just fine. You run the Food Bank, just a block from where you grew up. After going so far away for school these last 4 years, it's ironic that you have come back to where you started. People like and respect you, but you aren't satisfied just handing out food every day. The three of you are going to change things. You will start with unemployment, then do something about the violence and the drugs. That should keep you busy for, oh, a few weeks or so. After that, you'll see what else you can do.

REFLECTION QUESTIONS

1. Do the three of you have the power you need to accomplish your initial goals? Might there be some other starting place?

2. What power might you have now? What sort of power might you need?

3. What access might you have to other forms of power? How can it be built?

4. Who else seems to hold some power? What are they doing with it?

5. What assets seem to be available?

6. Who might be willing to work together to bring about some changes?

7. If you have no power at all, what do you expect you will be able to accomplish?

GROUP ACTIVITY: RECOGNIZING YOUR OWN BASES OF POWER

Often groups are locked in attitudes of powerlessness. One of the most important things an organizer can do is to help the group recognize that they have some collective power to begin with. Divide the larger group into teams of five members. Examine each team member's bases of power and consider how to use this awareness to help the group recognize the power they have.

1. Individually review the bases of power on pages 158–162 and check those that you have some access to. (3–5 minutes)

2. Think about a community that you are a member of, and jot down the bases of power that you have. (3 minutes)

3. As members describe their bases of power to the group, write down each base of power mentioned. (10 minutes)

4. Look at the list of power bases represented in this group, and discuss how you could use this awareness to help a group recognize that they have power they can use. (5–10 minutes)

5. Prepare to teach the larger group three things your team learned from your discussion that would be important for a community organizer to know. (5 minutes)

6. Present your lesson to the larger group. (3 minutes)

HELPFUL WEBSITES

Links to the organizations briefly described here are on the companion website at www.cengage.com/humansvcs/homan.

Empowerment Resources. Here you will find links to many organizations concerned with political empowerment and information on other resources such as books and networking. A number of empowerment topics and sources are discussed here, from the odd to the practical.

Empowerment. (You might have to scroll through a number of responses to "empowerment" if you are searching for this site.) Through this organization you can access numerous links to traditional topics such as intimate partner violence, homelessness, poverty, and activism and to more intriguing ones such as consensus decision making and anarchist activism.

Green Empowerment. This organization really is about power. It is committed to promoting renewable energy and sustainable development around the world by supporting community-based, renewable energy projects that are economically and environmentally viable, with a development goal of fostering self-sufficiency.

Vancouver Community Network's Citizen's Handbook. Self-proclaimed as the most complete grassroots organizing guide available on the Internet, this handbook provides a pretty impressive set of organizing principles and activities, along with a citizen's library. Check out "Grassroots Wilt," an article explaining how organizations harm themselves by not paying better attention to their members, including nine basic issues that are often overlooked.

Chapter 7

Powerful Planning

CHAPTER HIGHLIGHTS

- Planning as a waste of time
- Definition and description of a plan
- The process of planning
- Logic models
- Reasons for planning
- Degree of planning necessary
- Planning foundations: vision, mission, and values
- Four levels of planning
- Range of elements in an ideal plan
- Critical planning factors
- Values-driven planning
- Images of potentiality
- Brainstorming

- Criteria for good goals
- Relationship of systems theory to planning
- Force field analysis
- Asset identification and use
- Stakeholders
- Indicators of success and trouble
- Difference between monitoring and evaluation
- Evaluation steps
- 20/20 hindsight
- Obstacles to effective planning and ways to deal with them

Planning is a waste of time. You put in hours of endless discussion. You argue over subtle nuances of five-letter words buried in the middle of the third paragraph on the second page. And then, when you are finally done, the plan sits on the shelf, never to be looked at again. Planning is a waste of time. Don't you agree?

Well, if this is what planning is, then yes, it is a waste of time. Then again, lack of planning will almost certainly be a waste of time. Talking about what you want to do is not enough. You need to make decisions about what "better" looks like, and you must take actions to get you there. You know that you need to hear the voices of the people who have a stake in the outcome, particularly the voices of those whom the change is intended to benefit. So, what to do?

Let's start by recognizing that planning is necessary but that it also can be a colossal waste of time. To understand planning as a useful activity and to use it to increase the effectiveness of your change effort, you need the answers to a few questions. First of all, just what is a plan, and what, for that matter, is planning? Next, why should you plan at all? What benefit does it provide? Assuming you have gotten sufficiently good answers to encourage your further inquiry, you will probably want to know how much planning you need or don't need to do. Now down to brass tacks. How do you plan? What are some useful planning models? What are some basic obstacles to planning, and how do you confront them? And, finally, what else do you need to know or at least think about when you are getting set to plan? Let's take a look at each of these.

WHAT IS A PLAN? WHAT IS PLANNING?

The community is the context of your action, and power gives strength and purpose to your concerns. Planning puts that concentrated power to use by providing the approach and direction for your actions. The approach to planning described in this chapter refers to the steps you take to initiate and implement a community change. The procedures used in planning for the continued development of an existing social service agency may need to address other factors beyond the scope of this text, although certain perspectives offered here may be of some benefit in those situations as well.

A plan is a set of decisions made on actions to be taken to reach a goal. It is the product of the process of planning, an active process that is the opposite of simply allowing events to unfold. A plan can be said to exist when a point in the process has been reached where a coherent set of operations designed to meet a given goal has been determined with sufficient clarity that they may be acted on (Mayer, 1985; Perlman & Gurin, 1972; Weinbach, 1990). Let's take that apart.

Determining a coherent set of operations to reach a given goal means that you have made decisions on a number of things to do (and not to do) and that these actions are related to one another and are directed to whatever it is you want to accomplish. These actions need to be sufficiently clear so that you know just what to do. Therefore, you have a plan when you have proceeded far

enough in your consideration of possible courses of action that you know what it is you need to do to accomplish your purpose and you are ready to act.

A plan can be a very formal document, or it can simply be the clear understanding of the actions you are to undertake. If it is at all possible, it is helpful to write down your plans. Berkowitz (1982) pointed out that the very act of getting something down in black and white can clarify your thoughts. Seeing your ideas on paper also makes them seem more real, thus strengthening your own motivation.

Planning is the process, the series of steps you take to gather information and make decisions to determine your plan. Here are the steps in this process:

- Decide what you want to achieve.
- Identify what you have that you can use and what might be getting in your way.
- Select actions to be taken within a given period of time to use what you have to overcome obstacles and move you in the desired direction.
- Determine specific tasks.
- Assign responsibility.
- Analyze the outcome of your intentions and actions.
- Modify your plan.

I should probably clear up an important point about planning right now—you never stop planning. Of course, you are not going to spend all your time planning. Aside from the fact that such a prospect is dreadfully dreary, it isn't very productive. You are, however, going to continue to spend part of your time in planning. Planning is an ongoing process. The only way to get a plan "done" is to get all the information about your situation and then keep the world from changing at all. Of course, this is impossible. You have a plan as soon as you have decided what to do about the situation you are facing. You will always be tinkering with your plan, modifying it to meet changing conditions and additional information. Your plan is a living document. You can't plan for everything, so don't try to, and don't pretend to try to.

CAPTURING CONCEPTS
Logic Models

Logic models are useful tools in program planning and evaluation. In one page they describe the relationship between various aspects of the program and the results they are intended to achieve. Either an implicit or explicit theory of change directs these various aspects. Ask yourself: What do we think we need to put together to produce change? What does that change look like? and Why do we think this approach will work? A clearer theory of change will emerge when an open analysis of assumptions and expectations occurs. Logic models clarify the ideas and assumptions that go into developing the program and provide a road map linking one part of the journey with the next (Kagan, 1999; McLaughlin & Jordan, 2004; Osten, 2001; W. K. Kellogg Foundation, 2004). These connections are often presented in a visual display or "map." The specific component parts usually include these elements:

Resources/Inputs are those things dedicated to the program or used by the program or project, such as staff time, equipment, money, supplies, particular forms of community capital, and so forth.

Activities are what the program does with the resources, such as particular events, actions, processes, or technology. Of course you need to recognize that forces outside of your program or project will affect your success. So, you need to take some time to identify these as best you can as you determine your approach.

Outputs are the direct products of activities, such as the measurable amount of work accomplished or tangible things that are actually produced.

Outcomes are the changes that result because of all this work, such as changes in the skills or behavior of the target population, new policy, or the presence of some new identifiable element in the environment.

Impacts are the fundamental, long-range changes that occur in the organization or community as a result of the program.

Going from inputs to impacts follows a series of if-then statements that construct a theory of change. For example, if you have access to these resources, then you can use them to accomplish your activities. If you accomplish your activities, then you will deliver the amount and type of product that you intended. If you produce these things, then your participants will benefit in these certain ways. If these benefits to participants are achieved, then these significant changes in organizations, communities, or systems can be expected. This approach works very well with the participatory action research (PAR) process described in Chapter 5.

Like any kind of planning method, you will need to periodically update your model to incorporate what you see happening once you put your plan into action.

If you try to do your planning as one stage, and your action as the next stage, you will encounter several serious problems. First, group members want and actually need to do something to maintain and develop their interest. You can easily choke off the excitement by overemphasizing the need for a detailed problem analysis and a methodically detailed blueprint. You can only sell planning as action for just so long. A second problem involves the fact that you are always working with incomplete information. Once you think you are "done" with planning, it is much more difficult to incorporate new information into your

plan. And third, the ever-changing nature of situations means that the world in which the plan was originally developed is different from the world in which it is implemented. If you try to base all your actions on a plan that is somewhat out of date, you will be frustrated in your efforts to force the real world into the one envisioned by your plan. You may find this sufficiently irritating that you throw out the plan altogether.

Once established, your plan will be shaped and reshaped by new forces and new information you discover as you proceed with your action. Planning involves vision, discovery, decision making, and action. It is a purposeful way of looking at the future with the intent to shape it.

SOME BASIC REASONS FOR PLANNING

Why plan? Well, for one thing, it is almost impossible not to. Almost everything we do relates to some sort of plan, either implied or explicit. This morning when that blasted alarm went off, why did you get up? Why not just lie there in bed? Okay, so you did for a while, but why not just stay there? My guess is that lying around in bed would not have helped you accomplish your goals for the day. That is, it would have been incompatible with your plan. Somewhere along the line you decided to go to work or to school today, probably because that fits into an even larger plan. You determined a set of activities that will help you achieve your goal: Set the alarm at night. Get out of bed in the morning. Take a shower. Make the coffee. Grab your backpack or briefcase. Lock up. Go catch the bus. You get the idea.

Sometimes, especially when dealing with matters a little less routine than trying to get to work or school on time, it is easy to forget to do something important if you don't do a little thinking ahead. Look at this example again. Is there anything important you left out in your hurry? Good planning can keep you from overlooking an essential task, say, something like grabbing your keys so you can get inside when you come back home. Ever done that?

The importance of thinking ahead certainly applies to your change effort. If you want to achieve your goals, here, too, you need to plan. A plan will help you to use yourself and your resources in the most intentional manner. You simply will not accomplish your goals through a random series of actions. You know this. The actions you take must be those necessary and sufficient to accomplish the identified purpose, they must relate to the goals as well as to one another, and they must be in proper sequence. You don't have unlimited time and unlimited resources; therefore, you need to use these in the most effective way possible. You need to plan.

Powerful planning creates both a sense of urgency and confidence in moving toward your goals.

▶ Take a Moment to Discover ◀

Think of a time when a group you were involved with decided just what needed to be done, and then let it go at that. No one actually agreed to perform any specific task. Perhaps this occurred in your family, or where you work, or at school, or with a community action group. What was the result? Was the goal accomplished in a timely manner, or at all? How were the relationships among the members affected?

Simply by removing confusion, participants feel more capable. This feeling is further strengthened by the knowledge that they have made purposeful decisions from a range of alternative choices. Making necessary tasks clear and relating them to the accomplishment of important goals creates a tension that calls out for action. People feel the need to move, to get on with it.

As you move forward, things are going to get in your way. Your plan will help you see many of those twists, turns, and occasional potholes in the road ahead and prepare for them. Your plan will help you identify and marshal resources. One view of planning is that it is a way of solving problems by making the very best use of resources (Keller, 1983). Planning will guide your actions to be effective (productive in accomplishing your purpose) and efficient (done with the least time and effort) in achieving your goals.

Did you ever notice that in trying to solve one problem you end up creating another, perhaps even larger, one? Bad but unintended consequences are often the legacy of good intentions coupled with little forethought. A good plan produces thoughtful action and minimizes the likelihood that your efforts will simply generate new problems.

Good planning involves identifying both the promise and the difficulties that exist in any situation. Good planning goes beyond problems; good planning enables you to create opportunities.

HOW MUCH PLANNING IS NEEDED?

Basically, you need to know where you want to end up and how to get started to get there. The two most

CAPTURING CONCEPTS
Vision, Mission, and Values

Most planning processes for formal agencies, other organizations, and even whole communities begin with an examination of three foundation elements. Although the planning described in this chapter more directly addresses the concerns of a developing community organization anticipating a program of action, one that may remain less formal, an understanding of these planning components is helpful.

A **vision statement** is an energizing, positive view of a future condition made more possible because of the presence and work of the organization. It can describe either a result of the group's work or the condition of the organization itself. This vision should be compelling, energizing, challenging, attainable, and clear. Broad ownership of the vision is essential, so it should be developed by all of the active members of the organization. This is not just a statement jotted down by a couple of leaders. In a few words it captures the essence of what the organization intends to be and to do. All organizations, regardless of their degree of formality, should have a vision statement.

A **mission statement** essentially answers the question, "What business are we in?" It underscores the organization's basic priorities and what it will emphasize to achieve its objectives. Thus it describes the organization's products and services, along with its targeted market or key participants. It should differentiate the organization from other organizations, illustrating its uniqueness and particular niche in the community.

The **values statement** is a set of statements that respond to the questions, "At our core what do we hold dear? What do we believe is so important that it causes us to do what we do?" These values inform the work of the organization and the relationship it has to key internal (members, staff, and so forth) and external (consumers, funders, and so forth) constituencies. It also describes the importance of those relationships and how members relate to the organization's work and to one another. The behavior of the organization and its members will manifest these values if they truly shape the organization's culture. If not, another set of perhaps undeclared values are more powerfully operating. The value statements become the standard against which the most fundamental actions and decisions of the organization are measured.

If the organization is to become more formal, sustain itself over time, and effectively pursue an agenda of change, it will ultimately need to develop vision, mission, and values statements.

---

difficult problems most change efforts face are knowing what success looks like and actually taking the first step to get there. The less routine the challenge or goal, the more you will need purposeful planning.

Planning to implement community change is similar to the process of writing a paper. Most often, the most difficult words to write are the first ones, aren't they? If you don't really know what you want to say or what points you want to make, you are going to have a tough time getting started. You sit at your desk, fingers on the keyboard, stack of paper in the printer, beads of sweat on your forehead, the clock ticking away, closer to the date the paper is due. If you make things up as you go along, your paper may not cover the essential issues and may ramble on without focus. Using this approach, you are plain lucky if you hit all the important points because you probably don't even know what they are. Having a picture of what the paper should look like when it's finished, together with an outline to guide you, surely would help.

The time you put into your initial planning effort is important, but it should not be exhaustive. You do need to start with some planning. In fact, start with about as much as the participants in your effort can stand. No matter what stage of development your change effort is in, at the very least you need enough planning to know where you want to end up, where you are going next, and what you need to do to get there.

At some point you will notice that your planning efforts have become tedious. People may become bored with it. When this happens, they may agree to anything just to get the job over with. Planning then no longer serves its purpose and may become counterproductive. When you can't stand it anymore, stop doing it.

Participant interest is a critical driving or limiting force for your planning efforts. You may need to do a little educating on the importance of planning before you actually begin. If people don't see the value of planning, it will be hard to get them to do it with any enthusiasm. People often confuse "planning" with "inaction." (On the other hand, sometimes they do know that this is exactly what planning means.) If this is the case, don't use the word "planning." Call it something else, like "figuring out what we've got to do." Some people may be very willing to engage in planning as long as you call it something else.

You may also discover that some of your group's members value the contribution of planning and see it as a kind of game: outlining strategies; identifying enemies or other obstacles; looking for friends, alliances, and other resources; and figuring out how all these things fit together. As long as they don't get too carried away with overplanning, they can be very helpful in keeping your group looking ahead.

LEVELS OF PLANNING

You cannot make a detailed plan for everything, and you cannot be so vague that you don't really know what to do. Is there some sort of happy medium? Can you be a little detailed and a little vague? Yes, there is a way around this dilemma, but it is not by striking a balance between being detailed and being vague. The trick is to plan in levels—four levels to be exact (see Figure 7.1).

Your plan will proceed from the broad to the specific. You start with where you want to end up out there somewhere in the future, and then move closer and closer to the present, becoming more and more specific about what you need to do. When you have completed the four stages of the plan, you know not only where you are ultimately headed but exactly what you need to do tomorrow to start getting there.

Planning should be a creative activity, yet sometimes we get stuck trying to go from point A to point B in a pretty linear fashion. Yes, we may narrow the road by doing so, but we may narrow our thinking as well. One way to open up your thinking is to engage in

mind mapping, an approach to creative thinking developed by Tony Buzan (Buzan & Buzan, 1993; Quick & New, 2000). This is a simple, fun process that uses circles rather than straight lines. Start with a circle in the middle of the page and work out from the middle in all directions. Allow your ideas to jump all around, filling in circles extending from the core and creating new ones with various pieces of the project or action. Once you have all the circles splattered around, sets of relationships will begin to emerge. You may want to put your circles on index cards. Various techniques have been developed, from simple sorting of ideas into piles, linking related specific concepts to a broader concept, to more sophisticated cross linking concepts and statistical analyses. An approach called *concept mapping* looks to see how ideas can fit together and begin to align for action. Concept mapping software has been developed to help a group elicit ideas, note their connections, and display them as a visual map (Kane & Trochim, 2007; Novak & Cañas, 2008; Trochim, Milstein, Wood, Jackson, & Pressler, 2003). A mind map opens up your thinking and seeing, and concept mapping helps you to show the relationship of ideas. It is much more fun and comprehensive than a top-down only look at things, and it will help you identify each of the planning steps you need to pursue. No matter how you arrive at these basic components, your plan needs to include these elements:

- A sense of the ultimate desired condition

- A specific target that represents significant movement toward that condition

- The major activities you need to accomplish

- The specific steps to get you going

The first step is to establish the overall intent for your effort (Mayer, 1985). Here, you identify your vision for the future, the end result of what all your work is intended to achieve. For example, if you are concerned about prenatal care, your vision might be, "Every pregnant woman in Atlanta receives adequate prenatal care."

The next stage is to select an action-oriented target or goal that will help fulfill that vision. Using prenatal care again, your goal might be, "To establish a comprehensive prenatal care clinic by (a specific date)."

At the third level you establish the framework for your effort, breaking the goal down into the

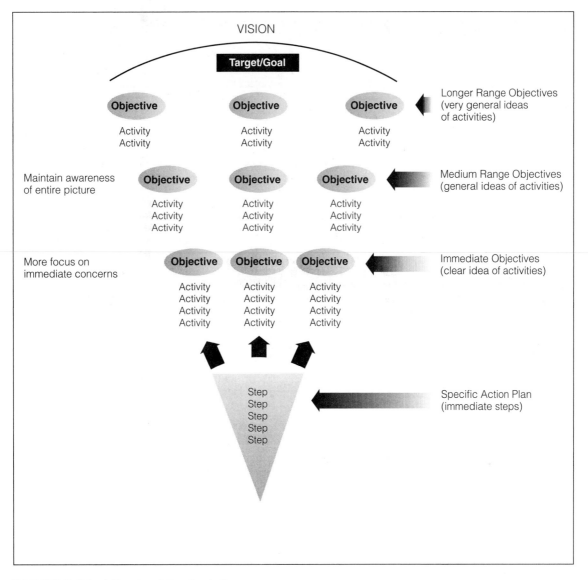

FIGURE 7.1 A Four-Level Plan for Action

major components of your plan. These describe the various sets of activities that must be undertaken to accomplish your purpose. Although you do not identify all the activities themselves, note what each set of activities is supposed to produce. This tier represents your best thinking of where in general you want to be headed and might include things like selection of the clinic site, determination of the range of services, initial staffing, securing grant funding, or establishing community support. Normally this list includes fewer than 10 items.

You can think of these as the major categories of the plan that you need to take care of. At this level you also want to get some idea of which of these categories you need to take care of in the early stages, which in the middle stages, and which are the last set of components you need to complete. Realize that even though a component may not need to be completed until the latter stages, there may be things you need to start doing early on. Let's say, for example, that writing a grant proposal is something you decide to do, but it isn't one of the first set of

A simple activity can help a group see the major categories of its plan and which set of activities need to be completed in the early stages and which are completed later. Ask the group, "What are the major things we need to take care of or get done to complete this project?" Begin listing them. You can pretty easily help the group distinguish between elements that are major components and those that are minute tasks. Usually about 10 things emerge as major items. Write each of these major components on a separate sheet of paper. Then have the group arrange these sheets of paper on a wall. On the top row place the items that are completed last in the project. On the middle row place those items that are completed in the middle stage. On the bottom row place those things that you need to get done first. You should have roughly the same number of items on each row. The group may rearrange items on the wall a few times before they feel that they've gotten it right. In the process the project comes more alive and the group more clearly sees the relationship among various parts of the plan. Although some components will be completed during the final stages of effort, you may need to begin to do some work on them fairly early in the process.

categories you need to complete. Still, you may need to begin gathering information fairly soon about available funding opportunities. Waiting too long to gather information such as application deadlines may set back your completion date.

The final level puts some meat on this skeletal plan, identifying what needs to occur within each set of activities. You are also figuring out a sequence for these activities and their relationship to each other. These specific action plans clarify what you are going to do over the next 1 to 3 months. For example, you may decide that you first need to build community support and that this will lead to involvement of people who can help you determine the range of services, which will set the stage for your fund-raising activities. Later on you can begin to identify possible sites.

Start by identifying steps you will take to gain community support, your most immediate concern. These steps could include contacting the Health Department for statistics you can use to describe the problem, identifying other individuals and organizations who have an interest in the issue, contacting a particular news reporter to do a story on the issue, and other specific actions. You want to make sure that you have identified the specific task that needs to be done, who will do it or be responsible for making sure that it does get done, the date it needs to be done, and what "done" looks like.

Plans at this level should look no further than 3 months ahead. In fact, the shorter the time frame the better. This level of planning represents actual, concrete decisions and specific steps. As a practical matter, these immediate plans can usually be determined in monthly (or, if appropriate, quarterly) meetings. Keeping in mind the major components you have already selected, at each meeting ask these questions: "Are there new or different pieces of this plan we need to take care of?" and "What do we have to do next?"

Planning for a relatively short but defined period of time enables you to be very specific and to keep the tasks close enough at hand so they have some sense of urgency or real purpose. When you plan too far down the road, you con yourself into thinking things are so far away you don't need to worry about them. So usually you don't, and they usually don't get done. At this final, specific level, the series of actions extend sufficiently into the future so that you have a sense of direction and progress, yet they are close enough at hand that you actually pay attention to them. As you execute your immediate plans, develop new information to incorporate into your next planning cycle.

As you begin acting, continue planning; keep looking ahead. This routine requires that you keep your focus on exactly what you are going to do over the next month (or so) and on making sure that those actions relate to the sets of activities (objectives) you need to be working on at the time. Continue to make sure that you have very clear steps to take and that each of these steps relates to movement toward the goal. With this ongoing, action-oriented approach to planning, you are constantly reexamining the relative importance and timeliness of each set of major activities, perhaps modifying them, perhaps eliminating

GLOBAL PERSPECTIVES

COSTA RICA—Unity, commitment, and energy grow strikingly in a group where there is a clear goal which all believe in (Maria, community worker, as cited in Kindervatter, 1983, p. 25).

NEW ZEALAND—Recently many of us in the community sector have come to better understand the difference between a complicated problem and a complex one. A complicated problem requires a lot of good management. If you get the details right, then you can usually sort it out. But a complex problem requires something else…something that is not as easily managed. Complex problems involve building relationships, trust, vision, and the engagement of communities…all the things that are messy and organic and usually out of your own direct control (Vivian Hutchinson, 2008, pp. 1–2).

GUINEA-BISSAU—Any group committed to working for development and social justice needs to build supportive structures and patterns…. Every new thing begins as a *dream* or vision. It is based on *values*. To make the vision a reality, the group must *set goals* and *find resources*. Committed

and trained people are among the most important resources. Setting definite *objectives* will help the group decide what to do to reach the goal, and a *planned program* will tell how to meet the objectives. There will need to be a *budget* reflecting the priorities of the group, and *organization* of roles and responsibilities for *implementation*. Finally, the members of the group must be willing to engage in self-criticism in a spirit of comradeship (Amilcar Cabral, 1982, p. 107).

GERMANY—Resistance to the steady dehumanisation of our lives is growing. It may slow things down here and there, but it is not of itself enough to turn the tide. Now is the time for those of us who at present allow this tide to sweep us along to generate our own visions of the future, to set against the schemes and projections of the powers that be….

The future belongs to everybody. But where are the opportunities for those wishing to articulate their feelings and aspirations to express them so loudly and clearly that, although they started out feeling alienated and off guard, they come to see themselves as effective fellow-architects of a world in which they

and their children would wish to live?

… [A "future workshop" can help people] criticize the existing state of things and work out how to reshape it….

The workshop itself begins with the critique phase, during which all the grievances and negative experiences relating to the chosen topic are brought into the open. All the points made are duly recorded and then amalgamated into a few main discussion areas. There then follows the fantasy phase, in which the participants come up with ideas in response to the problems, and with their desires, fantasies and alternative views. A selection is made of the most interesting notions and small working groups develop these into solutions and outline projects (often still of a rather utopian nature). The workshop concludes with the implementation phase, coming back down into the present with its power structures and constraints. It is at this stage that participants critically assess the chances of getting their projects implemented, identifying the obstacles and imaginatively seeking ways round them so as to draw up a plan of action (Robert Jungk & Norbert Mullert, 1996, pp. 8–12).

some and adding new ones. Your plan stays fresh, relevant, and clear.

BASIC PLANNING ELEMENTS

If you lived in a textbook world and could devote all the time necessary to develop the perfect plan, what could you do? You could explore each of the planning steps one by one, seeing each to conclusion before moving on. If anyone seriously suggests

that you really do this, tell him to go back to his reading because he certainly hasn't tried to produce change in the dynamic world in which both you and I live.

So, if things don't work this way in the real world, why learn about it? This is a good question. When you need to do some planning, you want to do as many of the right things as well as you can. As much as possible, you will select from the ideal to meet the demands of your current real-life situation. It helps to know what the ideal is. So open your textbook and step in. Look around; things are peaceful, quiet, and

CHANGE AGENT TIP

Regardless of how detailed your planning process, you must keep a number of critical factors in mind. Failure to incorporate any one of these matters can undermine all your hard work:

Clarity of your goal. All active members of your organization need to agree on and understand the goal and use it to guide decisions and actions. If each of these people were given a piece of paper and a pencil and asked to write down your group's goal, would each piece of paper say the same thing?

Inclusion. Do you know all of the necessary stakeholders, those who have a particular interest in the issue and are affected by it? Are they involved to their degree of interest and ability? Are you leaving any of them out? If so, are there valid reasons for excluding them? (For example, you may not want to include an opponent in your planning.) What do you anticipate will be the consequences for exclusion?

Availability of resources. Be on a constant lookout for people and things that you can use. Your ability to marshal resources is one of the most basic sources of strength.

Clear assignment of tasks. If people aren't sure what to do or how, they probably won't do it. Make sure people know what they are expected to do, how to do it, and by when these things should be done. Doing so moves you toward your goal and builds member and group confidence and capacity. Organization occurs when the variety of required tasks are done in a way that enhances the value of each.

Reward for work. Seeing progress is a good reward, but develop and use other forms of reward that are meaningful to the participants. Along the way, make sure people can recognize the progress that is being made. How will that happen?

Flexibility. Things will change, and unanticipated events will occur. Will you be able to make the adjustments necessary to keep your plans consistent with your goal accomplishment? Will you be able to make changes without getting flustered? Are you directing your action, or are you just aimlessly responding to events?

Monitoring, evaluating, learning, and refining. Routinely check to see if you are doing what you planned to do, and see if it is working. Use your reviews and your actions to keep learning. Use your learning to strengthen and refine your plan.

cozy here—and, yes, a little dull. Now that you have become acclimated, let's get to work.

These basic planning elements are present to one degree or another in all planning considerations. Sometimes, either because of other demands or the inattention of those doing the planning, they receive only a flicker of notice. However, each of these elements should be given some considered thought.

Identify Current Discomfort or Opportunity

Something brought you to this situation of change. Just what is it that people are upset about or dissatisfied with? What better is possible? By uncovering instances of irritating or harmful conditions or newly recognized opportunities, you give yourself a picture of the current situation that requires some changing.

Dealing with irritations, things that really bug us, is generally a good way to provoke initial action. Dissatisfaction, the feeling of being out of balance, is usually what gets a group going. However, you don't want to stay stuck with a focus on "what's wrong." You can start with feelings of dissatisfaction to get the ball rolling and then move to creative, exciting ways to put something new into place that better addresses the situation and changes the condition. Groups can move past dealing only with things that bother them to working on opportunities that inspire. Whatever the current condition is—anger or frustration with a problem or enthusiasm about an opportunity—you need to get a view of what better looks like. The appreciative inquiry framework, discussed in Chapter 2, invites you to see aspects of the situation that have worked or are currently working well that you can build on. Remembering that "organizations move in the direction of what they study" (Cooperrider et al., 2008, p. 30), looking at what you want to more fully develop gives you something to work toward and helps you identify your starting place or your focus.

CAPTURING CONCEPTS
Values-Driven Planning

A powerful way to bring people together, recognize shared interests, and affirm a common identity is through **values–driven planning.** Values—what we believe to be important and hold meaning—direct both our assessment of the world and how we act in it. Sometimes, though, we are not so clear about what our values really are, which ones might be in conflict, and which ones matter most to us. This is true for individuals and for groups as well. Often, people with common interests have not articulated the values that guide them. There may only be a blurry notion of what members of the group believe to be important. This can lead to a vague sense of direction or to misunderstandings. You can help a group arrive at a clearer picture of the current situation and make clear decisions about actions they want to take by first helping them to identify their values.

Often, groups experience a disconnection between what they value and what they are experiencing. Helping a group to clarify its values can bring into sharp focus this disconnect, revealing issues and opportunities for action.

Here are the basic elements. First, it is helpful to have a discussion of values: what they are, and how they shape what we understand and do. Next, in just a few words ask each member to privately write down three or four particularly meaningful values regarding the matter that has brought the group together: for example, strengthening a neighborhood, having children with disabilities feel welcomed and valued in the community, having a supportive work environment. You might ask each person to answer the question, "What's really important to me?" Members then take turns mentioning one of their values not already mentioned by another member. Do this until all values have been stated. You will probably end up with a list of 10 to 15 values, and each person is likely to have discovered values not previously recognized. These become the foundation for the group's analysis and action. A kind of "this is who we are and what we believe" identity emerges as the group recognizes a set of shared values. Members begin to see that they are not just individuals, but a community.

Once the group has determined what values are in operation in the situation, they can more readily assess what is going on. The shared values become a set of standards to measure their effort against. To begin to identify things that could be changed, you might ask, "What's occurring that doesn't seem to fit with our values?" To look at things that are working well and that the group may want to build on, you can ask, "What's occurring that we like to see and that fits with our values?"

The group can then draw upon its values and assessment of the situation to craft its vision for the future. You can open a discussion of visioning by asking, "What vision represents a better future that supports our values?" This leads to a vision that reflects what the members value while reaffirming the group's identity. The group can use its set of declared values to help make decisions regarding community projects. Not only will the group rank possible projects according to matters such as cost and feasibility but according to how well the proposed project mirrors and advances the community's values.

Values-driven planning helps members understand one another better, enabling them to better recognize different concerns and motivations. It helps to prevent conflict that can easily occur when there is just a vague assumption of what people value. Especially in difficult times, values can be a source of strength and guidance to draw upon. Values help connect people, promote group identity, and provide a firm foundation for action.

Identify Your Vision for the Future

What do you want to accomplish? What does "good" or "happy" look like? Your vision is your picture of what should be happening instead of what is now happening. It is the complete realization of your efforts stated in positive terms and clear, simple language. It is a strong declaration of your intent and gives direction and energy to your efforts.

Identify Your Target Using Images of Potentiality

What do you really want to make happen? Images of potentiality, a concept developed by Eva Schindler-Rainman (1977), provide a simple, yet powerful way to identify the specific outcome you desire. There is much truth to the saying, "If you don't know where you are going, you will end up somewhere else." A problem is simply the difference between where you are and where you want to be. Closing that gap is the intention of planning (Nutt, 1985). This method helps you see clearly just where you want to be. Using images of potentiality, you project yourself into the future and visualize what things will look like once you have changed things. Here is how it works.

- Pick an imaginary date in the future far enough away to give you sufficient time to work to accomplish your goals but not so far that the sense of urgency to act on the issue is lost. For some changes you seek, 2 months in the future would be appropriate. For others, a year or two would be fitting. Still others may require you to look 5 years down the road.

- Now, pretend that this future date is the present. So "today" is (whatever date you have selected). You are there now. Visualize the situation today. Go ahead; look around. What do you see?

- Describe everything you see now that the problem is solved and you have accomplished everything you had set out to do those months or years ago when you first started. Identify clear, visual images. For example, you can't really see "people getting along better," but you can see "people playing softball in the park." It's hard to know just what "things look better" means, but "all the walls have a fresh coat of paint" gives you a good picture.

If your group is just getting started, it should concentrate on turning only one or, at most, two images into reality. Trying to do more than that can fragment your group and stretch your resources past their limits. Or you can end up with the same bunch of people trying to do too much and getting burned out in the process. The images you select to turn into goals should present you with a moderate challenge. Using images of potentiality is a powerful way to make your goals for the future more real. When goals come alive, it is easier for people to commit to moving from where they are to where they want to be.

Select a goal that people are enthusiastic about and willing to work on to make happen. This may or may not be the "most important" item on your list of images. A common mistake groups make is to select the item everybody agrees is the most important. Often, this is something people really don't feel capable of dealing with, or even if the matter is important, it's not really very interesting. To start with, it is much better to pick interesting over important. Make sure everybody knows this from the start.

The criteria for a good goal should be kept in mind. First, it should be feasible; that is, the resources needed to accomplish the goal must be available. Second, it should generate some excitement. Third, it should be clear enough that it gets you all headed in the same direction and you can easily tell when you have reached it. Fourth, the goal should be something your organization will make happen. Finally, the goal should be consistent with the reason that brought you all together in the first place (Dale & Mitiguy, 1978).

Identify Stakeholders

Stakeholders are people who have a stake in what you do. In the broadest sense this means those whose interests your actions could benefit or threaten. Their influence is so powerful that they deserve their own category. Mason and Mitroff (1985) identified stakeholders as having purposes and strategies that support or resist your efforts. Those who are supporting have goals generally compatible with your goals and are moving (or would like to move) in the same general direction you are moving.

Resisters, whom they characterized as nonsupporting, resisting, or actually opposing, provide barriers to your success or move in the opposite direction. Take an extra minute or two to think beyond the obvious resisters to identify all those who have a stake in or benefit from the current situation. You cannot ignore them, for they will surely make life difficult for you as you pursue a change that threatens their interests.

Some people benefiting from the current situation may seem to have interests similar to yours, but they are currently getting something (for example, funding or good press) as they pursue their activities. Your presence can threaten their piece of the action, their turf. Remember that as soon as you enter the arena of action the scene changes. You may not be welcomed with open arms. This can be a surprise to you, so be prepared.

Now think about those with interests similar to yours but who would not be threatened by your success. Think for that extra minute or so about those who would be genuinely happy or who would breathe a little easier if you succeeded. You may be able to uncover some unanticipated backing.

It is essential to move supportive stakeholders to the role of investor by involving them in planning in a meaningful way (Benne, 1985; Ellsworth, Hooyman, Ruff, Stam, & Tucker, 1982; Kettner et al., 1985; Lewis et al., 2007). It is necessary that they develop ownership of the goal. When individuals have a strong attachment to the goal, their personal need to accomplish the goal leads to a strong commitment to the success of the entire group (Horwitz, 1954). Playing a role in the development of the goal is probably the best way to promote this strong acceptance. Key stakeholders cannot be limited to information-giving roles. They need to participate in strategy determination, task accomplishment, and decision-making capacities. Here, your attention to the foundation principle that everything happens through relationships becomes particularly important. No plan is perfect. You and those with whom you are working will find some smooth sailing and some choppy waters. You will make adjustments and move forward. This is much easier if you not only learn how to work on a plan, but you learn how to work together. As Bushe (2007) has observed, "strong relationships can overcome bad designs and plans, while good designs and plans usually can't overcome bad relationships" (p. 32).

Identify Factors in the Future Environment

You are planning today to institute something that will be in place some distant, or not too distant, tomorrow. You have an idea of what today looks like, but how about tomorrow? Consider how your efforts today relate to the future environment. Recall that any specific plan you prepare is somewhat out of date the moment it is "done." New developments will occur, and you will need to respond to some of these. Which forces will help or hinder your efforts at the time they are actually taking place, not today when you are thinking about doing them? What will occur in that future environment that makes it more receptive or more resistant to what you want to do? What new opportunities does the future hold for your organization? It is in this world, a month, a year, or 5 years from now, that you will be working. Do you know much about it?

Give yourself a glimpse of the future with an exercise called "creating the future." Select a specific date in the future, and act as if that future date were the present. Then ask participants to consider the following question: "What is going on today that can in some way influence our success in (whatever change you are attempting to implement)?" Some of these factors will be economic, some political, some technological, and some plainly off the wall.

Start with the broadest system (see Chapters 2 and 3) likely to have an impact on your efforts, and narrow your field down to the one in which your members participate. It is helpful to develop this picture of the future over two separate occasions. On the first occasion, create the future for the broadest arenas likely to influence your success. Then, about a week later, do the same for your more immediate spheres of action. (If you don't live in a textbook world, you may have only one opportunity to do this. If that is the case, reduce the number of levels you examine to no more than three.)

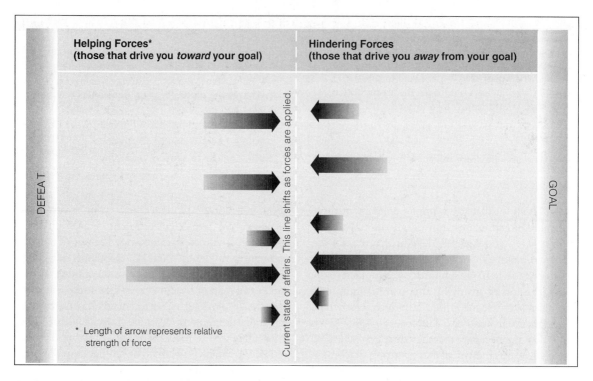

Helping Forces*
(those that drive you *toward* your goal)

Hindering Forces
(those that drive you *away* from your goal)

DEFEAT

Current state of affairs. This line shifts as forces are applied.

GOAL

* Length of arrow represents relative
  strength of force

FIGURE 7.2   Simple Force Field Based on Lewin's (1951) Technique

Identify Current Obstacles and Current Resources

You've dealt with the future; now you need a picture of the current environment—the arena of action in which you are going to promote change. These are the forces that have an impact on what occurs in the system in which you want to make changes. This requires your attention to its interaction with other systems that affect it.

Kurt Lewin (1951) described a technique known as force field analysis, which can help you visualize these interactions. Figure 7.2 diagrams a simple force field. A number of contending forces operate in your arena of action. Some of these forces drive you toward your goal; others drive you away from your goal. A state of tension exists, producing a dynamic situation as forces act on one another. At any given moment these forces are in relative balance; this balance represents the current state of affairs. (For an excellent discussion of force field analysis, see Brager & Holloway, 1978.)

Using this method of viewing the current situation can help you determine which forces you can mobilize and which forces you must counter. To get this snapshot, brainstorm all the forces now present that may help or hinder your success. These forces may be tangible items, such as people or meeting rooms or backhoes, or intangibles, such as apathy or personal connections or skills.

First, list all those things that may be getting in your way. Remember, you are listing currently operating forces, not those that may develop. Some common restraining forces include inhibiting policies or procedures, history of failed effort, lack of information, intimidating opponents, ingrained attitudes, and a lack of money. There are, of course, many more, some of which are unique to your circumstances. Generating this list will give you a good idea of the obstacles you are facing.

Next, list all those things that are going for you. Some common helping forces include the interest of a number of people, talents of the people you know, community or political connections, information, and tangible resources such as a plot of land. Many groups think only of the obstacles they must face or the difficulties they will encounter and fail to regard

CHANGE AGENT TIP

Brainstorming techniques help to generate ideas. Here are a few simple rules for brainstorming sessions:

- Write everything down
- Everyone offers an idea
- No criticism of any idea
- No discussion of ideas during brainstorming
- Stress the quantity not the quality of ideas
- It is acceptable to repeat an idea
- Build on one another's ideas

You can build on people's enthusiasm as they create the world they will eventually work to make real. While you are brainstorming, though, some people will catch on to the idea of clear images much better than others. In the spirit of brainstorming, you don't want to tell people that their ideas aren't good enough, yet you do want sharp images. To get around this obstacle, create two columns: one headed IMAGES and the other headed IDEAS.

Encourage everyone to offer their ideas, even if they are not yet sharpened into images. People will soon get the hang of things, and some good ideas that otherwise might be silenced will find their way into the IMAGES column. Planning that is purely rational is limited. Let your intuitive side come out of hiding and into the bright light of planning. Allow it to influence your actions as well.

---

equally the forces operating to benefit them. This leads to discouragement and lost opportunities as well. By examining your helping forces after you have considered your hindering forces, you generate confidence and build on the discovery of resources by beginning to look for them much more actively.

Force field analysis holds that driving and restraining forces are in relative balance. You do have a lot going for you. Unless the situation is rapidly deteriorating, some things present in the environment are keeping the situation from getting much worse much quicker. What are these things? The most obvious asset any community has is its people. This is so evident that it is frequently overlooked. Other common forces include dissatisfaction or anger, helpful laws and policies, leadership, money, talents, personal networks, and physical resources. What else is there? If you imagine the opposing forces as adversaries, what's holding them in check? These are some of your helping forces.

After the forces present in your arena of action have been identified, it is a good idea to get some notion of their relative power. You may, for example, assign numerical values to designate how much influence each force wields. This doesn't have to be a precise measurement, but it will give you an indication of the more important forces you need to think about. As you begin to move to action, remember that you can combine a number of smaller forces to make a more potent one. For example, a lot of people, a small room, and a couple of television cameras can add up to quite a powerful force.

Using force field analysis, you can discover a lot about your current situation in less than an hour. It is a good idea to repeat this exercise from time to time to keep your picture of the present, its dangers and its opportunities, up to date.

Identify Actions That Use Existing Advantages to Overcome Obstacles

Now that you have a picture of what needs to be changed, what the desired conditions look like, what future forces will influence your efforts, and what forces are now present that will affect your success, it is time to identify what you can do to get to where you want to go.

Decide which obstacle you want to overcome first. Often it is a good idea to pick the most powerful obstacle that you can do something about. Look over your list of helping forces or resources and decide which of these can be used to counteract whatever is working against you. Generally, pick assets that are easiest to use, although other criteria such as developing broader participation and keeping yourself from becoming too predictable should be considered. A clear picture of actions you can take will emerge from reviewing your assets. If there is time, test a number of alternative actions as you decide what to do. Sometimes less than the best is better. As you select actions that hold the best chance to get you to where you want to go, make sure these are actions you can actually see yourself doing. Selecting the best activities (as if we know what they truly are), but ones you know you are not really going to do, is about the same as selecting no activities.

Next, identify the particular steps that need to be taken (such as making phone calls, distributing fliers, or cooking tacos) to activate the resource.

Identify the Sequence and Time Frame of Actions

Which of these things do you do first? The best way to answer that is to consider what comes last. By working backward, you can better determine how the steps you plan to take relate to each other and to what it is you want to accomplish. You can also figure out how specific actions can bolster or interfere with one another.

The great philosophers of our time, standup comedians, understand that the secret to life is good timing. Deciding when something must be done is pretty important. Don't assume that this is commonly understood. Make your time frames clear.

One thing you will probably notice is that everything apparently needs to be done by tomorrow, if not the day before. Unless you are dealing with a scheduled event whose timing is outside your control, it is likely that you can pursue a less frenzied schedule. If a frenzied schedule is not really required, it won't be sustained anyway. People will normally do things about the time they think they need to be done. So don't drive yourself crazy worrying about getting everything done well in advance, and at once. If you jam up the first few months with most of your activities without rest or pacing, participants may feel worn out as soon as the first set of things is completed. You will probably discover that many things don't get done on schedule thereafter. This can lead to discouragement and to unnecessary conflict. Give yourself some leeway for things running over schedule.

Identify People Who Will Handle Necessary Tasks

Here's a radical thought: Things don't get done by themselves. Designate who is responsible for seeing that each task gets completed. There is a key phrase here—"seeing that a task gets completed." Individuals taking on the responsibility don't necessarily need to do the job themselves. They just need to make sure that it gets done. Sometimes no one in your group has the necessary time, talent, or interest to perform the task, but one of you can usually find another individual, perhaps from outside the immediate group, who does. This may result in bringing a new member into the fold. However you go about this, see that the individual has a sense of investment in the task and a sense of personal responsibility. Things no one is willing to commit to usually don't get done.

Sometimes no one is willing to volunteer to take responsibility for getting a certain job done, although everyone agrees that it is necessary. There follows an uncomfortable silence in response to the question: "Okay, who's going to take care of this?" Let's hope you catch yourself before you volunteer to take on another thankless job that nobody else wants to do. Otherwise you and the two or three other people who can't stand silence for an answer will come to be seen as the "main people" in the organization— the ones who really are going to worry about getting things done. The other people then get to become less "main" and understand that they have an acceptable role of being less committed. They can then come to expect less of themselves as they come to expect more of you "main people." Unfortunately, you will soon come to share these expectations.

So, what to do? The thing still needs to get done. If you have noticed a pattern developing, talk to the other "main" people beforehand. You can agree to take on your fair share of duties, but none of you will

CHANGE AGENT TIP

The Next Steps Action Chart is a simple form to keep track of the immediate next steps that your organization will take. Divide a piece of paper into four columns, and label columns across the top as follows:

Column 1: *Task*. This column has a clear, simple description of the task to be accomplished.

Column 2: *HDYTIGD*. This is the "How do you tell it got done?" column. Identify some simple, objective method to determine that the task was done. (For example, to determine that a meeting occurred, use minutes from the meeting. To

determine that an article appeared in the newspaper, use a copy of the article.)

Column 3: *Date*. This is the date by which the task gets done.

Column 4: *Person Responsible*. This identifies the person who will make sure that the task is completed. This person may or may not actually perform the task, but she will make sure the task gets done.

Refer to this chart often, and be sure to acknowledge your successes. This is an easy way to keep tabs on your progress toward your goal.

jump to rescue the organization by doing whatever no one else seems willing to do. The first thing you can try is to just sit there and accept the silence. It should be long enough that there is some noticeable discomfort. Eventually someone will speak up… maybe. If that hasn't produced an eager soul, something a little more direct may be in order. Try saying something like this: "Well, it looks like we don't think it's all that important that we get this done." This usually produces protestations to the contrary. If it doesn't, and people just sit there, then drop it, let it go. You may need to risk squandering a few opportunities before people get the idea that the work really is going to be spread around, or it's not going to get done.

If people agree that the job is worth doing and they say so, then ask again: "Okay, who's going to take this on?" After a second you may need to invite someone by saying something like, "How about you, Gus?"

An alternative approach is to ask: "What will happen if we don't get this done?" Then ask: "Is that okay with everyone? How about you, Gus?" These questions usually encourage some members of the group to agree to take charge of the task.

Identify Indicators That Show Planned Tasks Were Completed

It is sometimes difficult to determine whether a task is completed because we don't really know what "completed" looks like. By selecting indicators of job completion, you can more clearly determine whether or not you are doing what you said you

were going to do. These also help to clarify or make more specific just what the task involves.

If your task involves holding a meeting, one indicator could be the minutes of the meeting, another could be a sign-in sheet. If your task involves developing media attention, an indicator could be a record of news stories aired. If fliers are to be distributed, the fact that you have a flier and a list of the distribution points and numbers distributed could be indicators. Indicators are simply your response to the question, "How do I tell that I got it done?" These indicators help you monitor your efforts. You will be able to determine what you did and when. Not only will this help keep you on track, it will also help you determine your effectiveness. Evaluating your efforts is important, but before you can determine whether your effort is working, you need to determine just what work you have done.

Identify Measures of Effectiveness and Indicators of Trouble

To evaluate your endeavor primarily means checking to see if it is producing the desired results. When you evaluate, ask yourself: "Are we accomplishing what we want to accomplish? Why, or why not?" This is different from monitoring, which asks the question: "Are we doing what we said we were going to do?" Monitoring asks what is being done; evaluating asks whether or not it is working (Kettner et al., 1985).

Just as you have indicators of task completion, you should have indicators of task effectiveness.

These are your responses to the question, "How do we tell if this produced what we wanted it to produce?" If a meeting was to lead to increased money from a particular source, your indicator would be more money from that source. If your intent with the news media was to influence the vote of the city council, your indicator would be the council's actual vote.

These are pretty simple indicators, but they give you a sense of how you are faring. You also want to have some indicators of the effect of your overall effort. You need to identify clear signs to tell whether or not the change effort itself is producing the desired results. If you do not know what to look for to know if your efforts mattered, you don't know if they do. Some occasions demand a more sophisticated approach to evaluation. For example, you may need to clearly identify the relationship between actions and their consequences. You may need to determine not only if this particular action directly produced this particular consequence, but maybe also how or why. No matter how informal or thorough your evaluation procedures may be, you still need to know what your indicators of success are and what outcomes you expect to produce.

In any effort there are signs of your accomplishments, your growing success. By knowing what some of these are, you can recognize and celebrate their attainment. Maintaining an awareness of your victories great and small can keep you driving forward and help you overcome the myriad setbacks that can stymie you. Both indicators of success and indicators of trouble are important. If you have no warning signs, you may just drive off a cliff.

Perform Identified Tasks

All this planning doesn't amount to a hill of beans if you don't actually do anything. Although performing tasks may not technically be part of the planning process, let's not forget that action is what this whole business is about. Consider, too, that action and planning are occurring at the same time. You cannot just stop everything you are doing to plan, and you cannot wait until you are done planning to act.

Monitor, Evaluate, and Refine

Leave bread out for a while, and it gets stale. Leave plans untouched for a while, and they get stale too.

You need to keep an eye on your plans to keep them fresh, up to date, and relevant to your situation. Whenever plans no longer effectively relate to current conditions, they become deadweight. They also convince people that planning is a waste of time. To keep your planning useful for meeting current demands and giving direction to the future, you have to keep informed about current and likely future conditions and the effectiveness of your plan.

You set your plan in motion by acting on it. As you act, you change conditions and gather information. Your organization changes, and so does the rest of the world in which you are acting. You regularly need to acquire and use three sets of information.

One set of information to gather involves what you are learning from reviewing the indicators regarding task completion. This is your monitoring function. Are people doing what they said they would be doing? Are they not? Can you find out why things are or are not happening? What are you learning about how to do better? What's taking more time than you thought?

The second set of information involves your learning from the indicators of effectiveness or trouble. This is your evaluation function. Are you advancing toward your goal? Are you seeing flags of trouble? Are the things you are doing having the intended effect or not? Evaluation can be formative (looking at process) or summative (looking at end results). The clearer your goals and indicators, the more able you will be to assess progress and measure results.

The third set of information involves the new knowledge and information you come upon while you are engaged in the action. What are you seeing now that you didn't see before? What's new in the environment? New obstacles? New opportunities? What new information strengthens your cause?

What adjustments do you need to make as a result of what you are finding out? This is your refinement function. What structures are in place for incorporating this new learning into a fresh version of your plan?

Westley, Zimmerman, and Patton (2007) remind us that we routinely face three levels of problems, simple ones with some pretty basic steps you can follow, like baking a cake; complicated ones with a lot of different elements that need to come together, like landing on the moon; and complex ones in which the things you need to take into account are ever changing

▣ CAPTURING CONCEPTS

Throughout this book you have seen a number of references regarding the importance of learning. **Evaluation** is a critical step in your planning process because it promotes your learning and increases the likelihood that your change effort will be successful and meaningful.

Evaluation is not just counting up all the things you have done. It is looking at what has happened because of what you have done. You don't just "do" evaluation; you need to plan for it as you plan for any other critical element of work. This includes time frames for when you will evaluate. Recall that evaluation can be **formative**—looking at parts of your effort during the process—or **summative**—examining change as an end result. If you are using the PAR process described in Chapter 5 or following the logic model described earlier in this chapter, you have a great start on your evaluation. Each of these approaches involves if-then statements, creating a theory about change. Your theory is: If we do X, then Y will happen. Your evaluation asks: Did we do X, and did Y really happen? You have already identified both your outcome and your primary approach for achieving it. If you have followed the process described in the last few pages, you have also identified your indicators, so you have a very good start on your evaluation plan.

There are a number of approaches to evaluation; most stress having a planned approach, clearly identifying outcomes; and involving those who are to put the results of the evaluation to use (Coombe, 2005; Frechtling-Westat, 2002; Morley, Vinson, & Hatry, 2001; Penna & Phillips, 2005; Stoecker, 2005; U.S. Department of Housing and Urban Development, 2005).

An evaluation plan generally involves the following steps:

- *What immediate outcome or result do we intend to achieve?* This is the specific goal that you intend to accomplish.
- *What impact will that have?* This is what occurs because you have achieved your goal. It answers the "so, what" question: You accomplished your goal. So, what? Why does this matter? Here you

would also examine how accomplishing your goal moves you closer to your vision.

- *What are indicators that we have achieved this result?* These are the specific signs that your goal has been achieved. The clearer your goal, the easier it will be to determine what these signs are.
- *What are indicators that we have produced this impact?* These tell you what has happened because you achieved your goal. They are specific differences you can see or count because your targeted change has taken place.
- *How will we gather information to find out?* These are the methods you will use to get the information you need. Evaluation is about learning, and a number of the methods described in Chapter 5 for learning about your communities (guided personal discussions, surveys, focus groups, photo assessments, and so forth) can help you learn about the effect of your change effort within the community.
- *How will we analyze the information?* These are the methods you use for making sense out of the data you gather. For example, you may use some type of comparison, such as before and after comparisons, or some form of statistical analysis. You may identify different results for different groups of people.
- *Who will determine indicators and gather and analyze the information?* If you are using participatory approaches, members of the community and other important stakeholders will be involved throughout this process.
- *How will we use the evaluation to build on what works to increase our effectiveness and to inform others about our work?* Certainly, your organization will use the evaluation results to determine what you need to keep doing and what adjustments you need to make. In addition, you may provide results to other audiences such as funding sources, policymakers, and the media. Who might they be? How do you want them to respond to this information? How will you present it to them?

CHANGE AGENT TIP

When examining the impact of a particular change episode, you may miss some valuable information. Because your view is focused only on the planned change, you may not see other reactions to your efforts that are taking place. Nor may your funding sources. Looking only at the planned change gives a limited view and an incomplete understanding of what you are producing. Two evaluation tools can help you get a broader view.

The first is called Measurement of Planned Change, which looks at the degree to which your concrete goals were reached. Use this tool to chart your progress. The second is called the Signs of Impact, which lists, not the actions you are taking, but *the reactions you are seeing* that can be attributed to your work. This chart lists the signs that your efforts are making a difference beyond your immediate, planned change effort. Just as any

change effort has unanticipated setbacks, you will have unanticipated impacts as well. Recalling the idea of interconnectedness in systems theory, that changes in one part of the system produce changes in other parts of the system, you can understand that the changes you initiate may well have effects outside of your immediate intent.

At the beginning of every regular meeting, the facilitator should ask for a report on any Signs of Impact entries. This helps members refine their ability to recognize responses their work is producing as well as building confidence and motivation as awareness that the group is making a difference continues to grow. These are two different tools, showing different things. Project leaders should track both sets of indicators to get a truer picture of gains that are taking place (Hagberg & Homan, 2006; Hunter & Homan, 2006).

Measurement of Planned Change

Target area: The focus of your change effort	Measurement: The degree of change	Measurement method: How we know the change happened	Measurement impact: How we know this change mattered	Measurement date: When we're going to check and see	How to use information to effect action, or what action needs to be taken as a result of this information

Signs of Impact

Date	What was the reaction or response?	What important thing did that indicate?	Target area	Who was involved?	What did that mean?

and many parts aren't under your control, like raising a child. Promoting community and social change is complex. While your plan advances you forward, the scene is ever changing. Openness to learning from what you are doing and continuing to use your learning to refine what you are doing will advance you farther and faster.

From time to time get together with the people who helped develop the plan and are affected by it to

evaluate results, and use this evaluation to modify your plans. An appreciative inquiry orientation will invite you to examine what is working well, and what can be learned from that to accelerate the pace of progress. This is much more inviting than looking for failures or mistakes, which can be threatening and lead more to finding excuses than anything else. Involving key stakeholders in the evaluation can increase the validity of findings, promote learning, and "help community members understand and develop the knowledge and skills that will enable them to think evaluatively and conduct more internal evaluations" (Coghlan, Preskill, & Tzavaras Catsambas, 2003, p. 15). Like any other activity in developing the community, evaluation provides an opportunity to build capacity.

If you are in a fast-paced situation in which important conditions really do change daily, your plan will require constant attention and fine-tuning. The less rapidly changing your conditions are, the less frequently you need to review your plans, and the less likely you probably will. However, the less frequently you review a plan, the more thoroughly you need to review it. Don't wait too long between reviews, however. If you find that each review involves a rediscovery of your plans, then you have waited too long, and your plans have probably become documents that no longer inform your actions.

Review dates should be built into your planning process. Depending on your situation, this could be every afternoon, every 3 months, or every October. As I mentioned at the beginning of this chapter, you never stop planning. As long as you intend to learn and to act efficiently and effectively, you will continue to focus your plans.

OBSTACLES

Toward the end of your planning, take a little time to talk about the pitfalls in the road before you and how important it is to try to identify them. For example, an important one could be "We ran out of gas." If you think that might really happen to you (by the way, it usually does), think now of how you will recognize the signs that this is occurring and determine what you will do when you recognize those signs. You don't have to develop a strategy for dealing with each possible pitfall, but recognize them as warnings. Have some fun with the process. Take the lists out every now and then and look at them. If you are aware of possible pitfalls, they will be much easier to avoid, and you will be more confident because you realize what could have happened if you weren't looking.

You can employ a technique called projected 20/20 hindsight. Here's how it works. Take an imaginary leap forward to the date you have targeted for reaching your goal, or even an earlier date that is still some distance down the road. Then ask the group to look back from there on your effort…because you failed. Then ask: "From this vantage point, what did we miss in our planning? What happened that caused us to fail? What faulty assumptions did we make? What did we do that we shouldn't have done, or didn't do that we should have?" This will help you spot problems in advance, in time to decide how you will prevent them from happening.

Let's look at some of the things that can get in the way—and maybe even consider a thing or two you can do to face these obstacles.

An Unpredictable Future

One of the simple facts about the future is that you don't really know what is going to happen. By planning you increase the odds that you can predict and influence the future, but you cannot fully know or control it. Accept that simple fact, and be willing to be surprised. A misplaced belief that you are able to control all forces will leave you unnerved and unprepared when you discover that you can't. Anticipate the fact that some unanticipated things will occur. You can and should develop some contingency or backup plans. Most important, though, is to roll with the punches if you get hit by something you didn't plan for and be ready to take advantage of some unexpected opportunity.

Lack of Skill

Most planning situations in community change do not call for sophisticated skills. If you feel hampered that your planning process can't move forward because your data collection, data analysis, and consequent decision-making methods are not sufficiently complex, you might be overdoing things a bit. Hagebak (1982) called this problem the "bog of sophistication." Check also to see that this lack of skill is not simply a justification for not getting started. Large, highly complex change efforts require some sophisticated planning, but most changes are really not all that demanding.

Every day each of us answers the basic questions involved in planning: "What do you want to have happen? What do you have going for you? What is getting in your way? Knowing this, what

do you need to do?" We do this so often and so easily, whether it involves driving to the store or figuring out dinner, that we don't even notice we are planning, but indeed we are. You need to recognize that you not only have the fundamental skills but that you use them all the time. All you have to do is apply them in a different arena. What you already know is probably enough to get you started. If you need to know more, ask a planning expert for some direction or some time. Colleges, public agencies, and some social service organizations have planners. You can generally find someone pretty good who can give you a hand.

Lack of Interest

Most of us are not interested in doing things that are boring and have little value, especially if we don't think we are good at them. Planning is no different. If you want to involve people in planning, you have to confront these three obstacles. To promote a little more interest in planning, first of all you have to make it interesting. There is a natural excitement for doing or creating something new; capitalize on this. Don't wear people down with the mechanics of planning. Build on their enthusiasm. Also, give a little attention to the set-

ting. Consider doing this over pizza or in a cabin on a weekend retreat, or somehow making things a little different, a little unique, a little fun.

Second, you will probably have to confront people's previous experiences of fruitless planning. Invite them to point out how they will make sure that doesn't happen this time. You probably won't convince the reluctant by talking about the importance of planning. You have to approach the process as if it is important and clearly directed to improving the problem situation. Avoid making planning appear too grand. This often generates skepticism. When planning takes on a life of its own, it becomes irrelevant and cannot live up to its lofty promises. People realize this right away. They will go through the motions of planning, but they won't make an investment in it.

Third, the way you present planning will give people the message that this is something they can do. Calling planning "figuring out what we need to do," for example, will go a long way toward bringing things down to earth. Take your planning process one step at a time. Providing a rough overview of the process can be helpful. However, if you go through an exhaustive list of everything that needs to be done and all the things not to do, you will end up confusing people. Guiding people through the steps one at a time keeps them on track and gives them something specific to do. From time to time show how a particular step relates to what you want to accomplish so participants know why they are doing what they are doing.

Thirst for Immediate Action

When emotions are running high, people want to act. They don't want to mess around with this planning business. They certainly don't want to hear the learned voice of reason telling them to calm down and think this through thoroughly. That's all right. Plan a little bit. The energy they now have for action is probably more valuable anyway. (The exception to this is if what people want to do is clearly so shortsighted that they will cause more problems than they are solving. Then you might have to get them to stand back for a minute to take a broader look before acting.) If you can, get some agreement on where you want to end up, and then just worry about what you can do right now, and how you can do it. After a period of initial fervor, the group is usually ready to determine some longer-range strategy.

You do have a delicate balance to strike here. You don't want to get into the habit of not planning, but by the same token, you don't want to dampen enthusiasm and cut off spontaneity. Community change does require some discipline, and not everyone wanting to be an activist is ready to accept that. Over time, certain roles will emerge with some people acknowledged as providing strategic leadership whereas others can be counted on for taking needed action. As long as both aspects are valued, the group stands a good chance of achieving some success.

Problems occur if none of the activists want to seriously think ahead. Some people in leadership roles would rather be active than effective. They rather like their image as activists, and it is in serving that image that they are mainly interested. You will have to watch for this in yourself as well as with other members of your group. It leads to a resistance to considering the consequences of acting because the consequences are really not important, just the action is. It is vital to keep a sense of purpose. Planning will inform your actions with a sense of purpose.

If you are mainly interested in commanding attention, get into a gorilla suit and skydive onto the field in the middle of a big football game—you can scare a lot of people, it is exciting, and you will probably get on the news.

Planning to Avoid Action

At the opposite end of the spectrum are the *risk avoiders* who are hesitant to take action and so plan the thing to death. Risk avoiders want to make sure all risks are identified and minimized before any action is taken. Some want actions to come with guarantees. Sometimes the effort to plan is easier than the work involved in implementing the plan. After all, you can control the plan; you can't control everything that happens when you put things in motion. Testing your great ideas is a lot harder than declaring them. As the situation changes and new information becomes available, risk avoiders keep retooling their plans. They could do this forever, and probably would if something didn't come along to give them a push. (Something usually does.) The sad thing is that despite all their planning they aren't really prepared for action because they don't really want to act.

If you suspect that this is going on, you must confront it. Some of the following questions might be helpful for bringing the concern out in the open: "When will we have enough information to act?" "Are we more afraid of failure than we are willing to take a chance at changing things?" "Are we afraid of the work that we will have to do if we actually start acting on our plans, or are we afraid that our plans won't work?" This can lead to some productive discussion, and it can lead to action as you realize what you have been doing. Be careful not to demean or ridicule people for their fears. That approach will just lead to denial and divisiveness. It really is all right to feel uncertain. If that is what is going on, accept the fact that you feel that way, and accept, also, the fact that you still need to get going.

Belief That Plans Won't Have an Impact on Decision Making

There is a game that goes like this: person in authority asks subordinates for their ideas; gives them the impression that they are really being listened to; makes them feel part of this shared process; and then goes ahead and does what she wanted to do all along.

Has this ever happened to you? Probably. You feel like a dupe, don't you? It has probably happened to others in your group as well, so don't be surprised when you encounter this sort of skepticism. And don't encourage it by playing the same game yourself. Sometimes an idea someone else offers may be less perfect than your own, but it may still be acceptable. Accepting this "less perfect" idea may be the wiser course, especially if it is workable and others have a strong investment in the proposal. Broad ownership of the plan is usually more important than perfection anyway.

Encouraging people to take some responsibility for implementing their ideas (if the group agrees that they are worth doing) is one way to show that you take the suggestion seriously. With this approach, the person can make sure that the action will be handled in the way he wanted. If you ask people for information for planning, let them know how the information will be used and what purpose it will serve. Also, let participants know how the information will benefit them and the change effort.

Forgetting to Include People in Planning

Leaving people out of the planning process can be deadly. Some may passively or aggressively attempt to sabotage the direction you decide to take. Others may simply have little interest in pursuing a course they did not help set and that they may not fully understand.

Take stock of who should be and who would want to be included, or at least invited, to help determine your future goals and actions. Look at those who operate in the relevant systems your change effort engages, particularly those stakeholders in the benefit, action, and target communities. (These communities, which constitute your arena of action, are discussed in Chapter 5.) Try to figure out roles for those who want to be involved. Know that there will be a few people who did not participate in planning, even though they were invited, who will later raise objections. It is important for you to commit to actively inviting people and keeping open opportunities for participation. It may be appropriate to exclude someone from developing your plans. However, if you do, make sure you honestly examine your reasons for doing so, and also make sure you have considered the cost of their exclusion.

> ### ◄ Take a Moment to Discover ◄
>
> Can you remember a situation in which people making plans about something important to you could have involved you but left you out of the discussion? How did you feel about it? How did that affect your commitment to the plan or your trust in those making the plans?

Defining the Problem in Terms of the Solution

Defining the outcome you want to achieve and defining the means for achieving that outcome are two different things. For example, children in your neighborhood are threatened by cars speeding down a busy street they must cross on their way to school. This is something the neighborhood wants to take action on. Someone pipes up: "The problem here is that we don't have a streetlight at the intersection." The room positively flutters with the simultaneous bobbing of many heads. Hold it right there, don't move. You are in danger of defining the problem as a solution. Sorry, folks, but your problem is not the lack of a streetlight. The problem is that your kids may get killed. The streetlight may or may not be a good solution, but if that is all you think about, you will close yourself off from thinking about any other approach to achieving your goal. If you put in the streetlight and your kids still get hurt, you haven't accomplished your purpose. However, if your kids are safe without a streetlight (maybe you put in speed bumps or a crossing bridge instead), you have solved your problem. Which is more important, your children's safety or a streetlight? Now, which do you want to work on?

When you are defining the outcome you want to achieve, ask yourself: "If the situation were different only in this way, would we be satisfied?"

Groupthink

Many groups establish norms that prevent the free expression of ideas. In these groups, there is pressure to maintain an agreeable atmosphere free of dissension. The primary goal becomes promoting a shared perception of reality rather than discovering and shaping that reality. Conformity is stressed and accomplished more often by subtle than by direct pressure. Gentle reminders are given to members that the group has things under control and that expressions of doubt are expressions of lack of faith in the group and its leaders. The group conspires to ignore signs of trouble. Open disagreement is seen as an attack on the group and its prevailing wisdom. To suggest that there is a better way or that the group is overlooking something important is just not done.

Participants are not willing to be seen as deviants or troublemakers who upset the group's illusion of unanimity and control over events. To protect themselves and the group from this discomfort, participants censor their own thoughts. People keep their misgivings about a proposed course of action to themselves, sometimes taking potshots later on a failed course of action. Janis (1982) has labeled this process *groupthink*.

You can see how dangerous this process can be to a group. Their unreal view of reality can have some very real consequences. Agreements that are superficial can fall apart when put to the test. Things that have been ignored can rise up to knock down the group's efforts. The sad thing is that groups often aren't aware of their use of groupthink, and they are left confused about what went wrong.

Keep on the lookout for signs of groupthink, and bring it up if you think you may be closing off discussion to force group agreement. A good, simple question to ask is this: "Is there anything we don't want to look at?" When you have the time to use them, techniques such as brainstorming, force field analysis, and projected 20/20 hindsight should give you a good rein on groupthink tendencies.

CONCLUSION

Planning requires that you acknowledge and accept the fact that you will have to change your behavior. If planning doesn't help you figure out what you want, determine what to do, prepare you to do it, and keep you on track, planning is a waste of time. But if planning increases the chances you will do the right thing at the right time in the right way to get what you want, and you put it to use, then it has been time well spent.

Powerful planning not only gives you direction but builds commitment, enthusiasm, and confidence. Planning is a vision of a better future made more possible by the determination of purposeful actions. If you grab hold of that vision and make it yours, if you take those actions in the present to shape the future, if you continue to pay attention and keep your plans alive, evaluating and making adjustments along the way, one day you will look around at what you have accomplished—and it will feel good.

A LITTLE OFF KEY

The clatter of chairs being arranged on the concrete church basement floor provides the opening notes for tonight's meeting. For the past few months a few of you have been listening to people talk about "what needs to be done." Of course, you have been kind of prodding them by talking about what might be different, and even what they have that they can use to make things better. You and your partner Carrie have had a number of face-to-face conversations with individuals to get a sense of things and to stir some interest. You have identified some key stakeholders, but you have decided not to talk with those who seem to just want things their way. You don't have time for that.

You and the other members of the core group have gathered some good information from the conversations and from other sources. The flip charts are in place. You have the marking pens, little sticky dots for voting, and even a brief introductory PowerPoint presentation that gives a little background and identifies a range of issues that you have been hearing about. You have some provocative questions prepared and three other people to lead parts of the session. You're going to put together a plan.

"Come on, let's get going." It's Allan; you can hear his irritation. He's already told you that planning is what people who aren't willing to act do to waste time. Other people are getting a little fidgety too. You take that as a good sign. The energy is high. "Okay, says Carrie, "let's start."

After her introductory piece no one says anything. Uh oh. But then three people begin to talk at once, and things get going. Sounds like everyone has the same sense of what's important. You take

them through the *images of potentiality,* and their creativity begins to shape pictures of a better future that you'd never have thought of. They seem to enjoy brainstorming, though a few find it hard not to criticize or discuss ideas.

Five different things emerge as general goals, and you go through each one, looking for the obstacles you will face. Lots of obstacles. That early energy seems to be draining. Then, again, it's been a long night. Time to figure out what tasks need to be done. "One last step. Then we'll go home," you say to get the group back on track. "So, what are some of the things we should be doing this year?" you ask. No one says anything. Uh oh.

REFLECTION QUESTIONS

1. What parts are in place that will be helpful in putting together an effective plan?

2. What seems to be missing?

3. What is happening that might make things more difficult?

4. What planning steps are being taken? What other steps would you suggest?

5. What time frame for the plan has been established?

6. What is being done to promote interest? What else needs to be done?

7. What techniques are being used? How might they be used a bit better?

8. What information is present to help the participants? What seems to be missing?

9. Which planning obstacles are being faced?

10. How will this group determine if the plan is being worked and if it is working?

11. Who owns the plan? How can this be seen?

GROUP ACTIVITY: IDENTIFYING A NEIGHBORHOOD CHANGE

Planning should be a creative, fun, energizing experience fueled with imagination. Imagine that you all are residents of the same neighborhood, and that neighborhood has come up with this vision: The XYZ neighborhood is the most beautiful, safest, and most friendly neighborhood in Alphabet City. You are now coming together to bring that vision into focus and action.

Divide the larger group into teams of six to eight members. Each team will use its imagination to identify a change in the neighborhood, one that will be a *good start* for making the neighborhood

better. Using the images of potentiality method and the rules of brainstorming presented in this chapter, each team develops a list of images of what better neighborhood conditions can actually look like. Here are the steps:

1. Pick an imaginary date in the future far enough away to give you sufficient time to work to accomplish your goal but not so far that the sense of urgency to act on the issue is lost. You might want to select a date about 6 months from now. (2 minutes)

2. Now, pretend that this future date is the present. So "today" is (whatever date you have selected). You are there now. Visualize the situation today. Go ahead; look around. What does your team see? Using a flip chart or other large surface to write down ideas, brainstorm all the things the group sees that the neighborhood has accomplished. Do your best to identify clear, visual images. If you can take a picture of it with a camera, it is an image. It's hard to know just what "things look better" means, but "100 new trees" gives you a good picture. Remember your team is brainstorming, so list everything mentioned, perhaps putting some into an "idea" column, and some into an "images" column. Have some fun with this; really let your imagination flow. (10 minutes)

3. After the brainstorming is complete, see if there are some images that really are the same. Go ahead and combine these images into one image. (3 minutes)

4. See if anything else can be moved from the idea column to the image column. (3 minutes)

5. Give each team member five "sticky dots." These represent votes. The team first has to agree that they will support the neighborhood choice for a beginning project. Often a good starting point is to select something that is most

interesting rather than most important. This also has to be something the group thinks it can get done by the date your team has selected. Team members can use all five dots on one image, or they can spread them out on a few images. This lets members weight their votes for things they most care about. (You might want to pretend that a couple of team members are neighborhood members whose involvement you really want, but whose interests are often overlooked, for example, young people. If so, give them seven dots instead of five. This technique increases the volume of voices not often heard.) Team members then place their dots next to the images they want the neighborhood to start with. (3 minutes)

6. Now count the dots to see which image the group would like to start with. (3 minutes)

7. State a simple goal to complete the activity. For example, if your image is about a community garden, you might say: "By (state the date) we will have planted a garden at (name location) that is 500 square feet and has at least three different kinds of flowers and four different kinds of vegetables. At least 15 neighbors have been involved in this project." (5 minutes)

HELPFUL WEBSITES

Links to the organizations briefly described here are on the companion website at www.cengage.com/humansvcs/homan.

American Planning Association (APA). This nonprofit, public interest and research organization specializes in urban, suburban, regional, and rural planning. It has many local chapters and also has special divisions that focus on specific interest areas such as Planning and the Black Community, Small Towns and Rural Planning, and Gays and Lesbians in Planning. It provides guidance on neighborhood collaborative planning, kids and the community, and other special planning features. APA offers many useful publications.

World Future Society. This is an association of people interested in how social and technological

developments are shaping the future. It serves as a neutral clearinghouse for ideas about the future, including forecasts, recommendations, and alternative scenarios regarding what may happen in the next 5, 10, or more years. This information can help to guide your planning and decision making.

National Civic League. The league offers publications on planning, community visioning, and community building themes.

Centers for Disease Control. The Evaluation Working Group at the CDC provides a wealth of links to many very usable publications regarding evaluation.

Concept Mapping Resource Guide. Though this site has some proprietary interests, it is a good source for general introductory materials, research and case studies illustrating the use of the concept mapping.

Chapter 8

People—The Most Valuable Resource

CHAPTER HIGHLIGHTS

- You are not going to do it all by yourself
- Organization, a process and an outcome
- Six levels of participation
- Talents and assets the organization needs
- Personal characteristics of influential members that affect the organization
- Steps for getting people involved
- Ways to keep people involved
- Everyone has something to contribute
- Recognizing progress
- Special considerations for working with volunteers
- Cultural competence
- Observations on human behavior

You are not going to do it all by yourself. Any change that amounts to anything involves other people, maybe even a lot of people. Although few people will have sustained involvement over the life of the change effort, many people will play a role in its success. These people aren't just sitting around offering advice (well, maybe a few are); they are doing things to accomplish a specific purpose or set of purposes.

You will come to grips with the fact that the originators of an idea cannot keep it to themselves if they hope to get anything done. Not only do you have to share the idea but you need to share ownership of the idea as well. You will realize that success requires the time, talents, and perspectives of many other people. You will also know that all these people aren't going to flock to the cause. You have to go out and get them.

In previous chapters in Part 2 you have learned to better understand your community and how power operates within it, and you have been given some suggestions on how to plan your actions to produce the desired results. However, unless you are capable of being in several places at the same time, nothing significant is going to happen unless other people become involved. This chapter looks at how you involve people, how you develop and keep commitment, and how people's talents and energies can be put to work. Everything happens through relationships. That can't be said often enough. The three features of relationships are communication, trust, and mutual interest. Strengthening any one of these three will affect the other two.

Much of the work in a change effort is commonly done by people who are not paid to do it. This requires special attention. The nature of voluntary activity, particularly when complementing the work of paid staff, is an important consideration. Finally, as you work on various change attempts, you will find yourself reflecting on why people do the things they do to help or hinder.

Whether you need 2 people or 2,000 people, you need to understand them and understand how they can relate effectively to one another and to the challenges that beckon them in the process of change. Organization is fundamental to your success. Organization means people working in concert. It is both a process and an outcome. You do things through organization, and you build an organization as you do things.

WHAT DO YOU NEED?

As described in Chapter 5, three types of communities will be affected by your attempt to make a difference: the benefit community, the action community, and the target or response community. Taken together these communities within your arena of action are called your interest community. There are times when these are three different communities, and times when they are one and the same. Ideally, you want to have people from each type of community to aid you or even to make up your organization. There may well be conflicts among and even within these groups. Gaining a clearer understanding of these differences and how to negotiate among them will at the very least require some participation from those who will be affected by your decisions and actions (Patton, 1987). If the benefit, action, and target communities are all the same, this is a little easier. If they are all different, you face more of a challenge.

If you have decided to bring people together in a grand scheme to save the planet, or at least to clean up part of the neighborhood, does it matter whom you involve? If you just get a bunch of people together, won't that do to get started? The answers are yes and yes.

Yes, at first you make do with what you have. Enlist the support of anyone who is interested. From that group you will be able to get a lot of what you need.

And yes, it eventually does matter who participates. Over the long haul, any random group of people probably will not do. Unless your random group is so large that you are bound to find what you need within it, you need to be more intentional in your recruiting. In Chapter 7, the importance of involving those affected by plans and decisions in the process of making planning decisions was stressed. This notion applies to all of the organization's activities. This ethic is fundamental. As you consider the various ways of generating, utilizing, and maintaining the human resources of your organization, understand that those affected by the organization's actions, particularly members of the benefit community, play a critical role in determining actions and in taking them (Fawcett, Seekins, Whang, Muir, & Balcazar, 1982).

In a similar vein, your organization will benefit from the participation of those who have a role in implementing the change you are seeking. Without their involvement you run the risk of the change being sabotaged once agreement to establish new, more beneficial conditions has been reached among the parties who comprise the interest community. If the change does not make sense to those charged with implementing it, they will likely greet it with passive resistance at best. Conversely, if this group has an investment in the change, particularly through participation in its design and the actions to bring it about, there can be a substantial payoff. They will want to see the change work, and they may well extend themselves to see that it does. Because these are the people who will actually end up doing what needs to be done, it is their actions that ultimately determine the effectiveness of the change.

Involving people is a purposeful, ongoing process that addresses three essential considerations. First, the number of people and level of their commitment and participation must fit the demands of the situation. Second, particular talents and assets must be found among the participants. Third, participants who bring positive personality characteristics will be particularly valuable to the effort. Sometimes you will find one person who can offer all these things to the organization, but this is rare. Generally, if an individual can give any one of these things to the organization, it will benefit, and you should try to get her involved.

Let's take a closer look at each of these attributes.

Level of Participation

What does participation or involvement mean? Does everyone have to operate at the same level of intensity? No, involvement can occur in many different ways. Everyone does not have to have the same zeal. Making fervor a requirement of partnership would eliminate a lot of potential help and power.

Six different opportunities for participation are available to those who are interested:

- Leadership, the core group participants
- Workers, ongoing active participants
- Assisters, occasionally active participants
- One-shot participants
- Advisers
- Inactive, general supporters

As a matter of practice, people will change their level of involvement from time to time. Even if they move from a more active to a less active role, they may still feel a strong affiliation with the effort if communication with others in the organization continues to occur.

Leadership.   The core group, that handful of people who worry more, plan more, and provide more direction for the project than others, offers the most active level of participation. The organization and the changes it seeks are important in these people's lives. Even when alone they think about it, trying to understand more of the dynamics of the situation and what should be done to deal with them. These are the people who keep in close contact with one another to talk about what is going on. They meet more frequently than required by the routine schedule. They expect to participate in meetings, not just

attend them. They make many of the decisions about what needs to be done and understand, for the most part, why. These are the people for whom the organization and its agenda really matter, who want to keep things alive and moving. It is they who feel anxious about the organization's support and strength and who feel a real sense of loss should the effort dwindle and die.

The core group usually consists of 6 to 10 people, rarely more than that, especially for new organizations. The need for core group members to keep in steady communication with one another tends to limit its size. Members expect to be part of all major decisions and frequently feel a little hurt—or maybe even very angry—if left out.

Members may be elected, self-selected, or specifically recruited. They are often the products of the winnowing process that eliminated the initial big talkers and the only moderately interested from this role. The core group goes by a variety of names, including the steering committee, the planning committee, the Friday morning group, or the board.

Over time you may notice that members of the core group are no longer able or really interested in participating at this level. When this happens, it is common for formerly very active leaders to leave the organization altogether. The organization loses the wisdom, sense of history, and confidence that these individuals bring. It is important to find ways for these leaders to move "down" in their level of involvement, but not "out."

Workers.   Ongoing, active participants support the organization and its aims but choose not to take part in all the deliberations. They are willing to follow the leadership of core group members. These participants maintain a steady interest in the organization and take part in many of its activities. Along with the core group, they do much of the work of the organization and may even have particular responsibility for a major set of functions.

The difference between them and the core group is that participants at this level do not have as clear a picture of the overall program of the organization as it evolves, nor do they really care to. They either don't want to or can't currently attend all the meetings, consider and develop strategy, or worry about things in general. They only occasionally play a part in decision making. These workers may trust the members of the core group and the general direction things are taking, lack the self-confidence needed for deeper involvement, or be too busy or otherwise not that interested. You may well find potential (as well as previous) leaders among these workers. An effective organization will look for opportunities to groom new leadership and make sure that participation in the core group is open to people willing to make that kind of commitment.

Assisters. Occasionally active assisters do things when the mood strikes them or when they are specifically asked. Having a moderate interest, they would like the effort to be a success and will lend a hand, but they really don't want to get blisters.

Other occasional assisters have periods of high activity interrupted by stretches of apparent indifference. Their interest runs hot and cold. Organizational matters can hold their attention for only so long before their enthusiasm fades. Don't fuss over these members, but do maintain communication with them. Although their participation is sporadic, it can come in handy. It is often available when asked for, and over time some assisters develop a stronger affiliation with the organization once they discover their particular niche.

One-Shot Participants. This category includes those who do something only once or are involved for only a short period of time and then disappear from the scene altogether. These are people who soon learn that they have overestimated their interest or underestimated the cost of their participation. Some discover that the change effort isn't what they thought it was. Others simply flit from one thing to another, not quite sure what they are looking for, maybe never really finding it. Still others have a sneeze experience. Drawn by the excitement that a change effort offers, they step out of their ordinary roles to do some things, maybe even a flurry of actions they consider dramatic. Once they get this excitement or drama out of their system, they return to the safety of their normal routine. These sneezers get a big bonus. For the next 25 years (and perhaps well beyond), they can talk about the time they were "radical." Over time these tales can grow to rival the fabled "one that got away."

Even one-shotters can be a benefit to the undertaking. They may take part in organizational activities that require a high level of intense energy for a short period of time. Or they may be willing to join in a show of force and stand as part of a crowd. You may need people to do this. Although it would be nice to have more ongoing involvement, even these limited acts can be useful. Just don't waste a lot of your time trying to reenergize previous participants if it is pretty apparent that their batteries have gone dead.

Advisers. Advisers give little sustained attention to the workings of the organization, yet they can be valuable. These are people who can provide particular insights, ideas, or technical information. They are the people you go to when you want to hold a press conference but aren't sure how; or they might tell you how to get a particular action started or how to influence a particular official. Maybe they can give you pointers on how to strengthen your organization.

Most often you seek out advisers because of their experience in similar situations or because they have expertise in an area about which you know little. These supporters are usually more effective if you initiate their involvement by asking for some guidance. True advisers are different from those self-appointed saviors of the cause who just want to tell you what to do but don't want to sweat themselves. Frequently, members of the organization resist unsolicited advice as meddling or uninformed. Frankly, it is often just carping from the sidelines.

Many of those whom you will tap as advisers don't consider themselves to be members of your organization. In fact, their distance from the organization might bring some very helpful objectivity. Even though remaining somewhat detached, once they have contributed to what you are doing, they will develop an interest in your success, particularly if you report back on how their counsel was used. Due to the natural resistance most of us have to advice, you may need to legitimize the adviser's role within the organization before it can be used effectively.

Inactive General Supporters. You may enlist the support of community members who have a high degree of visibility and credibility but who may not do much actual work. Their assistance comes

DID YOU KNOW?   The Committed Visionary

Few, if any, people in the organization will be as committed as those (you?) who initially recognize and act on the need for change. Even in situations that might seem minor, the visionary, the originator of an idea and its required action, will be more dedicated than anyone else. The visionary sufficiently and personally felt the need to act before anyone else. That attachment to the reason for acting is not easily forgotten or dulled. It allows the visionary to weather the storms of doubt, confusion, and temporary setbacks better and longer than anyone else.

Moved unaided to action, the visionary has a greater fullness of involvement and often a greater need for success. Lack of success or abandonment of the effort comes much harder. Abandonment seems to repudiate or at least devalue those initial beliefs that were sufficient to risk rejecting complacency. Only success justifies the initial urge, the risk of taking action.

You need to understand this fundamental principle. Few will share, in quite the same way, your belief in the importance of what you are setting out to do. To ignore this invites misunderstanding and disappointment.

in the form of an endorsement of your effort. Questions regarding your intentions and legitimacy will be asked—not always out loud—and the support of influential community members can help calm these uncertainties and, in fact, signal particular groups that you should receive active support. Participation by these individuals usually comes in the form of an agreement that their name may be used in conjunction with your effort.

Other general supporters are people you may never know. They don't show up for any meetings or work assignments. They probably don't even feel that they are part of the change effort. They watch what you are doing and wish you well. As long as you make an effort to let people know what you are doing, you can trust that these supporters will be out there.

So what good are they? Even though they do not participate in any specific activity of the organization, they may contribute importantly to its success. Through many subtle means, perhaps talking to a friend, maybe writing an unsolicited letter to a public official, or simply voting a certain way, they help create a climate of change. Whoever makes decisions with regard to the change has to pick up signals that the change will ultimately meet with general acceptance, if not approval. Though inactive in your organization, these general supporters help transform the atmosphere in which it operates. Foster this support.

With six potential types of participants, how do you know who is going to be what type? You really don't. That clears things up a lot, doesn't it? Here are some clues that may point you to those who are likely to be more involved. Look for people who have made some investment in the effort or who have some special relationship to the issue the organization is working on or to the people working on it. Next, notice the ways people respond to requests to help out, as well as the extent to which they initiate actions or offer suggestions on what they can do. These are probably good candidates for active involvement. Those who don't follow through on their agreements or their own offers to contribute will probably be marginal participants.

Remember that only those who know about the organization can participate at all. Provide potential members with knowledge about your goals, activities, and other members. And be sure to provide clear opportunities for involvement. People unsure of your desire to include them or how they can be included may be hesitant to help out. You may mistake this hesitancy for lack of interest. Check to see that opportunities for involvement are real.

The best advice is to pay attention to people: listen, resist snap judgments, and be patient. When opportunities are real and communication is maintained, people will respond to their level of interest and self-confidence. Over time you will get a good sense of who wants to participate in a meaningful way and who is looking for something else. Those who are really not interested won't do much. Don't waste your time trying to change that. Figure out how their level of interest can benefit the organization and make use of it without pretending it is different from what it is. Those who really are interested will keep trying to help out if you give them half a chance. Help them discover how they fit into your organization.

Talents and Assets

At different stages of your organization's life it will need people to do different things. When your organization is just getting started, you need people who can inspire and motivate others. Later, when you are trying to overcome resistance from those who oppose you, you would benefit from people who have strategic skill or influence with the opposition. Although your group will more than likely have to meet most of the essentials on the following list, understand that you will not always have to have all these things available at the same time. Recruit what you need when you need it.

Numbers.   If you can hold all your meetings in a broom closet, you are in big trouble. The right number of visible participants will depend on the change you are working toward. Attempting to make a change within a private social service agency may require the visible involvement of only half a dozen workers. Making a change in a large public school system may involve hundreds or even thousands of people.

Numbers give credibility and a sense of confidence to participants and outside observers as well. People may have to see that others are making the decision to join in the action before they feel good about their own decision to become involved. Those you are trying to impress, particularly the opposition, will take you more seriously if they believe you are more than just a handful of idealists or complainers. Numbers also give you access to other resources your organization will require. People bring skills and talents and community connections that can benefit your effort.

Doers.   The people in your group will have to do things, not just talk about them. Some of these things are tedious and time consuming. You need people who are responsible in making commitments and following through. This includes those willing to take their share of the load without having to be pressured into it. Just as important, they have to let others take a share as well.

Opinion Leaders.   You have seen this happen. There is a gathering, maybe a staff meeting. Someone presents a new idea or suggests a different approach, and a number of eyes turn to look at the opinion leader. If she rolls her eyes, a collective belief that this is a bad or silly idea begins to emerge. If she nods her head, the suggestion is taken seriously. People, especially when unsure, frequently look to a select few to help inform and shape their perceptions. The opinion leader might be a person with formal authority, but often is not. You know who these people are in your arena of action. Get them involved in your organization, or at least on your side. They give you credibility and an avenue of communication to others who may be uncertain about joining in.

Potential Organization Leaders.   Leaders provide the organization with energy, confidence, and direction, along with a host of other things. Without leadership, nothing will be accomplished. The organization will fall apart. Leadership is an essential requirement for any organization.

Different types of leadership are needed at different stages of the change process, and not all leaders will sustain their interest. Further, leaders who were helpful in early stages may become difficult obstacles later on. As a result, your organization will experience a turnover of leadership, probably in the first 6 months if your effort lasts that long. This is natural; don't be surprised when it happens. Creating a pool of potential leaders and purposefully developing new leadership is absolutely essential if the organization is intended to have an extended life. You cannot develop the organization without developing new leadership. It is that basic.

One of your primary challenges as a change agent is to identify people who can perform leadership functions. Involve them in the organization and groom their leadership abilities. Remember, all current leaders were once potential leaders. Check to see who among those currently involved, perhaps in a minor way, has some potential for leadership.

A brief note here about leaders and leadership. Leaders aren't necessarily those people who are always in the spotlight. There are many different leadership functions. Some of these valuable roles include strategists, coordinators, public speakers, problem solvers, and those who help improve communication and understanding among the members. Trying to find one person who can perform all these actions will probably be a waste of time; find several people who can each perform a few of them.

Motivators.   Things will drag. There will be times when progress seems slow or nonexistent. People will lose sight of what they are trying to accomplish and why. People will become discouraged.

After an initial burst of enthusiasm, the newness and excitement will probably wear off. Other demands will be made on people's time and attention. Members will get distracted and maybe even lazy. You need someone to fan the spark of interest—to help participants see the chance for success and its importance and to encourage them not only to stay involved and working but to want to. Motivators know how to keep the energy going. They know how to have fun. Deadly serious organizations generally die. Motivators keep things lively.

Influence Connections.   You need people who have some influence in the benefit, action, and target communities. If you can recruit an influential person who is actually a member of the community to be influenced, your effectiveness will be enhanced.

Those with influence may act as translators. That is, they can explain your organization's goals to others, possibly resistant others, in a way that produces a response. They know the right code words and the right concerns and can better communicate within that frame of reference. Understand that this type of communication can require some special knowledge or skill. Some individuals with influence will be able to get people to want to go along. Others will make people (again, this usually means opponents) go along, even if they don't want to. Determine what kind of influence you need, and try to get people who have it.

Specialized Skills or Talents.   Any organized effort requires skills in certain areas such as writing, planning, negotiating, and running meetings. Chances are that these basic skills will be present in any group of a dozen people, so check first within your current membership to see who has these skills to contribute or who can more fully develop them. If your organization is large (or you intend for it to be) or the issue it is tackling is complex, you will probably need some additional skills.

This doesn't mean that one person always gets stuck doing the same thing. Some skills can easily be taught to others, or new members with particularly needed skills can be recruited. Generally, the most effective recruiters of new talent are current members who possess the same skill to some degree. They know what to look for, and they are often motivated by a desire to get some help. Perhaps one of the single most critical skills, and one which is often overlooked, is the ability to run a meeting effectively. Take pains to find someone who has this skill and let that person run your meetings or purposefully teach the "chair" how to do it.

Access to Other Resources.   In addition to people, you may need a variety of other resources (meeting rooms, printing, computers) to get the job done. Look for people well connected to a particular resource you need, to the community in general, or to a bank vault. These individuals may be willing to use their contacts or their own resources to help the organization get what it needs.

The Right Stuff

The organization cannot be divorced from the personal characteristics of its more influential members. They will affect relationships among the participants and shape the personality of the change effort itself. Look for these important attributes in the people you want to have actively participating in your organization. Hardly anyone will have them all.

- *Roll with the punches.* This ability is one of the most important qualities to look for in people who are going to play an important role in your organization. Every member of your core group should possess this trait. It may not surprise you now to know that not everything is going to go perfectly as you proceed to implement the change, but it may surprise you when it happens. Even if people are not purposefully resisting you, your plans will get knocked around a bit. That is one of the few things about the change process that I can guarantee. You want to have people working with you who know this and can handle it when the time comes. Stupid little things will happen: equipment will break down at a crucial moment; someone will forget to follow through on an important and simple task; it will snow on your Fourth of July rally. Big things may well happen too. When setbacks occur, many people get flustered. You need someone who can stand in there. People who roll with the punches have a sense of optimism. They believe that things will eventually work out and that they will help make that success happen. They are able to keep things in perspective and not get rattled by the unexpected. If you have a few of these folks involved, you will be able to make things happen. These individuals help others acquire this attitude as well. It kind of rubs off on them.

- *A good sense of humor.* A lot of what happens will be funny. People who can recognize this and help others to do so as well are extremely valuable. Humor energizes, releases tension, and gives us a clearer perspective on the situations we encounter. Along with this, you want to have people who are playful. You've got to introduce some play into your work, or people will find something more interesting to do. Just because what you do is important doesn't mean it has to be gloomy.

- *Tenacity.* Tenacious people won't let go of a project until it is finished. My mother used to call this 'stick-to-it-tiveness,' an antidote to the disease of 'give-up-itis.' Change very often requires that you keep the pressure on those who are improperly using their power (Alinsky, 1972). Tenacious people won't back off at a few (often empty) conciliatory gestures; nor will they let confusion or uncertainty defeat them. No one will be able to talk these people into quitting when things get tough.

- *Risk-taking ability.* Change means going from the known to the unknown. Risk takers are able to try something new, give unconventional ideas serious thought, and do things beyond what is ordinarily expected. Effective change often demands that this be done. An effective risk taker is neither ignorant of nor overly worried about possible consequences. He is personally willing to accept the same risks asked of others. This type of person usually has a healthy quality of irreverence. Some people are intimidated by the contrived trappings of power, but risk takers are not. They know that people are people, and they are not afraid of them. Risk takers are willing to stand up for themselves because they know that not doing so may involve an even greater risk.

- *Regard for others.* As people work on the issue, they will be working with each other. Careful attention to both the task at hand and the people working on it are requirements for success (Johnson & Johnson, 2009; Napier & Gershenfeld, 2004). People who can recognize and respond to what is important for other people are a must. Those who have true regard for other people have true regard for themselves. Because of this, they understand that some people will see things differently from the way they see them. This allows them to handle, even encourage, disagreement effectively. They can assert their own point of view without attacking people who think differently.

- *Self-reliance.* There are no blueprints, no handy guides to show you each thing that needs to be done. You need people who are aware of and trust in their own abilities to figure things out. People who can look to themselves and believe that they have some answers or can at least find them will give confidence to others. This is particularly true if they can acknowledge their own uncertainty and have the confidence to confront it.

- *Desire to learn.* The process of change is the process of discovery. Once your organization stops learning, it starts dying. People who are eager to learn more give your organization a better understanding of what to do. Learning is not only a prerequisite for action, it is the result of it. Action puts ideas to the test and produces new ideas. A true learner knows that you can't wait until you know everything before you do anything. You will be learning by doing. A learner delights in challenges, seeing challenges as opportunities for discovery. People who know everything can't evaluate or easily redirect their actions. They need to limit or ignore contradictory information; they need to make others wrong. This can get old very quickly. Learners know they don't know everything, so they don't have to limit themselves by pretending to know. Quite the opposite. Learners don't place artificial limits on themselves.

- *Responsibility*. Responsible people understand and accept the requirements of their participation. They get things done. They expect that they will take care of the commitments they have made. They don't expect other people to do it for them, nor do they expect other people to be incapable of following through on commitments. They make mistakes, but rarely make excuses. Responsible people take initiative and accept authority, knowing that both are requirements of responsibility. They make

and receive suggestions because they value what they do.

- *Decision-making ability*. Progress depends on a series of decisions. Indecisiveness leads to organizational stagnation. The organization needs to have people who know how to make decisions, who are aware of different styles of decision making, and who know when to use each appropriately. Some situations call for consensus, others are best served by a vote, and yet others may require an individual with authority to make the choice (Johnson & Johnson, 2009). In making decisions, these people recognize the requirements of the situation, including the importance of maintaining relationships among people in the organization and the members' willingness to support and implement the decisions that are made.

Participants will contribute other qualities to the organization, but the ones I have mentioned here are basic. Without them, or with too many people who act in the opposite manner, the organization will get nowhere and fall apart. No matter what else participants provide to the organization, they all give a bit (or a lot) of themselves. Who they are and the qualities and the characteristics they share will shape the character of the organization itself.

GETTING PEOPLE INVOLVED

Maybe you are thinking: "All right, so there are a variety of roles people can fill, but how do I get them involved in the first place?" Ask them. Although people may be expected to join something, the simple fact of the matter is that not many are clearly asked to do so. You may be surprised with the response you get when you take the time to ask.

According to a study by the Pew Partnership for Civic Change (2001), almost 90% of Americans believe that working with others is the way to solve community problems. They appear ready to take part in community efforts if they are effectively invited to do so. More than 40% of those who do not volunteer would like to get involved, but they don't know how or whom to call. This report reveals some differences on perspectives of community health, but there is a general sense of optimism. People who have strong linkages to the community are even more likely to become involved, as are those who have strong cultural or ethnic identity (Corporation for National and Community Service, 2007; Rubin & Rubin, 2008).

The Bureau of Labor Statistics (2009d) reported that 61.8 million people (26.4% of the population) volunteered for an organization in 2008, which is about the same number as in the previous year. These volunteers spent a median of 52 hours on volunteer activities. Almost 44% of those who volunteered did so because someone, usually a member of the organization, asked them to become involved. A smaller percentage, about 42%, became involved on their own initiative. The Corporation for National and Community Service (2008c) estimates that volunteers provided more than 8 billion hours of volunteer time in 2007. The Independent Sector has calculated the value of volunteer time at $19.51 per hour. That means that the value of volunteer time was more than $156 billion. Remember, these are only the volunteer hours for more formal organizations. This doesn't count the untold hours people provide contributing to less formal organizations and many other forms of helping. When people are concerned about their own financial situation, however, their financial contributions as well as their time declines sharply (Independent Sector, 2003). As the economic grip tightens for many Americans, we will see whether past patterns of decline hold or whether the shared sense of national crisis will continue to encourage citizens to take part in helping their communities.

Research by the Independent Sector (2002b, 2006) concluded that the best way to involve people is simply to ask them. If asked, 63% will volunteer, but only 25% will volunteer if not asked. Though different groups recognize different challenges, it appears that most Americans believe that challenges can be met, and most are willing to take part in meeting them. So ask.

To increase the likelihood that your approach will yield helpful, reliable members, follow this four-step process:

- Contact people
- Give them a reason to join
- Ask them to join
- Maintain their involvement

Contact People

For people to respond at all, you need to bring your organization to their attention. They need to know that you exist and want their involvement. If they don't know about you, they can't do anything with you. All active members, particularly the leaders, need to understand the importance of developing the membership of the organization. This is fundamental. One of the most important aspects of the leaders' job is to keep on the lookout for people who could be invited into the effort. Initiators of the change effort, in particular, need to fight the very real tendency to keep things to themselves.

Where do you find all these people? First, look around you. Your current contacts with individuals, particularly those with whom you work or who are involved in other community activities with you, will provide you with the best possibilities. When others working with you in the change effort also use their affiliations, the list of potential members can grow dramatically. This only works, though, if you are consciously seeking to recruit new participants. I cannot overstress that point. Regularly assess what you need, and stay on the lookout to invite those who can help to join your effort.

50/10 Rule

This is a simple, yet demanding rule; if followed, it will powerfully increase affiliation with your organization and its work. The rule is this: in the early stages of your organization's life, at least 50% of your time should be spent in one-to-one (or two-to-one), face-to-face conversation. At no time in your organization's life should this ever fall below 10%. This is more important than doing research, writing grant proposals, going to a meeting, or any other single activity you can do. Yet it is often an overlooked element of building an organization.

Making this type of contact brings you into direct relationship, not only with potential supporters, but with their networks as well. During the contact five basic things happen: you get to know the other person; you get to know their interests and abilities; they get to know you; they get to understand the issue you are working on; and you get to know whom they know. During these conversations a much deeper sense of understanding and affiliation will build. You move past intellectual discussions to gain insight into the person. You make connections between people, not just between people and issues. Remember, everything happens through relationships. You need to build relationships before you can ever hope to use them.

During these conversations you will find out levels of interest and readiness to help. You will discover how people can help out, and so will they. You will see how people understand and relate to the issue. There is no better way to do this. Even if the people are not ready to be active, they will be aware of what your organization is doing. They will likely talk about it to others. This is one of the best ways to affect community climate.

Many organizers call their first meeting much too soon. During meetings, especially initial meetings, people are in their meeting behavior mode. They may not reveal much of themselves, and they certainly don't readily reveal what they don't know. You need to build relationships and understanding before you hold your meetings, rather than during them. It is also much easier to build relationships among people if they already have a relationship with a few members of the organization when they get there.

This approach works best with two partners. This is helpful in a number of ways. First, people are just more comfortable and confident when they have the support of another individual. Next, partners can help each other remember what they had prepared to say. If you are a little nervous, it's easy to forget things, no matter how well prepared you are. Finally, two people convey the notion that there are a number of people with a shared interest. A single person can convey that only in words.

It is a fairly simple matter to draw up a list of people whose interest and involvement you would like to have. Then go see them. At the end of every conversation ask the question, "Who else should we be talking to?" This is likely to connect you to new networks of contacts and continue to spread your connections as you follow up. This is one of the most important rules of organizing.

Second, understand that you may need to make repeated attempts to contact people. You have to become part of their consciousness. People have many things to think about other than the change effort in which you are involved. If they do notice you, they may soon forget. More than one attempt will probably be necessary, particularly if your contact is not face to face.

Third, use more than one method to contact potential members (see Figure 8.1). Again, the more indirect your methods, the more likely that frequent as well as varied approaches will be necessary.

Fourth, when making contact with an individual, listen to their concerns as well. See if you can identify some problems or other circumstances you both have experienced (Max, 1980). Finally, the more personal and direct your contact is, the more likely you will be to receive a favorable response.

Give People a Reason to Join

First, people need to find the issue compelling. It needs to strike an emotional chord as well as an intellectual one. People also need to see themselves in the circumstances you intend to change. They need to see how their interests or the interests of people they care about are connected to what you are trying to accomplish. Further, they need to see that you have at least a decent chance of succeeding. If your goals are too impersonal or way too large, it will be hard to get a genuine commitment.

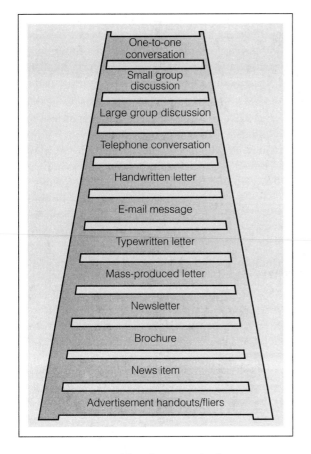

FIGURE 8.1 Ladder of Communication
Effectiveness

There are a variety of ways to reach people; the more direct ways will bring you greater likelihood of success.

SOURCE: Adapted from Howe, 1985.

In addition to believing in the importance of the group's goals and the group's ability to accomplish them, people join groups for a variety of reasons: they like the task or the activity of the group; they like the people in the group; or the group, though not directly satisfying their needs, can be a means to satisfying their needs elsewhere (Napier & Gershenfeld, 2004). People who believe in what you are doing, enjoy the activities you do, like some of the people involved, and see that participation can benefit them are the strongest candidates for membership. Understand that any one of these reasons could be sufficient to encourage a person to join. Both what you represent and the way you represent it are important. You have to

establish credibility with people before they will join your effort.

Ask for Participation

None of us likes rejection. Whenever you ask someone to do something or participate in something, you risk rejection. That's why some people don't ask at all. This is an entirely effective strategy for avoiding rejection. Unfortunately, it also avoids developing participation in your organization.

To want to soften the potential blow of rejection is normal. However, it is very difficult to soften the blow without sending the message that you expect it. If you tell people you expect to be rejected, that is probably what you will get. Another pitfall is the apologetic approach. It goes something like this: "I know you are real busy, and I hate to take up more of your time, but I want to ask you something, if you don't mind." Inspiring, isn't it? Usually, someone asking in this manner is simply unsure of the response she is likely to receive. Unfortunately, what this may be interpreted to mean is that the asker is not sure of the work she is doing or why. After all, why be apologetic? You are inviting someone to take part in something meaningful. That's a nice invitation to be able to offer.

There is no simple, handy way out of this. Recognize that many people are reluctant to take part in something that may cause them to alter their routines or their perception of "the way things are." They may have conceded to the burdensome conditions they currently face, and working to change conditions requires rejecting the investment they made in adapting to them. They may feel they cannot measure up to the demands involvement may make of them, perhaps exaggerating in their own minds just what those demands might be (Mondross & Berman-Rossi, 1992). Other people legitimately have other interests. They may genuinely be unable to give time now, and they may say yes later. Accept the fact that no matter how important the issue or how effectively phrased the request, some people will say no to you. This does not devalue you or your concerns.

Other members, ideally all members, need to be involved in recruiting. Depending on the size of your organization, you may want to have a group of members whose major responsibility is recruitment of new members. Here are some suggestions that should improve the likelihood that people will decide to work with you.

1. Decrease the distance. Many forms of distance can weaken the connection people have to the organization and its work—the distance between people and their understanding of the issue; the distance between people in the organization; the distance between understanding something needs to be done and knowing how to do it; even the physical distance between you and the people you want to have participate. The farther you are from face-to-face engagement and immediate experience, the less powerful will be the interaction. Of course, you can't have personal conversations all the time with everyone, but think of how you approach every aspect of this work. Where can you decrease the distance?

2. When you make a request of someone, make sure you provide an easy way for the person to respond to you. This is particularly important when the request is indirect, such as through a newsletter, because the response is not immediate. Ask yourself: "If people decide to say yes, how do they let me know, and how do they know I got their message?" Further, if they do communicate an interest in participating, ask yourself how they know what their next step is. Remember that involvement means action. If you merely say "thanks for your interest," you have not really promoted their involvement. You need to be certain they have received your response to their intent to take part and now know what to do.

3. Your request or "message package" should communicate the following elements: the purpose (aims or goals) of your organization; its importance; what it does; that it needs people; the types of things they can do; and the way they can let you know their decision to participate. Include in the activities they can do things that are fun (for example, social activities), things that are simple (for example, making phone calls, addressing envelopes, or giving money), and things that are "important"

(for example, meeting with legislators or appearing as a guest on a talk show). Based on your relationship and the nature of your contact (face to face versus a letter), you can modify these elements to best suit the situation.

4. Phrase your request (unapologetically) in the way likely to promote the best response. For instance, people may not want to join, but they may be willing to help. Joining may be perceived as involving endless meetings wrangling over subtle nuances in the bylaws. Helping may be perceived as doing some specific things to benefit the effort. Others may be willing to join by paying a few bucks to be a member, but may not be willing to help, which may imply doing a lot of work.

5. Ask specifically for what you need or for what you would like people to do. Make a clear request for a specific action or set of actions. Include clear options for participation. You may run across potentially valuable individuals who are only a little interested in participating at the present time but may well develop a stronger interest in the future. Ask them to do a few little things at first, and over time ask for more as their interest and feelings of competence develop. Even these initial simple requests should represent a level of participation slightly higher than these individuals would otherwise have considered for themselves. This will make their affiliation with the effort more real.

People's degree of participation relates to their interest and level of confidence, with confidence often being more important than interest. Confidence is related to three things: their comfort with the tasks or expected activities and obligations; their comfort with the people in the organization and their relationship with a sufficient number of people; and their comfort with the organization's culture.

There is an important caution here. Do not mislead people by saying, "The only thing I want you to do is ..." or "All you have to do is ..." if you have more that you intend for people to do. Stating one level of expectation while intending another will eventually create resentment. Though subtle, this is significantly different from increasing affiliation by making more important requests when there is more interest. Purposely misleading people tricks them when there is no real interest. Asking people for more participation should be based on developing interest. In this case, you are making a direct request for a new level of involvement. Don't ask people to do what they really are not interested in doing.

If someone you are grooming for greater involvement flat out asks you, "Is this all you want me to do?" you simply answer, "Of course, I'd like you to do more in the future, if you are interested, but this is how you can help out now." Expectations should be mutually clear and moderately challenging.

When you start out, there will be people aware of what you are doing who are not yet willing to make a commitment to join you. They may be waiting for you to prove yourself before they agree to work with you. These can be some of your future most valuable members. They are discerning people. They are only going to participate in something that means something (Von Hoffman, n.d.).

Then there will be others whose participation you would dearly love to have but who don't have any real intention of making a commitment. They may even lead you on a bit about helping. At some point you need to say to yourself that they know where to find you if they want to. If you have honestly made requests and created opportunities for participation that remain open and your desired recruits are aware of your organization, you probably have done enough. If you are spending your time falling all over yourself to get someone to participate, you have to stop and ask yourself why. You may want their participation because you somehow think you need their stamp of approval before you can truly take yourself seriously. When this is the case (as it really often is), you end up second-guessing yourself rather than doing the work you need to do. Believe me, you don't need the people who are just not interested. There will be plenty who are and plenty of things for you to do.

A number of people will simply seem to find their way to you and pitch in. That is encouraging, and you will experience it. Remember, though, that some people never help because they're never asked.

Maintain Involvement

Once people have expressed an interest and they're ready to go, you want to keep them going. You can talk people into joining, and you can talk them into staying one time, maybe twice. After that, there had better be more to it because they'll walk before you can do any more talking.

Several ways to promote continued affiliation revolve around some very basic human needs—needs for inclusion, control, affection, recognition, accomplishment, and altruism (Johnson & Johnson, 1997). Maintaining involvement is a matter of responding to these needs, recognizing that their importance varies with each individual and perhaps even with each cultural group (Latting, 1990). Further, personal contact to encourage continued involvement is critical, particularly for those whose personal networks may discourage participation (Rubin & Rubin, 2008). Here are some suggestions for keeping valuable members involved in the effort.

Make a special effort to help newcomers feel welcome (Dobson, 2003). Take a little time to introduce them to others in the organization and provide a bit of background on the issue and the work the organization has done and is currently doing. Make a purposeful effort to connect newcomers to the issue the organization is dealing with, the work of the organization, and the people in the organization. Don't expect people to make these connections on their own. How can you "decrease the distance"? Everyone who participates in the change process you are undertaking has something to offer, be it a skill, particular knowledge, personal connections, or other qualities that can benefit the organization. Keep an eye out to discover what each person can do, and be willing to ask her to do it when the time comes. Few things are as important for building your organization as your belief that every person has something to contribute. With this belief you will find ways to increase the investment of individual members and in doing so increase the cohesion and power of the organization. Without it you will use only the evident gifts of a few and dull the commitment of many, who may well become members in name only.

Most people feel uncertain in new situations involving strangers, so anxiety is the prevailing and dominant emotion at the start of any group setting (Napier & Gershenfeld, 2004). Change agents need to be aware of the stages of group development (see Chapter 11), particularly the uncertainty and wariness that accompany group beginnings (Mondross & Berman-Rossi, 1992).

Give people something to do, the sooner the better. When people respond favorably, put them to work right away. Give participants things to do that they can see as both meaningful to the undertaking and that generate a personal investment on their part. You will, or should, anyway, have a good idea of the types of things that need to be done. Often, you will have recruited someone with a specific task in mind. So, of course, this is what you will ask them to do. Still, it is usually a good idea to let them know about other things that need to be done that you would want their help on.

Wouldn't it just be easier to ask people what they can do? Certainly this question should be asked of each participant, but don't count on it to yield all the information you need. Some people may be new to participating in a change effort and simply don't know what they have to contribute. Even veterans of other change struggles often don't see how their skills in other areas fit with what the organization is trying to accomplish. And some are too shy, modest, or otherwise reluctant to let their talents be known.

Your aim here is to offer participants a range of tasks that to some degree match your perception of their level of skill, interest, and time. By the way, their interest and time will grow as their confidence grows. Self-assurance centers in three areas: confidence in knowledge of the issue, confidence in their relationships in the group, and confidence in task performance. Tasks that are short term and specific are usually better in the initial stages of involvement. Let members make the choice of what they want to do. They are more likely to do a better job on things they choose to do. Job satisfaction and involvement are important elements enhancing commitment (Dailey, 1986). Also, they become aware of other things the organization needs. This in itself communicates that they are needed in the organization, and it gives them things to think about doing in the future.

Give clear directions and adequate preparation. Even if you are working with people you already know pretty well, this change effort may be a different experience. It is new. By giving people the necessary background on the task they are to perform (for example, why these phone calls are

> **◼ Take a Moment to Discover ◼**
>
> Over the past year, if you stop and think about it, you have probably had the chance to join several groups or participate in some group activity. These may have been social groups or perhaps they involved more formal organizations. Maybe you were personally invited; possibly you just received a form letter or heard an ad on the radio.
>
> Which of these, if any, did you decide to take part in? What in particular attracted your interest or encouraged or discouraged your involvement? How did the way you were asked affect your decision?

important or a brief review of what the issues are) and making sure they have clear, complete directions, you will help people feel more confident in their abilities to do the job. They should also know whom to contact if they do have questions. This gives people permission to ask for added clarification if they need it.

Increase the responsibility of the work. Activities that are not sufficiently challenging or meaningful is one of the primary reasons that people stop giving their time (Corporation for National and Community Service, 2008d). Increased responsibility generally leads to an increased sense of ownership in the undertaking. It also increases the person's sense of value to the organization. You will constantly be amazed at how people undervalue their abilities. We are taught this devaluing process from kindergarten on. As a change agent, one of your most important challenges is to encourage people to unlearn those crippling messages and instead to acknowledge their competence, trust in it, and act on it. This means that you have to believe in the fundamental ability of people to do some things well—this includes you too.

If you are one of the initiators of the change effort, you have established a sense of ownership in the process. The mere fact (actually it is quite a significant fact) that you have gotten the ball rolling required a special investment on your part. You begin your participation in the group with a significant attachment to the organization and its purpose. This is not true of other participants. Their attachment will be different from yours, so you need to give theirs room to grow. Show how their work relates to the overall effort. People want to feel that what they do has a purpose. Develop leadership to provide more perspective, more energy, more personal fulfillment, more types of inspiration, and more shoulders to carry some of the load. You will need to include other people in offering all these things—welcoming, orienting, preparing, and so on. If you are the only one doing all this, you haven't paid enough attention to developing leadership, and you are probably getting pretty tired.

Give participants a chance to say no to some things. This is important, especially if someone has been doing a lot for the effort. Acknowledge the contributions the individual has made, and let the person know that someone else can do the job if she says no. This will strengthen the yes's you receive. By the way, giving people the right to say no while making them feel guilty about exercising that right isn't giving people a chance to say no.

Have people work together. Affiliation with others involved in the effort is important (Floro, 1989). Working together helps people get to know one another better. By relating to other people as well as to the task at hand, members strengthen their bond to the organization. On short-term projects, like addressing envelopes, it is often good to have people get together as a group. On long-term tasks, like doing background research, it frequently helps to have people work in pairs. Doing work with others increases motivation and accountability. Members are conscious about meeting the expectations of other participants, so they may do a little more than if they were doing things alone. Work doesn't have to be the sole focus. The social aspects involved in doing things with other people make the tasks more enjoyable and more attractive. Isolation diminishes enthusiasm and contributes to people feeling lost. Try to avoid this.

Help people to feel they are part of the group, an insider, not an outsider. To a large extent, working with others will accomplish this, but other steps should be taken or, in some cases, not taken. First, a "not taken." Watch out for inside jokes, stories, or perceptions that are mentioned in public but hold meaning for only a select few. Actions such as these convey that some people are more in the know than other people. The others feel less valued, less a part of things. It's no fun being an "other." Include others so they can join in the joke and in the group's shared history.

A number of steps can be taken to strengthen the sense of group affiliation and identity among the members. If your organization grows large, it may become less personal. Make a special effort to remember people's names and know how to spell them correctly. Invite participants to activities such as social get-togethers, parties, picnics, or going out for pizza. Members who are new or perhaps unsure of their status in the group (you will know who these people are) should receive a personal invitation in addition to any general announcement made.

Depending on the type of organization you develop, you may have membership cards, put together an electronic newsletter, post e-mail updates to a membership distribution list, or do any number of things that promote a sense of alliance.

Get to know people on a personal level. Personal relationships are the glue that holds the organization together. People are able to see that they themselves, not just their interest in the particular issue, are important to the organization. In turn, they communicate this to others. Ask for ideas and opinions. This brings members into the creative process of the organization, deepening their commitment. People value highly the things they create. (Don't forget those museum quality art projects you created in grade school.)

A couple of cautions are worthy of mention here. First, it is not a good idea to ask people for ideas about what other people should do. Most of us are quite happy to tell other people a lot of things that would seem sensible and easy to do—as long as we don't have to do them. When you invite suggestions about the direction to take, let members know you are looking for them to take part in putting the ideas into action.

Second, if you have an opinion or preferred course of action, don't ask someone else for hers. You may hear something different from what you were thinking. This can put you in a situation where you end up trying to discredit an idea you sought. If you want feedback or support for an idea you have, ask for it. That will put the discussion where it belongs.

Keep in contact. Out of sight, out of mind—out of action. This may stun you at the time, but the change effort you are working on isn't the single most important thing in the lives of other people involved in the organization. Believe it or not, other concerns will demand or distract their attention. You want to increase the chances that the effort is something they continue to pay attention to, so stay in touch. Information technology makes this pretty easy, but don't forget to use direct, personal contact as well.

True, people have a responsibility to maintain contact on their own, but matters of the moment can easily waylay the best of intentions. The organization has to do its part to communicate with its participants. This increases the chances that the effort is one of the many things they will give thought to.

Acknowledge people and their contributions. Recognize and thank people publicly for their interest and work on behalf of the organization. This doesn't demand an annual awards banquet (though that would be nice). In fact, informal methods can be more significant. During a meeting, for example, or in a newsletter, it is nice to mention an individual and the work he has done. Look for simple, sincere ways to draw attention to people and the value of their participation. In addition to public recognition, a private acknowledgment can be very powerful. This makes the message more personally offered and more personally received.

Routinely let members know the progress the organization is making. Gardens don't grow overnight unless, of course, we're talking about the weeds in

---

Take a Moment to Discover

Sometimes it is difficult to notice small gains as you labor to implement a change. Nothing is so discouraging as to put forth some energy with little to show for it. Especially if this involves taking a risk, why keep trying? If you have ever tried to master a new skill, you know what I'm talking about. Remember when you were trying to learn how to play the guitar, or use a computer, or cast a fly rod? From time to time you had to take notice of how you were improving. This helped you deal with some of the frustration, didn't it? Some of us couldn't see the progress quickly enough, so we still can't play the guitar worth beans. How can you use this experience to provide encouragement to others?

---

them. Each day's growth seems small, each month's significant, each season's wonderful. Until the first bloom of fruit appears, the waiting can be tedious. If you've grown gardens before and had success, you are patient and confident. If you haven't, you may wonder if you'll ever have a harvest.

Change usually results from a series of minor shifts rather than a sudden dramatic turn of events, although dramatic changes will occur and are exciting. However, these are not so much events in and of themselves as they are the culmination of the actions of the organization.

Every so often step back and take notice of how far you have advanced. This needs to be communicated clearly to those involved along with you. Identify specific achievements, whether that be meetings held, decisions reached, money raised, conditions improved, or whatever. Develop your ability to see these gains. You may have to look for them; they may not hit you in the face. Be able to compare how things were 3 months ago to where they are today. There will always, forever, be things not yet done. Give yourself and your organization a periodic break from those concerns. Learn to value and communicate to one another how far you have come. People like to be associated with a winner. They feel good about themselves and seek closer identification with the source of this good feeling. Paying attention to progress will keep a winning focus.

Progress involves a sense of direction. It is easier to go boldly if you have a good idea of where you are

GLOBAL PERSPECTIVES

ECUADOR—He was cross-eyed to the point of near blindness; a common occurrence, I'm told, when there is inbreeding over generations. He was unusually fat for a tropical village resident, and his voice was high pitched and gravelly. In short, he was perfect material for ridicule and scorn.

Victor Julio was anything but the village idiot. To the contrary, he was one of the more skilled and accomplished people in the community. He was the only person who read for pleasure and he read frequently. Nearly every day, in the fading light of late afternoon, he would read comics and laugh joyously to himself. Because of his sight impairment, he held the paper next to his face. It didn't seem to matter that the comics were old or that he had read them hundreds of times. He would sit there, day after day, with the parched comics right next to his face, laughing. He didn't care what others thought or were doing. He laughed and laughed.

His other avocation was sewing. Again, he would do this by twilight or limited light. He didn't sew a lot of things; only the pants in the crotch. He seemed to have two pairs of pants and both always seemed to have holes in the crotch, exposing his manhood. He would sew one pair, and the other would always obviously need mending.

More than reading and sewing, Victor Julio was a crafty businessman. He assisted his mother in the very lucrative business of selling cold bottles of beer from his house. Although near blind, he had an uncanny ability to make change by feel of the coins. Further, his retentive mind allowed him to keep track of how many bottles of beer

patrons had taken. This is a real skill when you're related to most everyone in the village and they feel they are owed some familial concessions. The entire village knew that Victor Julio was not mistaken in his count and his word was law. His other skill was tracking down used beer bottles. He seemed to know exactly where several hundred used beer bottles were scattered over the entire village.

Small villages are usually considered insular and parochial. Yet, they can have an expansive, sustaining nature. Most societies would consider this obese, nearly blind character an oddity. The people of Victor Julio's village, however, grew to respect his intelligence, exuberance, and vitality (Victor Julio, as told by Neil Vance, 1985).

ETHIOPIA—if the (an) objective of the organization is…to make community members support themselves working in the project, the (sponsoring organization) needs to avert problems. These problems are deterring participation of community members in the higher stages of planning and decision making…. In this participatory slum upgrading program, social workers as practitioners working at various levels can play crucial roles. The social workers as employees of the organization and working at the grassroots level can work on the empowerment of the community members to take part in the planning and decision making processes. The factors that restrain them from participation in the decision making are their socioeconomic status mainly education and economic problems. Hence,

empowerment of the community members is expected from social workers (Hussein Seid Hassan, 2007, pp. 78-79).

THAILAND—The task of the change agent is to help people reach their own conclusions and not necessarily always the conclusions of the change agent. By working and struggling together, the consciousness of the change agents and the people should change and reach higher levels. A change agent helps in starting a process of thinking, reflection, and action (Kamala Bhasin, as cited in Burkey, 1993, p. 134).

INDIA—The success of an asset-based approach to development depends on sustaining people's motivation to participate. The Self Employed Women's Association has years of experience of mobilizing women, discovering that success quickly builds on success and that highlighting these successes helps motivate others to join the movement….Organizers can generate positive energy and momentum by…asking people to tell stories about past successes where villagers have taken initiative and asking how these village resources can be used again to make a difference.

Exploring past successes generates pride among villagers and helps them understand why and how they have succeeded. Not only does this create energy and excitement as people tell their stories, it also helps people to start thinking about how they can mobilize in similar ways for new initiatives (Coady International Institute, St. Francis Xavier University, 2006, p. 31).

going. An uncertain future leads to hesitancy, which undermines commitment. As you report on the distance you have traveled, be sure to remind participants that they also know where all of you are going; your organization will move with a more confident step.

As you endeavor to maintain the involvement of those working toward change, remember to take into account basic human needs. See that the organization responds to these needs. Above all, promote the importance of the things people are doing and their value to one another.

WORKING WITH VOLUNTEERS

Most change efforts depend primarily on people who are voluntarily spending their time on the project (Schindler-Rainman, 1975). People are bound to the effort through their interest in the issue and the commitment that flows from this. They are not specifically paid to bring this change about.

Even if you are working with others in your agency or profession to promote some specific agency change or response to a community problem, you will probably be doing a number of things on your own time. Some activities will take place during nonworking hours or will be shoehorned in with other responsibilities.

Most of what has been said so far in this chapter relates to this typical situation. However, paid staff members are sometimes involved in the process of promoting change. Here are four situations in which this commonly occurs:

- A paid staff person (perhaps you) works in an agency and incorporates change activities into his job routine.

- An agency staff person has designated responsibilities for developing various projects aimed at community improvement.

- Paid staff are specifically hired to help coordinate and direct the change effort.

- The change effort may involve creation of a formal, ongoing organization or even a new agency, and in the process of institutionalizing the change, staff are hired to continue a change begun by volunteers.

In all likelihood, even these situations will call for extensive use of volunteers. When volunteers work alongside existing program staff, you need to be sensitive to a set of concerns particular to this situation.

Before you recruit your first volunteer, you should have a pretty clear idea of just what the volunteers will be doing. It is important to include staff in the determination of the role of volunteers and the identification of tasks volunteers will perform. If the organization is large enough to have administrators in addition to other staff, they should be included as well. It is necessary that staff and administrators be committed to using volunteers and that they know how to do it. Volunteers who feel unwelcome or who just show up and then sit around with nothing meaningful to do don't keep showing up (Corporation for National and Communty Service, 2008d; Lauffer & Gorodezky, 1977; Wilson, 1980).

It is easy for relationships between staff and volunteers to turn sour even when both parties are initially eager to work together. Volunteers sometimes begin to resent the fact that they are working hard to further the cause yet they don't get paid for their time, while others do. Or maybe they are relegated to jobs that are nothing but leftovers or seem too simple or are even demeaning. These are jobs nobody else wants to do. After a while they may come to feel like exploited, second-class citizens.

Paid staff sometimes feel threatened by volunteers. They may fear that their jobs may be given over to a volunteer some day, leaving them high and dry. Or, if volunteers are performing similar tasks, they may come to believe that the value of their work is undermined and that even their wages are affected by the available volunteer help. It is not surprising that an uneasy tension can develop if these concerns go unrecognized and unaddressed. Having volunteers complement paid staff requires thoughtful consideration.

Volunteers cannot be held accountable in the same way as paid staff. Rarely does a contractual obligation exist for people who donate their time. Because volunteering is a decidedly one-sided affair—that is, little of material value is directly offered to the volunteer for her services—the conditions that usually influence a working relationship don't exist. When agency staff work in conjunction with volunteers, make use of all the ideas previously examined for getting and keeping people involved in your change effort. In addition, you will want to pay attention to a couple of other matters.

If routine, predictable work needs to be done by volunteers, specific people need to be scheduled for specific times to do the work. Don't just hope people show up. That won't work. Also, expect that about one third of the people scheduled to help out will find themselves preparing excuses for why they "couldn't make it" when you expected them. Do overbook.

If a group of people is scheduled for a particular activity, be sure things are prepared so they can get started right away. Waiting until people show up before you figure out what to do can waste time and make you appear unorganized. Take a few minutes to prepare your directions and any necessary materials. Doing so conveys a sense of respect for the volunteers and the task they are to perform. It also gives them a feeling of confidence in knowing what they are to do.

Some orientation to the organization and to the role the individual is expected to fill can provide answers to questions that might go unasked (Lauffer & Gorodezky, 1977). Newcomers generally spend some anxious time guessing at things that veterans take for granted. For one thing, without trying to sound like your parents, do watch your language. Imagine walking into this conversation: "You know, Hank, with these cutbacks in WIC and the confusion over TANF, even stretching any FEMA funds we might use to cover only food purchases, we'll be in the red months before the end of the fiscal year. Then, if we can't come up with the matching portion of the foundation grant.... Well, you know what that would mean."

The level of people's intended involvement in the change effort and the complexity of their tasks will suggest how much orientation and training is required. Take care to see that people know what is going on and how they fit in.

Sometimes screening volunteers is called for. If this is the case, develop a clear set of screening criteria truly appropriate to the matters at hand. Then develop an effective method to determine whether or not the criteria are met.

As much as anything, a change agent is a manager. You want to bring together the talents and energy people have and direct these to the purpose of change. When you are working with people, recognize true good effort, even if (especially if) the outcome isn't all that good. If people make a good effort, that's usually a sign that they care that things turn out well. Attacking the results serves to discredit their intent. It is a waste of energy because you will have to go back and rekindle, reassure, and reestablish confidence in the relationship—not always easy to do when people are giving their time.

By acknowledging good intent and good effort, you are in a better position to discover what needs to be different next time. Respected people can more easily tackle tough problems, including their own mistakes. If you act toward people as if what they do matters to them, it most probably will.

Most of the people you will be working with, perhaps all the people you will be working with, are giving their time to something they believe in. Not everyone has the same amount of time; not everyone has the same strength of belief. Still, the relationship all these people have to the organization is a voluntary one. Nurturing this relationship requires careful attention.

CULTURAL COMPETENCE

Though this matter was addressed earlier, particularly in Chapter 1, it is worth reemphasizing here. One limiting phenomenon you may encounter is the difficulty you or others in your organization have crossing cultural lines to develop perspective and assistance. Bound by discomfort or ignorance in relating to whomever the "thems" might be (those in some way different from "us"), you may draw from a circle of support that restricts what the organization could become.

Perhaps a more insidious problem is not even seeing or regarding others as potential allies, rendering some members of the community invisible. If we only look to other professionals for collaboration or guidance, for example, our professional culture can blind and confine us.

So what will you do? Will you stick to your own group, leaving members of other groups as undiscovered allies? Will you label them as "uninterested" or

When arranging meetings, first try scheduling them for 7:00 a.m. Most of the time, the only conflict you will have at that time has to do with pillows or child care. People can usually make these morning meetings. People are also fresh at this time of day. By the time people get to the meeting, they have been up and going long enough to kick-start the brain cells. If the reason for the meeting is important to them, people will usually make it.

Just maybe, morning meetings will not be greeted with eager enthusiasm. Is there another option? Yes. It should work too. Using a simple method developed by Richard Fridena (1983), mark a sheet of paper with seven vertical columns, one for each day of the week. Next, draw horizontal lines across the columns for half-hour blocks of time, starting at 7:00 a.m. and ending at 10:00 p.m. Give each meeting participant a copy, asking them to darken the blocks of time when they cannot meet. Emphasize that this doesn't mean don't really want to meet, or would find it a little inconvenient—no, it means can't meet.

After you have collected them, put them all together in a stack. Now, here comes the tricky part. Hold them up to the light. Wherever the light shines through, that's a time when you can meet. This usually saves about 19 hours of trying to find the right combination by the "how about Tuesday at 4:00 p.m.?" method. You can modify this little gimmick to fit a variety of situations.

"uncaring" for not responding to an invitation not extended, or, worse, view them as enemies because they are not working on your side? Of course not, you say. I hope you are right, but don't be too hasty. In a confusing situation, one in which we are uncertain of our control, it is common to feel a need to affirm our particular construction of reality, and we often look to people who look like us or think like us to get that confirmation (Napier & Gershenfeld, 1989).

There are all sorts of cultural lines if you stop to think about it in a broad sense. Certainly you should be aware of any rationalizations you or members of your organization use to justify not involving people of a different ethnic group. That is pretty obvious. But how about people who occupy different economic positions in the community, different positions in the hierarchy of the place where you may work, or whose associations are distinct from yours? We all know that upper-level administrators are just do-nothing paper pushers, and the secretaries' biggest challenge is to see how long they can stay on break. Cops, they don't know anything useful, and when those church people aren't judging you, they are off hiding in the Bible. This knowledge should keep us from trying to include anyone from these groups, right? What other "highly enlightened" things do we know?

Do you treat some people with more respect than others because of the jobs they hold or their social class? Do you think that because a person is a member of an identifiable group, like the city planning department or the board of directors or maybe the police department, that she holds exactly the same views as every other member of that group? Napier and Gershenfeld (2004) call such mistaken notions attribution errors: "People committing an attribution error assume that the actions of the group reflect the particular attitudes of individual members and that knowing something about how a group behaves tells us something significant about subgroups or individuals within it" (p. 14). What do you know about the traditions, leadership, helping practices, and experiences of various groups that give life to your community? How will your knowledge, relationships, and ability to link networks enliven your change effort and bring it diverse forms of power?

It is normal to get used to being with a certain set of people, to stay with the familiar. It is simply easier to spend time with people who have similar interests, similar routines, and similar methods of communication. Some of us feel a bit inadequate dealing with people with whom we are not familiar. Yet the need for change probably touches people who aren't part of your familiar set. The ability to meaningfully respond to that need exists among them as well.

Don't be afraid of anybody. Don't be afraid, for example, to ask for or expect help from a bureaucrat, just because the person is a bureaucrat, or a mother receiving welfare, just because you don't know her experience. Don't immediately write off someone because of your own biases, fears, and practiced justifications.

When you begin to take action on things that need to be corrected, you will start with the people you know pretty well. For many of us the "people we know pretty well" is also a pretty homogeneous group. The questions are: Will you extend beyond this? Are you willing to challenge your own notions, level of understanding, and anxieties about people of different groups? Or will you remain comfortable with people of your own group, whatever group that might be?

Cultural competence requires that we value different cultures and expand our knowledge and communication and collaboration skills as well. We learn about other people, but we also learn about ourselves and how to interact in ways that promote effectiveness and affirm mutual dignity (Cross et al., 1989; NASW, 2001). Our ability to work with diverse groups is not an added benefit but a fundamental requirement. You may have to make a special effort to get to know members of your community with whom you don't commonly associate, learn with other members, and partner with them. Move from "them" to "us." The time to begin doing that is now, not because some special situation calls for your attention and their help but because you believe that this is a matter of basic importance.

THREE MOST DIFFICULT CHALLENGES FOR CHANGE AGENTS

Although change agents face lots of different forms of challenges in building strong organizations, in my experience three stand out. Each of these in some way touches on working effectively with members or potential members of an organization. The first job that change agents seem to ignore is making planned, purposeful direct contact with members of the community who could have an interest in the issue the organization is working on. The 50/10 rule described earlier in this chapter addresses this aspect of organizing. We seem to like having meetings, but don't seem so much to like going out and meeting people. It is not the fliers, announcements, and e-mails that will connect

people with the organization. It is the people making direct, personal contact that provide the organization's foundation. Indirect is insufficient.

The second area of responsibility that too often gets overlooked is developing leadership. Nothing is more necessary for growing an organization than increasing the number and effectiveness of leaders. Many aspiring organizers do not understand the distinction between an organizer's role and a leader. Chapter 11 has more on leadership. An organizer is constantly on the lookout for potential leaders and assists them in developing their confidence and skill. When organizers become leaders, they promote the organization's dependence on them, and they get in the way of others becoming leaders. They stifle the organization's growth. Each organization has multiple opportunities for different people to provide leadership. An organization with a strong set of leaders will be a force in the community.

The third aspect of an organizer's role that deals with common problems is helping to create an organizational culture that maintains good, productive relationships among members. Just like anything else in the organization, this is something that the organizer cannot do alone. Though by example an organizer certainly can set a tone for relating to others, developing leaders who understand this domain of an organization's life is important as well. Most organizations fall apart from the inside. Diverse interests, personalities, and skills can be a source of both tension and success. Most people want to do well and to contribute. Helping them do so along with others requires purposeful attention.

SOME REFLECTIONS ON PEOPLE

"Ultimately it is individuals who provide the leadership, commitment, and energy for social change" (Prager, 1999, p. 17). We don't spend enough time considering people—the raw material of the organized effort. What are they like? Why do they do what they do? What do we need to know about them? These are questions libraries of sociology and psychology texts attempt to answer, so I'll not presume any definitive conclusion here. Still, there are some things I think it would be helpful for you to consider. Many of these notions are based on my own observation and reflection on people with whom I have worked in the business of promoting change.

This sampler of observations includes some points that are plainly obvious, but don't be fooled. It is usually the obvious things we ignore or want to dispense with, and it is usually just such things that are in play. Here are some things to get you started. The statements offered here are about people in general. They refer to most people much of the time. There are ample exceptions to these generalizations, but in my experience they have been accurate often enough to be worth your consideration. See what you can add to this list.

- People are basically good and want to do good things. If given half a chance, they will.
- People are willing to provide help, given the right circumstances.
- People want to be accepted and liked.
- People fear being seen as incompetent, foolish, or stupid.
- People need to feel worthy and able, confident and competent.
- People need to save face.
- People need acknowledgment more than they need agreement.
- It is not easy for people to break out of routines.
- Lots of people won't ask for help, especially people who are generally competent, who want to appear competent, yet who need help with something they think others think they should know.
- People tend to take things more seriously when they are accountable to other people.
- You can't hold people accountable for things they don't know.
- People hear what they want to hear and remember what suits them.
- People need to feel connected with others yet prized for their uniqueness.

- All human behavior is designed to meet needs; it is purposeful, not accidental.
- People will do what they believe to be in their best interest to do.
- People need a sense of hope. To act, people need to believe that something beneficial will result from their actions.
- If people can't feel anything, they won't do anything.
- People operate within their immediate frames of reference, acting on what they can understand and what is important to them right now.
- People can only see what their vantage point allows them to see. Vantage points are shaped by culture, values, and experiences.
- People tend to wait until the last minute to get things done or at least do things relative to a deadline. It is the deadline that makes the task real.
- People fear the unknown. They are unwilling to commit to it. People who are confused will generally say no.
- People are spurred to action by enthusiasm and anger. They are immobilized by fear and confusion.
- People are open to influence when they are distracted (Johnson & Johnson, 2006).
- People are less open to influence when they have been inoculated against it (Johnson & Johnson, 2006).
- People who are unconvinced of an action or are in the initial stages of involvement need to see immediate results to justify their investment of time.
- People need to know their role and the importance of their actions in the scheme of things.
- People don't like to think their time is being wasted, especially by someone else.
- People want freedom and direction—simultaneously.
- People relate far better to a problem or an issue with which they have had a direct, personal experience.

??? DID YOU KNOW?   Everybody, Somebody, Anybody, and Nobody

This is a story about four people: Everybody, Somebody, Anybody, and Nobody. There was an important job to be done, and Everybody was sure that Somebody would do it. Anybody could have done it, but Nobody did it. Somebody got angry about that, because it was Everybody's job. Everybody thought Anybody could do it, but Nobody realized that Everybody wouldn't do it. It ended up that Everybody blamed Somebody when Nobody did what Anybody could have done!

SOURCE: From a cartoon titled *The Facts of Life.*

- Under stress, people will often vent their frustrations on the nearest available object, which might be a person, even a friend.

- Organizations, which are just collections of people, will act pretty much like people do.

What motivates you? Excites you? Induces fear in you? Anger? Action? What do you try to hide or show? How are other people the same as you, how might they be different? Are you ever truly unique? Watch other people. What do you see? What does that make you think about? What conclusions do you reach? Which should you challenge? Develop this practice. Think often about what you can learn from your own behavior, attitudes, and emotions.

Watch others and think about what you can learn from their behavior and what you guess their emotions could be. This is an imperfect process, but as you continue it, you will find that you learn quite a lot about people and what makes them tick. You will learn a lot about yourself too.

Fundamentally, this is what change is all about—your ability to work with or against other people to get something done. If you know yourself and other people better, you will get a lot more done.

CONCLUSION

Working with people to produce a needed change is a satisfying and sometimes exciting proposition. It will have its trying times too. To get through periods of frustration, notice the progress you all are making toward your goal. The work you are doing to improve conditions will by itself attract people and the skills they possess. Most of the time, though, you need to go beyond this natural attraction and actively seek the people you need. Learn how to involve people and how to keep them involved. Acknowledge and further develop the interest people demonstrate, thoughtfully strengthening their relationships to one another and their connection to the work that must be done. You need people to take action; you need action to get people.

Don't be intimidated by distinctions between groups of people. Seeing the value of people and what they can offer, you will reap the benefit of working with people from a variety of economic, social, or ethnic groups. Understanding that most people are giving their time, show respect for them and their contributions.

Continue to learn more about people; reflect on what frightens them, emboldens them, and moves them to action. Recognize that the human capital of an enterprise is its most valuable resource. With this understanding, you will promote change in a way that gives others a stake in the outcome and the efforts to achieve it.

The change effort requires the involvement of a number of people. Pay attention to the people who comprise the organization, and value them. As much as you value the work that must be done by the organization, as much as you value the goals it seeks to achieve, you know it is the people of the organization who will accomplish its purpose. Without the people, there would be no organization, no success. With them, so much is possible.

WHERE ARE THE CONNECTIONS?

Well, that was a great meeting. A whole 6 people showed up. Seems we have shrunk from the 20 that showed up the first time. At least we got one new person, but it didn't look like she knew what was going on. Something about the yawning made me think she wasn't too interested either. Where the heck is everyone? We put up fliers. We got on the news when this first started. The brochure looks good. What else do we need to do to get people?

We meet once a month to try to get something going and let people know about the issues so that we can build an organization. Don't people care about trying to get rid of poverty? Or is it that they just don't care for very long? Once again we are in the middle of an analysis of the problem of poverty when Harold speaks up and asks, "When are we actually going to start doing something about this?" Heck, he didn't even make a motion. We all looked at him like he said something profound.

I don't think we are going to get rid of poverty in Clayton County, Georgia, with 6 people. Only 6, but it was a good 6, or maybe 5, I still don't know about the new person, and I didn't get her name. You can count on Ron to get things done.

People will listen to Lisa, and she has a good head on her shoulders. Phillip keeps us going even when he looks around and sees more empty chairs than full ones. Sherill just knows people. Of course, there's Harold, who's tired of talking. Well, everybody has something to offer I guess. Now, how can we use that?

Maybe we need to think about how we got 20 people to that first meeting to begin with. Maybe we need to get back in touch with them again. Maybe they can do something other than attend meetings. Maybe we need to do something besides making up brochures, most of which are still in the box they came in anyway.

Why would someone really want to get involved in doing something about poverty here? What can we tell them—that there are more poor kids here than almost anywhere in the country—who are the "them"? When are we going to start doing something? Right, Harold? And what will that be? My guess is that we need to answer some other questions too.

So many children. What's going to become of the children?

REFLECTION QUESTIONS

1. How compelling and achievable is the goal?

2. Who needs to be involved?

3. What kind of message might you construct to invite people to participate?

4. How does that message get delivered?

5. Some people don't like to go to meetings. What else can they do to help build the organization or do its work?

6. How do you keep people involved once they do start to participate? How do you increase their level of involvement?

7. What do you think about trying to build an organization just through monthly meetings?

8. What might be some other questions that need to be answered?

GROUP ACTIVITY: CONTRIBUTIONS AND LEARNING

People are indeed the most valuable resources. However, we often don't know what each person has to contribute, and we often don't recognize our own abilities and interests either. This activity will help uncover knowledge, skills, and other assets available in your group, as well as things members would like to learn.

1. Divide the larger group into teams of two members and have each member interview the other to discover what that person might contribute. Remember that contributions can include things like enthusiasm. You can come up with your own questions, or you might ask some of the following questions: (5–7 minutes per person)

   - What are some things you know how to do? (for example, play a musical instrument, skateboard, garden, keep good records)
   - What are some other things that you know about? (for example, politics, current music scene, history of the community)
   - If you were given the chance to teach, what you would like to teach people? (for example, budgeting, nutrition, how to throw a curve ball)
   - What are some things you are passionate about?

2. Ask what two things your team member would like to contribute to the community. Write

each contribution, including the person's name, on a separate piece of paper. Use as many papers as you like. (5–7 minutes)

3. Have team members interview each other to discover what each person might learn. You can come up with your own questions, or you might ask some of these questions: (5–7 minutes per person)

   - What would you like to learn more about that might be useful to your community? (for example, how to run a meeting, fund-raising, carpentry skills, child care, storytelling)
   - If we were to meet a year from now, what new thing would you have learned that you are proud of?

4. Ask what two new things each person wants to learn. Write each contribution, including the person's name, on a separate piece of paper. Use as many papers as you like. (5 minutes)

5. Post the papers on a wall in the room, with contributions on one side and things to learn on the other side. (5 minutes)

6. What can you discover? For example, can anyone in the room teach what someone else wants to learn? What else do you notice? (10 minutes)

HELPFUL WEBSITES

Links to the organizations briefly described here are on the companion website at www.cengage.com/humansvcs/homan.

World Volunteer Web. At this global volunteer information portal you can find descriptions of experiences and programs for working with volunteers from around the globe. The site includes a list of research initiatives and studies on various aspects of volunteerism worldwide along with toolkits for working with volunteers.

Community Tool Box. Sponsored by the University of Kansas, this site has a wealth of down-to-earth infor-

mation for community development work. Check their Troubleshooting Guide for tips on dealing with some common problems you will face when trying to get people to work together to promote change.

Illinois Intergenerational Initiative. Some good insights for getting and keeping people involved in work with an intergenerational focus can be found here.

Families and Work Institute. Learn how to involve families in community mobilization efforts. You can download tips on working with busy parents as respected and legitimate partners in planning and implementing strategies for change.

Chapter 9

✳

Raising Other Resources

CHAPTER HIGHLIGHTS

- Money isn't always the answer
- Thou shalt hustle
- Budget development
- In-kind contributions
- Value of personal networks
- You will need to spend money
- When you should pay for staff
- Unanticipated expenses
- Money-generating approaches and organizational demands
- Two basic strategies: fund-raising and resource development
- Fund-raising in difficult times
- Steps to receiving money from individuals and groups
- Women as important contributors
- Resources within communities of color
- Making the request
- Membership development

- Build a donor base through prospecting and resolicitation, telephone solicitation, targeted mailings, direct mail, and events
- Sales of products and services
- Planned giving
- Fund-raising through the Internet
- Steps for getting money through public and private organizations
- Importance of identifying and targeting many sources
- Language of the funding process
- Elements for getting government money
- Grant-writing process
- Verbal presentations
- Collaborative resource generation
- Recordkeeping and Form 990
- All money comes with strings attached
- Record keeping

As you think about the change you are trying to create, many things may be involved. You find yourself asking, "How are we going to get everything we need?" Good question, well phrased—"everything we need," not "money for all of this." You may or may not need money. Granted, money can make things easier, at least it certainly seems that way if you don't happen to have very much of it, which is, of course, the case for most change efforts, especially in their early stages.

In Chapter 8 we focused on people as the most important resource available to the organization. In fact, the organization is people. It can get by without some other things, but it cannot exist without people. But the members of the organization may need other resources to aid them in their effort. In this chapter we look at what some of those other resources could be and how you can get them.

Most of the time people think that the first thing they must do is go out and get money. Some of the time this is true, but most of the time you can get a lot of what you need without spending a cent. How? "Thou shalt hustle" is one of the fundamental commandments of change. Hustling means to keep moving, keep probing, always being ready to gain ground. It also means getting things for free or very cheaply. Money is one way to get things you need. Hustling is another. A good change agent will know how to get things for free and how to get money for things that aren't free.

Before you can begin to do either, though, you have to decide what it is you really need. Determining just what resources you have to have is usually called building a budget, and it involves three fundamental tasks:

- Determining what you need
- Hustling what you can
- Getting money for the things you need to buy

BUILDING YOUR BUDGET

The English word "budget" comes from the French *bougette,* which is a small leather bag (Quick & New, 2001). Think of building your budget as filling your bag with the things you will need for your journey on the road to change. It is an ongoing process. You need some things to get the change effort under way. Next, you may need to find more resources to implement the change. Finally, you may need ongoing (and perhaps even greater) resources to institutionalize the change, to make sure that what

you started continues. A budget is a view of the organization's future (Hicks, 2001).

For example, a group of you may identify a need to develop a support system for students at risk of dropping out of school. You may need some resources to create an interest in the effort and select the best approach (getting under way). Next, you may need resources to establish such a system in a particular school (implementing the change). Finally, you may need to identify resources that will allow the support system to stay in place for years to come (institutionalizing the change).

In practice you will always be finding out that you need this or that to keep you going. Your budget needs will be somewhat different in each phase of your change process. Something that may be important very early in the game may not be needed at all later, and vice versa. Also, you may find that you only need some item or service for a particular occasion.

In the very early stages of your change effort, your focus is on generating enthusiasm and building support for your idea. You don't want to get bogged down in a lengthy analysis of the resource requirements of the change effort. You may not really even know enough at this point to determine what you need. At the beginning it is common to discover as many needs through your actions as through your planning. However, as time goes on, you will want to give more advance consideration to your organization's resource needs. Here are eight basic categories of things you may need now or in the future:

People: time, skills, talents

Communication: printing, postage, telephones, copying, software, Internet connection

Equipment: computers, video cameras, furniture

Supplies: pens, paper, coffee cups, refreshments

Space: meeting places, office, storage

Transportation: air travel, use of buses, rides to and from out-of-town meetings

Outside professional services: training or facilitation, accountants, attorneys, consultants

Special or miscellaneous needs: day care, raffle prizes, security, or a band for a fund-raiser

You may readily see needs in one area and not in another, or you may see ways of getting some things and not getting others. Go ahead and start with whatever categories you want. But don't stop there. You will need something, fairly early on, from each category. Bet on it. So start where you want to, but spend time on each category.

Take a look at what you need now or will need soon. Brainstorm the possibilities. You don't necessarily need to own anything or have exclusive access to it. You just need to be able to use what you need when you need it.

HUSTLING FOR THE THINGS YOU NEED

Hustling is just what it sounds like, moving around quickly and thinking ahead. In the broad sense, this means always looking for opportunities or ways to create them, being quick to make use of a change, thinking a few steps ahead, taking those steps while others sit back, and remaining ready for action. Rather than looking at the limits of your situation, see the possibilities. In regard to resources, make sure you get what you need free or at very little cost. You will get many things from places most people don't, generally because they don't even try. You will get people to give you things, often things that other people have to pay for.

When people, businesses, or organizations give you things or services you need instead of money, this is called an *in-kind contribution*. Soliciting in-kind contributions is an important part of the hustling process. Receiving contributions in forms other than cash might help you in your efforts to attract grant funding because in-kind contributions demonstrate community support (Robinson, 2004). Further, it helps establish a partnership between you and the contributing company, which may provide direct financial support later (Picker, 1997).

Businesses are encouraged to participate for their own benefit. In fact, many larger businesses have some sort of public involvement program. An effective public involvement program can benefit businesses by putting their internal resources to work at minimal cost, either as a supplement to or an alterna-

tive for cash contributions (Dove, 1983). In terms of marketing and measurable results, businesses may benefit more from in-kind contributions than from cash contributions (Walker, 1987). Companies may donate employee time and special expertise; some businesses may be able to save warehouse expenses by contributing unneeded or depreciated items from their inventory (Picker, 2001). In 2002 in-kind contributions from major U.S. corporations surpassed cash giving for the first time. This trend continues. In a survey of 197 larger corporations, who contributed $8.62 billion in 2007, noncash giving represented more than 54% of overall corporate contributions (Cavicchio & Torok, 2008). More corporations are providing in-kind support; see how your needs and the resources of businesses and corporations in your area match up (Sinnock, 1995).

You may be thinking, "I'm not a con artist; I can't do this." Right—and wrong. You are most definitely not a con artist, or at least you shouldn't be. A con artist tricks people into giving up something they usually can't afford to give up, often using misrepresentation. So, if you think you're not a con artist and you're not going to become one…Whew! That's where you are right. The world doesn't need more con artists, but a change agent does need to hustle.

True, the term *hustler* has some seamy connotations. If you prefer "go-getter," feel free to substitute. If you think you can't be a go-getter, you are mistaken. The fact is, everybody asks for things, and everybody gives things away. Most of the time you will find plenty of resources readily at hand, generally wherever you spend a good deal of your time—at work, home, school, places of play, and places of worship. You simply need to learn how to ask for things that your change effort needs, from people who have some reason to give them to you.

We in human services tend to act apologetic and even a little guilty when asking for things. If you stop and think about it, it's a little crazy to apologize for asking people to help out. To some extent this is a game, and it is fun to play. You'll enjoy being inventive, discovering creative ways of getting "something for nothing," despite what your Aunt Emma has said. Though practices may vary from one region to another, in general your organization will benefit from products and services you can obtain for little or no cost.

CHANGE AGENT TIP

There is a salesman in Texas who sells cars. He sells a lot of them. In fact, a number of years ago he sold more cars than anybody else in the country. He didn't even work too hard to do it. He just knew that people knew people, who knew people.

If you buy a car from Ol' Tex, he tells you to send your friends to him. If you do, and your friend buys a car, Tex will give you a very substantial finder's fee, cold cash. If you encourage a few friends to buy from Tex, you can make a tidy sum. Tex makes an even tidier one. Pretty soon everybody is buying cars, making tidy sums.

Tex operates on the principle that everyone knows 200 people. Somebody among those 200 people wants to buy a car. You and Tex are a lot alike. Tex needs customers; you need something else, say, the use of a backhoe for a weekend to help plant trees or a band that can supply a little music for your fund-raiser Friday night. Somebody from among the thousands of people the members of your group know is likely to be able to help you out.

Ask each person who is active in your organization to fill out a personal resources card. This activity is best done in a group, especially after some discussion of finding things for free. Provide opportunities at a later date to update your cards because people will always think of more to add, and they are also developing access to more resources. (Remember to put all this good information into your membership database.)

So what goes on this card? Names and resources; that is, names of people who can do something, and what they can do for your change effort. On the front of the card have members write their name, phone number, and e-mail address. Then in each of four columns (two on the front and two on the back), provide space to respond to each of these four requests.

1. Name the three most important people from whom you would be willing to ask a favor, especially a political favor, or the use of their influence.
2. Name the three richest people you'd be willing to ask money from to help this effort.
3. Name three people you'd be willing to ask to give something other than influence or money. (Write what you'd ask for.)
4. Name three skills or talents you'd be willing to contribute to this effort.

That's it. You now have an immediate resource bank.

You will have to offer some guidance on filling out this card. The immediate reaction of a few might be, "But I don't know any important people." Simply explain that you just need the three most important or richest or beneficial people that they do know. That may be a kid brother, a neighbor, or a local paint dealer. Any of these can contribute one dollar, one letter to a legislator, or help in painting the office. We all know people we can ask to do a little something for the cause. Take no more than 10 minutes to fill out the card. Any more time than that will make the process too tedious.

To give you an idea of how powerful this little resource bank can be, consider this: If you have only 10 people involved in your effort, and the average contribution they get from each of the "richest" people on their list is $10, you have immediate access to $300. Most attempts to get something accomplished don't start with that much in the kitty.

You can turn your need for certain items into an opportunity to develop support for your undertaking and an investment in your success. By making it easy for people to find ways to give to the effort, you increase your supply of investors. Whenever someone gives something, you get not only the particular resource contributed but a little bit of that person as well. By giving, people become a little bit more a part of the effort and a little bit more interested in its success.

When you and your partners in action have gotten to the point where you are looking for a particular service or item, ask yourselves whom you know who has it or has ready access to it. Those resources that are not immediately around you usually are not too far off, but you may have to ask someone outside the membership of your organization. If you don't have the resources you need at your disposal, you or the people joining with you in this effort probably know someone who does. In fact, if a group of you spend no more than 10 minutes talking out loud about this, you will almost always come up with at least two or three ideas.

To help you think about this further, consider some likely sources. First and foremost, consider who among the community you want to organize has ready access to the resource you need. Need a flier done? Is there a printing company in the neighborhood? Need some artwork? Is there an art department in your school? Need legal services? Are any of your colleagues attorneys or partners of one? Start within your own community. This strengthens the ties to the community, gives people a specific way to help out, increases the number of people who have a stake in success, and sets in motion a way for the community to begin thinking of and relating to itself. In fact, a lot of people will be miffed or feel left out if you don't ask them. They may be even harder to involve down the road if you overlook them now.

"Thou shalt hit them in their self-interest!" is another commandment that serves as the basis for a lot of what you do in promoting change. Your adherence to this direction will cause you to consider whose self-interest is or could be involved; this is the second group you look to. Two powerful motivators are economic self-interest and prestige.

Many times people will give you things free or at a reduced cost in hope of receiving some other returns later. These returns could include better access to a new group of customers, your continued business, and referrals for business.

People's sense of personal prestige can be used to your advantage as well. Does helping you out make someone look good? Does turning you down make someone look like a lout? Does anyone's stature increase or diminish according to whether or not that person responds to your request? People who see themselves (and are seen by others) as "doers" love to be able to deliver; they also hate thinking that other people think they can't get something done. Do you know any of these folks?

Other likely sources have some degree of self-interest but may have other motivations as well. People and organizations who are philosophically disposed toward you have resources of their own that they may be willing to share with you. In almost every community, at least one or two groups share your general concerns, even though their specific emphases may be different from yours. Consider how your success benefits the things they are working on. For example, if you are involved in developing a neighborhood tree planting program, consider the other environmental, conservation, and beautification organizations that exist in your area. If you are undertaking an effort to keep teen parents in school, think about the various organizations working on education, child abuse, economic development, mental health, or a host of other issues related to teen parenting.

Places where you spend your time and where you spend your money are places where you have built a relationship. They probably want to see you again. They may have something you can use. Ask for it. Among these are organizations to which you belong or that hold events you attend. These can be religious, civic, or social, from your synagogue to your aerobics class.

Also on your target list should be businesses or dealerships you regularly or have recently patronized. Where do you buy your insurance, where do you have your checking account, where do you get your tomatoes? Any or all of these might be willing to help you meet some specific need. Your presence or your hard-earned dollars are an investment in the success of these enterprises. You can certainly ask them to invest in yours.

Finally, there are relatives, friends, and acquaintances. Even if no one in this personal network of yours can offer what you are looking for, they might be willing to help find someone else who can.

The Foundation Center (2006b) has lots of good information for connecting with in-kind contributions. Some national organizations, such as *Gifts In Kind International,* serve as clearinghouses for connecting products with nonprofits.

Ask for What You Need

Now that you have determined what you need and considered who might have it, it's time to figure out who will be doing the asking and how. Then, you need to ask. Don't be afraid to ask. You and the issue you are working on are worth it. The worst thing that can happen is that someone will say no.

The simplest direction is that whoever has the best connection to the most likely source should do the asking. Most of the time this will work. However, sometimes you will need to spread the asking around a bit. Otherwise, you may find that you have the same two or three people doing all the asking. You might find a couple of people in your organization who enjoy doing this and become pretty good at it. See them as a resource for teaching others. Another option is to develop a small team for a particular event. Having a number of people involved in acquiring needed resources helps create an attitude that we're all looking for ways to add to the effort. Further, success in this endeavor will solidify the person's attachment to the change effort. This last point is particularly important. A person will usually take some particular pride in this accomplishment and feel closer to the organization that has benefited from it.

Exactly how you ask does depend on the situation. Regardless of the situation, though, there are a few things to keep in mind to improve your chances. First, the more personal the request, the better. Talking with someone face to face will usually get you a lot more than writing a letter. Second, be ready to show how the giving helps the giver. Everyone has some personal interest involved, even if it's not economic self-interest. Be able to identify and show how giving meets the giver's interest. Third, show how the giving benefits the recipient. Each of us likes to know that when we do something it matters. Be able to describe clearly what a particular gift will do for the change effort. Finally, close the deal. You are not asking someone to think about helping you. You are asking them to actually do it. Get a yes or a no when you ask. At the very least, get a time when you'll hear the yes or no. Then follow up.

After a while you will have developed a kind of go-getter state of mind, a way of thinking that believes that what you are doing is good and that there are lots of people out there who are able and willing to do something to keep things moving ahead. You won't think twice about asking for things you need. It will be routine. It will begin to affect the way you go about things in general. And, if you have gotten a good group of people to think and act this way, you'll be very hard to stop.

Get to Know Your Community's Resources

Many of the items and services your change effort will need can be found for free. The local bar association will help you find attorneys who will do pro bono work. Schools, hospitals, and faith communities can offer meeting space. People who sell, rent, or use the equipment you need will be a big help as well. Some, like auto dealers, may donate used cars. A construction company may donate the use of a front-end loader and an operator for a day. Some real estate offices may let you use their phones for a couple of evenings. You can probably find a rental company that has an extra set of posthole diggers to give you blisters.

And many companies will contribute computers that are outdated for their use but perfectly adequate for yours. Your success in finding these and other resources will depend in large part on how well you know your community, how many people you know, and how many people know you.

You're well on your way now to getting the things you need to change the world, or at least to improve your part of it. Will you need to spend any money at all? Yep. Hmm…you knew that was coming.

GETTING AND SPENDING MONEY

Yes, you will have to spend some money. Some things you can get for free or cheap look that way. Sometimes that's all right, sometimes it isn't. Your effort has a certain image it wants to project. Some of the things you may be able to get for free won't fit the image you are trying to project or just won't do the job, so you may have to pay for them. For example, maybe for one special all-day get-together you need a very stylish conference room and all you can get free is the church broom closet. Or perhaps you have reams of donated low-quality paper, but you want your letterhead to look classy. Some things are worth paying for.

Two additional warnings should be sounded here. First, don't ask people who can easily give a lot to give little. You can leave out the smaller contributors and lose out on some big items if some of the potential major givers feel they have met their contributing obligation. Second, refrain from the habit of taking a few bucks out of your own pocket to cover incidental expenses, unless this needs to be done in a hurry. Otherwise you (and usually others around you too) start using this approach as the way to get the things you need.

GLOBAL PERSPECTIVES

SCOTLAND—[I]t didn't take long for development officer Sian Langdon to realise that the Kickstart Programme is not about getting instant results....

Sian is one of a network of officers throughout Scotland helping voluntary and community groups develop the skills to make the most of funding opportunities....

Sian and the Inverclyde Voluntary Sector Forum organised an awareness-raising day aimed at people living in Inverclyde. "We brought in outside funders to tell people about what opportunities are out there....

People were delighted with the information on offer and lots said it had given them ideas.... I also work one-to-one with groups to help them find out about funding and go through the application process.... Sometimes you sit down with people and discover that their group hasn't yet got a constitution or a bank account, and you need both of these if you're applying for funding."...

In Glasgow, Kickstart officers... have put together a comprehensive funders' timetable—a regularly-updated, electronic list of funding opportunities for voluntary and community groups in Glasgow (Communities Scotland, 2002, p. 2).

TANZANIA—After nearly one year of fundraising and hard work six Maassai warriors took part in the Flora London Marathon to raise money for drilling water in their village, which had no access to clean, safe water....They saw it as a way to raise the nearly $120,000 needed to set up a permanent water well in their village.... Retaining their pride and dignity they ran in the Flora London Marathon, wearing their traditional clothing, jewelry and shoes made from old car tyres. They carried their shields and sticks just as they would if travelling across their homeland. After the marathon Green Force, a nonprofit travel company that works in Tanzania, established a website to plead for donations to help out the nearly 4,000 villagers who struggle with no clean water supply. The warriors did phenomenally well, raising enough money and beyond to get clean water to their village, but finding a source of water became a difficult challenge.... Finally, drilling succeeded and the water began flowing, as Maasai women and children celebrated in joy.... As one of the warriors who had run the marathon said, "... the finish line of the Flora London Marathon is not the finish. The finish is when we can turn on a tap in our village and get clean drinking water!" (Elisha Mayallah, 2009).

FRANCE—Here are a few tips for organizing. Beg or borrow the best equipment you can get your hands on—and if you are lucky enough to have some, share it with other groups. Unless you want to give a feeling of togetherness to people who are already convinced of your point of view, you have to remember that few people will trouble to read sloppily presented information, even if it is true. Good souls exist in every profession—advertising, journalism, and printing among them. Try to take advantage of their professional skills to make the information you want to get across really speak. Try also to recruit people with technical skills so your material can be well conceived, well presented and imaginative. It costs no more.... When people come to your meeting, don't let them get away without giving their names, contact information, and special skills and whether they would participate in future planning or action. Never waste a chance to find out who supports you.... Never be well-bred when it comes to talking about money. Working for change is usually volunteer, but it is never free. People should contribute (and be told specifically why they are being asked to do so) every time you get them together (Susan George, 1986, pp. 255–256).

GHANA—Beautiful beads are helping beautiful children connecting people from two different continents. Glass bead making is part of the Ghanian culture, but orphanages are not. However, with the AIDS epidemic leaving many children without parents something different needed to be done to care for the children. With the Bead to Feed program the Nyame Adom Foundation assists the orphanage where a grandmother and older sister and visits by a social worker help provide a home, education, and skill training for the children. Using skills that are part of the local culture, adult artisans make beads that are sold abroad to help provide the financial support needed to care for the children and to keep their new home open. The desire to help the children links the artisans and volunteers to strangers half way around the world (Nyame Adom & Tony Paniagua, 2009).

You cut yourself off from other investors, start feeling a little resentful, and out-of-pocket yourself right out of lunch.

Staff, an Expensive Item

One of the most important things you may have to pay for is people. Certainly people are the most valuable resource. They are also the most costly if you need to pay for them, and there are times when you definitely should.

This is an expense you normally don't incur until you are in the implementation or institutionalization phase of the change process, if at all. Paying for staff is the single most expensive item for almost any organization. Unless the organization is engaged in raising funds for things it gives away (for example, a food bank buying and then giving away food), most of the money it raises will be spent on people who work for the organization. All the other expenses taken together will rarely outweigh the expense of staff.

If we don't have to pay anyone to do the work, we'll save a lot of money, right? Absolutely. So the best approach is to get someone or even several someones to donate their time and work for free. Well, not necessarily. If all four of the following factors are present, the use of nonpaid staff for ongoing support makes pretty good sense. However, all four factors must be in place.

1. The work doesn't need to be done according to a tight schedule. Certainly, a specific amount of work doesn't need to be turned out every day.

2. The work doesn't place a high number of unusual, unpredictable, or inconvenient demands on the worker. People won't commonly be asked to go out of their way to do something.

3. You don't have to worry about the worker's ability to do the job properly. The work does not require a set of sophisticated skills, and there won't be much confusion about whether or not the job is being done right.

4. The worker is fairly easy to replace if she should lose interest or need to drop out for one reason or another.

If any of these things aren't true, there will probably need to be paid staff somewhere on the scene.

Although it may mean that you need to raise more money, hiring staff can make very good sense. Paid staff usually have a stronger sense of obligation. They expect to be and can be held accountable. Even if the contract is not written, both parties know that one exists. There is an agreement that provides mutual benefits. A paycheck not only provides benefits to the worker but also affirms the agreement he has made.

One of the key duties of the paid staff is to generate more support for the organization, including more funding. Generally, the position should be able to pay for itself and generate additional revenues. This certainly doesn't replace the use of volunteer help. The use of donated time will always be important. Paid staff should be able to enhance the effectiveness of this kind of contribution.

Your decision to hire employees will take into consideration the size, nature, and purpose of your organization. The intended length of the organization's life will also be considered. The longer you expect your organization to last, the more likely you will be to hire people to help run it.

Other personnel costs come in the form of specialized services you just can't hustle. These will frequently be in the area of legal or financial services; for example, bookkeeping and filing financial reports and documents. The more ongoing or pressing your needs for specialized services are, the more likely you will have to pay for them. Also, if the activity involves a significant use of one person's time (for example, an attorney pursuing a lawsuit or an accountant conducting an audit), you can expect to incur some costs.

Keep Some Money in Reserve

In addition to whatever personnel costs you have and the necessity to purchase items you can't or decide not to get as in-kind contributions, you will need money to cover a variety of unanticipated expenses. It is a good idea to have an adequate contingency fund available. You can't be certain when you will need to have some extra dollars on hand, just be certain that you do. It is a good practice to have enough money in the bank to provide operating costs for 6 months over and above any anticipated income. The size and the nature of your particular organization may dictate a smaller or larger backup fund. Still, you should plan to have something in reserve.

FUND-RAISING DURING DIFFICULT TIMES

It's no secret that the nation's, the world's, severe economic challenges harm the most vulnerable among us. It certainly affects the organizations that work with vulnerable individuals and families as well, making efforts to maintain financial sustainability all the more difficult.

Figures from the U.S. Department of Commerce, Bureau of Economic Analysis (2009a) and the International Monetary Fund (2009) show that the nation's and the world's economy is in the most severe recession in over 60 years. The Bureau of Labor Statistics (2009a, 2009b, 2009c) reported that unemployment rates and the percentage of long-term unemployment is the highest in more than 25 years and that the consumer price index experienced its greatest decline in almost 55 years. Tough times.

When the economy shrinks, so does giving. The Foundation Center reported that foundation assets declined by 22% in 2008 and that foundation giving will decrease in 2009 and even further in 2010 (Lawrence & Mukai, 2009). Corporate giving also falls off when profits decline (Warwick, 2009). Individual giving, which makes up 75% of all private giving to what is called charitable causes, also shrinks during recession years, especially during years when 8 months or more were in recession (Giving USA Foundation, 2008a, 2008b). Under more normal conditions giving continues to grow by more than 4% per year, so a decline is kind of a triple whammy (Center on Philanthropy, 2008b). First, there is a loss of normal growth. Second, there is an actual decline over previous giving. Third, demands for assistance increase.

Budget woes at all levels of government sour the mix as well. The U.S. Department of Commerce, Bureau of Economic Analysis (2009b) reported a decline in federal, state, and local spending in early 2009. The American Recovery and Reinvestment Act of 2009 (ARRA), often referred to as the stimulus bill, has boosted federal spending with particu-

lar help to assist those most affected by the recession. Still, 47 states are likely to grapple with budget gaps in 2010, and the ARRA provisions to help states will fill only about 40% of the shortfall the states will face by 2011 (Johnson, Oliff, & Koulish, 2009). Government funding provides about 66% of revenues for health-related nonprofits and just over 50% of the revenues of nonprofit social welfare organizations (Rushton & Brooks, 2006). So cuts in government spending add yet another challenge.

Might as well just pack it in, don't you think? There's just no money out there. Well, hang on. There is a lot of money out there. Even with reductions, individuals, corporations, and foundations gave more than $280 *billion* in 2008 (Lawrence & Mukai, 2009, Giving USA Foundation, 2009). Governments will still partner with local nonprofits, and creative organizations will be able to find new ways to attract dollars. Further, although overall contributions fall off, giving declines less than the economy as a whole, and individuals' contributions to human services and public safety actually increases during recessions. Donations do not keep pace with the shelter, food, and other assistance people seek during times of economic stress, but people do make a special effort to help each other (Giving USA Foundation, 2008a).

This is a time to use tried and true techniques, maybe providing some new twists on basic methods, while you conjure up some new, creative approaches. There are many ways for you to develop financial support. You may have to think ahead and work a little harder or a little smarter. When you do, you will cash in.

Here are some suggestions to help your organization make it through these difficult times from veteran fund-raiser Kim Klein (2009):

- Recognize that we are not in a crisis. A crisis is a temporary situation, and people step up knowing the situation will pass. We are in more for a long-term haul. So see this as an exciting period with lots of possibilities for whole new ways of doing business.

- "In all your communications, acknowledge, but don't dwell on, the economy. Focus on why the work of your organization is important and continues to be important." (p. 14)

DID YOU KNOW?   The CARE Test

Techniques for raising money must pass the CARE test:

Comfort for the donor in the cause, the solicitation method used, and how the approach is made.

Anticipation of the request and preparedness with adequate information that encourages a decision to give.

Readiness to give because of a conviction that the money will be well used for charitable purposes that serve the public good.

Enjoyment in the act of giving, and a welcome to the invitation to give again.

SOURCE: Greenfield, 2002, pp. 473–474.

- "Let donors know you are spending your money properly.... So give out a lot of budget information, and be as financially transparent as possible.... Publish your budget, expenses, and income on your website, as well as your audit, if you have one." (p. 14)

- "Focus a lot of energy on your mid-range donors—people who give $100–$1,500" (p. 14). Don't take them for granted. There are real growth possibilities here, especially if you give these people much more personal attention than you have before. They think that their gift can make a difference, and they are likely to be able to give more.

- "Examine you fundraising program for problems and solve them. Are personalized thank you notes sent out promptly? Is your database adequate? Is your website up to date and does the content change frequently" (p. 15)? What other aspects can you make better?

- "Make a list of the 50 most important people to your organization: Who are the people who would be very upset if we went out of business?...Make a note beside each name about what you are going to do with this person next." (p. 15)

The Giving USA Foundation (2008a) added that you should maximize the use of all fundraising tactics available. You will find quite a range of possibilities in the pages ahead.

FILLING THE COFFERS

Getting money to promote the cause is an essential matter for agents of change. It is not the root of all evil. Figuring out how to get money is a fun, creative, even exciting process. Granted, actually doing what you've figured out isn't always quite as much fun, but it can be made more so when you allow the enthusiasm of your imaginative planning to carry over. We need to treat money like any other resource that is critical to our success, valuing it appropriately and developing skills to acquire and use it wisely. Kim Klein (2000) provided a good perspective: "Nonprofits that work for social change must themselves be agents of change. The ways we think about money, raise it, spend it, save it, invest it, and plan for it are some of the most basic elements for modeling a world we want to create" (p. 155).

Your cause, your organization, and the things it needs are real. Money is simply an exchange mechanism (Mutz & Murray, 2006). Remember also that when you ask for money you are not taking anything away. You are giving someone a chance to do something meaningful and important. You honor a potential contributor with your request. Knowing just how important your cause is and how valuable your organization is, why would you hesitate to invite someone to take part? When you think of yourself as the giver rather than the taker, it changes how you approach this opportunity.

You might be thinking that there are lots of ways to get money, but nobody will give to you because you are controversial. Well, actually, good for you. Controversy is helpful, and the hotter the issue, the easier it is to raise money (Flanagan, 2000).

If you are so self-absorbed that asking for money is all about you and your insecurities, you won't build the relationships that are needed for change to occur (Klein, 2000). Greenfield (2002) made this point clearly, "fundraising is not about money—it's about relationships" (p. 4). Your fund-raising approach must be geared to the abilities of the members of your group who will be involved. Though all members should have a role, a few will take on greater responsibility. The design for dollars that you all come up with has to meet what people are willing to do. As their experience and confidence grow, people may be willing to do more and more risky things, including directly asking someone for money (Klein, 2002).

If, after all, you do need some money, how do you go about getting it? To answer this question you first have to answer a couple of others. The first critical question is how much do you need? A variety of techniques will yield you hundreds of dollars. These are great if you need hundreds of dollars; they are a waste of time if you need tens of thousands of dollars. The second question is, Do you need a steady income or an occasional infusion of funds? Generally, the larger your budget, say, over $10,000, the more predictable your income base needs to be. These two questions will set your general direction and help you decide on an approach. The two basic approaches to generate money are fund-raising and resource development. As you begin to select various options, you will need to ask more specific questions.

Fund-raising activities often occur on a smaller scale with the intent of an immediate payoff. Bake sales, raffles, and events fall into this category. This is appropriate for organizations that can get by with a short-term financial approach. Fund-raising usually involves a number of activities, each of which has a beginning and an ending point. When the need for more money becomes apparent, a new fund-raising activity is dreamed up and implemented. It is the sense of an upcoming need that spurs the fund-raising action. The organization lives off the proceeds from one activity to the next. Over time, you may plan so that these activities become more predictable, but you never really build a permanent financial base.

The *resource development* approach takes a longer and broader view. With this method, the intent is to develop a predictable and growing income base. Here, income is seen as the result of an ongoing process, not a specific activity. Expansion of donor lists, establishment of trusts, and planned giving are examples of the development approach. Organizations that plan to be in business for a while, that are visible in the community, and that have large budgets are usually better served by using resource development techniques.

One more proviso is worth mentioning. Getting money will cost you something. Whether that is postage, printing, hamburgers, or your time, it will cost something. Think this through. You want to be pretty sure that what you are likely to get is worth what you had to spend to get it.

Further, no matter how you approach the business of getting money, you will have to invest your own thoughts, time, and energy. You need to plan and to take action on your plan. You have to monitor activities to make sure that you are doing what you intended to do. Finally, you need to evaluate your approach to see that you accomplished your goals and that whatever investments you made in the process were worth it.

Two basic paths will get you to the rainbow's end. The first involves asking individuals to give you their own money. The second involves asking individuals to give you other people's money. In the first instance, people make decisions on behalf of their own interests. In the second, people make decisions on behalf of the interests of a group, organization, corporation, foundation, or government agency (Breiteneicher & Hohler, 1993).

Although the growing economic recession will certainly have an effect on your organization's ability to attract funding, contributions will not disappear. In fact, giving to human services tends to rise during times of recession and increase more quickly during longer recessions. If your organization continues to develop relationships with potential contributors, is prepared to make a compelling case for purposes meaningful to donors, and demonstrates good stewardship and accountability, you will likely weather the storm (Center on Philanthropy, 2008b).

Each change effort or organization will use a different approach based on the amount of money it needs, the types of activity in which it is involved, the current level of community acceptance, its need for short- or long-term support, its level of skill and interest in pursuing different approaches, and the time and money it can spend to raise more money. If you seek money from individuals, you will soon see that there is an almost endless assortment of ways to get individuals to give you money. You might even make up your own way.

Although getting money from corporations, foundations, and the like has its own twists and turns, these organizations usually share one thing in common: A written proposal or grant application will probably be required. The length and nature of these will vary, but it is likely that you will be doing some proposal writing for all sources other than individuals. Developing grant-writing skills is well worth your time.

CONTRIBUTIONS FROM INDIVIDUALS

Decisions made by individuals will determine whether or not as well as how much money you will get from any source. However, this particular category involves getting money directly from people with no intervening structure. I'm talking about people giving you their own money, not somebody else's.

This category deserves special attention not only because there are so many ways to go about it but also because more money comes from individuals than from any other nongovernmental source. According to the Giving USA Foundation (2009), about 75% of all the money given each year in the United States for charitable causes comes directly from individuals. It's not a paltry sum either. In 2008 individual Americans gave an estimated $229 billion to support causes they believed in, and more can be given. If you add in bequests, giving by individuals rises to $252 billion, a little more than 82% of total giving. In fact, Flanagan's research (2000) indicated that 38% of Americans said they wished they had given more money to charitable causes, and 14% would have given money but were not asked. Only 56% of households reported that they were asked to give in 2001, but 95% of them gave when asked (Independent Sector, 2002b). So ask. IRS reports of charitable contributions in 2003 indicated that most Americans donated about what they could comfortably afford (New Tithing Group, 2005). However, if affluent young and middle-aged individuals had contributed at the same rate as their less well-off counterparts, individual charitable

??? DID YOU KNOW?   The 11 Questions Every Donor Asks

Why me? If you remember that "me" is everyone's favorite subject, it will help train your focus where it should be: on the prospect and how his or her gift will make a difference in the world.

Why are _you_ asking me? For each donor, Why are you asking me? essentially means: What's in it for you? and Have you given yourself? and just what are your motives? If you have genuine passion for the cause, it'll show through, lending comfort to the donor and credibility to your ask.

Do I respect you? There is no more critical trait for a fundraiser than integrity. When people trust you, they're open to what you have to say. But trust takes time. You can't rush it.

How much do you want? Most donors want to give what they perceive as fair—not too much, not too little … you need to arrive at a dollar figure that challenges but is nevertheless seen as realistic by the donor.

Why _your_ organization? We all know there are wonderful causes. So how do you make yours stand out? … What makes you unique and different from every other organization are the stories you tell about the people you help.

Will my gift make a difference? Your goal as a fundraiser is to show donors, in practical, tangible ways, how their financial support will change and improve the life of a fellow human being, or a dog or a cat, or protect an environmental treasure.

Is there an urgent reason to give? While you can't manufacture it, there is some urgency for most organizations…. Deadlines, targets, and emotional stories are all your friends in this regard.

Is it easy to give? …You continually want to look for ways to make it easy for donors to give. That could be the convenience of a credit card, a toll-free number, having easy to fill out forms,…or a monthly giving program.

How will I be treated? Part of treating donors well is showing kindness at all giving levels. From placing their names on plaques, to site visits, to properly thanking donors, there are many ways to treat donors with consideration and respect.

Will I have a say over how you use my gift? While some donors want control, most will trust your organization to spend their gift wisely … IF you've first listened to, heard, and have fully appreciated any concerns they have in this regard.

How will you measure results? A certain percentage of donors, especially major givers, want measurable results. So in addition to having memorable stories to tell, as a solicitor you must know the numbers too.

SOURCE: McKinnon, 2008, pp. 99–101.

---

contributions would have increased by more than $25 billion.

Independent Sector's (2002b) study titled _Giving and Volunteering in the United States_ underscored the importance of building relationships with contributors. The study found that the average contributing household in which the respondent also volunteered gave almost twice as much as the average contributing household. It is not just the wealthy who give. Earlier studies have shown that those of modest means actually contribute a higher percentage of available income (Hodgkinson & Weitzman, 1996). What does this mean to you? Although middle- and upper-income individuals may give more total dollars, all members of your community are potential contributors and can be real financial investors in your effort.

Inclusive Fund-Raising

If you think of fund-raising as getting money from rich white guys, you are really missing the boat—or the bank. According to the Independent Sector (2002b), 89% of all households gave charitable contributions in 2000, and the Center on Philanthropy (2008a) found that more than 70% of American households gave to charitable causes in 2004, with an average contribution of $2,047 per donor household. Even at the lower percentage, that's millions of people and a lot of money. Few people are

Take a Moment to Discover

Here are some common, ineffective relationships organizations have with their money. Have you seen any of these?

- The organization insists on a level of financial security that few individuals could ever aspire to. It is afraid to use its money, keeping dollars locked away in various savings funds. It confuses fund-raising with fund hoarding.

- The organization keeps expenses very low, sacrificing quality of work and morale. It confuses fund-raising with fund squeezing.

- The organization drifts into financial security by changing the course of its work to attract funding for projects (and, as I might add, it limits or changes its work to appease a funding source). It confuses fund-raising with fund chasing.

Source: Kim Klein, 2000.

Connect: Women seek a sense of personal connection to the project.

Collaborate: Women like to work together as a group and do not respond well to competitive fund-raising appeals.

Committed: Women are committed to the causes they support and are more willing to volunteer time to these causes.

Celebrate: Women like to celebrate their accomplishments and have fun.

Although the opposite is not necessarily true about men, these six C's are particularly important to think about when you focus on contributions from women.

Nichols (2001) stated that women are more likely to give because of personal impact and are more concerned about privacy issues than men. Further, "women have less security about finances than do men and, as a result, often make smaller gifts" (p. 167). Kaminski (2001) pointed out, however, that women do not believe they are asked to give at the same level as men. The National Foundation for Women Business Owners (2000) found that women business owners are not only more likely to volunteer more hours for charitable causes than men but give at higher levels as well. The Women's Funding Network (2003b) found that women wanted to give their time as well as their money to see the impact their money had in their own communities. Two prominent vehicles for women in fund-raising are women's funds and women's circles.

Women's funds focus their grant making on issues that affect women and girls through organizations that are predominately governed and managed by women. The Global Fund for Women (2008), which began with a $500 donation by each of three women in 1987, gave grants totaling $8.67 million in 2008. The Women's Funding Network (2009), which is a partnership of 135 funds, with $465 million in working assets, focuses on issues that affect women, emphasizing investing in women's leadership. Many other women's funds exist and continue to be created. Although the focus is on issues particularly relevant to women and girls, Mary Ellen Capek and Molly Mead (2006) pointed out that all issues are women's issues, making over half the

unwilling or unable to contribute to a worthy cause, yet some fund-raisers overlook women and members of diverse communities.

Recognizing Women as Philanthropists. Women, particularly those who have participated in volunteer work, are ready to give (Sun, 2001). In 2008 more than 10 million firms, about 40% of all privately held firms, were owned by women, generating almost $2 trillion in sales (Center for Women's Business Research, 2009) and holding trillions of dollars in wealth (Kaminski, 2001). With women living longer than men, they will make key decisions regarding much of the $41 trillion expected to pass from generation to generation over the next 50 years (Center on Philanthropy, 2007). Yet women are often overlooked as a target group for fund-raising (Marx, 2000, Nichols, 2001). Kaminski (2001) pointed out that women and men have similar motivations for contributing but that "women respond to different 'triggers'" (p. 364). Shaw and Taylor (1995) described six C's important to women's giving:

Create: Women often give to create something.

Change: Women give to bring about social change.

??? DID YOU KNOW?   Time – A real investment

Time banking involves members of the community banking their volunteer hours in exchange for receiving help from others who have something to contribute. You receive some unit, like a time dollar, for every hour that you contribute helping your community, particularly by doing something for another person in your community. You can exchange this for someone doing something for you. This is a good way for a community, such as a neighborhood, to contribute and receive talents, strengthening community connections. No two time banking groups are exactly alike, but most involve setting up a list of people who have something to offer, some way of connecting people to exchange services, some unit that you can earn and then spend on what you want from the list, and some ground rules. Generally, the value of one person's hour is equal to every other's. Some groups have coordinators to help keep the process working.

---

population a special group somehow conveys the notion that women and girls receive some additional or particular attention, rather than essential attention.

Women's giving circles offer another opportunity for women's collective contributions to have a significant effect. They are more simply structured and easier to set up than foundations. In addition to providing funds, giving circles intend to develop deeper understanding and commitment to an issue. Fund-raising and social activism are inseparable (Women's Funding Network, 2003a). Typically, members of a giving circle contribute a set amount each year, say, $1,000, though a giving circle can be of any size. The pooled funds give the group the ability to make sizable grants. Although some individuals may find the $1,000 entry beyond their reach, the membership can be split among sisters or friends. One of the important aspects of giving circles is that the members are actively involved in the grant-making process, which enables them to become more attuned to community conditions and to further opportunities to provide leadership. No two giving circles look exactly alike. Some circles give time as well as money. That is a particular strength of this design. Each group decides what it wants to give and how (Bearman, 2007).

Fund-Raising and Philanthropy in Communities of Color.   The tradition of giving in communities of color is rich and vibrant. The tradition of fund-raising is not necessarily so. The whole matter of

philanthropy in communities of color is not well researched, but we are beginning to gain more understanding as fund-raisers reach out to all community members (Duran, 2001).

The Roper Center for Public Opinion Research (1999) analyzed participation in philanthropy among ethnic groups. This significant effort was described by Roper as "a relatively limited first investigation" (p. 2), and it was further noted that sample sizes for Native American and Asian American groups were too small to be included in the report. The Roper report observed that, generally speaking, African Americans and Hispanic Americans contributed less time and money to charitable causes than did non-Hispanic White Americans.

The W. K. Kellogg Foundation's (2000) Emerging Funds for Communities of Color (EFCC) Initiative conducted further research, adding interviews, focus groups, and networking meetings to their review of previous studies. They discovered that information on the giving practices of communities of color is not readily available, and furthermore, it is not the subject of much study. African Americans, Latinos, Asian American/Pacific Islanders, and Native Americans demonstrated less engagement in philanthropic activity, particularly endowments, and information on Native American and Asian American philanthropy was particularly hard to uncover.

New Ventures in Philanthropy was formed by the Forum of Regional Associations of Grantmakers to promote greater understanding of how to engage donors and grow philanthropy in communities of color (Lindsey, 2006). They extended the work of the Roper study and the EFCC, and numerous researchers (Abbe, 2000; Anft, 2001; Berry, 1999; Chao, 1999; Duran, 2001; Hunt, 2003; Mottino & Miller, 2004; Nichols, 2001; Polycarpe, 2004; Ramos, 1999; Reed & Dewees, 2005; Winters, 1999) who have shed some light on giving practices of members of diverse communities and the issues that those seeking a wider donor base must recognize. Several intriguing ideas emerged from these examinations. Let's look at a few of them.

How is "giving" defined? It is one thing to give to your community and quite another to give to your community through a donation of time and money to a formal agency. If the only "contribution" counted is the one you give through an agency, other forms of contributing are discounted or go unrecorded. Members of diverse communities give substantially in many informal ways (for example, for burials, to neighbors in immediate need, to community festivals, through informal networks of child care). Further, Latino and Asian American communities provide billions of dollars in remittances annually to family and communities outside of the United States. In many Native American cultures, giving is a notion of sharing, not charity, which affects how gifts are disbursed. The church has played a central role in many African American communities, redistributing contributions to both formal and informal networks and organizations to meet immediate needs as well as for advocacy. Many groups have been active in mutual aid giving. The African Union Society from the 18th century, the *mutualista* organizations among Latino communities, the many mutual aid societies among Asian American communities, and the support of tribal foundations by Native Americans provide glimpses of a long history of giving.

Are there barriers to institutional giving? Mistrust of traditional agencies and philanthropies and the culture they represent is common among members of diverse communities. Gordon (2007) has noted that some members of communities of color "see the funding process itself reinforcing much of the racism that has kept them disadvantaged and needing support in the first place" (p. 14). "Cultural competence, identification and empathy, sensitivity to race and 'knowing what you don't know'" are essential strengths of what-

ever organization is doing the work (Lindsey, 2006, p. 8). Many see these organizations as relatively inattentive or ineffective in dealing with the needs and issues of people of color. This is not surprising when the assets, staff, and boards of directors are disproportionately White. Why would these organizations deserve a contribution? Other factors such as overall financial net worth, unfamiliarity with planned giving, and ineffective solicitation methods also get in the way of greater institutional giving.

Who is being asked and why? The service orientation of many organizations corresponds with a view of communities of color as recipients, not contributors. Furthermore, one of the most significant elements in making a financial contribution is being asked (Independent Sector, 2001). Members of diverse communities may not be asked as frequently.

So what is there to learn? There's a lot. First, change agents need to recognize that increasing income among members of diverse communities has accelerated an interest in making financial contributions to organizations and causes members find valuable. Second, change agents need to challenge assumptions that they and traditional funders may hold regarding communities of color and their assets. Third, change agents need to learn that much is already occurring in the National Center for Black Philanthropy, the Asian Pacific Fund, the 21st Century Foundation, the First Nations Development Institute, the Potlach Fund, Native Americans in Philanthropy, Hispanics in Philanthropy, Black United Funds, the Chicana Latina Foundation, and other organizations. New endowments, foundations, and giving circles are being created, with donors and organizations gaining in sophistication and sharing their expertise (Lindsey, 2006; Martinez, 2005; Philanthropy.org, 2002; Reed & Dewees, 2005; Reed, Nuvayestewa, & Dewees, 2006; W. K. Kellogg Foundation, 2000, 2009).

Change agents need to learn about what motivates donors. Ferlinda Mottino and Eugene Miller (2004) pointed out a number of emerging themes in a study involving African American, Asian American, and Latino donors. The most substantial differences were not among groups but between older and younger generations. Older generations tended to focus more on their respective ethnic communities, whereas younger generations have a

---

??? DID YOU KNOW?   Ten Questions, Plus One

If you want money, you need to answer 10 questions, plus one.

1. Who has it?
2. Who is likely to give it to you?
3. Where do you have a connection with these people?
4. When are they in a giving or spending mood?
5. What message do they need to hear?
6. How do you send that message?
7. Who sends that message?
8. How do you make it as easy as possible for people to respond?
9. How do you acknowledge and nurture people for the future before and after they give?
10. What resources do you have to direct this effort?

Plus one:

• What other questions do you need to ask?

---

less racially and ethnically circumscribed view of the world. Younger generations gave more to support education efforts and see access to wealth as an important approach to empowerment. Both older and younger donors have a strong desire to effect social change, and both older and younger donors started young through volunteering. A personal connection with an organization was the most common reason for giving such as knowing that a family member or close friend had relied on the organization during a critical point in her life.

Change agents can explore new approaches that bring together the power of many individuals' giving to create a sizable source of funds that can make a significant impact. Giving circles are effective tools. So are focus funds, which are small grant-making organizations created by people who are not just connected by location but by shared experience and culture. They are attracting new donors whose wealth of community experience is coupled with financial contributions. By directly involving community members in grant making, providing a genuine connection that deepens giving practices, focus funds are attracting new voices and perspectives into investing in community change. Grants from focus funds are generally small and directed to groups and organizations that are often left out of more mainstream grant making. They also often become links between overlooked communities and outside institutions (Kasper, Nielsen, & Chao, 2004; Lindsey, 2006; Ross, 2006).

Helping those in need, giving back to society, and enhancing the moral basis of society appear to be similar among all Americans (Roper Center for Public Opinion Research, 1999). Yet different histories, attitudes, and methods of giving prevail among different groups of Americans. Like any other endeavor, a better understanding of the community, its perspectives, resources, and practices will increase your effectiveness. Developing the capability and leadership of members of the community will lead to more relevant and appropriate action than will reliance on others whose perceptions and agendas may be different from the community. Most of all, change agents need to learn better how to act on a belief that every member of the community has something important to contribute. Self-reliance and partnership are much more powerful goals than grateful dependence.

Six Basic Steps

Getting money from individuals involves six basic steps no matter what approach you use. By breaking it down into steps, I run the risk of making the process seem pretty complicated. In actual practice, you will be able to mentally check off each step (and you should do this) once you have repeated the procedure a few times. The more experience you gain in asking for money, the simpler and more routine this process will be for you.

First, it is helpful to know whom you are asking. *Identifying your prospects* is a fundamental step: "Who" comes before "how" (Breiteneicher & Hohler, 1993). Understanding how much you need and when as well as whether you are looking for a nonrenewable gift or building a substantial base of income will guide you in your selection.

Second, you need to *nurture these prospective givers*. Once you have identified the prospects, establish some type of relationship with them. This includes developing their awareness and interest in your efforts (Baird, 1997; Brakeley, 1997; Flanagan, 2000; White, 2001).

Third, think about and *prepare a message* that will be most effective in producing a favorable response. You need to take into account what this particular individual needs to know and feel to decide to contribute money. You need to put together a message that will provide that information and stir those emotions.

Fourth, you need to *deliver that message*. Think of how and in what circumstances you can most effectively communicate your message to the people who need to hear it. The more direct your communication and the clearer your request, the more effective you will be. Recalling the "ladder of communication effectiveness" described in Chapter 8 should give you some ideas on techniques you can use (Breiteneicher & Hohler, 1993; Freyd & Carlson, 1997; Klein, 2000; Reinhart, 1990; Seltzer, 2001).

Fifth, after you have sent your message, *follow up* to see that your message has been received, you fulfill any expectations, and that any pledges made were kept (Baird, 1997; Mutz & Murray, 2006).

Finally, *say thank you*. In many situations, particularly when you have made a direct personal request, a personally written thank-you is an important step, even if you did not receive a contribution at this time. Remember, there is always tomorrow (Baird, 1997; Flanagan, 2000; Klein, 2004).

Direct Requests

The most effective way to ask someone for money is to do it directly, face to face. The more money you are asking for and the less experience the prospect has in giving to a cause like yours, the more you need to be prepared when making your request. Even if you are making a minor request from a friend, don't assume that preparation is unnecessary

(Klein, 2000). Here are a few things to know and do that might help you.

Know Your Prospect

- Gauge how much the prospect is capable of giving.
- Determine the prospect's likely motivators and to what facts and emotions he is likely to respond.

Prepare Yourself for the Contact

- Know in advance what you will say. Be able to clearly and simply describe what you need and why. Practice out loud so it doesn't sound awkward.
- Describe why you think the undertaking is important to the prospect and what her contribution will mean.
- Be willing and able to answer questions.
- Determine whether anyone else needs to be involved in making the request.
- Arrange the right time, place, and people to ask the prospect.

Make Contact

- Make your request.
- Get the money then and there, or at the very least arrange a time when you can pick it up.
- Thank the prospect.

Tips for Direct Requests

- People give to people. The asker's relationship to the giver is important (Breiteneicher & Hohler, 1993). We respond best to an appeal from someone who is trusted for some reason other than her link to the organization asking for the money. A request or recommendation from a friend tops the list (Roper Center for Public Opinion Research, 1999). Many studies and surveys have explored why people give to charity. Tax advantages are almost never near the top of the list. The donor's relationship to the organization or its mission is far more important as is a recognition of the organization's needs and a belief that the money will be spent wisely (White, 2001).
- Identify the predisposed. These are the individuals, businesses, or others whose interests and actions suggest an inclination toward your organization's mission. These are people who have raised their hand in some way (Ahern & Joyaux, 2008).

- Promote personal involvement. Some ways to do this include inviting prospects to take part in lectures or public meetings, personal issue discussions, presentations to other groups, and to volunteer. Nonprofit agencies particularly want to make sure they are grooming a new generation of investors (donors) and that their fund-raising techniques increase civic engagement rather than keep donors distant (Hall, 1996; Reinhart, 1990).

- People are more likely to respond when asked to give an immediate contribution than when a delay between the request and the receipt of the donation exists (Reeves, Macolini, & Martin, 1987).

- People are more willing to help out someone who has done them a favor or who has given them something (Regan, 1971). Consider buying your prospect dinner, lunch, or a soda. Have you done anyone a favor recently?

- Discuss common opinions and values at some point in your conversation. This provides a shared frame of reference and a recognition of affiliation that makes the request easier to state and easier to meet.

- Ask for a specific dollar amount (Flanagan, 2000; Mutz & Murray, 2006). You might ask: "Is this an amount you are comfortable with?"

- Smile. Lawyers teach witnesses to smile at the jury because research shows juries believe a witness who smiles more than a witness who does not (Flanagan, 2000).

- Major donors will often contribute to exciting programs with their hearts more than their heads. Exciting means bold or visionary more than controversial (Panas, 1989).

- You never offend a person by politely asking for too large a gift. Most are flattered that you think they could give that much (Reinhart, 1990).

- Reward or in some way recognize contributors, paying careful attention to provide special rewards to major givers (Baird, 1997).

- Using emotion can help. Pride, outrage, guilt, affection, and fear are common emotions that promote a response.

- You may get a no, but a no in fund-raising may be a "not yet." To deal with a no, you might ask: "Is there something that concerns you about whether this would be a good use of your money?" This allows you to continue relationship building and explorations of other options while creating an opportunity to answer unspoken questions (Mutz & Murray, 2006). If you receive a no to a specific dollar request, you can also ask: "How much can you give?" You want to create an option between your requested amount and zero.

- Keep in contact with donors, especially major donors. Maintaining attention shows donors that you take their interest, not just their money, seriously (Klein, 2006).

Take a Moment to Discover

Many of us are uncomfortable when asking people for money, so we tend to put a lot of distance between the asker and the giver. We are often more concerned with taking care of our discomfort than with getting what we're asking for. We usually end up with good protection from discomfort when we do this but with not many more dollars than we started with.

Think about how often we ask people, friends, relatives, coworkers, and the like for money for routine requests. We commonly ask for money for stamps, gas, snacks, and pop—or at least we expect people to chip in. Sometimes we also ask people to spend money to go out on a Saturday night to attend a basketball game or a movie.

Reflect on last week or last month. How many times have you asked or expected someone to give you money for something, regardless of what it might have been? How many times have they asked you for money?

Think about the circumstances surrounding the request for money. What can you learn from thinking about the times you ask people to give you money, or to spend money to be with you, or when they ask you to give money? How would you ask any of these people for money to support your change effort? Today, ask one person to give you money for something, ideally for some worthy cause you support.

Pitching to Groups

If you can't directly ask an individual to give you money, your next best bet is to ask them in a group, the smaller the better. Groups can achieve a shared or group view of a situation and exert peer pressure on their members to respond appropriately. Groups can be addressed as a unit to solicit funds from the group itself as a single contribution, or contributions can be requested from individual members of the group.

When preparing to make your pitch to a group, consider many of the same things about the group as you did with individual donors—estimate their ability to give, their giving history, and get some background information on the organization itself. Understand, also, that most groups are worried about your legitimacy, especially if you are a new organization. Your approach to them must take this into account.

Receiving money from the group itself, rather than from the members of the group, requires a different process. Many groups and organizations, especially those that routinely make donations over $1,000, have a formal process established for handling requests. The larger and more formal an organization is, the more extensive the process is likely to be. The more you know about the process, the greater your chances of receiving funds. This process generally requires a written proposal together with a short verbal presentation in support of the proposal. Follow the guidelines described later in this chapter on funding from organizations.

Tips for Pitching to Groups

- It is sometimes helpful for you to have a couple of people present in the audience who have already agreed to give you money. Yes, you may call them shills. These shills should demonstrate their support and their contribution in a way that best stimulates participation by other members. For example, if you are "passing the hat," these supporters can be among those who first receive the hat. Seeing their friends drop in their checks or dollars can encourage others to do so as well.
- You can find various lists of civic clubs and organization online. Check to see which of these may be interested in your cause.

Memberships

Requesting an annual membership fee from participants in the organization is a simple, effective way to raise money and increase commitment (Greenfield, 2002). This approach tends to make your organization a more formal one, bringing more expectations and responsibilities.

In your effort to "recruit" members, start with individuals who by word or action have expressed an interest in the organization or its goals. Each of these people should receive a personal request that they become members.

It is easier to ask for a membership than for an outright donation. You are acknowledging interest and inviting participation as well as asking for money. Potential members have the opportunity to gain a sense of affiliation. They have a choice to belong. As members, they are not considered nor do they consider themselves outsiders who are asked to give to "you." Instead, they become part of "us" and to some extent become recipients of the contribution as well as makers of it. By asking every person who has expressed an interest in your effort to become a member, you can quickly add to your coffers. Even though the amount you raise from this group is likely to be relatively small, it's worth the modest effort.

After asking everyone who has shown some support for the effort, the next step is to contact those who are potential beneficiaries of the organization's work. Again, a personal, face-to-face request is far more effective than any other method. A simple plan should be worked out to reach as many people in this group as possible. At the very least, when anyone from the organization has contact with another person who could gain from what the organization is doing, that person should be asked to be a member. This is a habit that should be consciously developed among the members of your core group. If only a handful of members routinely recruit and you have no other plan for approaching these potential contributors, you will still steadily build the organization and provide new income.

Tips for Annual Memberships

- Keep membership dues low, below what people are able to give. Membership dues simply get people involved in the organization; you can ask them for other help later.
- Consider having several levels of membership with different privileges and benefits for each level (for example, voting and nonvoting). The higher the level, the higher the fees.
- Your membership form should be simple to fill out and return. If you can collect it on the spot, you will get a much higher rate of return.
- Keep an accurate database of your membership, including key information that allows you to contact members for education, mobilization, or fundraising. Once a year print it out, and with a small team of you who have been around for a while, go through it line by line to make sure everything is accurate. Make corrections if someone has moved, become divorced, or died (Klein, 2000).

- Include the line "make your check payable to" on the form. If the donation is tax deductible, say so.
- You can also ask for other information such as special knowledge, skills, community contacts, or interests. Don't require this information, otherwise the form may become irritating to fill out.

The third step in developing a member base is to invite people to join whenever your organization contacts the general public. This, too, should become a habit, and it is an easy one to acquire. Membership forms should be available at all public events, appear in all newsletters, and be on your website. Each public speaking opportunity should be accompanied by a call for people to become members. Pass out forms toward the end of your talk, right after you make the request. If you can work it in, take a moment before you conclude your remarks to allow people to fill out the membership form. Use a modified form for presentations that requires only essential information. Also have a box that says, "I can't pay you now, but I will later." You may lose a few dollars that you could get then and there, but it will rope in enough fence sitters to more than make up for it. Members should receive something in return for their contribution (Hicks, 2001). Membership cards are easy and inexpensive to produce. They should not look cheap. Attractive, plastic laminated cards that fit easily into a wallet or billfold are the best.

Newsletters are important in reaffirming participation. Each membership organization should have one. It is important to remind people that they are members and why. If it is easy to provide other benefits, do so. Special event invitations, discounts, or other rewards available to members only are helpful. However, do only what is easy to do. If you make the process too complicated, you turn a simple technique into a time-consuming one.

Members become the source of future funds and friends. Each year you ask members to ante up. Although not all continue, most will, providing the organization with a predictable source of income.

Periodically you should make a special appeal to members for additional donations. This should be tied to a special situation or challenge to the organization. Although you don't want to barrage members with these requests, you will be able to draw money as well as goods and services from members in addition to their membership fees.

Indirect Requests

Indirect requests from individuals include all techniques other than a face-to-face request for a contribution. These are primarily requests through your website, e-mail, over the phone, or by post mail. Indirect methods produce a much lower response rate but have the advantage of reaching many more people. Even if individuals don't respond to one particular indirect request, their awareness of the organization is increased, and they may respond at another time.

Further, those who do respond become part of your donor base. You will resolicit these people from time to time for additional contributions. Most people who give once will give again, usually at least two more times. A good yardstick is that as long as you cover the initial costs of your solicitation campaign you will eventually make money if you have a planned resolicitation campaign. An exception to this would be large mailings of tens or hundreds of thousands that may actually lose money on the first round. Campaigns of that sort really understand that initial costs are an investment in a high future return. Ideally, you want to do more than just cover your costs. You want to make money the first time. Understand, though, that *resolicitation of identified donors is where the real money is.* Your rate of return on resolicitation is a great deal higher than that on your initial request.

Some groups do what is called prospecting. This means that their initial contact is done mainly for the purpose of discovering prospects (the gold in this game) to add to their base of donors for future contacts and additional dollars. Keep accurate and thorough records on all donors. Building your donor base is a basic concern. You don't want to start from the beginning each time you go out to ask for money.

Telephone Solicitation

This method involves calling people at home and asking them for money to support what your organization does. The better your organization or the problem it deals with is known, and the better you know the people you are calling, the better will be your results. Get lists of people who will be likely to give. Contributors to organizations similar to yours, names of potential beneficiaries of your efforts, friends and acquaintances of your members, and memberships to exclusive clubs and organizations are good places to start. This method has the benefit of involving members of your organization in making direct requests and reaching a large number of donors.

Tips for Organizing Telephone Solicitations

- Finding ways to maintain the enthusiasm and esprit de corps of your callers is essential. It is far better to have too many callers for the number of calls to be made than vice versa. A good standard is to expect that each caller can complete 40 calls per night and be willing to work for two nights of calling. Therefore, it will take 12 committed callers for you to complete about 1,000 phone calls.

- Spend about 20 to 30 minutes on training. This will help build confidence and reduce mistakes, but don't overdo it and make it tedious (Freyd, 2001; Greenfield, 2002).

- Make sure lists are neat and are complete with names, addresses, and phone numbers before you start.

- Develop a short, written script that will guide what you say. The script should include your responses to the things the person at the other end is likely to say. The script should mention your name and the name of the person you are calling early in the conversation. Read the script out loud a few times before you make the first call. This will get you comfortable with the message and help make sure that it sounds natural, not phony. You will also be able to hear if your request is clear. The script should have the respondent answer yes to a couple of short-answer questions before asking for the contribution (for example, "Are you aware of _____?" "Do you think _____ is a problem in our community?"). If calling friends and acquaintances of members, use the member's name in the script. Get permission to do so.

- Arrange for a small group of people (six or so) to call from the same location. The location should have a phone line for each caller. Social service agencies, insurance agencies, and real estate offices are likely candidates. It is important to do this as a group. Individuals who call from home hardly ever complete the task.

- Complete all calls before 9 o'clock.

- Have letters and any related materials available in advance to follow up each call. One letter goes to those who have agreed to send their contribution, thanking them for their contribution. This letter should include the amount pledged. Another letter goes to the people who are thinking about contributing, thanking them for their interest. The third letter goes to those who have said no, asking them to consider it at a later date. Make sure envelopes and stamps are available and that a letter is prepared after each call and sent the next day. A personal handwritten note is included from the caller on each letter.

This approach has the advantage that you speak directly with the potential contributor. It has the distinct disadvantage of pestering people at home along with a host of other callers offering dance lessons, water softeners, and tickets to the local police ball. Because of this, most organizations do not do cold calling (that is, when people are not expecting you to call). You run the risk of turning them off to your organization. You also have to be concerned about the volunteers doing the calling. They may be treated rudely. You could lose a few this way. Although many people feel annoyed by telephone calls requesting contributions, others are comfortable giving by phone. Using this method to reach people who are already supporters reduces potential problems.

Telephone fund-raising campaigns come in all sizes. You can call 100 people or 100,000 people. The number of telephone lines at your disposal will play a large part in this decision. Equally important is the number and the enthusiasm of your volunteer callers, and the amount of time you have for planning, recruiting volunteers, and administering the program (Freyd, 2001).

It is important to check rules regulating telephone solicitation from both the Federal Communications Commission and the National Do Not Call Registry, run by the Federal Trade Commission. Your state may have "do not" call regulations as well.

Tips for Telephone Solicitations

- Acknowledge any likely resistance to the call.
- If the request is met with a noncommittal or a no response, suggest a small amount.

- Consider having the volunteers get together for dinner before the calling begins; after dinner meet for a half-hour training session. These activities can stimulate group spirit and help give callers confidence (Ardman & Ardman, 1980).
- Have fun. Have refreshments. Most people are reluctant to make phone calls, so add as much social enjoyment as possible to the task. For example, set pizza goals. Whenever the group achieves a certain total in pledges, send out for a pizza. Keep a scoreboard of totals, and cheer when certain amounts are reached.
- There are firms specializing in telemarketing. Check the percentage of money that goes to you and to them before you decide if you want to hire them. Check on the reputation of the firm by getting a list of clients and talking to them.

Telephone Support for Small Mail Campaigns

The telephone can be a useful tool to increase the impact of a letter sent to a select group of potential donors. A mailing of 500 can easily be followed by three nights of calling. This will measurably increase the number of contributions the letter could generate on its own. This approach incorporates features of broader telemarketing and direct mail methods. Due to its smaller scale, it is simpler to do and easier to manage.

The letter should be signed by an individual who has some favorable status in the eyes of those receiving the letter. Ideally, the letter signer should be a member of the group receiving the letter, known personally by members of that target group, and be identified with the issue. For example, a successful homebuilder who has spoken publicly on the issue of homelessness could be a good letter signer for other homebuilders asking them to contribute to an effort that works with people who are homeless.

Sometimes an individual who is outside the immediate target group but held in high regard by those in the group will make an effective letter signer. The highly popular coach of the university basketball team, writing to those same homebuilders, or a nationally respected environmentalist, writing to a local environmental group, may produce a good response.

Tips for Support of Mail Campaigns

- Write the letter for the signer. Most signers don't want to take on the job of composing a letter. Provide an opportunity for the signer to review and modify the contents to reflect his personality. Make sure the essential elements are retained.
- Use facts and emotions in your letter to which the target group is likely to respond. Frame the message in a way that makes the most sense to them. This is usually not the time to get people to agree with your political or philosophical view of things. Your main purpose here is to get money.
- Mention that this mailing is going to only a few people.
- Include a P.S. on the letter saying that someone will be calling in a few days.
- Include a self-addressed return envelope with the letter.
- Ask the signer if he would be willing to make a few follow-up calls. If so, you can indicate this in the P.S.
- Follow the same procedures involving telephone solicitation discussed earlier. Additionally, make sure you remove from the calling list names of those who have responded to the letter before you begin your calling. There's no need to bother them again. Also, include a copy of the original letter when you send your follow-up letter to those who are undecided.
- Personalize your outside envelope. Handwrite or type the address. Save mailing labels for some other time (Brentlinger & Weiss, 1987).
- Use an envelope of high-quality paper.
- Have the signer's name and mailing address as the return address, or use a mailing address with no name. Do not use your organization's name in the return address. After all, they are responding primarily to the contents of the letter and the signer, not to your name.
- Send your letters with first-class postage. Use stamps, not metered mail.
- Handwrite a code number or the person's name on the return envelope you have inserted. This reminds people that you are paying attention to who is responding, and who is not.
- Have the letter signer actually sign each letter and write a personal note on as many letters as possible. Something like "Don, I hope to hear from you" would be sufficient.
- Using another name, have your own address and phone number included on the list so you can see how the process is working.

On some occasions, particularly if your organization is not well known, you may want to have several people sign the same letter. Having several signatures on the same letter gives the impression of broader support and increases the chances that those receiving the mailing will respond to the name of a person they trust. The disadvantage to this is that you can lose the more personal touch that a single signature provides.

It is particularly important to get good lists when using this technique. The names you select should be those who are much more likely than the general public to respond to both the issue at hand and the person or persons signing the letter with the amount of money you need.

Direct Mail

Direct mail is effective for prospecting and resolicitation. Unless you have a hot list, one that is likely to provide a high percentage of contributors, or a huge mailing, you will probably not make a lot of money on your first general request. In fact, you may well lose money on the first go-round; a return of 1 or 2% is considered acceptable (Klein, 1992). However, continued resolicitation of the contributors who do respond can bring you a profit in the long run (Lautman, 2001), so don't give up on your donor list too quickly.

Direct mail is best used as part of a long-term process for building a constituency base and keeping your donors connected with you (Klein, 1992; Lautman, 1997; Mutz & Murray, 2006). Of course, if you are holding some lists that just sizzle in your fingers, you might want to give this a try. The quality of your list is the most important ingredient in this type of fund-raising (Barnes, 1989; Lautman, 2001). Also, be aware households received more than 13.5 billion pieces of direct mail from nonprofits in 2007. That's well over a hundred solicitations a year (U.S. Postal Service, 2008a). It all gets tossed in the trash, right? Well, actually, no. Almost half of those who receive direct mail do read it, and another 33% at least scan each piece (U.S. Postal Service, 2008a).

In addition to costing you money, direct mail requires considerable time and energy. You need to gather lists, design your mailing piece, stuff and address all the envelopes, gauge the best time for sending all this out, and check your supply of aspirin. For these and other reasons, most smaller or new organizations do not use direct mail. Larger, well-established organizations do find this profitable. They have the resources to put into it.

This method exists because if you have the resources and you do it right, it can make money, lots of money. Some companies specialize in direct mail and can run your whole campaign for you. Others specialize in renting lists (for example, the list of all subscribers to a nationally syndicated magazine who live in a certain ZIP code area). Others, including sheltered workshops and organizations serving people with developmental disabilities, will take your addresses, envelopes, and materials and prepare the mailing.

Direct mail techniques have become increasingly sophisticated. If you believe your organization would benefit from pursuing this method of fund-raising, check to see which firms in your area can help you. Again, see if you have any special connections that could lead to some free or low-cost consultation. Remember, it is important to be sure the firm is reputable before you do business. Do your homework.

Events

Need money? Hold an event. It's almost a knee-jerk response. Imagine a small group sitting around fretting about money. Before too long someone will very likely pipe up with, "Hey, let's hold a (dance, fun run, basketball game, concert, all of the above)." Be sure that your community, especially likely donors, and your members who are to organize the event have sufficient interest. Special events are becoming increasingly more difficult. In many communities both donors and organizers are getting burned out on them (Sinnock, 1995).

According to fund-raising experts Harry Freedman and Karen Feldman (2007), given the time, energy, and often money that it takes to produce an event, there are only three good reasons to have one:

- to raise money
- to raise the group's profile
- to attract new members or donors.

Event fund-raising usually means that you are introducing an activity into the community calendar that is interesting enough that people will want to give you money to join in the fun. And it should be fun. Events can attract attention and energize your members and supporters, affirm your connection to the community, and showcase your organization's leaders (Greenfield, 2002; Hicks, 2001). They can offer a clear focus for activity and help members and others in the community learn how to work together.

Your awareness of the community calendar, by the way, is important. You want to make sure that you have taken into account religious holidays, sports events, cultural festivities, long holiday weekends, and other potential conflicts. Monday and Friday evenings, for example, could conflict with religious groups. The best days for special events, particularly major evening events, are midweek or Saturday (Allen, 2000).

Less risky than creating your own event is to capitalize on an existing community activity. The work and worry is much less in this case, though the money may be as well. Though you can just sit back and collect the profits, your early involvement in planning will give you the chance to see that the event is handled in a way that supports the image of your organization. Also, you want to make sure up front just how much you will receive from the revenue generated by the event. Generally about 10% of the gross revenues is a fair amount (Allen, 2001a).

There are five basic types of events: those requiring attendance and ticket sales, those requiring participation and registration fees, those that other groups do on your behalf with a select community of potential contributors, those that are small select gatherings, and those that serve as a promotion of your organization as well as some other product or service.

Regardless of the approach you take, make sure that you use the opportunity to tell your organization's story as well as provide some activity and raise some money. Set aside time in the program and provide organizational materials and displays to help participants connect what they are doing with why.

Some events can be considered as much people-raising events as fund-raising events. In this case, you try to get as many people to take part in the activity as possible while making just a little bit more money than you need to cover your costs. Here, the cost to the participant is very low because you are more concerned with bringing out a lot of people than bringing in a lot of money.

If you use this approach, you had better make sure you know what you want to do. Many groups are disappointed when they have a great turnout and little money to show for all the work. If you make a $2 profit on every person who shows up, you will need 500 people to attend to make $1,000. Making $1,000 after many, many hours of work can be deflating. Getting a crowd of 500 people can be a tremendous boost to your organization. Just make sure that your purpose is clear.

You have to have a number of things going for you to hold a big event that raises a lot of money. First, you have to have a lot of resources to put into planning and organizing and promoting the event. This usually means people (and their contacts) and money. Second, you need to have plenty of time in advance of the scheduled date to work on the project. Six months or more lead time is a good standard for larger affairs (Allen, 1997; Greenfield, 2002; Ulin, 2001). Third, your event should be sufficiently unique or attractive to a large group of probable respondents. This requires that you have access to a lot of people who would truly consider taking part. Finally, your organization, or at least the issue on which you are working, must have strong credibility in the community. The members of the community have to know about you and your issue and care about your success.

Smaller events are obviously much easier to organize. However, even small events have the same four demands, just on a reduced, perhaps a much reduced, scale.

Make sure that you check any legal requirements, such as permits, and consider what insurance, if any, you may need (Allen, 2001a; Greenfield, 2002).

Remember to collect names, e-mail and post mail addresses, and phone numbers of those attending each event. These names can be added to your contributor or support list, which you may resolicit for future income (Klein, 1992).

The event isn't really over when it's over. There are a number of things to take care of after the big day has come and gone. Of course, you will want to make sure that all necessary expressions of thank-you are sent. You also want to do an assessment of the event to see what worked well and what needed more attention. If you plan to repeat the activity, make sure all your records are in order: guest lists, budgets, expenses, actual revenues, printed material, assessment notes, and other artifacts you can use to guide your next affair (Ulin, 2001). Establishing an event as an ongoing activity can be beneficial. Repetition allows you to continue to improve its quality while introducing a fairly predictable source of funds into the cycle of your fund-raising activities.

There's no doubt about it. Events require creativity, attention, and hard work. They can drain an organization's resources, deflect from its primary work, and set members up for disappointment. Events can also energize and excite members, provide a clear set of activities for members with the promise of tangible results, provide a vehicle for attracting new members, help communicate your organization's presence and work to the community, and raise money to boot.

Ticket Events. Paying, usually in advance, to attend something a little bit out of the ordinary is the essence of this approach. Contributors don't have to do anything but be there. Food and entertainment are the common features of these fund-raising events. Dinners, plays, concerts, famous and semifamous speakers—all are used as ticket events.

This is another area in which competition and costs are increasing. Some communities have literally hundreds of these events per year, and it is not surprising to have costs run up to 80% of your total take (Freedman, 1996). This fund-raising method requires some sort of drawing card, some enticement for people to add yet another activity to their day-to-day routine. Not only are people asked to put something else on their schedule, they are asked to pay to do this as well. They need to buy a ticket.

There are two important elements for success. First, select a drawing card that is sufficiently interesting to prospective contributors. This may include the other people in attendance. People may not want to miss an important social occasion that all the "right" people attend. It's fair to say that social-

izing is the main event at a major benefit (Brentlinger & Weiss, 1987). The more out of the ordinary your request, the more special it should be. For example, coming up with something to lure people out on a Tuesday night is more challenging than getting people to eat a midweek lunch.

The second necessary component involves selling all those tickets by setting the right price for the event and getting those tickets into the hands of contributors and getting the money out of their pockets. Although tickets are frequently sold at the door, it is the advance ticket sales that normally determine your success.

Tips for Ticket Events

- Don't count on your drawing card or invitation to sell most of the tickets. Ticket sellers usually sell far more tickets than the event itself would. Ideally 80% of your tickets will be sold before the first invitation is sent (Greenfield, 2002).

- Get a very detail-oriented event manager to coordinate the work (Allen, 2001a; Freedman & Feldman, 2007; Ulin, 1997).

- Consider getting corporate sponsorship to underwrite the event or a significant portion of it, but recognize that sponsors need benefits such as visibility or high-end clients attending the event (Freedman & Feldman, 2007; Ulin, 1997).

- Promote your event to groups and individuals most likely to attend. A good invitation list is essential. Any advance publicity about the event is helpful. Figure out how your drawing card is newsworthy. Fliers, mailings, telephoning, and newspaper notices should be used. The strategy here is to keep the event in the public eye and build a sense of anticipation (Brentlinger & Weiss, 1987; Ulin, 1997). This is particularly important for major events.

- Make it easy for contributors to buy a ticket even if no one asks them to purchase a ticket. Have a phone number they can call, an order blank they can fill out, or some other way of getting in touch with you.

- Ticket sellers should be grouped into teams of five, with team leaders. Team leaders check weekly on team members' progress. This need not and should not be heavy-handed. Each member should expect to be contacted about progress. Team leaders need to follow through.

- Team competitions motivate ticket sellers, and especially team leaders. You'll be surprised to learn how important it is for some sellers to get "credit" for a sale. Winning teams should get some prize or recognition.

- People often buy tickets mainly to please the ticket seller. The nature of the event and the cause are important, but the ticket buyer's relationship with the ticket seller or the organization the seller represents is usually more important.

- Encourage some people to buy a block of tickets, not just one. For example, businesspeople sometimes buy an entire table of tickets for a dinner event, giving seats to employees or clients.

- Send "save the date cards," a notice mailed as much as 6 months in advance, to prospective patrons. Their purpose is as much to stake a claim to the community's attention as it is to reserve a spot on the calendar (Brentlinger & Weiss, 1987).

- Whenever possible, get news coverage of your event. You will have to determine some newsworthy angle that will attract coverage. Remember, your event can give more than money. Milk it for all that it's worth.

- Get meaningful donated items to be used as door prizes, and include a mention of these on printed tickets and in your promotions. A weekend for two at a nice resort is a good door prize.

- Publicly, formally, and clearly recognize all volunteers who made the event a success. This includes acknowledgments in the event program, a personal letter, and mention to the audience on the day of the event.

- Make sure members of the media get special attention and that they know whether or not they are to be treated as regular guests. If not, provide a media room with plenty of food and beverages, a media kit, and someone to show them around and introduce them to key attendees. Help them get the story you want told (Allen, 2000).

- Prepare and follow a checklist of things to be done. This requires advance planning. Have a checklist for things you need to do in the months, weeks, and days leading up to the event. One organization has a 101-item checklist for one of its major events, including everything from developing the planning committee to checking the room temperature on the day of the event. The length of your checklist will be determined by the size and complexity of your event (Allen, 1997; Brentlinger & Weiss, 1987; Greenfield, 2002; Ulin, 2001).

- Do what you can to keep your expenses down. The lower your costs, the higher your return. Know what all your expenses are, and find ways to reduce them. Shopping around will lead you to bargains. One caution: Don't look cheap and tacky. A fancy, high-class event should look and feel that way.

- Using celebrities may be a good idea for your event. Many celebrities will waive their appearance fee if they believe strongly in the issue. They will also attract immediate attention to your organization and issue. Be careful of hidden costs, however. Airline tickets, hotel rooms, and fees to members of the celebrity's entourage can be very expensive. Make sure you know all the costs in advance (Fisch, 1989b; Freedman, 1996).

- Many people who buy tickets to the event don't show up. This varies with the type of event, but it is not uncommon to have a third of the ticket purchasers absent. It is acceptable to oversell the event. It will probably make you nervous, but go ahead and do it anyway.

Registration Events. These events are similar to ticket events, except that the contributor is asked to do more than just attend. The contributor pays to become a participant, not just an attendee. Such events usually provide some benefit that lasts beyond the event or the opportunity to engage in an enjoyable activity. Workshops, conferences, and seminars are examples of the first type. Bicycle tours, fun runs, and golf tournaments are examples of the second.

Tips for Registration Events

- Most registrations will come in during the week prior to the event. Don't sit back and wait for this to happen, but don't get panicky too early and call off the event.

- Figure out in advance how to make the event look and feel successful even if you only get half the registrations you expect. How you arrange seating in a room and how you design where people congregate at the beginning of the event are two ways to do this.

- Make sure you have direct access to your target group, and involve them in planning the event. You shouldn't try to attract librarians if no one in your group has ever shelved a book; don't try to involve basketball players if you all think King James is only a British monarch who had something to do with the Bible.

- For conferences, you can make money by renting space to vendors who hope to sell products or services to those who attend.

- If your event involves something measurable, ask participants to "sell" pledges or sponsorships. Participants ask their friends, neighbors, and innocent passers-by to contribute a certain amount, say 50 cents or $5, for every run scored, every mile run, or every basket made. Sponsors can also contribute a flat dollar amount. This can be as high or low as they please. Participants who bring in a certain amount in pledges above the entrance fee may have the fee reduced or eliminated.

- Send a letter to prospective participants. Enclose with this letter two sponsor sheets for the participant to fill out. The reason for sending two is that the participant may need more than one if she fills the first sheet with sponsors. If the participant does not need the second sheet, suggest that it be given to a friend (Petersen, 1979).

- Understand that you'll need to devise a simple money-collecting mechanism and that not all those who have pledged will make good on their promises.

- Send a thank-you letter acknowledging your receipt of the registration fee.

- Provide participants with some mementos of their involvement. Baseball caps, T-shirts, and pens printed with the name of the event are good souvenirs. These can serve as enticements as well.

- Get high-profile people to take part in your event. Featured speakers, local elected officials, or local athletes can serve this purpose.

Registration events are commonly targeted to a specific group such as counselors, day care operators, golfers, subatomic nuclear physicists, and other everyday people. This makes it somewhat easier to select an attractive activity. The challenge is to design the activity in such a way that it stirs interest and effectively meets expectations.

Registration events have a further benefit in that they capitalize on what people do anyway. Professionals attend conferences as part of their work routine, golfers golf, and runners run. Registration events don't ask people to do much out of the ordinary or to add much to a busy schedule.

You won't have to go through all the bother of selling tickets, but you will have to promote registrations. Except for the ticket-selling process, registration events require about the same things as ticket events. You need to promote the event, do advance planning, make a checklist, and keep your costs down. Because registration events deal with a narrower potential contributor group, they are often a little more manageable.

Events Coordinated by Other Groups. Many groups hold activities for their members that serve as fund-raisers for community service activities. This often involves something like an athletic tournament, a barbecue, or some modest entertainment. The sponsoring organization will usually split the proceeds with you. They do most of the work, and the event is directed to their members. The community service orientation of the organization is fulfilled in a way that gives their members something enjoyable to do.

Tips for Supporting Other Groups

- Get out your list of local clubs and organizations, and send a letter to each group on the list whose assistance you would want. The letter should include examples of things the group could do to benefit your organization and how the two of you would work together. Follow up the letter with phone calls to the organizations most likely to respond.

- Have clear, written agreements about what each of you will do and how money is to be collected and divided. Keep this simple; after all, they are doing you a favor.

- Unless the sponsoring group has a well-established community activity they do as a community service fund-raiser, you should shy away from events that go beyond the membership of the sponsoring group. These are usually pretty small-scale events and are best kept that way by having the sponsoring group work with the people and the activity they know best.

Private Entertainment Events. Special receptions, private parties, and small, exclusive dinners are examples of this approach. Generally there is a select invitation list of people who can write a significant check. The event is hosted by a prominent individual or an institution, and attendance is seen as a sort of privilege (Hicks, 2001).

Tips for Private Events

- Have the host extend a personal invitation in addition to the formal written invitation.

- Select a site that is unique, one that most people commonly do not have access to.

- Let it be known that someone of celebrity status will be attending. The person only needs to be in attendance. She does not need to perform or give a talk, though, of course, that could be an added attraction.

Small events like these can generate a lot of money at relatively low cost, particularly if the host will underwrite expenses. Further, this activity has the added benefit of allowing you to do some donor education about your organization and your cause (Hicks, 2001). You will have to decide whether the exclusive nature of this type of event conflicts with your organization's culture and purpose.

Promotions.   Take advantage of what is going on in your community. Is there a grand opening about to happen? Is the attendance at the movie theater down during the middle of the week? Can you help the local nine attract more fans to the ballpark?

Often businesses will include an organization in a special promotion to boost their product and their image in the community. This usually involves your organization getting a percentage of the sales; for example, 25 cents from every Morty's Mega Monster Burger sold today will go to your organization.

This is a form of cause-related marketing, in which a business and a nonprofit organization develop a short-term or ongoing partnership that benefits them both. This usually involves more established and less controversial organizations, but check to see if such a partnership is possible for your group (Goldstein, 1993; Marconi, 2002; Sinnock, 1995).

Tips for Promotions

- Prepare in advance to describe your ideas to the sponsoring business or organization, and be able to show how both parties can benefit.
- Ask your Chamber of Commerce about any grand openings or other special events businesses are scheduling.
- Watch for new construction of business and commercial complexes, and talk with the owners.
- Keep the type and amount of work you do reasonable compared to what you are likely to gain and consistent with your own organizational goals and image. After all, you want to be seen as more than a hawker of Morty's Megas.

- Periodically send a letter and follow up with selected phone calls to likely sources. They may not bite the first time, so give them other opportunities to think about a mutual project.
- Don't be pushy or demanding or riddle prospective partners with guilt.

Nonevents

As a variation on the direct mail and registration event approaches, some organizations find that asking people not to do something works well. Using a lighthearted approach, contributors are told they can participate in an event without having to do anything, without even having to leave their homes.

A nonrun for people who hate jogging, a stay-at-home tea for people who just can't get the hang of holding a teacup with their pinky just so, or a don't-weed-the-garden Saturday can hold a lot of appeal.

Tips for Nonevents

- Hold the nonevent at the same time every year.
- Do some buildup. As the time approaches, let people know that the nonevent is coming up so they can plan not to take part.
- Send humorous thank-you letters with your receipt of the registration fee or contribution.
- Have fun!

You will act as if this is a real event, but, of course, no "participant" has to do anything. Registrants should receive something to acknowledge their involvement. A packet of flower seeds or a tea bag can be enclosed with the original letter. Or a T-shirt claiming that the wearer definitely did NOT run on the hottest day of the year can be sent to those who send in the registration fee.

Sales

Selling a service or a product is a pretty standard way of raising relatively small amounts of cash. Bake sales, car washes, and yard sales are the most frequently seen examples of this approach. Each of these could be the subject of a booklet describing "How to hold a successful _____." A variety of little tricks can increase your profits.

If you're holding a yard sale, begin collecting items early from as many sources as possible to make sure you have a lot of good things to sell. Hold your yard sale at a house in an affluent neighborhood. (Yard sale junkies are inclined to shop where they think rich folks are getting rid of some good stuff, cheap.) If it's a bake sale you're holding, make sure you have a variety of goodies at a range of prices. Then select a spot where people who have the munchies are likely to pass by. Outside the college cafeteria or right outside the church or temple after services are good bets. If it's cars you wish to clean, try to corner the busiest intersection in town.

Selling products made especially for you (for example, T-shirts or baseball caps) is a little trickier. You usually have some initial investment to make, or you get a small percentage of the overall price of the object. If you think you can sell a lot of these, it may be worth doing. The best strategy is to sell these items on a variety of occasions to a captive audience of potential supporters. Rallies, conferences, and other special events provide captive audiences.

Sales of candy and nuts and other dentists' delights also require a high volume to make a profit. Items that sell for a dollar or less make it easy for someone to "contribute" to the organization and get something in return.

Organizations that have a lot of kids have, along with them, immediate customers—the kids' relatives. Kids are usually more willing than adults to go to neighbors or to stand in front of the local grocery store to sell their goods.

Because success requires a lot of people selling a lot, a lot of organization is required as well. Sales teams with team captains and clear accounting methods to keep track of the product and the money are essential. The companies that provide the products can usually instruct you on how to set up your promotion and keep track of your sales.

Holding an auction is another method of sales. You have to spend time and energy locating quality donated items for sale, promote the auction effectively to attract a good number of buyers, and then conduct the actual auction so it runs smoothly and gets you as much per item as possible. This includes selecting the best order for auctioning the items, holding an auction preview, and preparing a program. A professional auctioneer is generally well worth the money for the directions he can provide as well as his skill in working the buyers. Some auctioneers will volunteer their services for nonprofit organizations. Many professional auctioneers are members of the National Auctioneers Association (NAA); search their directory online or contact that organization's local chapter for help in obtaining the services of an auctioneer. Before you hold an auction, attend a few on your own to see how, and how well, they work.

If an auction doesn't suit your fancy, how about selling pizza? Occasionally you will be able to find a restaurant or stadium concession that will let you have a large share of the receipts in exchange for providing workers. The work usually involves working the cash register, waiting on tables, or bussing tables. You don't have to do the cooking. You may not make a lot of money, but this is quick and easy. About all you have to do is schedule some of the members of your organization to show up to work and make sure that they do it.

Although you may be able to use this method on a routine basis, say once a month, make sure more than enough of your members are willing to work before you agree. People can quickly get tired of this duty, so it is generally better to make this a fun, special occasion. Generally speaking, the smaller or younger your organization, the more likely you will benefit from a project that is short term and involves selling a product or service you have readily at hand. What you choose to sell and how you choose to sell it are limited only by your creativity, the resources you have to put into the effort, and, of course, the legal restrictions you may face.

Well, how about that bake sale? You might promote the idea as a baking contest, getting lots of sponsors, like grocery stores, bakeries, or companies that sell kitchen supplies or baking goods. Charge a fee to compete, and have some cooking related prizes, like quality cookware. Bring in some high-profile judges, like a local television personality or coach. When the competition is over and the prizes have been awarded, auction off the creations (Loewe & Mould, 2007).

A newly emerging source of funding is through a much more comprehensive earned income program.

These are ongoing entrepreneurial enterprises that make use of sophisticated business practices to provide a steady source of funds for the organization. Social entrepreneurship is part philosophy and part business, with the emphasis on using business approaches to change conditions. Let's say you are a small, volunteer organization with more modest means and goals, wanting to make money to support the work of the organization. What might you do? Whether it is a cupcake or a full product line, the basic notion is to put a product or service in front of as many people as possible who are likely to spend money on it. Some examples of social entrepreneurship include auto repair, restored bicycles, plant nurseries, thrift stores, creating and selling posters, educational tours, self-defense classes, and gift baskets. You get the idea. You might find yourself anywhere in the yellow pages.

Social entrepreneurship extends beyond the notion of just finding new ways to generate funding. The goal of transforming conditions is far more important than the goal of making money. The intent is to address complex social problems in a way that empowers people who have been left out or kept out of the mainstream (Hartigan & Billimoria, 2005).

First, stop and think whether you may already have enough work to do. Is this something that you really want to take on? How will this affect your attention to your fundamental mission? What are the potential tax liability issues? Do you really have the up-front capital that is required? Have you thought about the fact that these enterprises sometimes lose money? If you think you have good answers to these questions, you may want to forge ahead and see if you can craft your niche within the marketplace. Some organizations that take the plunge bring in not a hundred dollars but a hundred thousand.

Fund-raiser Andy Robinson (2002) has captured a number of sound ideas for developing an earned income program and offered a number of cautions for organizations considering entry into the world of social entrepreneurship. Here are some tips from Robinson:

- What assets—goods, services, intellectual property—do you have that someone might buy? This could include training and publishing.

- Get some outside help from your local business college, nonprofit resource center, local or regional community loan fund, local businesspeople, local economic development agency, or Chamber of Commerce. National organizations such as the National Center for Social Entrepreneurs, the Institute for Social Entrepreneurs, and Community Wealth Ventures can also be helpful.

- Develop a sound business plan and a marketing plan based on market research.

- Keep your expectations modest.

- Most commerce is conducted business-to-business, not business-to-customer. How can you best serve area businesses, including government and nonprofits?

- Seek funds from social lenders such as credit unions or community loan funds.

- Lead with your mission, but don't forget your customers.

Planned Giving

The concept of planned giving means a gift that is of sufficient magnitude that making it is integrated with the donor's personal financial plan or estate plan. The way the gift is made is designed to benefit both the giver and the receiver. Obviously, gifts of this type usually come from the more well-to-do. This method of developing an organization's resources is on the rise and can provide tremendous financial stability for formal organizations. Much of the information on planned giving provided here is drawn from the Nonprofit Counsel (1986) and from Moerschbaecher and Dryburgh (2001).

Generally, planned giving has been seen as an avenue only for older and larger organizations. Experts are now saying that every formal organization, no matter how small or how new, should have a planned giving program. Planned giving, through endowments, for example, is not limited to the elderly and the wealthy. Many people of modest means, as well as younger donors, are creating endowments (Leher, 2000).

What does such a gift look like? Probably the most common is a bequest in a will. However, the gift can take on many forms such as trusts, pooled income funds, or other mechanisms designed to increase both the ease of making contributions and their value. Some of these methods will provide income to your organization soon, whereas others will have an impact many years down the road.

This all sounds pretty technical, doesn't it? Well, it is. That is why you should seek the assistance of an attorney, a bank trust officer, an accountant, or another professional knowledgeable about planned giving if you intend to pursue this approach.

The income potential of a planned giving program is huge, but confusion over how to get started causes many organizations to ignore this approach altogether. It can also be a source of conflict and tension between the staff of an organization and those whose job it is to court wealthy donors. A clear understanding of the role planned giving can play within an organization, even a small organization, should be developed before you pursue this option. If you can afford to ignore thousands and thousands of dollars, you can disregard this source of support. However, if you are an incorporated organization that plans to be around for a while, you'll probably want to see how you can get some of these gifts directed your way.

Looking in Nooks and Crannies

A broad range of options for relieving your money woes should be explored. Did you know that placing coin collection canisters by the cash registers of 100 restaurants can bring you $20,000 a year? Or that you can easily make $75 just by having 20 members of your organization save aluminum cans for about a month? Hard work, isn't it?

How about pennies? There are untold creative ways for collecting pennies. A local bank might sponsor a "bring us your pennies" week on behalf of your organization (Goldstein, 1993), or a radio station could promote a penny week. Other ideas include a "collect the mayor's weight in pennies" drive or a "mile of pennies" promotion (that would be 84,480 pennies). You can dream up all sorts of ideas. In addition to all the pennies you get (which, of course, do turn into dollars), you can get tremendous publicity, lots of dimes and quarters, and, yes, even dollars from people who want to support your creative cause (Lynn & Lynn, 1992).

How about a donation of commercial property, a huge untapped resource for nonprofits?

Millions of dollars of commercial real estate may be available for donations, and the IRS has ruled that nonprofits can freely accept these gifts and turn them into cash (Martinez, 2002).

Is there a sports franchise in your area? Many have foundations, and some plan to expand their contributions to help their communities (Join Together Online, 2000).

Look for every chance you can to raise money. If pursuing a particular opportunity does not distract you from your main purpose, take advantage of it. Some things should become routine, second nature. Every one of your newsletters should include a way for people to give you money. Many a community presentation will provide you with an opening to ask for financial help. Make use of it. As you incorporate this perspective in your continued efforts to strengthen your organization, you will worry less and be able to spend more.

USING THE INTERNET AS A FUND-RAISING TOOL

The Internet is essentially a communications tool. It allows you to reach more donors more quickly in more ways. Donors are way out ahead of fundraisers when it comes to use of the Internet. Though disaster relief prompted a great number of new online donors, many more people are finding the Internet to be an easy way to make contributions, and the numbers are increasing each year (Wallace, 2006, 2008; Watkins, 2006). About 1 of every 10 donors gave online in 2007, mainly because of the speed and ease of giving. An organization's online presence is important for donors in all age and income groups. Other than not having a computer, the main reason people do not give online is that they are unaware of online options (Center on Philanthropy & Innovative Research Group, 2007). Help them find options.

With more people every month connecting to the Internet, this medium has become a more and more routine aspect of daily life. According to Nielsen Online, more than 228 million Americans are hooked up to the Internet at home, and those who visit the Internet connect to the world through their computer screens more than 40 hours a month on average (Nielsen Online, 2009). It would be a mistake to think you can only reach younger audiences through the Internet. Most of the growth in Internet use is coming from older age groups (Media Audit, 2004).

While you are reading this, potential donors are online gathering information and transacting business. Though organizations have not done much asking through the Internet, this is how a growing number of donors want to be asked (Flanagan, 2000). The *Grassroots Fundraising Journal* (2006) is a good source for learning about fund-raising software. They have a comparison chart that lets you examine different features of leading software. You may want to work with an application service provider (ASP) to add sophisticated features to your website such as donate now buttons, shopping carts, event registration, and many other useful highlights. Though there is usually a set-up fee, this can be a simple solution to a complex problem.

Websites and E-Mail

Two essentials for Internet fund-raising are a good website and a usable database. Your website not only helps to establish your credibility and the importance of your issue, but it can offer your viewers many opportunities for affiliation. Show visitors to your site just how you are using funds that you receive, and be sure to provide a link for contributions on every page. Make sure members can easily provide you with updated addresses and other contact information (Fox-McIntyre, 2001; Grobman, 2008; Hart, Greenfield, & Haji, 2007). Keep your friends and donors close at hand. Collect e-mail addresses. Not just once in a while—always. Your database of supporters is your most fertile ground for growing stronger commitment and harvesting continuing financial support. Everyone on your list is a potential contributor. Think of them that way. Treat them that way.

You can keep in contact and encourage more active involvement through your use of e-mail, but first, a gentle reminder about courtesy. Let people both "opt in" and "opt out" of your list (Flanagan, 2000; Greenfield, 2002). Though you will find different ways of asking for addresses, send solicitation or invitation mailings only to the addresses that have been given to you by the person who holds the address. At the end of any mass mailing, provide the receiver with an opportunity to unsubscribe or be removed from the list. Do develop a privacy policy, and post it on your website (Poley, 2001).

Charity Portals, Online Malls, and Affiliate Marketing

An emerging number of charity portals are partnering with nonprofit organizations to reach large numbers of contributors. These are essentially websites that provide their viewers with a list of nonprofits and encourage them to contribute. They accept credit card contributions on your behalf. While it may not cost you anything to be listed, the portal may charge you a small percentage of each contribution. You won't be the only organization listed; you will be competing with many others for attention—and contributions (Stein, 2003). Do a little comparison shopping when considering a portal to provide this service. You will want to check a number of things including the portal's history, set-up fees, fees for donations, support, and donor form appearance (Quinn, 2005).

A growing number of organizations are gaining new funding and even donors by adding online malls to their websites. Most online malls, often called charity shopping malls do not charge nonprofits that list with them. When someone buys an item from a network of online retailers, a percentage of the profit from the sale goes to the selected nonprofit organization. Encouraging your supporters to shop through your mall site can provide you with ongoing funds, with little cost. You may choose to set up your own charity mall so that you are able to receive the total commission from all purchases. However, this could require a lot of time and energy in set-up, design, and maintenance (Murray, 2005).

Affiliate marketing, such as the Amazon Associates program, can track customers directed to them through your website and pay you a commission each month for purchases made (Grobman, 2008).

Online Auctions

Ah, the staccato pulse of the auctioneer's voice. It is exciting and adds urgency to purchasing decisions. You will miss some of this with an online auction, but you have quite a lot to gain. An online auction allows you to keep items, many items, in front of the public, a much bigger public than can fit in any event room, for a longer period of time. You can get into that game by using online auction software to run your own auction or contracting with a company that administers online auctions. (See Grobman, 2008, for a number of pointers for online auctions.) Of course your supporters will want to support you and bid on some items, but many people who have never heard of you will bid as well, just because they want the item. You can offer a range of products, from celebrity donated items to works of art contributed by supporters. Because your auction can last 24 hours a day for weeks or months, people from all over the world can participate. The design and administration of your auction can provide a great way to bring in computer savvy volunteers who may enjoy this way of helping out the cause.

A number of companies want to host charitable auctions, and some do this free of charge. You can work with organizations such as MissionFish, working with E-bay Giving Works, to guide you through the steps. Of course, you will want to do some research on any company before you contract with them.

Social Media Sites

With billions of visits per month, social networking sites generate a lot of connection. How would you like even a tiny portion of those monthly visits to provide a connection and contribution to your organization? Many of the most popular sites such as Facebook, MySpace, and LinkedIn have methods for their users to connect with causes and the organizations affiliated with those causes. Members can find an existing cause or create one of their own. This includes you and your supporters. Beneficiary organizations can create pages or profiles as well for involving the network's participants with their work. This provides a good way to tell your story, raising both awareness and funds, along with contributions of volunteer time and expertise.

This is a fairly easy process. The networking sites that provide this option have pretty clear directions for you to follow. Donations, limited to incorporated, tax-exempt, 501(c)3 organizations, are processed through an organization like Net-

work for Good or Just Give, who mail out checks to receiving organizations every month.

Options are being developed for providing "charity gifts," essentially allowing one person to give the gift of a specific item needed by an organization in the name of another. Other developments include features such as changing your home page to something like the SmallAct Network, which provides a very small contribution to an organization of your choice every time you open your home page. These small contributions can add up if not only you but many of your supporters do the same thing.

Text Messaging

Okay, this is not the Internet, but it is another approach to make use of what people are already doing rather than trying to get them to do something different before they can support you. Working with a phone company, you can create and promote a text number to give cell phone users a simple way to make a donation. A good example of this is Atlanta's Salvation Army, which has provided a holiday giving program that lets donors give $5 to the organization by sending a text to a specified number. The donation is added to their phone bill (Walker, 2008).

You can imagine how integrating these opportunities into your website and e-mail campaigns can lead to increased awareness of your cause and your organization, along with some increased financial support. It is important to keep up to date with new trends and shifts, but the Association of Fundraising Professionals (2008) stressed that building a great website and using e-mail to engage your constituency provides the foundation for much of your online fund-raising.

Regulations

If you have a solicitation request on your website, or send solicitation requests to donors in another state, you may be subject to charitable solicitation registration and reporting in more than just your home state. There is no national consensus regarding reporting and registration, and regulations among states vary (Johnson, 2007). Some fax or text messages sent to solicit donations may run afoul of the Telephone Consumer Protection Act of 1991 or Federal Communications Commission

Many cities have a professional fund-raising group that meets monthly, such as a chapter of the Association of Fundraising Professionals. Attending their get-togethers can give you some good ideas and some profitable contacts. There are many ways of using the Internet to reach potential contributors (Christ, 2004; Fox-McIntyre, 2001; Greenfield, 2002; Grobman, 2008; Hodiak, 2001; Johnson, 2001; Network for Good, 2009; Poderis, 2006; Stein, 2001; Wallace, 2008). Here are a few ideas.

Uses of Website

- Calendar of events
- Event registration
- Membership renewal
- Secure means of giving with a credit card
- Online pledge form
- Opportunity to provide an "In Memory" or "In Honor" gift (called commemorative or tribute giving)
- Donor recognition
- Sales of items
- Promotion of your organization's income-producing enterprises
- Online auctions
- Educate supporters; show video to make your message come alive
- Build relationships with interactive features and staff directory with photos.

Search engines rank websites by content, so give a boost to your site by making sure it has lots of key content words and phrases. You can purchase keywords from major search engines.

Uses for E-Mail

- Bring content to your audience, keeping them informed of issue developments and your group's successes with periodic brief messages.
- Follow up shortly after people have given their e-mail address to the organization, when they are most likely to give.
- Distribute your online newsletter with organization news, issue information, key contributors and recognition of outstanding work, specific needs, and ways to contribute.
- Send personalized updates, thank-you notes, and special invitations.
- Send direct requests for contributions at a critical point in an issue campaign.
- Create a personal fund-raising page to support an activity, like bowling so many games or walking or biking so many miles, to benefit an organization, asking recipients to click on a link in the e-mail. A number of application service providers (ASPs), like Active Giving Solutions or Justgiving.com, will help set up these personal pages.
- Send a general solicitation letter.
- Direct readers to visit your website.

regulations (Tupper, 2007). Nonprofits that send advertisements or promotions of products or services may well be subject to Federal Trade Commission provisions of the CAN-SPAM Act (Welytok, 2008). Do check with an attorney to see which laws governing fund-raising using information technology apply to you. Almost all states and many local governments have passed laws regulating solicitations by nonprofits. For example, some auctions or raffles may be considered gambling. Your Internet message reaches beyond the borders of your state, so these laws may apply to you (Greenfield, 2002). Consult the guidelines for regulating Internet fund-raising

developed by the National Association of State Charity Officials (2001).

Relationships Are Still Important

Relationships are the key to any organization's work, whether through active participation in planning and action or through making a financial contribution. Internet methods do not replace the importance of developing relationships with contributors. If you think of these methods as ways to begin relationships or to further deepen them, you will develop a solid base of support.

SECURING FUNDS FROM PUBLIC AND PRIVATE ORGANIZATIONS

You now have a pretty good idea of how you can get money from individuals. If you want to consider all the options, where else can you look? Getting money from other groups and organizations, including the government, is another potentially valuable approach. This involves negotiating an intervening process, which serves as a kind of barrier or filter between you and the people who make the decisions. Almost every potential funding organization has some process you must follow.

This means at least two things to you. First, understand the procedures for each particular funding source and follow them well. Second, understand that, even with this approach, it is people, acting as individuals or as a group, who make the final decisions. Their decisions will be based on objective reasoning as well as a variety of other influences. Get to know the funding procedures and get to know the people as well as you can.

The process for approaching funding organizations for money has many similarities to the way you approach individuals. First, identify prospective sources of funds, and then target those that are most likely. Second, establish contact and nurture prospective sources. Third, prepare and submit a written proposal to the funding source, and follow up on that submission. Fourth, prepare and offer a verbal presentation to the funding source, and follow up on that presentation. (Though this step is not always required, it is helpful to be prepared.) Fifth, say thank you and nurture future relationships.

Identifying Prospective Sources

Increasing your awareness of all the possible sources of funds is an ongoing process. First of all, look at groups whose interests or goals are compatible with yours. Next, consider professional groups that may be interested in your concerns. Third, find out all you can about community service groups and their funding priorities. Next, think about the businesses and corporations that serve your area. Federated funding programs, such as the United Way, would

be the fifth set of potential contributors. Foundations are another possible source to consider. Finally, get to know how the various levels of government can be involved in funding your operation.

Spend some time brainstorming the possibilities; then make some educated guesses on what your best bets are. Follow that with some research on the sources you consider most likely. After that, keep your eyes and ears open to other possibilities. You may discover something that changes a low-ranked source into a suddenly hot prospect. Maybe your best friend's brother just got elected chair to a wealthy community service organization. Maybe the county government just received a federal grant to fund organizations such as yours. Things change. Be aware, and be flexible. This will provide you with a lot of opportunities.

It is helpful to know a little more about each type of funding source, from those whose processes are likely to be informal to those whose procedures are increasingly formalized. The more formal and large the funding source, the more formal and complex their process is likely to be; also, the more likely they will be to fund formal, incorporated organizations. Smaller, local funding sources tend to be more flexible.

Like-Minded Groups. These are groups that share values similar to yours. They may well be promoting an issue that is similar to yours. Groups that see themselves as working on the same issue, trying to mobilize or influence the same constituency, will also see themselves in competition with you. If this is the case, they will probably be more interested in protecting their turf than in giving you money. However, groups that have a related political or issues agenda may welcome another group into the playing field by making a contribution to get you going or to help with a special situation.

The process is likely to be informal, usually involving your making a direct request to the group during one of their meetings. Ask for a specific amount for a clearly identified purpose, and show how their contribution promotes your mutual concerns. Do your homework before the meeting by getting to know a member or members of this group. Find out how much the group would be willing to give. Ask for an amount in that range when you make your pitch.

CAPTURING CONCEPTS
Understanding the Terminology of Funding

Knowing the common language of the funding process is important. Here is a brief overview of the terms you are likely to hear.

An **RFP** is a request for a proposal. If a funding source, often some branch of government, is sending out an RFP, it is seeking proposals from community groups to provide a particular service. Often, your proposal will be in response to an RFP.

Matching funds are dollars given to an organization if it can come up with some additional dollars elsewhere. Often, the match is expressed in terms of a ratio. For example, a 3:1 match means that for every dollar you raise elsewhere the funding source will give you $3. If you raise $250, the source would give you $750, for a total of $1,000. There are frequently minimum and maximum limits on matching funds.

Pilot programs and **demonstration projects** are somewhat experimental. Usually, a funding source will give you money for just a couple of years to get the program up and running. The premise is that other funding sources will pick up the tab after the initial funding has run out if the program has merit. It may also be intended that the program be used as a model for others to follow. **Seed money** is given to start up a new project, usually covering initial expenses and salaries. **Start-up funds** do about the same thing.

The **funding cycle** is the time during which a funding source accepts new proposals and awards grants. Different funding sources have different funding cycles. A **fiscal year** is a budget year. It describes a 12-month period during which money is spent on an organization's program. Different funding sources use different fiscal years. Some follow the normal calendar year, beginning January 1 and ending December 31. Another common fiscal year, one often used by state and local governments, begins July 1 and ends on June 30. The federal government's fiscal year runs from October 1 through September 30. As you can see, receiving funds from various sources that use different fiscal years can create some complications for your organization.

When a government source awards a **grant** to another organization to provide funds to enable the receiving organization to perform a specified set of functions for an agreed-upon dollar amount, it usually formalizes the relationship through a **purchase of service agreement** or **contract.** This contract sets forth the terms of the relationship, including the nature and extent of the services the receiving agency will perform, the amount of funding the purchase agency will provide, and a schedule of payments.

If your organization is incorporated and pays staff, you may want to prepare a **case statement,** which describes your organization's needs, goals, objectives, strategies and tasks, staff, facilities, budget, institution plans, financial history, and staff competence to serve the mission or the cause the organization represents. It is a database. This is a massive document, requiring many hours of staff and volunteer time. Aside from its helpfulness in organizational management, it is an essential tool for seeking large contributions, especially from corporations. If your organization is not pursuing this type of major funding, your time is probably better spent doing something else. Putting together a good case statement requires a lot of work. Do it when it is worth all the effort.

IRS Form 990, the Return of Organization Exempt from Income Tax, or some version of this form must be filed with the IRS each year by almost all tax-exempt organizations. It is the primary source of information about your mission, governance, finance, and programs. A number of potential donors review an organization's 990 to help them decide whether or not to contribute. The IRS established new rules for filing the 990, beginning with returns filed in 2009. Many smaller organizations do not know they are now required to file a version of the 990, and they will lose their tax-exempt status if they fail to file (Coffman, 2009). Form 990 and the new rules are described later in this chapter.

Though the contribution is likely to be modest, rarely over $250, this can be an important step in fostering alliances that will be helpful down the road. Be willing to return the favor to other groups when your ability to help out is developed.

Professional Groups and Associations. Some organizations promote the interests and issues relevant to a particular profession. Dentists, nurses, accountants, social workers, and turkey farmers all have professional organizations. Many of these will have local chapters in your area. Some of the things you are working on will be a natural for two or three of these groups to support. If your request can reinforce the group's issues, its image, or the self-interest of its members (ideally all three), you will reinforce your chance for a favorable response. If you are developing a program to assist people with AIDS and their families, for example, check to see if any of these groups has expressed a particular interest in this topic. These would be the first groups to approach.

Professional associations normally want you to put your request in writing. Most often this works to justify to their membership any support given to you. The decision to give you money will probably be based more on your initial discussions and verbal presentation than on your written proposal. The organization's local board or steering committee will hear your request. Try to get a commitment from them at that time. A delayed decision or one routed through their committee structure may mean that enthusiasm for your request is lacking. This may be a signal for you to develop more support.

The amount of money you receive will probably be less than $500. Even associations of the wealthier professions don't often give more. There are exceptions to this. Some organizations see their support of community efforts as a routine function. Where this is the case, you may receive more money. However, the process is likely to be more complex, with your written request carrying more weight.

Community Service Clubs and Organizations. Clubs and organizations such as the Lions or the Soroptimists are formed to give their members status, opportunities for socialization, a mechanism for providing service to the community, and recognition for that service. Take these factors into account when approaching service organizations.

Most of these groups have a pretty well-defined area of interest, and the recipients of their help must be seen as worthy of support. Therefore, children, the physically challenged, or those struggling to overcome serious obstacles may be favored.

Getting the support of the organization's leadership beforehand will smooth the way. A well-prepared, factual, and emotional presentation will play an important part. It often helps to include those who would benefit from your organization's work in making the presentation. It is sometimes useful to make a purely informational presentation to the general membership that spurs interest several months before you make any request for money.

These groups will give by taking on something as a project, making a modest one-time contribution, or by "passing the hat" at a meeting, usually a breakfast or luncheon. If your request clearly falls within the group's special project interests, you may be able to receive up to a few thousand dollars. If not, don't count on more than $200.

A main purpose of some community service groups is raising and dispensing money. Chief among these is the Junior League. Other groups that are unique to a particular community serve this function as well. These organizations follow a fairly structured funding process. Their grants can range into the tens of thousands of dollars.

Businesses and Corporations. Larger corporations that are major employers in your community will almost always contribute to the community in the form of donations. Smaller businesses frequently will as well. Corporate giving is big business. In 2007, corporations contributed about $15.7 billion to charitable causes (Giving USA Foundation, 2008b). Corporations give through their foundations, through direct corporate giving programs, or use both vehicles (Geever, 2007). Although some product in-kind giving is part of this total, corporations provide additional, valuable technical in-kind contributions as well. Providing funds, goods, and services to support community efforts demonstrates social responsibility and is good business practice as well. There are a number of directories on corporate giving. *Corporate Giving Directory,* the *Foundation Directory Online, Hoover's Online,* and the *National Directory of Corporate Giving* are four excellent resources for identifying corporations that contribute money. Information about the corporation, its funding priorities, and the number of dollars it contributes is provided. A contact person for each source is identified as well. Periodicals and newsletters such as the *Chronicle of Philanthropy* and the *Corporate*

Philanthropy Report are also helpful resources. These can be pricy for a small organization, so check to see if your library subscribes.

Strategic philanthropy, a term coined more than 30 years ago by Nina Kaiden Wright, describes an approach corporations use to evaluate the most effective way to spend their donations (Ferguson, 2006; McKay, 1988). The intent is to promote the corporation that promotes the community project. While corporate giving is likely to decline as the economic recession deepens, corporations continue to align contributions with business objectives and corporate reputation (Boney, 2008). Some observers characterize corporate giving as enlightened self-interest, a belief that contributions benefit the businesses in the long run by promoting a healthier community and business climate (Ferguson, 2006; Picker, 2001; Zippay, 1992). Further, customers are more likely to purchase from companies that supported a cause (Boney, 2008; Burlingame, 2001; Riley, 2000). John L. Mason (1988), former president of the Monsanto Fund, used the phrase "investing for results." Those responsible for fund investments must be able to demonstrate that the fund supports the objectives of the corporation.

Contributions are often tied to corporate marketing strategies, with many donation dollars coming from marketing budgets (Hunt, 1986; Picker, 2001). *Cause-related marketing* has become common. This generally involves contributing a certain amount to an organization for every product sold. Cause-related business sponsorships, which usually involve the financial support of an organization's event, increased from $120 million in 1990 to $1.57 billion in 2006 (Klayman, 2009). This type of business support of a community cause not only brings in more money for the business and community organization but attracts greater public awareness and involvement as well (Burlingame, 2001; Cone, 2009).

Many corporations are going beyond giving away dollars to actually making a conscious investment in strengthening the community. Three comprehensive surveys on corporate philanthropy found that companies are making increased efforts to support employee volunteer involvement (Committee to Encourage Corporate Philanthropy, 2006; Muirhead, 2006; Streeter & Jordan, 2008). A report by the Conference Board (2002) showed that this approach

produces far more in return for the community than the cost of the investment. For example, General Mills developed a partnership with the Stairstep Foundation, a center for development of initiatives in the Minneapolis African American community. Together they have supported Siyeza Foods and created a new manufacturing business employing inner-city neighborhood residents.

Corporations usually have special priority areas (for example, education, youth, and family issues), and they tend to target their contributions to projects that address these interests (Streeter & Jordan, 2008). Often, the chief executive officers or members of corporate allocations committees determine funding priorities based on their personal interests and social contacts (Sheldon, 2000; Streeter & Jordan, 2008; Zippay, 1992).

Another important concern is geographic (Morth & Collins, 1996; Picker, 2001). Corporations with large numbers of employees in regional offices or plant locations throughout the country tend to target their giving in local areas (Webb, 1982). Remember to mention any volunteer support your organization receives from the company's employees (Breiteneicher & Hohler, 1993). Corporations invest in communities to support the strategic goals of the business while addressing important community issues. This allows them to align their competitive strengths with the focus area of the organization receiving their funds (Coady, 2008).

The larger the business and the more distant the ownership from the community, the more complex the sequence of activities to secure funding is likely to be. The reverse of this is true as well. The smaller the business or closer to the community the ownership, the simpler your request can be. This includes, believe it or not, just walking in and asking.

Newspapers in many communities publish an annual list of the largest employers in the area, with a description of the company and the names of the chief executives. This is an excellent source of likely prospects. If your newspaper does not have such a list, check with your Chamber of Commerce. Also check company websites. Look on the community relations pages if you can't find information on funding on the home page (Schladweiler, 2001).

Your case statement will serve you well in approaching businesses, particularly large ones. A large request should be based on a well-thought-out strategy. Identifying and wooing the right corporate officer with the right people is a must. This is an above-board process that promotes donor understanding and involvement with your organization and its request. Whenever possible schedule a personal, face-to-face meeting. Chances of receiving funding are estimated to increase by 70% if a proposal is preceded by personal contacts (Picker, 2001).

Recognize the potential benefits important to the contributing corporation (Breiteneicher & Hohler, 1993; Morth & Collins, 1996). Strengthening its ties to the community and boosting employee morale can be major considerations (Allen 2001b; Burlingame, 2001; Flanagan, 2000; Stannard-Friel, 2004). Explore the tax advantages to the corporation as well. Though this is normally not the compelling reason for the contribution, particularly from small businesses, tax benefits can add to its attractiveness. Be aware that some donors are insulted by the implication that tax write-offs are their only concern. Also, understand that the paperwork necessary for the business to get some tax breaks may not be worth the trouble.

Employee matching programs can be a valuable source of funds for your organization. In these programs the company matches gifts given to you by their employees (Coady, 2008; Committee to Encourage Corporate Philanthropy, 2006; Picker, 1997; Sheldon, 2000). Ask each contributor if her company has such a program. Don't assume that the contributor has thought of this.

The number of nonprofit organizations competing for corporate dollars will undoubtedly increase. Though corporations are more conservative than individual donors, don't assume that you are too controversial for corporate funding (Flanagan, 2000; Sheldon, 2000). As Sheldon (2000) pointed out, "there are many doors to company giving" (p. 91). The organization that does its "homework" properly—research, cultivation, and planning the best approach—will be the one that gets its share (Boney, 2008; Sheldon, 2000; Webb, 1982).

Labor Unions.   In many parts of the world labor unions are involved in serving their communities. Labor unions provide a variety of resources to support community efforts. Not surprisingly, unions frequently contribute labor—particularly skilled labor.

Plumbers, electricians, carpenters, and other workers donate valuable skills that you may not be able to afford to purchase. Not only do union members and their organizations donate time, but they give money as well. Just as you would with any other prospect, it is important that you do some research to see how your project links with the interests and giving ability of a particular labor organization you might approach for a contribution. A good starting point is the Central Labor Council in your community. Check also with the state federation of the AFL-CIO, which is likely to be headquartered in your state capital city (Seltzer, 2001).

Cooperative ventures between labor unions and foundations provide an intriguing and potentially valuable alliance. Though characterized as "unlikely partners" by Richard Magat (1998), over the years there have been many instances of collaboration between foundations and labor unions to serve working families. These partnerships continue today, particularly through the Working Group on Labor and Community. Part of the national Neighborhood Funders Group, an association of 250 foundations, the group supports and educates funders on how they can assist collaborative efforts between organized labor and community organizations, particularly those engaging the working poor (Neighborhood Funders Group, 2009).

By including labor unions in your resource development plans, you establish a connection with a group of workers already organized for action and with a history of giving. This is a pretty potent way to extend your resources.

Federated Funding Programs.   Federated financing refers to campaigns conducted by one agency for others or for a particular group of contributors. Usually, the fund-raising group is itself a nonprofit agency or an arm of another body such as a corporation (Mirkin, 1978). Federated campaign organizations commonly have four functions. First, they develop membership from participating agencies. This involves screening new applicants as well as monitoring current members to assess the appropriateness of their continued involvement. Second, they raise money for their members through a combined appeal. Third, they assess a range of community needs. Fourth, they allocate funds to their members based ostensibly on the determination of community needs and the members' ability to meet them.

Catholic Charities, Federation of Protestant Welfare Agencies, federal government employees Combined Federal Campaign, and United Jewish Appeal are federated campaign organizations. The largest and best-known federated campaign in the United States is the United Way of America, the parent organization of local United Funds. It has been in existence since 1887 and operates in more than 1,000 communities throughout the United States.

Because of the tremendous amount of money and publicity it generates, the United Way demands your attention. The United Way has been moving toward incorporating community building and development principles in the last few years with an emphasis on building on community assets. In addition to funding direct services, many United Way affiliates are supporting community change efforts and public policy advocacy efforts (United Way, 2006). There are two primary ways to get money from the United Way. The first is through the traditional grant process. The second is through donor designations. In this case, donors to the United Way designate the particular organization that they would like to support. Some United Ways have a process in place to assist donors in making designations.

It is important to understand that each United Way organization has its own policies and approach to funding. In some communities, for example, receiving United Way dollars might mean accepting some limitations. Pursuing other sources of funding (for example, approaching corporations) may be restricted. You may also be prohibited from soliciting funds from the community during the months of the United Way campaign. An agency's appeal in the community and its consequent ability to help the United Way attract funds may be an important reason for its inclusion in United Way membership. A number of United Ways are moving toward more open funding, rather than just funding a set of member agencies. Some United Ways have shied away from supporting organizations that actively confront the community's power elites. You may want to explore whether United Way participation might dampen your organization's approach to dealing with issues of social justice.

The United Way has a very formal process, including submission of a written proposal and a verbal presentation, sometimes two. Get as many members of your agency's board as you can to attend these presentations. Those individuals who make funding decisions like to see clear demonstrations of board involvement and support.

Begin building social relationships between members of your organization and volunteer members of the United Way funding committees. Though you should properly stay within the prescribed process when making a request for funds, it doesn't hurt to have people who like you make the decisions. Few awards from the United Way fall below $5,000, and typically they are several times that amount. Since there are 1,350 United Ways, each with their own personality and funding priorities, it is a good idea to do some research and get to know United Way staff to learn more about how this important source of funding works in your community.

Foundations.   Foundations exist to give away money and promote certain interests. In the 10 years between 1997 and 2007 the number of foundations increased from 44,146 to 75,187. In 2008 foundations gave out an estimated $45.6 billion, though this figure is likely to decline in 2009 and 2010. Foundation assets dropped almost 22% in 2008, more than $150 billion was lost, and giving to foundations may decrease by more than 10% in 2009 (Lawrence & Mukai, 2009). Still, foundations will be giving away billions of dollars. You won't be the only one who knows this, so you are likely to face stiff competition.

Foundations generally give to organizations with some sort of track record. Rarely do they give to start-up organizations, though they may give to an unincorporated group that links with one that is incorporated. They like to fund specific projects rather than provide general funding for ongoing programs (Geever, 2007).

A lot of homework on your part is essential prior to approaching any foundation. This point cannot be overstated. Between 40 and 75% of proposals don't fit the funders' guidelines (Robinson, 2004). Using the resources of the Foundation Center, other publications, computerized databases, and indexes in your library, you can narrow your search to perhaps half a dozen foundations that make grants in your field and your geographic location (Geever, 2007; Lewis, 2002; Robinson, 2004). Similar to most any funding source, your ability to form a relationship with contact people at targeted foundations will enhance your prospects. The ability to work in a supportive way with potential partners is one of the most important dimensions of their work (Geever, 2007; Huang, 2006; Mahoney, 2006).

Foundations can be divided into six categories (Allen & Regional Youth Project, 1981; Lewis, 2002; Pendleton, 1981):

General purpose foundations. These are the particularly large and well-known foundations. They have a wide range of projects and operate with relatively few restrictions. Generally, they are interested in very large projects.

Special purpose foundations. These foundations restrict their funds to a geographic area or to a specific field of interest.

Corporate or company foundations. These foundations are established by corporations or companies to handle most of the funds donated by the company. There are almost 2,500 corporate foundations, which in 2008 granted $4.4 billion, much of this amount is in the form of in-kind contributions of medicine. Not surprisingly, over half of corporate foundations expect to decrease giving in 2009 (Lawrence & Mukal, 2009). In addition to medicine, corporate foundations provide other forms of in-kind support. Some corporations donate funds through the corporation in addition to their corporate foundation. Also, many corporations will match an individual employee's contribution to a charity of the employee's choosing, but only if the employee brings it to the attention of the corporation by filing the proper forms.

Family foundations. These are usually small foundations, but a few are quite large. They operate under the control of the family that set them up. Their grants fall within their areas of personal interest. Many of the smaller family foundations are not included in published listings.

Operating foundations. These organizations use their resources to conduct research or provide a direct service.

Community foundations. This type of foundation operates with many small funds centralized under community management. There are more than 700 community foundations in the United States, so it is likely that you will find one in your community or close by (Council on Foundations, 2008). Community foundations gave an estimated $4.6 billion in 2008, for the first time outpacing corporate foundations. Community foundations also are feeling the economic pinch, and almost three quarters of these foundations anticipate a decline in 2009 giving (Lawrence & Mukai, 2009). Grants are usually restricted to a particular geographic area. However, many of these local community foundations do have large assets and a broad range of interests, and they are particularly focused on local issues and draw from a broad range of primarily local donors. In many communities the local community foundation takes a leadership role in identifying issues and motivating community support to address them. In addition to providing funding, they help connect local organizations with technical assistance around fund-raising and management practices. This makes them an excellent source for your community change effort.

What if you are just getting started? Would a foundation help fund your new organization or project? Though most foundations prefer to work with existing organizations, more than 2,000 foundations do provide start-up or seed money. Here your challenge is to establish your credibility with the funder, demonstrating that your leaders are well qualified, your board members are committed, and your cause is compelling. Look for foundations that provide seed money and the best match of geographic location and demonstrated interest in the

CHANGE AGENT TIP

One of the most helpful organizations to assist your fund-raising efforts is the Foundation Center. The Foundation Center offers a huge amount of information through its website at foundationcenter.org. In the last few years the Foundation Center has expanded their free online training and education, now offering more than 15 interactive web-based classes covering grant-seeking, proposal writing, and nonprofit management. They are offering many resources in Spanish. Here are some other resources you can find at their website:

- Nonprofit-related news and research through *Philanthropy News Digest*

- *Catalog of Nonprofit Literature*, an online bibliographic database of more than 27,000 listings, updated daily, many with abstracts of books and articles relating to philanthropy

- *PubHub*, a searchable catalog, updated daily, of annotated links to foundation-sponsored reports and the most recent publications on specific issues from across the full spectrum of philanthropic activity in the United States

- *Nonprofit Literature Blog,* which spotlights key books, pamphlets, articles, and other resources acquired by the Foundation Center Libraries

- *Spanish language resource list* on nonprofit governance, fund-raising, and proposal writing, including links to nonprofit websites providing information in Spanish on the nonprofit sector and on possible sources of funding for nongovernmental organizations in Latin America, as well as Spanish language grant-seeker training both in person and online

- *Foundation Center's Online Librarian,* responds to questions about foundations, philanthropy, and fund-raising research via e-mail or chat

In addition, the Foundation Center provides resources and assistance through its four Field Offices and its more than 400 Cooperating Collections throughout the country, at least one in every state. Check the Foundation Center's website or your local library to see which Cooperating Collection is nearest you. These collections are housed in public libraries and other public centers. In addition to providing a wealth of resources, they provide excellent guidance

to assist your efforts. Here are some things you can find in the Foundation Center's Cooperating Collections:

- Reference librarians experienced in finding information on funding sources

- Free orientations to the collection

- Copying facilities for a nominal charge

- Copies of valuable Foundation Center publications (such as *Foundation Fundamentals, Guide to Proposal Writing,* and *Grantseeker's Guide to Winning Proposals*), directories of funding sources, newsletters, fund-raising journals, guides to fund-raising and grant writing, program planning, nonprofit management, and almost anything else short of the exact combination to the bank vault

- Foundation and corporate annual reports, press clippings, and application guidelines

- The *Foundation Directory Online Professional,* a collection of databases that provides access to an unprecedented wealth of timely, comprehensive information on grant makers and their grants

The Foundation Center has free interactive online classes to teach you how to use *Foundation Directory Online Professional.* You can access information on more than 96,000 foundations, corporate giving programs, and grant-making public charities in the United States; a database of over 3,600 sponsoring companies, offering a quick pathway to corporate funders; a database of more than 1.4 million recently awarded grants; and a keyword-searchable database of 533,000 recently filed IRS Forms 990 and 990-PF.

This is a very easy-to-use tool that will help you customize your search, and a well-targeted search is the key to grant seeking. Even first-time grant seekers will easily figure out how to use this database to narrow the search to the likeliest prospects. And remember, there is a reference librarian at all Cooperating Collections especially to help you. The Foundation Center's online database is the Crown Jewel; this is a *fantastic* resource. If you are looking for grant funding, you just have to check this out!

SOURCE: Karen Koevary (2009).

work you will be doing and the issue you will be addressing (Margolin & DiMaio, 2008).

Your approach to foundations starts by sending a letter of inquiry to each foundation on your target list. Express your interest and describe your organization, including a list of other groups that support you. Demonstrate that you have read their guidelines and want further clarification to see if your project fits (Geever, 2007). After about 2 weeks, follow up your letter with a personal phone call. Always make personal contact unless you are explicitly told not to. You should quickly acknowledge receipt of any information from the foundation with a personal response.

The decision to make an award to you will generally be based on the strength of your proposal. Verbal presentations are not often required. Gifts range from hundreds to hundreds of thousands of dollars. Many foundations provide matching grants as well, giving you money to match what you have raised elsewhere. Not only does this often make your proposal more attractive, but it may provide incentives for members of your organization to raise more money (Klein, 2000).

Keep contact with the foundation throughout the process of fund seeking and project implementation. Find out what level and type of communication is appropriate and use this knowledge to maintain relationships. "Philanthropy's open secret is that relationships matter" (Garonzik & Harris, 2008). Remember that the process isn't just about getting one particular grant. Future funding from a particular source may well depend on how you handle all aspects of your work together. This includes letting the foundation know the impact that their support has had on your organization and its constituency (Geever, 2007).

Public Funding

Government funding provides a good percentage of the budget of most social service agencies. Some private agencies are almost totally publicly funded. Though government agencies rarely give money to organizations that are not incorporated, small agencies and new programs in existing agencies do receive government funding. Similar to foundations, public funding can go to a small organization operating under the umbrella of an established, incorporated nonprofit.

"Government" really means governments. Your organization may work in an area that cuts across various city and county government lines. Each is a potential source of funds. These local governments sometimes combine to form a *council of governments,* which serves as a mechanism for funding community

programs. State and federal governments are certainly potential sources of funds. So when I say "government," the term does not refer to just one government body. Different layers or levels of government exist, each with its own organizational structure and procedures.

Strings are usually attached to public funding. The higher the level of government, the more and the stronger those strings may be. Some might be considered ropes. Some programs become addicted to government money and the resulting government control. They stop looking to other sources of funds from the communities they serve. This can turn into a bad habit. Think about it.

How do you get money from the government? Good question. The answer is complicated by all those various levels of government and the various programs each government operates. Here are a few guidelines that point the way.

- *Get information.* Find out what funds various levels of government have to deal with social concerns such as yours. Discover through which mechanisms, departments, and programs they give this money. Explore Grants.gov, which allows organizations to electronically find and apply for more than $400 billion in federal grants. USA.gov for nonprofits is another federal source rich with information, specially geared to nonprofits. (It also provides a wealth of other information, such as access to surplus government property, tax information, and even information on incorporating.) As New (2001) stressed, "virtually every department, agency, and division of the United States Government has grant funds to offer" (p. 693), so find out as much as you can.

  Establish contact with people in government funding agencies. Call them. These individuals know what is going on and can alert you to upcoming opportunities. Also, agency policymakers can help you discover money stashed in various bureaucratic hiding places and find ways to make this available to you. This could be done, for example, in the form of a highly specialized proposal request directed to your organization.

  If you don't know anyone in a particular government agency of interest to you, start with the community information or community relations department and go from there. Discover and make use of notification procedures used by government agencies. Get on a list to receive requests for proposals. Then start building those contacts.

Develop a rudimentary understanding of the budget, particularly the budgets of local governments. Some local governments have a standing practice of funding outside (nongovernmental) organizations whose programs benefit the community. The more you know, the better. You don't have to drive yourself crazy, but do understand where and on what the money is intended to be spent. Review the most likely budget categories. This will give you some indication of how much money is available in your interest area. Also, you can use your agency contacts to find out if and how some of this money can be directed to support your organization's endeavors.

- *Get help.* Develop a relationship with politicians and their staffs. They are helpful in identifying possibilities and supporting your requests. Politicians who can get credit for delivering the goods to their constituencies have additional motivation. Supportive administrative staff in government agencies can give you information and direction. Government operations should be public knowledge, so this will not compromise public service. Keep in contact with the program coordinator, and if you have a question, don't guess—ask (New, 2001).

- *Get public attention directed to your issue.* This will be helpful in making requests to state and local governments. One of the functions of government funding is to keep people quiet. Attracting community awareness and concern to your issue can attract government money as well. Another role of government is to promote and support helpful private efforts. If your organization becomes recognized as a valued community resource, government funding sources may be happy to show their investment in your mutual success. State and local government funding tend to respond to political influences within the community (New, 2001).

- *Get involved in the budget-building process.* Find out how the various departments of your state and local government participate in development of the budget, and work with them to include funding in the new budget to deal with your area of concern. It is easier to get money if it is there in the budget in the first place. The submission of a formal proposal is usually part of the funding process. Get a well-written proposal describing an effective approach to addressing a recognized problem into the right hands on time. Don't be afraid to ask for guidance as you are preparing your proposal.

If money is available in the budget to respond to a recognized community need, if timely and valuable information regarding the funding process is given to you, if you have internal, political, and community support, and if you describe an effective approach in a well-written proposal, you stand a good chance of getting government funding. Purposefully work to put all these elements in place.

Get to Know the People Involved

Regardless of the type of organization from which you are seeking funds, be it the federal government or the local PTA, you will be dealing with people. You cannot overlook this. The personal relationship that develops might be the most important factor affecting funding (Webb, 1982). Establish a good, friendly, and appropriately personal rapport with the individuals who serve as your contacts within the funding sources you court (Browning, 2009; Geever, 2007; Golden, 2001; Mahoney, 2006; Schumacher, 1992; Sheldon, 2000). Follow their advice and direction. Ask questions. This gives your contacts a little bit of a stake in your success.

Yes, politics is involved. The process isn't pure. Yes, it is often whom you know. Yes, people do help one another with favors. This isn't as seedy as it sounds, though. Frankly, most of us would rather work with someone we know, in whom we have confidence and trust. Grantors are no different.

Inside advocacy is a big part of the game. Make use of opportunities to meet grant makers, and cultivate those relationships. Treat them as colleagues; do not act subservient. Some foundations or groups of foundations have a "Meet the Grants Makers" event. Take advantage of this. Also consider attending the National Network of Grantmakers conference to get to know the people who may give you money (Robinson, 2004).

GRANT WRITING

I have frequently referred to a written proposal. You have probably sensed that this item must be important. It is. Whether your intended funding source is a corporation, a foundation, or a unit of government, some sort of proposal will probably be required. Skill in proposal writing is a valuable asset in your organization's efforts to acquire money. Local colleges, agencies, community foundations, and professional fund-raisers offer grant-writing workshops and training courses. Take advantage of these resources.

When I say "grant writing," what I really mean is *proposal writing*. Your proposal is your record of what you want to do and how. It is the passkey to many a treasure vault. On many occasions, it will be the one element that gives all the others meaning. But it does not stand alone.

A critical aspect of any grant-seeking process is making sure you have done an adequate amount of research on possible funding sources. Narrow your list to only those whose interests, resources, and requirements match your organization's goals, abilities, and characteristics. Some funders place lots of restrictions on the use of their dollars; others require that you do extra work for which no funding is provided. Make sure you can live with the conditions of the grant (Burke & Prater, 2000; Geever, 2001; Quick & New, 2000).

Once you have identified a possible funding source, then, to the extent possible, prepare that funding source to receive your proposal favorably. The quality of your relationship may be as important as the quality of your proposal (Garonzik & Harris, 2008; Golden, 2001). Next, clearly think through just what the program or activity you are describing in your proposal is intended to accomplish. After this, figure out just what you actually have to do to meet that goal; that is, effectively plan your activity or program, including its likely costs and evaluation proce-

dures. Your initial planning is crucial. These steps warrant a significant investment of time and creativity. What you write in your proposal is the product of this effort. Consequently, it is well worth your time to take this preparation phase seriously.

Given the complex nature of some proposals, you may well want to assemble a team to guide both the planning and the proposal preparation. This includes members of your organization and your community partners as well. If you do not do this work up front, you are much less likely to be awarded a grant. If you do somehow get lucky and get a grant, though, your project may well fall apart because you haven't built a proper foundation. Future funding is affected by how well you handle this project (Browning, 2009; Golden, 2001; New, 2001; Quick & New, 2000).

When you have clarified your purpose and approach, sit down and write your proposal following the guidelines provided by the funding source and organized in the way most meaningful to the funding source. If more than one person is involved in writing the proposal, make sure that you check to make sure that both the voice of the proposal and the information are consistent (Clarke & Fox, 2007). After the proposal is written, packaged in an attractive, easy-to-read manner, and submitted (on time!), you need to muster the appropriate support to reinforce its positive reception.

Written proposals vary in length according to the requirements of each funding source. In some cases, a written proposal of one page will suffice. In others, you may need more than 100 pages to provide all the information requested. Some organizations hire professional grant writers to actually put the grant proposal together. There are some pros and cons to hiring someone outside the organization to do this work. It is a good idea to check with other organizations about their experiences to see if this would work for you or be an expensive waste of time.

Although each funding source will have its own preferred format and areas of emphasis, there are some pretty standard components to a proposal. Your written proposal essentially responds to four questions.

- What problem are you trying to resolve?
- How do you intend to solve this problem?
- How much will this cost?
- How can you tell if your program works?

These four questions can be broken down into as many as 15 distinct proposal categories. These categories and many of the tips that follow have been drawn from my own experience and the guidance of numerous authors who describe the grant-seeking process (Browning, 2009; Burke & Prater, 2000; Clarke & Fox, 2007; Coley & Scheinberg, 2000; Davis, 2006; Dutro & Coffman, 2006; Flanagan, 2000; Geever, 2007; Golden, 2001; Morth & Collins, 1996; New, 2001; Picker, 2001; Quick & New, 2000; Robinson, 2004).

The complexity of your proposal will be governed by your particular funding source. Most funding sources provide a clear set of guidelines for you to follow in preparing your proposal. Do follow these precisely (Smith, 1989). One of the major reasons proposals are rejected is simply their failure to follow prescribed guidelines (New, 2001). There is no need to make your proposal more complicated than required, and doing so may work against you. Your proposal may include some or all of these pieces.

- *Cover letter.* Keep this letter brief, rarely beyond one page. Tell the funding source who you are, what you intend to do, why, and how this relates to the funder's interests. This should be on your official letterhead, addressed to a specific person, and be signed by an officer of your organization.

- *Title page.* This states the title of the project, to whom it is being submitted, the date of submission, the name and address of the organization submitting the proposal, along with the name of a contact person (or proposal author) from the submitting organization.

- *Abstract or proposal summary.* This brief summary is one of the key elements of your proposal. In it you clearly and concisely describe your response to the four basic questions mentioned previously. In addition, tell the funding source a little bit more about your organization. To some extent, this is an expansion of your cover letter. Still, this should be kept short, no more than two pages, generally much shorter than that.

- *Introduction/organization information.* In this section describe your organization in more detail. The purpose here is to demonstrate your credibility as an organization capable of pursuing a project. You may also include particularly interesting aspects about your organization as they relate to the project you are proposing.

- *Problem statement.* In this section provide some background information on the problem you intend to address. You may describe how long the problem has persisted in your area, how this problem is manifested (symptoms), and other efforts that have been undertaken to solve it. Address a problem that is the same size as your efforts to resolve it, not something sweeping such as hunger or war. Describe the range and depth of the immediate problem, both through your use of statistics and in narrative discussion. You want to communicate to the funding source that this is an important issue that demands attention.

- *Goals or proposed response.* Here you describe what needs to be done to address the situation or what long-range goals you seek. Do not describe your specific activities in this section; instead, clarify the broad accomplishments expected by your effort. You may also phrase this section in terms of solutions; that is, what broad solutions does this problem require?

- *Statement of objectives.* A program objective is a statement of a concrete, measurable result of your program within a specific length of time (Cavanaugh, 1980). These objectives relate to your goals. You cannot be vague here; clarity is important.

- *Implementation or methodology and management.* In this category tell the funding source exactly what you will do, and when, to accomplish your objectives. Tell the funding source how you will use your resources, including facilities, equipment, and personnel, to achieve your desired results. You may also include a description of how those affected by the problem will be involved in the activities. You will also describe how you will oversee the effective use of these resources, how you might disseminate information about the project, and your work to make ongoing improvements.

- *Personnel involved.* The people who will be working on your project are important. Provide a brief background description (one paragraph will usually suffice) on each person who will have an active role in the project.

- *Budget.* The funding source needs to know on what you intend to spend the money you receive. Prepare a line-item budget reflecting the various expenses required to undertake this project. Often, the budget section lists other sources of revenue and indicates which expense or portion of expenses will be covered by the source from which you are seeking funds. Either here or in a separate income section, describe any income the project is intended to generate.

- *Budget narrative.* In this section briefly describe the expenses listed in the line-item budget. You may also provide a brief explanation or justification of the importance of these expenditures. Don't be shy about pointing out the amount and type of support the project will receive from your organization.

- *Future funding.* If your project involves more than a one-time activity, the funding source will probably want to know how you intend to continue the project after this particular grant runs out. Commonly, funding sources provide money for a limited period of time. If they intend to make an investment, they will want to know that you are currently preparing to keep the program (and their investment) alive. Organization sustainability is of particular interest to funders (Geever, 2007).

- *Monitoring.* It's important that you keep track of your activities to see that you are doing what you said you were going to do. In this section, clarify how you intend to keep tabs on your proposed activities.

- *Evaluation.* The funding source will want to know how you will go about determining whether you have met the stated goals, and why or why not. Have a clear description of outcomes and the impact your project will produce. Show how you define "success" (Browning, 2008, 2009; Clarke & Fox, 2007).

- *Appendixes or addenda.* Put any information in this section that does not fit into any other category but is still important for the funding

source to know. This could include endorsement letters from other organizations or noteworthy individuals, the names and titles of members of your board of directors or other active community supporters, a letter from the Internal Revenue Service verifying your tax exempt status, news clippings regarding your organization, affiliations with other organizations or other funding sources, and additional statistics or other supporting data.

Many organizations find it helpful to develop a boilerplate proposal that addresses all 15 proposal categories. A variation is to prepare some beginning proposal information for a number of projects that you would like to have funded. Keep all of your grant or proposal materials in an accessible file. This way you will be well prepared to respond to requests from potential funding sources. Do not merely send along your boilerplate proposal. It is simply a background document that will assist you in preparing a unique proposal to a particular identified funding source (Browning, 2000; Geever, 2007).

Tips for Grant Writing

- Do your homework on prospective funding sources. This can never be said enough. At the very least, know the key players, what the source is looking for, and how they want you to relate to them.

- Serve on a grants review panel. There may well be local funders who would welcome your assistance, and it will help you better understand how grant makers evaluate proposals.

- Brevity beats verbosity. Keep your writing short and to the point. If you are not sure that something belongs in your proposal, it probably does not belong. Proposals to corporate givers and small foundations are typically short.

- Write in a straightforward, person-to-person style. Remember, these are people reading your proposals, not computers. Use active voice.

- Send your letter directly to the proper person, and do double check the correct spelling of names. Do not send "To Whom It May Concern" or "Dear Sirs."

- Avoid jargon, bureaucratic language, and acronyms. Funding sources are more impressed with what you can do than with how you can sling the lingo.

- Humanize the proposal. Let the voices of those who will benefit come through.

- The cover letter and proposal summary are the first things most reviewers look at. These are your keys. Make them work.

- The title of your proposal should be clear and grab interest. Don't make it cute.

- Ask questions. If any part of the guidelines is unclear, no matter how small, be sure to ask for clarification so you know exactly what to do.

- Throughout your proposal, make sure you clearly demonstrate how your project effectively furthers the goals of the funding source. Your goals are important, but so are theirs.

- Point out the strengths of your organization, not just the needs it has. While it is usually helpful to show how dire the situation you are facing is, you want to leave the impression that you are capable of dealing with it.

- Only ask for as much money as you had originally discussed.

- Avoid the common problems that lead to proposal rejection: not clearly identifying and substantiating a significant problem, and lack of clarity about how monies will be used for project activities. Other common problems include methods not suited to the scope of the problem, no clear evaluation plan, objectives not clearly measurable, and an unreasonable time schedule (Coley & Scheinberg, 2000).

- The proposal will be reviewed by several people, so don't make them tear apart some fancy binding to make copies. Most prefer that the pages of your proposal be clipped together. Some don't even like staples.

- Make sure your proposal is easy to read, with lots of white space and type not smaller than 12 point.

- Use charts, graphs, and pictures to help reviewers clearly see what you are saying.

- Many funding sources include their review criteria, showing exactly how they will rate proposals. Use these as a guide.

- Have at least two other people read and comment on your proposal, including using review criteria to score your proposal. These should be people who are not familiar with your work. It must make simple sense to them.

- Follow up. Do not sit around for weeks or months waiting for a reply. Unless you are instructed to do otherwise, contact the funding source about 2 weeks after you have delivered your proposal. Then ask when would be a good time to recontact. You want the funding source to know that you are taking the proposal seriously, but you do not want to be a pest. Also, this provides you with an opportunity to offer additional information that would be helpful in securing the grant or to clarify any misunderstanding. Further, this strengthens the personal relationship between you and your contact person at the granting organization. Strong personal relationships are often as important as strong proposals.

- If you do not get the grant, find out why. This communicates purposefulness on your part. Do not complain or criticize. You may have another opportunity. How you handle your learning and relationships now may affect the next opportunity.

- Say thank you (yes, again). Even if you do not get the grant, it is important to express your appreciation for having been considered for this grant. You do hope that you will have an opportunity to work together in the future. Your "thank-you" helps foster future opportunities regardless of the outcome of this particular proposal.

- Stay in touch once you have received the grant. From time to time send project updates, news clippings, letters from people who have benefited from the project, and other indications of your project's success. Pick up the phone for conversation on occasion too.

VERBAL PRESENTATIONS

Occasionally a verbal presentation may be required. Sometimes groups believe their work is done when the written proposal has been completed and submitted. They spend little time on the presentation figuring that "we know all this stuff, and anyway it's only a 15-minute presentation." After spending weeks writing a proposal, some aren't willing to spend a couple of hours preparing a verbal presentation as compelling as possible. Then, again, some are.

Some presentations will occur before the proposal submission. These may provide you with an opportunity to receive an invitation to submit a proposal. Others follow upon delivery of your proposal. These presentations allow the grantors to meet with you and discuss the merits of your project.

I have seen groups turn a probable no into a yes with a well-handled presentation. I have also seen the reverse happen as a result of a poor presentation.

◧ Take a Moment to Discover ◨

A proposal can have a number of elements. The complexity of a proposal is related to the complexity of the project for which funding is sought and the requirements of the funding source. The following list reviews seven different elements for a standard proposal. Put yourself in the place of a proposal evaluator. Critically look at each element of your proposal. Score each element from 1 (very poor) to 6 (superb). What would your total score be? What weaknesses did you discover? As it stands, would your proposal be funded?

Summary	Clearly and concisely summarizes the request
I. Introduction	Describes the agency's qualifications or "credibility"
II. Problem statement or needs assessment	Documents the needs to be met or problems to be solved by the proposed funding
III. Objectives	Establishes the benefits of the funding in measurable terms
IV. Methods	Describes the activities to be employed to achieve the desired results
V. Evaluation	Presents a plan for determining the degree to which objectives are met and methods are followed
VI. Future or other necessary funding	Describes a plan for continuation beyond the grant period and/or the availability of other resources necessary to implement the grant
VII. Budget	Clearly delineates costs to be met by the funding source and those to be provided by the applicant or other parties

SOURCE: The Grantsmanship Center.

Tips for Verbal Presentations

- Use an interactive process. Ask for questions. Two-way communication helps build a relationship and allows you to discover and respond to what the grantor is thinking.

- Anticipate objections, even draw them out. This gives you a chance to openly discuss whatever reservations may exist in the grantor's mind. If you don't do this, your side may never be clearly heard (Crompton, 1985).

- Know your program, what you intend to accomplish, and how.

- Be straightforward. If the grantor feels you are being deceptive or beating around the bush, she may think you really do not know what you are talking about, or worse.

- Be well organized. Your presentation should flow logically from one subject to the next. Rambling around may cause the grantor's interest to wander away.

- Bring audio or visual enhancers to your presentation. These would include films, PowerPoint presentations, charts, or photographs. Use these to support your presentation, not substitute for it.

- Put materials into the hands of the people who are hearing your presentation. Again, this could include charts and graphs or photographs. You may want to do this toward the conclusion of your presentation so that during your presentation the audience is looking at you, not the materials in their hands.

COLLABORATION

The notion of organizations working with one another rather than against one another to get funding goes against the grain of common practice, but it may truly be beneficial. Your organization can benefit from forming partnerships with other organizations, using your combined resources to seek out and secure funding. By dividing the work, both in getting funding and in completing the project, a lot more can get done. Many donors, from individuals to foundations and government agencies, look favorably on collaborative efforts (Klein, 2000; Quick & New, 2000). By demonstrating community leadership on an issue as sensitive as funding, you can enhance the image of your organization to funders, constituents, and other key community players. More important, it may help stimulate a new way for organizations in your community to relate to each other, allowing you to accomplish much more (Fallon, 1993).

RECORD KEEPING AND REPORTING

Keeping your financial records straight can help you make better plans and decisions and may even keep you out of jail. A number of personal money manager programs (such as QuickBooks for Macs and PCs or even free open source software like GnuCash) meet most routine needs for a typical community change project or organization. For example, you will be able to monitor the income received from various sources, including grants, individual donors, or specific income-generating activities. Further, you can note the dates you received or expect to receive the funds. You can use this information to make projections and to make decisions: Can we buy that fax machine? If so, when? What is costing so much money? Where can we reduce expenses if we need to? Can we afford to hire some staff?

With good record keeping you can account for how you have handled all the funds you have received from whatever source. Sloppy record keeping has been the source of many, many rifts in organizations, and it has led to the loss of valuable dollars from external funding sources. Organizations involved in controversial issues are always open to attack. A favorite tactic of opponents is to point to financial mismanagement as a way of destroying a group's credibility. Smaller organizations often do not keep track of their money very well, and most cannot afford professional book-keeping services. With a little training and conscientious dedication to putting in the necessary data, your use of simple personal money manager software will provide a good picture of your organization's financial health and protect you from unnecessary vulnerability.

Ah, the smell of freshly baked cookies, the lure of banana bread still looking tasty under its cellophane wrap, and, of course, the little squares of marshmallow krispies to remind you of your younger years. Ready for the rush of customers, these and other goodies are set out on the folding table behind which you and a few other members of your group sit ready to take cash and make change. Another bake sale. By day's end you have raised $73.12. (Where did that 12 cents come from?) How much did this cost you?

Record keeping can be helpful in increasing the effectiveness of your fund-raising efforts. Some organizations put a lot of time and some actual money into projects that produce a pretty small return. Using your personal money manager program, or a spreadsheet program, you can get a better sense of which endeavors seem to work best for you. At the very least you can identify each fund-raising activity and note how much you spent (or are spending) on each, how much you have received, and the different rates of return on your investment in each activity. Much of the cost of fund-raising efforts for volunteer organizations is the use of volunteer time. Assign a dollar figure for each hour of volunteer time to get some measure of cost. Then you can make some comparisons of the value of the return you get from different activities related to the value of what you put into them. For example, you might decide that volunteer time is "worth" $8 an hour.

So, if 10 volunteers put in 2 hours each for a particular effort, that effort "cost" you $160 (10 volunteers × 2 hours × $8 per hour). How much did you really "make" on that bake sale? Could other activities bring in more dollars for the same cost, activities that are just as easy and that people actually will do? Some fund-raising activities have purposes beyond producing income—attracting community attention or establishing a sense of camaraderie among participants, for example—but you should know the costs of these activities as well. Good financial data can help you figure out which efforts need more attention and which should be discontinued. If your organization gets too large or too complex, you can add more sophisticated accounting or spreadsheet software.

Keeping accurate records gives you a good handle on what you have done and where you have been. This will help you decide where you can go from here.

Form 990

If you are a tax-exempt organization, you need to report to the IRS. You do this by filing IRS *Form 990,* the Return of Organization Exempt from Income Tax. The 990 is the primary source of information about your mission, governance, finance, and programs. It allows the IRS and the general public to evaluate your organization and how you operate. Some potential donors use the information provided on this form to help them make decisions about contributing.

Beginning for returns filed in 2009, almost all tax-exempt organizations must file some version of Form 990. This represents a big change from previous rules. Previously, organizations with gross receipts under $25,000 did not need to file. Many small organizations, which make up three quarters of the nonprofit sector, are unaware of the new rules. The IRS estimates that half a million small nonprofits will lose their exempt status by May 2010 because they have failed to file for 3 consecutive years. Though some of these are organizations that have closed shop, many are operating organizations that just don't know about the new rules.

The new form, which is now an 11-page core form and 16 schedules, also requires more disclosure for larger organizations regarding potential conflicts of interest, compensation of board members and staff, and other information related to financial accountability. Organizations that have annual receipts of more than $1 million must file the full Form 990. Those with annual receipts between $25,000 and $1 million could file the shorter Form 990-EZ in 2009, but in 2010 the threshold for filing the full Form 990 drops to $500,000, or $1.25 million in total assets, and in 2011 the thresholds drop further to receipts of $200,000, and assets of $500,000. The smaller organizations, with receipts under $25,000, file the much simpler electronic postcard, Form 990-N. Churches and organizations included in a group return are exempt, but everyone else must now file. If you lose your tax-exempt status for not filing, you have to go through the application process all over again (Coffman, 2009; Foundation Center, 2009; GuideStar, 2009; Independent Sector, 2009a; Internal Revenue Service, 2009a).

STRINGS ATTACHED

There are many treasure chests out there: some are large, some are small, and some are very well hidden. To discover any of these requires work (sometimes a lot of work), some ingenuity, some fiscal accountability, and some entanglements with the inevitable strings attached to each. Don't kid yourself. Each source of funds comes with strings attached. Some are threads, some steel cables. If you depend on contributions from the general public, you must keep the trust of that public and continue to demonstrate your worthiness. If you receive money from the federal government, you may find the regulations governing the use of those funds make sense in Washington, D.C. but seem a little crazy in Tacoma. Some funding sources may expect you to avoid controversial activities, especially those aimed at them.

Acknowledge that the strings are there and that you'll have to keep on good terms with the puppeteer, or be willing to run the risk that some of what you want may be left dangling.

CONCLUSION

No matter how big or small, old or new your effort is, you will need to generate additional resources. Many times you will be able to directly receive needed goods or services. Sometimes you will need to raise money to acquire them. Regardless of the approach you use, you will be asking other people, either as individuals or as representatives of organizations, to provide the resource support you need. Target your efforts to those most likely to respond favorably. Develop and nurture relationships with those who may be able to invest in your success and ask them to do so. Your request may take any number of forms: a direct person-to-person request, a letter, an organized pre-sentation, or even a formal written proposal. Thoughtfully and purposefully prepare and deliver your request to increase the chances of a rewarding response. Acknowledge and thank the people who have considered contributing to the realization of your goals.

The various techniques described in this chapter should give you some direction toward your pot, or at least your cup, of gold. More than that, however, they should spark your own thinking, your own ingenuity. In your own unique fashion, refine the methods described here and come up with some creative ones of your own.

SOMETHING'S BREWING

Your agency works with people in the community who have been labeled chronically mentally ill. You are tired of just using meager service approaches to assist this population (bless you). While working with your clients, you realize that they are capable of much more than they are given credit for or expected to do. So you have begun talking with them, and you have developed a group of clients who want to do something to direct their own future, using their abilities. Many have family members who have close ties to the members, and a few are well connected in the community.

Your small community has a fairly high unemployment rate, and hardly any employer will hire one of your clients, not even the new national chain sporting goods store scheduled to open soon. So

your group has decided to open its own business, a coffee house/restaurant. Wouldn't it be great to host the Rotary Club meeting there?

Some members have some skills in meal preparation, customer service, and other restaurant matters, but others do not. Further complicating things is that you have no money to open and capitalize the venture. Your group's hopes are high, especially because the city just donated a closed restaurant for your use. Well, that's great, but you still have no money. You know that the community foundation can give you some guidance, and you have heard that the United Way is interested in building community capacity. You still have no money, but you have convinced your agency to allow you to spend time on the project. Nice again, but you still have no money.

REFLECTION QUESTIONS

1. Which budget categories might be important to you now and in the near future?

2. What in-kind resources might be available to your group? How would you go about looking for them?

3. How might your clients become involved in raising resources for this undertaking?

4. Do you think individual members of the community would contribute to this effort? How would you ask them?

5. Where might you find support from other organizations? Which ones might be interested in this enterprise, including organizations that are not social service groups?

6. Why might a local United Way or community foundation see this as an interesting opportunity?

7. Which fund-raising or resource development approaches fit best with this creative response to a community issue?

8. How would you check out funding possibilities from granting organizations?

9. What could you say about this project that would make a strong proposal?

10. Who might give you guidance? What might you ask for?

GROUP ACTIVITY: GO OUT AND GET IT

This activity will give you some experience in asking for things from members of the community and help you get over some hesitancy about asking. Divide the larger group into teams of five or six members each,

and collect as many of the items on the following list from strangers, or at least from people who are not members of this group or class. Feel free to modify the list of items to fit your particular circumstances.

Item	Contributor Signature	Solicitor Signature
Pen		
Matchbook or lighter		
Item from the cafeteria (3 extra points if it is an edible item)		
A book from the library that is not checked out to you (2 extra points if you get a book that you can keep)		
A wrapped stick or piece of gum		
A U.S. quarter featuring a state on the East Coast		
An item of value that exceeds one dollar		
The business card of someone who promises to provide some specific help to your class or organization		
Additional creative items that your team chooses (1 point for each additional item up to three items)		

In normal circumstances you would prepare more and target your prospects more, and the things you would be seeking might be somewhat more valuable. Still, there will be some preparation and targeting even in this game. Here are the rules of the game.

- Each person on your team needs to successfully get an item from a stranger.

- Each time you get an item you must have the stranger sign in the *contributor* box, and the person who got the item sign in the *solicitor* box.

- You cannot pay money for any item.

1. As a team, review the items that you are to gather and develop some sort of strategy for how you will gather these items. (5 minutes)

2. Your team has 22 minutes to search for items. The clock starts when the facilitator says "Start" and runs until teams are back in the room with their items. (22 minutes)

3. Scoring (winners receive our praise and admiration):

- +2 points for each item collected
- −2 points for each team member who does not obtain an item
- −1 point for each minute the team is late returning to the classroom

4. One of the most difficult aspects of fund-raising is actually doing the asking. After returning from hunting and gathering, teams prepare to teach the larger group what they have learned from the experience by answering the following questions. (10–15 minutes)

- What personal hesitancy did you have in asking?
- How did you overcome this?
- How will you use this learning in future community change efforts?
- How did you target your prospects?
- What strategies seemed to work better?
- What happened that was unexpected?
- What three things that your team learned would you like to teach to the larger group?

5. Teams take turns teaching their lessons to the larger group. (5 minutes each)

HELPFUL WEBSITES

Links to the organizations briefly described here are on the companion website at www.cengage.com/humansvcs/homan.

Foundation Center. This is an extremely valuable resource. The center has resources on how to write proposals, a directory of grant makers on the Internet, and links to many other valuable sites. Its Cooperating Collections can be found in public libraries or other public centers in each state. It provides access to many publications, such as *Diversity in Philanthropy,* a comprehensive bibliography of resources related to diversity within the philanthropic and nonprofit sectors (Bryan, 2008).

Grantsmanship Center. The current day's grant announcements from the *Federal Register* and links to grant-making organizations are available here. You can also access the full text of the *Grantsmanship Center Magazine.*

Grants.gov. This is the single access point for more than 1,000 grant programs offered by all federal grant-making agencies. It keeps a running post of grant opportunities for the last 7 days and provides an online newsletter to keep you up to date with information about the federal granting process. You can search various grant opportunities, get proposal information, submit your proposal, and track your submission through this site. Although the federal government has other sources of information, such as the *Catalogue of Federal and Domestic Assistance* and the *Federal Register,* this site is probably your best and easiest way to find what you need.

National Council of Nonprofits—Nonprofit Economic Vitality Center. The center assembles key information from across the country, presenting information about the economy and the nonprofit sector and analyzing how the economic downturn is hurting nonprofits in different geographic regions, as well as different types of nonprofits, such as the arts and health care. The site also identifies various action steps that nonprofits can take and illustrates some of those options with examples of proven programs. The site also recognizes grant makers who are making extra contributions to help nonprofits meet their missions.

Time Banks. Helps you understand the notion of time banking and connects you to existing time banks.

Join Together. Regular updates on funding news, particularly regarding initiatives for dealing with substance abuse and violence, are provided by this organization.

Funding Exchange. This network of community-based foundations throughout the United States is "committed to change not charity."

Arizona State University Lodestar Center for Philanthropy and Nonprofit Innovation. The center produces and disseminates research related to nonprofit leadership and publishes the *Lodestar Center Nonprofit News.* In addition, you can get your questions answered through their Ask the Nonprofit Specialist service.

Grassroots Fundraising. Useful articles from the *Grassroots Fundraising Journal* on topics such as direct mail, special events, major gift campaigns, and phone-a-thons are available through this organization. You can access links to many other good fundraising sites, and sign up to receive regular e-mail updates, including tips from professional activist fund-raiser Kim Klein.

Idealist.org Action Without Borders. This organization has a huge set of resources online for community organizations in 11 different languages.

Non-Profit Guides. You can access free web-based, grant-writing tools for nonprofit organizations, charitable, educational, public organizations, and other community-minded groups here. The site also provides tips, sample proposals, and links to other resources.

National Committee for Responsive Philanthropy. This organization works to encourage philanthropy to fundamental issues of social and economic justice. They engage in research, publication, and advocacy to further this aim.

Women's Funding Network. This network of more than 145 organizations provides funding and information to assist women around the world to work for social change.

Association of Fundraising Professionals. News and articles on a broad range of fund-raising topics are available through this organization. The have a good section of frequently asked questions and provide access to members through regional and collegiate chapters. They also sponsor a Youth in Philanthropy project.

Chapter 10

✳

Getting the Word Out

CHAPTER HIGHLIGHTS

- Awareness promotes interest; ignorance inhibits action
- Education alone is insufficient for action
- Credibility is essential to your success
- The three Holy M's: message, medium, market
- Word of mouth
- Interaction with other groups and organizations
- Newsletters, brochures, and position papers
- Effective presentations and using a speakers' bureau
- Fliers and posters
- Multiple uses of information technology
- Other organizations to communicate your message
- Public service media and PSAs
- Radio and TV talk shows
- Get in and on the news
- Editorials and letters to the editor

Some things just shouldn't be kept secret. The need for the change you are seeking and the attempts to make change fit nicely into this category. Getting information to people and getting information from them are crucial activities in your march toward change. Using information and communication technology to raise awareness, make connections, and mobilize action and support expands your reach and accelerates your efforts.

To get on the community's agenda of issues, the community needs to know you exist. As a change agent, you need to go beyond your professional circle of supporters and begin to foster community awareness and dialogue. To build needed community support, you must also reach out and inform people who don't know much about the issue and may never even have thought about it.

Earlier, we looked at ways to get information from and about your community. In this chapter we look at reasons to get information out as well as some of the ways you can reach people who can use the information to aid the cause you are working on.

Regardless of the size of your community—a social service agency, a neighborhood, or even an entire city or beyond—your ability to effectively inform others is a great asset. Some methods described in this chapter (press conferences, for example) are more appropriate for informing larger audiences. Yet you can apply the basic concepts for reaching people with your message to all the different communities you focus on in your change efforts.

IMPORTANCE OF MAKING YOUR EFFORTS KNOWN

Drawing attention to your actions and the need for them serves several purposes. Why you are communicating to people will affect how you choose to do it. Remember that everything happens through relationships and that relationships are built on communication, trust, and mutual interest. Your ability to effectively communicate is a critical factor in building the relationships that you need. Let's look at several other major reasons you might want to get the word out.

Let People Know You Exist

Your organization is a new force in the environment. It will move people in new directions, sometimes in directions they do not want to go. This movement occurs when people react to what you and other members of your organization are doing. But you will have no reaction—you probably will have no members—if no one knows you even exist. This is the starting point and the first reason to publicize your intent and your action. People have to know that there is an interest in changing things before they can decide what to do about it. If people don't know you exist, they can't work with you or oppose you. Spreading the word will give some people hope and enthusiasm and other people worry.

Stir Interest

People hear that old ways are going to be challenged. People start talking. People start thinking. In some cases, people even start acting. Provoke people. You don't have to get people mad, but you do have to get

them thinking differently and thinking about behaving differently so they will begin to believe in the possibilities.

You have to overcome the inertia of inaction or acquiescence. The rumblings of interest begin to alter the circumstances in which you are operating. With your help, interest will build on itself, setting things in motion.

Expose the Issue and Educate for Action

It is easy, and fairly common, to take refuge in ignorance. The security that comes with not knowing is a powerful force in keeping things as they are. Bringing the issue into focus shakes people out of their complacency.

It is sometimes safer to pretend a problem doesn't exist, especially if you feel powerless to do anything about it. When people begin to see what is really going on (at least from your perspective), they begin to understand the various aspects of the issue and, most important, how it affects them. Awareness makes it harder to tuck things away out of consciousness.

Ignorance is not always a purposeful choice. Sometimes people simply don't know. So many things compete for our attention that we scarcely notice some things, but we might be willing to do something about them if we did.

Those who are responsible for maintaining the problem would just as soon keep other people unaware. They especially don't want their own roles noticed, nor do they want to be held accountable for their actions, or lack of them. By exposing the ramifications of the problem and who is involved, you can agitate people and counter the very powerful process of ignorance.

Education, however, is not sufficient for action. Don't be fooled into thinking it is. Too many groups make the mistake of assuming that if people know about a problem they will act on it. They even have "education" as the major goal. Education may be a precondition for action, but it is not action. Merely knowing about something does not guarantee action on it.

Once people have a clearer picture of a situation, you can introduce them to ways of putting their awareness into action. Help people see that they can act, and probably should. Show them how and what steps they can take. This is a necessary part of the process of educating to promote change. People who are aroused want to know what they can do. Don't leave them hanging. Take advantage of the opportunity you have created.

Education through strategic communication will help shape the political and organizing environment, creating a climate for change (Minch, 2005). Not everyone will be so concerned about an issue that they will want to spend their time working on it, but they may be supportive of those who do. You need this kind of support. A hostile or insensitive environment will make things harder for you and aid those resisting change. A more knowledgeable, supportive atmosphere affects the tone of the contest. Potential resisters may see the handwriting on the wall and make a less than concerted effort to maintain the status quo.

Attract New Support

Building the organization involves building membership in it. The message you send out regarding the need for action will bring people into your organization. People who care enough to move ahead will be glad to know that others are involved in the issue. Your organization gives them a way to express their interest.

Strengthen Affiliation

The notoriety the organization receives increases the attachment of those who have already enlisted. It helps build an identity, which contributes to a feeling that participants are part of an alliance to be reckoned with. As members of such a group, they feel more important or more powerful. As other people come to regard the change effort more seriously, its participants are reinforced for their commitment. This bolsters resolve and enhances motivation to press forward with the work of the organization. This shapes people's sense of themselves. Once a person or a group has an identity, it becomes difficult to break.

Credibility

I will frequently mention credibility or allude to its importance. It is a central element necessary to your efforts to promote change. Are you real? Do you have the power you say you have? Is your information accurate? Your credibility will be challenged both directly and indirectly by supporters and opponents alike throughout the life of the change effort.

At first you are asking people to believe in what doesn't yet exist. This is not easily done. Whether for members, those you hope to influence, or the public in general, uncertainty is hard to act on. For you or me to commit to something, we need to let go of some fairly natural restraining tendencies. We require at least some evidence that letting go is a good idea. The less credible or believable something is, the more reluctant we are to affiliate with it. The more we are able to believe that something is for real, the more willing we are to respond to it.

If handled correctly, your efforts to communicate your presence, your purpose, and your progress will provide you with this most powerful benefit. Credibility establishes the foundation for all the other benefits. It makes them possible.

IDENTIFYING THE PEOPLE YOU NEED TO REACH

You will be communicating different types of information to at least three different groups:

- Your supporters, whether active or general
- The target or response community
- The general public

It is most important that your membership be kept informed. Your participants should be apprised of the progress of and particular challenges to your operation. Tell them what's going on. Be sure your direct supporters are well informed about the issue or problem you are trying to rectify. Keep the issue before them to keep them in touch with the purpose you share and to deepen their understanding and commitment. From time to time provide a motivational piece. These are intended to maintain, and periodically heighten, enthusiasm. Finally, let participants know about specific organizational needs they may be able to meet.

Continue to educate other constituents of the action and benefit communities regarding the problem, the goals, the activities of the organization, and the

CAPTURING CONCEPTS
Social Marketing

Many organizations, particularly public organizations, are using **social marketing** as a means of transforming community attitudes and behaviors, often around issues of public health. Social marketing uses the same marketing principles that have been successful in selling products to consumers to get consumers to "buy" new ideas or behaviors to benefit the target community and society in general. Practitioners use the four P's of marketing: **product, price**, distribution or **place**, and **promotion**. Breast cancer screening, smoking cessation, condom use, and immunization campaigns all employ social marketing techniques (Weinreich, 2003).

---

sources of resistance. Keep them aware of roles they can fill.

Positive change results when people who have a good idea also have the power to implement it. Two fundamental things you need to communicate to the target community are the strength of your ideas and the strength of your support. Whether the target community actively opposes the changes or not, you will have to overcome some forms of resistance, even if that just happens to be old habits.

The target group should know what it is you expect them to do; that is, what and how they are to change. Extend opportunities to them to participate in improving the situation. Finally, they should be aware of the important activities of your organization, including large and small victories that enhance its position in the eyes of other community members.

On some issues it is important to have the general public take notice. There are times when even relatively small changes would benefit from broader community awareness. When you communicate with the general public, you usually do so either to gain broad approval and sanction for your activities and concerns or to rouse it to action. Inform the public of the validity of your concerns and the unreasonableness, if not the downright perfidy, of any opposition. The more general public onlookers there are, the more difficult it will be for resisters to get away with things that they shouldn't. You want the public to understand how your success will benefit them and that your failure will be their loss. Finally, you want the general public to know that you are alive and kicking. Let them know some of the things you are doing, and periodically remind them of your issues and successes.

THE THREE HOLY M'S

The basic reason you communicate with people is to get a reaction from them. You want them to think or to know something, do or not do something. Therefore, you take care (or at least you should) to prepare the proper message. The disappointment of many change efforts can be traced to a lack of attention in preparing and sending an effective message. To prepare an effective message, pay homage to the Three Holy M's (see Figure 10.1):

- *The market:* the recipients of your message, the people from whom you want to get a reaction

- *The medium:* the technique or device you use to get the message to the market

- *The message:* what the market needs to hear to respond

When we fail, it is often because we start by saying what we want to say without giving adequate consideration to who is going to hear it and how. We get things backward. The message is the last thing we should consider. The market is the first. The medium fits in between.

The entire process of getting the word out is driven by the reactions you want to get from the market. It is as simple and as complex as that. Your actions do not produce change. It is the *reactions* to your actions that do. So be clear about the reactions

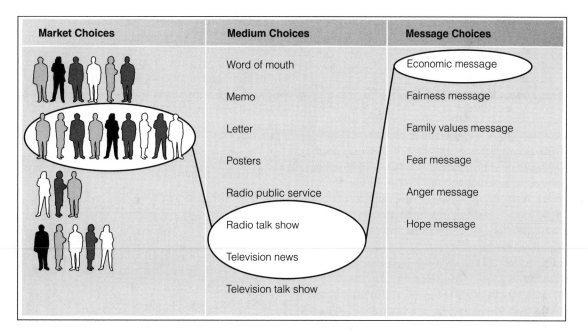

FIGURE 10.1 The Three Holy M's

Example of relationship between the Three Holy M's: Pick the right market, select the right medium, and craft and send the right message.

that you intend to provoke. The more that other things become important, such as feeling self-righteous, the less effective you will be. Paying attention to how the message, the medium, and the market relate to each other will strengthen the impact of your communication. Just who are these people you want to influence? What response do you want from them? What do they need to hear to trigger that response? Do they respond to facts, demonstrations of power, emotion, or intellectual argument? In what ways do they receive information? Which methods do they trust? Which of these can best carry the message you want to send? Which methods would the market consider to be appropriate for your message? You will probably want to consider other things as well, but this is enough to get you started.

The market—the people you intend to influence, and therefore the messages you send—will no doubt vary from one change project to the next; so too will the vehicles you use for delivering the message to the market. You may even have different markets or sets of responders within the same change episode. Nonetheless, you will more than

likely use some standard methods. You will be more effective if you understand how to use these methods to your advantage.

TECHNIQUES FOR SENDING THE MESSAGE THAT YOU CONTROL

Some methods for getting the word out are under your control or largely under your control. That is, your group is responsible for preparing and sending the message rather than having to convince or rely on someone else (such as the news media) to do that for you.

As you prepare to send your message, think about how you will *receive* messages from the people to whom you are sending your message. If your communication is only one way, you will not build much of a relationship with those you hope to influence. You really have only a few ways to see if your message was received and understood. Ask yourself, how can we not only communicate *to* our market but *with* our market as well?

Word of Mouth

Talk it up. People involved in your effort should tell everyone they know (and a few they don't) just what they are doing and why. It has long been said that word of mouth is the best form of advertising because people regard as truth or near truth the things they hear from those around them. Think of the power of gossip or the rumor mill. If something is repeated often enough, it becomes true whether or not it actually is. Presumably, you will be spreading the truth, which should increase the believability of what you say.

When you talk with people about the situation you are facing, especially people who are unfamiliar with it, be sensitive to their level of interest. Plant seeds; don't give lectures. Build curiosity; don't assume it. Avoid turning people off by giving them more than they want to know. It is usually better to tell people a little less than they need to know rather than a little more. The type and number of questions they ask will let you know how interested they are.

One effective technique involves asking questions and then listening. Get people thinking about how they feel about the issue, and see if they can relate it to themselves in some way. Try to pick up on that feeling. Guide people to reach their own conclusions on the matter. People become more attached if these judgments are their own beliefs, not just yours. You should have a few standard points you want to make. You can even have a few standard phrases handy to rely on if you like.

Consider a more formal campaign in addition to spur-of-the-moment conversation. This may include a planned strategy with specific individuals "assigned" to those you particularly want to influence. Or you may assign teams to directly contact individuals in certain groups or areas in your community. A door-to-door approach in a neighborhood is an example of such a campaign. Using some of the forms of communication technology discussed later in the chapter is another.

Meetings

Obviously, the people involved in your project will be meeting from time to time to plan, exchange information, and make decisions, but other people meet too. This provides you with an opportunity to spread your message. Concentrate on groups and organizations whose support you would like to cultivate. This is a good way to build allies too. Most groups will give you the 5 or 10 minutes you ask for to make a presentation. Make your points clearly, using examples and facts to back them up. That is, be prepared. Using a little emotion often helps, even with the stuffiest groups.

Let the members of the group know what you want from them. Ask for it clearly. Then be quiet. Wait for the response. Remain for any discussion by the group on the matter. You may be able to inject some insight, and it will be a lot harder for them to turn you down when they are looking at you.

Always leave some written material behind. A one-page summary of your points or a brochure and your request are usually all that is necessary. Make sure that whatever you leave has your organization's name and a way for people to contact a specific person in your group.

Newsletters

A regular means of communicating to your members is necessary to keep everyone linked to the effort. If your organization has more than a handful of members and these members don't see each other regularly, you might want to develop a newsletter. Your computer may well have a publishing program that can help you create an attractive piece. Newsletters enhance the feeling of legitimacy and permanence of an organized group. They help supporters keep in touch with the organization and its agenda. But newsletters take time to produce, and if you need to pay for printing and mailing, they can cost money. Sending an electronic newsletter can reduce cost and expand the number of recipients, but it does not have the same effect as hard copy that people will touch.

A few simple suggestions will help your newsletter accomplish its purpose of communicating to

CHANGE AGENT TIP

You can save money by using bulk mail to send a large number of similar mailings. There are specific provisions for using bulk mail, such as sending a minimum of 200 (or 50 pounds) of identical pieces. The more work you do up front to reduce the load on the Post Office, the more money you can save. Further, the Post Office has special provisions to reduce mailing costs for nonprofit organizations. United States Post Office Publication 417 can give you a good start, but schedule some time with a local Post Office representative so you understand the rules, permit costs, and so forth. If you do a lot of mailing, this can definitely save you some cash.

supporters and strengthening their sense of affiliation: Keep it simple and personal, keep it regular, and put one person in charge.

First and foremost, someone, a responsible someone, needs to take on preparation of the newsletter as his major contribution to the organization. If nobody really wants this job, don't try to put out a newsletter. You would only get a couple of issues out before it would fizzle. Fizzled projects aren't good for organizations.

Next, make sure it is published on a regular basis, preferably monthly, or quarterly. Sporadic or hit and miss publications give the impression that other efforts by the organization are sporadic or halfhearted.

Finally, remember that you want people to read the thing. Rarely should it exceed four sides in length. (There are, of course, exceptions to this, particularly for newsletters whose purpose is to examine a range of community issues or whose intended audience extends beyond the organization's members.) A basic line-up of articles would include these regular columns: news, editorials, featured personality, and upcoming activities or events. That's about it.

Don't forget that your organization is made up of people, not just issues. People like to see their names in print. So print lots of names. Look for ways to spread credit around when describing gains the organization has made. When featuring an individual, profile the personal side, not just the professional side, and always mention some reason the individual is supporting the cause. Use humor, cartoons, or simple graphics, and keep the articles short. Solicit articles from supporters to distribute the workload and promote a sense of ownership.

Newsletters are good for reaching outside your organization as well. Include people on your distribution list who are not active in your effort but who should be kept informed about your organization, particularly members of the news media. Features in your newsletter can become the basis of news stories.

Brochures

There seems to be a natural desire for some people to want to develop brochures. They can provide credibility and also present a brief picture of your organization's purpose, its history, including accomplishments, and methods for people to participate along with you, along with methods for contacting you. Here again, your computer may well have tools for making it easy to design your brochure. However, before you rush off to the printer, stop and ask yourself: Who is supposed to read this brochure, how will they get it, and what are they supposed to do once they have read it? If you can't come up with good answers that justify the time and possible expense of printing a brochure, you shouldn't produce one. Unless your change involves establishing a permanent program or alliance or organizing a significant conference, you probably don't need a brochure.

If you decide you need a brochure, there are some basic things you should know. Most brochures are made from a standard 8½ × 11-inch sheet of paper folded in thirds. This arrangement gives you five panels for graphics and information and a back panel for an address if it is to be mailed. You can design and print out a brochure quickly for an immediate need, but for wider distribution and ongoing use, have your brochure printed on high-quality paper.

The purpose of your brochure will be either informational, answering questions and conveying pertinent details, or invitational, arousing curiosity

🔁 Take a Moment to Discover 🔁

Today you will probably pass by quite a few signs that beckon your attention to a community event or to an item of information someone thinks you should know. Will you read any of these? Maybe a few, but not most. What do you think determines this? What can you learn from your answer?

and encouraging some steps toward participation in something. Decide which emphasis you want, and stick to it. If you want people to read it, keep these tips in mind as you develop your brochure:

- Think space; brochures with too many words are rarely read.

- Keep your sentences short and avoid jargon.

- Use a hook to grab attention and get people to peek inside; bold statements or questions often do the trick.

- Work with an experienced printer; most will provide you with valuable guidance.

- Consider using a union printer; aside from philosophical reasons to do so, some groups will scrutinize your literature wanting to see the union label.

Position Papers

If your group has taken an official position on a particular matter, you may want to prepare a clearly written statement that convincingly articulates your position. Sometimes called a white paper (because most government reports had a blue cover), this is particularly useful in communicating your point of view to government bodies, community task forces, and the news media. A position paper provides an explicit statement of your beliefs and protects you from people who want to misconstrue your position. It also provides you with a good tool to help shape the development of policy, especially if you are trying to influence the decisions of a working group looking into the matter. Other groups will rely on the work you have done, sometimes using your work in place of work they would otherwise

have to do for themselves. If you only offer your viewpoint verbally, you have to trust that your comments will be remembered, and remembered accurately. Quite an act of faith. A position paper can serve as a backup to amplify the points you make when using other forms of communication.

The length of a position paper will vary according to the complexity of the issue you choose to address. It may be as short as a single page, or it may be 25 pages long. The paper should outline why the issue at hand is relevant to your group, what your position is, and how you support your position. Your support should demonstrate philosophical, rational, and factual justification.

If you are preparing a paper that exceeds five pages, provide an abstract that summarizes the entire paper in two or three paragraphs. Use headings and subheadings to highlight key sections. Supply a bibliography showing the sources you used to develop your position. Make sure that your organization's name, logo, and contact information are on the first page. For particularly long papers, it is also generally a good idea to include a table of contents. As with any written material, make sure it is attractive and free from errors of spelling, grammar, and punctuation.

Speakers' Bureau

Making presentations to other community groups or at a community forum is a useful way to shape the community's perception of your organization's concerns and establish the climate for change. It helps make your organization visible as well. This affords you the opportunity for a face-to-face discussion with people who are themselves part of an organized power base or who are interested in community affairs.

To make a speakers' bureau work, you need to identify people who are interested in making presentations, train them, and solicit invitations to speak. Each of these elements is important.

Not everyone is interested in public speaking, and certainly not everyone is good at it. Ask your supporters to volunteer for this assignment and also ask them to identify people they think would be good speakers. Then make a particular effort to recruit people who have a special expertise. This is not something you want to talk people into doing. Only use people who like, or at least don't mind, this type of activity. They won't back out of engagements and will probably represent you more effectively.

Training is an important component of your program. Each speaker should be comfortable with her standard presentation, be well versed in the organization's goals and positions, and be practiced at handling questions, particularly the tough ones. Each speaker should learn how to relate your group's concerns to the concerns of the audience.

Seek out opportunities to make presentations. Many groups use guest speakers. This includes college classes, civic and fraternal organizations, community affairs groups, religious groups, and others. Libraries, hospitals, and major employers often sponsor community lecture series. Look in the community events calendar in the newspaper to get an idea of the type of speaking possibilities typical of your community. Then send out a letter to appropriate groups announcing your availability and respond quickly to the invitations you receive.

Your speakers' program should be part of a purposeful campaign. It is more effective if you target particular constituencies you want to influence. Personally arrange opportunities to address specific groups whose members may play a role in any community debate on your concerns.

Fliers and Posters

Fliers and posters can be inexpensive ways to notify a lot of people or foolish ways to waste a lot of paper. By giving thought to just a few things, you can improve the quality of the ones you produce. The first point to think about is how you are going to distribute your material. If you produce 500 fliers, you want to make sure that 500 end up in public, not neatly stacked on somebody's desk. You can't hand people a fistful of fliers and expect that they will distribute them for you. The process must be more purposefully managed. This matter should be cleared up before you print your first piece.

The next point concerns where you post your information so people will notice it. Places where people go to look for information are obvious, though not always the best, choices. Too many bulletin boards are so cluttered with outdated information that nobody really pays attention to them. Most of the time people will not stop to read a poster, so it is a good idea to put them in places people are moving toward or where they are already stopped.

Your message has to capture attention. Striking design and sharply contrasting colors do this. One dramatic word or picture will command more attention than several. Think space. A few easy-to-read words is far better than an essay. Finally, tell people what they need to know. If you can do this in a provocative or clever way, all the better; the reader will remember more.

CYBERORGANIZING

You can spot them. They have sleek laptops and even sleeker mobile devices. Dare we call any of these things phones? Their nimble thumbs tap away at the tiny keyboard without even looking, reaching out to their friends and followers and the world while standing still dash or driving. They are Generation V (Generation Virtual). They follow Generations X and Y, and they may be pushing 24, maybe 25? Right? Well, maybe. Adam Sarner (2008), analyst at the respected

CHANGE AGENT TIP

Someone in your organization, maybe you, will be talking to groups of people to help educate them about your issues and to draw their support. Here are a few tips that can increase your effectiveness and comfort.

Two Essential Questions

- What do you want from this group?
- What do they need to hear or know in order to respond?

Basic Outline for Presentations

- Describe what you are going to talk about overall; introduce key topics.
- Describe the specific topic or subject of your presentation; define the topic if necessary.
- Identify who you are to be able to talk about this subject.
- Describe why this subject/issue is important.
- Present information on the issue.
- Give examples of what this subject/issue looks like in everyday life.
- Describe what you would like the group/audience to do; specify the nature of your request.
- Describe who will benefit from the group's action; particularly identify how the group can benefit or how the people they directly care about can benefit.
- Summarize key points.

- Thank the group for the opportunity to present, their attentiveness, and their response.

Some Tips

- Be yourself.
- Build a common connection between you and the audience and relate your message to what is important to them.
- Get the audience involved by asking questions to get them thinking.
- Personalize your message; tell it through the eyes and voices of those most affected.
- Provide concrete data and the views of other experts.
- Provide a simple handout; one page is generally best.
- Using PowerPoint or a similar tool, show a few text slides, pictures, or graphics to enhance your words; this can even be one word or one sentence.
- Make eye contact; just looking at foreheads works.
- Use humor; don't force it though.
- Have a standard story or phrase you can use.
- Compliment the audience whenever possible.

information technology and research firm Gartner Inc., has this to say about Generation V: "Unlike previous generations, Generation V is not defined by age, gender, social demographic or geography, but is based on demonstrated achievement, accomplishments (merit) and an increasing preference toward the use of digital media channels to discover information, build knowledge and share insights" (p. 1).

The "digital divide" refers to the gap between those who do and do not have access to digital and information technology, know how to use it, and see its benefits. Organizers should recognize this as an issue and help community members get connected to technology that provides access to information, creativity, and other members of the community. Differences in access and use of digital technology can be found among older people, those with low incomes, those with less than a high school education, and people living in rural

areas, but this divide is shrinking in the United States. The Pew Internet and American Life Project (2009) found that 87% of those 18 to 29 years old use the Internet, but 82% of those 30 to 49 years old do as well. Almost 75% of Americans age 50 to 64 are also spending time online.

Generation V is more about behavior than age. Sarner identified three behavioral attributes that characterize this generation. First, they use technology as a day-to-day tool to facilitate communication. Although they are familiar with the use of the technology, they may not understand how it works or even care to understand. Second, Generation V members demonstrate an overwhelming desire to participate through involvement in global communities to gain information. They don't rely on broadcast media to shape their views of the world. Further, they value "two-way participation—an active involvement in the community rather than a passive consumption. Generation V expects a conversation rather than a communication" (p. 1). Finally, they value collaboration, believing that " 'we' is more powerful and valuable than 'me' and that sharing increases the value of something rather than diminishes or erodes it" (p. 1). Sarner concluded that the changes brought by Generation V—driven by a desire for creativity, belonging, self-actualization, and self-determination—will lead to huge opportunities for those who can accept the signs and react to the new forces shaping the technological landscape.

Obviously, lots of people are catching on to the benefits of multiple forms of communication. Community organizers are, or should be, too.

Community organizer and candidate Barak Obama and his team certainly understood. The campaign raised half a *billion* dollars online with 3 million donors making a total of 6.5 million contributions. More than 90% of those donations were in increments of $100 or less. After Alaska Governor Sarah Palin famously dismissed the value of community organizing in her acceptance speech at the Republican National Convention, Obama raised $10 million within 24 hours (Vargas, 2008).

Obama maintained a profile in more than 15 online communities, including BlackPlanet, a MySpace for African Americans, and Eons, a Facebook for baby boomers. On Facebook, where about 3.2 million signed up as his supporters, a group called Students for Barack Obama was created in July 2007. It was so effective at energizing college-age voters that senior aides made it an official part of the campaign the following spring. And Facebook users did vote: On Facebook's Election 2008 page, which listed an 800 number to call for voting problems, more than 5.4 million users clicked on an "I Voted" button to let their Facebook friends know that they made it to the polls, a good example of online peer pressure (Vargas, 2008).

So, what are these various ways of communicating, and how *do* they connect with organizing something a bit more modest than a presidential campaign?

A basic digital organizing approach consists of a number of components. The core of your program will most likely be the development and use of your website and your e-mail system, along with the various methods of connecting that these support. Next would be your use of social media, particularly social net-

working sites. Your work will be further accelerated by making use of various tools for specific purposes. Finally, you can extend your reach using blogs and finding more effective ways for your members to make decisions and work together. You don't have to have all these elements at once, and you can certainly add more features. The more ways you connect people to the issue, to the organization, to the action, and to each other, the more power you can generate.

Just like all the other forms of communication, how you use online and other communication technology will fit with your understanding of the Three Holy M's (message, medium, and market) described earlier in the chapter. Here, too, you will communicate both within your organization as well as with other members of your community who are not participating in your organization. With your members you will have discussions about the issue, current activities, and the work you are doing for the purposes of moving your organization forward, helping it to achieve its goals. With those outside your organization you will communicate about your organization and the issue and your work or activities for the purposes of raising awareness, recruiting active participants, and developing general supporters. Some of your communication will be directed to those in your local area, and some will include those outside your area, potentially throughout the world.

Websites

If you intend to go public, you will be expected to use routine ways of communicating your presence, your issue, and your purpose, and for most organizations a website is now considered routine. Far beyond the matter of credibility, a website serves a number of valuable, practical purposes. It can draw attention to the issue or set of issues you are working on as well as to your efforts to deal with them. Through your site you can promote community discussion, build membership, mobilize people to action, generate revenue, and direct people to services or other resources your organization has to offer. Your website should be considered the core of your Internet presence (Stein, 2001).

There is a lot to learn about operating a website, and a basic overview will help guide your thinking. I have drawn the following information from what

I have learned working with organizations as well as from a number of experts in the field (Christ & Fignar, 2005a, 2005b, 2005c; Flaiz, 2009; Fox-McIntyre, 2001; Hill, 2009; Osten, 2001; Stein, 2001; Sturm, personal communication, September 2, 2009; Sullivan, 2002; Vernon & Lynch, 2000).

Setting up a Web page can be a fun, creative exercise that is no longer a very difficult task. Sophisticated website designers learn Web formatting specifications, scripting, and markup languages, but you can now layout text and graphics as well as create links to other pages within your site without learning these underlying programming commands by using available software. You use this software much like you would use your word processing program, creating the words and pictures you want. The program automatically converts this into a language that can be read by any Web browser. Web page programs such as Microsoft Expression Web 2 and Adobe Dreamweaver are fairly easy to use and enable you to build a professional-looking website.

The quality of your website depends most on the quality of your planning. This planning is best done with the team that will oversee the creation and refinement of your site. Carefully think through how you want your site to accomplish your mission and promote your identity. For your site to be useful to you, it must first be useful to your audience. Who is your potential and desired audience? What are they trying to accomplish when they contact your site? Why would they want to stay there? For starters, have each team member identify the three most important things a visitor to your site wants to achieve, and go from there. You can even do a full-blown workshop on the topic. It's that important.

As you begin construction, consider how technologically sophisticated your audience is likely to be. Also think about who is *not* your audience, including any group that you would not want to receive certain information.

The site is like a book with individual "pages" serving as chapters or sections. Your home page provides the introduction to your organization and the site, so it should convey your philosophy and fundamental message along with easy guides to information that can be found on the secondary pages. Spend some time examining other websites for features and organization that you like.

First develop your basic content, then add more sophisticated features such as forms, animated graphics, counters, and the like. Providing advanced features makes your site look professional and polished. If these are overdone, however, your site may look too cluttered and be too slow.

If possible, add metatags (which are hidden descriptions or keywords) on your home page. This will increase your chances of being noticed and listed by search engines. All search engines have a set of rules (called an algorithm) that produces the ranking of sites in response to a query or search that some interested soul initiates. Some search engines rank according to variables such as how frequently the site is updated, how often it is viewed, and the number of other sites that link to it. Most look for keywords at the top of the page, along with the number of times the keywords are mentioned. If your keywords are right up top and mentioned several times, your site may be deemed more relevant and get ranked higher on the list and your target audience will quickly find what they are looking for and stay there.

Most people who are searching don't go past the first page of a list of sites, so the higher your rank, the more likely you will be seen. Make it easy on your visitors. Provide clear, simple titles to each page, and avoid complex graphics that slow down response times. Here are some tips from the experts:

- Make sure that you make a good first impression and include the search phrase you're targeting in page titles, header tags, or called out content (think bulleted lists). Make it easy for visitors to quickly see what's there. Headers should be succinct, usually under 55 characters. Sentences are best kept to around 10 words. Paragraphs that take up about four lines are ideal. Let searchers make an immediate connection between what they're looking for and what you're offering (Flaiz, 2009).

- Have an initial welcome paragraph that greets visitors and tells them what they need to know, provide a "contact us" page that is linked to every page, and make sure your home page is linked to every page.

- Use commonly accepted terms such as "home," "about us," and "contact us," to help people find their way through your site. Avoid trying to give such basic terms more clever names.

- Provide a brief and interesting tour of the site and a tour of the organization: history, current efforts, vision and goals, and major activities.

- Make the most important thing the easiest thing for visitors to do on your site. That might be signing up for your newsletter, contributing to your organization, or volunteering time. Whatever it is, make it easy to do.

- Make it readable by using dark text on a light background.

- Create site modules by grouping major departments and organizational functions and providing links not just from the home page but from secondary pages as well. You may want to use a site map, which you can call an index or table of contents, to link to other pages; this further helps get your site ranked higher.

- Have a site search feature that allows visitors to find information quickly.

- Show how people can find you on Facebook, Twitter, or other social networking sites.

- Build interest and visitorship by developing a single question survey that changes every month. Provide last month's results along with the date this month's results will be posted.

- Post your IRS Form 990 and your annual report, if you have one, to show donors that you are a transparent organization.

- Have a secure means for contributing, especially money, and make sure that every page has links to the donations page.

- Allow members to update their e-mail and other contact information so you don't lose them if they move.

- Bring things to life with audio and visual clips.

- Advertise your electronic newsletter.

- Use news headlines, questions, or riddles to direct visitors to other pages you would like them to see.

- Provide a feed to which readers can subscribe to keep them updated on current information about your issue or your organization.

- Pay attention to diversity issues, providing affirming elements and eliminating potentially offensive ones.

- Use gender-neutral language.

- Provide an informative, even entertaining FAQ (frequently asked questions) page.

- Keep pages to fewer than three screens.

- Use more than one proofreader.

Once your website has been put together, introduce it to the world. First, choose a trademark domain name that reinforces your identity and is short and easy to remember, one you will keep. You will probably need to renew your domain name every year or two. Then host your site on a server, which is connected to the Internet 24 hours a day. Most small organizations don't have the money for the hardware and software and staff to run their own server, and it is generally easy to copy it onto your account with your Internet Service Provider (ISP). Your ISP can show you how to copy your creation to a space within your account so that your Web page is now available to the world. You can also contract with a hosting service that will charge you a monthly fee for keeping your website accessible and performing some routine management tasks.

Now that you're online, you want to make the acquaintance of as many search engines and portals as possible. Portals are search engines or sites that serve as gateways by directing visitors to other sites. Most portals provide ways to contact their editors. Build relationships with these editors and keep in contact with them.

Though you can sit back and let some search engine discover you, it is better to introduce yourself to your worldwide audience by making a posting to a search engine. Most have a simple way to invite you to add your website to their list, providing an icon or button to click on. You click on to that spot, follow the directions, and you are now on stage. Registration services are available, but most are set up for businesses, and you can do much of what you need yourself.

DID YOU KNOW?   What Can We Do with a Website?

If you keep asking that question, you will be fine. As your organization grows and your experience using the Web does as well, you will think of new ways to make use of your worldwide exposure. Here are a few ideas to spark your imagination.

- Keep visitors up to date and intrigued with current organizational news and activities.
- Conduct an auction of donated goods and services.
- Provide a calendar to announce events, along with an annual calendar.
- Offer online event registration.
- Create a page with information and talking points on an issue and create an action alert button, which visitors can click to send a prepared e-mail (which visitors can modify) to public officials.
- Provide an easy way for visitors to contribute financially.

- Highlight successes.
- Showcase outstanding work of members or staff or supporters or partners.
- Educate with issue briefs and statistics.
- Provide more detailed analyses with white papers and reports (you might need Adobe pdf files for these).
- Offer a virtual library of sources covering topics of interest.
- Do online surveys to develop consensus or gather data for advocacy efforts.
- Collect e-mails to add to your database for mobilization through e-mail or for sending your electronic newsletter.
- Publish fliers for your supporters to print, copy, and distribute.

SOURCE: Fox-McIntyre, 2001; Grobman, 2008; Quinn, 2005; Stein, 2001; Vernon & Lynch, 2000.

One final suggestion is that you put a number of Web links in your site that connect your visitors to similar sites. Web linked pages are among the most visited sites on the Web. Once you have featured someone else's site, you want them to do the same for you. Getting agreements with other sites to link to yours gets you into the club pretty quickly. Because some search engines even use this as a factor in ranking, it is worth the effort to make these connections.

Your ISP or hosting service should provide you with access logs and referrer logs to let you know which of your pages are viewed and when, as well as where visitors from your site came from before they stopped at your place. You can use this information to continue to refine your site and your links.

Putting all this together and, just as important, keeping it together requires the investment of time. Your credibility is strengthened and your purposes are served if you keep your site updated and maintained. While this could be a great way for volunteers, particularly younger members, to participate in the

development of your organization, remember that volunteers may drift away or may not really have the skills you need. Weigh the benefits of volunteer contributions and commitments against getting a sponsor to underwrite the operation of your website, including the service of a webmaster.

Include the fact of your Web page and its address in all your printed material, your voice mail, your e-mail signature, and in any slow-moving conversations. Your organization will soon reach farther than you had ever imagined.

Caution: If you ask people to contact you, they just might. You can get swamped with e-mail and other requests for your time and attention. Are you prepared for that?

E-Mail

The most basic and versatile means of reaching people is e-mail. If someone is interested in your cause and willing to support you, even if just by word of mouth, is there any reason you should not keep in touch?

Collect e-mail addresses from your website with a "we'd like to keep in touch with you" request or a "refer to a friend" button (Grobman, 2008). In fact, think of taking an e-mail address with you after every contact with a supporter. Make sure you create e-mail databases of supporters and members.

If you are a small organization, preparing a distribution list—a list of people to whom you want to send the same message—using the simple feature on your e-mail program will do the trick. Collect as many e-mail addresses from supporters as possible. Use the blind carbon copy feature whenever you send a note to a large distribution list. This avoids having a huge stack of addresses that gets in the way of your message. Also, people will appreciate that you're not announcing their addresses to everyone in the world. To avoid irritation, ask permission to place someone on your distribution list, or send a note to the entire list and ask people if they would like you to delete their names. Do check with your ISP to see how many addresses you can include in one mailing.

You may use e-mail to send and receive messages and bad jokes, but change agents can use this tool in a number of additional ways. You can use your distribution or mailing lists to e-mail brief news bulletins or (less frequently) calls for action or (even less frequently) special Action Alerts. Sending a regularly scheduled electronic newsletter to your list boosts interest and connection with the organization. A newsletter lets you provide more detailed information on aspects of the issue, development of the organization, any successes, and featured personalities. You continue to build an informed and potentially active constituency.

Develop different distribution lists from all the names you have. Some lists will be just the core, active members. Others may involve people who are working on a specific project. Maintain a list for your entire membership, and one that includes all members and supporters. Tailor your lists for the kind of information you want to communicate. Some information you only want members of your organization to see. Some will be geared to a larger audience. Some might be directed to a targeted group in the community such as elected officials.

It is helpful to have someone in your organization fill the role of list manager to make sure that all of your

lists are up to date with new participants and address changes. Another helpful tip is to put the name of your organization as the first item in the subject line, followed by the particular topic of the discussion. Not only does this help receivers of the message to recognize your e-mail, separating it from all the others that may flood their in-box, but it also helps receivers more easily organize your information into folders.

Mailing Lists and Discussion Lists and Web Groups. If you want to reach a lot of people, consider using a mailing list of your own in the same way that national organizations do to keep people informed of their efforts or to carry on discussions. Essentially there are three kinds of mailing lists: discussion, where every subscriber can post a message; moderated, where a moderator reviews each message before it gets posted; or announcement-only, where only the moderator posts messages (Levine, Baroudi, & Young, 2007). Unless you have a person who can actively moderate the discussion, you probably want either the first type for an open discussion or the last type for just sending information, like your newsletter.

To create your own mailing list operation, contact your ISP or contract with one of many companies that specialize in setting up mailing lists. GNU Mailman has free software for managing electronic mail discussion and e-newsletters. It also comes with a discussion list to help you solve problems. LISTSERV is a product, a brand, not just a process. It has become somewhat like Kleenex to be the generic name of the thing itself. LISTSERV Free Edition is a freeware version of LISTSERV Lite, limited to organizations that do not derive a profit from using the software. Yahoo! Groups and Google Groups also operate both as e-mail mailing lists and discussion forums, helping you to manage your list and how it is run. These are free services that provide a number of features, such as voting and calendaring, that can help your members talk with each other and work with each other.

The mailing list provider company can maintain your subscriber list and help manage the operation for you. You invite people to "subscribe" to—that is, participate on—the list. They don't pay anything to subscribe. All they have to do is send a simple, standard message (usually just a few words) to the mailing list address indicating their interest in joining.

With a mailing list, your organization can send a message to all the subscribers on your list. You can choose to have subscribers become recipients of updates or information, but this is really one-way communication. You can also create options for any subscriber to send a message to all other subscribers on the list; in this way discussion can occur. You can extend your mailing lists functions to include discussion groups of varying degrees of sophistication. Here you can have simple exchanges or threaded conversations about a particular project or issue that the organization is facing, develop methods for decision making, and increase member participation. These are usually intended for members of the organization itself.

Social Media

Sitting on the beach just outside of a small fishing village on the Sea of Cortez on the west coast of Mexico, I watched a fisherman cast his net over the side of his small boat, hoping he could pull in dinner for his family and some extra fish to sell at one of the fish markets in town. Not far off another fisherman was doing the same, and yet farther away, another. What would happen, I thought, if these nets grew bigger and continued to grow? How many fish could each catch? What, then, if these nets, still growing, got connected to each other, and to those of other fishermen beyond my view? And if these linked nets could be used efficiently, what then? Poor fish.

Welcome to social networking, one component of social media, which includes a number of Internet and mobile-based tools for sharing and discussing information. We are both the ones doing the fishing and we are the fish. While we are using these technologies to bring people together to support our issues and our work, others are casting about for our participation as well. Using social networking tools, our sets of contacts continue to grow as do the sets of contacts of those with

whom we are connected. Social networking enables us to communicate within and across networks, reaching an almost unimaginable number of people.

This kind of organizing has been with us for a long, long time. More than 50 years ago Saul Alinsky was organizing around churches in Chicago, connecting networks within and across congregations (Breckenfeld, 1960). Organizing has always been about generating awareness about an issue, finding people who are passionate about that issue, connecting them as a way of building power, and then putting that power into action to make change. You find people and their connections where they are. Today many people are online and their friends and associates are as well. In just one month in early 2009, for example, Compete.com (2009a) reported that Facebook alone had over 1.6 billion visits, up from 357 million just a year earlier.

One of the benefits (or consequences) of social media is that these tools encourage people to "live in the now." We are all living, breathing, and working in this new real time, and there is value in knowing what is happening right now, and knowing what is going on all over the world (Pendrys, 2009). Social network sites make visible the often invisible connections among people, so reaching all these people has become a whole lot easier and much more efficient. Alinsky (1972) taught us to work within the experience of the people we are organizing. Using online methods to build and maintain relationships is within the experience of many of the people we are organizing. They must be within our experience as well. I imagine that online networking is well within the experience of many who have just read this paragraph.

If you don't have your own Facebook page and are not tweeting or LinkedIn, you might dip your toe or keyboard into one of these sites to find out what people are doing and see firsthand how you can use these media for organizing. Most sites have good guides to help you learn about the site and how to use it. Take some time to explore and see how a site's particular functions fit with your organization's mission, goals, and activities.

The number of social media sites grows every day. This is not just an American phenomenon; it is international in scope. Each country or region has its favorite sites, but a number of sites have participants from all over the globe. Some sites have specific purposes, and others have unique audiences. A number of sites, such as Change.org, MoveOn.org, or Care2.org have been developed to promote social change. Ning.com helps you create your own site for free.

Each month new sites are developed and old ones fold. Some, like Twitter, were barely on the radar (itself a cool, new technology, once upon a time), and others, like MySpace, now perhaps fading, were emerging when the previous edition of this book was being prepared. Google Wave is a new communication tool being unveiled today that will merge your e-mail, Facebook, Twitter, and other avenues of communication into one browser. You soon may be sending waves, not just tweets or e-mails. Other features allow you to work collaboratively or play games, if you get tired of all that working. The next hot new phenomenon may well be on the way, just under today's radar. Who knows, it could be your site.

Many people participate in a number of different sites, and it can get complicated or time consuming to keep on top of all the information. Social network aggregators can help. They let users consolidate their profiles and pull together their friends and messages from across the various network sites they might participate in. OpenId, for example, allows users to log in just once to gain access to a number of sites rather than logging on to each one separately, and OpenSocial is being developed to provide more interoperability among sites.

Communicating through cursors, clicks, and keyboards may seem pretty impersonal for human services professionals. The central feature about social media, though, is the social impact. Social media promote relationships, which particularly for networking sites is the purpose, not just the by-product. Whether your online presence is as an individual or as an organization, you don't just send out information, you engage in two-way conversation. Communicating through profile-driven pages where the topic discussion is mixed with photos and tidbits of personal life humanizes the discourse.

Social media has a democratizing effect. People are learning from one another, gathering information, exchanging ideas, and giving feedback. They are actively engaged in both sending and receiving. They are shaping one another's views of the world, not just

accepting deliveries sent by broadcast distribution channels (Sarner, 2008). This makes social media enormously important for organizing.

Sometimes you will converse as an individual through your personal online presence and at others from your organization through its distinct online presence. In addition to your personal profile, Facebook, for example, gives you the opportunity to create your own groups, whose participants you select or approve. You may use this feature to work with those who are already part of your organization, affirming group identity, or you can create a group around a topic to recruit people to your organization, or to generate awareness and general support. In addition to group pages, you might consider another option, a fan page. While fan pages have been used by public personalities, they are also available for organizations to communicate with their fans or supporters. Assuming that your ego is in check, this is something that you may want to create for your organization. With a fan page you can target your messages, for example, by age or location. You can put a URL on your website or on your Facebook page to get people connected to your organization's fan page. When someone becomes your Facebook fan, she may suggest to her friends that they become your fans as well, and the connections continue to grow. Fan pages also let you add your blog feed, Twitter feed, and other outside content. Just like user profiles, fan pages have a wall, a central location where your organization's fans can post messages to you and where the organization can post news, information, and other messages as well. Whatever you publish to your page's wall can appear in the news feed on your fans' pages. You can go directly to them; they don't have to go find you. Other features let you organize information about your organization. There are other differences between group pages and fan pages to consider in determining how your organization can best become part of a social network.

> Twitter—A social networking tool to stay
> in touch, via brief updates, w/friends,
> acquaintances & interested strangers as you
> go through your day.

That tweet checks in at 139 characters.

Twitter is a form of micro-blogging, where users send very brief messages or "tweets" to other users known as "followers." These text messages are short

DID YOU KNOW?   Social Media and Standard Social Network Service Features

Social media sites fall into four general categories:

Social news: Digg, Sphinn, Newsvine, and BallHype let you read about news topics and then vote or comment on the articles. Articles with more votes are promoted to a more prominent position.

Social sharing: Flickr, Snapfish, YouTube, and Jumpcut let you create, upload, and share videos or photos with others.

Social bookmarking: Delicious, Faves, Stumble-Upon, BlogMarks, and Diigo allow you to find and bookmark sites and information of interest. You can save your bookmarks online and access them from anywhere or share them with others.

Social networks: Facebook, LinkedIn, MySpace, and Twitter allow you to find and link to other people. Once linked or connected, you can keep up to date with that person's contact information, interests, posts, and so on. Many people are connecting to friends and business associates with whom they had fallen out of touch. It's bringing the world together like nothing else has (Jones, 2009a).

The following features are pretty common for most social network sites:

- Post a profile and a picture.
- Control whom you accept as a friend and who can view your profile.
- Build a list of friends connected to your profile page; find friends in a variety of ways (name, school, e-mail addresses, ZIP codes, common interests or groups); friends are displayed on your profile.
- Become friends with others; connect to their page.
- Start your own group around a special topic, issue, or geographic area.

- Affiliate with a cause or group and invite others to affiliate; find out when they join a cause or group; make contributions to an organization.
- Post to your page or to others' pages and respond to postings on any pages you are connected to—ideas, current activities, notices of community events or issues—you can usually post in text or with attachments.
- Prepare and share photo albums.
- Send information automatically to all who are linked to you.

Many sites offer features that allow you to chat, using instant messaging, create events or organize get-togethers, share videos, import blogs from blogging services, offer your own blog, create a forum page for comments about a specific topic, provide a personal URL, open your own Internet store, and use your mobile device as well as your computer.

Think about how an organizer could put these to use. Here are just a few ideas.

- Get quick help or guidance on a project or a task.
- Bring issues to the attention of others.
- Provide information and news and event notices.
- Encourage financial support.
- Mobilize for action.
- Organize interest groups.
- Organize events.
- Continue to build your organization's base of supporters; you can track who is most visible in supporting your efforts, provide additional, more personal contact and invite for greater levels of involvement, including online leadership roles.
- Create broader community interest with buzz and viral communication getting broader notice.

and to the point, no more than 140 characters. Twitter is a unique form of social networking. It started as a way for friends to stay connected, answering the question, "What are you doing?" It has evolved to become a platform for news stories and for the exchange of social commentary (Stewart, 2009).

With its rapid growth and incorporation into the commerce of everyday life, it deserves some special mention here. Twitter is a social networking medium; users provide a personal profile, so it is used to build relationships as well as to exchange information. You select people you will follow. This could be a news reporter, a friend, a professional colleague, or someone who has written on a topic of interest to you. People may choose to follow you as well. Users can easily "unfollow" each other too.

According to Nielson Media Research, the number of unique visitors to Twitter increased 1,382% in one year: from 475,000 a year earlier to over 7 million in 2009 (McGiboney, 2009). Just 2 months later Compete.com noted that visitors had increased from the 7 million mark to more than 19 million. Lots of people are going to Twitter, but they may not be staying there. In 2009 more than 60% of American Twitter users failed to return the following month (Martin, 2009). This is a common phenomenon for a new social platform. MySpace and Facebook also experienced some departure of users in their early stages (Stewart, 2009). Twitter provides a quick way for you to gather and send information, keep your personal network alive, make new connections, and help brand your organization. At least at this stage Twitter is becoming a common way for more and more people to get the word out.

Text Messaging

Of course, you don't have to be online to send and receive messages. Texting is an increasingly popular form of communication to reach people no matter where they might be. In the United States more than half of cell phone users regularly text, and in Europe and Asia more than 70% use it (Covey, 2008). Certainly many young people have grown up with text messaging. When timely communication is necessary, texting enables you to communicate very quickly with members of your organization. Twitter uses the Internet to send messages, so you can send links and pictures with your message, but texting is just that—text. Though your message is likely to be limited to 160 characters or so, you can get your point across very quickly to a number of people at a time. They, of course, can spread the word by texting to a list of their friends. Mobilizing scores of people can be done in very little time.

Young Americans between the ages of 13 and 17 sent or received almost 2,900 text messages per month in 2009. This is an increase of more than 1,000 texts per month over the previous year and up 566% from 2007 (Nielsen Company, 2009).

Others are catching on as well. Those between 35 and 44 are approaching 250 texts a month. In fact, Americans are using their mobile phones much more often to send texts than to make phone calls (Covey, 2008). The wireless information trade organization CTIA (2009) reported that by the end of 2008, Americans were sending about 110 billion messages a month, 10 times the number sent just 3 years earlier.

Instant Messaging

What if you want to have a back and forth conversation with one of your buddies, maybe even do some work together online without your words being restricted to a limited number of characters? Instant messaging is one way to do this. To open this option for communication, you first have to connect with a messaging service such as AIM through America OnLine (AOL), ICQ (cute for "I Seek You,"), Skype, Google Talk, Yahoo Messenger, or Windows Live Messenger. You may already have software for an instant messaging service loaded on your computer. Then you create a "buddy list" or a "contact list." The service, which is free, alerts you whenever one of your buddies is online at the same time you are, and it lets your buddies know that you are online. You can also leave a status message that lets your contacts know what you are doing at the moment, and most services will let you connect with your Twitter account. Buddies can simply contact each other and begin working or just chatting. Some services let you send a message to one of your selected partners who is offline, saving it, like e-mail, for when she goes back online. Most also provide options for using your mobile phone, including texting, and some instant messaging services now offer video conferencing as well.

Competition among major companies has interfered with using a common standard for this technology. You may not be able to contact people who are not using the system that you use.

Blogs

A blog, short for Weblog, is a website used for an ongoing discussion of a topic of interest. The author or authors post information to the blog in the form of articles that are listed chronologically,

??? DID YOU KNOW?   Twitter Tools and Tips

A number of tools and related resources have been developed to help your tweeting. New ones are being created all the time. Here is just a sampling.

Tools

Twitter Search: keyword search that brings up anyone throughout the world who has tweeted about a topic. You can also find people by their company or organization. This is a quick way to make connections.

Tweet Deck: a personal browser that allows you to see all of your friends' tweets and keeps you connected with your contacts across Twitter, Facebook, and other sites. You can group friends into different columns to keep things organized and create a column for the results of your keyword search. The browser can help you craft your tweets to shorten them and even help translate them into a different language. (Seemic DESK-TOP, which allows you to manage multiple accounts, and Twhirl are other similar tools.)

URL shortening services: helps to shorten those lengthy URLs that take up a lot of characters. TinyURL, bit.ly, and Snipurl are examples of these services.

Tweetscan: sends you an e-mail when one of your keywords was mentioned on Twitter.

Tweetbeep: lets you know when you, your organization, or any other keyword you want to track is mentioned on Twitter.

Twittonary, Sitemasher, and Twictionary: can help you understand and sling the lingo.

Twitter Site: has information on other tools on the Applications page, and the Twitter Support page provides a helpful guide.

Tips

*   You can follow your tweets on your iPhone or other smartphone.
*   You can send Twitter updates through your Facebook account.
*   Generally use your real name for your Twitter ID, and make sure to put your organization's name in your profile. Consider using your organization's name instead of a nickname to help brand your organization and help people find you.
*   Remember that your Twitter name counts within your 140 character limit.
*   Include a "follow me on Twitter" signature on all of your e-mail accounts or for your social media e-mail signature.
*   Follow people with similar interests to help you understand how Twitter conversations work. This will help you learn the etiquette. Don't be afraid to ask questions.
*   Remember that you are building relationships. Provide things that people like, such as statistics, links, opinions, and tips.

SOURCE: Evans, 2008; Jones, 2009b, 2009c; Pendrys, 2009.

with the most recent article on top. Blogs not only send out the author's views on the topic, but most also provide a way for other people to leave comments about the articles. Blogs create the possibility for generating interest through two-way communication. An energizing element of a blog is replying to comments or feedback. Responding to others' ideas and opinions and posing questions of your own keeps the conversation going. You build a following and attract attention to your personal or organization's blog when you create a commenting culture.

Though most blogs are mainly text, they can use a combination of text, pictures, and links to other Web pages and to other blogs. Successful blogs update content frequently. That is a key feature of this communication tool. Though most often blogs are personal publishing tools, organizations can make use of this approach as well. You can include your blog on your organization's website as another way of promoting awareness and analysis of your issue.

It is pretty easy to set up a blog that has a good layout and the features that you want. Free blogging software and publishing platforms, such as WordPress, can provide what you need to get started, including an understanding of this medium and tips for effective use.

CHANGE AGENT TIP

E-mail lists, social networks, tweeting, and texting are powerful tools to quickly notify your members of an action that needs to be taken immediately. All of these are useful tools for action alerts. Maybe you need a large number of supporters to contact an elected official just before a key vote or to turn out for a public demonstration of solidarity. At times it may be important to flood a local television station with protests over unfair coverage. A strong immediate response capability will impress opponents and supporters alike.

Bloggers reach out to their particular audience, but through their ability to interact with other bloggers they can extend their point of view to other audiences as well, providing another form of viral communication. You may decide to use blogging to contribute to a broader understanding of your issue, helping to promote a climate for change. You can link your blog to your social networking site, like your Facebook page or Twitter account. Bloggers have had a significant effect on national debates, even influencing how the more traditional press handles issues.

Tools for Working Together

How about Tuesday at 9:00? No, okay, Wednesday afternoon? Can't do Wednesday? Thursday morning is booked for me. Any other morning? Let's try.... You have been in that conversation, haven't you? You can spend a lot of your time together just trying to arrange for the next meeting or conference call, or you could try a simple, free online service to help you discover that break in the clouds when the sun shines on a time available for most of you. Maybe you are trying to get your members to make a decision on something other than meeting time, or you want to gather opinions on a community issue. There's help online for you as well.

Getting Together and Making Decisions

- *Outlook Calendar* is a simple tool for exchanging calendar information among those who share the same server and are using the same software. It has limited features, but it is a good start for finding a common time among people, such as workers in the same agency, who share this tool.
- *Meeting Wizard* is available to anyone connected to the Internet. Meeting Wizard

automatically invites participants to the meeting or event, sends alternative times, summarizes results, and communicates them to you. You review the responses, confirm the time, and Meeting Wizard lets everyone know. It will also send reminders. You can add personalized notes and make changes if needed. The service lets you make arrangements for up to 50 people, and it is free. Meeting Wizard also works with Outlook.

- *Doodle*, like Meeting Wizard, is available on the Web. This free service helps you arrange a meeting or events by conducting a poll offering different choices. This is a simple matter of creating a poll and forwarding the link to all participants. There is no maximum number of participants in a poll. You could try to arrange a meeting or an event for a thousand people if you want to. Doodle can be used for a number of other purposes as well. Anything involving doing something together, such as sharing rides to an out-of-town activity or choosing the name of a new neighborhood park, can be done with Doodle. You can access Doodle with Outlook, from your mobile phone, or through your Facebook account.

- *Survey Monkey* provides another option to help with decision making. This service helps you to design and send surveys that look professional and include a variety of different question forms. You can send your survey through e-mail or put a link on your website. Many features are free for up to 100 respondents. Using added custom features and sending your survey to an unlimited number of respondents still only costs a couple hundred dollars a year.

Communication and collaboration are important elements for any enterprise. A number of companies have products that will let people working at different locations help craft a written document, prepare a presentation, exchange ideas by creating a wiki, or create group "to do" lists, complete with reminders. *Zoho*, for example, provides a suite of about 20 different applications to help members of your organization work more efficiently and effectively. Some are free for personal use, and discounts are provided to nonprofits.

Conferencing.   You and your colleagues can meet or work together without ever having to get in that car—or on a plane. In addition to the conferencing options previously mentioned, video and audio conferencing can help you and your members and constituents join talents.

Video conferencing allows you to see everyone you are working with. Each person has a window on the monitor. You can talk, see reactions, and get things done, just like a face-to-face meeting. Of course, it is a face-to-face meeting, but one where participants can be thousands of miles apart. Such a conference is called a multipoint conference.

To conduct a video conference, you need a webcam, a microphone, and some software. You can get the camera and microphone for $100 or less. Your computer may even come equipped with these features. Software programs such as Skype, ooVoo, and SightSpeed, or iChat for your Mac are free for groups of five people or fewer. Many companies provide video conferencing for larger groups, with numerous features. There is quite a range of prices. With a little homework you can find something affordable.

Audio conferencing is like having a telephone conference call without the expense. You can also use the audio component of your video conferencing software to connect members by voice if they don't have video equipment. You may need a headset with earphones and a microphone to turn your computer into a phone that can connect people from around the city or around the world with no long distance charges. Many companies provide audio conferencing, and quite a few offer free versions.

If it is difficult for people to get together because distances are too great or schedules too hectic, and conferencing over the Internet is not an option, a simple telephone conference may be in order. If your organization's work involves a public agency, you may be able to use their teleconferencing services. By searching the Internet you can find a number of companies who specialize in telephone conferencing. Some firms charge you a per minute fee to set up an 800 number or provide you with a free connection, with those calling long distance paying normal long distance rates.

Constituent Relationship Management.   You are feeling pretty good. You have managed to gain attention for your organization and the issues on which it is working. A number of people have given you money or their time, attended events, and shown other forms of support. Don't want to lose track of them, do you? You want to keep your base of support strong and continue to build that base. Constituent relationship management (CRM) is built on customer relationship management methods used by businesses. CRM is "the set of processes and supporting technologies used to acquire, retain, and enhance constituent relationships. Constituent refers to all people with some relationship to the organization—donors, funders, volunteers, clients, and all other people who help the organization achieve its mission or are benefactors of the mission" (Hagen, 2006, p. 1). You may have names and contact information in various files, lists, even on scraps of paper. Maybe some in your organization's leadership has a set of constituents, and others have some of these and a lot of different ones. Or, you may have things in one place, easy to find and easy for key members of your organization to work with.

Hagen (2006) contrasts organizations and their relationship with constituents. Some are in constituent chaos, with information scattered all about. Some are self-centric, focusing their attention inward, and like those in chaos, miss many opportunities to engage supporters and cross-promote different aspects of the organization. Others are in the enlightened Stone Age, actively seeking to have high-quality interactions with their constituents, but with many different forms of data collection and storage that makes this difficult. Organizations that are relationship-centric have constituent information that is reliable and easy to access, and they regularly make use of information to cross-promote different aspects of the organization involving constituents in fund-raising, mobilization, awareness, and other forms of support.

A number of companies offer CRM products. CiviCRM is a freely downloadable Web-based, open source CRM that is designed specifically for advocacy, nonprofit, and nongovernmental groups. Others provide discounts or even free licensing for nonprofits. Don't be surprised if you have to customize the package to best fit your organization's requirements.

You might explore techniques like webinars or podcasts to help you bring knowledge about your issue and support to your organization or find some other tools to promote awareness, connection, and action. Tools we have discussed in other chapters, like mapping technology or online fund-raising, can also be put into your digital toolbox. New technology is not new for long. Soon another new wrinkle or brand new tool will open up more possibilities. We may not know what that will be, but we do know that more and more people are finding new ways to exchange information and ideas, and build relationships. As organizers we need to find people where they are. As organizers we are always eager to find better, more effective ways to connect people to the issue, to the organization, to the action, and to each other. As organizers we understand that as a matter of cultural competence we need to communicate within the frameworks of the people we are organizing.

MESSAGE METHODS OTHER PEOPLE CONTROL

Some people are in the business of communicating information, and at times you will use them to help get the word out. You can pay public relations and advertising companies to help you with this. Among other services, they will help you design materials and develop and buy advertising. If you

have oodles of money, you may want to buy their expertise. Check around to determine what professional assistance and paid advertising can do for you and which agency can best serve your needs.

Most change efforts, however, aren't beset by the problem of what to do with all that extra cash. They need to figure out how to do things for little or no money. Some people in the communication business will help you publicize your concerns for little or no cost. These fall into four categories: other groups and organizations, public service advertising, entertainment and public affairs programming, and news media.

Again we get into this "you" business. As I have pointed out, *you* includes you and all the other people in your organization as well. This is particularly true when it comes to communicating outside your group to the rest of the community. If your mug is always in front of the cameras, if your words are the only ones quoted in the press, people outside your organization and, sadly, also those within it, will begin to think that the organization is pretty much just you and a bunch of followers. Worse, it can affect you this way too.

Make a special effort to have a number of faces for the public to see and a variety of voices who can speak on the issues you (all) are facing. To establish easy access to your group, identify a particular individual as a contact person for those outside the organization who want to get your group's views and reactions to issues or events. The contact person may then help connect those who have such requests with any one of the organization's members who is prepared to respond. It may be appropriate to have one contact person, but it is most definitely not right to feel that only one person really knows what is going on, that only one person should have the limelight. A number of people can represent you well if representation becomes an expectation and a responsibility. Some members will be better than others, yes, but some are definitely better than one.

Other Groups and Organizations

The main ways other groups can help you are by allowing you to make a presentation to their members and by providing you space or coverage in their publications and links on their website. Think

GLOBAL PERSPECTIVES

PAPUA, NEW GUINEA—Real dialogue (or deep mutual personal speaking and listening)…is not just telling, it is listening. It is not just teaching, it is learning *with*. It is not extending knowledge, it is discovering the richness of knowledge already present in the life of the people…. As the animator listens and shares in the life of the community, he/she will become aware of the discontents, the worries, the deep and nagging questions of the people, the social, economic, and political affairs. As the animator begins to see and understand, then his/her role becomes more concrete because now the animator can help the people to see. This can be done by re-presenting to the people the life situations they are having difficulty seeing. Their condition is like being inside a box and therefore not being able to see the box. A representation can help the people to get out of the box to see it (Melanesian Council of Churches, 1977, p. 220).

BRAZIL—The Community Empowerment Network (CEN) is attempting to foster an environment of empowerment in target communities. Coordination between the communities is a vital step toward this goal. The people best qualified to address the issues facing these communities are those who live there. As such, facilitating easier communication, coordination, and collaboration between these populations is one of CEN's main objectives. CEN has created Rede Amazônia (the Amazon Network), an online and off-line network for collaboration between rural communities. Activities have included introducing individuals with similar interests over e-mail and Skype and community exchanges between communities (Community Empowerment Network, 2009).

CROATIA—Anti-government protests organized on Facebook fizzled Friday when roughly 3,500 people turned out for a demonstration that organizers hoped would draw 60,000. About 2,500 people gathered in the capital, Zagreb. Several hundred turned up in Croatia's second-largest city, Split, and a few hundred more in five other cities to protest government austerity measures.

"It's easier to click a mouse, in the safety of your home, than show up in public," said Jaksa Matovinovic, a spokesman for the group that organized the protest.

Still, the protests demonstrated that online social networks have began to have some political impact in this former Yugoslav republic, where only 2 in 5 households have access to the Internet.

The Facebook group, called "Tighten your own belt, you gang of knaves," criticized Prime Minister Ivo Sanader's measures to fight a potential financial crisis, saying they would hurt the average Croat while politicians and the rich would be unscathed. It also blames the government for failing to fight crime and corruption.

"Only united we are becoming a force that no one can ignore," the group's leader, Josip Dell Olio, told the crowd in Zagreb (Vukic, 2008).

---

of all the publications in your community in addition to the regular newspapers: church bulletins, employee newsletters, social service newsletters, and community interest group mailings, to name a few. Most of these are potential vehicles to carry your message to a specific constituency. This is particularly true if the group's interests are similar to yours or if a member of another group is involved in your project.

Personally contact the individual in charge of the publication. Be ready to explain how information on your project would be valuable or of interest to their readers. Ask for publication guidelines and deadlines. You will be surprised at how frequently your request for publication is accepted.

Groups who share a similar viewpoint can assist you in other ways. On some occasions, say, at a news conference or a public hearing, other organizations may offer public statements on your behalf to lend emphasis and credibility to your assertions. They can also help by making routine announcements for you to their own constituencies. When you thank assisting organizations for their help, let them know of any reaction or benefit you received as a result of their assistance.

Public Service Advertising

Many change efforts use this form of communication to enhance their efforts to reach the public. The standard approaches include free billboard space, newspaper community announcement columns, electronic bulletin boards, and radio and television public service announcements.

HALFWAY THROUGH HIS PRESENTATION MYRON WAS STRUCK BY THE FACT THAT HIS AUDIENCE DID NOT SEEM IMPRESSED WITH THE NEED FOR FAMILY PLANNING.

TODAY'S LECTURE: FAMILY PLANNING

Billboards. Outdoor advertising companies often donate billboard space to community groups for special projects or events. Usually, this also includes the cost for putting up the signs. The signs are posted on a space-available basis. This means that some of your signs may stay up for a long time in some very out-of-the-way location or for a short time in a prime spot. Customarily all you have to pay for is printing. The billboard company can direct you to printers who handle this type of work, and the outdoor advertising company will show you how to design a billboard, including some tricks that will help you reduce your printing costs. Be aware that your sign should have no more than 10 words on it. Also, the sign company may not be sure just when there will be free space to hang your sign, so make sure you give them plenty of lead time. There may be a nominal cost, but even in this case it will be a fraction of normal retail costs.

Newspapers. Newspapers run several community announcement columns. Typically, one column provides information on upcoming community events, whereas another describes services or resources available in the community. Each column appears regularly on a certain day, perhaps every

Sunday or every Thursday. Watch for the section in which the columns run, and then contact the editor for that section. The editor will let you know what you have to do to get your information printed.

Many newspapers have an online events column listing more community activities than appear in the paper. You can go to the paper's website and add your event to the list there as well.

Electronic Bulletin Boards. A number of communities have their own bulletin board and allow groups to post events and other activities. Some larger organizations, such as the United Way, also provide bulletin boards offering a community calendar.

Public Service Announcements. Some of the following suggestions are drawn from information prepared for the United Way by Ruby and O'Brien (1978), Smucker (1999), and Communications Consortium Media Center (2009). Public service announcements (PSAs) are not the same thing as news stories. They are, in effect, commercials for your project. They are handled by different departments at the television and radio stations and are seen as a service to the community and to the organization featured. They usually describe a service the organization offers, a need the organization has, or an upcoming organization activity. Because of the growth of cable networks and media presence on the Internet, there are a growing number of outlets for PSAs. Local television and radio are still the most common on-air places to run your local organization's PSA.

Print media. In addition to mainstream newspapers, community newspapers and shopping guides are good places for your ad. If your ads are produced digitally and you use a common graphics program, the publication can easily reformat the ad to fit the space available (Davis, 2009).

Radio PSAs. Radio PSAs are pretty easy to prepare. It is helpful to contact each station to find out if any particular format is preferred. This serves a number of purposes. First, it establishes contact between you and the station. Second, it helps you provide the station with material that is easy for it to use. Third, it gives you a good reason to do a follow-up contact with the station to ask if your materials were in the proper form and if they have any questions regarding the content. You are really doing a follow-up to remind them of who you are and to reinforce the importance of your announcement. Follow-up contact is important whether or not you made a previous contact. Now, most public service directors will tell you this isn't necessary, that they will air whatever they can fit in. In actual practice, though, they do develop certain preferences, whether they know it or not. They tend to air more frequently those announcements that are easy for them to handle, that are well written and well prepared, and that help people they know and like. I have seen significant differences in results between groups who simply send out material and hope it gets played and those who put in a little extra effort to establish contact and prepare their material well.

Make no mistake, this is a very competitive business. Radio stations routinely receive many requests for "free advertising." You need to do something to make yours stand out from the rest. Here are some guidelines to help increase the odds that your message will get on the airwaves.

- Write your message in a way that sounds good when it is read out loud. Most radio PSAs aren't prerecorded, though some are. The deejays don't want to read a statement that sounds too awkward or stilted. Read your announcement over a few times and modify it until you get the right sound. Though the deejays will probably change it a bit themselves to suit their own style, the less work they have to do, the better.

- Time your announcement. Standard spots are 10, 15, or 30 seconds in length. Often stations just want their deejays to describe your announcement in a sentence or two. Each station will have its preferred standard. At the end of each announcement, note its length. Remember that professional announcers can read with emphasis faster than you can. A general guideline is two and one-half words per second.

- Type your announcements in large type using capital letters only. If you have proper names, spell them out phonetically as well. Use double or triple spacing and wide margins. Some stations that use shorter PSAs prefer that the announcements be typed on index cards.

- Include some sort of hook to get the listeners' attention. People don't remember boring messages. Probing questions, humor, and dramatic statistics are good devices. Some stations like announcements that have some emotional content (but refrain from being too melodramatic); others prefer messages that are purely descriptive or factual. If you haven't discovered preferences while doing your "homework" on the stations, then send two versions of the same announcement.

- If you include a phone number in your announcement, it should be the last thing in your announcement. Repeat the number if you can.

- Some stations will let you record your own PSA. This personalizes the message more. Using your own name in the announcement ("Hello, I'm Carl Kadukey of…") further individualizes it.

- If you have an ongoing need for public service airtime, consider using a 3 weeks on, 2 months off airing schedule. Periodically rewrite your messages. This schedule keeps your messages fresh with both the audience and the station, and it gives the impression that you are always around.

- Enclose a brief cover letter with your material. This should describe who you are, mention the importance of the announcement to the community and your program, and ask the station for their help in informing the public.

- If you can make the time (and you really should try), it will help your cause to hand deliver your announcements to the station. This is particularly true the first few times you work with a station before you get to know the people at the station and they get to know you.

- Send a follow-up thank-you to stations that aired your message. Note any response you received from the community that could be related to their support.

Television PSAs. The process for television public service announcements is similar to that for radio except that television PSAs have both the benefit of, and the requirement for, visual support. You can make your production as simple or as complex as your time, skill, and budget will allow. Television stations prefer to air announcements that are well made, so even if your production is simple, avoid looking cheap.

There is a lot of help available to assist you in producing your spot. Community access cable television stations will train you in the use of video equipment. Students from the media or public relations departments of the local college may be able to help you as part of a class project. Advertising companies occasionally donate their services to the right cause if requested to do so by the right person. Even the local network affiliate station may produce your announcement at very little cost if a key person at the station takes a real interest in your project. Here are some suggestions to help you get your message across.

- Get to know the public service director at each station. The person who fills this role will also have other duties at the station. She will give you helpful directions on how to work effectively with the station. Because each station may have some unique procedures, ask for directions and follow them.

- If you are using still pictures and artwork instead of video, remember that a television screen has a 3:4 ratio, so any artwork you prepare should conform to that ratio. Pictures that convey action are usually better than those showing someone's face, unless the face communicates a certain drama or elicits an emotional response. Use one picture for every 8 to 10 seconds of audio. Too many different visuals are distracting.

- Having a local personality as a spokesperson can give you credibility and recognition. It also makes producing the spot a relatively easy matter. (Do not use a media personality or your spot will only run on the station for which the individual works.) Avoid the talking head approach; cut away from the speaker a couple of times to show some other action, or have the speaker involved in the action. Get a signed release from each person seen in your announcement.

- Your visuals will tell your story. Thoughtfully consider what you want your viewer to feel. Then choose images that will produce that response. In fact, turn the sound off when you are reviewing your PSA. If you are getting your point across well by the visuals alone, you have done a good job.

- Prepare an audio script, perhaps including music that evokes a response from the viewer and complements the video portion of your spot.

- Include your phone number and website address.

- Standard television PSAs are 10, 15, or 30 seconds in length. Many PSAs are 30-second productions, but 10-second or even 9-second spots have a better chance of airing. There may be more open time slots for this length, and you will probably be competing against fewer spots.

- You may have a better chance of getting your spot aired on independent stations. Though their audience may be smaller, this may be offset by the fact that your announcement is shown more often. It is worth it to make a special effort with these stations.

- Many stations are willing to make a dub (a copy) of your PSA and to send the dub to other stations.
- Get to know the traffic manager at each station. This person slots the paid commercials and the PSAs and, in some cases, has discretion in deciding which PSAs get aired and when. If there is some open time that can be filled with PSAs, and they know you and like your project…. Well, you get the picture.

Entertainment and Public Affairs Programming

Essentially this approach involves appearances on talk shows. Community talk shows have long been the staple of local Sunday television programming, competing with the roosters for the attention of early-morning risers or the drowsy late-afternoon viewer after all the day's games have been played. The weekday midmorning slot also finds an occasional audience. Not exactly prime time. The main thing, though, is that there is an audience. You will reach some people who have an interest in your community, and you have the opportunity to educate and build a relationship with one of the station's on-camera personalities, even if he is not yet one of the stars. An additional benefit is that it makes your supporters feel good. There is something about being on TV that makes people seem and feel important. It also hones your skills in representing your project to the public. What you receive from an appearance on one of these programs is certainly worth the small effort they require.

Radio talk shows are quite a different matter. These programs continue to hold popularity and influence. Often looking for controversial topics, they provide an ideal medium for your message. Since many of these shows are of the call-in variety, you have the chance to interact with your audience to directly influence some perceptions and to get people talking about what you are up to and why.

Knowing something about your audience is helpful. The Pew Research Center for the People

and the Press (2008) reported that the audience for political talk radio is more conservative and more Republican than the public at large. Of the regular listeners, 44% describe themselves as conservative, which is more than twice the only 19% who consider themselves liberals. More conservative Republicans, 28%, regularly listen to radio shows that invite listeners to call in to discuss current events, public issues, and politics compared with only 17% of the general public. Your talk radio audience is more likely to be men than women.

A number of simple steps can help you take advantage of the potential these television and radio programs offer you.

- *Do a little homework on the show itself.* Watching or listening to the show a few times before your appearance will give you a sense of the program's flavor and an understanding of how the host approaches topics and works with the guest. You may pick up on the host's biases, way of asking questions, or a propensity to do most of the talking or to let the guest have a free rein. Most hosts want to set their guests at ease because a comfortable guest is a talkative and engaging guest.

- *Get the facts straight.* Your use of statistics or ability to cite a particular study communicates that you are well informed on the subject and deserve some consideration. A simple technique is to prepare an index card that outlines the points you want to address. Next to each, note a statistic or reference to jog your memory. When doing a radio show, you can keep your index cards right in front of you as well as any other material you want to use. If you are doing a call-in show, you are likely to hear from people who disagree with you or who don't fully understand your perspective. This gives you a wonderful opportunity to show the strength of your ideas. While preparing, review your list of points and imagine that you are on "the other side." What would your objections be? Consider how your facts and reasoning could counter those objections. You can add these notes to your index cards as well. This exercise will help you communicate to supporters and opponents alike.

CHANGE AGENT TIP

Orchestrate call-in shows. This is a simple way for you to influence the direction of the conversation in a way that puts your efforts in the most favorable light. You have taken some pains to get airtime and to prepare yourself well. Now complete the job. Use the airtime fully to your benefit. I am surprised at how rarely this is effectively done.

You need just a handful of supporters, each prepared with two questions. Each person has a primary question and a backup question in case an "unscheduled" caller phones in with a question that is close to one of your prepared ones. Use good judgment. Don't overdo things, and don't ask a question that has already been asked by someone else.

When you prepare your questions, include some that appear to be hostile to or in opposition to your point of view, but ones for which you have a good answer. Also, write them in the way that people really talk. Perfectly proper grammar and a two-dollar vocabulary are not commonplace on call-in shows. Establish some kind of order or time schedule for your supporters to call in.

"I'd feel a little silly doing this," you might be thinking. Don't worry, most people do. In fact, that's usually enough to get them to waste this golden opportunity to communicate their ideas and shape a part of the community's perception. Is that important to you? It's your call.

- *Provide background material to the show host.* When you schedule your appearance, ask the host how much in advance he would like this information from you. Usually a week in advance is sufficient. You can suggest this. Provide the host with a small packet of information regarding your effort that includes a one-page description of your group, what it intends to accomplish, and why. Also, provide a set of sample questions that address points you would like to have emphasized and that can guide the host in developing additional questions. Clearly indicate that these are sample questions; don't imply that the host is incapable of coming up with inquiries of his own. (The less controversial your project, the more comfortable the host will be in using these questions.) Other elements can include newspaper stories on your project, position papers or statements you have produced, a list of your goals and objectives, a list of your accomplishments, general project descriptions, or brochures. Don't overwhelm the host. Just pick from whatever you have that would give someone a good understanding of your concerns and your organization, and use a marking pen to highlight key sections.

  You want to make things as easy for the host as possible. A well-prepared host invigorates the discussion and helps you emphasize important topics. The easier you make the host's job, the more willing he will be to work with you. It is also more likely that you will be invited back.

- *Be interesting.* Use stories, examples, and humor to illustrate your points. Data in monotone is the scourge of the talk show. The only demon nearly as scary is the guest who can utter only the words yes and no. You don't need to be Chris Rock, but you do want people to take an interest in what you have to say. The simplest direction is to tell your story in human terms. There is a lot of truth in the saying that the death of a thousand people is a statistic; the death of one man or woman is a tragedy. How can your audience see themselves, their family or friends, or the things they value in what your organization cares about or what it is doing? What can they find funny or frustrating or moving? Guests who are engaging, well informed, well prepared, and who make the host's job easy are welcome ones.

Talk shows give you an opportunity to personalize your organization and its concerns. They give recognition to your efforts, a boost to your supporters, and help you reach people with whom you would not ordinarily have direct contact. They can attract a few new supporters, quite a few opponents, and encourage the climate for change.

Local News Media

She lowered the microphone from my face, and then paused so I could fully appreciate her point. "Mark," she said after a moment, "this is a news interview, not a public service announcement. If you want to make a public service announcement, contact our public service department. If you have a news story, we can keep talking." I wonder if my red face, which did fortunately make an appearance on the news that evening, caused people to adjust the color on their set.

What is news, and how do you get the people in the news media to report it, preferably in a way that furthers your interests? News is something that has just happened or is about to happen. It is unusual, affects a lot of people, affects someone generally considered to be important, or affects someone the audience can identify with. If it happens in the immediate vicinity of the audience, it is especially important. Some of the information in this section was drawn from Rathbun (1986) and materials developed by the editors of the *Arizona Daily Star* (1988), Daun (1991), Kimble (1991), Johnson (1991; personal communication, 1999), Cross (1992), Lefton (1992), Buckholtz (2001), J. K. Lesher (personal communication, 2002), Kornmiller (2005a, 2005b), Minch (2005), SPIN Project (2006, 2008), and Bonk, Tynes, Griggs, and Sparks (2008).

The number of Americans who get their news online continues to grow. Overall, 37% of the public say they get their news online, which is more than triple the number 10 years ago (Pew Research Center for People and the Press, 2008). This has led to changes in local media with newspapers reducing staff, increasing their online presence—some offering Internet chats with reporters, or closing altogether. Local television stations are also cutting back and promoting their online sites. Some newspapers are moving to including more columnists from the community, which creates more opportunity for your organization to gets its views into the public discussion (Bonk et al., 2008).

News is something you would be interested in even if you were not involved with the story. If you don't think you or the people you know would be interested, it probably isn't news. Publicity isn't news either. Publicity is designed to promote a person or a group, not to inform the public. True, there are gray areas, and promotion does on occasion pass for news. However, an organization that is intent only on promoting and not informing will soon wear out its welcome with members of the news media.

Some of these items can be news for an organization:

- Election of officers
- Opening of an office or headquarters
- Issues and events
- Significant projects
- Actions that attract attention or have consequences for the community
- Significant community meetings
- Benefits
- Important speakers, important visitors
- Release of the results of studies or fact-finding activities
- Special awards won or given
- Member participation in national or world affairs
- Unusual fund-raising ideas
- Community classes offered

The size of your organization and the significance it has in your community will determine the extent to which any of these items will pass as news.

During the fall some media, particularly print media, begin planning projects for the next year. These are ideas that take a while to put together and consume the time of several departments. They are likely to be investigative and have broad appeal. This is a good time to contact your local paper (which may well be part of a national chain) to offer story ideas for the upcoming year. Typically, the ideas need to answer three questions (Kornmiller, 2005a):

- What?—define the issue.
- So what?—why anyone should care.
- Now what?—what could happen.

For news to be reported it must meet the criteria of interest and accuracy. News needs to be of interest to a good portion of the audience, and the facts must be correct. What you read about in the paper, hear on the radio, or watch on the 6 o'clock news is a combination of hard news and feature stories. Hard news mainly includes events and occurrences, whereas features touch on stories of human interest or offer more

CHANGE AGENT TIP

The SPIN Project (2002) suggests that organizations create an Online Press Room to support their media relations efforts. Your Online Press Room can provide the following for access by reporters:

- breaking news
- previous news releases and press clips
- background information on your organization

- background information, briefings, and context for complicated issues
- data, charts, and graphics
- subscription to a LISTSERV that sends out weekly e-mail alerts to reporters and interested readers.

Provide easy-to-find contact information so a reporter can call you for an explanation or more information.

---

in-depth information on a subject rather than on an incident.

News coverage can accomplish a variety of purposes. Eric Weltman (2004) has outlined a number of benefits for your group:

- Educate the general public about a problem.
- Pressure decision makers.
- Show levels of support.
- Provide public visibility for your organization.
- Promote an event.
- Show donors the work you are doing.
- Involve people in your work, for example, by inviting important local officials or new coalition partners to an event, like a press conference.

For news to be reported in a way that furthers your group's interests, you must provide good, accurate, informative facts that put your group's concerns in a good light and respect the professionalism of the people in the news media. Your major local newspaper or journalism society, or perhaps a public interest group, may publish a manual to assist you in working with the media.

Getting in or on the news is essentially a business of form, of information, and of relationships. I'd have to say that good relationships are surely as important as anything else. Let's take a look at how these relationships are built.

Building Productive Relationships.   Just who are these news people, and how do you get to know them? Almost anyone who makes decisions on what gets printed or aired as news is a potentially valuable person to know. For the print media, mainly

newspapers, the key people are the city editor, the assignments editor, feature and editorial page editors, editorial writers, and reporters, both the beat reporters and the general assignment reporters. The beat reporters will probably be the most important among this group. Of course, it doesn't hurt to know the managing editor and the publisher either, but they are not as immediately involved with writing and preparing stories and editorials.

For radio and television the cast is about the same. Most radio stations have pretty lean news operations. In addition to the news director, radio stations also have people who read the news, and a few have full-time reporters. The news and talk stations have larger news departments, but even these are pretty small except in major news markets. Local affiliate television stations and some independent stations have standard news departments. You will notice different levels of commitment to the news operation even among stations in the same city. The most important personnel for you to know in television news are the assignments editor and the producer. Also helpful to know, but of lesser importance to getting your story on the air, are the reporters, the news director, and the anchor people. Both radio and television stations have station managers who set the general policies of the station, but they are not typically involved in the day-to-day production of newscasts.

Editors make the basic decisions in news operations. For example, they decide what types of stories they are looking for, which stories will be covered, the amount of attention the story will merit, and which reporter will be assigned to a particular story. Editors have most of the formal power, but they work behind the scenes. The people with whom you will have the most face-to-face contact and with whom you will most likely develop a relationship are the reporters. Reporters can influence editors' decisions, and they do the most critical job on the news team—they report the story. Reporters gather information, decide what is important (the angle), and communicate their impressions through the story they prepare. Television news producers are becoming more influential in deciding what they want to air and the story angles. Though the editors decide which stories get covered, reporters can and do suggest story ideas. Don't forget that your current reporter friend may one day become an editor.

To identify reporters who may be interested in your issues, watch the news and read the paper. Don't overlook community, ethnic, and independent media as well. Notice which reporters seem to cover which types of stories. Newspapers have some reporters assigned to a particular beat. These reporters look for and report stories on particular subjects; for example, the goings-on at City Hall, crime, health, or economic matters. They also have general assignment reporters who are not tied to a specific area. However, even these reporters do have some areas of interest, though they may not always be free to pursue them. A few television reporters have a specific area on which they concentrate, but most work on general assignment with some particular areas of interest and expertise. By paying close attention to the reporters and the stories they cover, you can begin to get to know them.

Of course it helps to meet them. The basic ways are pretty routine. The most likely way you will meet a reporter is by contacting her directly about a story. Let the reporter know who you are and something about your organization. Indicate your knowledge of the reporter's prior work. Recognize that it is usually an editor, not the reporter, who makes the decision about stories. So give the reporter a good story to sell and a way to sell it. This may result in an interview, which gives you the opportunity to get to know the individual better. If the work you are doing in your change effort has attracted media attention on its own, you may be contacted for an interview by the reporter. Another opportunity is the talk show. Some reporters also serve as hosts of talk shows. Your appear-

ance on the show gives you an excellent chance to begin building a relationship with the reporter.

Once you meet them, how do you build a relationship? Essentially you do this the same way you would with anyone else you would like to know better. Being friendly is a good start. Yes, there is a bit more you can do.

- Be well prepared for your interview. Assist the reporter in getting a good handle on the story. Have your facts straight and at your fingertips and be able to convey the essential elements of the story. If there is an opposing view, acknowledge it, but show how yours is better by comparison.

- Be straightforward. Evasive people don't gain much favor with reporters. Certainly you will represent the facts in the way that best supports your position, but don't misrepresent them. You want reporters to be able to count on your information. You will only burn somebody one time.

- Be polite. Even if the reporter seems unfriendly, maintain your courtesy. This does not mean you should be apologetic for your concerns or your actions, nor does it mean you have to act as if you are in any way less important than she is.

- Though you may make suggestions about things, like other people to contact or ways to visualize an issue, never tell reporters how to do their job or imply that they don't know how.

- Invite reporters to make a presentation on the news media to a group in which you are involved. This could be a college class, a professional organization, or a church group.

- Get together with reporters for lunch or after work for some refreshment. Get to know them on a more personal level. You may ask for a meeting for the purpose of discussing an issue or a potential story. This allows you to help the reporter more fully understand the complexities behind a situation. It also gives you the chance to get to know one another better. If the invitation was purely social, do not use this time to discuss your particular agenda, except in the broadest of terms. If the reporter wants to bring up a particular question, fine, then you can talk about things more specifically.

- Be seen as a good resource. Let reporters know the things you are involved in, but don't be a name-dropper. If you have expertise in particular areas, let them know. Call reporters from time to time with potential stories they may be interested in. You will find that you will be contacted for assistance with other stories. Often this will involve helping the reporter identify a person with knowledge of a particular subject. Or it may involve some specific information. If you don't have the information they need but you think you might be able to get it, tell them you will work on it for 10 minutes and get back to them. Then you make some quick phone calls. This is much better than giving the reporter more phone calls to make or saying "I don't know." Don't, however, call just for idle conversation, you will be wasting the reporters' time and be seen as a pest. Make sure that reporters can contact you easily with both your e-mail address and cell phone number. They want to reach you easily, and if they don't, they will just try someone else.

- Put reporters on your organization's mailing list. This keeps them aware of what you are doing and gives them some story ideas.

- Never, ever ask reporters to do you a favor by running a story, and never tell them that they have to do a particular story.

- Yes, reporters make mistakes. Only ask for a correction on a serious error. When asking for a correction, explain why you believe it is necessary. This is a touchy matter, so be particularly respectful when making your request (Kirst-Ashman & Hull, 2009).

- Once you have gotten to know a particular reporter, keep in touch.

Providing Good Information. Good information is, first of all, accurate. The facts you provide are reliable and give a suitable representation of the situation. Assuredly, you want to paint a picture that serves your purposes. Draw attention to factors that support a point you want to make or that distracts notice from a situation you don't want examined. Though you may stress certain details over others to emphasize a circumstance, do not exaggerate your case by overstating specific facts. For example, if 100 people showed up for an event, you may say that you were excited that so many people attended, but do not say that the crowd was more than 250. Don't be surprised if you are challenged about your information, and be prepared to back up what you say.

Good information is interesting and relevant. Try to draw a connection between yourself and the reporter's audience. The audience should be able to see themselves in what you experience. Stories related to recent news items are easier for the audience to associate with.

Good information is unusual. Show how the condition you are describing is not commonplace or not acceptable.

Good information is important. Demonstrate that what is happening or has happened affects a lot of people or some particular person or thing the audience highly values. An increase in taxes or the destruction of a historic landmark could be considered important information.

Good information is thorough, yet concise. The information you provide touches on the classic "five W's and an H": Who, What, Where, When, Why, and How. Address these fundamental points in as succinct a manner as possible. Clearly stress important factors, but do not lecture on them.

Many times you provide information through an interview. When responding to a reporter's questions, try to give distinct, direct, 10- to 15-second answers, and throw in a few quotable lines. Long responses with no pauses make it harder to hold the reporter's attention and leave you to the mercy of the reporter or the editor who must capture the chief points of your message.

This is particularly true of television, where news stories are rarely more than 90 seconds long, and usually less. Before taping your interview, spend a couple of minutes going over the essential aspects of your story with the reporter. This will assist the reporter in asking you the right questions, and it will help you get oriented so you can distill the main ideas you want to communicate.

Remember that anything you say to a reporter can be used in a story unless you clearly state beforehand that what you are saying is "off the record." Even then, some reporters will try to figure out how they can use the information. Don't say it unless you can handle reading it. If the reporter cannot use the information, you have to ask yourself why you are bringing it up in the first place.

You may be called and asked for an interview or asked a question that you are not really prepared to answer. If this happens, one of the worst things you can say is "no comment." Remember that you don't have to talk to a reporter until you are prepared to do so. You may tell the reporter that you are right in the middle of something, ask for her deadline, and promise to get back before then. Take some time to prepare yourself and compose your thoughts (Buckholtz, 2001). A reporter may ask you a question that is based on an accusation from your opponent. Avoid just responding to your opponent. Show that you are more reasonable, using your response to underscore your main message themes.

Whether your interview is a spur of the moment event or one that you have arranged, prepare yourself by going through your notes and asking yourself the question that would make you cringe—and answer it. Then ask yourself another and another. This will help you feel comfortable handling the most difficult questions. During the interview you still may be asked a question that is worse than you expected. You don't have to answer the question as asked. You can rephrase the question, addressing broader issue themes that refocus your message. You can also answer a negative question with a positive answer, without repeating the negative comment in your reply (Buckholtz, 2001).

Using the Proper Form and Style

Initial Contact.   Knowing whom to contact for a story is the first step. If you have established a relationship with a reporter or an editor, that is a good starting point. If you haven't, it is proper to start by speaking to the appropriate editor. When contacting a television station, ask for the assignments editor. For newspapers, talk to the city editor or the city desk when you have a story involving hard news. If you have a feature story, speak to the proper feature editor or tell the city desk that you

have a story intended for the "feature side." They will direct you to the right person.

It is appropriate to use e-mail to get information to the media. Include the name of your organization or event in your subject line. Attach photos, but include your text in the message area of your e-mail. Make sure to include the names of people in your photos, along with who took the photo and where, as well as the date and name of the event (Kornmiller, 2005b).

Selling your story involves thinking about it from the editor's perspective. Why would the audience care about this story? What makes this unique or different from the daily routine? How does this idea relate to recent news? You would also want to know what the caller has available to help get this message out. Dealing with these concerns will help you sell your story. Remember that you have two audiences. You must convince your first audience, the media, that your story has merit to get to your second audience, the general public.

Many reporters have seen it all. The ways that most groups present information is so routine that when reporters or editors see something new they flock to it. Further, if you can convince reporters of the validity of your position on the issue, they will make your point for you.

Objectivity is a rarely achieved condition in news reporting, and it may be rarely intended. Here are some ideas that will help you get your story noticed:

* Always think visually, especially for television. Find a way to tell or reinforce your story using images.

* Tell the story through the eyes of the person most affected. If there is a victim, let her voice tell the story.

* Don't lay it on too thick.

* Jar the media out of their preconceived idea of who you are. Show a side of yourself that they don't know.

Carefully study the newspapers and the TV news for a week or two. You will learn quite a lot. You will see how stories are handled and what gets attention. Most of all, you will see what reporters are looking for. Give it to them.

News Releases. Communicating with the news media by means of a news release is common practice. So common, in fact, that an editor may have to wade through dozens before getting to yours. It is important to recognize that you are in competition with others who want attention. Taking a little extra effort to prepare your release properly may help yours stand out from some of the rest. Write the release as if you were the reporter. Pay particular attention to the headline and the lead or beginning paragraph. It should sound like news. You need to grab attention with your headline and lead paragraph. If it doesn't, the next person who might see your release will be a member of the cleaning crew.

Generally, a news release has four essential elements: a title and date, contact information, release date, and text. Figure 10.2 provides an example of a standard news release. When writing your release, put all the important information in the first paragraph, ideally in two sentences. This includes the who, what, when, where, why, and how. This is your "lead." Your lead should entice the reader to want to know more. Since editors cut from the bottom, make sure that your most important information is at the very beginning of your release. Each subsequent paragraph should have information that is of decreasing importance. Use short words, short sentences, and short paragraphs, usually no longer than two sentences. News releases are straightforward pieces, so avoid humor and cute phrases. Using direct quotes from individuals can spice up your release, but clear the quote with the person before using it. Try to keep your release to one page.

Unless there is some reason you want to work exclusively with one particular news outlet, distribute your release to all news providers. It is far more effective to hand deliver your release. If your release concerns an event, you should deliver it 7 to 10 days before the event. Then follow this up with a fax and then finally with a call within a week of the event. When you call, don't ask reporters if they got your release. This will irritate. Simply remind them of the release and use your time to sell your story.

You may want to send a photograph along with your news release. Newspapers use black-

NEWS RELEASE

(The words "News Release" should appear in large, bold print at the top of the page.)

Name of your organization: *(if you don't have stationery)*	Contact person(s): *(with titles)*
Address:	Phone, fax, E-mail:
Today's date:	For Immediate Release *(or For release: date)*

SAMPLE NEWS RELEASE FORMAT

(Start almost halfway down the page with a 3- or 4-word slugline that says what the story is about.)

Stack Headlines to Highlight Important Points

**It Is Acceptable to Have
More Than One Stacked Headline**

Begin the rest of your story a few spaces below your slugline. Remember to use your five W's and your H in the first paragraph. You should double or triple space your text and use wide margins. This enables the editor to make changes.

Use standard 8½-x-11-inch white paper.

If you have to go to a second page, write the word "MORE" three times across the bottom of the page.

MORE   MORE   MORE

Sample News Release Format/Page 2 of 2

Start the new page with a new paragraph. At the top left of the second page write the slugline and "Page 2 of 2." Do not exceed two pages for a news release.

At the conclusion of the release, put a series of pound marks ###### or put the word "END" three times across the bottom.

Because your release goes to the electronic as well as the print media, use the words "news release," not "press release."

END   END   END

FIGURE 10.2 Sample News Release

and-white glossy photographs. Attach a "cutline" to the bottom of the picture describing the photograph. If you are identifying people in the picture, do so from left to right. Attach the cutline to the picture by taping it on the back near the bottom so that the words appear just below the picture. Put some time into planning your headline and your photo. Make them so irresistible that the editor cannot pass them up. Editors know that most readers look only at the headline and the photo, and maybe the first couple paragraphs of the story. If you can tell your story in a headline and a photo, you have a real advantage.

With the rapid growth of information technology, more and more editors are relying on e-mail. In some newsrooms, editors don't even check the fax machines frequently. In fact, a fax machine can go through an entire load of paper before anybody notices. Call the news outlet before you send your release to alert them to the fact that it is coming.

If your organization has a website, put your news releases and news stories there in addition to sending your notices by e-mail. Some newsrooms have individuals who comb through local Web pages for stories.

News Conferences.   When your organization has a particularly compelling story or announcement to make, a news conference may be in order. This is an effective approach for attracting a lot of attention to your concerns. News conferences are for special occasions rather than routine stories, so use them sparingly. Giving attention to a few special details can help your news conference run successfully.

Send a teaser media advisory, a short piece advising of news to be made, a week in advance. This short release announces the news conference and promotes interest in it. All the essential details regarding time and location are included, along with a description of the purpose and the participants. In describing the purpose, state things in a way that will spark the curiosity of the editor receiving it. For example, you might say that information will be provided showing that a major state agency is operating in violation of federal law and is in danger of facing millions of dollars of sanctions. Or you might promise to show how more than 100 children died last year because of the inadequacy of prenatal care services and how this problem is costing the state millions of dollars. You want to whet their appetite without giving away your story.

Call the media people you have invited on the day after they received the advisory. Again, don't ask if they have received your advisory. The stated reason for calling is to answer any questions regarding the arrangements for the conference. Do not answer any questions about the substantive issues you plan to discuss at the conference itself. Of course, the real reason you are calling is to heighten their awareness and interest. Call again the morning of the event as a reminder.

There may be times when you want to call a quick news conference to rally attention to an immediate issue. The sense of urgency can promote reporters' interest in the event. These types of conferences may be useful in calling attention to a controversial community development before an opposing side has determined how it is going to handle public discussion on the matter.

Don't answer questions about the subject of the conference before it takes place. You may get a call from a reporter who is trying to pry the story from you. Resist the temptation to give it away. Once the story is out, there is no reason to hold a news conference, and no one would attend anyway.

Generally, the best time to schedule a news conference is Monday morning at 10 o'clock. News builds during the week as stories develop and compete with new stories. Things start more or less fresh on Monday; it is a slower news day, and all the news crews are at full strength. Ten o'clock is the beginning of the workday for many reporters. Scheduling your conference at this hour draws their attention before other stories emerge throughout the day.

Hold the news conference at a familiar or particularly significant and visual location. Reporters and editors don't want to waste time figuring out how to find some out-of-the-way place. They want a location they can get to easily and that underscores the issues being discussed. This adds to their ability to cover the story. A strong visual image captured in a photograph or on videotape can heighten the impact of your words.

Have adequate parking and easy access. This may strike you as pretty self-evident and a little silly, but I have seen film crews drive around a location for a news conference a couple of times and then keep on going because there was no place to park their van. I have also witnessed reporters wandering around a complex for a while before figuring out which building and which room the conference was being held in. They were not in a good mood when they finally arrived. Don't let this happen to you. It's a simple matter to take care of.

Prepare news packets. Include in the news packet the text of your presentation along with a news release describing the conference. Also provide a one-page fact sheet and any supporting information that may help reporters understand the issue more fully or give them an additional angle on the story. Pass these out halfway into the conference. (You don't want to give them the story before the conference starts or have them sit there reading, not paying attention to what you are saying.) Personalize the packet. Make labels with the reporters' names, and stick them on the packets right before you hand them out. It's a small detail, but it is one of those things that show you are a class act.

Start the conference 15 minutes late. Even reporters arrive late to functions. You want to have as complete an audience as possible, and you want people to mill around a bit to increase anticipation. This is also a good time to begin to set up postconference interviews.

Have a prominent speaker. A familiar and important face lends credibility to your cause, attracts attention, and makes your conference more newsworthy. Do not have more than three speakers.

Make the presentation brief, followed by questions and answers. The main prepared remarks should not exceed 15 minutes. Shorter is better than longer. Prepare yourself to anticipate reporters' questions so you have good, pointed, concise responses. If attendance by nonreporters, supporters, or the general public could be considered appropriate (and it usually is), have them sitting or standing where they will be caught by the camera.

Arrange for interviews immediately following the formal presentation. Let the reporters know who is available for interviews. More than one person should be prepared to be interviewed.

Give some thought to the setting. Have about 12 feet between the speakers and the first row of chairs (if seating arrangements are necessary) to give

photographers enough room to operate. If you are indoors, the photographers may need to set up lights. This means there must be an adequate number of outlets and sufficient space to set up their equipment.

Have good visuals. In addition to what the location has to offer, you may have models, displays, large charts, or other visual aids to help with your presentation and to reinforce your comments.

Make sure that your audio system is clear and sufficiently powerful. This is particularly important for news conferences that are conducted outside.

Have good munchies. Coffee and donuts go a long way toward establishing goodwill.

Provide dramatic information. You have a captive audience; send them a strong or provocative message. Have them leave wanting to tell other people what you had to say.

Keep a list of who attended for possible follow up.

Event Coverage. Your organization will be involved in other newsworthy events. Protests, important meetings, and community service functions might be good events for calling out the news media. Many of the steps involved with a news conference apply here as well. Send out an advance news release or media advisory, give thought to the location, have people prepared to be interviewed, and have printed material to distribute to reporters. You can probably forgo the donuts.

Your material and your comments should focus on the purpose of the event, not the event itself, because event activities should be self-evident. Show how the activities relate to the purpose; don't just emphasize the activities themselves. Although reporters may not use the news release you hand out at the event, they may well feel naked without one. So do have one available, and remember to keep it to one page.

Reporters value their time, just like you do. They like the concept of "one-stop shopping"— that is, all the people who they want to talk to are there: the public official, the victim, the organization's spokesperson, and so on. Make sure you know what the story is. Don't make the reporters try to figure that out. In advance, think about what's really going to get in the story and concentrate on that. Keep it simple. And remember those visual images.

Weekly and Specialty Newspapers.   In your efforts to work with the news media, remember that there are many players, not just the major ones. Although daily newspapers continue to struggle, weekly newspapers are generally thriving, particularly alternative weeklies or those that serve suburban or rural communities (Bonk et al., 2008). In addition, a medium-sized city will probably have a dozen or more newspapers that reach smaller or specialized markets. Many of them have small staffs and are starved for news and attention. It is common for smaller papers to allow you to submit your own articles for publication. Get a list of the ones that exist in your community, and make use of those that can help you spread the word.

Editorials.   Editorial support, particularly from the community's major newspaper, is extremely valuable. It says that what you are doing is not only important to know about but also that it merits approval. Contact the editorial page editor or one of the editorial page staff about their writing an editorial in support of your concerns or allowing you to prepare a guest editorial. (Guest editorials,

usually up to 500 words, are becoming a more common feature in both daily and weekly newspapers.) Arranging a face-to-face meeting is preferable, though not always necessary. Unless the editorial board is very familiar with the topic, spend some time educating them about the importance of your issue and the strength of your position. Providing documentation of your points is particularly important. It is helpful to understand the editorial slant of the paper and to be able to show how your agenda relates to specific positions they have taken in the past.

Letters to the Editor.   One of the most widely read sections of the paper is the letters to the editor. They offer you a useful vehicle for generating community discussion of your concerns and for influencing community opinion. Most papers have an e-mail address just for letters to the editor. Not all newspapers print all the letters they receive, and the ones they do print are often edited. A few hints will strengthen the likelihood that yours will receive attention. First, keep your letter under 150 words. Next, recalling that editors cut from the bottom up, put all your essential details in the first few sentences. Refer to some story that has recently appeared in the newspaper or the letters to the editor column. Make sure that any fact that you use

Using a few carefully placed letters to the editor, you can generate plenty of community discussion and turn a small issue into an important one. You can also keep an issue going, preventing it from fading from public view. In addition, you can stimulate the interest of the news media and generate further coverage of the matters you are working on.

Here is how it works. Invite people over for a letter writing party. You only need about five people. Each person writes a letter addressing the basic subject. This is the first group of letters. These are mailed a couple at a time, with a few days between each mailing. Then, on the assumption that a couple of those letters from the first group will be published, a second group of letters is written as responses to the first. These are drafts that await only some specific references to the published letters to which they refer.

These response letters are written in a way that they can apply to any of the letters in the first group; a few can even take oppositional points of view.

A couple of these are typed up and sent soon after the first letters appear. Then the process is repeated in response to the next letters published. Make a few of your letters provocative so they will stimulate this additional community response. You will notice that other people in the community will begin writing letters as well.

You want different signers to the letters you have generated, so get permission from several people to use their names on letters your small group writes. Read the letter to the person whose name you are using for his approval before it is sent, and send the person a copy, especially since the paper may call to confirm. Notify the "writer" when the letter is published. Also use different types of stationery and vary the typeface a bit.

By the time you are finished, it will look like this issue has sparked a great deal of community reaction. And all it really took was five or six people having fun working together for an hour or two one evening.

---

can be verified, particularly by providing a source that can be easily checked. When providing your name, also add any title that can lend credibility to your words. Send your letter neatly typed and free from grammatical or spelling errors. Finally, include your phone number.

Deadlines and Other Details. The more you know about how to make the job easier for members of the news media, the more they will want to work with you. You will learn many of these things by doing. You will learn when you have to reach a reporter to make the evening paper. You will learn that two thirds of the people get their news from television and that television news gets many of its stories from the newspaper. You will learn that it is not really a community issue until it has been in the paper.

You will learn by your mistakes too. You will learn, as I did, not to call a reporter just before the evening news airs. She was busy putting the final touches on a story and.... Let's just say that my phone call was not a welcomed diversion.

You will learn that timing is important. Get to know the deadlines for the newspapers and

the broadcast schedule for television. Generally speaking, you can call in a breaking news story at any time. However, for planned events or to drop a tip, call television stations between 9:30 a.m. and 3:30 p.m., but do not call within 45 minutes of a newscast. Deadlines for morning newspapers are around 9 p.m. and 11 p.m. (for early and later editions); for afternoon papers, 7:30 a.m. and 10 a.m. are probable deadlines.

You will learn to provide brief, written material emphasizing important facts and views whenever you are working on a story. This is particularly helpful when working with television news because the station may send only a photographer to capture your event. When there is no reporter on the scene, your written material will help the station put the story together more easily and more effectively, increasing the chances it will be aired and covered well.

You will learn that you enjoy working with the news media. You will learn how good it feels when your message goes out and the community begins paying attention to the importance of the things you are doing.

CONCLUSION

People should know about you and what you are doing. If you remain unknown, your road will be difficult, if not impossible. Good skills in publicity will make it much easier for you to accelerate your progress toward success. You cannot take advantage of the potential benefits if you rely on a haphazard approach. You need to manage this task with a sense of purpose.

Take purposeful steps to communicate with your supporters, your targets, and the community at large. The means of communication you choose and the messages you send will be geared toward your understanding of the market, those people you intend to influence, and how you want them to respond.

There are many methods at your disposal. Some, such as word of mouth, newsletters, brochures, and position papers, are largely within

your control. Information technology advances provide many new avenues for getting your message out. Other methods require assistance from people outside your organization. These may include the use of billboards, public service advertising, appearances on talk shows, or getting your efforts and issues described in the news.

When you get the word out about your organization, you attract much more than just attention. You pave the way to new supporters and the resources they can provide. You establish the credibility of your issue and your efforts to resolve it. You awaken the community's interest and get it to recognize the need and that the possibility to improve the community exists. You start moving the momentum for change in your favor and in so doing make it much harder for others to try to make your organization and its concerns go away.

SOME IMPORTANT NEWS

Friday morning, yesterday's coffee still in the pot, phone ringing down the hall, no one answering, of course, and Ben sitting at his desk, more drooping than sitting, poring over the box scores, with his fancy new computer glowing with the beach scene screen saver. Friday morning, everything is in its place. Setting her purse down, Melanie peers over Ben's shoulder. "What are you up to?"

"Just reading the paper." He looks up. "There was an article I saw earlier that started me thinking. It's about a report the university just released on health care costs related to prenatal services. It says that insufficient services cost the taxpayers millions of dollars."

"That's pretty surprising, Ben."

"Well, it shouldn't be, Melanie, that's what we've been saying all along."

"No, actually, I meant the fact that you were reading the paper and that you started to think. But the stuff about the report is pretty impressive too."

"Thanks. You know, I was thinking, here we are putting together something that will deal with just what this report is talking about, and nobody called to ask us our opinion. I get the feeling that a lot of people don't even know we exist."

"Well, we certainly have been talking to people, Ben. What do you want us to do? Get on the news?"

"Yeah, I think so. Or at least find some way of reaching more people than we have. Maybe we can get all those who say they are interested to show up at a news conference, or some sort of event, or heck, just write some letters to the editor. We have to get a hold of them somehow. You are on Facebook, aren't you? How about we create a little buzz there or start tweeting. I bet some reporters will pick up on things if we get enough conversation going."

"I don't know anything about the news business, Ben. I'm not even sure who it is we're trying to reach."

"So, we learn. And people learn a little more about how important prenatal care is and what we can do about that as a community."

"Well, it wouldn't hurt to get to know Jeff Johns from Channel 7. Maybe there's a way we can use the attention that report is getting."

"I know this sounds a little out of character for me, but let's think this through for a little bit, even come up with a plan. What could we do?"

REFLECTION QUESTIONS

1. What might happen if the community is better educated about this issue? What might happen if it is not?

2. Which parts of the community do they want to target with their information? What different messages might they construct? How will they send them?

3. How will they receive messages back? What will they do with those messages?

4. Is anything in place right now that would help Melanie and Ben communicate quickly with all those people they have been talking to?

5. What might they have had ready before they even began these conversations? What might have been put in place to keep people connected?

6. How might they reach the people they want to reach?

7. If you were helping to develop the plan, what would you include in that plan? What might be your first steps? What communication method would you use as the effort begins to grow?

8. Does anyone else need to be involved with the plan?

9. How might they build relationships with reporters?

10. How would you make use of the attention that the university's report is getting?

11. What else do Melanie and Ben have going for them?

GROUP ACTIVITY: MAKING A HOME IN YOUR COMMUNITY FOR YOUR ORGANIZATION

You are building an organization to address issues of homelessness in your community. Right now there are only a handful of people in your organization, including a few people from government agencies, some people from the neighborhoods, and a couple of people who are homeless. You need and expect this organization to grow.

Divide the larger group into teams of four or five members. Imagine that you are members of this emerging organization. Identify your individual roles and determine who will represent people who are homeless, the agencies, and the neighborhoods in your organization.

How will you communicate your organization's existence, its purpose, its importance, its needs, its capabilities, and its activities? What is the starting point for answering these questions?

1. Using specific topics addressed in this chapter, decide what steps your organization will take to get the word out. What else do you need to think about? (15 minutes)

2. Prepare a brief report explaining your starting point and including the steps your group will take and what you believe each step will produce. (5 minutes)

3. Present your ideas to the larger group. (5 minutes)

HELPFUL WEBSITES

Links to the organizations briefly described here are on the companion website at www.cengage.com/humansvcs/homan.

The SPIN Project. With an excellent set of tutorials, publications, and other resources, this organization guides activists on how to work with the media and bring issues to public attention. *SPIN Works!* is an activist-friendly and extremely useful media guidebook that provides tips to help you make good use of electronic communication with members of the media. SPIN Project also provides consultation to grassroots groups working for social change. This is a tremendous resource.

TechSoup. A wide range of very useful instructional articles and worksheets on emerging technology for nonprofit organizations is available. Aimed primarily at those who do not have much experience using technology, more advanced information is also available. The site offers message board support and explains social networking applications that can strengthen your organization and connect you with others to change the social environment.

Community Media Workshop. Started by a reporter and a community activist in Chicago to help increase awareness of oft-neglected parts of the community, this organization has helpful articles on media relations strategies, techniques, and tricks. They also produce *Getting on the Air and into Print*, both on CD and in a print version that can be used as a workbook. Though this publication and other resources have a definite Chicago focus, you will find a variety of resources that will help you in your community

Common Cause. This organization helps reporters find useful information. The Press Center section of their website includes their latest press releases, advisories, reports, statements, letters, and testimony. If you're a reporter and have a question, you are provided with a Common Cause contact and can sign up to receive news releases.

FAIR (Fairness and Accuracy in Reporting). This media watch-dog group promotes activism to address media bias and censorship. They provide guidance and a number of tools for spotting unfair reporting and responding to it.

Society of Professional Journalists. The society offers helpful resources on issues involving access to government records and activities and freedom of information education. This is also a good site for understanding the ethics of journalism and other matters pertinent to professional journalists.

Weinreich Communications. A number of useful articles explaining social marketing are available at this website.

Center for Community Journalism. Sponsored by the State University of New York, Oswego, you can connect with community journalists and others.

Learnthenet.com and **Learnthat.com.** Lots of good information and tutorials on website development are available at these websites.

Search Engine Watch. While the site touts itself as the authoritative guide to search engine marketing and optimization, it is much more. Here you will find articles, news, white papers, and blogs about a range of topics related to communicating through the Internet.

Communications Consortium Media Center. Working to empower diverse and underrepresented communities to participate more fully in decisions about their lives, CCMC supports collaboration among nonprofit groups sharing policy goals as an effective and efficient way to gain credibility and to influence public policy. A range of tips for working with media is available on the site along with contact information for other organizations that will help you get your message out.

Chapter 11

✳

Building the Organized Effort

CHAPTER HIGHLIGHTS

- Structure, flexibility, and organization
- Structure and organizational needs
- Issues and action
- Types of issues
- Issues and organizational development
- "Good" and "bad" issues
- Compelling issue themes
- Sequence of "typical" change activities
- Leadership development and key leadership roles
- Strenthening identity with the community and organization
- Unearned dividends
- Beyond reaction, promoting your own agenda
- Donut hole—structural limitations
- Stages of organizational development
- Small group processes
- Common pitfalls for groups promoting change
- Organization types, characteristics, benefits, and cautions
- Benefits of incorporation and how to become incorporated
- Development and purpose of bylaws
- Organizational sustainability
- Four essential responsibilities of an organizer

"Some assembly required." Daunting words, these. You begin to feel a little gnawing uncertainty in the pit of your stomach. You open the box. Pieces spill out over the carpet, and you wonder if any got swallowed by the deep pile. Oh, well, if you want to go anywhere, you have to start putting this bike together. You look at the pieces, sigh, and reach an uncertain hand for the directions. They're written in Korean. Since you speak only English, this may be a bit of a challenge.

Putting together an organized change effort can be a similar experience. You have to have enough of the right pieces to begin with, a few tools, a fair amount of patience (it doesn't come together all at once), and an understanding that those who write the directions may be using a different language. The challenge is to get all the pieces working together so that the thing, bike or organization, moves forward with those who climb on board.

Over time you will move past complaining, to seeing issues, to taking action. You may even be the person to get things started. However, a successful change effort needs much more than a couple of initiators. It needs a number of people working together, using their knowledge and talents and time in an organized way, and it needs issues to get and keep things moving.

To build your organization, you first need to gather some of the parts: people, information, other resources, issues, and some time. Then you put these parts together in a way that enables them to work with each other, using the potential of each to produce a desired result with the least amount of wasted energy. Making this happen requires organizing, structure, and flexibility.

Organizing is the process of obtaining and putting together the necessary pieces to accomplish your purpose. *Structure* refers to the deliberate, agreed-upon methods for handling predictable or routine activities and tasks. *Flexibility* is the ability to change tasks, responsibilities, and structures to better achieve your goals according to the particular demands of your set of circumstances. It is the lubricant that keeps the whole thing running smoothly. Together, all these elements comprise the organization. Building an organized effort brings into focus all those matters we have discussed in previous chapters. Information, community, power, planning, people, resources, communications—all of it. Your organization fits all those pieces together and puts them to use. You will build the organization as you are doing the work of the organization. If you are just doing the work, but not building the organization, you will still have lots of work, but pretty soon you probably won't have much of an organization. The work will beome more burdensome and your base of power, and therefore your ability to influence, will remain small.

But how much organizing do you need to do, and how much structure needs to exist? These two questions have the infuriating answer of "It depends." Some of the factors on which these depend are your purposes for organizing in the first place; the number of people involved; the nature of the issues on which you are working; the number, complexity, and relationship of your tasks; and the intended longevity of your organization.

If your intent is to develop an organization that will provide a large number of people with a permanent base of power to contend with a range of fundamental issues, you need to pay a great deal of attention to the organizing process and the development and maintenance of supportive structures. But if your goal is to rectify a specific concern, and you are bringing people together only for as long as it takes to deal with this particular matter, less attention is needed for crafting your process and establishing your structure.

A handy way of thinking about these differences is by asking yourself the question: "Is the organization itself more important than the particular problem we're working on, or is resolving the problem itself more important than putting together an organization?" Or to put it another way: "If we lose on this matter but strengthen the organization, is that good or bad?"

A word of caution about structure—keep looking for the right balance. Too much or too little structure can scuttle your efforts. If you "just let things happen," you may end up spending a lot of time going nowhere until a few more compulsive or impatient souls start telling everyone else what to do or end up doing it themselves. This is not a good prescription for organizational success. However, if you assume you have to create procedures for any eventuality, you are going to bog your work down with a lot of unnecessary rules and regulations that don't fit the situation you are facing, and you will not know how to handle unpredictable or unplanned occurrences.

As your organization develops, you will start feeling a need to make certain matters more routine. For example, you may need to determine who calls meetings, who runs them, and who keeps track of what you are doing. Having people agree to hold certain positions within the organization may be a way to provide some management of these items.

As you grow, more separate tasks need to be done, and you may notice that having everybody doing everything gets confusing at the very least. Maybe it would be better to work in teams, each with certain areas of responsibility. If each decision—from the color of your stationery to the menu for your community luncheon—must be fully approved by every member, you won't be making many decisions. Perhaps you need to agree on who needs to make what type of decisions, and how they are to go about doing so.

Generally, a good practice is to allow your structure to emerge in accordance with the emerging needs of your organization. This means that you have to be attentive to the needs of your organization. Some of these needs can be easily anticipated; some have to be discovered. When you notice things that require routine attention, clarify responsibilities or develop procedures to take care of them. Be willing to modify and improve those procedures. This may mean getting rid of them altogether.

Becoming more organized helps you build and focus the interest of participants and other resources. However, organizations are not built out of thin air. They must have a reason for being. When enough people are concerned about something to move toward action, there is the beginning of organization. Organizations are brought to life by issues and are built by working on them.

ORGANIZATIONS ARE BUILT AROUND ISSUES

Something has to demand your interest and grab the attention of others. Something has to spark a surge of effort to overcome the many reasons not to bother to make things different. Something must sustain your drive and give meaning and purpose to your use of power. You need issues. Issues provoke action. Issues give you energy and a reason to move. You are not just serving the community; you and the community members are changing it. What should change?

What Are Issues?

Issues help us see and get a handle on the problems or conditions we are facing. It is usually some source of irritation that leads to action. Issues are rooted in controversy (Williams, 1989) and disagreement (Kettner et al., 1985). They focus on a proposed solution to a problem (Staples, 2004) or underscore the consequences of not acting. Issues bring an undesirable situation into focus in a way that leads to action. An issue is tied to something specific; it is not just a general dissatisfaction with the way things are. Issues serve to crystallize feelings by attaching them to a specific circumstance, condition, or set of behaviors. Issues give people something specific to work on.

Issues are different from problems. As Robinson and Hannah (1994) explain, "problems are common gripes which are discussed in general terms, characterized by overall agreement that they need to be addressed, but in fact, lead to no action. Issues, on the other hand, are specific, selected aspects of a concern dissected into manageable parts of solutions that can be acted upon" (p. 82).

Issues are developed by change agents to attack a problem or improve a condition. They come in layers—from superficial indications of things not as good as they could be to fundamental sources of chronic destructive conditions. Issues have a number of basic elements.

- Issues are a way to define, perceive, understand, or give focus to a situation.

- Issues are an expression of dissatisfaction about a situation.

- Issues are produced by obstacles or resistance to improvement.

- Issues imply action or contain proposed solutions to difficulties.

- Issues shape people's responses to the situation and serve as rallying points.

Though issues may contain the seeds to solution, they also hold some traps for the unwary problem solver. Understand that the way you analyze a problem suggests methods for solving it. Be careful of defining the problem in such a way that only a limited set of solutions can be seen. You can overcome this potential shortcoming by discovering how other people see the issue. It also helps to have a clear understanding of the kind of issue you are working on.

Types of Issues

Not all issues are created equal. They come in a variety of types and serve various purposes. Though you will be more concerned with developing particular issues for the direct purpose of generating action, issues also commonly describe extensive concerns. Certain *fundamental issues* provide the starting point for consideration and action. Hunger or poverty or crime circumscribe a set of problems or questions that appear on the social landscape. They provide the broad context for action and speak to basic concerns we have as citizens. Because they are so broad, they are not sufficient to provoke action. But they do provide the foundation on which more specific issues are built. They give us a framework to identify, examine, and give meaning to these more specific matters.

Specific issues are those clearly identifiable sources of frustration or barriers to accomplishment that call for purposeful, distinct action. They are compelling and exciting (Staples, 2004). Specific issues fit into three categories: mobilizing or recruitment issues, long-range issues, and maintenance issues.

Mobilizing or *recruitment issues* strike people's self-interest and attract people to the organization (Staples, 2004). They seize attention, generate dissatisfaction with current conditions, and spur people to action. Mobilizing issues help to illustrate the problem and give people something to do about it. They act like a magnet by showing people that joining with others is a good way to work on the things that bother them. These issues tend to be immediate and pressing. Action on them can produce direct results in a relatively short period of time.

Long-range issues require sustained effort on several fronts over a span of time. Although they are still specific, people are less inclined to jump on board either because the payoff is too far in the future or because the challenge just seems too big or difficult. Still, these issues are important to nourish the organization and help it to achieve more significant benefits for the community it serves. Mobilizing or recruitment issues can be used as building blocks for achieving success on a long-range issue.

Maintenance issues are aimed not so much at drawing people out or resolving a particular matter as they are directed toward promoting the organization itself. For example, this may involve taking a strong public position on a community controversy or endorsing another group's stand. Maintenance issues can provide mileage by establishing new allies, increasing visibility and credibility, and developing new skills (Staples, 2004). They can also be short-term matters that the organization deals with as a kind of energy booster while it is engaged in dealing with a long-range question.

Working on the fundamental issue of having all children, regardless of their degree of disability, included as contributors to your community, you may have a long-range issue of inclusion in the schools. You may tackle the immediate issue of accessibility of playground equipment or the degrading treatment of families in the process of developing individualized education plans (IEPs) as a mobilizing issue. Your public endorsement of a civil rights group's report charging patterns of racism in a particular school's special education program can provide a good maintenance issue.

Issues and Organizations

What kind of issue is used and how it is used will depend on the kind of organization promoting the change. Management of the issue will vary with the purpose of the organization, its intended longevity, and its current stage of development. Different types of organizing efforts result in different relationships with issues.

Temporary, single-issue organizations. Some organized efforts are temporary ones. They deal with a particular situation and bring about a distinct and limited change. This is a fairly typical approach to promoting change. Once the issue that has prompted a group to form has been concluded, there is nothing to keep the group active, and people return to their routine activities. Most temporary, single-issue groups don't give much thought to developing the organization beyond the resolution of their particular problem.

Ongoing, single-issue organizations. Some groups work on a rather large "single" issue over a long period of time. Usually this is a more fundamental issue such as hunger or education. They are not so much single-issue organizations as they are organizations with a limited focus restricted to a set of related issues. Their primary purpose is to deal with a persistent community condition. They draw people interested in this one issue and make no real effort to attract people with other interests. Because they intend to be around for a while, they must address two distinct continuing goals. First, they must accomplish the purpose of the organization to rectify certain community problems. Second, they must build and solidify the organization itself in the process. Their use of issues must further both these ends.

Multi-issue, power-based organizations. Even though multi-issue organizations attract a lot of attention in the literature on community change, they are probably less frequently developed than other types of organizations. They are established to contend with an array of issues affecting people in a similar constituency. Multi-issue organizations cast their nets much farther than single-issue groups, hoping to snag a broader array of issues and bring in people who are attached to them. These organizations use issues as a way to achieve progress by improving conditions while at the same time attracting new members. Alinsky (1972) said that "the organization is born out of the issues and the issues are born out of the organization" (p. 121).

CAPTURING CONCEPTS
Good Issues, Bad Issues

Distinguishing good issues from bad issues is important. Good issues will move people to action; bad ones won't. Here are some characteristics of issues to keep in mind when you or your organization define issues for action.

Good Issues...

- Are simple to comprehend
- Suggest concrete action
- Suggest immediate action
- Are ones you have a stake in, where self-interest is involved and that relate to people's experience
- Involve emotional and intellectual attachment
- Offer the beneficiaries a way to participate
- Promote community unity
- Respond to the needs of the organization
- Provide a moderate challenge
- Limit the risks of failure
- Capture the imagination

Bad Issues...

- Are vague, abstract, or theoretical
- Have no clear resolution
- Have future or delayed action
- Are outside the community's frame of reference
- Involve only an intellectual attachment
- Limit participation to a few individuals
- Promote divisiveness in a community
- Respond only to an immediate situation, ignoring the needs of the organization
- Are difficult or insignificant
- Entail high costs for failure
- Are dull

Pick your issues carefully and be sure people have enough power to act on them. Power is a precondition for action. An issue is not a real issue until the group has the power to act on it.

Issues are beneficial in building the organization so it can confront other issues down the road and fortify its ability to be an ongoing community influence. Although these groups confront a range of issues, at any given moment they are likely to have a particular focus. In addition to improving specific community conditions, these organizations intend to alter the established balance of power in the community. They are concerned not only with firming up the organization but also with expanding the power base by attracting new members and giving those members a real feeling of power.

Issues and Organization Development

You will use issues to move the organization along. A good issue will attract people to your effort and help your organization gain in credibility. Different types of issues are called for at various stages of an organization's development. A newer organization requires a more immediate and compelling type of issue than a more mature organization does. (Though it is important to remember that immediate issues should not long be absent from the scene.) Your community assessment, described in Chapter 5, is a tool for uncovering issues.

The way you assess a situation, select issues, and take action is similar to the shape of an hourglass (Figure 11.1). You may proceed from the very broad to the specific as you conceptualize the problem and focus on an issue, preparing to move people to do something about what disturbs them. Those narrow, specific issues will propel people to action. Then, as members gain some experience and confidence grappling with immediate issues, they become ready to take on broader challenges.

In a similar hourglass fashion, some change agents float a number of issues, purposefully blurring the boundary lines between distinct issues to attract a greater number of people to the change

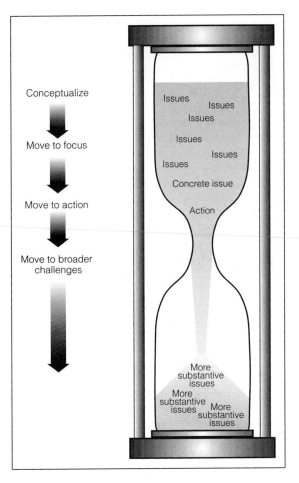

Conceptualize

Move to focus

Move to action

Move to broader
challenges

FIGURE 11.1 Issue Hourglass

As with any hourglass, you can flip over the issue
hourglass to repeat the process on increasingly more
substantive issues.

effort (Gates, 1980). This broader array of issues is used
in a mobilizing phase to stir interest. As the group
moves to a decision-making phase, a clear, concrete
issue must be defined. If this specific issue can represent
an array of concerns, the organization has a better
chance of maintaining the enthusiasm of its various
members. If the issue relates only to a narrow set of
concerns, the organization runs the risk of losing members who may become disenchanted, feeling that the
organization has been unresponsive to their problems.
Once the group successfully tackles the specific action
issue, it feels more capable of addressing other, perhaps
more substantial problems.

Selecting Issues for Action

What is it about an issue that will cause people to
change their habits? A number of factors affect how
people respond to issues. Issues should be *immediate*,
something that people are currently bothered
about; *specific*, something clearly identifiable; *action-
able*, there are some specific things people can do;
and *realizable*, people are encouraged by the prospect of victory (Alinsky, 1972). The most important
principle to keep in mind in the selection of issues is
that good issues move people to action, whereas
bad issues don't (Kahn, 1991).

To start with, any issue you decide to act upon
needs to meet five criteria. You need to give a
strong yes to the following questions:

- Does working on this issue clearly connect
  with our vision?

- Does it fit with our mission, that is, the kind of
  work that we do?

- Does it reflect our values?

- Are people excited about it; do they feel some
  passion? Does it move people to action?

- Can we take sufficient action with our current
  resources or with just a few more that we can
  get pretty easily?

The whole point of developing issues is to get
people doing something, or doing something differently, to make things better. You have to shake
them out of whatever they are doing that keeps
things the same. Things will be different only
when a sufficient number of people start acting differently. The issue will challenge people to do just
that. How you frame an issue brings certain aspects
of the matter into clearer view, helping people see
what is there and making it harder for them to
ignore it (Rubin & Rubin, 2001). People engage
the world through the frameworks they have
created to make sense of what is happening. They
are "mental structures that shape the way we see the
world. As a result they shape the goals we see, the
plans we make, the way we act, and what counts as
a good or a bad outcome of our actions" (Lakoff,
2004, p. xv). Your ability to frame the issue in a
way that resonates with the values and interests of
the community you want to mobilize will help

CHANGE AGENT TIP

Once a group is really rolling with their litany of complaints, you want to get them to think about acting to make things different. A few key comments can turn the conversation from impotent frustration toward action. Essentially, you want to get the group to focus on a choice between hanging onto their frustrating situation or acting to make it different.

There are many different things you can say to change the direction of the conversation. The point is to keep your comments or questions short. Here are some examples:

- I guess we could hang onto being so frustrated, or we could do something. Which should we do?

- Now that we have gotten all this off our chests, are we going to just sit back and let things stay the same?

- It feels good to finally get this all off our chests, doesn't it? Maybe it feels so good that we can keep meeting like this without ever doing anything to make things different.

- I don't suppose we actually want to do anything about this?

- Sounds like we are ready to make some changes around here.

- Where can we start making changes?

---

crystallize their view of the situation that leads to action. Here are some ideas on how to get the ball rolling.

- Highlight aspects of the issue that make people feel angry, guilty, excited, or almost anything. People won't do anything unless they feel something, so—get them to feel.

- Challenge people with the issue. Show how it puts something they value on the line or provides a test.

- Increase the discomfort with the present situation by emphasizing the negative side of the issue. Bring out the irritating details or the harmful consequences of current conditions.

- Rub raw the sores of discontent. Use the issue to prod and poke at the things people are already upset about (Alinsky, 1972). Prevent people from salving their discomfort. Keep people upset. Remind them that they are upset, and remind them why. Grind. Irritate. Do this until almost any action toward change is a relief.

- Thou shalt have a quick initial victory. Take action on one simple aspect of the issue that people can identify as a success. Giving people a taste of accomplishment can whet their appetites for bigger challenges. They begin to believe in their capability and are encouraged to continue their efforts.

- Thou shalt hit them in their own self-interest. Help people see how the issue affects them.

Point out details that show they have a stake in the outcome.

- Make them live up to their own rhetoric. People with high-sounding phrases and low-level actions are hard-pressed to keep ducking the issue when you persist in holding them to their words. This method can be a withering tactic when used on opponents or a kind of kick in the backside to sluggish supporters (Alinsky, 1972).

- Stimulate a vision of what can be accomplished to replace the reality people have to deal with today. Get people to consider the possibility of an ideal alternative to what they are currently experiencing (Schaller, 1972).

- Adjust the issue to reflect the fact that people's values are inconsistent with the current condition and their own behavior. Clearly show the difference. Communities, like individuals, sometimes just drift along in their routines not realizing that they have developed habits out of sync with their important beliefs. At one time or another we all plod along like this, not noticing, at least not until something or someone hits us pretty squarely in the face with the disturbing truth. This approach is complicated by the fact that competing values are often present in any situation. To use this technique, take the high road, and take it first. Accentuate overarching values that emphasize people's goodness as well as their tradition of fair play and active help for one another. Paint your issue with the brush of these values, and show that they are superior to petty or mean-spirited notions that may also be operating. This helps to put your opponents on the defensive.

- Use your own language and terms to shape perceptions. Don't use the language of your opponents to describe the issue, and don't just negate the other point of view. Reframe the issue to highlight values that you and your community share (Lakoff, 2004).

- Personalize the issue. Use a particular victim or villain in the present situation who characterizes the elements of the issue you want to underscore. You can, in fact, make a person the issue. It may be easier to get worked up about little Joey Balefuleyes or rude Carl Callous than about the Department of Health Services. This can dramatize the concern or put people on the spot. Don't let scoundrels hide behind anonymous regulations, corporations, or vague consequences. It is much simpler to take note of and monitor the actions or the plight of an individual than of some impersonal system.

- Plant seeds if the situation is not yet ripe for action. Sometimes you need to be patient. Nurture a developing interest by bringing up the issue from time to time. Ask people for their ideas and opinions on it. Let them stew on it for a while. After some time of sorting things out on their own, potential participants may become more attached to the issue and more receptive to pursuing it further.

- Keep the issue in front of people's faces. Issues not seen or felt are easily ignored. Don't mistake an initial burst of enthusiasm for long-term commitment. It is too easy to get distracted, lose heart, or forget the original provocation. Keep the issue and what it means clearly in focus to serve as a motivator and a guide for ongoing activities. By the same token, don't get too discouraged if the early response is underwhelming. People practice ways to insulate themselves from a difficult reality. It may take a little while for them to shed their reluctance to take a chance that things could be better. By keeping the issue before them and keeping it from growing dull, you begin to wear down that resistance.

Regardless of the approach you take, use the issue as a tool to force the hand of the opposition and to move the minds, hearts, and, if need be, the hindquarters of those who could support you. Find the edge of the issue that cuts. Cut through the excuses. Cut past the fears. Cut down through layers of defenses until you pierce a nerve. Cut so that people can feel.

The most fundamental method for getting a response aims a message at people's immediate self-interest. With this as your reference point, a number of particularly compelling themes can be used to communicate your issue and prompt a reaction:

- Children
- Pocketbook issues
- Family issues
- Fairness
- Beating up the bully
- Frustration
- Prevailing values

Whichever theme—and there are many others—you find useful to frame your issue, remember that your concerns not only make sense but are just and good as well. If you take the high ground, any opponent will have an uphill struggle.

A direct or personal affiliation with the problem is the most fundamental reason people respond. In fact, it is fair to say that some degree of personal attachment to the issue or the change effort is necessary for an individual to maintain involvement. If everything else is equal, the more directly the issue affects you, the stronger your attachment will be to the effort to resolve it. Whether the connection to the issue is direct or indirect, it must be a personal one. People with little investment in an issue will probably not ride out the rough spots.

By selecting an issue, you give people a way to identify what is troubling them. You help people begin to get a handle on the problems they face and to grapple with them.

Once you have focused people's attention on an issue, you can begin to build an organization that

CHANGE AGENT TIP

Building on community assets is the foundation of development approaches, generally, but it is the feeling of irritation that leads to initial action. You may want to get a sense of what is bugging people. Maybe, though, you or other folks in your group find it a bit hard to just walk up to people, especially if they are strangers, and ask them what's bothering them. How do you start this conversation? How do you get people to open up? There is a simple method to break the ice and get good information.

Construct a simple survey asking people to respond to three specific issues you have selected. (Make sure you leave off a couple of good issues.) You can use a simple ranking system from "extremely upset" to "don't mind at all." The point here is to keep it short. The survey is mainly a tool for getting at other things that are annoying people.

Once you have your survey put together, go knocking on doors, sitting in laundromats, stopping by offices, or wherever you will find the people you need to talk to. When you make contact with people, ask your three questions to get them started. Then ask them to identify two other things that aggravate them and why. Talk about these items, and ask a few follow-up questions. You will find that people like to give their opinions, especially if they don't have to prove they are correct.

This approach will accomplish four basic purposes. First, and most important, it will help you discover what is on people's minds. Second, you can use it to stir them up a little. The discussion will bring some irritants to the surface, prompting people to recognize that everything isn't just hunky-dory and getting them a little restless to do something. Third, it will help you and the other participants make contact with people and get to know them better. Fouth, it will help you recruit new participants.

---

will take action. Although each organization is unique in some ways, most organizations progress through some basic phases.

BRINGING THE ORGANIZATION ALONG

No two change efforts are quite the same, so it is with some hesitance that I suggest a "typical" set of organization-building activities. Yet it is helpful to have guidelines that can provide some sense of how to go about the process. Keep in mind that although an organizing effort generally follows these steps, your particular situation may demand a slightly different order or timetable. Remain flexible, and tune in to the needs of your change effort.

Identify What's Bugging You

What is it that you seem to keep coming up against? What is it that sets your blood to boiling, makes you shake your head in disgust, or leads you and your associates to complain? Or, what could be a lot better if people would just do something? Try to put your finger on what it is that you wish were

different. Recall that identifying the issue is not the same as identifying the solution, which refers to how you can make things different.

This step particularly relates to change episodes you initiate as someone who has a personal interest in an issue. If your intent is to organize people rather than to solve a particular problem, you will need to identify what is bugging them. So, as you read the following steps, remember that "you" includes all of you who are organizing and acting.

Think About It for a While

Now that you have a good idea of what is irritating, see if you can figure out why. Think about what makes it so annoying to you and maybe to others. Now is a good time to sit down with one or two people who might feel the same way you do.

Based on what you know, try to diagnose the situation. What seems to cause it? What seems to keep it going? Who gains from keeping things the way they are? Who would be inconvenienced by a change? Spend some time mulling it over. Try to focus in on the issues you want to address. At this point, those who are initially interested in or affected by the issue need to take part in this preliminary assessment. Not only does this spread work and affiliation, but more discovery about the issue affirms conviction and builds confidence. Though you are a very small group at this time, the commitment of a beginning core group helps you to move to the next stage of expanding your base of change initiators.

Do a Little Homework

Test your assumptions. Doing some sort of preliminary community assessment is beneficial. If there are facts and figures to be gotten, get them. The more your small team knows about the issue, the better you can communicate your concerns. You will also be more credible to those who must consider whether or not they will respond to you, and you will feel more confident about what you are doing. (As your organization grows, your command of the issue needs to grow as well.)

Express yourself clearly and succinctly by organizing your thoughts. There is nothing wrong with jotting down a few phrases and saying them out loud to hear how they sound. You don't want to prepare a script, but you do want to be able to make some poignant comments. You will never really stop doing homework, but you should not wait until you know everything before you act.

Identify Other Interested Individuals

Remember the 50/10 rule described in Chapter 8. At least 50% of your time in the early stages of organizing needs to be spent on one- or two-to-one, face-to-face conversations, and at no time in your organization's life should this ever drop below 10%. Thinking about the issue and the homework you and the team have done will help you identify groups of people as well as specific individuals who are affected in one way or another by what is going on. First, approach those you feel most comfortable with and who will take the least amount of convincing. Find out not only what they think about the issue but also how they feel it or experience it. Make a prospect list of these candidates, and add to this list as your change effort evolves. Don't be dismayed if someone you think should care about the issue just doesn't. That will happen.

Much human services work, whether individual therapy or community change, occurs through development of effective relationships. Spend some time getting to know potential partners a little better if you do not know one another well already. Gaining confidence in each other and firming your understanding of what you each think and feel about the problems you face will help you deal with the uncertainty inherent in working for change. Throughout this process, you need to strengthen the belief that you can actually do something to improve your situation. The less well you know each other, the more time you should put into building these relationships. This is a crucial time in building the organization. Your ability to attract initial encouragement and actual support will probably persuade you to continue your efforts or convince you to forget the whole thing, at least for the time being.

Identify Those Who Are Willing to Do Something

Eventually you do need to ask for a commitment. Something like "Let's do something about this, okay?" followed by, "What do you think we should do?" is helpful not only to get people to agree that they will somehow be involved but also to get them thinking about what they will do. They must put themselves in the picture of action.

Every conversation should include this question: "Who else should we be talking to?" Remember, you don't just want a small group of friends who tell you how right you are, you want to build some sort of an organization. Go back to your original prospect list. Are there any individuals on that list to whom you should now be talking?

By this time you may have only a handful of accomplices. You and your co-conspirators should each agree to get a commitment from one or maybe two additional people. Letting these new recruits know who else is involved usually provides some reassurance. You don't need to go from 2 people to 200 overnight. You can get quite a lot done with even 6 or 8 people.

Have a Small Group Meeting

The main purposes of this first meeting are to rein-force your feelings about the issue as you currently see it and to strengthen your commitment to each other and to solving the problem. Other important concerns include shaping and clarifying the issue you will address, providing leadership opportunities for people other than yourself, and figuring out what your next steps should be.

Two potential dangers should be avoided at this initial get-together. The first is just sitting around complaining about the situation and not making any concrete decisions on what to do about it. Although this may help confirm your own intelli-gence and moral rectitude, it releases energy that should be spent working on getting rid of the prob-lem. The second is trying to make detailed plans for all the work that needs to be done, with an implication that it all needs to get done right away. This can lead to a beginning burst of creative energy followed by a feeling of being overwhelmed. Members may feel drained just thinking about all the additional work and spend the next few days crafting excuses as to why they can't be involved after all. The fact is that you survived this week without all the work being done. You will probably survive the next one even if things are not markedly different. There is a lot you can do to improve this situation; you don't need to do it all at once.

Do the simple things right away. Generally, it is more difficult to start doing things than it is to actually do them. So make it as easy as possible for people to start. By the way, simple does not necessarily mean unimportant.

You need to find some balance between confir-mation of your beliefs, directions for the future, and specific tasks to complete in an identified period of time. In fact, all meetings should include identification of *specific tasks* to be done by *specific people* by a *specific date*. Keep the number of things to do reasonable and useful. They should yield some clear perception of progress. Further, all meetings should allow you to get to know each other better and to enjoy each other's company. (If you don't, you probably won't keep working together.)

Finally, two items for consideration at your first meeting will become routine matters for future discussions: Who else should we involve, particularly someone with leadership potential; and what else do we need to know?

Recruit and Do Your Homework

During the time between your first and second meetings, you should be active in moving the effort forward on your immediate objectives. Sounds pretty evident, but you would be surprised at how many change agents use this time to wait for the next meeting. Complete any assignments you agreed to do.

You and your team will now extend your recruiting activities by continuing to interview pro-spective participants, particularly drawn from those who are experiencing the situation that needs to be changed. Now that things are beginning to roll, you can say "join us" in a clear, simple way. Even though some people may hesitate to "get involved," they may be willing to help out with some identifiable job. It is a good idea to ask new members to help you or another team member with a particular task. This gets them involved quickly and easily and helps make connections by giving them someone to work with.

Continue doing your homework on the issue and the community, especially the community in your arena of action. Find out how similar commu-nities or groups have dealt with this problem. Obtain a more accurate understanding of who is likely to support or oppose you and why. Begin to discover who benefits from the current situation and how they profit. You also want to uncover the costs involved in maintaining these conditions and who has to pay them. Do they pay in dollars, in anguish, or in lives? This is the time to more fully develop any needs or asset assessments that may be required.

Hold Your Next Get-Together(s)

In addition to the ongoing purposes of strengthen-ing your resolve and continuing the development of leadership, this meeting should focus on an anal-ysis of the situation and movement to taking action. You are now growing larger, beyond the original initiators. Define your issue focus and plan for action. Begin to develop broader strategies and tactics. A lot of the homework you have been doing will be used during this meeting, so information sharing is critical.

The answers to some basic questions should help you understand what you are facing and provide some direction for your action. The first set of questions centers on principal members of the community. Who are the actors in the play? Who makes decisions on this issue? What are the nature and consequences of these decisions? Who feels the problem? Who else needs to feel the problem; that is, whose behaviors need to be different? Who is likely to oppose you and why? Who is likely to support you and why?

The next set of questions relates to the actions you would consider taking. Knowing who needs to feel the problem, how can they feel it? To what will they respond? What do you need to do to get the right people behaving in the right way? You may not get complete answers to all these questions at this meeting, but you should make substantial headway. Answering these questions will help you develop strategies and tactics.

Your planning efforts should start taking shape, moving forward with the processes outlined in Chapter 7. If your objective is to resolve problems rather than to establish a broad power-based organization, focus most of your planning attention on actions to produce the desired change, not (for now) on building the organization. Look for opportunities for some easily completed miniprojects or quick, initial victories.

Depending on the issue you are tackling, all this may be a lot to accomplish at one time. If you notice that members are getting weary of the process, take a break until the next time you get together. This next meeting shouldn't be too far off anyway if you want to sustain the momentum and complete some basic work. In the meantime, make sure there are a few specific things you and your associates can do to keep a sense of progress. For example, this may be the time to begin raising other resources or exploring alliances with other groups.

At the completion of this stage, you have clarified your goal and the major areas or sets of activities you need to work on. This will suggest some areas on which members can concentrate their energy. This is a very important development. By breaking the overall enterprise into practical packages, participants can better understand and manage what they have to do. With the emergence of this division of labor, you can help participants make sense of what needs to be done and how their efforts fit into the overall picture. The result is less confusion and more efficiency.

Although it is helpful for members to have a clear set of tasks on which they can focus, allow for the fact that members may want to take on new duties from time to time. The fact that members have particular responsibilities does not mean they should always be stuck doing the same things. Members should always have opportunities to develop their skills and commitment by undertaking new responsibilities.

Do What Needs to Be Done

It is a good idea to work together in teams, even if the team has only two members. Working in teams allows for a creative exchange of ideas, helps prevent members from being disconnected from the effort or from each other, and provides motivation as individuals usually want to be seen as responsible contributors to team success.

Members and teams need to keep in communication with each other. Many of the tools of information technology can help you keep in touch as you do your work. Make sure the various teams get what they need from one another and that their work fits together. If there are four or more teams or if the group is large enough, it is usually necessary to have a liaison committee or a steering committee to serve this function. Members of this group regularly communicate with each other to be sure that the work of the teams is coordinated and that necessary information is exchanged in a timely way. Also, they are commonly empowered to make decisions that don't require full discussion by the entire organization or that need to be made within a very short time frame. With each team having an identified liaison, any member of the organization has easy access to other teams. (Notice that a structure is starting to emerge.) It would be a mistake, however, to require that teams only communicate to each other through the liaison. Such arbitrary rules can become a source of unnecessary conflict and can hamper communication.

It is also about time to appoint a "Nag." Finally, you should start thinking about what you want to call yourselves. Understand that most of the work of the organization does not occur at meetings, but between them. Teams should get together as needed.

Get Together Again

Celebrate your accomplishments and your victories. This is a valuable exercise. If you only look at how far you have to go or the work you still need to do, you will soon feel worn out. By this time in your organization's development, you have come a considerable way. Turn around and look at the ground you have covered. Paying attention to your gains is energizing.

Look for ways to incorporate some easily arranged social activities into your work. Perhaps a "no business" get-together is in order about now, or maybe a combination potluck/working session.

Although you need to continue refining your action plans, you now begin seriously discussing matters pertaining to the organization itself, not just to the work of the organization. Make decisions on formalizing the organization. Are there any positions that need to be formalized and filled? Do you need a treasurer, a secretary, a chairperson? Do you need a bank account? Do you need routine meeting schedules, agendas, minutes, and other formal procedures? Do you need to establish bylaws that delineate the formal procedures of the organization, particularly who gets to vote on matters affecting the organization? The answers to some of these questions rest with the decision on what kind of organization you want to be. Later in this chapter I describe various types of organizations.

If you anticipate that your organization will grow so big that all the members can't get together to discuss concerns and make effective decisions in a timely manner, a specific policy-making group will be needed. Usually called a board or a steering committee, this group makes the fundamental decisions that determine the direction of the organization and the way it is to function. It also oversees the activities of any staff hired to carry out these policies on a day-to-day basis and makes decisions regarding significant expenditures of funds.

These are all items you may discuss during this meeting, which is mainly given over to matters of the organization's growth and development. A special team should begin working on those mechanisms critical to enabling the organization to operate smoothly while aggressively pursuing its goals. This team's recommendations should be proposed for adoption at the next general meeting.

Hold a Formalizing Meeting

The purpose of this meeting is to adopt recommendations regarding key aspects of structure and procedure, familiarize new members with your purpose and program, and reinforce your collective will to succeed. It is here that you approve the bylaws and elect officers to formally establish yourselves as an organization. Prepare to work on a set of more formal vision, mission, and values statements. Not every organized change effort needs to reach this stage; only those requiring sustained action over a period of time will need this degree of formality.

During this meeting you have to strike a delicate balance between having things well organized and ready for decisions and remaining open to suggestions. Because there are likely to be new members who aren't really certain about what is going on, leave some clear opportunity for them to ask questions and contribute ideas and leadership. You cannot simply allow for this, you must encourage it. Otherwise it all looks like a "done deal" cooked up by a few insiders who will reduce everyone else to the role of spectator. Provide background on what has occurred to date, who has been involved, what you intend to achieve at the meeting, and why. Leave some non-pivotal leadership positions open to nominations from the floor, and solicit the participation of newcomers to fill them. By taking steps such as these, you can let both new and old members know how they fit in without having to throw all the work you have done out the window and start over from scratch.

Though this meeting will emphasize matters pertaining to the organization, it must not be devoid of action items. Decide on a number of actions to further your agenda to keep you directed to your business and to sustain your momentum.

CHANGE AGENT TIP

The Nag

Most of us intend to do the things we commit to do, but the distractions of the everyday world often leave our well-intended promises locked in the I'll-get-to-it-when-I-can closet. How can action groups deal with this very normal dilemma? Appoint a **Nag**. Or if the members of the group haven't developed a sense of humor yet, you can call this person the **Follow-up Coordinator**. This is an extremely valuable position and one that every group should have. The key point is that this role must be understood, formalized, and mutually accepted; that is, the group needs to clarify what the job is and agree to select a particular person to do it. Basically, the Nag does three things:

1. Records everyone's commitments during the meeting.

2. Reads back the commitments (along with completion dates) at the end of the meeting to make sure everyone has the same understanding.

3. Calls the responsible person a few days before a task is to be completed to check on her progress. Phone calls with real conversations are much better than e-mails for this purpose. Although the Nag may help the responsible person figure out how to complete the task, the Nag does not assume responsibility for doing the work. This is really a very friendly reminder call; it brings people's commitments back to their attention so they can act on them.

When the role is agreed upon and understood, the Nag's duties help reinforce the idea that the organization is working and that people are doing what they are supposed to do. This job is so important that the Nag should rarely take on any other responsibilities for the group.

Go Public

If you haven't already done so, select a name. A name gives you identity and solidifies you as an organization. It signifies to you that you have actually brought something to life. You become more than "a bunch of us who want to do something." Your name should be easy to say and to remember, and it should let people know what you are about.

Go public. Promote the fact of your existence. You now have built a strong foundation for your organization, and it has momentum. Announcing yourselves puts your name and purpose into people's awareness. Proceeding quietly can be counterproductive and confusing to potential participants. Are they being encouraged to participate or not? People are a little suspicious about secretive or unknown groups. Regardless of whether they are supporters or opponents, it is hard to reckon with something they don't know much about, which appears to have little broad support, or which perhaps doesn't have enough confidence in itself to clearly, publicly state its case. Going public will make an opponent more worried about the attention, interest, and support you will draw. A supporter will be encouraged to see that helpful actions are being taken and that you are real.

There are different levels of going public. Some of these, like purposefully spreading the word, being open about your intentions and your actions, and posting fliers promoting the issue and inviting participation, might be done at an earlier stage. Press conferences, public demonstrations, and other acts can be used as forceful coming-out events. Any activity that seeks recognition of your group as an entity in the community should stress what the issue is and what you have been doing about it. Plans for future actions and invitations for participation should also be announced.

Begin Indirect Recruitment

Up to this point, recruitment efforts have been personal, generally face to face. If the issue you are tackling requires a larger organization, you now need to reach out beyond your personal networks to a larger audience, inviting the participation of people none of you know. Although your personal efforts will continue, extend your welcome much further. The suggestions in Chapters 8 and 10 will help you attract and use new members.

Hold an Annual Meeting

Most of the organization's meetings will focus on making decisions, sharing information about emerging matters, and refining plans for action. Although relationship building and noting progress

GLOBAL PERSPECTIVES

AUSTRALIA—We want less talk and more action. But uncoordinated, poorly planned action can get pretty messy. The future is in the hands of the people who are willing to sit through meetings, more meetings, more meetings. The right meetings, of course: meetings which lead to action (Ruth Lechte, 1983, p. 3).

THAILAND—Capacity building of farmers and their institutions is essential for achieving a balance in economic, social, and environmental development goals. The main components of capacity building may include: Farmer-centered development. An enabling environment was created to facilitate farmers to self-improvement. Development to us means not only improvement in farmer's knowledge and capacity but also in their morale. Participation of farmers. Active participation to us means that farmers assume the major role in decision making and managing affairs…. Participatory Learning Forum or interactive learning, which is a methodology developed to

enable farmers to gain more control of their lives and businesses as farmers (Trasnee Attanandana, Russell Yost, and Patreep Verapattananirund, 2007, p. 89).

ZIMBABWE—We want to be helpful in groups, to learn to work as a team. There are some animals we don't want to imitate in our group behavior: donkeys, stubbornly refusing to change their opinions; fish, sitting there with a cold, glassy stare; rabbits, running away when there is conflict or tension; peacocks, showing off and competing for attention; ostriches, burying their heads in the sand and refusing to face problems; lions, fighting whenever others disagree; monkeys, fooling around and chattering; snakes, hiding in the grass and striking unexpectedly; chameleons, changing color according to the people they are with; or rhinos, charging around upsetting people unnecessarily. (From Training for Transformation by Anne Hope & Sally Timmel, 1992. Reprinted by permission.)

UNITED KINGDOM—If community networks are to support the diversity of social realities in community then they must provide safe and welcoming spaces that encourage and facilitate participation and engagement. Enabling people to tell their stories and interact with one another in ways meaningful to them and in comfortable environments is central to effective community networking (Peter Day, 2008, p. 2).

CHINA—Go to the People
Live with them,
Learn from them,
Love them.
Start with what they know.
Build with what they have.
But with the best leaders
When the work is done the task accomplished
The people will say,
"We have done this
Ourselves" (Lao Tsu, 700 BC).

BURKINA FASO—In rural Upper Volta (now Burkina Faso), the village chief and his council decided that

---

are important aspects of any get-together, these meetings are more focused on the organization's work and immediate goals. In addition to these ongoing meetings, it is important to bring all members together at least once a year with a special gathering to reaffirm the organization's purpose, celebrate its accomplishments, promote member relationships and their identity with the organization, and look toward the future.

A number of members who are not that active in pursuing the organization's goals may still feel some sense of connection. Newsletters and e-mails might help remind them of their affiliation, but actually spending time with others who are in some way involved in the organization makes the connection stronger. Quite a number of people

don't show up to routine meetings because they feel a bit out of touch and unprepared to take part. An annual meeting makes few demands on members, as it is more social than anything else.

Typically, functions for the annual meeting include the following:

- Celebrating the organization's accomplishments over the past year.

- Giving awards or special recognition to organization members and other community supporters for special contributions.

- Bringing people together to remind them of their shared interests and purpose; letting them see that they are a part of things.

they desperately needed a solid and safe footbridge built over a small gully that filled up with raging water about 2 months every year and cut the village off from its fields and access to a nearby market town. The village had managed to construct a rickety log bridge, but every year there was at least one fatality from someone falling into the gully.

Good decision, but there were many challenges. The local government dismissed the village request because a new paved road and bridge were "imminent." The villagers lacked reliable advice on their options for getting a footbridge built—what needed to be done and the resources required. The village itself had great difficulty pooling village resources due to animosities stemming from family feuds that went back several generations.

Sometimes difficult challenges are not enough to stop an idea. The village family heads unanimously expressed a deep-felt need for the bridge. They had all suffered from the current situation. The turning point came when family leaders promised to lay down their differences and cooperate to have a dependable bridge. A spillover benefit was that three other villages downstream would also benefit from the bridge as a dependable access to the nearby market town.

The village was able to draw on the assistance of a Peace Corps volunteer, who found another, who had training in civil engineering. Good to have some help, but you need real materials to build a bridge. The chassis of an old junked truck would be the bridge frame. Wooden boards would need to be bolted to the bridge frame. Small causeways would need to be built up with clay and rocks, and masonry cement walls would need to reinforce the gully walls up and downstream from the bridge. The boards and cement would cost about $500.

The labor would require seven-person crews working over a 3-month period. The women and children carried the rocks, sand, clay, and water to the site. The men built the causeways and mixed the cement. The village also needed a mason to supervise the work. Fortunately, one of the village men had recently learned some masonry skills.

The village found a source of "self-help" funds for the materials, and the local governor agreed to transport the truck chassis to the village. The village council organized the labor by family and by week in such a way that members from feuding families did not have to work together in the same crews!

The bridge was completed 2 weeks ahead of schedule. The Peace Corps volunteers provided some early guidance, and after the initial planning stage, the village took over. When the village volunteer did venture over to the site, he found that he was just in the way.

Fifteen years later the volunteer received a letter from a villager saying that the bridge was still in great condition and had been faithfully kept up by the village. He also indicated that the paved road was still not built (John Scheuring, 2002).

- Strengthening social ties.
- Fostering member enthusiasm and confidence.
- Drawing community attention to the organization and its issues.
- Electing new officers.
- Preparing to identify the organization's focus for the upcoming year, which will be decided in subsequent working meetings.

Keep Working, Monitor Progress, and Confirm the Actuality of the Change

Continue to move your agenda forward by identifying and completing tasks, particularly those that institutionalize or make permanent the changes you seek. Understand that once the change has been agreed to you will need to monitor its implementation. You may discover that you will need to keep the pressure on to ensure adherence to agreements that are to result in changes.

Implementation will not be easy. Unanticipated problems and other setbacks will occur. Those who resisted the change may attempt to undermine its genuine realization. It is not uncommon for changes to be temporary. A situation that appears to have been changed may well revert to the previous condition once the pressure to pursue new directions has been removed. Maintain vigilance and an unmistakable willingness to take action until changes are incorporated into the day-to-day life of the community (Kettner et al., 1985).

DEVELOPING YOUR ORGANIZATION

You cannot separate building an organization from developing leadership. This is one of the very most crucial and most often overlooked aspects of organizing. Even if your effort involves only 10 people working together for 6 months, this subject requires your purposeful attention. The larger you aspire for the organization to grow and the longer you intend for it to be around, the more critical this concern becomes.

In the very early stages of the organization you will likely provide some leadership, but your leadership role will diminish steadily. In a fairly short time you will understand that it is your job to develop leadership, only on rare occasions should you provide it. If you are always in the leadership chair, no one else can sit there. Invite others into the chair, and get more chairs. This is a critical understanding for a true change agent. It is *not* your job to be the leader. It *is* your job to develop leaders.

Develop Leadership

Leadership is the ability to draw forth the ideas, energy, and commitment of members to define goals, achieve them, and to strengthen the relationships among members. Leadership provides a sense of confidence to members of an organization or a group.

Developing leadership entails more than looking for the one leader to replace you. It means looking for several leaders to work alongside you, some of whom may assume aspects of your role when it is appropriate for you to leave the scene. Leaders are those people who routinely demonstrate the ability to influence others in an attempt to move the group forward. Leadership more accurately refers to the behaviors that provide the influence. The reason for making the distinction is that by seeing leadership more in terms of behaviors than as people you open up the possibilities for leadership to be expressed by any number of members in the organization. This keeps the group vital and self-reliant rather than dependent on a few.

Particular types of leadership roles are important to the organization. At least six basic needs for leadership exist in organizations:

- Guiding strategic and tactical decisions
- Inspiring and motivating others to encourage accomplishment of tasks, including modeling task performance by assuming your responsibility to get work done
- Providing direction and coordination of efforts
- Representing the organization to the public
- Negotiating the organization's interests with other individuals, groups, and organizations
- Addressing internal relationship issues

Different people can fill each of these roles; you don't have to worry about finding someone who can play them all.

Potential leaders possess some degree of commitment and capability. Both of these attributes can be strengthened over time. You can start developing leadership by encouraging the people who are currently participating in the organization who demonstrate a willingness to provide some leadership. Some of these individuals will turn out to be effective leaders, and some of them won't. Some potential leaders will hold back, so you may not notice them at first. Perhaps they are a little unsure of themselves, or perhaps they are a little unsure of the organization, its sincerity, or its prospects for success. These potential leaders may take a little while to survey the scene before deciding whether making a greater effort would be worth it. There will also be some individuals who are not currently members of the organization, but whom you will deliberately recruit because of your awareness of their leadership capabilities.

One implication of this is that you will probably experience a turnover in leadership. The people who are eager to get something going may not be good at sustaining their own efforts, much less the organization's. The organization has different needs in different circumstances and at different stages of its development. Don't be disappointed if the early leaders drift away from the organization. In fact, it is very likely this will occur. That is one of the reasons you need to be on the lookout for new leaders.

How do you develop these potential leaders into actual ones? A good beginning is to let other members know that you don't have all the answers, that you are finding your way too. One of the best ways to kill off emerging leadership is to convey that it is not needed or not wanted. To counter that possibility, actively encourage others to take a greater role, see to it that opportunities exist, and then get out of their way.

A beginning means of encouragement is soliciting ideas, especially as they relate to the six basic areas of leadership. Leadership involves some degree of risk taking. The potential leader must feel sufficiently safe before he or she will demonstrate real leadership. Safety levels vary among people. Some establish confidence pretty easily, whereas others take a while. By asking for ideas, you get some gauge of capability while inviting a small leadership commitment in a nonthreatening way.

You may notice that one or two members of your group, perhaps including yourself, are seen as the arbiters of which ideas are good and which aren't. If this pattern persists, your efforts to develop new leadership will seem phony and remain superficial. You need to demonstrate your trust in the judgment of emerging leaders if your efforts to develop leadership are really going to mean anything. By deferring judgment to others and following their lead, you send a message to everyone that there are more than just a handful of people capable of providing direction.

You may need to do more than provide encouragement and opportunity. You may need to provide some conscious mentoring, working closely with those who seem capable of and interested in assuming a greater leadership role. Pass on what you have learned through your own training and experience, particularly your experience in this effort.

Strengthen Identity with the Community and Organization

On the rare occasions when you see him without his Cubs hat, you know that somewhere—on his shirt pocket, his pen, or someplace you would rather not look—you will see the team logo, that big C with "ubs" tucked neatly inside. He has canonized longtime, long ago revered player Ernie Banks, even if his regular church for some reason has yet to do so. You know that he still agonizes about how close they came in '84 and '03 to finally, finally winning a pennant. Something that still has not happened since 1945. You look at his mood today and you can tell what happened on the field yesterday. He doesn't just root for the team. This man *is* a Cubs fan.

An important aspect of organizational development is creating a sense of member identity with the community and the organization it represents. You probably have had that feeling. Maybe you are a die-hard fan of a particular sports team. Maybe you don't just belong to a political party, it's part of how you see yourself. Maybe your profession isn't just what you do, but what you are and where you work is more than just a place of employment. When participants not only feel that they are a part of a community or organization, but that it is a part of them, they will take care of it.

What contributes to that sense of identity? For starters, the organization itself having an identity, perhaps with a name and a logo. Beyond these, an organization creates its own artifacts—posters, brochures, letterhead, statement of values, collection of newspaper stories, and many other things—that note its existence and history.

A good organizer will find and foster many ways to draw a member into closer connection with the community and organization. Although frequent contact from the organization through newsletters, e-mails, and calls for action are important, more powerful is bringing members into contact with each other and with the work of the organization. Shared experiences and stories that keep these alive create a bond. Deeper participation, such as involvement in decision making and having some degree of responsibility, promotes a feeling of ownership and strengthens ties. Being recognized by others as a member, whether that be in welcome at a meeting, having the member's name on a published committee list or in a newsletter article, or being the proud owner of a membership card, affirms the individual's belonging to the group. An organizer will also help members to see threats posed by outside forces to the community or organization as a way to have members stand together.

Somewhere along the line, when members identify with the community or organization and feel that it is theirs, what happens doesn't just affect their interests, it affects them.

Take a Moment to Discover

Think back to a time in your experience with someone who was a leader, especially after the leader had been absent for a while. Maybe this was your teacher, a member of your choral group, or your star pitcher, someone in whom you all had confidence. How did you feel and perform when that person was gone? How did you feel when that person returned? All of you in the class, in the group, or on the team had work to do or contributions to make that the leader didn't take away from you. Yet in that person's presence you all seemed to perform better. Who could offer that type of leadership in your organization?

Expect Natural Turnover

After an early period of enthusiasm, a few of your number will disappear. Don't be surprised if half of your initial group is gone after 6 months. Don't be worried either. (Well, do be worried if these individuals haven't been replaced by others or if overall interest and participation is steadily dwindling.) Some loss is natural. There are many reasons. It is harder to keep something going than it is to start something. Some people get discouraged by not seeing immediate results. Others may find that they are not really very interested in the issue after all or can find nothing very meaningful to do about it. Some would rather talk a good game than play it. Yet others will move away, get a new job, fall in love, fall out of love, or have some other experience that takes them away from the action.

As long as your issue is sufficiently important and you make an honest effort on some basic fronts, your numbers will be sufficient to do the work. Here are some things you can do to cut down on the loss of membership:

- Help members find specific ways to contribute.
- Offer encouragement to the unsure.
- Provide opportunities for leadership.
- Establish a sense of overall direction.
- Make it very easy for members to recognize progress the group is making on getting work done, on moving toward your goals, and on making an impact in the community.

- Strengthen relationships.
- Keep in frequent communication, including personal communication between leaders and others in the organization.
- Recruit and involve new members.

Things to avoid doing are wasting energy worrying about who is no longer active and wasting time chasing after people who really aren't going to maintain their involvement. Although some absences could have been prevented, and you can learn something by doing some reflecting, most of your turnover can be accepted as natural. You will continue to grow if you focus your energies in a positive direction.

Get People Doing Something Right Away

All that early energy and enthusiasm needs some focus to keep it from dissipating. An activity that is a stimulating change from the routine can serve important functions of unifying the participants and providing them with an opportunity to enjoy working together. A specific project or event people can undertake quickly works best. This is not an activity that is carefully thought out and then patiently explained to the group. No, these activities are best born of the spontaneous ideas that just seem to pop out of group discussion. The best ones are tangible, like painting a mural, creating a banner, conducting a food drive, or digging in for a Saturday neighborhood tree planting. Even something social like a barbecue, a weekend campout, or a fun-filled retreat could work. Really, almost anything that will get people going and confirm their identification with the effort will do.

This focal activity becomes an enjoyable experience that attracts the interest of new members, becomes part of the group's history, and, by moving the group forward, introduces it to a range of other possible activities.

Know That Things Will Take Longer Than They Should

We all know that change takes time, but we tend to throw that understanding out the window when dealing with our own efforts to make change. Though your work should and will accelerate the process of change, maybe even significantly, it will not make it immediate. Sorry. If you can maintain the odd state of eager patience, you will be effective while still being pleasant to be around.

Decide Whether an Easily Achieved Gain Is Better than One Gained from Struggle

You may be able to pick up the phone, call someone you know well, like the mayor or another influential community member, and easily solve a problem your budding organization is facing. Is this the best thing to do? Not always. Often it is more beneficial for the organization to gain a sense of accomplishment by achieving something through hard work. Your decision is based on what, at the time, the organization needs most.

Accept the Reality of Unearned Dividends

An improvement in the community will benefit everyone, not just those who helped to bring it about. If a neighborhood park gets built, people who never worked on the project will swing on the swings or play a little three-on-three on the basketball court. This can cause resentment and create divisiveness. Do not presume to know why each nonparticipant does not become involved. Instead, focus on those who are involved, and create honest, ongoing opportunities for people to become involved according to their abilities. Then just accept unearned dividends as a fact of life.

Move Past Reaction

During the early phases of building your organization, you may be responding primarily to some discomfort experienced by the members of your community that is caused by an outside authority. You may initiate action by trying to stop something from happening or by trying to end a harmful practice. These can be effective motivators.

At some point, if your organization is to grow beyond an immediate issue, you will need to promote your own agenda. Go beyond a series of essentially defensive struggles to assert your own program of action. When this occurs, you are much more in charge of your own destiny. You are provoking reaction rather than acting provoked.

THEORY OF STRUCTURAL LIMITATIONS

Most community action organizations are developed and run by people who saw or felt a need to act and were unwilling to sit still. Most of these people are volunteers. Their attraction to the organization is rooted in the goals and action agenda of the organization. Participants may join an organization for a number of reasons (see Chapter 8), for example, liking the people involved with the organization, but most leaders' level of commitment is related to what the organization is about, what it is trying to do.

That's great for providing energy and direction for action, but it may not be all that great for handling the nitty-gritty details that keep the organization running. Organizations, like any other system, require routine maintenance and attention to many little chores that help it survive and grow. This is not too difficult when the organization is fairly small, but taking care of a larger, growing organization is something that many volunteer leaders just don't want to do. As the organization expands, it reaches the limits of the structure that volunteers have put into place to manage organizational activity and development. There's often not enough to hold it together, and the effort more or less collapses from its own weight (Guerra, 1999).

I refer to this as the donut hole theory. Maybe not the most apt term because donuts stay pretty small, and the batter is cooked all at once. Organizations keep getting bigger, and their parts are "cooked" in fits and starts. Still, the picture of a hole in the middle of an expanding mass is the picture I get whenever I see this happening.

To survive its own growth, an organization needs to specifically recruit and develop leaders who will undertake the management of routine organizational tasks, or they must be able to hire staff to perform those activities. This will be essential to sustain your organization. It cannot be overlooked.

GENERAL STAGES OF ORGANIZATIONAL DEVELOPMENT

It is normal for your organization to go through certain stages in its development. Though these periods of growth are fairly predictable, the length of time it takes to pass from one stage to the next will vary with different organizations. At every stage, your organization has the opportunity to move forward toward growth or stagnate and eventually pass away.

The appreciative approaches described in Chapter 2 will help you continue to move forward. When an organization hits a snag or begins to stall, disappointment and fear can lead to withdrawal of commitment and to bickering among members. Understanding that these challenges are normal, that they can be expected, can lessen the threat. Being able to use the group's experiences of success as guides for continued growth and development will move you through difficult times. An organization that can remember and use what works will find that what doesn't work will go away (Hall & Hammond, 1998). If you are a strengths-based organization, one that will "obsessively notice and employ each partner's most valued strengths every day" (Cooperrider, 2008b, p. 8), you will have a lot to work with.

The seven common stages of organizational development and maturation are introduction; initial action; emergence of leadership and structure; letdown, loss of members, and floundering; recommitment, new tasks, and new members; sustained action; and continued growth, decline, or termination.

Introduction

This marks the very beginning of your effort. You recognize your (or the community's) frustration with current conditions and begin to talk to each other about it. You begin to understand the issue more clearly, get to know one another better, understand your feelings about the situation, and decide to do something to make a change.

Initial Action

This stage is characterized by a handful of original members doing an armful of tasks. Common tasks include contacting potential supporters, gathering information, preparing written statements, and holding meetings to figure out what it is that you want to do and how to go about doing it. Enthusiasm, energy, and regard for one another are usually high.

At this stage, groups often make their first presentation (often unsuccessful) to those who are in a formal position to do something about the problems the community faces. They soon realize that more work needs to be done to secure significant change.

Emergence of Leadership and Structure

As the next steps are being considered, members frequently turn to a few leaders for direction, clarification, and encouragement. A need to make decisions and organize work more efficiently is recognized, and procedures are established. Work proceeds as members gain a clearer picture of what they need to do. A clearer sense of purpose begins to take hold.

A few of the original cast drop out as the early period of inspired activity gives way to more routine work. Another common deterrent to maintaining participation is the tendency for some early leaders to focus on their own agendas, seeing only their own solutions to problems, and generally ordering others around. Even though these "leadership" actions may be done with apparent politeness, they soon wear thin. Leadership struggles may well occur as the group continues feeling its way.

Letdown, Loss of Members, and Floundering

It is common for organizations to go through a period of doldrums. The early energy has waned, and nothing seems to be happening. Members may become emotionally fatigued. If no concrete gain can be seen or if no interesting action has taken place, people may lose focus and question whether the effort is going anywhere. The organization will lose some members, and those who stay may vacillate between being angry at the defectors and struggling to keep their own faith.

This is a critical time for the organization. If no visible activity involving a substantial number of members occurs or no identifiable victory can be claimed, the effort is likely to wither. An appreciative orientation will be an important asset to help the group refocus and shore up confidence. If the organization can make it through this period successfully, it can take future occasions of listlessness in stride more easily.

Recommitment, New Tasks, and New Members

Leadership asserts itself during this phase to motivate members and assure them of the value of their involvement. Work is broken down into coherent, manageable assignments, and members feel good knowing what they have to do and how their work fits in with the overall scheme of things. New members are recruited, and they bring vitality and new ideas. If members can point to a particular accomplishment, they begin to feel good about themselves again and renew their belief in the organization. A more genuine sense of purpose is realized.

Sustained Action

The organization's program moves forward, and members can readily acknowledge gains on several fronts. Setbacks are seen as temporary, not terminal, and a sense of confidence, and perhaps even pride, takes hold. Many of the early leaders play less active roles, and new leaders step forward. New projects are considered and undertaken. These new ventures occupy the time and devotion of only some of the members. Everybody doesn't have to be involved with everything.

As the organization continues to grow, more formal means of communicating among members are developed.

Continued Growth, Decline, or Termination

Scenario 1. The work continues, but nothing new or interesting seems to happen. Leadership remains in the same hands, and the same verses keep getting repeated to the same songs. Those who have the most investment in the effort struggle for a while to put the best face on things while not really doing much to refresh and restock the organization. They may work harder on their own responsibilities and take over other people's jobs. After a while they, like the rest of the members, run out of gas. People stop showing up, work is done sporadically and less well, and for all practical purposes the organization exists in name only, if at all.

Scenario 2. The work of the organization is completed, and it is time to go home. Sometimes when this occurs, the members aren't quite sure what to do with themselves. There is a little restlessness as members still get together to try to figure out what to do next before it finally dawns on them that they are, in fact, done. This is a good time to deliberately recognize accomplishments. Holding an event that celebrates the group's successes and declares an end to the effort allows members to feel a sense of achievement and completion, enabling them to move on to other things. In the absence of a commonly proclaimed conclusion, members just drift off into other interests with vague feelings of being unfinished.

Scenario 3. New projects and new challenges bring more members and continually recharge the interests of participants. Periods of stagnation or confusion are recognized and managed. New leadership urges the organization forward. The authority of the organization's reputation paves the way to further accomplishments. The community and the individual members feel strengthened by their affiliation with the organization.

SMALL GROUP PROCESSES

The work of organizations is largely the work of groups. Most of the stuff of organizing for change—discussing, plotting, planning, decision making, and camaraderie—occurs in groups. Building a successful organization demands an understanding of the functioning of successful groups. Purposefully building around the support and close communication a small group affords can be a helpful method of organizing (Breton, 1994; Gutiérrez, 1995). The information in this section dealing with small groups has been drawn from Tuckman and Jensen (1977), Tropman, Johnson, and Tropman (1979), Alle-Corliss and Alle-Corliss (2009), Konopka (1983), Brown (1991), Home (1991), Sachs (1991), Mondross and Berman-Rossi (1992), Zastrow (2001), Lumsden, Lumsden, and Wiethoff (2010), Napier and Gershenfeld (2004), and Johnson and Johnson (2009).

Task and Relationship Dimensions

Two basic levels of group operation require continuing attention. The first of these, the *task* or *goal* component, is directed toward accomplishing the group's purpose. The group puts forth energy to determine which steps must be taken to accomplish the goal, to take the necessary steps, and to keep moving forward. All those actions that conduct the group toward these achievements are called task or goal actions. If the task component receives little attention, the group won't accomplish very much.

The second principal element of a group's operation is the *relationship* or *maintenance* component—the ability of group members to work well together, to effectively manage their conflicts, to maintain their involvement, and to feel good about themselves as individuals and about the group as a whole. All those actions not directed at the goal or work of the group but directed at enhancing harmony among individuals and between the individual and the group are called relationship or maintenance actions. Maintenance activities are most important for organizations that intend to stay together for a while. Taking care of relationship issues after a sequence of intense task activities is especially vital to the organization's continued health. If the relationship component receives little attention, the group will probably fall apart.

Any action that strengthens the group on either the task or relationship level can be considered a leadership action. Johnson and Johnson (2009) identify a number of specific leadership task actions that can promote group effectiveness:

▶ Take a Moment to Discover ◀

Imagine a situation in which a group of you are trying to accomplish something. This may be planning a party, preparing for a class presentation, or even cleaning the house. Review the lists of task and maintenance leadership actions, and put a check next to those you see yourself routinely providing. Next, put a star beside those you seldom do. Now look at what you have marked. What does this suggest to you about your leadership style and what you think is important?

Information and opinion giver: offers facts, opinions, ideas, feelings, and information

Information and opinion seeker: asks for facts, opinions, ideas, feelings, and information

Direction and role definer: calls attention to tasks that need to be done and assigns responsibilities

Summarizer: pulls together related ideas and suggestions and restates them

Energizer: encourages group members to work hard to achieve goals

Comprehension checker: asks others to summarize discussion to make sure they understand (pp. 188–190)

Relationship or maintenance actions include these roles:

Encourager of participation: lets members know their contributions are valued

Communication facilitator: makes sure all group members understand what is said

Tension reliever: tells jokes and increases the group fun; helps members with perspective taking and recognizing common interests

Process observer: uses observations of how the group is working to help discuss how the group can improve

Interpersonal problem solver: helps resolve and mediate conflicts

Supporter and praiser: expresses acceptance and liking of group members (pp. 188–190)

TABLE 11.1   Characteristics of Effective and Ineffective Groups

Effective Groups	Ineffective Groups
Goals are clarified and modified so that the best possible match between individual goals and the group's goals is achieved; goals are structured cooperatively so that all members are committed to achieving them.	Members accept imposed goals; goals are competitively structured so that each member strives to outperform the others.
Communication is two-way, and the open and accurate expression of both ideas and feelings is emphasized.	Communication is one-way, and only ideas are expressed; feelings are suppressed or ignored.
Participation and leadership are distributed among all group members; goal accomplishment, internal maintenance, and developmental change are underscored.	Leadership is delegated and based on authority; participation is unequal, with high-power members dominating; only goal accomplishment is emphasized.
Ability and information determine influence and power; contracts are built to make sure that individuals' goals and needs are fulfilled; power is equalized and shared.	Position determines power; power is concentrated in the authority system; obedience to authority is the rule.
Decision-making procedures are matched with the situation; different methods are used at different times; consensus is sought for important decisions; involvement and group discussions are encouraged.	Decisions are always made by the highest authority; there is little group discussion; members' involvement is minimal.
Structured controversy in which members advocate their views and challenge each other's information and reasoning is seen as the key to high-quality and creative decision making and problem solving.	Disagreement among members is suppressed and avoided; quick compromises are sought to eliminate arguing; groupthink is prevalent.
Conflicts of interest are resolved through integrative negotiations and mediation so agreements are reached that maximize joint outcomes and leave all members satisfied.	Conflicts of interest are resolved through distributive negotiations or avoidance; some members win and some members lose or else conflict is ignored and everyone is unhappy.
Interpersonal, group, and intergroup skills are stressed; cohesion is advanced through high levels of inclusion, affection, acceptance, support, and trust; individuality is endorsed.	The functions of group members are stressed; individuality is de-emphasized; cohesion is ignored; rigid conformity is promoted.

SOURCE: D. W. Johnson & F. P. Johnson, *Joining Together*, 10th ed. Allyn & Bacon, Boston, MA, p. 26. Copyright ©2009 by Pearson Education. Reprinted by permission of the publisher.

Effective and Ineffective Groups

Johnson and Johnson (2009) identified characteristics of effective and ineffective groups (see Table 11.1). Ongoing attention to factors present in effective and ineffective groups will help you monitor the functioning of your own group and identify specific areas where improvements can be made. Johnson and Johnson's simple, valuable model will help you maintain awareness of essential issues.

Four other critical factors for group effectiveness have been identified by Kaner, Lind, Toldi, Fisk, and Berger (2007):

Full participation: All members are encouraged to speak up and say what's on their minds.

Mutual understanding: Members need to understand and accept the legitimacy of one another's needs and goals.

Inclusive solutions: Members take advantage of the truth held by all members, not just the quick and the powerful but the slow and the shy as well.

Shared responsibility: Members recognize that they must be willing and able to implement the proposals they endorse.

Stages of Group Development

Napier and Gershenfeld (2004) describe six stages in the evolution of working groups: the beginning, movement toward confrontation, compromise and harmony, reassessment, resolution and recycling, and termination. These stages are built on the classic work of Tuckman and Jensen (1977), who described the five stages of group development as forming, storming, norming, performing, and adjourning.

Before members ever enter the group they have some idea about what is going to happen. These ideas color their perceptions during the *beginning* stage, which is a time of watching, waiting, and testing out how to act. Members try to find their own identity in the group and determine how much they will allow themselves to become involved (Alle-Corliss & Alle-Corliss, 2009). Gradually, people become more comfortable in the group, drop their polite facades, and begin acting more like themselves. This stage is characterized by *movement toward confrontation*. Questions arise over who makes decisions and how. Concerns over matters of control and freedom are expressed, and leaders are criticized. Members try to firmly establish their place in the group, seeking prestige and influence. This is bound to cause some conflict. After a while, members realize that if this continues the group will disintegrate.

This recognition ushers in a period of *compromise and harmony*, during which the group tries to reverse destructive trends and reopen communication, drawing members together. A period of goodwill ensues with tolerance for different behaviors and more acceptance of individuals. Collaboration increases, and competitiveness is reduced. Though openness and honesty are encouraged, members are careful not to step on one another's toes, and there is a subtle pressure to preserve the spirit of harmony. As a result, resistance goes underground, making it harder to make decisions. Feelings of confidence and relief give way to increased tension. The group realizes that a kind of superficial fellowship needs to be replaced with some other approach.

During the period of *reassessment*, the group may try to impose greater restrictions in an attempt to streamline procedures and increase efficiency. Or it may delve more deeply into its problems. This can lead to the group realizing how vulnerable it is to personal needs, suspicions, and the fears of its members. Members come to see how these issues affect the ability of the group to accomplish its goals. By establishing mechanisms for appraising its operations and making adjustments, the group can build on the foundation established in the previous phase. It legitimizes the expression of feelings that are not always positive or that may produce conflict. The group realizes that its survival depends on increasing shared responsibility as well as personal accountability. This, in turn, increases trust and individual risk taking.

During *resolution* and *recycling*, the group realizes that periods of conflict and periods of harmony are normal, and conflicts are handled easily and quickly.

The final stage is the *termination* or *adjournment* stage. At this point the group has decided to finish its business and members go their separate ways, though some may retain some level of connection.

Groups can get "stuck" at various points as they move toward maturity. Also, they may regress from time to time to earlier stages of development. It is helpful to understand these phases so you can recognize events occurring within the group as signs of normal group development. With this understanding, you can help guide the group as it matures and be patient with events that might otherwise appear disturbing.

Common Pitfalls for Groups Promoting Change

Not surprisingly, every organization experiences some problems as it tries to get organized. A number of probable trouble spots can make the road a little rougher than you would like it to be. Keep your eye out for these problems. Each problem is followed by a list of symptoms to watch out for.

Inflexibility

- Overinvestment by individuals in their ideas, positions, and plans; unwillingness to see how changes to ideas, positions, and plans offered by others can help the group achieve its goals.

- Failure to see early plans as tentative.
- Inability to "roll with the punches" and take setbacks in stride.
- Defining problems in terms of solutions instead of in terms of actual conditions.
- Lack of contingency plans; no "spare tire."

Intolerance for Confusion

- Belief that things won't or can't work out all right.
- Premature need to have complete answers to all questions; belief that these answers will never arrive.
- Need to know what everyone else is doing, and why.
- Lack of belief in one's own ability to figure things out.
- Need for guarantees.

Poor Group Process

- More talkative members not actively withholding comment and inviting or allowing less talkative members to participate.
- No purposeful effort to assist less talkative members to develop confidence in their ability to make verbal contributions.
- Less talkative members not accepting invitations or opportunities to contribute.
- Lack of clear, mutual understanding about what the group intends to accomplish; lack of clear and agreed-upon expectations.
- Members' inability to state what is important or what needs to be done to achieve success.
- Lack of summarization; lack of checking to see that members understand decisions.
- Development of a "repository of all knowledge"; that is, an individual who is supposed to know everything so other members are relieved of their responsibility to know.
- Over- or underemphasis on task demands.
- Lack of purposeful attention to group process, or too much attention to matters of group process (including the "heavy duties"; that is,

every little problem becomes a "serious issue that I think we need to discuss").

- Expecting someone else to solve something you see as a problem.
- Not taking time to enjoy each other's company.
- Believing that having fun is a waste of time; viewing tasks as work only.

Inadequate Communication

- Exaggerating or understating the importance of issues, concerns, or problems.
- Inability or unwillingness of members to declare needs in a way that people can act on them.
- Belief that everyone thinks things are as important, as good, or as bad as you do.
- Ignoring cultural variants and assuming that everyone wants to be treated the same way you want to be treated; not considering how others would want to be treated.
- Inability to listen to what is important to other members; inability to "go past the words." (*Hint:* Could you write down two things that are clearly important to each person with whom you are working and clearly state how each sees that these are being met?)
- Making inexplicit agreements.
- Not understanding how the actions of one team or group within the organization affects the agenda, matters, or concerns of the others.

Lack of Distributed and Developed Leadership

- Decision making by just agreeing with me (or with you).
- Current leadership is too directive.
- Current leadership states opinions as facts.
- Leadership invested in "experts."
- Unwillingness by members to assert leadership.
- Whining by members who are less involved in leadership actions.
- Inability of leaders to promote leadership skills of others; lack of purposeful distribution of leadership tasks.

DID YOU KNOW?   Twenty Tips for Productive Meetings (Plus One)

1. Know why you are having a meeting, and design your procedures to accomplish your purpose. If your proposed meeting doesn't clearly and logically relate to action or increased group cohesion, don't have it.

2. Pay attention to matters of scheduling. First, select a date that gives you enough time to implement the decisions you make at the meeting. It does no good to come up with a brilliant idea that you just cannot act on because you have left yourself too little time to do anything. Second, select a date and hour that allow for as many of the key participants to attend as possible. Next, give yourself enough time during the meeting to take care of the needed business. Finally, select a site that is convenient and appropriate for the nature of the meeting and the size of the group.

3. To the extent possible, make sure participants know and understand the purpose and type of meeting beforehand. Send out pertinent information in advance of the meeting so individuals can start off mentally prepared. (Though you should encourage participants to read over the material you send, don't expect that everyone will do so. You had better briefly review the key points of the material before you begin a discussion on it.)

4. Prepare yourself well with material, information, and any supplies needed to conduct the meeting. Review minutes of previous meetings and reports related to the topics under review to get your bearings straight before the meeting begins.

5. Develop an agenda that allows for the major items to be discussed. It is generally better to place important issues at the beginning to make sure they

receive their due attention rather than rushing through them in the closing minutes. Know how much time should be spent on each item. If more time is needed as the meeting progresses, negotiate for it, clarifying that other items may get little or no time. Do not have the meeting go longer than advertised unless you have negotiated for the extra time. If more time is needed on an issue that can wait for resolution, ask a few people to work on it and provide a recommendation for action at the next meeting.

6. Decide how long the meeting should last. People can usually meet for about an hour and a half before their minds begin to wander to things more interesting. Marathon meetings that go on for hours can be useful at the beginning stage of the organization when enthusiasm and a sense of mission are running high or when preparing for some critical event in the life of the organization. They can make the circumstances seem more dramatic and the people involved in them more important.

7. Don't try to do too much at one meeting. Your preparation for the meeting should include a review of the topics for presentation and an assessment of participant interest as well.

8. Establish group sizes appropriate for the degree of discussion necessary. A large group may be broken into smaller groups for discussion with time allotted for reporting back to the entire group.

9. Pay attention to matters of structure and space. Whenever possible, participants should sit in a circle. Leave an extra chair open for a

Lack of Follow-Through on Tasks

- Lack of honest understanding that "didn't have the time" often really means "didn't take the time."

- Inability to break tasks down into manageable units. (*Hint:* You can make phone calls in 10-minute blocks.)

- Too many excuses. (*Hint:* If you "hear" yourself fashioning or rehearsing an excuse

to other members, let that be a signal unto you.)

- Frequent statements that things are "in process" or "being worked on."

Turning Fears Into Anger

- Communicating that less involved members are not concerned or not intelligent.

late-arriving member, but otherwise try not to have too many open seats. Too much space between people decreases the energy and the potential for group cohesion.

10. Have fun. Meetings that are deadly serious can be deadly. A little playfulness can be an important element. For example, asking participants to bring snacks can contribute to a more congenial and relaxing atmosphere and increase involvement.

11. Use the talents and the interests of the participants. Unless you are simply giving information to a passive audience, remember that each participant is a resource.

12. If all members do not know each other well, take time for introductions. "Icebreaker" activities may be helpful in building new relationships. These can be as simple as having each person say a little about herself and state what she intends to get out of the meeting.

13. Clarify the intended outcomes at the start of the meeting. During the meeting, periodically check with the participants to see how you are progressing toward their accomplishment.

14. As you begin the discussion of items, bring people up to date with recent developments. This can be particularly helpful to new members.

15. Purposefully keep the discussion on track, periodically summarizing the key points and identifying areas of emerging agreement. This can be done gently. Don't be heavy-handed.

16. Make explicit, specific decisions that are clearly understood by everyone. Don't let a lot of talk about something that needs to be done substitute for definite decisions and assignments about doing it.

17. Follow the general ground rules for effective discussion: Pay attention to spot those who are trying to speak and encourage them to do so; invite comments from the more quiet members; acknowledge contributions of members; encourage controversy in a climate of respect, recognizing that which is important to one another.

18. Use decision-making methods that are appropriate to the importance of the topic; for example, consensus on important items and majority vote on minor ones.

19. When a matter is settled, move on.

20. Close the meeting. Summarize the main points and decisions made during the meeting, identify the next steps to be taken, and recognize progress being made by the organization toward its goals.

Plus One. You've just concluded a successful meeting; give yourself a pat on the back. But are you done yet? Not quite. Jot down your understanding of matters immediately after the meeting, including impressions, next steps to take for the direction of the effort, and specific tasks. Make sure you write down your own assignments.

- Intolerance of another's peculiarities or well-intentioned mistakes.
- Your fears are greater than your faith in others.
- Making up problems that don't really (or as yet) exist.
- Assuming or imposing arbitrary limitations on what you can do.

Poor Development Efforts

- Lack of purposeful recruitment efforts.
- Lack of purposeful fund-raising and other resource-raising efforts.
- Lack of purposeful development of new leadership.

Most of these problems can be nipped in the bud if members recognize them and decide to handle things differently. A group that routinely assesses how it is working is able to acknowledge and deal with its internal problems. With such an orientation established from the very beginning, periodic general reminders will take care of most of the problems.

Still, some individuals don't get the message. Even after a group discussion of behaviors that can promote or hamper the ability of people to work together, they persist in acting in a counterproductive way. This needs to be brought to the attention of the errant members, ideally in a way that does not cause embarrassment. You can call direct attention to things when they happen without attacking an individual. You can help by saying something like "Hang on for a minute, Ed. You just interrupted Sandy. He may not be finished." Or, if need be, it can be discussed in private. If it is truly a problem, though, it cannot be neglected. Dealing with these situations in a matter-of-fact manner before they get to be persistent problems will minimize the chance that an angry confrontation will be needed to clear the air.

Two final points are worth making here. First, you aren't the relationship sheriff who has the job of keeping everyone on the cooperative straight and narrow. Every member should be encouraged to deal with things that are getting in the way. Second, obviously, not every little mistake needs to be pounced on. Some things that are really not part of a pattern can be ignored.

Meetings That Keep the Momentum

Meetings that produce nothing but future meetings can be the death of the movement (O. M. Collective, 1971). A seemingly endless series of reports, hit-and-miss conversations that randomly address items of importance, discussions that spend too much time on minor concerns and too little on major ones, matters routinely held over for yet another meeting—you have been to this meeting, haven't you? You have seen these characteristics in "action," and you have winced at the thought that tonight you have another meeting to attend. You may well have attended more bad meetings than good ones. This shouldn't and doesn't have to be

the case. Too many meetings accomplish too little, waste time, or are just plain dull. One of the great ironies is that most of us have frustrating experiences at meetings most of the time, yet the notion that just anyone can run a meeting persists unquestioned. The title of "chair" does not by itself confer magical powers that enable its holder to handle a meeting well. A poor conductor will inhibit the performance of an orchestra; an ineffective chair will hamper the productivity of a meeting (Tropman et al., 1979). Meetings should provide or revive energy, not sap it.

Actually, learning how to run a meeting effectively is much easier than many people make it out to be. By using your time, your participants, and yourself purposefully, you can accomplish quite a lot by bringing people together. Keep your focus on the goals for the meeting, pay attention to both the task and maintenance needs of the group, use a little common sense, and you will have meetings that maintain interest and inspire action.

Running meetings will quickly become routine for you. The danger is that it can become so routine that you become sloppy. Going over a mental checklist before each meeting is a good habit to get into. The more you are primed to get the most out of your meetings, the more you will produce, the more time you will save, and the more momentum you will build.

TYPES OF ORGANIZATIONS

Not all organizations are the same. Distinctions are based on type, design, and purpose. You have a variety of organizational configurations from which to choose to bring people together to work for change. Some common types of organizations include membership organizations, open organizations, coalitions, and networks.

Membership Organizations

While all organizations have members, membership organizations are characterized by having a prescribed method for individuals to establish their affiliation. Normally this consists of paying dues.

Organizations may establish other criteria as well. These can include setting minimum qualifications for membership, nomination and selection procedures, written agreements detailing the rights and duties of membership, a code of ethics or conduct, and other policies that more strictly define membership. In addition to codifying requirements for membership, some organizations develop a number of symbols and rituals that serve to further strengthen the members' identification with the organization and their bonds to one another. These range from a Shriner wearing a fez to the Girl Scout promise sign to a member of the Lions Club having to pay a fine for not shaking everyone's hand before the start of a meeting. Use of special signs is more commonly the case when group affiliation itself is a particular value.

Of course, all organizations develop some set of symbols or norms that convey a sense of uniqueness. Yours will too. You most likely want to cultivate a broad membership in a welcoming atmosphere, so more restrictive admissions practices and elaborate customs are probably both unnecessary and unhelpful.

Dues are perhaps the simplest and the most effective method to distinguish formal membership. One of the main reasons for establishing dues is that in so doing you ask someone to explicitly declare support and affiliation. You literally confirm the member's investment in the organization's goals. Because your intent is to both strengthen and increase participation, it is a good idea to keep the cost of dues relatively low, but high enough to create a sense of real participation from members (Beckwith, 2004). There are some exceptions. In some circumstances, for example, a membership coalition, high membership fees can be used to affirm commitment. Though you can raise money through the payment of dues, doing so is usually a minor consideration.

Because they have taken steps to confirm the individual's connection to the group, membership organizations can generally depend on a stronger commitment from their participants than can less formal groups. Defined membership makes it much easier to identify, contact, and mobilize proponents of an organization's point of view. These organizations also have a better gauge on the degree of support they have and, if need be, can point to their roster as evidence of that support. They can unequivocally assert the fact that they are speaking for a genuine constituency.

Open Organizations

Most membership organizations intend to be permanent, and over time they will pursue an array of interests. In contrast, open groups tend to be more focused on current issues and often do not plan to solidify the organization's development. Those involved are more likely to identify with the issue than with the organization. Building the organization is done primarily to accomplish a specified purpose rather than being a goal in itself. Thus, codifying membership policies is less of a concern. There are few barriers to membership. In organizations of this type, whoever says he or she is a member is a member.

Open organizations readily accept new participants. With concerns related more to the organization's agenda of change than to its procedures, prospective participants find it easy to become involved in the organization and its work. This can be an asset for a group working on a specific concern, especially one that can be resolved in a matter of months.

Participants have little actual commitment to the organization itself, so it is often difficult to sustain allegiance. Members tend to come and go unless the program of change is very specific and time limited. It is pretty common for work to be fragmented and for many projects to be dropped before completion. Of course, this can also be true of membership organizations. It is just more likely to occur when the participants' ties to the organization are loose and when no one is quite sure who is really involved. Open organizations certainly can structure their procedures, though a spirit of informality is more common to these groups. If members of an open organization intend to move beyond a short-term, restricted agenda, they will have to pay more attention to developing the organization itself.

Some open organizations have a very specific focus and concentrate most of their energies on accomplishing a defined objective. A group formed

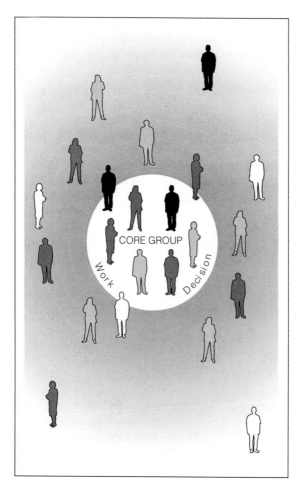

FIGURE 11.2   Model of a Core Group

A core group is an action-oriented organization with little formal structure. An "inner circle" of highly committed members does most of the work and makes most of the decisions. Membership in the inner circle is open to anyone willing to do the work.

to deal with a specific community crisis or to change a particular agency policy are examples of such groups. Groups that work to resolve very limited issues are often called *ad hoc* groups. Another type of organization with a narrow focus is a *task force*. This variation describes a temporary collection of people who commonly have some special expertise that is particularly helpful in dealing with the problem at hand. Both ad hoc groups and task forces are often called together by some sponsoring organization, such as a City Council or United Way.

A *core group* is another variation of an open organization (see Figure 11.2). Core groups are made up of a small group of dedicated activists who are able to mobilize others to action. They usually have a narrow focus and little structure. If the number of active members of the organization stays small, it is likely that those who function as the core group will serve as unelected directors of the effort, probably without declaring that they comprise any formal decision-making body of the organization. Core group members usually do not hinder others from becoming involved in the inner circle, but they don't actively encourage it either. If relative outsiders are willing to jump in and work, and at the same time try to figure out what is going on, they can do so. However, core group members are commonly too impatient to spend time preparing new members for more active roles. This, of course, is a condition that can be remedied if acknowledged. Core groups can be highly efficient and can successfully address a limited agenda, but it is difficult for them to sustain enthusiasm for long periods. With little effort directed to building for the future, groups like these tend to come and go.

Coalitions

An organizer assembles resources, brings them together. This could include bringing together supporting groups or those with a shared interest. Coalitions are organizations of organizations (see Figure 11.3). They have a tremendous potential for bringing together immediate power. They are created when a group realizes that its power base is too small for it to successfully pursue an important issue, so it joins forces with others who are affected by the same issue. When these various organizations agree to work together, the coalition is born. Collaborative efforts are gaining increased attention from funders and activists alike, and attention to coalition building practices have grown as well (Chavis, 2001; Mizrahi & Rosenthal, 2001; Wolff, 2001).

Many coalitions are of the ad hoc variety, formed to address a particular concern and disbanded once that particular matter is resolved. Others become more permanent organizations, usually with a single broad focus such as health care, hunger, or reproduc-

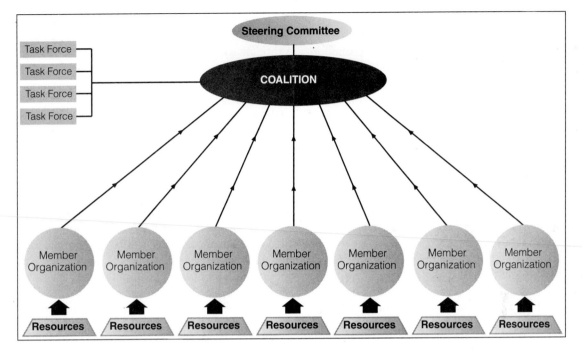

FIGURE 11.3 Model of a Coalition

tive rights (Checkoway, 1987; Cox, 1987a; Dale, 1978; Kahn, 1991).

Putting a coalition together provides a number of benefits to the change effort. One particular advantage is that the coalition has ready access to resources that have already been organized. Each member has something already in place that is of value to the coalition. This may be volunteers, money, good relationships with lawmakers, or leadership ability. Also particularly important is the ability to inform and mobilize a large number of people in a fairly short period of time. Each member probably has staff, a board of directors, and a constituency it serves. That could represent quite a horde of partners. Coalitions often have an easier time gaining identity and acceptance in the community. Many of the participating organizations bring established community credibility; their names and their leaders are recognizable to the media and to other members of the community. Finally, involvement by a variety of groups working on the issue gives it an almost immediate degree of legitimacy (Jansson, 1994).

Coalitions, however, have some built-in conflicts. Among them is the protection of turf that often characterizes relationships among groups operating within a generally similar arena. Participation in a coalition requires members not only to divide their time with yet another group but often to divide their loyalties as well. There needs to be clarity about the self-interests of the organizations involved (Sampson, 2004). If the coalition is the result of a funder's directive rather than a participant initiative, commitment to the new organization may be restrained, and if a lead agency is designated in this arrangement, power and control imbalances can threaten relationships. As the coalition gains strength, one additional concern is that the power and voice of smaller, emerging grassroots organizations may be muted. Dealing effectively with these conflicts promotes the coalition agenda and can markedly increase community capacity as well.

Assembling a coalition involves a series of steps somewhat similar to bringing new members into any organization. The first step is to determine whom you would like to have involved in the coalition. The second is to contact them, emphasizing how the issue affects their self-interest. The third is to secure some commitment to the coalition from each organization. Next, you need to involve the member groups in the work of the coalition. Of course, throughout the life of the coalition, you need to maintain communication with those who are involved.

You will take several things into account in selecting potential members. The best starting place is to enlist the support of organizations with whom you have already established a relationship. After this, a little critical thinking is in order (Kahn, 1991). The first question you should ask is, "Who is most likely to join?" Organizations that serve people who are affected by the issue or that have compatible philosophical positions are likely candidates. So, too, might be those whose particular interests, talents, or knowledge relate to your issue. Could the carpenters be interested in your community renovation efforts? Could the insurance brokers help you curb drunk driving? Coalitions working on a legislative agenda may want to present a mainstream face to legislators (Berg, 1999).

The next question is "Who has what we need?" In addition to the more obvious resources of expertise, numbers, and money, make sure you have members in your coalition who can relate to the different publics you intend to influence.

Contacting potential members is best done through a face-to-face discussion. This allows you time to answer questions and clarify how the aims of the coalition fit the interests of the organization whose involvement you seek. Additionally, explain any benefit the organization could receive through participation in the coalition. If possible, bring along an individual who is well regarded by the targeted organization to help you make the pitch.

It is important to get a written agreement from those who are willing to be publicly involved. It is always a good idea to first ask the organization how they may help the effort. You can build on these ideas for further commitments. The easiest way to obtain a record of agreement is to develop a simple commitment form that spells out various general categories of commitment. Another approach is to ask for a letter of support written on the organization's stationery. Whichever way you choose, it is important to at least secure permission to list the organization as a member of the coalition. Although some organizations cannot, for reasons of their own, become official members of the coalition, they can publicly endorse the coalition and its goals. This should be offered as an option to those who decline membership.

From the very beginning, enlist other members to help with the recruitment effort. This increases their commitment as well as the coalition's field of contacts. Once you have a number of organizations signed up, it is time to hold a general meeting. Take this opportunity to build further enthusiasm for the undertaking and strengthen cohesion among members. Also, clarify members' roles and expectations and underscore the value of participation and the potential for significant accomplishment that exists as a result of those now present in the room.

You will find that a relatively small percentage of member organizations will be regular active participants. However, this core can accomplish a lot by using the many resources at the coalition's disposal. This may range from asking one or two members to perform some specific activity to occasionally mobilizing the entire membership. It is important, though, that these resources be used. Making direct requests of member organizations increases their feeling of involvement in the effort. Organizations rarely asked to do anything will lose interest and will most likely not follow through when they are finally asked. One important thing to remember is that each participating organization is concerned about many other things. One of the consequences of this is that requests for action should be made directly if at all possible. General requests of the membership are likely to go unheeded.

Communication among member groups is a crucial concern for the coalition. From simple matters like sending a follow-up note to those who agree to become members to holding coordinating meetings or sending out periodic progress updates, matters of communication must be given a high priority. Communication from the coalition to the broader community is important as well. A silent coalition is an invisible one. This can present a challenge because coalition members have different styles and different constituencies. There needs

DID YOU KNOW?   Building a Successful Coalition

Mizrahi and Rosenthal (2001) surveyed more than 40 coalitions in an examination of factors that affect their success. Here are the top 10 internal factors that respondents reported as contributing greatly to their success:

- Commitment to the issue, goal, or cause
- Competent leadership
- Commitment to coalition unity

- Equitable decision-making structure and process
- Mutual trust, respect, and tolerance
- Broad-based constituency of members
- Achievement of interim victories
- Ongoing contributions of resources by members
- Shared responsibility and ownership
- Provision of benefits to coalition members

to be one unified, core message that all members agree on and communicate. Different members can communicate the same core message, but in ways that feel authentic to them. One suggestion is to have groups in your coalition that are on the very activist end of things. Those activist groups can more freely voice concerns that more moderate groups feel they cannot speak to (Minch, 2005).

Coalitions commonly form committees or task forces organized around various functions to which the coalition needs to attend. These may include fund-raising, membership development, media communications, lobbying, and research. A coordinating committee composed of committee leaders and other interested members should be set up to manage the affairs of the coalition. This committee also helps plot overall strategy and direction. Open access to participation in this committee is vital. A general rule is that anyone who wants to be on it can be. Clear and meaningful opportunities to be involved in decision making will check the growth of divisive fear and mistrust.

A coalition is a form of collaboration. Successful collaborations have shared ownership of goals and results, relationships among members that are kept active, appropriately distributed work, and shared recognition of each other's interests and efforts. These features are based on clear agreements and kept strong through ongoing monitoring and communication. Lack of attention to any one of these will stress the ties among members and diminish commitment.

The League of Women Voters (1976, pp. 1–2) offered several tips for forming successful coalitions:

- The goal should be clearly defined and stated; no one is empowered to speak for the coalition on any other issue.

- Each organization is free to act for itself outside the coalition, but not in the name of the coalition except with appropriate authorization from other members. What is required for authorization should be delineated.

- All participating groups should be encouraged to speak out in their own names, as well as under the coalition umbrella, in support of the goal.

- If everyone can agree from the beginning that success is more important than individual or organizational prestige, later conflicts will be minimized (though seldom eliminated).

Coalitions can be very effective and can provide you with credibility and resources very quickly. Keep in mind that with so many varied interests involved, coalitions require a high degree of attention to maintenance matters.

Networks

Networks are distinct types of organizations that link people through a series of interconnected personal relationships (see Figure 11.4). The intent is to establish and nurture these relationships so that each member is connected in some way to all others.

Network

FIGURE 11.4 Model of a Network
Members of a network are connected to all other members. Each member can contact any other member to make a request. Members bring personal and professional resources to the network.

Networks are not created to deal with a particular problem; rather, they are established to promote very broad goals. Networks put like-minded people in touch with each other so they can share resources and further common interests. This arrangement, which provides an accumulation of social capital, dramatically increases the availability of support and practical assistance.

Whereas a coalition is a collection of organizations, a network is fundamentally person centered. Some networks involve people who hold leadership positions or are fairly active in the community; others just bring together people who share a certain situation, helping them to get to know each other, develop trust, and create opportunities to work together. A network can be drawn from various sectors of the community, or from a particular interest area. For example, participants could include members of human service agencies, faith communities, local businesses, schools, neighborhoods,

or health providers. The assumption is that these individuals are able to activate resources other network members could use. This can be something tangible, like providing space for a meeting; it may be a service, like conducting a presentation on discharge planning; it may be a skill, like helping to set up new computer software; or it may simply be helpful in cutting through the red tape.

A network is built on the idea that people are more willing to be helpful to someone they know and trust than to a stranger. So, a principal aim of a network is to have as many people with similar interests get to know, trust, and commit to help each other as possible. Therefore, an individual is invited into the network not so much to help with a particular problem as to be available to help in general.

In addition to the emphasis placed on building personal relationships and sharing resources, networks stress the importance of circulating information. The assumption is that many of the network participants are "in the know." Members help one another keep current on developments within their areas of interest. They also assist in putting the word out when one of the members needs some special help. A particular organization or agency usually serves as a clearinghouse of network information. Websites, regular newsletters, and routinely updated membership lists (which identify particular resources members have committed to share) add to the storehouse, as do frequent get-togethers among members.

Dosher (1977a, p. 6) identified four main functions that networks provide:

- Communication linkages and information channels for the exchange of needs and resources.

- Participants support systems and resource sharing.

- A means for coordination, cooperation, collaboration, person and program actualization, training, and capacity-building.

- A means for collective action.

One way to get the network established is at an initial meeting conducted in a workshoplike atmosphere. These key network concerns should be addressed at this first gathering (Dosher 1977b, p. 1):

- The purpose(s) of the network
- Network function or goals
- Recognition of personal values
- Deepening and strengthening interpersonal relationships
- Structure and member roles
- Identification of member resources
- Future plans and responsibilities

A network is a process for bringing people together to advance a particular public policy or practice (advocacy network), to assist one another and to serve mutual needs (exchange network), or to change community conditions (development). Members of a network are committed to sharing information and resources (Langton, 1982).

Some networks are structured simply to facilitate the connection between individuals and serve advocacy, exchange, and development purposes. They provide many points of entry for bringing participants into a relationship with one another, with members reaching out to their own personal networks to help people feel more connected in the community (Tranynor & Andors, 2005). Such a network is not formed to take a position on specific community issues, but the process does facilitate network members getting together to take action, though not in the name of the network. Because of the many connections members have made through the network, it is easier for people to join forces to organize a legislative action program, a workshop, or a bake sale. Those who want to be involved in any given project can do so, and those who do not can just sit back if they like.

Valdis Krebs and June Holley (2006) described the process of network weaving. It is a purposeful strategy for strengthening communities based on the assumption that communities are built on connections. Network weaving is the intentional development of networks, along with the linking of various community networks. This usually starts with a small project to bring people together so that they get to know each other and learn to collaborate. This can create valuable connections, but it is not enough. If left unmanaged, networks result in small, dense clusters in which everyone knows everyone else and no one knows what is going on in other clusters. The isolation and lack of diversity limits the vitality and influence of any network. Finding matters of shared interest and linking diverse community networks brings in new information, new ideas, greater access to resources, and greater power. Weaving these networks together requires an active leader, or network weaver, who has the vision, energy, and social skills to connect diverse individuals and groups. One of the weaver's key roles is to identify and develop new weavers who will eventually take over much of the network building and maintenance. Otherwise, the network, like any other type of organization, will become dependent on the central weaver and the organization that might have originally sponsored the network weaving effort. Network weaving is community building.

Every one of us has our own personal network—those people we know and for whom we would do a little extra. An organized network simply brings all these networks together so people can ultimately benefit from one another's particular abilities and "connections."

INCORPORATING

If you want to stake a claim for permanence, you may consider formally incorporating your organization. By so doing you create a separate legal entity with its own identity.

Benefits of Incorporating

Incorporation creates a psychological effect on the membership that all of you, working together, have created something with substance. It also provides you with recognition in the community beyond your immediate supporters. It can provide other, more practical benefits as well. A corporation can serve as a buffer between the members and an uncertain world. As a separate entity that can sue or be sued, it can provide some protection to its members in the event of a lawsuit. In fact, many states provide for exemptions from or a limitation of liability of directors of nonprofit organizations. (Nonetheless, it is a good idea to check into insurance, particularly corporate general liability and directors' and officers' liability insurance.) Taking the step to incorporate will help you get money, either by giving you greater access to funding from government organizations and private foundations or by aiding your efforts to solicit contributions from private individuals (Hicks, 1997). Incorporating means that you really are in business to pursue your mission.

You may work with a community coalition or small organization that does not want to go through the steps of formal incorporation, yet your group may want to seek grant support through foundations or government sources. In some instances an established, incorporated agency may be willing to let you affiliate with them under an arrangement that allows you to use their incorporation status. Check to see if an agency you work for or others within the community will sponsor the community group and its activities (Hicks, 1997).

Basic Steps of Incorporation

The decision to incorporate brings with it a series of additional decisions that will shape the future of your organization. It will also bring some additional paperwork. Following the guidance of an attorney and an accountant familiar with incorporation procedures is a wise step. Most incorporations are routine matters, so it should not be difficult to find a professional among your community contacts who can provide you with help for free. The process of incorporating includes the following activities.

Identify Your Purpose. Spend some time thinking about your reason for existence. Write down, in very broad terms, your areas of interest and service. In many states, a statement of purpose is required in the Articles of Incorporation. This serves to set forth your area of legal operations.

Identify the Incorporators.   These are the people who will take initial responsibility for getting the incorporation under way. They will play a significant role in shepherding the process until the board of directors is formally established. Frequently, the incorporators become the first board of directors.

Develop a Board of Directors.   Though you do not need much of a board to incorporate, you do need substantial help from your board to stay in business. Most new organizations need a working board. Having a few board members who serve as window dressing to enhance your image may help, but you need to have a good group who will be active in helping to determine the direction of the organization and securing community support.

The board you establish at this time is a policy board, which is different from an advisory board. Policy boards hold the ultimate power in the organization. As their name suggests, they set the formal policies governing the operation of the organization. In addition, other routine duties include approving the budget, approving contracts, approving significant expenditures, and hiring or firing executive staff. By contrast, advisory boards hold no formal power within the organization. Their main responsibility is to provide community input into the direction of various programs. Although some advisory boards are very active in support of their programs, they have no formal decision-making authority.

Give some careful thought to the development of your board. One basic decision involves the size of the board itself. A board with 15 members is about average. (The laws of your state may set some limitations on the size of your board.) You will probably want to hold a couple of slots vacant in case you identify an outstanding individual whose participation on the board could make a strong contribution to the organization.

When selecting board members, start by looking for individuals who can provide one of the three W's: work, wealth, or wisdom. Then meet specific needs of the organization by recruiting community members who possess certain expertise

or resources or who have access to a particularly important population. For example, do you need an accountant, someone from the construction industry, a wealthy individual with wealthy friends, or members active on diversity issues? Paying careful attention to the ethnic and gender balance of your board almost goes without saying (almost, but not quite). However, many organizations fail to include members of the constituency they serve on their boards of directors. This is an inexcusable oversight. Attention to the composition of your board is one of your most important tasks.

Select Officers.   You will determine which individuals will fill the positions you designate. The typical positions are president, vice president, secretary, and treasurer. These offices are normally filled by election. Some organizations have replaced the board offices of president and vice president with chair and vice chair, making the president and vice president paid staff positions.

Prepare Articles of Incorporation.   This legal document establishes your organization as a corporation and sets forth basic principles. It covers issues such as the organization's name and purpose, its place of business, the handling of any assets in the event of its dissolution, its status as a profit or nonprofit corporation, as well as other matters. Obtaining the assistance of a professional is important to help you draw up these articles.

One of the important issues you should discuss with your attorney or accountant is the tax status of the corporation. You need to determine first whether or not you intend to be a nonprofit organization, and if so, whether or not you intend to be tax-exempt. The two common types of nonprofit corporations are those designated as either 501(c)(3) or 501(c)(4). These numbers refer to classifications within a section of the Internal Revenue Code. These are 2 of 28 different types of tax-exempt organizations under 501(c) of the code, which represents quite a range of concerns (IRS, 2008). Some of the tax-exempt categories allow for a number of creative approaches that may well relate to interests in your community. You may want to take a look at them as well. For the purposes of our discussion, I will focus on the types of organizations referred to as 501(c)(3) or 501(c)(4).

Though both types are nonprofit, there are important distinctions between the two. Contributions to 501(c)(3) organizations can be tax deductible for the contributor, whereas contributions to a 501(c)(4) generally are not (IRS, 2008; Phelan, 2002). Further, claiming tax-exempt status as a 501(c)(3) organization saddles you not only with more paperwork but with certain limitations on the amount of lobbying activity your organization can undertake. However, a 501(c)(3) organization most definitely can participate in lobbying. (This is more fully discussed in Chapter 15.) Activities such as voter registration and candidate forums are permissible if conducted in an unbiased and nonpartisan manner, but 501(c)(3) organizations are strictly prohibited from engaging in political campaigns (IRS, 2006). Consider incorporating as a 501(c)(4) organization if you intend to engage heavily in lobbying. Such an organization can take part in lobbying and some political activities as long as the principal purpose of the organization is to advance social welfare (IRS, 2008, 2009e; Phelan, 2002; Zack, 1997).

If you find it in your interest to be heavily involved in election activities, you may want to form an organization that is expressly political. Section 527 of the tax code covers these organizations. That section provides for limited exemption from income taxes for political organizations such as political action committees (IRS, 2002; Zack, 1997).

Congress frequently considers legislation relating to nonprofit advocacy, so it is a good idea to check with organizations such as the Alliance for Justice and Center for Lobbying in the Public Interest to see if any modifications have occurred that would affect your plans. Before you make any decisions regarding these various options, consult a professional who is familiar with choices for incorporation so you fully understand the restrictions and the benefits each choice provides.

Agree to a Set of Bylaws. The basic rules describing how the organization is to operate are declared in your bylaws. Their purpose is to prevent problems by establishing and making clear the basic procedures for running the organization. Here are some matters commonly addressed in bylaws:

- Leadership roles and duties
- Election procedures
- Quorum policies, voting methods, and voting rights
- Determination of criteria for membership
- Establishment of committees
- Schedules for various types of meetings (annual membership meetings, regular board meetings)
- Notification of membership regarding organization action
- Expenditure of funds
- Procedures for amending the bylaws

No set of bylaws can anticipate every possibility, but they do prevent problems stemming from misunderstanding or misuse of power. Bylaws should be written clearly so they are easily understood. Professional assistance can be valuable in developing your bylaws.

File with the Appropriate Government Agency. So the public can know what you are up to, state incorporation laws will probably require that your Articles of Incorporation be officially filed with the appropriate government office.

> A sample set of articles of incorporation and bylaws is provided on this book's companion website at: www.cengage.com/humansvcs/homan.)

Publish Your Articles of Incorporation. To give the public even more of a chance to learn about your corporation, in most states you are required to publish your Articles of Incorporation in a newspaper published in the area of the primary location of your operation. This may well be the major expense in incorporating, so before you give your money to the major daily, check to see what your publishing options are. Frequently, smaller newspapers in the area, maybe even in a nearby small town, can publish to fulfill your legal requirement. Their advertising rates may be a fraction of what the larger papers will charge you.

CAPTURING CONCEPTS
Features of Movement Capacity Building for Nonprofits

There have been significant resources dedicated to the development of nonprofits' organizational capacity. However, less attention has been paid to the capacity of groups to support movement for social change. Below are nine areas the Building Movement Project identified as important building blocks of *movement capacity* of nonprofit organizations.

Vision: The organization has a statement of the world it wants to create and a theory of how change is made, including the role the organization plays in the larger social change arena and to whom the organization views itself as accountable.

Principles: Based on its vision of social change, the organization develops values that are applied within and outside the organization.

Learning and Reflecting: The organization allocates time for its staff and constituents to learn and reflect on the organizational vision through presentations, readings, discussions, or arts and culture. The organization reflects on its own work to refine its vision and strategies.

Issues of Race and Power: The organization considers society's "dominant culture" and how that culture is, often unconsciously, replicated within the organization itself. The organization analyzes how the effects of race, class, gender, and other cultual factors affect its work.

Work Across Boundaries: The organization builds relationships with other agencies, groups, and individuals to create a movement, and supports other groups without trying to "own" every issue or campaign.

Work Across Generations: The organization has a mechanism for transferring trust, power, and responsibility from older leaders to younger ones, while educating younger leaders about the complexities of social change work and inspiring their involvement in these issues.

Constituent Involvement: The organization has a mechanism by which to promote meaningful constituent involvement that goes beyond just staff, board, and funders. The organization also directs resources toward constituency involvement, within and outside the organization.

Structure: The organization creates a system of effective leadership, management, and accountability while remaining creative and flexible in internal and external problem solving. The agency collaborates with other organizations to bring about social change.

Funding: The organization recognizes and has transparency about the impact that funders' priorities have on the organization's work. The organization also examines how to maintain accountability to its constituents, particularly when funding comes from sources other than the organization's consituent base.

SOURCE: Building Movement Project (n.d.).

File Necessary Reports.   You will be required to file periodic reports with various government agencies. For example, if you are a tax-exempt organization you are most likely required to file IRS Form 990. Some smaller organizations can file a shortened Form 990-EZ. (Chapter 9 discusses Form 990 in more detail.) These forms must be made available to the public, so some organizations have posted them on their website—not only to fulfill the law but to present the information on the form to serve marketing purposes (Sechler, 2000). It is another way to get your accomplishments and your program out to the public and to potential funders.

Now you are a full-fledged corporation doing important business in your community. You have come a long way from the days when you just sat around and grumbled about problems. You have accomplished something meaningful for today, and you have done something for the future as well.

SUSTAINING THE ORGANIZATION

Getting an organization up and running is quite a feat. Keeping it alive and growing stronger may be even more challenging. It is rare for an organization just to keep going on its own. Seven key factors affect an organization's sustainability. Each of these has been discussed in this or previous chapters. Each deserves thoughtful, purposeful attention.

Membership

Your membership is your organization. Without members you do not exist. You can look at three facets of this aspect of your organization to bring you a strong and diverse membership base.

Not long after your organization begins to develop, it is a good idea to *establish numerical targets*. If you have no idea how big your organization needs to grow and who needs to be involved to give it what it needs, your membership development activities will be haphazard, if they exist at all. Here are some key questions to guide your thinking and acting.

- How many people do we want to have involved? At 6 months? In a year? In 2 years?

- How many do we need at the various levels of involvement that were discussed in Chapter 8?

- How many might be relatively inactive but could be mobilized when needed?

- How many from different sectors of our community need to be involved? Do we need businesspeople, those from faith communities, educators, or perhaps political officials? How about age and ethnic diversity?

- Are there particular interests that need to be included or people from different neighborhoods, different parts of the neighborhood, or other different areas?

From the very beginning you will engage in *intentional recruitment*. Early on the small group of initiators will likely involve those whom you know. Then you will reach out to the people in the networks of those whom you first contact. Your later recruiting efforts will be guided by the numerical targets you have developed. You will put together both a recruitment plan and a retention plan. Your recruitment plan will include a number of routine, ongoing ways to bring in new participants. It will also have some special recruitment activities. You will grow stronger when each member of the organization looks for opportunities to invite new participants. Your retention plan will include methods for keeping people connected with each other and involved in the organization's life. You will allow for different levels of interest while providing opportunities for interest, confidence, and commitment to deepen.

You will make sure that *new members immediately have things to do*. These will match the individual's initial interest and available time. If you wait very long at all before you involve a willing person, you may find that the person is no longer willing. Decrease the distance, or in this case the time, between a person's agreement to take part and your invitation for that individual to actually do something.

Leadership

Remember that there are different forms of leadership. Leaders influence or inspire others to help the organization achieve its goals or enhance the relationships among members. People who just like to tell other people what to do aren't what you are looking for. I've never seen an organization with too many leaders. I've seen very, very many with too few.

Your attention to leadership occurs in three areas. You are always on the lookout for *new leadership*. In fact, it is a good idea to identify the number of new, active leaders you will develop each year or each 6 months. Provide opportunities for new leadership to emerge, and identify individuals who seem to have leadership potential. For a number of reasons a few of these will not move into leadership roles, so look for potential wherever you can. Mentor new leaders to help them become more effective and more confident, which includes their helping to develop a new set of leaders as time goes on. Your organization will depend on *ongoing leadership* to move the organization forward. Some of these leaders will have responsibility for broad organization matters; some will have leadership in a particular area. While they continue providing leadership, good leaders will reflect on how to increase their leadership skills. Some leaders will want to decrease their level of involvement. A strong organization will recognize and support those wishes and find ways to include *emeritus leadership* in the life of the organization. Former leaders who move out of the organization take their knowledge, experience, and the confidence they engender in others with them. Provide avenues for emeritus leaders to move down in their level of involvement, but not out of the organization.

Structure

The structure of your organization will emerge to meet the demands the organization is facing, but some form of structure will help to focus energy, keep people connected, and get the work done. Typically, you will build five different aspects of structure as your organization grows.

You will establish *meeting schedules*. These include regular meetings, such as monthly meetings, special project meetings for parts of the organization that are working on a particular matter, and annual meetings that bring all members together and serve as a time for celebration and renewed commitment to the vision. As the organization's work begins to settle into place, it is a good idea to have a schedule of times when people will get together.

Meetings are generally not the place to build the organization. They confirm the process of organization and draw attention to it. The organization is built outside of meetings in the relationship building process, the connecting process, and the steady work on projects that advance the organization's agenda. Some of this occurs in small group task-oriented meetings; some in small group relationship building get-togethers. Most of it does not occur in the general monthly meetings of the organization.

You will put *communication methods in place*. Keeping people connected to each other and to the organization and its work is critical for your success; make sure communication among members is routine. There are numerous ways for groups to keep in regular communication, and you will select the ones that work best for your organization at its stage of development. Organizations need to communicate for sharing information, making decisions, building relationships, and affirming organizational identity. Newsletters, e-mail distribution lists, telephone trees, and websites are just a few of the methods that can serve different purposes.

As the organization continues to grow, you will *identify and fill key roles*. This provides opportu-

nities for leadership development. Typical roles may include officers or designated leadership roles, the Nag (or follow-up coordinator), a meeting facilitator (a chairperson doesn't have to run all the meetings), and task performance roles. Roles related to task performance can include any specific, ongoing responsibility that a member accepts, such as newsletter editor, Web page editor, plan monitor, or meeting reminder.

You may decide that *formal incorporation* will solidify the organization, bringing it credibility and access to other resources. Formal incorporation is not needed for all organizations. This will be a decision that the organization will make as it actively considers its future.

An organization that is well linked in the community is likely to have more recognition and more access to power. *Creating alliances and collaborations* with other organizations will become part of its structure.

Program or Issue Agenda

Your organization will have a vision, a goal, and an immediate focus. Your success in improving conditions in your community calls for planful action. This factor of sustainability has five components. You will select a *major* or *focus issue* that will guide your work for the upcoming year. You will develop and implement an *annual plan*, which you will refine at least every 3 months. You will routinely prepare a *next steps action chart* or make use of a similar tool to identify specific tasks and responsibilities for shorter periods of time, for example, one month. You will attend to *maintenance issues* and monitor their progress.

You will determine a process for handling *emerging issues*. Even though you have a major issue that provides most of your organization's focus, things will come up that you did not anticipate or that a particular member wants the organization to address. If you are not careful, this can become the "issue of the month." That is, each month someone brings up a new issue and you set aside your agenda to talk about this new concern and make a few gestures toward it, until next month when another new issue calls for your attention. If you are a network organization, this may not be a big problem.

However, if you are like most other organizations, you will find that you have divided your energy among lots of different matters without accomplishing very much at all. You will probably just run out of gas. Some emerging issues are important and can give the organization a boost in activity. For this to occur, you need to have a way to decide how to handle them. One method is to accept only new issues that can be resolved in less than a month, or to actively decide to stop working on a current issue, replacing it with the new one. Whatever approach you use, acknowledge that there are many things out there that could benefit from your attention, but overloading the organization and its members will accomplish nothing.

Effective Relationships

Everything happens through relationships. How members relate to one another and to the vision and work of the organization will be a critical factor in its success and longevity. Most organizations fall apart from the inside. It is not that the work itself is too difficult; it is that working with one another becomes too hard.

Organizations with effective relationships share a number of features. There is a *high level of cohesion* among members. Group cohesion is the glue that holds the group together. It is the result of all the things that attract members to the group, to each other, and to the group's work and purpose. Cohesion helps us get through the setbacks and disappointments as we pull together. People feel like they belong. They have a strong identity with the organization, and they are much more willing to contribute their knowledge, skills, and time.

Conflict is inevitable. People will have different opinions and interests. *Conflict resolution* is a skill that can be learned. Members can learn how to gain from dealing with their differences. Knowing that the group handles differences well will help people feel relaxed and open to offering their ideas and talents.

It is common for some work not to get done. Someone will not follow through on a commitment that was made. This happens. The team needs to have a *process for dealing with a lack of follow through* in place up front—one that everyone knows about

and supports. If possible, the process should be in place before you have to deal with the problem. Trying to deal with it while you are having the problem is hard. People can be upset and defensive. Setting up a process beforehand will make this likely challenge a little easier to handle.

Much of the work of change occurs first in small groups. When you are aware that each group works on two levels simultaneously, you can better understand what is occurring and act to improve the group's functioning. A strong organization pays attention to both the *task* and *relationship* dimensions of the group and the organization itself and provides leadership necessary in each dimension.

Monitoring and Evaluation

You left the interstate a few hours ago, traveled a succession of roads that seemed to get smaller and smaller and more lonely, and the pavement has just ended. Somehow, you think, this might not get you to Louisville, where you should have been by now. Most change efforts will take you into new territory. Planning will give you a sort of road map to guide your way. It usually helps to check that map to see if you are headed in the right direction. Monitoring and its close friend evaluation are kind of like checking that map. Monitoring lets you know if you are doing the things you planned to do. Evaluation helps you to see if what you are doing is producing the intended results. People often give up when they are feeling lost or not seeing any progress.

Plans are great, but only if they are used to make your action more efficient and effective. It is important to monitor your plan to see that you are actually doing what you said you would be doing. If not, look at what that is telling you. Maybe your plan was too ambitious, not sufficiently interesting, some unexpected opportunities developed, or something else is occurring. It becomes an opening for ongoing learning. Without monitoring you may have that anxious feeling of drifting, or worse, failed expectations.

Monitoring and evaluation (see Chapter 7) are necessary activities to help you stay on track, use the learning from your experienes to make needed

CHANGE AGENT TIP

Some Tips for Dealing with Interpersonal Conflict

- Preventing is easier than fixing.
- Build relationships; find multiple connections with the other person.
- Reflect on your own view of the world. Do you believe the world is generally friendly and cooperative, or that it is generally hostile and harmful? Is life an adventure or a struggle? Your beliefs about the world will affect what you draw to yourself. What you truly believe you will create.
- Remember that conflict is normal.
- Differences in expectations create tension and conflict. Clarify expectations for each person in the relationship and arrive at a set of shared expectations.
- Be able and willing to say what is important to the other person, not just what is important to you.
- Bring irritations up the second time you experience them.

- Realize that most people operate on good intentions most of the time.
- Seek common interests and overriding truths. What do you each value?
- Picture a good relationship, even a time when you had a good relationship with the other person you are now in conflict with. What is occurring in that picture of a good relationship? How can you bring that picture into your current reality?
- Be able to describe how you want to act in conflict, not how the other person should act. You can only control yourself; in fact, nobody can control your actions and decisions but you.
- We all re-create history to serve our present purposes and think our story is the only accurate view. Remember that you are the "other person" to those you are in conflict with, so consider how the other person would tell the story of a difficult encounter.

refinements to your plan, and help you recognize progress. Any effort needs to be reinforced in order to continue. If you don't know that what you are doing is working, you may stop doing it. On the other hand if you can see where you are being successful and how to make adjustments to increase your effectiveness, you are likely to become even more confident and motivated.

Funding

Notice that this is the last factor of sustainability. Far too often funding and sustainability are used as almost synonymous terms. This is a misunderstanding of sustainability. If your organization has the first five factors but does not have funding, it still can accomplish quite a lot. If you add funding, it may accomplish a tremendous amount. However, if it has funding but misses any *one* of the other five, it will eventually fail. Of course, having money is important and helpful. It does make possible a number of opportunities, which is why it is on the list of critical factors. Still, it is the least important of them all.

Three considerations for funding are important. A strong organization has *local funding*. Whether that be from local government, membership dues, local fund-raising, in-kind support, including volunteer time, or any other source, investment from the local community is necessary to establish relevance and partnership. A basic rule is that at least 40% of your funding should come from local sources. If the community isn't really owning the organization, who is, and why? Many local communities do not have a strong financial base. *Outside funding* from foundation grants, state or federal grants, website-generated contributions, or other funders from outside your area can add to what the organization is able to do. Your skill in attracting ongoing local and external funding partners will accelerate your efforts, as long as you do not allow fund-raising to become your organization's primary goal.

Many organizations fall into *primary funding source dependence*. When this occurs, the organization looks to one main funding partner and does not develop other revenue streams. This poses a number of problems. First, this dependency opens the possibility that the primary funder can have too strong an influence on the organization's action agenda and methods. The organization may pull back from some issues or may engage in a limited range of strategies and tactics to achieve its goals in order not to risk losing funding from its primary partner. Second, if the primary funding source stops funding the organization, there may be too little left in the coffers for the organization to continue to function. It may die, or it may begin chasing any funding just to keep the doors open. Finally, dependence may produce a kind of laziness that keeps the organization from creating new collaborations and bringing new partners into the work. This can keep an organization isolated from having a much greater influence.

Funding is a valuable contributor to the life of an organization. See how you can use it to extend your efforts rather than distract you from your goals.

When you put together all of the information in this and other chapters, you will build an organization that becomes an integral part of your community. It will be of the community, not just for the community. It will use its knowledge of the community and its assets, its ability to act purposefully and powerfully to change conditions, and its skill in communicating to continue to become stronger and more relevant. The way that it does its work will attract new resources. How it takes care of those resources will help it to do more work and do it better, bringing in even more resources to help the organization sustain its growth and bring its vision more fully to life.

FOUR FUNDAMENTAL RESPONSIBILITIES OF AN ORGANIZER

You could lose a lot of sleep worrying about each little thing that you could be doing as an organizer. By keeping yourself open to learning and using what you are learning from your experiences, you will be fine. Paying active attention to four fundamental responsibilities will give you a good framework to help you make decisions as an effective organizer.

Connect. An effective organizer will connect people to the issue, the organization, and to each other.

Develop leadership. An effective organizer will understand a variety of leadership skills. An effective organizer will continually look for potential leaders and nurture their talents, giving opportunities for leadership and helping them learn from their experiences. An effective organizer will support current leaders' growth and recognize their contributions. An effective organizer will find ways for leaders to continue to be involved with the organization when they want to step away from providing active leadership.

Inspire confidence. An effective organizer will recognize that commitment, motivation, and healthy risk taking are strongly influenced by confidence. An effective organizer will help members appreciate their abilities, realize the contributions they are making, and help them see the organization's progress toward goals. An effective organizer will find many victories to celebrate.

Develop and maintain a culture of learning. An effective organizer will help members draw learning from each experience, particularly by modeling her own openness to learning. An effective organizer knows that mistakes and setbacks are part of the game as are moments of brilliance and success. An effective organizer will turn blame into inquiry, make note of good intentions, and put learning into practice.

CONCLUSION

There is a lot to complain about. Sometimes it just feels good to let off steam. Sometimes it feels even better to use that steam to accomplish something. You are probably not the only one around who thinks things could be better than they are right now. When you set your mind and energy to finding some of those other people and working together to actually make a difference, change is inevitable. Your very decision to join forces and to act transforms the nature of things. The chances are that you will also accomplish some, maybe even all, of the specific changes you seek. You are moving from hoping things will change to making changes.

Every person in your organization always has some energy, but like batteries on a store shelf it may be just sitting around. Maybe all that energy is going in different directions and is being wasted. Acting together in an organized manner will bring more resources to bear on the situation and make your energy much more efficient, more focused, and more powerful.

Your recognition that problems don't have to be tolerated will move you through a series of actions that will result in coalescing forces directed toward change. Identify others who are willing to work alongside you. Gather more information on the community and the issues that affect it. You and your partners will come together to determine which steps you will need to take, and you will take them. You will experience bursts of enthusiasm when all things seem possible, and you will hit the doldrums and question the probability of your success. And you will keep moving forward.

You may start with just a handful of people, but your organization will grow. It will become more structured to meet the emerging demands it faces, yet it will remain flexible to ensure that procedures make your work easier rather than getting in the way. Some of the people working with you will drop out of the effort, but you will add new members to strengthen your numbers. Recognize that developing leadership and developing the organization are inseparable.

Since most of the planning and work will be done in small groups, pay attention to group dynamics. Particularly, help the group perform the tasks it needs to perform while enhancing relationships among members of the group. Know that conflict and controversy are not only inevitable but hold the potential for strengthening the group and its efforts. Recognize and deal with those pitfalls that predictably face any group working for change.

And you will have meetings, large ones and small ones—many meetings. Make sure all these meetings have a purpose, that you all know what that purpose is, and that you take practical steps to see that the purpose is accomplished.

The type of organization you become will reflect the demands of your situation. It may be a small, temporary alliance of individuals working to achieve a modest improvement in the community, or it may develop into a formal enterprise that becomes legally incorporated.

You will be able to help the organization grow and to sustain itself. Keeping in mind your fundamental responsibilities as an organizer will guide you as you go.

This process of putting the pieces together to build an organized effort will be a challenge. You will be exasperated, and you will be excited. You will be doubtful, and you will be confident. You will get angry, and you will laugh out loud. Perhaps above all, you will take a degree of satisfaction from the fact that you were able to get something done, and that this mattered.

A SMALL SPARK CAN START A PRAIRIE FIRE

You succeeded in getting Carla on the waiting list. Of course, they don't call it a waiting list because it would be flat wrong to put someone dealing with mental health challenges on a waiting list. It will just be a few weeks until she can be seen.

In some ways you are glad that Carla's mom stopped by to talk with you. In some ways you aren't. It's nice that your neighbors call on each other when they need help, and it's good that Carla's mom thinks you can help. "You work in mental health," she said, "maybe you can help us. Nobody else seems to do anything."

Carla was in the hospital for 3 days after her third suicide attempt in 3 months. You find out that the hospital didn't know much about her previous attempts. Carla was sent "home" to the place where she lives with two other women, roommates selected by the agency that arranges people's lives on behalf of the state's mental health division. You also find out that no worker is scheduled to visit Carla at home even though the medication they gave her takes 3 weeks to benefit her. What would happen if you didn't light a fire under somebody to get things moving? What would happen if Carla's mom never talked to you? What happens to all those other Carla's out there? You work in this system. You live in this community. You think it's going to take more than lighting occasional fires to make things better. This is making you angry.

You begin to do a little homework. You find an article in the paper about a lawsuit filed against the hospital that involves something very similar to Carla's situation. You find that local mental health agencies can't find workers to fill open positions and that some they do hire are barely qualified and don't last long on the job. You know you and Carla's mom aren't the only ones who are frustrated. In fact, one of your friends at work and a colleague at another agency feel pretty fed up with what's going on.

Your first instinct is to call a meeting of human service agencies, faith community leaders, and the school district to discuss this situation. You even think about calling a press conference to bring this whole matter to the community's attention. Then you have a second instinct. This tells you that by being organized you can be powerful, not just noisy.

So you, your colleagues, and Carla's mom get together after work and come up with a list of names of other people who might be interested in making some changes. You find that even though there are just a few of you involved right now, you have lots of connections in the community. You feel pretty good to be doing something other than complaining or apologizing. It seems that this has lit a fire under you.

REFLECTION QUESTIONS

1. What types of issues do you see emerging? What might be a fundamental issue that brings people together? What might be some long-range issues? What issues might be used to mobilize or recruit people?

2. Which steps have been taken so far? What might make this a good start?

3. What will your next steps be?

4. Who is the "you" in this story? Who in your community is most likely to be involved? Who else do you want to make sure to involve?

5. What type of organization might you build?

6. If this effort were to build and really make significant changes in your community, what would you need to pay attention to? What might be some obstacles you will face in building the organization? How will you deal with them?

7. What needs to be in place for the organization to remain a powerful presence in your community?

8. What role will you personally play in building this organized effort?

GROUP ACTIVITY: MAINTAINING AN EFFECTIVE ORGANIZATION

ACME Organizers Inc. has been hired to assist a community group that is beginning to organize. ACME has impressed upon this group that most efforts fall apart from the inside rather than failing because of strategic or tactical errors. The group has taken this message to heart and asked ACME to prepare a brief training/workshop session to deepen their understanding. In addition, the group wants to leave the session with some specific actions to take to make sure that they build a sustainable organization.

You are all members of the famous ACME Organizers Inc. Divide into teams of four to six members and come up with a plan for the workshop for this community group. You can decide within your team what kind of group has hired you.

1. Develop a brief training session that addresses issues of sustainability discussed in this chapter. In addition, consider other factors that affect sustainability and how you would help the community group address them. (20 minutes)

2. Present your session outline, rationale, and any other information regarding your work with the community group to your colleagues at ACME Organizing, Inc. Ask your colleagues for their feedback. (10–15 minutes)

HELPFUL WEBSITES

Links to the organizations briefly described here are on the companion website at www.cengage.com/humansvcs/homan.

Alliance for Justice. This is a national association of public interest advocacy organizations, and its website has many good links to advocacy, law, and government organizations. In addition, its Nonprofit Advocacy Project provides a wide range of assistance to organizations, including a network of advocacy attorneys and accountants, clear and practical publications providing legal guidance, and even one-on-one technical assistance via phone, letters, and e-mail.

Building Movement Project. The Building Movement Project works to strengthen the role of U.S. nonprofit organizations as sites of democratic practice and to advance ways nonprofits can significantly contribute to building movement for progressive social change. Here you'll find tools for how to transform service organizations and their larger networks to include social change/justice activities. The goal is to build communities where citizens are engaged, empowered, and assertive, and service organizations are more inclusive, transparent and responsive.

Independent Sector. A diverse collection of more than 600 charitable, religious, educational, health, and social welfare organizations, its numerous publications and services help organizations find answers to basic questions that affect group growth and development.

Center for Community Change. The center assists in the development of organizations, especially for low-income people who want to make a difference in their communities. The center makes onsite visits to grassroots groups to help in all phases of organizing and connects organizations with similar missions, or those within the same state or region, to encourage them to work together and learn from each other.

Idealist.org/Action without Borders. This group can connect you with more than 87,000 organizations in 165 countries. It has links to interesting community involvement opportunities and provides assistance on finding project funding, getting volunteers, developing publicity, becoming incorporated, help landing a job, and much more. The global reach of this group will give you exposure to many different projects and perspectives.

About: Nonprofit Charitable Organizations. Part of the *New York Times* online, this site provides lots of online information, from one-stop information for starting a nonprofit to fund-raising, public relations, and more.

Hauser Center for Nonprofit Organizations. Part of the John F. Kennedy School at Harvard, the center provides information and research on nonprofit leadership and management, political and community engagement, and other topics through a network of 50 scholars. Information on international experiences is available as well.

Grassroots Organizations Operating Together in Sisterhood (GROOTS). This group nurtures relationships of mutual support among women engaged in redevelopment efforts in their communities. GROOTS helps urban and rural grassroots women's groups share their successful development approaches and methods globally.

Guidestar. This organization keeps an excellent up-to-date tutorial on IRS Form 990 questions and provides comprehensive data on more than 1.5 million nonprofit organizations, connecting them with donors, foundations, businesses, and governing agencies.

Chapter 12

✳

Taking Action—Strategies and Tactics

CHAPTER HIGHLIGHTS

- Temptations for inaction
- The will to act
- Cycle of empowerment: decision, action, involvement, communication, decision
- Relationship between situation, organization ability, goals, and strategy
- Strategies and tactics
- The definition, strengths, limitations, and use of five basic action strategies: confrontation, negotiation,

- collaboration, co-optation, and advocacy
- Importance of ethics
- Mutual benefits
- Education as a strategy
- Effect of a receptive environment
- The right people in the right place
- Tricks for special occasions
- Strategies and tactics used against you
- Factors necessary for action
- Commandments of change

It's time to put your money or, maybe more important, your time where your mouth is. It's time to stop talking about what you would do, or what you are going to do, and to start doing it.

Many good efforts die aborning. The frustrations with present conditions or the excitement of creating new ones run smack up against the reality of taking action. Antennae—in search of reasons not to make a change or why it can't be done—suddenly sprout. And these are very sensitive antennae. They can pick up the murmur of a potential difficulty and magnify its volume until it can shout down the tentative notion to act. Good intentions wither into halfhearted attempts accompanied by strains of "I'll see if I can..." or "I'll think about doing..." or the death knell: "I'll try to..." If you look for reasons not to take action, you will find them. You just have to decide whether these are more important than the reasons to act.

If you have actually read this far, either you have to take a test on this chapter, or you really intend to make a difference. Maybe both. If you intend to act, accept the fact that uncertainty comes with the territory. Acknowledge the misgivings that tug at you to hold back. Oh, yes, there will be many little voices saying:

- You can't act until all the details are covered.

- You can't act because you might not succeed.

- You can't act because you don't know exactly what to do.

- You can't act because no one has done this before.

- You can't act because there will be repercussions, you may get into trouble, someone may not like you, or you may have to do some real work.

Those voices may fret at you, but they won't keep you from moving forward. By your action, you talk back. You are saying:

- All the details will never be covered; I can accept that.

- I do expect to accomplish something important.

- Most of what I know I have learned by doing; this is no different from anything else, and I certainly have enough basic skills and knowledge to at least get the ball rolling.

- Sure, there will be repercussions, including the fact that I can take some pride in what I am doing, I'll get to know some good people even better, and I may even have a little fun.

- There will be hassles; I can handle them.

Understand, the best you can, the realities of the situation, good and bad, and accept them. Then you can start doing things that lead to changes. It is not lack of money or support or authority or skill or any similar thing that coaxes people into sitting still. These certainly are barriers, but ones that can be dealt with. It is the lack of will to confront the barriers, real and imagined, that preserves conditions that should be changed. It is the will to act—and to keep acting—that makes the difference, a will built on the belief that things should and can be different. You can

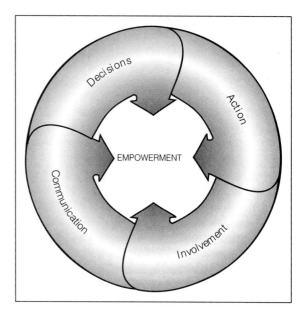

FIGURE 12.1   The Process of Change and Empowerment

start without resources, and you can proceed when they are in short supply, but you can't do much with meager will.

The decision to act and to succeed is the precondition to accomplishment. The more clear that decision, the stronger your actions will be. This decision depends on two things: that chances to gain something meaningful are sufficiently high and that dissatisfaction with the current state of affairs is sufficiently strong. To sustain action, you, as the change agent, must keep these two factors in focus, at times emphasizing the prospects for success while at others intensifying the discomfort over current conditions. You need to do this both for yourself and for the other participants in your change effort. If one or the other of these ingredients is irretrievably lost, it is time to stop beating your head against the wall and move on to something else.

Your decision to act is made real when taking action. Taking action is the final step and the first one (see Figure 12.1). Every change effort requires that someone begin doing something different. Every successful change is the result of action. Distilled to its essence, the process of change involves taking goal-directed action, strengthening your organization

DID YOU KNOW?   A Checklist for Action

The questions on this checklist will frame your perspective of any setting for action. Your need to answer these questions will guide everything you do, and your ability to answer them will powerfully increase the likelihood of your success. Check your checklist often.

- From whom do we want to get a response?
- What response do we want to get?
- What action or series of actions has the best chance of producing that response?
- Are the members of our organization able and willing to take these actions?

- How do the actions we decide to take lead to the needed development of our organization?
- How do our actions produce immediate gains in a way that helps us achieve our long-term goals?
- Is everything we are doing related to the outcomes we want to produce?
- How will we assess the effectiveness of our chosen approach to help refine the next steps we should take?
- What are we doing to keep this interesting?

through the effective involvement of others, maintaining communication to keep the reality of the change effort and the relationships among members strong, and continuing to make purposeful decisions, building power and skill as you repeat the cycle. Action. If you remember no more than this and adhere to it, you can look forward to numerous successes.

It all boils down to this. None of your ideas, desires, or plans amount to a hill of beans unless you act on them. Once you have decided to act, here are some approaches that can make your actions more effective.

MAJOR ACTION STRATEGIES AND TACTICS

I once worked with a group of social workers who were trying to make changes within a major state agency. They kept talking about how they needed to cooperate with this person or that department. It was apparent that all their cooperating was getting them nowhere. When I questioned why they were pursuing this strategy when it clearly was not working, the person sitting next to me patted me on the knee and said, "Mark, I shouldn't have to remind you, we're social workers, and social workers

cooperate." Aside from the dubious premise of the remark, it showed how a group of people had gotten locked into a strategy that was determined out of context with the demands of the situation they were facing. Though generally it is nice to be cooperative, it is hardly virtuous to be ineffective, especially if important real-life needs of members of the community are at stake.

"Thou shalt have the situation dictate the strategy" is a fundamental commandment of community change. Each situation you face will provide you with a set of unique variables that recommend one strategic approach over others. Be sensitive to these cues as you decide on your strategy. The selection of the approach you take must be based on your organization's ability to take the best advantage of your strengths and the openings the situation offers you. The choice is driven first by what exists in the situation, which is then matched to your group's temperament and available resources. Both the temperament and available resources can be changed to some extent.

Avoid the trap of becoming limited in your choices, which is the result of never allowing yourself to consider different methods. Doing the same thing all the time leads you into yet another trap, that of being predictable. Especially in a conflict situation, if the other side always knows what you are going to do, they can more easily prepare to control how they respond, and you could lose an important advantage.

As Alinsky (1972) pointed out, "the action is in the reaction" (p. 129). It is not the actions that we take that make the change; it is the reactions we get to our actions that set change in motion. The person or persons from whom you seek a reaction are members of the target community. I refer to them as the *target* or the *respondent*. My use of the word target is not meant to imply opposition. They may or may not be in conflict with you, although in most cases there is some degree of hesitancy or resistance. The target is simply the focus of your efforts. Be cautious about your expectations. You can make a mistake by presuming that a target is either hostile or eager to respond favorably.

A strategy is the general framework of, or orientation to, the activities you undertake to achieve your goal. It is not a particular action but rather a series of actions that take into account the anticipated maneuvers of your organization as well as those of other parties, particularly the target. It is the overall approach to action that sustains your effort by giving it a coherent direction. Erlich and Tropman (1974) referred to strategy as the "orchestration of influence attempts" (p. 175) that brings together and consciously blends a variety of different components of action. They add that a strategy "takes into account the actions and reactions of key allies and adversaries as they bear upon achievement of the proposed goal" (1987, p. 258). In my experience, five basic strategic approaches can be pursued:

- Confrontation
- Negotiation
- Collaboration
- Co-optation
- Advocacy

Tip

- The purpose of any strategy or tactic is to provoke the target into a reaction helpful to your cause.

Confrontation involves bringing the demands of one party to the attention of another and forcing compliance. *Negotiation* is the process of bringing parties with different interests and perspectives to an agreement. *Collaboration* occurs when parties contribute resources to accomplish a common goal. *Co-optation* results when parties share common beliefs about matters and when the success or failure of one party produces feelings of success or failure in the other. Finally, *advocacy* is the process of presenting an issue to the target for attention and action. This approach may use any of the first four strategies to gain needed attention and to resolve the matter though confrontation and negotiation are more likely.

The essential outcome of the change process is the institution of new agreements that create a change in the environment and alter the relationship among various parties. In practice, these basic strategic approaches may represent stages in an overall attempt to forge and maintain agreements between parties. Each succeeding approach envisions the parties in closer relationship. For example, when parties are in confrontation, they are usually far apart on the matter at hand; when they are collaborating, they are working together. So you may use one approach to set the stage for activities in the succeeding one if you intend to move the other party into a closer relationship with you. That is, you may use confrontation to get the other party to negotiate, which may lead to collaboration, which in turn may result in co-opting your former opponent (Figure 12.2). Your advocacy efforts can utilize these stages as well.

Of course, you may neither need nor want a closer relationship. You may confront and force the other side to agree with you with little or no negotiation, and you can negotiate a settlement that does not include a subsequent series of collaborative activities. So the agreement you reach by employing one or another of these strategies is based on what you are capable of producing given the factors present in the situation at hand, the current nature of the relationships among parties, and the relationships you ultimately wish to develop.

Tactics are specific activities designed to elicit a particular response from the target within the context of a discernible strategy. They can be further defined as "an action or phase of a strategy implemented to attain a limited objective which is instrumental to the attainment of a desired end state or goal" (Conner & de la Isla, 1984, p. 245n). In

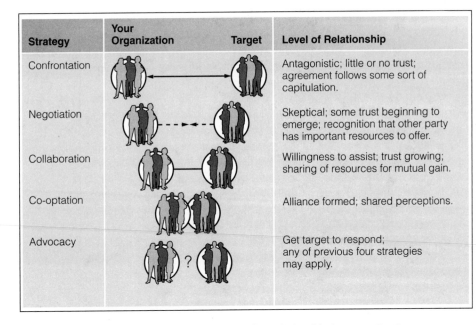

Strategy	Your Organization	Target	Level of Relationship
Confrontation			Antagonistic; little or no trust; agreement follows some sort of capitulation.
Negotiation			Skeptical; some trust beginning to emerge; recognition that other party has important resources to offer.
Collaboration			Willingness to assist; trust growing; sharing of resources for mutual gain.
Co-optation			Alliance formed; shared perceptions.
Advocacy			Get target to respond; any of previous four strategies may apply.

FIGURE 12.2   Linking Strategy Choices to the Relationship between Parties

selecting tactics, you need to know who the target is, what response you want, what will influence the target to respond in the desired manner, and how that response fits with your overall strategy to accomplish your purposes.

All of this means you have to do a little homework before you launch into action (Figure 12.3). Here are the major elements you need to study:

- The issue
- The target
- Your members
- The resources at hand.

Using the process of force field analysis described in Chapter 7 is helpful. You need to have enough information so you can act with intelligence and confidence without getting sucked into the quagmire of paralysis by analysis.

- *Assess the issue.* Know the issue better than your target does, including the basic facts of the matter and the causes and effects of problems. Know it well enough that you can communicate it in clear and perhaps even dramatic terms. Know how the problem or issue is addressed elsewhere or what solutions have

proved effective. Know the rights and obligations of the parties involved.

- *Assess the target.* Know the target system, how it acts and reacts. Know who the principal decision makers are and their particular interests. Know if the target is likely to be generally supportive or opposing of your efforts, and why. Make sure you have, in fact, selected the right target. Determine where the target has strengths to assist or resist you. Does the target have strong community or political support? Does the target have interests that are compatible with yours? Has it shown an interest in collaborating? Is it a master at manipulating the media? Does it have a lot of money? Recognize the target's vulnerabilities. Is it overly sensitive to its public image? Is its funding source willing and able to exert pressure? Are there superiors to which it must answer? Each system has its own Achilles' heel, a vulnerable spot in a seemingly invulnerable structure.

- *Assess your members.* Where are your sources of strength? Do your members have a high degree of commitment and confidence? Do you have numbers? Where do you have expertise? Are there important cultural norms that will inspire or

Elements	Things to Know
Issues	Basic facts; causes and effects of problems; solutions applied in other places; rights and obligations of parties
Target	Probable reaction to specific tactic; principal decision makers; degree of and rationale for support or opposition; strengths and vulnerabilities; cohesion
Your members	Degree of commitment; numbers; probable reactions to target's tactics; cultural norms; strengths and vulnerabilities; cohesion
Other resources	Awareness of needed additional resources; availability and location of resources; steps required to gain access to resources

FIGURE 12.3 Considerations for Your Selection of Tactics

impede certain actions? Do members recognize their assets? Where is your Achilles' heel? Are your members easily intimidated? Will they lose interest at the first sign of difficulty? Do you work together well or fight among yourselves?

- *Assess your other resources.* Know which resources are vital for your success. Which of these are at your disposal or can be developed fairly easily? Is there community sympathy for your situation? Do you have access to money or to the news media? Will other groups lend you active assistance?

Many of these homework items are easily known; some take a little digging. Be careful to avoid taking important items for granted. With the understanding you gain from your investigation, you will be well prepared to consider a variety of options for action.

Confrontation

Confrontation is the strategy you use when you need to compel a target to change its position or behavior. In these cases, the target becomes the opponent.

Situations for Which Confrontation May Be Appropriate

- The target engages in actions that are unjust or harmful.
- The target refuses to meet with you.
- The target is unresponsive to your call for change.

- The target doesn't expect a battle from you.
- The target cannot effectively defend itself from your attack.
- The target doesn't want attention.
- You need to show that the target is vulnerable.
- You want to dramatize the issue.
- You want to draw attention to your group.
- You need to energize your group.
- Your members need to feel a sense of power.
- Your members are especially angry.
- You need to show that you are willing to fight.
- You need to attract allies.

In confrontation you pit the power of your organization against the power of the respondent on a particular issue, in a particular context. Rarely will your organization be more powerful overall than your opponent, but you can be more powerful in a specific instance. Define the extent of the conflict, and focus your power on a fixed area of operations. For example, you may not be more powerful than the state government, but you may be able to force the manager of a local welfare office to change procedures.

To employ this technique, set the vulnerability of the opponent against the strengths of your organization. The more carefully contrived this match is the better. It starts with understanding what the respondent is likely to be sensitive to. Your tactics increase the opponent's discomfort to the point that it becomes more palatable to agree with you than to maintain resistance. You must be able to devise an operation so that either the degree of disturbance or its duration is something you can sustain much better than the opposition can.

Confrontational methods are usually showy because you must get your adversary to notice you and to respond in some way. Also, the added attention increases the perception of community pressure and contributes to a climate of controversy that is often bothersome for the opponent.

Strengths of a Confrontational Strategy

- The presence of an external opponent that is the focus of your organization's attention significantly strengthens cohesion.

- By picking your fights purposefully and beating a formidable foe, you increase the perception of your group's power.

- You can intimidate targets, making them less likely to give you problems on other matters or more likely to be agreeable to your concerns in future situations. The mere threat of confrontational tactics in the future may be sufficient to accomplish your purposes.

- Winning provides your group with a tremendous emotional uplift.

- You may be able to catch the other side off guard, especially if they are not accustomed to being met by planned, organized confrontation from groups such as yours... or by those cooperative social workers.

Limitations of Confrontation

- This strategy requires a strong commitment by your members. Their commitment can be put to the test, exposing possible weak spots in your organization. Remember, some people are much more willing to talk a good game than to actually play one.

- A loss can be discouraging and emotionally draining. It can lead to internal bickering as members look to blame someone, often those close at hand, for failure.

- The other side, whether they win or lose, may become less willing to work with you in the future and may become passive-aggressive in their implementation of agreements. (This is much more likely if you don't keep the heat on them.)

- You may discover you enjoy this approach so much that you engage in confrontational methods just because you like the show, not because they are effective, and become more impressed with developing tactics than with producing outcomes.

- You may discover that you so dislike the emotional investment this strategy requires that you look for ways to avoid its use, even when it is clearly indicated.

Confrontation requires a sharply defined opponent. This can result in an oversimplification of the situation in which assigning blame becomes the easy answer. When you blur lines of responsibility to intensify the focus, you run the risk of ignoring other relevant factors that may impinge on the problem. You may forget that a major reason for confrontation is that changing your target's behavior disrupts established patterns, allowing you to move aggressively on related aspects of the situation. Your supporters may become disheartened to discover that they may be just getting started; they aren't done. Further, if you think changing your target's behavior solves all your problems, you can lose sight of your own areas of responsibility and capability. This blurred view may reinforce a belief in your own powerlessness. After all, if the target is fully responsible for the situation, you are fully dependent on its actions or nonactions for your own welfare.

Tactics and Tips for Confrontation.   *Freezing the target.* Keep your focus clearly on the target. Refuse to be distracted by others, often allies or subordinates of the target, who try to get your attention. When using this approach, your concentration is sometimes riveted to a single individual. Keep this one target in your sights and attempt to isolate it from its buffers or bases of support. You may need to engage in a series of actions to get and keep the target interacting with you.

This tactic is especially useful when the target is easily identifiable, when the target tries to get you to deal with others who have limited authority to act, or when attempting to respond to a number of allied opponents would diffuse your energy and dilute your efforts.

Personalizing the issue. This is related to freezing the target, and it essentially involves linking a particular person with the problem you are trying to rectify. The intent is to make life miserable for someone whose actions or inactions make life miserable for others. Pressure is brought to bear on the individual through a variety of means. Commonly, the target is cast as the cause or the maintainer of the problem and the suffering it produces. The target comes to symbolize all that is wrong with the situation. Typical methods can include public ridicule, constant interference with the target's routines, as well as exposing the target's arrogance, ignorance, incompetence, or the difference between the individual's public statements and private actions.

This tactic tends to cause the target's tentative supporters to shy away for fear of becoming targets themselves or of being painted with the same brush. It will, however, tend to solidify the target's hard-core support. This may strengthen resistance, but it may also result in a small group of particularly nasty opponents becoming cut off from their support and going down together.

Your actions may result in removal of a particularly offensive individual from a position of power. However, simply removing one person from the scene rarely removes the conditions that cause the problem. Personalizing the issue sends a message to the target system regarding the seriousness of your intent and your willingness to hold those who perpetuate the problems accountable for their actions.

This tactic is particularly effective when the target has little strong personal allegiance, is arrogant or offensive, and is prone to hasty or imprudent reactions.

Holding accountability sessions. Hold em accountable. Public officials may want to hide from your organization's demands. This tactic keeps them firmly and publicly on the hook. An accountability session is a large public meeting where elected officials or public administrators are faced with publicly supporting or opposing your organization's specific demands. You ask for their response on the spot. Because these sessions rely on political pressure, they are most useful for public officials rather than corporate targets (Midwest Academy, 2001).

This is not a public hearing, discussion, or education session. This is a call for support for your positions. The target is literally on stage in front of hundreds of people, subject to a show of the massed power of your organization.

Careful and detailed planning must be put into such an event, starting with making sure that your target (or small number of targets) has some meaningful power to do something about the issues. Matters such as making sure you have a written acceptance of your invitation, inviting the media, arranging the facility, preparing a step-by-step production of the show, and clarifying and rehearsing specific roles for your members are required. Because the target's responses are recorded on a highly visible, large chart and scored as "yes," "no," or "waffle" (or similar term), members need to be prepped as to how to react to what the target is really saying. All this suggests that you need to do a good bit of organizing and power building before you attempt to hold an accountability session (Midwest Academy, 2001).

This is a chance for public officials to shine and receive the dramatic and boisterous support of a large group of organized constituents or to feel the anger of those whose concerns have just been rejected. Because the members of your organization get a big boost from the energy and their show of power, it is helpful to have some public officials stand on stage and agree with you.

Getting outside help. This procedure involves seeking the assistance of others, particularly organized groups, who are outside your immediate arena of action and who are sympathetic to your cause. Ask potential allies to endorse your concerns and provide you with specific acts of assistance, such as making public statements on your behalf, loaning you volunteers, or arranging meetings with key individuals. Outside allies have access to different audiences than you do and may well have direct access to some decision makers who won't give you the time of day. It is particularly helpful to draw the assistance of a group that has broad public approval or credibility.

This tactic tends to demonstrate the breadth of your support and the legitimacy of your position. It helps you to keep from becoming isolated yourself, aids in keeping a resistant opponent distracted, and increases the resources at your disposal. If your organization is small, new, or relatively unknown, outside help will be beneficial.

Using disruptive tactics. These activities generally fall under the rubric of direct action. According to Staples (1984), direct actions occur "when a group of people take collective action to confront a designated target with a set of specific demands. The group action involves people directly with the issue, using their numbers as a means of pressuring their opponent" (p. 3).

Procedures for handling disputes are the turf of those who control the procedures. Standard approaches may give the opponent the upper hand as these are usually designed to protect those in power rather than to accelerate needed change. So you may well be playing their game, and they are probably just as good at it as you are, if not better. You may need to change the game so your opponents have to respond to your procedures. This puts them on unfamiliar ground. They are not so sure how to react, and they will probably make some mistakes.

You can take a variety of actions to throw an opponent off balance and out of the comfort zone of the predictable. Sit-ins or occupations, picketing, boycotts, and mass demonstrations are among the most common forms of attention-getting activities. Because they are familiar, your opponents may know how to respond, so you may need to add some new wrinkle. However, even though they may know how to respond, they usually don't want to, and they generally would like to avoid trouble.

Often the most effective disruptive tactics emerge from the situation itself. A busy office may be frustrated by an endless series of phone calls that tie up the lines and prevent any work from being done. A public agency may be hamstrung by countless requests for different public documents. Rush hour commuters may become angry at a traffic stoppage, become incensed with everyone (this includes you), and demand that something be done to settle this. Convention proceedings may be interrupted by staging a guerrilla theater act. Be creative, and be willing to do the unpredictable.

One of the worst things that can happen is that you are ignored. Actions that attract notice at the outset may quickly become part of the landscape. Take pains to make sure this can't happen.

The usual process for engaging in disruptive tactics is to escalate the disruption in accordance with the resistance you meet. This conveys a sense of mounting pressure. However, as Kahn (1970) pointed out, reversing the practice by directing a major action on a relatively minor issue may prove effective by catching the other side off guard.

Civil disobedience. Defined by Rubin and Rubin (1986) as "intentionally and publicly disobeying a law and the passive acceptance of the consequences of disobedience" (p. 261), civil disobedience may take a number of forms. It may involve diverting the water from an irrigation canal, setting off building fire alarms, or refusing a court order to return to work. Perhaps the most common example is unauthorized occupation of a building or a site. If you are going to engage in civil disobedience of any kind, preparation is extremely important.

You should be well aware of the possible and probable consequences of your action and be prepared to accept them. Participants need to be well rehearsed for the actions they are to take or not take. If those taking part are likely to be harassed or taunted by those opposing the action, they should have experience role-playing this situation prior to the event. Should arrest be likely, or even desired, participants must know how to conduct themselves throughout the arresting and booking process. Arrangements for bail or legal representation must be worked out beforehand. Organizers must have undertaken a reconnaissance of the area to maximize the effect of the operation and avoid problems. It is a good idea to get some special training from those who have experience conducting these actions. If you and your members know what to expect, you will be able to stand firm and make an important statement.

Use this approach when you need to grab attention from an unresponsive or delaying target or when the broad community is tolerating or refusing to take a hard look at problematic conditions. If you want to provoke people into taking sides, dramatic actions help. These methods are effective at revealing opponents as oppressors or calling attention to an unjust or absurd law, ordinance, or regulation. They can energize the members of your organization and strengthen their commitment to the cause.

Threats of action may be sufficient to produce the response you want. Often the image of the event in the opponent's mind is more fearful than the event itself. If you do make a threat, be sure you are ready to back it up with action.

Diversionary issues. Remember the old movies where captured GIs plot to escape from prison camps? They always come up with the idea of starting a fire somewhere on the compound, and while the bumbling guards scurry about trying to put out the blaze, our heroes make good their escape. Using diversionary tactics is not much different. You get the respondent worrying over a set of secondary concerns or alarming actions you might take. In their distraction, they agree to your primary point or allow you to institute a change before they can move to stop you.

One community group attempting to establish a much-needed community agency was being thwarted by established agencies that felt their turf was threatened. The community had just conducted a special drive and raised a large sum of money to deal with the problem. Representatives of the various community agencies and government bodies gathered together to address the problem as a body officially appointed by the mayor. Immediately, the advocacy group demanded it receive all the money raised. This precipitated an onrush of arguments as each agency vied with the others to lay claim to a share of the pot. In the midst of all the commotion, the advocacy group asked that the decision on divvying up the funds be put on hold for a moment while design of the proposed new agency was approved. So concerned were the participants to get back to the business of dividing the spoils that they unanimously endorsed the proposal in a matter of minutes. This was done in a packed community hall before news crews of three local television stations and both major daily newspapers. The advocates gave interviews describing the new agency and its benefits, and the event received strong media coverage. By the time the opponents realized what had happened, it was too late to go back on their agreement to support the new agency, to which they had even decided to award a token amount of money.

This tactic can work when your target is concerned with a number of issues. Exaggerating one issue may increase the target's feelings of vulnerability to that issue and keep it so preoccupied that other matters seem less important. Resistance to other matters then breaks down.

Encirclement. You can overload the target by forcing it to respond to a variety of different tactics at the same time instead of one at a time. Confront the opponent with a lawsuit, picketing, investigations by government agencies, letter-writing campaigns, boycotts, or other actions to the point that the target is overwhelmed. You must have sufficient resources to pursue this method (Booth & Max, 1977).

Developing dependency on a pet project. This is somewhat like a diversionary issue. In this scenario your organization undertakes to help the respondent accomplish something of major importance to it but of minor importance to you. Because of the particular assets your group possesses (for example, credibility within the benefit community), you can assist the respondent a great deal. After the respondent has made an investment and the project is under way, ask the respondent to make a commitment to something important to your organization, usually on an unrelated matter. Knowing that you can withdraw your support and ruin its special project, the respondent may be willing to go along with your request.

For this technique to be successful, the respondent must care more about the pet project than about the matter you want changed. Further, you have to be emotionally and ethically prepared to withdraw your support from the project and allow it to fail. This tactic functions well with a target that has been passively resistant to your efforts or that acts in a paternalistic manner toward your group.

Partners in collusion. This gambit is a variation of the good cop, bad cop routine. In that game the bad cop

berates and generally mistreats a suspect. With a threat and a flourish, the bad cop then exits the room, leaving the suspect alone with the good cop, who is sympathetic and kind. The good cop then asks for cooperation so that the suspect won't have to deal with the bad cop. The good cop may suggest a dislike for the bad cop and his tactics and may even hint that the suspect's assistance can be a way of getting at the bad cop. The suspect decides to cooperate with the much more reasonable good cop.

The good cop in your case would be an advocacy group that appears to be reasonable and well mannered, especially in contrast to the inflammatory rantings and public displays of a different, apparently more radical community group that fulfills the role of the bad cop. The role of the suspect in this little drama is played by the target of your intentions. Just like the cops, the two groups are acting in accordance with a planned tactic. The "bad" group can be picketing, while the "good" group, with respectable representatives carefully chosen, asks for a meeting. After agreements have been reached, both sides can claim victory while making sure not to discredit one another. After all, you both have constituencies you need to keep happy and possibilities for future mutual actions to protect.

This tactic can be effective in bringing together two groups with similar interests but different action orientations. The target may be able to rebuff either group's approach, but the purposeful combination of the two changes the situation significantly. This approach may move the target toward co-optation by the "good" group.

Lawsuits. Being sued is almost as much fun as root canal surgery. Most people would prefer to avoid both if they could. Enter the threat of a lawsuit to get the target to pay attention to you. Although large companies and government organizations often find themselves the subjects of lawsuits, being sued is no trivial issue to them either.

Many individuals, especially those who have come to tolerate, if not accept, a condition of powerlessness, are unaware of their legal rights and their opportunities to assert them. Participation as plaintiffs in a lawsuit can bring members a sense of strength and power. Legal action allows them to assert their rights in a forum that must take their concerns seriously. The courts have been an important mechanism for social change. They have forced progress when those in power have resisted acknowledging legitimate fundamental obligations (Kirst-Ashman & Hull, 2009). Your willingness to seek redress through the courts demonstrates that your organization refuses to be pushed around. It shows that you are willing to make your claims and to back them up. It forces the target to reckon with you.

If you do threaten legal action, make sure you can back it up. Determine that you are on a strong legal footing before you make your threat, and follow through by filing a suit if your issues are not resolved satisfactorily.

Once you are in court, the proceedings can drag on and on and on. And on and on…especially if your opponent decides to try to tie you up or simply to outlast you. Meanwhile your members' enthusiasm can wane if there are few other fronts on which you are working. This can lead to discouragement. So, as you consider this tactic, take care to become well versed in what you can expect. Know the type of resolution you are seeking, understand your opponent's options and likely responses, and ascertain the probable costs in terms of both time and money that this commitment will require.

You don't want your members just sitting around during the time it takes to settle the suit, so rarely will pursuit of legal action be the primary focus of your activity. Still, there are ways members can participate in the process. They may actually serve papers on your opponent, a rather empowering action; they may take part in the deposition process, allowing them to directly confront the target; and they can perform some research and information-gathering tasks (McCreight, 2004).

Using legal tactics requires a close coordination between the organization and its attorney. Decide whether you will include the organization in the action, use small suits to focus your case, or file a class action. You may also need to sensitize the attorney to the developmental needs of your organization and their relationship to the lawsuit (McCreight, 2004). Having an attorney as a member of your organization is a definite asset, especially if she agrees not to be compensated until you prevail in your litigation. If this is not available to you, there still may be ways for you to receive representation without a great deal of financial strain. Organizations such as the Alliance for Justice, which is a group of advocacy organizations, the National Lawyers Guild, and the American Civil Liberties Union may be able to connect you with legal resources to support your cause.

Be prepared for the fact that as soon as you mention the possibility of litigation (or most any conflict tactic for that matter) the target will accuse you of being disruptive, as if you are the problem, not the target's policies or actions you intend to change. If they respond this way or in similar ways, such as acting as if you have harmed the warm relationship between you, take it as a good sign. You have made them uncomfortable. Still, be careful about how you present your legal options. You don't want to make wild threats, nor do you want to prematurely close off exploration of other avenues.

Lawsuits can be effective when the legal rights of your organization or its members are being abused. It can also be the tactic of choice to accomplish some other purposes. Lawsuits may be an effective way to attract attention from diverse audiences. Your action may gain the interest of regulators, the media, legislators, and other potential targets (League of Women Voters Education Fund, 1977). Legal action, or the threat of it, can motivate the target to work more seriously with you on the matter at hand. Through the discovery process of litigation, you may be able to acquire some valuable information about your opponent that would normally be unavailable to you. The publicity or attention your suit attracts can increase your organization's credibility (McCreight, 2004). Involving the courts can draw attention to issues, opening up even larger discussions of fundamental rights. As the light begins to shine a little more on these matters, the climate surrounding the change effort begins to change (Steinman, 2005).

Use appropriate channels. The use of institutionally designed appropriate channels is anathema to some change agents. Generally, they fear that this lets the target control the process and that it threatens to bog down their efforts. These fears are well founded if all you do is concentrate your efforts on trying to make these channels work.

There are some valid reasons for pursuing officially designed procedures, while not fully relying on them for your success. First, they may work. The shock of this may cause some major coronary damage, but it does happen. Second, by not following procedures you give the target an out for not dealing with you.

CHANGE AGENT TIP

The simplicity of current communication methods can allow your group to make its presence felt in a big way, with very little work on your part. For example, you might want to try a redial party or a fax flood.

A redial party is a fun way to make a big impression. Essentially you gather a group of people who each leave a voice mail message saying the same thing. Each person also gives the names of two other people who support this position. If you have 20 people making the phone call, the names of 60 supporters are registered. The whole process of calling takes less than 15 minutes. Here's how it works.

First, select a target whose attention you really need to grab, probably someone who has been resisting your group. The target needs to have an answering machine or some voice mail service, which you call during non-business hours to be sure you can leave a message rather than actually getting a live person. Next, invite a number of people over for a potluck dinner and a phone call, asking each to bring the names and phone numbers of two other people who would be willing to support a message on behalf of your organization.

Then prepare a very simple, short script for each person to read when it is his turn to make the call. The script goes something like this: "Hello, (target's name), this is (your name). I'd like you to (state the action you'd like the target to take). Two of my friends (or neighbors or colleagues) also want you to do this. Their names and phone numbers are (state the names and phone numbers for the two other people). You can call them if you need to. Thank you for helping us make progress on (state your issue in just a few words)."

Once everyone has gathered, spend a little time enjoying each other's company and talking about the issue to heighten enthusiasm. When it's time to start, one person goes into another room where it is likely to be quieter, dials the target's phone number, and reads the prepared script into the voice mail. This person hangs up, walks out of the room, and hands the phone to the next in line. That person hits the redial button on the phone, and repeats the process. Pretty simple. All anybody has to do is hit a redial button, read a script, and pass the phone to the next person.

A couple of hints to make things go smoothly: Use a phone (preferably portable) with a redial button. Have each person practice the script out loud before making the phone call. Finally, to keep track of progress, have each caller check his or her name off a list once the call has been completed.

It is helpful to prepare a one-page background sheet for each person whose name is going to be used. They should know the issue and be able to state a position in the very unlikely circumstance that they would be asked to.

A fax flood accomplishes a similar purpose. Collect signed, two-sentence statements regarding the issue from members and supporters of your organization. (Collect a dollar or two from each person to cover expenses and to have them feel more a part of the activity.) Once you have a good number of statements (25 or more), take all your messages to a company that sends faxes. Have the company fax all of your messages, preferably at a particular time, one after another. This has the effect of interrupting the recipient's flow of faxes from other sources, adding to the pressure. (A fax company that is friendly to your cause will work with you a little better.) You can increase pressure by having each statement request a reply. You can combine a fax flood with a redial party by having participants each bring a couple of signed fax messages and dollar bills.

In my experience these tactics work best when directed at someone who has some other person she needs to report to or to buffer from public pressure. You let this person know that all these calls or faxes are a sample of what you can do. Tell the target that you are directing this activity to her with the hope that progress can be made, otherwise you will use this tactic on the person the target does not want contacted.

The target can easily represent itself as the victim of an ill-informed if not insolent group. Such a response may be generally accepted by less involved members of the community, which may be most of the community. You may end up undermining some potential support. Third, by taking the appropriate steps, you can clearly demonstrate that you have acted in good faith but that the procedures just don't work. You can show that the target is insensitive, arrogant, or incompetent in dealing with your legitimate issues. The target is now on the defensive.

It is important to develop a backup plan for what you will do when the prescribed procedures fail. However, don't wait until the breakdown has been proven before you try to figure out what your next steps will be. Have some point in mind at which you can declare the process to be a failure. This allows you to be prepared to emphasize your message about the ineffectiveness of the system and to switch quickly to your backup plan. This quick change in the game is likely to catch the target off guard. This tactic is particularly appropriate when you are dealing with a bureaucratized organization.

CAPTURING CONCEPTS
Good Advice on Conflict Tactics

Greg Speeter (1978b) summarized some good advice on conflict tactics from Alinsky that will serve you well.

1. **Rule 1.** Power is not only what you have but what the enemy thinks you have.

2. **Rule 2.** Never go outside the experience of your people.

3. **Rule 3.** Wherever possible, go outside the experience of your enemy.

4. **Rule 4.** Make the enemy live up to their own book of rules.

5. **Rule 5.** Ridicule is your best and most potent weapon.

6. **Rule 6.** A good tactic is one that your people enjoy. If your people are not having a ball doing it, there is something very wrong with the tactic.

7. **Rule 7.** A tactic that drags on too long becomes a drag. People can sustain militant interest in any issue for only a limited time, after which it becomes a ritualistic commitment, like going to church on Sunday mornings.

8. **Rule 8.** Keep the pressure on with different tactics and actions and use all events of the period for your purpose.

9. **Rule 9.** The threat is usually more terrifying than the thing itself.

10. **Rule 10.** The major premise for tactics is development of operations that will maintain a constant pressure on the opposition. It is this unceasing pressure that results in the reactions from the opposition that are essential for the success of the campaign. It should be remembered not only that the action is in the reaction but that action is itself a consequence of reaction and of reaction to the reaction ad infinitum. The pressure produces the reaction, and constant pressure sustains action.

11. **Rule 11.** If you push a negative hard and deep enough, it will break through to its counterside. That is, every negative can be converted into a positive.

12. **Rule 12.** The price of a successful attack is a constructive alternative. You cannot risk being trapped by the enemy in his sudden agreement with your demand and saying, "You're right; we don't know what to do about this issue. Now you tell us" (p. 108).

Cutting off support, particularly financial support. You may be able to weaken an opponent not only through direct confrontation but also by eroding some of its major assets. Take some time to analyze factors critical to the opponent's operation. It may be more profitable to focus your actions on these critical supports than directly on the opponent itself. A good starting point is money. Generally, reducing the opponent's ability to get and use money will force it to change its behaviors. For example, a bank needs depositors and a store needs customers. If you can influence depositors or customers, especially one or two major ones, to change their practices if the target doesn't change what it is doing, you can strike a severe blow. Your members are customers. They can use their purchasing power for leverage. Maybe a recalcitrant agency counts on United Way funding, which you can hold up with negative publicity and direct lobbying. Find out where the money comes from, and you will usually find a good wellspring of power.

Other important sources of support include people whose endorsement is necessary for the target's success. Drawing these people away from the target or reducing the enthusiasm of their approval can seriously shackle an opponent.

This tactic is most appropriate when engaged in confrontation with a powerful opponent. It sends a strong message to other potential targets that you are willing to implement tough measures to achieve your goals. Consider making an example of one particular opponent if you are fighting several similar opponents. Don't forget the other side can play hardball with your support base too.

An excellent description of a host of additional nonviolent confrontational tactics is described in the series *The Politics of Nonviolent Action* by Gene Sharp (1973a, 1973b, 1973c). Confrontation requires acceptance of risk, clarity of purpose, and a high level of emotional energy. If handled well, it is capable of producing dramatic changes.

Negotiation

Negotiation is a good strategy to use when the response community is willing to work toward an agreement and your prospects for working out a favorable settlement will not be significantly improved in the practical future. Though all strategies call for an understanding of your target, negotiation, which involves a distinct type of relationship, places a premium on your understanding of the cultural and political frameworks of your negotiating partners.

Situations for Which Negotiation May Be Appropriate

- You can neither convince nor force the respondent into full compliance with your demands.

- Your organization can no longer effectively sustain confrontation.

- Your group needs to see progress toward accomplishing some gain.

- The respondents have indicated an awareness of the legitimacy of your concerns.

- You have identified something both sides can exchange to meet your interests.

- You can provide the other party with a gain that assists them and serves your interests.

- You want to build a working relationship with the respondent.

Negotiation is a process of reaching an agreement between or among parties through a discussion during which each agrees to use or withhold available resources or to perform or refrain from performing certain acts. (For this discussion, I will consider negotiations between two parties, although more parties could be involved. The same principles generally apply in situations involving more than two parties.) The decision to enter into negotiations rests with the perception by the parties that there is something to gain from participating or something to lose by not doing so. To negotiate, the parties have to be willing to come to an agreement. Further, there must be an overlapping range of acceptance (Rubin & Rubin, 1986); that is, what is at least a little acceptable to one party is at least a little acceptable to the other. If the ranges do not overlap, if the parties cannot find mutually acceptable items, then negotiation is not possible.

During negotiation, be aware of the interests of both parties as well as the relationship that exists between you. This helps you identify possible short- and long-term costs and benefits. For example, you may negotiate an agreement beneficial to you that harms the other party and weakens the relationship between you. Or you may be so concerned about maintaining a relationship that you make an agreement that provides you with very little immediate benefit.

The relative power of parties affects the negotiation process. Of the many forms of power involved in the negotiation, two are particularly significant. The first is the extent to which one party depends on the other to accomplish its goals or meet its needs. The second, and related, concept is the extent to which a negotiator has desirable alternatives to the negotiation. The ability to walk away from the negotiation to another attractive alternative will dramatically increase a negotiator's power. Research by Tenbrunsel and Messick (2001) revealed that negotiations among parties of dramatically unequal power tend to be less productive, take longer, and be characterized by more competitive behavior. Further, these authors pointed out that differences in power lead to increased uncertainty, producing more self-focused interpretations of the situation and less shared understanding. If you are in a generally low power position with regard to your target, you will want to be able to focus your power or develop alternative choices to equalize power in a specific situation.

Negotiation takes two basic forms. Negotiation can be *positional*, a process in which parties declare their positions and try to go as far as they can with their position. For example, you think you and your friend should go out for hamburgers, and your friend thinks you should eat pizza. Your position is hamburgers, your friend's is pizza. You try to convince your friend of the merits of hamburger while acting in a way intended to get the decision to go your way. Meanwhile your friend is doing the same about the glories of pizza. You are both locked into your positions, and your bargaining will likely take on a win–lose quality.

The other basic form of negotiation is *outcome oriented*, a process in which you identify the broad outcomes you want to achieve based on the parties' respective interests, not their positions. Alternative choices are generated based on a clear understanding of the needs of the parties. Neither party has to devalue the other's interests. Each merely needs to value an agreement that meets the needs of both parties. Using this approach, you and your friend determine that you really need to eat something pretty soon that tastes good, fills you up, and doesn't cost very much. This opens up the possibilities. Who knows, maybe you decide to go to a restaurant where you can eat different things.

Regardless of the approach you use, both parties should be operating from similar orientations. You cannot assume that the other party will understand negotiating in the same way that you do.

Strengths of a Negotiation Strategy

- You are likely to end up in a more favorable condition, even if you don't get everything you want. Getting only half of what you want is probably an improvement over what you have now.

- You set a precedent that negotiation can occur. Your foot is now firmly in the door. When you were little, did you ever try to talk your mom into letting you stay up an extra half hour to watch something "real important" on TV? Even though she agreed to do this "for this time and this time only," I bet you knew you would be able to negotiate again.

- You might get more than you expected.

- The other side's ability to gain something makes them more accepting of your gains.

- The opening discussion allows you to bring issues to the table that have not been formally acknowledged. Even if you don't immediately gain much on some of them, you have put them into the awareness of anyone who observes the negotiation.

- You begin to develop a relationship with the other party that is much more within your control.

Limitations of Negotiation

- You can negotiate away some nonnegotiable items.

- By focusing on the wrong agenda or spending too much time on peripheral issues, you can accept the appearance of gain while gaining

Take a Moment to Discover

Have you ever lost sight of the importance of a relationship as you bulldozed ahead to get something that seemed important to you? Or have you ever been so afraid of losing someone's favor that you did something that went against your grain? What did you learn from these experiences? How can you apply that learning to your role as a change agent?

nothing of real value. For example, you may find yourself discussing where the road will cut through the neighborhood rather than whether it should be there at all.

- You can settle for too little and weaken the legitimacy of your call for future concessions from the other party.

- You can look like dupes to your own constituents, weakening their support and confidence. You can look like pushovers to the other party, which may lead them to take you and your concerns less seriously.

- You can damage future relationships by selfish or subservient actions.

Tactics and Tips for Negotiation. Some minor or simple negotiations require application of only a few of these suggestions. Determine the degree of importance the outcome of negotiation holds for you as well as the degree of difficulty you are likely to encounter in achieving your goals, then treat the negotiation process accordingly.

- Be prepared. Have an agenda. Know your facts and figures and have them written down. Select an advantageous time and place for conducting negotiation sessions. If the negotiations are particularly important or difficult, clarify the various roles members of your team will play, and rehearse some of the probable negotiation scenarios.

- Have a clear goal in mind.

- Be willing to renegotiate.

- Find out what the other side wants or needs, and see if you can give it to them. You don't have to, but see if you can. If you do, determine when and how you will do this, and possibly in exchange for which benefits you seek.

- Be willing and able to package items or issues to provide a wider range of negotiating possibilities.
- Acknowledge that the other party may need to blow off steam from time to time. You don't need to respond to everything that is said.
- Identify how agreements will be monitored and what sanctions, if any, will be applied for nonconformance.
- Get a third party involved if you are in a decidedly less powerful position.
- Confirm agreements in your own words.
- Be fresh, well rested, and eat right. (This does matter.)
- Be willing to break off negotiations or to take a break.
- Get to know the people on the other side; let them know you and your concerns. Be aware that people need to save face and will go to great, often unreasonable lengths to avoid losing face.
- If you spot a problem with the negotiation process, bring it up for discussion.
- Summarize frequently.

Methods for Win–Lose Negotiation. If you decide it is in your best interest to pursue positional negotiations, these suggestions can help you gain an advantage over the other party.

- Ask for more than you need, but be sensible; don't exaggerate to absurdity.
- Prepare a retreat plan that delineates how you intend to use various items in your negotiation. To do this, you must clearly identify your nonnegotiable items, your important items, and your giveaway items.
- Ask more questions than you answer. Generally, let the other side do more of the talking.
- As time goes on, people sometimes become more willing to agree, if only because they want to move on. You can use this to your advantage by dragging on or exaggerating minor issues, moving to more significant ones when the other side is worn down.

- Spend detailed time on items you are willing to give away. This draws attention to the item, making it appear more important than it really is. As a result, you may more easily get something important to you because the other side now "owes" you one.

A number of authors have provided additional insights on the negotiating process, for the most part reflecting a bargaining perspective. Brager and Holloway (1978, p. 196) offered these points:

- Relate your concerns to the other party's frame of reference.
- The more you can demonstrate commitment to a position that is credible to the other party as irrevocable, the more you are likely to win your point in the settlement. (Many others expound on this point, including Schelling [1963], Pruitt [1981], and Rubin and Rubin [2001].)

Rubin and Rubin (2008) made these suggestions and observations:

- Negotiators should remember that they speak for a constituency, not just for themselves.
- Make sure you get specific commitments, expressed in verifiable terms, not vague, unenforceable promises.
- Before the negotiating session, your team should simulate or role-play the negotiation, including having some of your team play the parts of the opponents.
- Make sure that you have mastered the facts.

Fisher (1972) suggested that bargainers attempt to find negotiating issues by fractionating or separating the issue into subissues to discover some points of possible agreement.

Splain (1984, pp. 166–170) recommended the following guidelines:

- Insist that your organization is dealt with as the only bargaining agent.
- Formalizing the bargaining committee and thoroughly preparing for the negotiations represents a critical set of tasks. It requires a more serious detailed effort than preparation for any single action or leadership meeting.

- You must lay the ground rules. Five key ones are that all relevant information necessary to bargain in good faith must be made available; agree on the timetable (dates and times) as well as the location; identify the other side's bargaining team, and clarify any questions of authority and accountability; agree on whether bargaining is open to observers or closed; and agree whether or not any nonbargaining activity (for example, using the media) will be allowed during the bargaining period.

- Be capable of demonstrating flexibility in your range of styles. Be able to employ soft (friendly) or hard (abusive) tactics.

- Avoid getting publicly locked into a position.

- Use informal conversations to break an impasse, or let neutral third parties define a beneficial compromise.

Chester Karrass (1981, pp. 44–45), an expert in business negotiations, found the following tactics profitable:

- Set up a negotiation schedule that allows you time to think about issues.

- Refuse to permit items that are considered nonnegotiable to be discussed.

- Never answer until the question is clearly understood, and do not hesitate to answer only part of a question. Allow the other person to interrupt; it gives you more time.

- Lead your opponent into examining your counterposition: "We seem to be on the same track except for...."

- Place the blame for errors and oversights on past policies, data processing systems, outside consultants—anybody but the person opposite you.

- If a sensitive issue has to be negotiated, save it for last, after successful resolution of some other issues.

In addition, Karrass recommends that you take steps to make concessions without coming off the loser. Some techniques include getting the other party to put all its demands on the table first; don't be baited into item-by-item negotiations and concessions until you are sure of all the other party's demands; never be the first to make a major concession; when your opponent makes one, don't assume you have to make one of equal importance; get something in return for each concession you make; conserve your concessions, give a little at a time, make your opponent work for what he or she gets; don't hesitate to say "no" to a key demand, say it often enough, effectively enough so the other party knows you mean it; don't agree to "split the difference," try for 70–30 or 60–40 first; don't be afraid to back off from a concession you've already made, but don't try to back off once the deal is concluded; keep track of all concessions made, take notes on yours and the other party's.

Methods for Outcome-Based Negotiation. One of the most significant contributions to the art of negotiating is contained in the gem *Getting to Yes*, by Roger Fisher and William Ury (1991). Their approach, called *principled negotiation*, involves starting with a clear understanding of the *legitimate interests* of the parties. It proceeds to the generation of alternative strategies to serve those interests. The selection of the subsequent course of action must meet the tests of fulfillment of the parties' requirements in a way that can be measured by objective criteria.

Fisher and Ury contrasted this with traditional negotiation, which starts from a *limited set of positions* designed to meet the interests of only one party, irrespective of the other's interests (see Figure 12.4). Such a process is characterized by a test of wills, not merits, and results in invalidating the other's interests (which are tied to its positions) rather than exploring issues to discover possibilities of agreement.

As a general practice, principled negotiation has a number of advantages, especially when you are dealing with a more powerful competitor. This style of negotiation helps to even the playing field and keep you in control of factors in the situation that are more likely to be in your favor. Items irrelevant to the issues and over which you may have little control carry much less weight in this process.

The methods Fisher and Ury outline enable you to fully commit yourself to necessary actions. As long as you think you have the right and the capability to insist on being treated respectfully— Do you?—you need not have any hesitancy about acting in a principled manner, whereas you may be reluctant to fully engage in a process that relies on

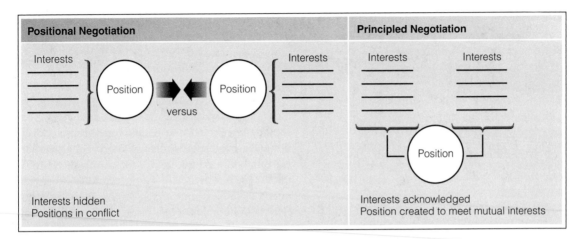

FIGURE 12.4 Differences between Positional and Principled Negotiation

being devious and clever or undermining the other party. By insisting on dealing only with the facts and merits of a situation, you don't have to accept illegitimate interests as legitimate.

Negotiation requires preparation, purposeful attention to detail, and an ongoing awareness of alternative choices. Further, it requires an intentional decision regarding the methods you will use to reach agreement. When used effectively, negotiation can bring about a solution to current problems in a way that fosters opportunities for future problem solving.

Collaboration

Collaboration occurs when two or more parties share resources to accomplish a goal important to them all. They go beyond the mutual acceptance of a course of action; they "co-labor." That is, they each perform some measure of work to accomplish the goal.

When the strategy of collaboration is used, the target becomes a *partner* in a common enterprise. The shared goal need not be equally important to all parties, nor do they necessarily pursue it for the same reasons. For one group the particular, observable end to be accomplished may not be all that important, but the ability to establish a working relationship with their partner may be. Or perhaps collaboration offers relief from accusations of callousness through the appearance of sensitivity that participation in a cooperative venture can bring. In fact, the partners don't even have to like each other to collaborate, although it makes things much easier if they do. Whatever the reason, the common goal unifies their respective motives and provides the impetus to work together.

Too often community groups think they are collaborating merely because they go to the same meeting, maybe even month after month. This is co-attending; this is not collaborating. Collaboration requires that each partner actually do something to promote the common enterprise.

Situations for Which Collaboration May Be Appropriate

- The respondent has resources you need and from which you can benefit.
- You have resources to offer.
- You need to carry forward the results of negotiated agreements.
- You recognize you can give the respondent a way to meet some of its needs if the respondent helps you meet yours.
- You want to develop a working relationship with the respondent.
- You want to show that you can get the respondent to react to you, and you are looking for ways to make it easy for that to happen.
- You want to increase the respondent's dependence on you.

- You want to educate the respondent through close or ongoing contact.

- You recognize that the respondent is agreeable and wants to work together.

- You want to establish new attitudes and practices in the community.

We talk a lot about cooperation, but most of us aren't really skilled at developing and maintaining collaborative relationships to meet community problems. It is hard enough to work together on a class project or to get five families (especially if they are related) to go on a camping trip together. Getting groups who are nervous about one another's motives or dependability to join forces is a formidable task, though it is possible if thoughtfully done.

As one strong advocate of collaboration pointed out, agencies and organizations don't cooperate, people do. Collaboration is people deciding to work together (Hagebak, 1982). Yet these people are tied to organizations each with their own policies, procedures, traditions, and formal and informal goals. These and a host of other barriers interfere with the purposeful attention to matters collaborative relationships require. Still, as Hagebak pointed out, "when it gets right down to basics, the decision to cooperate—or become a barrier—is a *very personal decision*" (p. 33).

Before a group can begin to work together, it really must be able to work together. Standing disagreements, jealousies, and rivalries cannot coexist with a commitment to work for change. How many times have you seen this in a family, a group working on a class assignment, or a congregation in a faith community?

The presence of conflict will erode commitment and eat away at the foundation for building a better future. There are only two exceptions to this. The first is when the competing groups face a common enemy. That shared interest in an opponent will move antagonisms to the background, but it won't get rid of them. Though the parties may temporarily set differences aside, they are there, lurking beneath the surface. The fear and mistrust are never too far from the work. Resources are warily shared, and the awareness of a temporary truce weakens the relationships on which success depends. If the common enemy appears to be getting the upper hand, competing groups may turn on each other in frustration and blame. They become unwitting accomplices with their opponent. The second exception occurs when collaboration is around a very specific matter and expectations of collaborative behaviors are fairly limited.

For true development to occur, internal conflict must be relatively low. Although development activities can help bring people together, the development or community change work can exacerbate existing conflicts. So, before real work on community change can begin, some work on reducing internal conflicts must take place.

If development activities are to be a form of conflict reduction, even resolution, the parties involved must recognize and agree to this strategy. Otherwise, they will undermine the effort in order to confirm their perceptions and positions. That initial agreement itself requires some reduction in conflict.

Some of your partners will be coerced or convinced into collaborating with you. Others, with interests and motives similar to yours, will be eager for the opportunity. For collaboration to be effective, even the most well-intentioned partners must confront a number of matters that threaten to weaken their relationship or scuttle it altogether. Doing so successfully can provide for creative, powerful relationships and a cooperative spirit, which can ultimately extend to other matters.

Strengths of a Collaborative Strategy

- The resources that can be brought to bear on the situation automatically increase.

- You may be able to move your partner into a greater appreciation of problematic conditions and their ability to have a positive impact on them.

- You can teach your partner more effective ways of assisting the benefit community.

- You may increase your partner's dependence on you, thus altering the balance of power.

If carefully nurtured, collaborative relationships can establish a whole different way of addressing community dilemmas. Collaboration makes future problem solving much more efficient by taking energy away from maintaining battle lines and putting it toward improving the community.

??? DID YOU KNOW?   Some Advice on "Getting to Yes"

1. "The most any method of negotiation can do is meet two objectives: first, to protect you against making an agreement you should reject, and second, help you make the most of the assets you do have so any agreement you reach will satisfy your interests as much as possible" (Fisher & Ury, 1991, p. 97).

2. The stronger the other side appears "in terms of physical or economic power, the more you benefit by negotiating on the merits. To the extent that they have muscle and you have principle, the larger the role you can establish for principle the better off you are" (p. 106).

3. "Separate the people from the problem" (p. 106). Be hard on the problem, soft on the people.

4. "Negotiators are people first" (p. 18). "People's desire to feel good about themselves, and their concern for what others will think of them, can often make them more sensitive to another negotiator's interests" (p. 19). "On the other hand, people get angry, depressed, fearful, hostile, frustrated, and offended. They have egos that are easily threatened" (p. 19). "To find your way through the jungle of people problems, it is useful to think in terms of three basic categories: perception, emotion, and communication. The various people problems all fall into one of these baskets" (p. 22).

5. "Interests define the problem. The basic problem in a negotiation lies not in conflicting positions but in the conflict between each side's needs, desires, concerns, and fears" (p. 40). "Behind opposed positions lie shared and compatible interests as well as conflicting ones" (p. 42). For a wise solution, reconcile interests, not positions. Insist on objective criteria. Don't try to settle differences of interest on the basis of will. "Negotiate on some basis independent of the will of either side, that is, on the basis of objective criteria" (p. 82). These criteria should be legitimate and practical and should apply to both sides.

6. Hold people personally accountable for their actions and their information.

7. Acknowledge the interests of the other party as important to the negotiation.

8. "Look forward, not back" (p. 52). "You will satisfy your interests better if you talk about where you would like to go rather than about where you have come from. Instead of asking the other party to justify what they did yesterday, ask, 'Who should do what tomorrow?'" (p. 53).

9. "Invent options for mutual gain" (p. 56). "Four major obstacles inhibit inventing an abundance of options: premature judgment; searching for the single answer; the assumption of a fixed pie (the situation is seen as essentially either/or; either I get what is in dispute or you do); thinking that 'solving their problem is their problem'" (p. 57), an orientation that creates reluctance to think up ways to meet the interests of both sides.

10. "Never yield to pressure, only to principle" (p. 88); that is the integrity of the process.

11. "If you have not thought carefully about what you will do if you fail to reach an agreement, you are negotiating with your eyes closed. The reason you negotiate is to produce something better than the results you can obtain without negotiating" (p. 100). Therefore, determine your BATNA (Best Alternative To a Negotiated Agreement). "That is the only standard against which any proposed agreement should be measured. That is also the only standard that can protect you both from accepting terms that are too unfavorable and from rejecting terms it would be in your best interests to accept" (p. 100).

12. "Apply knowledge, time, money, people, connections, and wits to devise the best solution for you *independent of the other side's assent* [emphasis added]. The more easily and happily you can walk away from a negotiation, the greater your capacity to affect its outcome" (p. 106). This is really all about power. In other words, you will be stronger by the extent to which you do not depend on the negotiation.

13. If the other side refuses to focus on the merits, just don't respond to the game they are playing. "In effect, you change the game simply by starting to play a new one" (p. 107). Still, the other party may attempt to engage in trickery. Three basic tricky ploys that may be used are those intended to

(continued)

Limitations of Collaboration

- Jealousies and other difficulties often cause partners to pull back in a posture of self-protection as soon as complications emerge. This undermines cooperative intent, rendering the effort practically ineffective and emotionally dissatisfying.

- You may become less willing to bring a partner to task on other matters for fear of reducing their collaboration on your shared undertaking.

- The partner may take all the credit for success, and blame you for failures.

- You, who may be more committed to the success of the actual project, may end up doing a far greater share of the work.

- Energy, sometimes a great deal, is required simply to maintain the relationship.

- You may lose some autonomy as you provide your partner with a degree of control.

- A breakdown in the collaborative relationship can make it much more difficult for parties to work together in the future.

Tactics and Tips for Collaboration. A collaborative relationship needs to function on both the task and relationship levels. Each of you should be clear and reasonable about what you expect to get from the venture and what you expect from your partner to achieve your goals. People aren't going to magically grasp and remember your expectations. You are going to have to tell them, perhaps

more than once, and hold them accountable. Though many aspects are unique to each of these relationships, a number of general topics should be carefully examined. You need to proceed with a steady and mutual recognition of the importance of each of these items.

Communication. You need to keep talking with each other throughout the life of the project. Generally, the more personal your communication (preferably face to face) the better. Each partner should have a primary communicator who has the authority to give, receive, and act on information. If you just want to get work done and iron out differences, keep the number of participants at any meetings small, probably no more than three per participating partner. (Information exchange meetings can be much larger.) As the size of the group increases, the opportunity for members to participate declines, and people start playing to the audience, especially if there are difficulties in the relationship. When you think you need to put on a show, you can bring in more people.

Clear agreements. You can prevent a multitude of problems by explicitly delineating the tasks to be performed and the type and extent of resources to be shared. Clear, mutual understandings also help coordinate efforts and resources. Hagebak (1982) warned that memory is imperfect, perceptions differ, and forces affecting our decisions change. So even when working with partners who are friendly, it is best to put agreements in writing.

Decision making. You and your partner need to determine over what issues each can make its own decisions and which require joint approval. If there are multiple partners, you also need to determine which style of decision making you will use. Consensus usually works best. Essentially, consensus exists when two conditions are met: Each party is able to clearly state what the decision is, and each party agrees to support and implement the decision. Other methods, such as majority vote or decisions by an executive committee, may be appropriate.

Monitoring and evaluation. Believe it or not, all good intentions and wonderful ideas don't pan out. Keep track of how partners are living up to their agreements and how well plans are working. Clear agreements and plans will aid in this process. Since you cannot foretell the future, accept the fact that refinements and renegotiations are part of the game.

Recognition. Each of you needs to receive some acknowledgment from your constituencies that you are serving their interests. Stories in the local media, personal letters acknowledging your work, or appearances from other partners before your group are likely ways to get this recognition. Quotes from your partner regarding how your contributions help them and how the project helps your constituency can be useful. Be willing to provide the same sort of recognition to your partner.

Trust. A sufficient amount of trust in each other or in the strength of some external mechanism that holds parties accountable (like a contract or an oversight body) is a prerequisite for collaboration. Acting in a trustworthy manner yourself is the first step in promoting this quality. In situations in which there is some hostility between partners, the other party might suggest that you refrain from some legitimate activities that party just doesn't like. They may be using the relationship to get you to cut back on some of your other activities. You need to assess for yourself whether or not you are living up to the specifics and the spirit of the agreements you have made on the matter at hand.

Leadership. There has to be a force to keep the ball rolling, and rolling in the right direction. An ability to spot potential problems, bring issues and opportunities to the fore, and effectively coordinate activities is necessary. The strength of the agreements themselves is not sufficient to accomplish these requirements. People from your organization, and ideally from the other's as well, need to clearly understand the necessity of providing a leadership function within both the work and the relationship realms of the program.

Here are some additional points to help make collaboration work.

- Make sure the timetable for task completion, and especially the pay-off period, is realistic and mutually understood. Make sure partners know when certain activities need to be done and that they have a sense of progress. Sometimes the more tangible benefits take a while to realize. It may take some time to complete a ball field or turn a profit on a business venture. You don't want partners getting discouraged and giving up because they had an unrealistic idea of when they would achieve returns.

- Provide opportunities to create a sense of ownership in the venture. This is especially important for reluctant associates. Involve partners in things such as naming the project or designing a logo. It will be hard to undermine a project they have christened.

- Provide public acknowledgment of the respondent's participation in the combined venture. This lets many people know the expectations your partner is expected to meet.

- Use vehicles, such as the letter to the editor column, to call attention to your partner's contributions and to encourage future ones.

- Give tangible awards, such as plaques or certificates, at a presentation before your group as well as your partner's. You can do this while you are working together in a way that suggests a future productive relationship. Don't leave recognition until everything is completed.

- Privately acknowledge good work. You can do this with a comment or in a personal letter. It is better to make reference to something specific than to make general statements.

- Work together on tedious or demanding tasks like letter stuffing or digging holes for a tree planting. You can easily introduce a social component into these activities that strengthens the relationship as you really do work together.

- If your partner is creating a problem, bring it to his attention in a direct, matter-of-fact manner. Nip it in the bud. You can say something like this: "Jim, I've noticed _____. As a result, _____. How do you think that could be corrected?" Avoid the "Jim, we need to talk" approaches that introduce a degree of uncertainty, which introduces defensiveness and burdens the matter with excess emotional baggage. Wherever possible, let your partners make corrections to the problems they have created.

- Take note of what is working and the advantages each partner is reaping. It is a bad practice to focus on problems while taking good things for granted, yet it is a common one. When you pay attention to things going in the right direction, you emphasize a positive focus and build confidence in the relationship. This also helps you keep problems in perspective and deal with them more effectively. Failure to deal constructively with problems is often a sign that there is little confidence that the relationship can handle any conflict.

- Get to know one another personally. The less we know about people, the more we have a tendency to make up things about them, especially if we begin to encounter problems. Though you don't have to become fast friends with your partners, a more personal, informal relationship can help cut through artificial barriers common in more reserved relationships. Further, a built-in accountability exists among people who know each other well, as long as one party doesn't use the relationship to take advantage of the other.

Collaboration requires attention to maintaining agreements and relationships. By greatly increasing the resources available, a more comprehensive improvement in a situation can occur more easily, and the experience of collaboration can establish progressive methods for understanding and acting on future challenges.

Co-optation

Many years ago, a social psychologist by the name of Muzafer Sherif (1936) conducted an experiment in which individuals observed a fixed point of light in the darkness. Because of a perceptual phenomenon, the light appeared to move. Sherif asked the participants to note how far the light moved. When individuals worked with others to form a group decision on the amount of movement, individual judgments were replaced by the group's perception of reality. What the group decided became "true," and the individuals' judgments were discarded in favor of those of the group. Even when no other group members were around, the individual still relied on the group's perception as being correct.

People's perception of reality is strongly shaped by their affiliations. You may decide you can accomplish more by bringing certain actors or groups of actors into the fold than you can by keeping them at a distance. Through continued exposure to your perceptions, even opponents can begin to see things your way. In fact, this strategy is especially geared to opponents. Barker (1999) described co-optation as a "strategy for minimizing anticipated opposition by absorbing or including an opponent in the group's membership" (p. 105). Kirst-Ashman and Hull (2009) described it as "eliminating opposition to a cause, plan, or organization by assimilating opponents into the group favoring the cause, plan, or organization" (p. 444). Co-optation occurs when the beliefs and attitudes others hold about a situation conform to yours.

Co-optation usually begins when a formerly antagonistic party changes its manner in regard to its opponent. This party will often appear to be more accepting of its previous opponent and in some way invite the adversary into a relationship of greater congenial contact. This may even include offering a means of formally joining the inviting party's ranks.

This gambit is frequently used by powerful resisting groups to undermine their more grassroots opposition, but it is available for use by grassroots organizations as well (Crowfoot et al., 1983). It is not uncommon, for example, for key leaders of the opposition to be offered jobs in the competing organization. Or perhaps appointment to a special committee that appears to carry some status or special privileges is arranged. Such tactics are intended to weaken an opponent's resolve by giving those who make the offer an appearance of being fine folks after all . . . and, in fact, their positions don't seem to be that unreasonable either. Those who have been co-opted will begin to soften their opposition or risk losing this newfound acceptance by their former enemy. They may begin to justify this new moderation by finding merit in a previously scorned point of view. When this occurs, a former opponent accepts, usually unwittingly, a position of furthering the interests of the co-opting party.

People are susceptible to this approach for a variety of reasons. They may be so tired of the antagonism that they are eager to pick up on any change in attitude. They may believe the new, more amiable relationship provides greater opportunities for influence. They may be flattered, or even simply relieved. The strategy of co-optation is usually purposefully manipulative. Your ethics will direct you to use it not as a way to deny a party's legitimate interests but rather to bring legitimate interests of your members into easy recognition.

Situations for Which Co-optation May Be Appropriate

- The opposing group is uncooperative and is not a good target for confrontation, perhaps because it is highly regarded by most of the community.

- Maintaining an adversarial stance will result in only isolated gains or a standoff.

- A few key individuals who have some influence within the opposing group are amenable to some sort of affiliation.

- There is a particularly vocal critic you would like to silence.

- Your group doesn't have the capability for effective confrontation, nor does it have the resources needed for collaboration.

- You can weaken opponents by bringing them into your organization where their opinions will be in the minority (Barker, 1999).

- You will probably be in an ongoing relationship with the respondent, and you believe that a productive, working relationship can develop if purely antagonistic positions are changed or not adopted at all.

Some people are uncomfortable with the notion of co-optation. It somehow doesn't seem quite right, as if beating an opponent over the head (not literally, I hope) were a lot better. The fact that co-optation is more covertly than overtly influential makes it different from most other strategies. It does not make it better or worse. This strategy is simply another way of bringing an opponent over to your way of seeing things. You are choosing to work more closely with an adversary, and you are providing the adversary with an opportunity to better understand your needs. Ultimately, any strategy is intended to persuade the respondent to accept the legitimacy of your beliefs. Co-optation is a more subtle form of persuasion in which you invite respondents into your perspective rather than directly countering theirs.

Others may not like this approach because it does not strike directly at problem-causing policies, nor does it maintain a clear distinction between conflicting camps. Points that can be made through open confrontation may be obscured; and it appears to blur the lines between good and evil.

There are times when distinctions need to be emphasized and the nature of the conflict dramatized. At these times, co-optation is the wrong strategy to pursue. However, not all opponents must always be seen as evil and kept at arm's length. The notion that opponents can never accept and act on the validity of your interests is a fairly limiting one. The question is, How do you ultimately get them there? Pursuit of this strategy is based on the belief that greater understanding and at least a partial alliance will lead to more change than the more direct use of coercive power.

Strengths of a Co-optation Strategy

- You can defuse a potentially harmful critic.

- You can maximize a former opponent's commitment as she identifies with your self-interests.

- You can gain some insights into the workings of the competition.

- You gain access to a community or organization that has been closed to you. The co-opted party can serve as a kind of translator, communicating your interests with an understanding of the codes and perceptions of the other group. This person can also act as an introducer, helping members of your group gain some degree of acceptance in the other group.

- This strategy requires little investment of energy or resources.

- An obstructing group can become an allied group.

Limitations of Co-optation

- You can let a fox in the henhouse. That is, those whom you invite in may have no interest in working with you and may use information they obtain against you.

- You may inappropriately soften your stand and become reluctant to hold your newfound friends and their organizations as accountable as you should. (You become a little co-opted yourself.)

- You can be transparent in your attempts and come off as insincere and manipulative, further damaging relationships.

- You can get caught up in the game of co-opting people, thereby diminishing your own personal integrity.

Tactics and Tips for Co-optation

- Co-optation is a process that works over time. The target of your intentions is eased into a greater appreciation for your point of view. Be aware that respondents are likely to be at least a little cautious, so go gently. Avoid the temptation to put people down for past sins or to prove that they or their organization are wrong, or you will just promote defensiveness and maintain existing frictions.

- Absorb some of the target's concerns by making selected and acceptable changes in your organization (Mason & Mitroff, 1985).

- It may be helpful to place the target on one of your key committees, even your steering committee or board. Though the degree of responsibility you give will be based on the nature of the relationship with the group the

target represents, some degree of importance must be attached to the role to ensure the individual's interest and involvement. Also, greater responsibility deepens and accelerates the process of cultivation.

- Targets should get the message that they are seen as team players.

- Once targets have had some time to become acculturated to the needs of your organization, invite them to help seek solutions to the problems you face, particularly as these relate to working with their own constituency.

- Don't attempt to co-opt too many people at a time. Two important targets are plenty.

- Whomever you attempt to co-opt must have credibility within the opposing community.

- A good person to target is one who has cooperated with you in the past.

- Remember that the purpose is to draw in and build support, not to set someone up as a patsy who will suffer some loss because of your actions. Aside from the obvious ethical problems with harming someone, it will probably come back to haunt you.

Co-optation requires patience and a belief in the possibility that someone who has previously interfered with your success can become an advocate for your cause. It can curtail resistance and establish valuable links to key constituencies.

Advocacy: Giving Voice

In advocacy we give voice to our knowledge and values on behalf of and in partnership with those whose voices are not often heard. Roughly translated from its Latin roots, advocacy means just that: to give voice. Advocacy more commonly refers to speaking out for the interests of others. It is different from organizing, which brings people together to develop their own voices and power, but may be an important step toward organizing or may use organizing in concert with other activities to change conditions.

Advocacy is generally expressed in four broad forms. *Policy advocacy* is directed to making changes in public policy, often in the form of laws. *Cause or class advocacy* involves action on behalf of a class of people who are affected by shared conditions (Ezell, 2001). *Professional advocacy,* a form of cause advocacy, furthers the recognition of a profession's skills and contributions and asserts its particular interests. *Case advocacy* focuses on a situation affecting an individual or small group, such as a family. Jansson (2008) further distinguishes four styles of policy advocacy: "ballot-based advocacy, to change the composition of government or to get a ballot initiative enacted or defeated; legislative advocacy, to secure the enactment of—or the defeat of—specific legislative goals; analytic advocacy, to make policy choices that are based on hard data and structured analysis; and troubleshooting advocacy, to increase the effectiveness of operating programs (p. 92).

Case advocacy is the most common form of advocacy practiced by health and human services workers. Hardly a week will go by when you are not faced with a situation that calls for you to intervene to help people get the assistance they deserve. While this creates change in a particular situation, the change may not be long lasting or may not benefit others who do not have the aid of an advocate. However, if you and your colleagues make a habit of advocating within your particular field of practice, it is likely that you will set forces in motion that will lead to more enduring change. It can even begin the process of more macro-level advocacy.

In addition to your work with individual cases, you may become an advocate as a member of an agency board of directors or a community advisory group. Of course, you can help organize or participate in an advocacy campaign to achieve a specific goal. Policy and cause advocacy requires access to and credibility with policymakers and other decision makers, research capability, and a base of organizational power (Minieri & Gestos, 2007).

Advocacy can take place in conversations among agency workers or through more formal administrative processes such as fair hearings, grievances, and complaints (Kirst-Ashman & Hull, 2009). Advocates also may use public hearings, media attention, private pressure in back room negotiations, and legislative action.

Like any other tool in our professional repertoire, advocacy allows us to effectively fulfill our professional responsibilities and purposes. More specifically, advocacy reaffirms the value of the constituent, the value of our relationships with the constituent, and our professional values. In fact, our professional identity and ethics require us to advocate for the rights of members of society (Council in Rehabilitation Education, 2008; NASW, 2008; NOHS, 2000; Public Health Leadership Society, 2002). "Advocacy and human services are intertwined" (Wark, 2008, p. 69). Our own ability to function in accordance with our knowledge and values is hampered by conditions we may need to change. Further, advocacy prevents avoidable losses and discomfort and the additional expenditure of resources (including personal time and energy) required to restore the loss that occurs when attention is not appropriately given. We have a choice to become silent partners in maintaining conditions that exploit and demean—or not.

Situations for Which Advocacy May Be Appropriate. Although there are many different circumstances that call for someone to perform the role of the advocate, these are likely to fall into one of five categories.

1. The rights community members are unacknowledged, ignored, or denied. Harmful attitudes and practices lead to conditions in which benefits, information, and other resources are blocked or withheld. People are treated with disrespect or prejudice. People are deprived of opportunities for development and contribution.

2. The helping system is unable to respond effectively because little or nothing is in place to benefit community members.

3. The individual's or group's crisis situation does not fit routine response procedures.

4. The responding institution (for example, the human service agency) does not have a meaningful relationship with those community members as a people. They and their issues are not real to the institution.

5. The people lack sufficient knowledge, skill, confidence, or power to meaningfully assert concerns without assistance.

Strengths of an Advocacy Strategy

- Participating in advocacy efforts can strengthen your network of professional connections, advance your skills, and enhance your personal credibility and reputation.

- You can help change how health and human services systems operate by advancing new policies, programs, attitudes, and practices.

- By partnering with community members who are affected by the situation, you help create opportunities for their skill development and empowerment. Futher, collaboration reinforces the beliefs among both community members and professionals of the potential for other future partnership practices.

- Professionals sometimes find it more comfortable to complain or preach from the safety of the sidelines. Getting into the game signals that the profession must be taken seriously, expanding its influence and credibility.

- In both cause and case advocacy, the willingness of community members to assert their interests may protect them from future disregard or abuse.

Limitations of an Advocacy Strategy

- Advocacy often involves representing and acting on the interests of those with less political, social, and economic power, so the process can diminish the role of those distressed by the matter, pushing their participation to the background. Advocates may be more interested in organizing other professionals or well-connected citizens.

- There can be a subtle, and sometimes not so subtle, message that professionals are the ones who really know the system and how to get it to respond. This can reinforce patterns of apathy and dependence among community members.

- The change agent's professional identity may serve as a hindrance to assertively challenging colleagues. There may be a lack of willingness on the part of advocates to make demands that create discomfort for peers or others in authority, particularly if these individuals are members of the advocate's profession or reference group. Advocates my settle for more modest gains than could be achieved by more insistent approaches. Professionals and agencies may fear being seen as confrontational (Kirst-Ashman & Hull, 2009).

- Case advocacy can put people at risk of passive or active retribution even if the particular advocacy effort succeeds.

Tactics and Tips for Advocacy.   Building an organized advocacy effort requires attention to the various elements described throughout the text: building power, developing an organization, effective planning, and taking action. Advocacy efforts may also employ the strategies of confrontation, negotiation, collaboration, and co-optation. In addition, here are some specific pointers to help you become an effective advocate.

- Know your issue well. Be aware of areas where your knowledge is fuzzy. Do something about that. *Don't* pretend. Develop your "argument." Link facts and examples with a rationale for action.

- Know the relevant rights, rules, and regulations. Be able to cite chapter and verse. Know how procedures work, such as a formal complaint process. If you choose to ignore them, do so on purpose and have a rationale for so doing.

- Get a partner. You will feel more confident if you have a knowledgeable, friendly co-advocate with you.

- Ask for help. Get information and possibly involvement from relevant advocacy organizations and other organized groups.

- Develop a picture of what "better" looks like. Have a clear idea of how you would like the matter to be resolved. Stay open to alternative ways to solve the problem. Focus on interests, not just positions. Be creative.

- Focus on the outcome. Do not get lured into a discussion of peripheral issues. Acknowledge them perhaps for a future discussion, but return to the matter at hand and keep attention there.

- Recognize and communicate awareness of legitimate interests. Be able to identify both your (and the constituent's) interests and the interests of the party to whom you are advocating (the target). Communicate this awareness in a way that the target knows you understand those interests.

- Link the issue. Be able to connect the issue and its resolution to the mission, goals, and statements of the target as well as to commonly held human values.

- Use emotion appropriately. Be willing to inject emotion so that the target better feels the issue as well its importance to you. Avoid being purely rational or overly emotional.

- Get clear agreements with timetables. Any agreement lacking in specific outcomes to be produced by specific actions of specific people according to a specific timetable is fluff. Do not fall into the trap of accepting a promise to "take action" or "look into" the matter.

- When agreements are made, determine what actions you should take if agreements are not kept by the other party. Keep the record straight by recording agreements.

Your decision to engage in advocacy will energize and deepen your professional commitment. Your decision to continue learning how to do it well will bring rewards that no attempt at accommodation can ever bring.

OTHER STRATEGIC AND TACTICAL CONSIDERATIONS

Adhere to a Firm Code of Ethics

Consider the ethical dimensions of your action or inaction. If you set up an opponent, have you unfairly or unnecessarily abused another human being and cheapened yourself in the process? If you allow a serious problem situation to persist because you will only engage in polite tactics, how does your mannerly approach honor those whose suffering is prolonged?

From time to time you will hear the complaint: "That's just the ends justifying the means." Recognize these statements as specious. The fact is that all behavior is purposeful. All behavior is a means to secure some valued end. That is, all ends are purchased by, and may be used to justify, the choice of some means or actions. For example, if I choose not to engage in a certain behavior to preserve my sense of professionalism, I am simply selecting a different end, preserving professionalism, and using the importance of that end to justify whatever action I decide to take or not take.

Don't get caught up in meaningless arguments over whether the ends are justifying the means. Your time is much more wisely spent firmly rooting yourself in a fundamental code of ethics. Review your commitment to ethics and keep it alive. Do examine whether or not you are justifying your unethical behavior. "The more justifiable an unethical action is, the more individuals feel that it is okay to engage in that action" (Tenbrunsel & Messick, 2001, p. 211). Your behavior may very well change from one situation to another, not, one hopes, because you lack ethics but because your ethics inform and drive every important decision you make. Your steadfast commitment to integral ethical principles will guide you to act differently as you face different challenges to your beliefs.

Recognize Mutual Benefits

Along with basic concerns regarding selection of a strategy mentioned at the beginning of this chapter, three overriding considerations should be kept in mind. First, you need to think about how a certain approach will help your organization accomplish its particular goals. Next, you need to consider how the strategy will aid in the continued development of the organization. But that's not all. You must also take into account the benefit the target perceives from pursuing a course of action you desire. If you have given thought only to what you want them to do and not why they will want to do it, you have only thought things through halfway. You need to consider why the target will respond, from their point of view—not yours.

People do things because it will get them something they want or avoid something they don't want. People don't readily act against their *perception* of their self-interest. So your deliberations

GLOBAL PERSPECTIVES

NIGERIA—(July 15, 2002) Unarmed village women holding 700 ChevronTexaco workers inside a southeast Nigeria oil terminal let 200 of the men go Sunday but threatened a traditional and powerful shaming gesture if the others tried to leave—removing their own clothes.

Most Nigerian tribes consider unwanted displays of nudity by wives, mothers, or grandmothers as an extremely damning protest measure that can inspire a collective source of shame for those at whom the action is directed.

About 600 women from two nearby communities are holding ChevronTexaco's giant Escravos terminal. They range in age from 30 to 90—with the core group being married women 40 or older.

The women want the oil giant to hire their sons and use some of the region's oil riches to develop their remote and run down villages—most of which lack even electricity. The people in the Niger Delta are among the poorest in Nigeria (Associated Press, 2002c).

(July 16, 2002) The unarmed women holding 700 ChevronTexaco workers in a southeast Nigeria oil terminal agreed Monday to end their siege after the company offered to hire at least 25 villagers and to build schools and electrical and water systems.... "We have to do a much better job of having communities involved in our business. We now have a different philosophy, and that is do more with communities," [ChevronTexaco executive Dick] Filgate told the women (Associated Press, 2002a).

(July 18, 2002) Hundreds of unarmed women seized control of at least four more ChevronTexaco facilities...even as the 10-day occupation of an oil terminal by other village women ended....

The women involved in the latest takeovers, all members of the Ijaw tribe, were refusing to leave until they had met with senior company executives to press their demands for jobs and community improvements (Doran, 2002).

(July 26, 2002) Village women chanted jubilantly Thursday after ending their weeklong occupation of

ChevronTexaco oil pipeline stations in exchange for jobs, business loans, schools, and hospitals (Associated Press, 2002b).

SOUTH PACIFIC—Change rarely takes place when people are "comfortable" or think they are comfortable. A tension must develop before people or groups can have meaningful change. These tensions are often expressed as a felt need, and are finally articulated in one way or another.

Community development workers who merely help people to become "comfortable," who do things for people—identifying and analyzing their problems for them and "doling out" answers—are part of the problem, not part of the answer (Melanesian Council of Churches, 1977, p. 220).

ISRAEL—We had a group of community workers in the city, in the neighborhoods, a staff of young street workers, and also the Golden Age Club participants.... We organized a committee of aged people and some other

---

on strategy must include not only what you need but what they need as well. This raises a number of questions. What's in it for them? Or, what's important to them? Will the target readily recognize a benefit, or will you have to sell them on it? Remember, in many cases the change may require that the respondent move onto unknown territory or even accept a loss of power. Remember, also, that although a course of action "makes sense," it may have little bearing on the response you will get. What makes you think the target will respond in the way you want it to?

Another fundamental commandment of change is, "Thou shalt hit them in their self-interest." The more clearly you can focus your actions on the things (rational, normative, and emotional) that are

important to the respondent, the more direct and meaningful the response will be. Although this may very well mean that you select a strategy that will cause the respondents discomfort for resisting, you will generally find that the more easily the other party is able to recognize a benefit by pursuing the action you desire them to take, the less resistance to change you will encounter. The more convincing you need to do, the more resistance you can expect. By discovering a course that can provide direct benefits to each party, you weaken both the interest in and the legitimacy of opposition.

If you can identify some things each party is eager to accomplish and select an approach that provides for that accomplishment, the change effort will be fairly smooth. If, however, you are the only volunteers. We started organizing them to fight, to get health coverage for thousands of people in Jerusalem.

First of all we had a real problem, because the elderly were afraid to confront anyone. So we started working with them. We did role-playing. Because when we took them to the Mayor and to the rabbi, they suddenly became passive—they couldn't even talk. So I told them, "I am the Mayor. Oh, you are very nice people…" And little by little they became more aggressive. They learned how to be more and more aggressive, and they started going to people in the newspapers. They started learning how to present their problems. That took about five or six months of work.

The municipality ignored the problem of reopening the centers because it would cost a lot of money…. So we decided to move on to other tactics. We issued a warning that the funeral of the next man to die would leave from the house of the Mayor…and from the home of the Minister of Health. We realized that behind every position,

or agency, there is a man with his weakness. You have to find the weakness. We found that such threats were very effective.

Next we came with around eight hundred aged, and we demonstrated in [the Mayor's] office. But [the Mayor] was quite clever. He brought the demonstrators Coca-Cola and other things to drink, and that was not helpful to our conflict. He treated them as guests.

Then we went to the Ministry of Health. They were less clever than [the Mayor], and they closed the doors, so the aged threw stones at the office….

Later this same night…they came to an agreement to give many, many people their health insurance…without paying money, like socialized medicine. That was the result of this fight (Avner Amiel, 2001, pp. 105–106).

NAMIBIA—Illegal squatters living in Windhoek's Havana 6 settlement yesterday emerged victorious from the High Court, after appealing to have the Windhoek municipality's actions of evicting them and demolishing their shacks stopped.

High Court Judge Petrus Damaseb yesterday granted the shanty residents an interim interdict, declaring the law whereby the City of Windhoek is allowed to remove them off its property, the Squatter's Proclamation of 1985, declared invalid and of no effect.

This will remain the case until at least August 14, when the case will return to court. The municipality did not oppose the group's application; something Damaseb said was noted to the local authority's credit. The City is one of four respondents sighted in the case, the others being the Windhoek City Police who enforced the evictions, the Attorney General's office and central government.

Yesterday's court appearance was pre-showed by a demonstration by part of the group in front of the high court in the morning. The Havana squatters, who reportedly number around 400 currently, have been embroiled in a to-and-fro battle with the City of Windhoek, erecting structures and seeing them torn down, since at least February (Denver Issacs, 2009).

party to receive a direct benefit, the change effort is likely to be a more difficult undertaking.

Education as a Strategy

If the only thing in the way of positive change is a lack of information, then education is an effective method to use. Frankly, a simple lack of information is rarely the major stumbling block. Too often those who wish to promote change have their sights set on educating people (frequently focusing on the already sympathetic) as if all that anyone needs in order to act is more awareness of the situation and its consequences. When education becomes the goal, change agents too often stop short of doing all they need to do to move the

process forward. There is an assumption here that knowledge is sufficient for corrective action, that if people just knew more they would automatically act to change things. My guess is that you already know the importance of a number of things—changing the oil in your car, balancing your checkbook, studying routinely, not just the night before the test. Is knowing these things enough to get you to act on them the way you should?

Do you really want people to know more, or do you want them to act differently? Education is an important and often a necessary part of any change effort, but it is only a part. Certainly, people need to know about problems, their effect, and what an individual can or should do about them. Yet they generally need more. Education must be complemented by other methods that will motivate people to act in a meaningful manner.

Create a Receptive Environment

A host of elements and actors are present in any situation. In most cases, only a few of these will be directly affected by your efforts to bring about change. Those who must respond to your attempts will look for signals in the environment that favor or oppose new directions. Prior to taking action directly related to the change you intend to make, you may take steps to help create a climate supportive of or at least non-resistant to change. This could involve an information campaign, inclusion of specific opinion leaders in your planning efforts, or other approaches.

As Julian (1973) observed, change comes about when a "significant number of people—or a number of significant people" (p. 9) agree that a problem exists. By creating this impression, you encourage acceptance of new ideas and make it easier for decision makers to respond favorably.

Get the Right People in the Right Places

The quality of many decisions is directly related to the quality of the decision maker. If the actions of a particular decision maker are going to be crucial, it may be important not only to attempt to influence that decision maker but to influence who holds the decision-making position in the first place. Your organization may decide to actively participate in processes to determine who will hold pivotal decision-making positions. This may mean taking part in political campaigns, search or selection committees, or confirmation proceedings.

The simple fact is that it is a lot easier to influence those whose beliefs are similar to yours than it is to influence those with whom you have some fundamental differences. This is especially true if you contributed to an individual's successful effort to obtain the position. Working to get the right people in the right places could be an efficient investment of your time.

TRICKS FOR SPECIAL OCCASIONS

A limitless number of special techniques can be used to strengthen the effectiveness of your organization. Remain aware of the little things that are important to your success, and see if a little twist here or there can give your project or cause a boost. Be inventive and have a little fun while you're at it. Here is a sample of particular tricks to address common hindrances.

Stacking a Small Room

The conference room where you are to make your presentation is located on the ninth floor. You could use the exercise, but it's quicker to use the elevator. Six people get on the elevator with you. At the third floor, two more people step aboard. One more squeezes in at the fifth. "What brought this crowd?" you wonder. By the time you have made it to your ninth-floor destination, you are beginning to feel claustrophobic. All 10 of you tumble into the same conference room. It is a very nice, comfortable room with a large table surrounded by plush seats. Additional chairs line the walls. The place can easily hold 50. After their passage on the crowded elevator, the people separate into three little groups seeking their own places in the room apart from the others. They find seats along the walls as you go to the head of the table. You doodle on your note pad for a while. No one else enters the room. Finally it is time to begin. You look up, notice all the empty chairs, and think to yourself, "Hardly anybody showed up. What's wrong?"

The use of space can give an impression of community disinterest or create the sense that there is a movement afoot. You may want to convince dubious members of the community that everyone is on board with the project, or you may want to demonstrate overwhelming community support to an opponent. If you expect 30 people to show up, schedule your function in a room that can comfortably seat about 20. Set up only 15 or so chairs to start off. Have a few stacked up in the room and the rest easily accessible in the room next door. As people arrive and chairs are being set up, you can be "amazed" by the tremendous turnout. If people have to stand along the walls, so much the better. Even those who aren't in on the ploy won't mind having to stand as long as the show is good.

Defusing an Opposing Argument

Preempt the opponent's argument or plan by releasing it first. Let your audience know just what is coming, and then discredit it. This leaves the opponent offering something people have heard before and about which they have at least some suspicions. They have been inoculated against its impact. This approach allows a group to be forewarned and thus forearmed. The opponent is put on the defensive and may even be forced to abandon or alter a favored position. Of course, you may even anticipate and announce this likelihood.

Keeping the Record Straight

Amnesia seems to strike some targets when it is time to make good on promises made. It seems as though they were "misunderstood," and they didn't really mean what you thought they meant. In the course of a discussion, some outrageous statements may be made, ones that, especially if made politely, may go unnoticed or, if noticed, be tolerated. These common occurrences can be dealt with by having a member of your group volunteer to serve as a secretary and take minutes of the meeting.

Nobody actually likes to be the secretary, so rarely will anyone compete with your volunteer for the honor. Yet the secretary is one of the most powerful people at any meeting. During the meeting, the secretary can record, confirm, and note the confirmation of promises. The secretary also has the authority to interrupt the proceedings at any point to "ask a question for clarification." This gives the secretary the chance to call attention to a comment or ask a speaker to further explain some objectionable statements. By acting in his official capacity, the secretary can expose points without being argumentative. As long as the individual doesn't overplay the role, the secretary can control the meeting.

The minutes should be widely distributed, making sure that key points confirmed during the meeting are underscored. You need to anticipate that some of the targets will object to the record, so be ready to effectively counter these gripes. The "volunteer" should be well prepared to perform the function. Spend a little time discussing and perhaps even role-playing this position.

Individualized Petitions

A petition provides a simple way for people to voice their opinion. Twenty-five people can sign a paper attesting to their support for an idea or a statement. Still, it is only one piece of paper. Much better to have 25 pieces of paper, each one asserting the same support for the desired action. This is not the time for conservation.

In addition to the printed message and signature, each person could be encouraged to write a one-sentence personal note on the bottom of the page. Most people are willing to do this, especially if you are prepared to suggest some topics about which the individual may want to comment. You can even suggest some comments when it seems appropriate.

If you put a fold in each sheet and then stack the opened sheets on top of each other, it makes for a more impressive pile. You can present two pieces of paper with 50 signatures or a fluffed-up batch of 50 papers, many with personal statements. Which do you think will have the greater impact?

STRATEGIES AND TACTICS AN OPPONENT MAY USE ON YOU

You are not the only group considering the actions it can take to gain an advantage or head off a threat. When the target has become an opponent, it may be trying to provoke a response from you that would advance or protect its interests. It is helpful for you to consider a few common schemes you are likely to face.

Buffer Groups

Beware the formation of a committee established to "explore and seek resolution to shared concerns." Though I suppose a few of these things really work, most of them are set up by those under attack to diffuse energy. They become part of a pseudo problem-solving structure that simply adds an additional layer between you and the target while allowing the target to establish some control over the action setting (Crowfoot et al., 1983).

First of all, recognize the process for what it is, and even if you do participate, place your trust in other activities you control. Refuse to accept limitations on your actions as a condition of membership. Be willing to declare the process a sham and walk away from it. The opponent is likely to want to hang onto the appearance of cooperation, so you may be granted some concessions to appease your threats.

Divide and Conquer

In a conflict situation, the target is likely to try to drive a wedge between you and your partners or among the members of your organization itself. This is usually done by granting some temporary favor to one group over the other, spreading rumors, or promoting an agenda likely to bring dispute to your ranks.

Discuss this probability among yourselves in advance, and see if you can guess what your opponent will try to do. By making a game out of it, you can strengthen your resolve for unity and belittle your opponent's methods.

Absence of Decision Makers

As a variation of the buffer group game, the target may serve up a variety of individuals who can "transmit your concerns" to those in authority. You can transmit your own concerns. If people don't have the authority to act, don't waste your time meeting with them.

Vague Agreements

Any agreement lacking specific outcomes to be produced by specific actions of specific people according to a specific timetable is meaningless. Common "agreements" include those to "take action" or "resolve the problem," or worse, "to look into the matter." There are a number of ways to dress up delays or inaction as agreement. Be careful to make sure that what you are agreeing to is meaningful.

Acknowledge that the "agreement" represents a good starting point, but not a real agreement. Then specify the steps and the time frame acceptable for forging a true agreement.

Telling You What You Want to Hear

This is one of the most effective tricks in an opponent's arsenal. It can deflate the energy from your drive more quickly than air can escape from an untied balloon. This ploy is especially effective with those who are uncomfortable challenging authority, don't really want to do any more work, or who yearn to be "right" over being effective. Be prepared to hear a variety of pat responses that by themselves mean nothing. "I agree with you." "Yes, you're right." "You have raised some valid concerns." These are some of the standards. Be mindful not to let these statements reduce your impetus for useful action. Use the apparently favorable response to push for actions to back it up. You may answer by saying something like this: "That's great to hear; now let's focus on exactly what you are going to do."

Endless Meetings

Much, if not most, of your work will be done during volunteer hours. By calling meeting after meeting, the target can simply wear you out. The time spent at a meeting is increased by the time spent thinking about and preparing for the meeting. This can add up. Quite often the people who call these meetings are paid for their time, so they may be happy to meet forever. If you suspect this is happening to your group, first confront the target about it. Then start placing strict requirements on the justification for meeting. Make sure the intended outcome of the meeting is realistic and logically related to movement on your goals. If there is no real need to have a face-to-face conversation, tell the target you will discuss matters over the phone.

You can play this game too. Have a good supply of "alternates," so any number of people can attend meetings rather than just a few. If the alternate is not sufficiently versed to make a decision, state that decisions reached at the meeting must be ratified by the membership. If an alternate needs to be brought up to date with the current state of the proceedings, make sure the target is requested to do so during the meeting. The need for the target to regularly reorient new participants, who may be no more than message transmitters to your organization, can dampen enthusiasm for this ruse.

Don't be shy about scheduling a meeting at a time and in a place that is convenient to you but inconvenient to the target.

Requests for Volumes of Information

Check to see how the target intends to use the information you produce. If they cannot clearly demonstrate that information leads to action, tell them you prefer to spend your time in more constructive ways. Another response is for you to request payment for producing certain kinds of information. If they are not willing to pay for a "study," ask them how this information can be so valuable.

Withholding Information

The target may promise to provide you with necessary information that is rightfully yours. They promise, but do not act. They may continue to delay to drain your momentum and to keep you from being able to move or make decisions. Do not wait. At the time you request information, establish deadlines and methods for ensuring accountability. Be willing to make an issue over the broken promises, invoking the intervention of third parties or other parties who have power over the target. You may be tempted to withhold information or action until the target gives you what you need. This may work on some occasions, but inaction on your part may play into your opponent's hands.

Especially when you are dealing with a public institution, learn how to request information under the Freedom of Information Act, and be willing to exercise that right.

Overwhelming You with Information

There may be some truly important data provided in the volumes you get, but you will have to wade through mounds of relatively meaningless information to discover it. An opponent may use this tactic to say that they were more than forthcoming with their information and that they did in fact tell you of their plans, so you should not be surprised by the unfolding of events.

Your tendency will be to set things aside until you have time to read it all. It may gather an inch of dust before that time ever comes. By then it may be too late. To protect against this, have someone in your group prepared to critically pore over any information you receive. You could end up with a lot of ammunition.

Providing You with Special Attention or Offerings

Be wary of opponents bearing gifts. Although you want to allow for the fact that people do change their attitudes, it is wise to consider the context in which special favors are offered. If there is an expectation that you will back off on your pursuit of issues or if you are to be seen as more important than other members of your organization, your benefactor may not be operating from the most kindly of intentions. You may decide to accept the gift and pass it along to someone else. Or you can decline altogether.

Feigning Injury or Hurt Feelings

Avoiding accountability is important business for some opponents. Unable to deal with the facts of their behavior, they may try to gain some sympathy by acting unjustly accused or unfairly harmed. What they are really trying to do is change the agenda and put you on the defensive. You don't need to explain yourself, nor should you feel apologetic or guilty for adhering to the importance of the facts of the matter. You can defuse the opponent's tactic by giving your opponent a clear, specific way to be a partner in problem resolution. Their refusal to do so can become an enduring symbol of their insincerity.

COMMANDMENTS OF CHANGE

As I have reflected on the diverse types of change efforts I have been involved in over the years, I have come to recognize some fundamental ideas. These principles achieve "commandment" status if their importance is consistently borne out under varying circumstances. Here are Homan's Thirteen Commandments for promoting community change. Remember them, and use them to further your own change efforts.

1. Thou shalt hustle.
2. Thou shalt keep the cycle of empowerment rolling.
3. Thou shalt do thy homework.
4. Thou shalt hit them in their self-interest.
5. Thou shalt have those who feel the problem play a significant role in resolving the problem.
6. Thou shalt have the situation dictate the strategy.
7. Thou shalt have a quick, initial victory.
8. Thou shalt prevent unintended consequences.
9. Thou shalt keep thy options open.
10. Thou shalt do things on purpose.
11. Thou shalt roll with the punches.
12. Thou shalt commit thyself to learning. And the final one, should you forget everything else.
13. Thou shalt laugh and PEA,[1] and thou shalt be relieved.

DO YOU HAVE WHAT IT TAKES?

As you get ready to move from talking about doing something to actually doing it, take stock of the assets your group brings to the scramble. Be sure the basic factors crucial for action are clearly present in your group. This will help you detect any weak portions in your foundation that may need some shoring up before you press the issue. Check to see that you are well supplied with the following ingredients.

Clarity of purpose. Your issue is clear and compelling, and your sense of purpose certain and strong. You are able to articulate both your issue and your purpose.

Commitment. You and the other members of your group have made a conscious commitment to do what it takes to achieve success. You are determined not only to take action but to adequately prepare for it as well.

Interest. There is sufficient interest in the issue from a sufficient number of people.

Workers. There are enough people willing to take on whatever time-consuming tasks are necessary so that one person doesn't get stuck with it all.

Leadership. Tasks are accomplished, members are motivated, relationships are strengthened, and an appropriate range of leadership has developed so one person doesn't try to do the things other people could and should do.

1. Have *Persistence,* generate and use *Energy,* and take *Action.*

Information. You know what you need to know to act and to prevent unintended consequences.

Risk taking. You and the other participants are willing to take risks.

Power. Your organization has enough power to get a response from those from whom you need a response at this particular stage in your change episode.

CONCLUSION

You won't put up with things the way they are. You have acknowledged a need to take action. You involve more people, giving you the power and resources you need. You keep talking to each other, and you make decisions. With a clear sense of what you intend to accomplish, you have assessed the situation to determine the most effective strategies and their accompanying tactics to advance your goals. You have determined how the ideal selection of actions fits the real capabilities of your group. You have actually gone out and implemented your actions purposefully and evaluated their effectiveness.

You have committed yourself to the success of your venture. You are determined to be persistent. You enjoy the company of your partners. And you do not take yourself so seriously that you cannot recognize and benefit from the humor that comes as a welcome visitor to most any situation. Though maybe you are just starting out, you smile. You have probably already won something pretty important.

AN AGREEMENT GOING TO WASTE?

You are working to assist a neighborhood that is threatened by a change in land use that could really harm the neighborhood, or perhaps improve it.

A year ago, after months of negotiation, the City promised the neighborhood that it would buy an unused parcel of land in the neighborhood and, working with the neighborhood, turn it into a park. The owners of this land had agreed to sell the land to the City for a low price because they owed a lot of back taxes on the land and they really didn't have a use for it. Now, after the City has acquired the land, it wants to sell the parcel to a chemical waste company. The company will process various forms of chemical waste on the site to prepare the wastes for disposal elsewhere. The City is interested in both the increased tax revenue and the possibility of providing some jobs to neighborhood resi-

dents. Some of the residents like the idea of jobs also. Further, the City has assured the neighborhood that the new business poses no dangers.

The neighborhood's previous experience has given it some confidence, good leadership, creativity, and good skills in organizing. Although most of the neighbors haven't been involved in the life of the larger community, a few have some pretty good connections. They have built good relationships with the media, and city elections are coming in a few months. Some of the neighbors are really angry now, and some are just tired of dealing with things.

The neighborhood association has come to you to help the association develop strategies and tactics to stop the chemical waste project and to restore the park. How will you help the neighborhood figure out what to do?

REFLECTION QUESTIONS

1. What is present in the situation that will guide your choice of which strategy to use? What opportunities exist? What dangers?

2. What tactics do you think this group can and will use to make that strategy work? What makes you think so?

3. What reactions from whom will your strategy and tactics produce? How will these reactions help the group achieve its goal?

4. What sort of internal conflict might you expect? How will you deal with that?

5. Who needs to "own" the selection of strategies and tactics? How will you act to create ownership?

6. What might be some unintended consequences that could result from your choice of strategy and tactics? How might you act to reduce these?

7. What strategies and tactics might be used against the neighborhood? By whom?

GROUP ACTIVITY: THE ACME ORGANIZERS HELP PREPARE FOR ACTION

Divide the larger group into teams of five members. You and your team, members of the famous ACME Organizers, have been hired to organize your college community to improve conditions that affect community members. Of course, you know that selecting a good organizing issue is an important step, but taking action on that issue is what makes things real.

1. Discuss how your team is going to discover issues that are important to members of your college community. (5 minutes)

2. Go out into the college community and gather information on potential issues. Team members may decide to look around, talk to people, read bulletin boards, take pictures on their phone, or investigate in other ways. (15 minutes)

3. When the team returns, discuss potential issues members have discovered and select one issue

your team thinks could bring people together to take action. Prepare an action plan that covers the following points. (20 minutes)

• Describe your issue.

• Use information from the chapter to determine the strategy that would work best.

• Explain the the rationale for the strategy you have chosen.

• Describe what you think will happen when you take action.

4. Present your plan to the larger group. (5 minutes)

5. Open a discussion in the whole class regarding how learning from this activity can be used to link issues to action in the broader community.

HELPFUL WEBSITES

Links to the organizations briefly described here are on the companion website at www.cengage.com/humansvcs/homan.

COMM-ORG. Supported by the University of Wisconsin Department of Community and Environmental Sociology, this organization provides information organizers and scholars can use to learn, teach, and do community organizing and has resources on a variety of topics including funding, training, action, research, and Internet activism. A moderated listserv discussion group of more than 1,000 members from 12 countries links activists and academics from around the world.

Links to many community organizations and a host of training materials are also available.

Kentuckians for the Commonwealth. A good look at an organization that helps to develop leaders to build organizations in communities across the state of Kentucky. The site provides a number of publications on statewide issues as well as information on local chapters. You will get a good glimpse of issues and the people working on them.

Midwest Academy. One of the best-known training organizations for direct action tactics; many useful tips are available as well as information on jobs and training opportunities.

National People's Action. This is a network of hundreds of community organizations throughout the United States that commonly employ direct action tactics on a range of issues, including neighborhood safety, immigrant rights, and affordable housing. The site offers links to many grassroots organizations, which may be a source of insight on strategies and tactics for your group.

National Lawyers Guild. The guild is committed to using the law as an instrument for the protection of the people rather than for their repression. The organization provides a member newsletter and quarterly journal, along with a number of helpful articles and books on legal issues. There are local chapters in many communities.

USAction. A collection of activist organizations working on social, racial, health, and economic justice issues, this site includes an action blog, numerous issue campaigns, and a list of state affiliates and partners. TrueMajority, a project of USAction, organizes activists online.

Center for Substance Abuse Prevention (CSAP). This is part of the Substance Abuse and Mental Health Services Administration with a wealth of information on a variety of approaches to substance abuse issues in local communities, including tools for capacity building and prevention education.

✳

PART III

A Closer Look at Typical Change Contexts

Not far from where you are sitting right now, there are people who are frustrated by circumstances that seem beyond their control. Opportunities are hidden or denied. Services don't work. Insensitivity has grown from indifference to erode hope.

Not far from where you are sitting right now, people are deciding to take action to direct their future. Somebody started the process that brought these people together. Maybe somebody who 2 years or even 2 months ago never thought about challenging "the way things are."

How will it turn out for these people? Will they fail? If so, why? What will get in their way? Will they succeed? If so, why? Will they just be lucky, or will they do the right things right?

Today, what do they know about producing change? Do they know much about the community that will be affected by their efforts? How will they generate the power they need? Will they waste their time trying to plan for every possibility, or will they fail to plan at all? How will they attract others to their cause, and will they work well together? Will they be able to raise the money and other resources they will need? How will they spread the word about what they are doing and why? Will they be able to define issues to produce the reaction they want? What steps will they take to become more organized? Will the strategies and tactics they select fit the situation they face?

You know something about each of the questions they will have to answer. You are probably much more prepared to begin the process of promoting change than most people who actually take the risk to do so. If you were meeting with those people today, you would have important contributions to make.

As you engage in professional practice, you will encounter many systems that have an impact on the people you serve. You will have many chances to initiate changes to remove barriers people face or to create new resources or new promise. Different arenas of action were covered in a general way in Chapter 1. In the chapters in Part 3, you will get a closer look at three different settings in which you may very well have the opportunity to develop and use your skills to promote change.

Neighborhood change efforts may take you out of your office and into the places where people live. What occurs or does not occur in neighborhoods has a tremendous effect on the quality of life of the residents. Neighborhood change can take on many forms, ranging from more fully developing the natural helping systems that already exist to establishing neighborhood self-government and economic vitality.

In Chapter 13 we explore the meaning of neighborhood and gain an understanding of the importance of neighborhood functioning. You will see how neighborhoods change over time, and you will learn about neighborhood organizations. You will discover various ways to strengthen neighborhoods, and you will be given some insights on important factors that will affect your chances for success.

Organizational change skills are particularly important for professionals working in human services. Our organizations can be vehicles for fostering beneficial change or mazes in which good ideas and good service get lost. The process of improving existing services or developing altogether new approaches involves some change in service organizations. For many of us service organizations are our workplace—our work community. Their degree of effectiveness or ineffectiveness has an impact on our own ability to render quality assistance. The satisfaction we derive from our work is closely related to the functioning of the organization through which we do it.

In Chapter 14 you will gain a clearer picture of the characteristics that influence the behavior of organizations. You will consider several different types of changes organizations can make in the community and you can make in organizations, and you will learn more about the obstacles and opportunities that affect the change process. You will be introduced to key ingredients of organizational change, and you will be provided with a number of specific tactics that will increase your effectiveness. You will be asked to consider ethical questions regarding your responsibility to develop a workplace that promotes respect for workers and the community they serve.

Legislative change is increasingly recognized as a critical activity for social workers, health care workers, and human services workers. Policies that emerge from legislative bodies can set in motion an array of forces that limit or expand opportunities for the people with whom we work. The extent and availability of public resources is directly related to legislative decisions. Community conditions and even the way services can be provided are shaped by the actions of those who set public policy.

A variety of legislative assemblies, from town councils to the Congress of the United States, pass laws that affect our communities. A number of avenues exist for influencing these legislative decisions. One of the most effective of these is the practice of lobbying. Specific lobbying activities become far more productive when made as part of an organized lobbying effort. Social service agencies and other nonprofit organizations certainly can and, I believe, should take an active role in lobbying to influence policies that affect them and their constituents.

Chapter 15 focuses on efforts to influence the actions of state legislatures because these bodies are more accessible to the average worker and because the policies they establish have significant consequences. You will learn how to prepare yourself to take part in the work of affecting legislation. You will gain an understanding of the legislative process, and you will see how the essential components of a legislative action campaign work together. Basic lobbying activities and methods are explained, and you will be given a number of tips for increasing your effectiveness. You will learn about the rules that apply to lobbying by nonprofits and see that these organizations are permitted to engage in this activity.

At some stage of your career you may well find yourself working to strengthen a neighborhood, improve an organization, or influence the passage of laws. Whether you respond to the challenge of change by working in these arenas or others, you already have a strong base of information to strengthen your efforts. Some people burn with a desire to make things different, whereas others, who have forgotten even how to feel angry, make daily concessions to survival, having given up and given in long ago. What will your actions mean to them, and to you?

Chapter 13

Enhancing the Quality
of Neighborhoods

CHAPTER HIGHLIGHTS

- Definitions and perceptions of neighborhoods
- Effects of neighborhood quality or stress
- Characteristics of neighborhoods
- Factors affecting neighborhood health
- Dakota experience
- Models of neighborhood change
- Choices for human services workers
- Types and purposes of neighborhood organizations
- Activities of neighborhood organizations

- Characteristics of successful neighborhood organizations
- Neighborhood revitalization components
- Change-related tasks
- Tools for neighborhood development
- Principles for neighborhood empowerment
- Neighborhoods as economic systems
- Diverse perspectives and interests
- Ideas to increase the prospects for success
- Neighborhood action, a way to confirm dignity

Most of us who live in a village, a town, or a city live in a neighborhood. Neighborhoods are a common environment in rural, urban, suburban, and exurban communities. For most Americans, the quality of our lives is strongly affected by the conditions that exist in the area captured by the view from our front doors (Ahlbrandt & Cunningham, 1979). Our neighborhood may be a densely populated place where row houses snug against each other or a tract of suburban single-family dwellings that try to hold the urban cacophony at arm's length. The boundaries of a trailer park might mark our neighborhood. The houses clustered together in our small Native village can give us our neighborhood. Or the neighborhood might be our apartment complex.

WHAT IS A NEIGHBORHOOD?

At its very core, a neighborhood is made up of the interaction of three things: residents, residences, and land uses that either support these or coexist with them. Though it would be hard to have a neighborhood without residents and residences, land uses among neighborhoods vary. Parks, streets, stores, offices, factories, open space, and other natural or constructed features help to shape and define the neighborhood.

Neighborhoods exist to provide their residents with security, comfort, and neighborliness. Security has to do with feelings of protection from the elements, safety from attack, and escape from the hustle and bustle of daily life. Comfort includes the provision of amenities that make life easier as well as taking pleasure in the physical appearance of the place. Neighborliness refers to the residents' awareness of one another and their positive interdependence. We are not just bodies in search of a warm, dry place to spend the night.

Who are the neighbors? Of course, they are the people and things that call the place home—whether or not that home has a front door. To some extent, anyone who spends a significant amount of time there or who has property there—a worker or a business owner, for example—could be considered a neighbor. The degree or sense of affiliation neighbors feel toward the area and toward one another has consequences. It can bring the neighborhood together as a community or render it nothing more than a coincidental occupation of a plot of land.

Neighborhoods come in many shapes and sizes. Wide variations of neighborhoods exist not only among cities but within the same city. To some, a neighborhood is home to hundreds of people. To others, the term may describe an area of 75,000 people (Downs, 1981; Hallman, 1984; Kotler, 1969). Barker (1999) described a neighborhood as "a region or locality whose inhabitants share certain characteristics, values, mutual interests, or styles of living" (p. 252). Schwirian (1983) defined a neighborhood as "a population residing in an identifiable section of a city whose members are organized into a general interaction network of formal and informal ties and express their common identification with the area in public symbols" (p. 84).

Neighborhoods have been distinguished by social class, race and ethnicity, psychological unity among people who feel they belong together, family status and lifestyle, housing conditions, and social characteristics that describe the interactions of people within the neighborhood and between the neighborhood and the wider community. Various neighborhoods have particular norms and values. They hold beliefs about acceptable displays of wealth, noise, home upkeep, lifestyles, and attitudes toward outsiders (Hallman, 1984; Keller, 1968).

Schwirian (1983) combined these and other factors into descriptions of neighborhoods as natural areas, social areas, and interaction systems. *Natural areas* are characterized by a particular geographic area, a unique population, a social system with rules and norms, and distinguishing emergent behaviors or rules of life. *Social areas* are marked by different combinations of status, family form, and ethnic specialization. *Interaction systems* describe a series of social systems and relationships. Our place and how we have arranged it tells us something about who we are. Rubin and Rubin (2001) pointed out that "control over space permits a definition and expression of culture, especially a culture that stands in opposition to dominant groups" (p. 102). Ahlbrandt and Cunningham (1979) have summarized a neighborhood as a community, a market possessing purchasing power, a service area, a provider of shelter, a political force, and an actual or potential level of government. A neighborhood is made up of both tangible and intangible elements. Anything that either enhances these or detracts from them affects the quality of the neighborhood and the lives of the people experiencing it.

Different observers recognize different dimensions in their view of the neighborhood. For example, residents are more likely to see a much smaller neighborhood than will urban planners (Coulton, Korbin, Chan, & Su, 2001). Downs (1981) described four expanding dimensions of the concept of neighborhood:

- The *immediate neighborhood* (sometimes called the "face block") is the cluster of houses around one's own.

- The *homogeneous neighborhood* extends to where the market value of housing or the mix of housing types and values noticeably changes.

- The *institution-oriented neighborhood* describes an area in which residents share common relationships with a local institution such as a school, church, police precinct, or political ward.

- A *regional neighborhood* comprises a much broader area such as an entire suburb or township.

As you can see, neighborhoods resist clear definition. In fact, Downs (1981) stated that "no one definition has come into widespread acceptance among neighborhood residents themselves, neighborhood organizations, or academic analysts" (p. 13). Who defines the neighborhood and how it is defined does have consequences for the effectiveness of community change initiatives, though. An initiative may not reach or have an effect across an entire target area that nonresidents may define. Using smaller units named by residents may produce a more effective arena for organizing (Coulton, Cook, & Irwin, 2004). A couple of the most meaningful observations are in some ways the simplest and in some ways the most complex. Wireman (1984) said that "a neighborhood is the area named by residents when asked: 'Where do you live?'" (p. 38). The National Commission on Neighborhoods (1979) offered this explanation: "In the last analysis, each neighborhood is what the inhabitants think it is" (p. 7).

Although academicians, city administrators, and professional planners may argue over the proper determinants of a neighborhood, it is the residents for whom the concept has the most meaning and who ultimately define their own boundaries. Researchers have found that members of specific neighborhoods do have definite ideas about what constitutes their neighborhood, suggesting that "neighborhood" is a "vivid reality in people's lives" (Ahlbrandt & Cunningham, 1979, p. 14).

We each have our own personal neighborhood. Essentially, your neighborhood is what feels like your neighborhood. This, however, is a dynamic perception. Your understanding will be affected by your age, how long you have lived in the area, how much time you spend in it, whether and how far you have ventured on your walks, and other factors that influence the type and degree of your interaction with the various elements of your neighborhood. Think about your own neighborhood. What pictures do you see?

Neighborhood as a Focus of Attention for Professional Workers

The neighborhood is the smallest operating unit in a community above the level of the family (Doxiadis, 1968), and what goes on there seriously affects its members. Efforts to strengthen the quality of neighborhoods command the interest of those who deliver human services. This is not a new phenomenon. While attention to neighborhoods as a way of addressing a range of social, economic, political, health, and environmental issues waxes and wanes, neighborhood organizing, revitalization, and planning have a long and rich history (Fisher, 1985; Rohe, 2009).

Why should we care about strengthening neighborhoods? First of all, the people living in them matter. The character of a neighborhood affects all its residents, perhaps especially its children (Acevedo-Garcia, Osypuk, McArdle, & Williams, 2008; Annie E. Casey Foundation, 2002; Coulton, 1996). Growing up in a distressed neighborhood has a strong impact on a child's well-being (Federal Interagency Forum on Child and Family Statistics, 2002; Tyler, Johnson, & Brownridge, 2008). The social environment of the neighborhood influences human behavior in many ways. Child development, family stability, socialization, education, and social control all respond to neighborhood conditions (Fellin, 2001). The physical, emotional, and mental health of residents is affected by neighborhood conditions. Differences in neighborhood social capital affect childhood obesity rates (Singh, Kogan, & van Dyck, 2008). Perceptions of neighborhood safety may even affect obesity rates of mothers of preschool children (Burdette, Wadden, & Whitaker, 2006) and reduce rates of children's physical activity, contributing to this growing health problem (Molnar, Gortmaker, Bull, & Buka, 2004). Environmental factors such as the presence of parks can lead to collective efficacy, neighbors' feelings of mutual trust and willingness to help each other, which is associated with positive health (Cohen, Inagami, & Finch, 2008). Neighborhood conditions certainly affect elders. Perception of neighborhood disorder, for example, discourage older people from walking (de Leon et al., 2009), whereas architectural features such as front porches can increase feelings of social support and reduce psychological distress (Brown et al., 2009). Researchers in London have linked neighborhood problems to chronic stress and increased health risks among residents, particularly in lower income neighborhoods (Steptoe & Feldman, 2001). A neighborhood stress index, the City Stress Inventory, indicated that neighborhood characteristics can influence depression, anger, and self-esteem (Ewart & Suchday, 2002). You can see how an increase in social capital can benefit the millions who live in our neighborhoods. It is not surprising that an analysis of residents' self-rated health has led researchers to call for efforts to improve neighborhood safety and promote residents' involvement in organized social groups (Rohrer, Arif, Pierce, & Blackburn, 2004).

Further, underdeveloped and impoverished neighborhoods can affect the entire community, harming a city's image and its economic health. Deterioration tends to worsen and spread. By increasing the health and vitality of neighborhoods, we expand residential choice, provide for a better distribution of population and jobs, and contribute to the tax base rather than drain resources from it (Suchman, 1994). We promote conditions that encourage security, interaction, and the growth of social capital (Wagner, 1995).

Martinez-Brawley (2000) noted that "despite modernization, the daily round of life for millions of people is carried out in relatively small, circumscribed, local settings. Modern dwellers draw a manageable radius around their homes, at least as a mental referent" (p. 210). With the exception of the commuting suburbanite, this is true for most of us. She further elaborated, "primary ties and local sentiments give real direction, though not always positive, to the daily activities of most people. People live day to day within the intimate confines of a locality. The most universal of all human experiences happen 'at home,' where one's deepest emotions are revealed" (p. 227).

The neighborhood is a close community where intervention can have a significant impact. The nature of social services may well change in response to the challenges of an information or knowledge society. Agencies that can incorporate a more integrated approach to serving their communities will become increasingly relevant. Wagner (1995) has pointed to the emergence of a Fourth or Community Sector, which may well replace the traditional Third (nonprofit) Sector, which he says favors maintenance and survival over client change and social impact. This Community Sector is defined as "a loose amalgam of existing and yet-to-be-created non profit organizations (self-help groups, neighborhood and member-based organizations) that develop new approaches and financing mechanisms to address neighborhood concerns. They link three activities: social service, economic development, and capacity building, and create a local vision and renaissance of activity" (p. 12).

Training for social work, human services, and other helping professions should place students in neighborhood networks rather than isolating them in single-service agencies. Morrison and colleagues (1997) argued that differentiation among the roles of caseworker, group worker, and community organizer is not functional to a "holistic approach that emphasizes the environment as well as the person in the environment" (p. 533). Community psychologists have pointed out the connection between individual and neighborhood well-being, calling for psychopolitical literacy, an understanding of the relationship between political and psychological factors that enhance or diminish wellness and justice, and psychopolitical validity, research and action to improve the human condition that takes these factors into account (Prilleltensky & Fox, 2007). Maury Nation (2008) sums up this challenge well, saying, "embedded in this concept is a call to move beyond diagnosing and treating the consequences of disadvantage to challenge the sources of disadvantage" (p. 195).

Almost any issue that change agents might address can be worked on at the neighborhood level. Certainly housing issues will have a neighborhood focus, but other matters affecting the community are played out in the neighborhood arena. In Aiken, South Carolina, community health workers and police have teamed up to increase prenatal care in high-risk neighborhoods with impressive results. A shockingly high infant mortality rate of 13.5% has dropped to 4.9%, well below the national average. Other health benefits have followed. Cases of sudden infant death syndrome have all but disappeared, and a full-time health clinic has been established in a local housing project. The police have learned more about the neighborhood and its residents, and a trusting partnership between police and residents is being built (Nonprofit Pathfinder, 2002).

The Family Violence Prevention Fund (2002) began a neighborhood organizing project in Philadelphia to mobilize neighbors to plan and implement approaches to stem intimate partner violence. The proven success of this effort has led to the Community Engagement for Change Initiative to mobilize community members to prevent family violence in 18 community groups (Mitchell-Clark & Autry, 2004). The University of Dayton's Fitz Center for Leadership in Community in collaboration with the Dayton Foundation, the Dayton Public Schools, local government, and numerous foundations and corporate partners is connecting five public elementary schools to their neighborhoods after more than 30 years of court-ordered busing. Through more than 40 programs at each site and with an emphasis on youth and community assets, the initiative promotes wellness, the arts, civic engagement, parent and neighborhood participation in learning, financial literacy, and many other improvements in neighborhoods surrounding the schools (Ferguson, 2009). Sacramento is promoting the health of older people by creating walkable neighborhoods (Hooker, Cirill, & Geraghty, 2009). The United Way of Tucson and Southern Arizona (2006) is providing funding and training to help community agencies move from a preoccupation with providing services to harnessing the power of neighborhoods to address a variety of issues. Many community problems find their way into neighborhood streets and homes. The capital to solve problems and build a better life can be found there as well.

Some Fundamental Challenges to Neighborhood Health

Neighborhoods should offer security, comfort, and neighborliness to their members, and most Americans are fairly satisfied with their neighborhoods: 88% of owners and 76% of renters rated their neighborhood a 7 or better on a scale of 10. Still, that means that millions of people were less satisfied. Though crime, litter, and poor street conditions concern some residents, renters experience these troubles much more than do homeowners (U.S. Census Bureau, 2009). Although overall 80% of parents consider their neighborhoods supportive for their children, only 68% of those living below the poverty level feel that way (U.S. Department of Health and Human Services, 2005). Crime, housing affordability, civic infrastructure, and segregation remain major challenges to healthy neighborhoods. Only about half of the nation's families believe that their children are living in safe neighborhoods (Annie E. Casey Foundation, 2006). This may reflect anxiety-raising news reporting as much as true conditions. According to the FBI's *Uniform Crime Report* (2009), each of the specific crimes measured by the Uniform Crime Reporting (UCR) Program continues to decrease. The Federal Interagency Forum on Child and Family Statistics (2006), a collection of 20 federal government agencies involved in research and activities related to children and families, found that the number of youth victims and perpetrators of violent crimes has declined not only steadily but dramatically since 1993.

Home ownership is part of the American Dream, but many people are finding that just having a place to stay consumes so much of their income that they have little left over for other of life's necessities. The National Low Income Housing Coalition calculated the national median housing wage—what a person needs to earn to afford a two-bedroom unit—and found no county in the United States in which a renter earning the prevailing minimum wage can afford even a one-bedroom apartment (Wardip, Pelletiere, & Crowley, 2009). Even renters earning an average income have a hard time affording housing as 49 hours of work are required to pay the rent on a two-bedroom apartment. The situation is even more dire for extremely low-income households, those earning less than 30% of an area's median income. Based on the coalition's research, there is a shortage of 5.5 million units of affordable and available housing. In the last 2 years many families have lost their homes as a result of foreclosure, contributing to the increase of

DID YOU KNOW?

Four factors not so common a generation or two ago pull apart the connections to the neighborhood as a place and lessen connections among neighbors.

Mobility: About 14% of the U.S. population moves every year with more than 46 million address changes (U.S. Postal Service, 2008b). With that many people moving each year, it is hard for neighbors to get to know each other.

Women in the workplace: In 1950 about 34% of women participated in the labor force; in 1975 the figure had risen to almost 46%; it is now almost 60%, with mothers accounting for most of the rise over time (Hayghe, 1997; U.S. Department of Labor, 2000; U.S. Department of Labor, Women's Bureau, 2009). As a result, there are fewer adults at home during the day who have family, home, and area as a more immediate focus.

Increased disposable income: Even in the current economic climate, people have more disposable income than in previous generations. In the last 40 years, per capita disposable income has more than doubled (U.S. Cenus Bureau, 2005; U.S. Department of Commerce, 2009b). Having more money to spend draws people away from neighborhood-generated recreation and other neighborhood activities. For example, children are more readily engaged in recreation and activities away from the neighborhood, which limits the connection their parents have with one another.

Easy access to non-neighborhood relationships: More affordable travel options are available, such as air travel, and Americans own more cars: almost 40% of all households now have two vehicles and another 20% have three or more (U.S. Census Bureau, 2008c). E-mail, social networking sites, and other kinds of Internet interest groups make it much easier to develop and maintain relationships outside of the neighborhood.

2.2 million renters and making an even greater demand on affordable housing units (Wardip et al., 2009). According to the U.S. Department of Housing and Urban Development (2001), except for very large units, monthly housing costs have been greater for renters than for homeowners. What impact do you think this has on families?

In some poor neighborhoods, efforts to serve and strengthen the community come and go, making it difficult for residents to trust in and commit to organized groups. A high turnover of community groups leaves a fragile and transient civic infrastructure (De Vita, Manjarrez, & Twombly, 1999). Though our nation is becoming more culturally and ethnically diverse, our neighborhoods continue to confine many of us to cultural isolation. High levels of racial segregation persist among U.S. neighborhoods. Since 1990 there has been only a slight decline in segregation. Although many middle-class families of color have moved from the cities to the suburbs, those suburban neighborhoods are not necessarily integrated (Kent, Pollard, Haaga, & Mather, 2001).

Dealing with these challenges means that we must become skilled at recognizing and using the resources we have around us.

Neighborhood Assets and the Dakota Experience

The empty lot that could be a garden. The carpenter who can teach you how to fix a broken door hinge. The church choir who might open a neighborhood meeting in song. The purchasing power of a dozen organized families. The retired librarian who is well liked by her nephew, a member of the City Council. The recipes from a hundred countries that can perfume a dinnertime evening. Sources of neighborhood wealth are all around us, if only we would develop an eye (or ear or nose) to recognize them.

As with most forms of community development, meeting the challenges and enhancing the quality of neighborhoods involves the identification, mobilization, and connection of neighborhood assets and community capital. Once you begin to look at common things with new eyes, you cannot help but see what is there. A friend of mine bought a new Dodge Dakota not too long after they came on the market. Anxious to show off her new acquisition, she went tooling around town to, well, show off. She came back surprised. "There are Dakotas everywhere," she told me. "I must have seen a dozen in 2 hours." At first she was a little disappointed that she wasn't all that special, but soon she discovered a special kinship with other Dakota drivers. They nodded at each other. A few waved. One or two even honked. Soon she was on the lookout for more Dakotas. She'd never seen a Dakota before she bought one. Now, tuned in to their existence, they were "everywhere."

If you have ever bought a new car, you have probably had the Dakota experience—seeing something special that you'd never noticed before. This can even work for new cell phone features, clothing styles, or anything else you have newly come to value. Once it becomes real for you, you see it all over the place. I've worked with community groups who've had the Dakota experience. They started to see resources all around them once they became able to spot something of value among the traffic of common things. When you begin to look, it's hard not to notice that Dakotas are everywhere.

QUALITY NEIGHBORHOODS

The quality of neighborhoods is surely affected by the quality of their housing stock, but there is more to a neighborhood than just houses (Ahlbrandt & Cunningham, 1979). It is naive to think that families are completely self-sufficient, particularly in this highly mobile, highly specialized nation. Assistance is not as readily available through extended family systems as it once was. Most families meet their needs through their interaction with other systems.

Clearly, the neighborhood is one of those valuable systems. Neighbors can provide one another with a range of practical and emotional support. Borrowing a cup of sugar, helping out in times of emergency, establishing social contact over a cup of coffee, or helping to fix a leaky toilet are some of the common forms of assistance neighbors

provide to each other. The benefits of these commonplace activities, of course, extend beyond eggs and coffee and functional flushing. These connections provide psychological benefits by strengthening our attachments to a wider human community and by helping us recognize the reality and importance of our interdependence. More effectively functioning neighborhoods are more likely to offer their members the benefits of "neighboring" (Keller, 1968). The most important contributor to neighborhood satisfaction may well be a shared sense of neighborhood trust (Grogan-Kaylor et al., 2006).

These neighborly activities are complemented by institutions that may provide jobs as well as a variety of commercial, educational, religious, and social services that benefit residents. Wireman (1984) described this set of social functions that would be provided in an ideal neighborhood (p. 39):

- Effective schools responsive to neighborhood needs.

- Attractive, clean, safe play places close to home for casual, unstructured play. (For small children, these areas must be within sight or calling distance.) Places and appropriate supervision for more formal play, including cultural activities.

- Adult control over neighborhood children's behavior.

- Fast access to emergency health care.

- Locally available or convenient transportation to other support services—normal health care, family counseling, special educational services, and so on.

- A variety of provisions for child care, including preschool, after school, and care during summer vacations.

- An opportunity for children to know a variety of adults as friends, neighbors, and role models.

- An environment relatively safe from crime, physical hazards, and racial or ethnic tensions.

Other important functions include the following:

- Opportunities for members to interact, build relationships, and offer mutual support.

- Preservation and enhancement of important neighborhood features (land, homes, flora, streets, etc.).
- Shielding members from intrusion by exploitive external interests.
- Providing a familiar place of safe haven.

Of course, not every neighborhood is blessed with an abundance of developed internal resources. If the needs of their residents are to be met, neighborhoods must work to develop internal resources and collaborate with external institutions to obtain needed assistance. They should have the flexibility to shape a range of responses to best fit the area's particular requirements. These neighborhoods can be further strengthened by attracting resources that enable them to create and develop their own institutions (Suchman, 1994; Wireman, 1984).

Hallman (1984) developed a checklist for assessing the presence of needed resources in the neighborhood and the organizations involved in providing them (see Table 13.1). Reviewing this checklist will help you see how, by whom, and where these basic requirements are being met or not being met adequately. Observe that a combination of individuals or groups based both inside and outside the neighborhood contribute to the health of the neighborhood. By partnering with residents to take advantage of opportunities to strengthen basic neighborhood elements, health and human services workers can significantly benefit the families who reside there.

NATURAL PROCESSES OF NEIGHBORHOOD CHANGE

Like any system, neighborhoods are always undergoing some degree of change. People move in and out. Some dwellings deteriorate; others benefit from the attention of paintbrush and hammer. Some trees, if there are any, wither and die; others bloom and, perhaps, new ones are planted. Forces outside the neighborhood, such as the general economy, attitudes of lending institutions, and changing local ordinances, help or hinder neighborhood improvements. Of course, the rate and direction of change can also be influenced by the presence of a purposeful change agent.

Several authors have observed the way neighborhoods change over time. Some of these models of change focus on factors related to neighborhood decline, whereas others explain forces working in the direction of neighborhood revitalization.

Invasion-Succession Model

The invasion-succession model views changes in the neighborhood as a result of conflict that occurs when a natural area is "invaded" by socially or racially different individuals. If some accommodation between the newcomers and the established population is not reached, one of the groups will withdraw. This will lead to changes (Schwirian, 1983). If the withdrawing group takes valuable resources from the community (for example, family income, shop ownership, political clout) before these can be effectively replaced, the neighborhood is likely to decline.

Life Cycle Model

Various life cycle theories describe the changes in neighborhoods. One of the major proponents of this point of view has been Anthony Downs (1981). According to Downs, neighborhoods have a life cycle from birth to death, but they may reverse the "aging" process through various forms of revitalization. Further, they may resurrect themselves. From an abandoned, lifeless space, a neighborhood may be born anew.

The life cycle model includes five different stages of change:

- A stable and viable neighborhood
- A minor decline
- A clear decline
- A heavily deteriorated neighborhood
- An unhealthy and nonviable neighborhood

A stable and viable neighborhood exists when no symptoms of decline have appeared and property values are rising. A period of minor decline may follow in which some minor deficiencies in housing units are visible and density is higher than

T A B L E 13.1   Organizations and Groups Available to Benefit the Neighborhood

Assets	Based within Neighborhood				Based outside Neighborhood		
	Local Association	Private Nonprofit	Private Profit	Government	Private Nonprofit	Private Profit	Government
Employment							
Services							
Jobs							
Commercial							
Sale of Goods							
Services							
Income Support Programs							
Credit							
Housing							
Utilities							
Food							
Clothing							
Safety							
Transportation							
Education							
Recreation							
Arts							
Health							
Social Services							
Governance							
Civic Participation							
Communal Events							
Religion							
Social Support							

*Individuals, families, and informal groups also provide resources.

SOURCE: Adapted from Hallman, 1984.

when the neighborhood was first developed, but property values are stable or increasing slightly. A neighborhood in clear decline is marked by populations from lower socioeconomic groups. Renters are dominant in the housing market, and landlord–tenant relations are poor because of high absentee ownership. Other factors, such as higher density, low confidence in the area's future, and abandoned buildings, are also associated with this stage. In heavily deteriorated neighborhoods, housing is very run down and even dilapidated. Most structures require major repair. Subsistence level households are numerous, and profitability of rental units is poor. Pessimism about the area's future is widespread. An unhealthy and nonviable neighborhood is at the final stage of change. Massive abandonment occurs, and those residents who remain are at the lowest social status and incomes in the region. Expectations about the area's future are nil.

At any stage the neighborhood can be declining, stable, or improving. At the time Downs made these observations, he noted that although images of severely blighted urban landscapes have been burned into our perceptions, most U.S. cities do not contain any neighborhoods in the latter two stages of decline.

Downs and his life cycle model have been criticized as contributing to policies that encouraged redlining, a practice by lending institutions to withhold loans to residents living in "redlined" sections of a community, and other practices that contributed to the decline of urban neighborhoods (Metzger, 2000). Others have rejected this argument, saying that this theory had little impact on policy and practice or that other factors contributed to urban decline (Downs, 2000; Temkin, 2000).

Political Capacity Model

The physical and economic conditions of a neighborhood send messages to the residents and to outsiders as well. Residents may see daily confirmation of the enormity of their struggle to cultivate a safe, healthy, and attractive environment. It may erode confidence in their hope of achieving personal success. Outsiders may see an area not worth saving or one easily exploited. Although these perceptions may be accurate, they may mask a vibrancy of interpersonal relationships that may exist in poor areas and be absent in more affluent ones.

Departing from what he sees as an overemphasis on physical and economic factors affecting neighborhood change, Rick Cohen (1979) has focused on a political analysis and presented his stages from the point of view of development rather than deterioration. Accordingly, a neighborhood can be economically rich while remaining politically poor. The first of Cohen's stages is a *disorganized neighborhood*, one in which there is no organization capable of providing leadership. In these neighborhoods a change agent should act as a catalyst while nurturing people with leadership potential. In *primary institutional neighborhoods* a few basic organizations exist, such as churches, schools, and fraternal and social clubs. Here the change agent acts as a mobilizer, strengthening the linkages among families and neighborhood institutions, changing the orientation of residents from inward to outward, further developing leadership, and developing neighborhood resources. *Civic neighborhoods* are beginning to deal with issues of neighborhood interest. A group claiming civic concerns as its primary purpose is developed. The organizer's role is that of process facilitator, assisting the neighborhood by helping to get its resources and groups to work in harmony. A *networked neighborhood* has a civic group with strong support, and nearly every block is represented in the organization. There is a danger that the organization may become too centralized and bureaucratized and that it may engage in nonproductive political tests of wills with municipal officials. The result of these conflicts could be stalemate and inaction. By assisting the organization as a strategist and negotiator, the change agent can help the neighborhood group navigate through some stormy waters. In a *mass communal neighborhood*, everyone is a member and participates in a neighborhood organization or civic group. The neighborhood is concerned about a wide range of issues, and it delivers services. High voter turnouts, widespread participation in organizational activities, many different people in leadership roles, and an increasing control of neighborhood resources are indicators of a mass communal neighborhood. The change agent acts as a maintenance assistor to help keep the neighborhood from slipping into stagnation.

As you can see, the development and status of a neighborhood organization is a stimulus to and a reflection of the state of political organization of the neighborhood. Each stage of neighborhood development presents new challenges to the neighborhood organization itself. For example, Cohen pointed out that many neighborhood organizations are born of controversy and opposition. The group starts off in an underdog role. When their political capabilities significantly increase and successes mount, the organization may be set adrift as it realizes it has outgrown its original identity. It may experience some aimlessness as it searches for a new identity. A further challenge confronts successful neighborhoods. Mastery of political influence may result in the neighborhood pursuing its own interests at the expense of other neighborhoods. A lack of awareness of the interdependency among neighborhoods may lead to the NIMBY (Not In My Back Yard) phenomenon, producing destructive, selfish conflicts ultimately harmful to all.

Additional Models of Neighborhood Change

Other models have been developed to explain neighborhood change (Schwab & Ringel, 1991; Schwirian, 1983). Demographic and ecological theories describe changes in demand for housing supply and the changes in economic base (for example, from heavy industry to service) to identify forces that produce neighborhood change. Creation of attractive, additional dwellings outside the neighborhood may draw people away. Development of employment opportunities in the area immediately surrounding the neighborhood may lure new residents to the neighborhood. These theories also deal with issues related to the effects of crowding and residential design.

Sociocultural approaches look at changing values related to urban living. The purchase of a home is related to the availability of a number of benefits, such as cultural facilities, recreation, and social diversity. If the neighborhood provides an attractive package of elements that have current cultural value, the area is likely to grow. If these elements are missing, the area is likely to decline.

Political-economic explanations of neighborhood change emphasize forces at play beyond the neighborhood boundaries. These include the actions of a variety of monied interests (such as developers, banks, and construction companies) who work together to influence property values and government decisions regarding revitalization efforts. Their manipulation of broader community decision making results in assistance to some areas of the city and inattention to others, with the ultimate beneficiaries being the monied interests themselves. Domhoff (2005a) believed that power is vested in land-based growth coalitions that seek to intensify land use. Struggles over land resources are at the core of a community's power struggles. Other forces, such as rising or falling mortgage rates, taxation policies, and availability of land for development, also have relevance for neighborhood growth or decline.

Social movement explanations for neighborhood change focus on the effects of neighborhood organizing, including issue identification and development, action to achieve neighborhood goals, and citizen participation in municipal decision making. The effect of these organized activities (if successful) is certainly change. These changes may make the area more attractive to current residents as well as to a host of newcomers … some of whom may be considered to be "invaders."

You can recognize some relationship among these more commonly presented views on neighborhood change. Each should give you some clues for assessing the conditions in your neighborhood and the route you may take to improve those conditions. Though neighborhoods may undergo some "natural" stages of growth or decline, movement in any particular direction is obviously not inevitable. Purposeful action on your part could bring about changes that would improve the quality of the neighborhood and the lives of its residents.

UNDERSTANDING NEIGHBORHOOD ORGANIZATION

Your efforts to improve neighborhood conditions will trigger development of a neighborhood organization or assist the progress of an existing organization.

GLOBAL PERSPECTIVES

UNITED KINGDOM—[I]t is important not to see the neighbourhood as just a territorially bounded entity but as a series of overlapping social networks. We should not underestimate the importance of physical change, physical boundaries and local landmarks in creating a sense of belonging and identity, but the differences between neighborhoods may perhaps best be understood as the differences between the form and content of social networks. It is these residentially based networks which perform an important function in the routines of everyday life, and these routines are arguably the basic building-blocks of social cohesion—through them we learn tolerance, co-operation and acquire a sense of social order and belonging. Who and what we are surrounded by in a specific locality may also contribute in important ways to both choice and constraint and, less tangibly and more indirectly, to notions of wellbeing and social worth (Ray Forrest & Ade Kearns, 2001, p. 2130).

ARGENTINA—The new neighborhood associations have organized community purchases of food at reduced prices, as well as volunteer brigades of skilled workers who reconnect homes to the public service grids when their electricity, household gas or water supplies are cut off for failure to pay their bills.

The assemblies' projects range from a community vegetable garden to a neighborhood bank in which people can put their savings....

Neighborhood associations on the west side of Buenos Aires successfully pressured the Edesur power company to consider the possibility of a 180-day suspension of cutoffs due to delay in paying bills. Assemblies in other neighborhoods are demanding discount electricity rates for the unemployed (Marcela Valente, 2002).

TAIWAN—One summer afternoon in June 1995, a college student on the way home after classes walked, as she did each day, through a neighborhood park. Since she had been walking this route since childhood, she was shocked to see a newly minted sign posted at the gates announcing the demolition of a section of the park to make way for a new road. In disbelief, she went to ask local officials about the sign. They told her that a decision had been made and that there was no way of altering it, since the project had been publicized earlier and nobody had objected to it then. Undeterred, the young woman then turned to several of her classmates for help, and they began a petition effort. Six days later, after they had gathered some five hundred signatures, the hastily formed group held a public hearing, to which they invited the director of the Department of Urban Development. More than a hundred residents of the area showed up. Seeing the strong opposition, the department director declared that the plan would be reexamined and promised that in the meantime construction and demolition would be suspended (Ya-Chung Chuang, 2005).

VENEZUELA—Misión Barrio Adentro (MBA: "Inside the Neighborhood Mission") in Venezuela is one of the most striking examples of Latin American social medicine (LASM).... LASM scholars and practitioners endorse collective rather than individual approaches to health care, stress the importance of political-economic and social determinants of health, and promote holistic approaches to health-disease-health care processes.... For example, rather than observing that rates of infant mortality are higher in a particular minority group and analyzing individual risk factors, LASM and critical epidemiology scholars would document race- and class-based differences in access to health care, sanitary infrastructures, employment, and political representation and how they might produce higher levels of morbidity and mortality.... Community workers assisted residents in forming neighborhood health committees.... (Cuban physicians anwered the call to live and work in poor neighborhoods.) When the first 58 physicians arrived in April 2003, they were placed in homes and used the same space as a living area and examining room. Two additional groups of physicians followed. Health committees accompanied physicians on afternoon house-to-house visits—meeting families, assessing health needs, treating patients, and conducting censuses—as well as on emergency house calls. Committees, whose members included many individuals without previous leadership experience, assumed active roles in fostering prevention, enhancing health infrastructures, and procuring resources (Charles L. Briggs & Clara Mantini-Briggs, 2009).

You will bring people together to undertake a partic-ular project, or you will aid in developing a perma-nent organization that itself will undertake diverse projects and provide other functions. Regardless of the nature and extent of the changes you seek, some sort of neighborhood organization will be involved.

As you begin to gain a better understanding of what the neighborhood needs and has, you may come to the conclusion that a concentrated and comprehensive approach to organizing is ultimately needed. If your primary professional responsibilities do not lie in the area of community organization, you may not be able to make the type of invest-ment that the thorough approach to organizing would require.

What to do? Well, you could go out for pizza and forget the whole problem. This is probably not the most effective approach for assisting the neigh-borhood. At least four other choices are available to you. One course of action would be to initiate a modest but meaningful change with a definite begin-ning and end for your involvement. The neighbor-hood receives the direct benefit of the change, itself an important accomplishment, and it may awaken the residents' recognition of their capabilities and spur some of them to take some further actions. Even if no subsequent action directly follows the change epi-sode, it may indirectly contribute to efforts further down the road.

Recognizing that continued resident action may not happen of its own accord, you may decide to take the second option, which involves purpose-fully using the change to develop leadership and continued interest. If you can further link the nascent neighborhood organization to other support systems (for example, a successful organization from another neighborhood that can serve as a mentor), the effect of your particular change episode may be more long-lasting. This second approach requires greater involvement than the first.

Your third alternative is to get help. There may be individuals or groups in the community who can sustain a deeper level of involvement in working with the neighborhood. Your main contribution is to discover the particular resource and help estab-lish the relationship between the neighborhood and those who will provide organizing assistance.

Your fourth choice involves convincing your agency to become more actively involved in the life of the neighborhood.

Whether your participation is modest or sub-stantial, an awareness of neighborhood organizations is useful. In addition to the authors specifically iden-tified, the ideas in this section were also drawn from and shaped by Anderson, Homan, and Lawson (2001); Aspen Institute (1999); Bratt (1987); Brueg-gemann (2006); Burghardt (1982); Clay (1979); Dupper and Poertner (1997); Fantini and Gittell (1973); Fellin (2001); Institute for Community Eco-nomics (2002); Kennedy (1996); Kotler (2005); Kretzmann and McKnight (1993, 1997); Kretzmann, McKnight, Dobrowolski, and Puntenney (2005); Mayer (1984); National Center for Economic and Security Alternatives (2002a, 2002b); Rich (1979); Saegert (2006), Scheie, Williams, Mayer, Kroll, and Dewar (1997a, 1997b); Suchman (1993, 1994); Suchman and Lamb (1991); Thomas (1986); Wagner (1995); Warren and Warren (1977); Williams (1985, 1989); Wireman (1984); and Wolpert, Mumphrey, and Seley (1972).

Types of Neighborhood Organizations

Neighborhood organizing is by no means a new phenomenon; neighborhood organizations have been recorded for more than a hundred years. In more modern times, federal programs in the 1960s and 1970s provided the impetus and support for development of neighborhood organizations. For a period of time these organizations flourished. Even after federal support diminished, many of these groups continued and new directions in neighbor-hood action were taken, sometimes encouraged by municipal governments. Neighborhood organiza-tions formed as a result of government programs certainly were influenced by the goals of the pro-gram as much as by the residents themselves.

Currently, residents seem to be showing renewed interest in their neighborhood organizations. For example, the number of neighborhood associations in the Phoenix area grew from 52 in 1990 to more than 1,000 by 2009 (City of Phoenix Neighborhood Services Department, 2009). Results from the annual Metro Survey by the Metro Chicago Information

Center showed increased participation in neighborhood organizations for all ethnic and income groups surveyed (Garth, 1997).

Fisher (1984, pp. 9–16) described three approaches to organizing that are based on how neighborhoods are envisioned:

Social work. The neighborhood is viewed as an organism. Efforts are made to build a sense of community, particularly by providing social service organizations. This method lobbies for and emphasizes delivery of social services.

Political activism. The neighborhood is viewed as a political entity or power base. The absence of power needed to defend the neighborhood is seen as the basic problem. Efforts are made to give people more control over their lives. Strategies are rooted in the presumption of a conflict of interest between the neighborhood and those in power outside of the neighborhood.

Neighborhood maintenance. The neighborhood is viewed primarily as a residential area. Efforts are vested in protecting property and its values. Neighborhoods using this style of organizing are usually free of major problems.

Many neighborhood organizations regularly interact with their local governments. Such a relationship may provide benefits to both the neighborhood and the government in the form of decentralization of government services or decision making. Though this may only involve opportunities for an exchange of information between the two groups, more significant collaborative efforts also occur. Some neighborhood groups receive contracts to deliver public programs in the area, and others work closely with units of government to create, develop, and operate programs benefiting neighborhood residents. Neighborhoods can move beyond being a place where outside forces plant externally controlled public institutions or drop by to provide services. Kotler (2005), a strong advocate of neighborhood self-governance, sees neighborhoods as political units of settlement that are either self-ruling or dominated. He advocates transferring existing public authority and institutions to the control of the neighborhood. In his view, "the purpose of neighborhood action today is to regain self-rule and representation in municipal government" (p. 47).

Simpson and Gentile (1986) identified three forms of neighborhood organizations related to governmental processes: advisory councils that are officially established by the municipal government, independent neighborhood groups that have claimed governmental or political powers, and groups that have been organized by or incorporated into an official government neighborhood program.

In addition to these general categories, Hallman (1984, p. 265) described a number of other neighborhood organization classifications.

Neighborhood association: used for two purposes, advocacy or low-budget, self-help activities; has individual members, representatives from other organizations, or a combination; ranges from block clubs to multi-issue neighborhood organizations. (*Note:* A neighborhood association is *not* the same as a homeowners' association. These associations are described later in the chapter.) A neighborhood association is the most common way that neighbors come together to strengthen the neighborhood and advance its interests. Participation in a neighborhood association is voluntary, not mandatory like a homeowners association. Some neighborhood associations have membership dues, and some incorporate as nonprofit organizations.

Neighborhood congress: an organization of organizations; tends to concentrate on advocacy and neighborhood organizing but might sponsor a neighborhood corporation or program operations.

Neighborhood advisory committee: usually set up by a government agency to deal with issues related to its mission; has an advisory role in program planning and possibly in program implementation and evaluation; selection of members might be by an administrator, nominees of specific organizations and interests, or a combination.

Neighborhood council: a unit with official recognition by the city or county to deal with policy issues in a number of program areas; mainly advisory authority rather than final decision making; members usually elected by residents; in some places, existing associations have gained recognition as neighborhood councils.

Neighborhood corporation: funded and staffed to operate specific services or undertake developmental activities; incorporated, usually as a nonprofit organization but might have a profit-making subsidiary (or vice versa). (*Note:* Similar activities, especially as they relate to economic development, are performed by neighborhood development organizations and community development corporations.)

Neighborhood government: has legal power and authority equivalent to that of a municipality to make policy and run specific programs; has access to financial resources necessary to carry out its responsibilities; democratic selection of governing officials. (*Note:* Some neighborhood government groups might more accurately be referred to as quasigovernmental organizations in that they have some, but fairly limited, policy-making authority, often related to zoning issues.)

Neighborhood organizations may also take on other forms. *Community development corporations* (CDCs), a significant type of neighborhood organization, were started in the late 1960s with the intent of linking inner-city communities with broader economic and political opportunities. CDCs focus on a specific urban or rural area with a broad agenda of development issues, including job training, commercial and industrial development, and, particularly, housing development. They receive public and private funds, and they are run by professional staff and guided by citizen boards. In addition to neighborhood residents, board members typically come from business and lending institutions. The profits from the various enterprises run by the CDC stay in the community to provide for services and further development. Through CDCs,

"the community plans and develops its own economic future" (Brueggemann, 2006, p. 175). CDCs run the risk of catering to private sector interests. To be truly effective, CDCs must engage in community organizing to mobilize various forms of community capital for true development to take place (Lowe, 2008).

Almost 60 million Americans now live in one of 300,000 *association-governed communities*, including homeowners' associations, condominiums, and cooperatives. This is up from just over 2 million in 1970 (Community Associations Institute, 2009). Almost 80% of all new housing starts since 2000 have been in association-governed communities (Community Associations Institute, 2006). Although many of these are concerned with rules proscribing or prescribing behavior, many others provide avenues for neighbor interaction. Some smart growth communities such as Irvine, California, and Anthem, Arizona, are full master-planned communities whose management company does much more than oversee the enforcement of rules.

Again, it is important to distinguish neighborhood associations, which are commonly organized to bring neighbors together and assert their common interests, from homeowners' associations. A typical *homeowners' association* (HOA) concerns itself primarily with the maintenance of neighborhood facilities (for example, a community pool) or the preservation of the physical attractiveness of the neighborhood. Participation as a voting member is usually limited to property owners, so renters rarely have any real voice. Homeowners' associations are sometimes more concerned with regulating residents' behaviors, often done through enforcement of deed restrictions, than with advocacy on behalf of the neighborhood. They are often set up and even managed by the corporation that built the housing development. Advocacy issues are commonly related to protection of property values. It is common for the original developer of the tract to establish the association and transfer authority to the homeowners once most or all of the lots have been sold. An HOA is governed by a volunteer board of homeowners, who are elected by the residents. Some HOAs are very large and assume many of the responsibilities of local government, such as road maintenance.

Tenants' associations may be considered as a type of neighborhood organization if you consider an apartment complex or similar housing configuration to be a neighborhood. Certainly these organizations at the very least exist within neighborhoods. Tenants' organizations are primarily developed to secure and protect the rights of renters to receive well-maintained, safe housing.

Social service agencies, both public and private, may assist in the development of a *neighborhood service center*. (If the center is not developed, established, and operated by the neighborhood, it would not technically be a neighborhood organization.) Although the operators of the center usually defer to the authority of the sponsoring agency, center staff will, from time to time, engage in advocacy or development efforts on behalf of the neighborhood. These activities complement the provision of direct services such as counseling or job training programs. As a social worker or human services professional, you may have the opportunity to help develop such a center or to refine the nature of the programs it offers.

As you can see, no one basic neighborhood organization type exists. Organizations are shaped not only by the particular circumstances of the neighborhood but also by the interests of the organizers. Factors such as the extent of the organizers' interest, awareness of organizing options, and availability of time may well be reflected in the design of the organization.

Activities of Neighborhood Organizations

A brief rundown of common activities undertaken by neighborhood organizations provides some examples of the things you may be able to accomplish by bringing people, both residents and individuals and groups from outside the neighborhood—particularly local government, schools, religious institutions, social service agencies, and private foundations—together in the effort to strengthen the vitality of a neighborhood.

You can accomplish a great deal to enhance the quality of life for neighborhood residents simply by encouraging and supporting the further development of natural helping networks that exist in the neighborhood. Here are some ideas that you might try:

- *Strong identity*: attractive, identifiable neighborhood boundary markers; emblems on windows of collaborating businesses; special neighborhood signage
- *Events*: potlucks; carnivals; fairs; art shows; holiday lighting; activities emphasizing area

culture; entertainment, such as sporting events, dances, or drama

- *Facelifting*: neighborhood cleanup; minor housing rehabilitation or beautification; tree planting and other landscaping; community gardens; beautifying commercial corridors; streetscape improvements; pocket parks

- *Social interaction*: newsletters providing information on resources, neighborhood personalities, and neighborhood and community events affecting the neighborhood; intergenerational mentoring; exchange of resources or services for mutual assistance; participation in neighborhood organization decision making, operation, or activities

- *Resource exchanges*: tool banks within or among neighborhoods; toy libraries; recycling of building materials; co-ops such as babysitting or food purchases; skills banks

- *Community education*: forums; speakers; credit and noncredit classes

- *Sponsorship of groups*: Girl Scouts; Little League; Alcoholics Anonymous; performing arts group

- *Involvement of youth and older neighbors*: young people on neighborhood council; partnership in service learning; neighborhood history project; youth-run training and information programs; home repair projects for older persons; storytelling projects

- *Monitoring services of local government*: garbage pickup; fire protection; police protection; street maintenance and repair; sewer maintenance and repair

- *General improvements*: traffic; zoning enforcement; neighborhood planning

- *Security*: identification of household items for burglary protection; safety and security inspections; foot patrols; neighborhood watch; community policing in collaboration with neighborhood crime prevention efforts; neighborhood-based public defender and mediation services; cadre of community youth workers working with service agencies and law enforcement

- *Service delivery*: day care; visitation of elderly; shopping services; provision of emergency food; substance abuse counseling; services designed for particular groups such as children, young people, older people, or single parents

- *Administration of public programs*: garbage pickup; job training programs; GED preparation; collaboration with public sector for program design, development, implementation, and evaluation

- *Housing and economic development*: anti-redlining actions; property management; property development, for example, with Community Land Trusts; housing rehabilitation, for example, working in partnership with the HOPE VI program; acquisition of personal assets through home ownership programs such as HOME and savings plans such as Individual Development Accounts; small grants program, loan funds, business incubators, and business assistance centers to promote economic vitality, including development of resident businesses, such as home repair and maintenance, landscaping, house cleaning, house painting, computer services, typing services, restaurants, and retail

- *Political empowerment*: voter registration activities; voter turnout activities; candidate forums; public hearings; participation in coalitions; organization of power base

- *Improvement and redesign of local schools*: family resource centers, providing an array of wellness and human services; schools to function as activity and community learning centers with increased hours of operation; schools serve as resource attractors for community development efforts; schools transformed into community development and education centers; neighborhood involvement in classroom activities, service learning, and school decision making

- *Neighborhood government*: zoning; permits; licensing; traffic and parking regulations; code enforcement

Many of these activities can easily fit into more than one category. As you become more involved in the neighborhood, you will intentionally develop activities that serve a variety of purposes. The "spillover" effect of programs often produces additional positive benefits, such as intergenerational or interethnic contact, development of leadership, or increased commitment to the neighborhood.

Elements of Successful Neighborhood Organizations

One of the most important contributors for bringing people together and keeping them together is their sense of identity with the issues, the organization, and each other. Helping members to develop a strong identity with the neighborhood, their neighbors, and conditions that affect them builds the foundation for action. Features of identity include a community name; community artifacts; feeling of community *membership*—not *visitorship;* sense of shared values; recognition of shared experiences; and convening occasions.

If a group of people can frame issues and goals in a way that underscores a feeling of connection, they draw strength and commitment from one another. Deborah Martin (2003) described the importance of place identity for energizing activism: "place-frames" highlight the relationship between a place, like a neighborhood, and people's experiences there. This links activism with something people care about, understand, and share. The way we think about a place, or whether we think about it at all, has powerful consequences for how we act about it.

So creating a sense of identity and affiliation is important. What elements are important to building an effective neighborhood organization? One study identified a number of factors that helped neighborhood groups during their first year of organizing (Laird & Hoover, 1993). These neighborhood organizations:

- Felt connected to other resources, such as community agencies, schools, churches, and other grassroots organizations.

- Participated in community networks that led to an increase in confidence, competence, and access to other resources.

- Continued to involve more people.

- Trained and empowered new leaders.

- Became recognized by elected officials and were contacted by them.

- Held celebrations tied to the neighborhood.

- Recognized and exchanged resources within the neighborhood.

- Received and made use of technical assistance.

- Received modest financial support from a funding source interested in nurturing their success.

A COMPREHENSIVE NEIGHBORHOOD REVITALIZATION PROGRAM

Many of the neighborhood activities described in the text can be integrated into a *comprehensive neighborhood revitalization program.* This is a long-term process that requires sustained commitment from a number of parties working in partnership with the neighborhood in accordance with a community plan. Neighborhood leaders and residents drive the process through neighborhood organization and governance, changing the way they relate to powerful people and institutions outside the neighborhood.

Basic activities in such a comprehensive approach could include efforts to improve physical appearance; upgrade community facilities and infrastructure; rehabilitate existing housing and add new housing stock; revitalize neighborhood commercial assets; provide ongoing economic development and job training for residents; integrate and ensure relevance of social services; improve the effectiveness of public services, particularly schools and public safety; promote resident interaction; and develop leadership. In essence these comprehensive approaches address the interaction of the full range of community capital discussed in Chapters 2 and 5: environmental, physical, human, economic, political, informational, cultural, spiritual, and social. These themes resonate with the ideas of many others as well (Annie E. Casey Foundation, 2002; Aspen Institute, 1999; Chaskin, Joseph, & Chipenda-Dansokho, 1997; Kennedy, 1996; Naparstek & Dooley, 1997; Suchman, 1994).

Basic Change-Related Tasks

Neighborhood change is similar to any community change endeavor. For the community to act on the possibility of change, two conditions need to be present: The residents must be sufficiently unhappy with current circumstances, and they must have a sufficient degree of belief that their actions can produce a successful outcome. For the change to be made, the neighborhood must have sufficient power and resources to introduce the change and to sustain it.

The information in previous chapters provides you with a solid foundation for building and sustaining an organized neighborhood change effort. A brief review of important elements geared specifically to neighborhood change, with suggestions from Gatewood (1994); Hallman (1984); Kretzmann, McKnight, Dobrowolski, and Puntenney (2005); Schwab and Ringel (1991); Suchman and Lamb (1991); and Suchman (1993, 1994) underscores the key phases.

To get off the ground, a neighborhood organization needs an initiator, someone to get the ball rolling. This could well be you or the person who brought the interest for improving the neighborhood to your attention. In addition, a neighborhood organization needs to do the following:

- *Promote communication.* Neighbors need to talk among themselves to recognize dissatisfaction, stir up interest, and begin building some level of trust. This may occur through informal conversations with residents, a door-to-door resident contact campaign, informal small group meetings, block-by-block organizing, or by other methods.

- *Do its homework.* A better understanding of neighborhood characteristics, concerns or sources of irritation, community capital, leadership figures, institutions, and other elements should begin in the early stages. Continue to develop a good information base, especially an asset inventory. Essential here is the recognition, documentation, and use of the wealth of assets of individuals (including "strangers"; that is, the marginalized members of the community—the young, the old, and the labeled); local associations and organizations from stamp clubs to neighborhood organizations; local institutions, including parks, libraries, and community colleges; natural attributes such as vacant land, proximity to downtown, trees,

rivers, scenic views, and historic sites; and local community leadership. Using mapping technology can give you a good picture of where to find what you have.

- *Develop issues.* The ability to define and articulate concerns will help build momentum.

- *Hold initial meetings.* You need to introduce the idea of an organization, begin to formalize the organization, identify beginning plans and related actions, and make decisions. Remember not to call your first meeting too soon. You need to begin building relationships with other neighbors through face-to-face contact before you bring people together for a meeting.

- *Take initial action.* Do something to help confirm the reality of your organization and its capability. Usually these are specific, visible actions such as placing a stop sign. Or they are beginning actions that lead to further actions such as inviting an elected official to meet with your group.

- *Celebrate accomplishments.* Draw attention to the gains you have already made.

- *Recruit additional members.* Attract new participants to your effort.

- *Further develop plans.* Plans can become more comprehensive. Remember to include not only the people who live in the area but those who work or go to school there as well.

- *Further develop organizational leadership and structures.* Identify potential leaders and provide them with opportunities for demonstrating initiative, influence, and direction. Clarify organizational issues through development of various committees, promulgation of bylaws and, perhaps, preparation of Articles of Incorporation.

- Remember that most organizations fall apart from the inside because people haven't learned how to work well together. Neighborhood organizations are particularly vulnerable to this. There may be some history of bickering among neighbors, people involved with the organization may not feel that they are getting the credit they deserve, or a few people try to run everything. Keeping people focused on the issues and spreading around the work and the glory will help. So will having fun. Develop activities where small groups of people spend some time together just to enjoy each other's company.

- *Engage in fund-raising and acquisition of needed items.* Obtain the resources needed to operate the organization and to pursue its activities.

- *Take further action.* Engage in actions or tackle projects that have a more significant impact on the neighborhood.

- *Expand power.* Create linkages with other sources of power, join coalitions, create media attention, or undertake other activities that promote your group's ability to influence decisions affecting the neighborhood.

This rough sequence of activities offers an overview of some of the basic tasks you will need to perform. This process is not really a step-by-step guide; some of these actions will overlap with one another or even occur simultaneously. Also, although some of these activities have a beginning and ending point, most will be ongoing throughout the life of the organization.

Tools for the Neighborhood Builder

You can put a number of models and programs to use in building a strong neighborhood. Here are some that you may want to learn more about.

- *Community Land Trusts (CLT).* This is a powerful way for neighborhoods and even broader communities to keep control of a valuable resource—land. This is a nonprofit organization that owns real estate in order to benefit the community, generally to provide housing and land for development. Over 160 CLTs are operating in the United States today along with a handful in Canada and the United Kingdom as well (Institute for Community Economics, 2009a). Land is usually held by the CLT, though most often homes or buildings are owned by those who live in them or use them, with the land leased by the CLT to the resident. This way the land always remains available for its intended purpose, while at the same time the homeowner can make a profit on the sale of the home. It also keeps homes affordable: because the land is not sold, rising land values don't affect the price of the home. Residents who sell are usually required either to sell back to the CLT or to sell to another low-income household. Residents are truly residents, not absentee landlords. Those who own CLT homes are required to live in them as their primary residence. CLTs have the added benefit of keeping money in the neighborhood to further economic development. First, residents typically own their homes, rather than sending rent money to a landlord who may not live in the neighborhood nor spend money there. Second, as CLTs engage in development work, the value of properties in the area increase. This value is retained in the community, not transferred to absentee landlords. CLTs are membership organizations, and their boards usually are comprised of those using the property as well as those who represent the broader community. Income from real estate holdings are used for both neighborhood programs and further development work (Institute for Community Economics, 2009b; PolicyLink, 2006; Webster, 2000). Although the efforts of motivated individuals have been the main force in developing CLTs, local government and public officials have provided a growing impetus for CLT growth. Local community groups, foundations, and support from the private sector are all contributing to the formation of CLTs (Greenstein & Sungu-Eryilmaz, 2007). This gives you a variety of potential partners for using this tool.

- *Community Development Financial Institutions (CDFIs).* These institutions include community development loan funds, community development banks, community development credit unions, and micro-enterprise loan funds. They are private sector financial institutions whose main mission is community development. CDFIs provide access to credit in specifically targeted areas for individuals and organizations often denied financial services by traditional banks. Funds are often geared to small entrepreneurs, helping to increase the number of locally owned businesses. These institutions also invest in neighborhood facilities. Currently there are more than 1,000 CDFIs, with billions of dollars in capital. Although CDFIs draw resources from depositors and investors, most also receive support from the CDFI fund administered by the U.S. Department of Treasury. These institutions provide another way for neighborhood members to establish bank accounts and have access to funds to make improvements in their own lives and in the life of the community (Coalition of Community Development Financial Institutions, 2009a, 2009b; U.S. Department of the Treasury, 2007, 2008).

- *Renewal Communities Empowerment Zones and Enterprise Communities (RCEZ/EC).* These areas were created by the federal government in 1994 to promote business development and job creation in economically distressed cities and rural areas. By the end of 2009 Congress is likely to decide on proposals to extend the program. Employers in these designated areas enjoy some significant tax benefits related to equipment purchases, environmental remediation, and hiring of area residents. Housing, health care, and education also have been provided through this program. Seventy communities in 41 states share an $11 billion federal tax incentive package. This is a highly competitive process, requiring active local government involvement (Salkowski, 2002; U.S. Department of Housing and Urban Development, 2009a, 2006).

- *Community Reinvestment Act (CRA).* Originally passed in 1977, the CRA states that regulated financial institutions have obligations to meet the credit needs of the local urban and rural communities in which they are chartered. The act monitors levels of lending, investments, and services (such as ATMs) in low- and moderate-income neighborhoods that have traditionally been underserved by lending institutions. Institutions must meet tests based on the size and type of institution. If an institution is not adequately serving the neighborhood, the institution may incur penalties such as denial of

approval for expansion or merger. Since passage of the act, more than $6 trillion in reinvestment has been committed, and since 1996 more than $407 billion of community development loans have been made (National Community Reinvestment Coalition, 2008). Community groups can be involved in the evaluation process. This is a powerful tool that neighborhoods can use to see to it that capital and other financial services are available in the neighborhood. Advocacy groups, such as the Neighborhood Community Reinvestment Coalition, can give you information and guidance to make best use of the CRA to strengthen your neighborhood, and each chartered lending institution has a CRA officer (Federal Financial Institutions Examination Council, 2009a; National Community Reinvestment Coalition, 2008).

- *The Home Mortgage Disclosure Act (HMDA).* Enacted by Congress in 1975, the act requires financial institutions to report public loan data. Almost 9,000 financial institutions must respond to these requirements. This is another tool to determine whether financial institutions are serving the housing needs of their communities. Data are also used to help public officials distribute public sector funds to attract private investment to areas where it is needed. The Federal Financial Institutions Examination Council (2009b) creates disclosure reports for each metropolitan area, and they are available to the public at their website.

- *Individual Development Accounts (IDAs).* These accounts are matched to the savings accounts of individuals and are used primarily for home purchase, job training, education, and business start-up. Though typically the match is $2 for each dollar saved, it may go as high as $8. You might think of them as similar to an employer match for a 401k contribution. Thus, they are seen as asset-based approaches to working with individuals and neighborhoods, based on the idea that asset ownership, not just income maintenance, is necessary for economic opportunity (Lombe & Sherraden, 2008). Participation in an IDA contributes to individuals' gaining more assets beyond savings and bulding toward the future, which has a positive effect on their communities (Han, Grinstein-Weiss, & Sherraden, 2009; Lombe, Nebbit, & Buerlein, 2007). Both family and neighborhood stability is affected by asset accumulation. For low-income households, home ownership is the most important component of net worth. From the beginning of 2007 to the middle of 2009, more than 4 million homes were lost to to foreclosure (Foreclosures.com, 2009). Low-income households have been hardest hit by foreclosure and declining home equity. Preliminary information, though, suggests that IDA participants have low default and foreclosure rates (CFED, 2008a).

IDAs are funded by public and private sources, are held by local financial institutions, and are managed by community-based organizations. Organizations that offer IDA programs often combine the match incentive with financial literacy education and other supports (Buchholz, 2005; CFED, 2009b; Sherraden, 2000). CFED (Corporation for Enterprise Development) is committed to expanding economic opportunity and estimates that there are more than 500 community-based IDA programs, with new programs being added each year. A CFED-conducted survey found that IDA participation is spread among age groups, with a little more than 20% of the account holders under the age of 20, and almost half of these under the age of 12 (CFED, 2008b).

IDA programs must be designed to respond to different community settings. With high rates of unemployment, travel time to attend classes or meetings, and lack of a strong economic infrastructure in rural areas, rural households face particular challenges. When provided with opportunities, such as well designed IDA programs, these households show a willingness and ability to save and accumulate assets (Grinstein-Weiss, Curley, & Charles, 2007). The First Nations Development Institute, First Nations Oweesta Corporation, and CFED have developed a training and technical assistance program to help Native communities design and implement IDA programs that take into account the unique

challenges and opportunities for these communities (CFED, 2009a). A number of participants drop out of IDA programs, but those who are very low income or who received welfare are not necessarily those who drop out. It is not necessary to inculcate these participants with "savings habits," assuming that they wouldn't save unless forced to. Other factors, such as the presence or absence of debt and of assets such as education and more life experience are more likely predictors. In fact, the design of the IDA program has more to do with persistence or dropout than do characteristics of the participants. Factors such as higher match rates, automatic transfers to the IDA, higher limits on matchable deposits, and longer time to make matchable deposits help promote participation (Grinstein-Weiss et al., 2007; Putnam, Sherraden, Lin, & Morrow-Howell, 2008; Schreiner & Sherraden, 2005).

- *HOME and HOPE VI.* These are programs operated by the U.S. Department of Housing and Urban Development (HUD) to provide affordable housing, upgrade public housing units, and deliver social and community services for residents. These two different programs offer a number of program options and partnership possibilities with local business and neighborhood organizations (U.S. Department of Housing and Urban Development, 2008, 2009a).

- *Small grants programs.* A number of neighborhood-supporting community organizations have developed partnerships with community foundations, local governments, and even the United Way to provide small grants for neighborhood projects. Typically these pay for materials but not for personnel.

ADDITIONAL FACTORS RELATED TO SUCCESSFUL NEIGHBORHOOD CHANGE

Attention to a number of general principles that apply to neighborhood change and empowerment will give you a better understanding of this arena and strengthen your effectiveness.

Sources of Strength

Membership development is a key matter. Groups with large memberships are taken much more seriously by actors outside the neighborhood and by residents as well. More members mean more resources, more clout, more potential leaders, and so on.

Revival, even in deteriorated areas, is possible. Though in some cases a significant infusion of external resources is required, each neighborhood has some capacities and resources that can be mobilized to promote neighborhood renewal (Clay, 1979).

Interaction develops commitment. Neighbors' interaction with one another, and with neighborhood services such as the local grocery store, will increase favorable sentiments toward the neighborhood. Sentimental attachment to the neighborhood is further increased when residents can participate in networks that not only meet their own needs but that help them recognize that they have important contributions to make to others within the network. This has implications for building a sense of community. Neighborhood changes that increase these positive sentiments may be accomplished through rather small, low-cost efforts (Kretzmann & McKnight, 1993; Morrison et al., 1997; Putnam, 1995; Roach & O'Brien, 1982; Wagner, 1995).

"The level of satisfaction of citizens with a neighborhood and their perceptions of the direction of neighborhood change are critical in determining the commitment of people to their place of residence" (Ahlbrandt & Cunningham, 1979, p. 13). Additionally, "for revitalization to occur, residents must have confidence not only in the physical elements of the community but also in their neighbors" (Clay, 1979, p. 79).

A shared perception of threat can move people to action. Mobilization of neighborhood resources is more likely when the neighborhood is perceived as threatened (Thomas, 1986). "Neighborhood organizations, regardless of the income of their constituents, share a single overriding goal: defense of their turf" (Williams, 1985, p. 112).

Residents need incentives for action. It is not sufficient to sustain members' motivation with a focus on general neighborhood benefits. Residents need to understand their personal connection to the "common good" (Rich, 1979).

Economic Considerations

The neighborhood is an economic system. It has wealth, enterprises, and a flow of money, goods, and services in and out, and circulation within. Its wealth may be seen in buildings and physical facilities, land, equipment, and machines (ownership can be near or distant), as well as in the personal wealth, talents, and skills of its people. It has commercial and industrial enterprises and public and nonprofit organizations. All these have capital investments and goods. They hire people and give out money through paychecks and public welfare programs.

All neighborhoods have a cash flow. As an example, a neighborhood with 2,000 people with a per capita income of just $10,000 has an annual income of $20 million. How much of this circulates in the neighborhood or goes out of it determines how much the neighborhood is benefiting from its money input. "A net in-flow of dollars adds to prosperity, a net out-flow leads to decline" (Hallman, 1984, p. 83). A study by the U.S. Department of Housing and Urban Development (1999) found more than $331 billion in retail purchasing power in inner-city neighborhoods. If harnessed efficiently, that's a lot of economic power. Organizations like the Initiative for a Competitive Inner City (ICIC), which has successfully promoted the development of enterprises based in numerous low and moderate urban neighborhoods, have found that there is more available income than traditional methods for uncovering wealth have reported (McLinden, 2006). The Small Business Administration and ICIC have recognized the potential for new employment from the development of small businesses in the urban core (ICIC, 2005). Capturing both the local income and the income-generating capacity of often overlooked neighborhoods can create an economic engine to help transform neighborhoods.

Lending institutions must disclose lending records. The Federal Home Mortgage Disclosure Act requires records disclosure. Neighborhood organizations have used this act and the Community Reinvestment Act to work with lending institutions to encourage lending in the neighborhood (Federal Financial Institutions Examination Council, 2009b; Hallman, 1984; Naparstek & Dooley, 1997; National Community Reinvestment Coalition, 2008).

Diverse Perspectives

Skepticism may be the order of the day. Many neighborhood residents will take a "wait and see" attitude toward your new organization. They may have been disappointed by past attempts at neighborhood change, or they may be mistrustful of claims that "I'm from the government (or social service agency), and I'm here to help you."

In poorer neighborhoods, residents may have learned that they fall way down on the local government's and the wider community's list of concerns. They may have developed an outlook of impotence, and they certainly don't have much faith in pursuing matters through "appropriate channels," which more often lead to a runaround rather than to resolution (Williams, 1985).

A number of different interests affect the community. The individual resident wants some things that conditions in the neighborhood influence. Perhaps she wants security, maybe protection of property values, possibly social relationships. The neighborhood residents in common, as a community, also have things they want. Many of these will be the same as individuals' wants—good schools, police protection, and well-maintained streets. Some may be different. The community may want all single-family homes, whereas an individual might decide to make some extra money by dividing a dwelling into several apartments. The community may want an attractive environment, whereas the individual may want to decorate a front yard with the remnants of 1978 Oldsmobiles.

Other actors also have intentions in and for the neighborhood, some compatible with community preferences and some in conflict. The most likely other interests are absentee landowners; businesspeople from inside as well as outside the neighborhood, such as developers or store owners; lending institutions, such as banks; service institutions, such as churches, schools, or social service agencies; and local government (Ahlbrandt & Cunningham, 1979; Wolpert et al., 1972).

There are a range of cultural perspectives in most neighborhoods. Change agents need to recognize that cultural backgrounds and different patterns of interaction among groups can affect what people see, value, or dislike in current situations or proposed actions.

ENHANCING THE PROSPECTS FOR SUCCESS

Neighborhood change and empowerment is a process of discovery and action. The suggestions provided here should help to build successes, establish neighborhood potency, and increase your awareness of this arena of action.

Tackle issues that are within your capability. Remember that the specific problems on which you intend to take action cannot be larger than your base of power and resources. If you are not faced with an immediate critical problem, gain some experience and develop a track record on smaller actions before you deal with bigger ones. If you do not have that luxury, expand your power base by establishing connections with community institutions and other community groups, or attempt to partialize the issue.

Many of the issues confronting neighborhoods are related to more fundamental community and social problems occurring beyond neighborhood boundaries. Your organization can ally itself with others as a way of making inroads to more fundamental problems while it takes action in the neighborhood to counter their effects. For example, you may participate in a movement promoting economic justice while undertaking economic development activities in your neighborhood. Understand that as you address larger issues you are likely to need support, assistance, and actual resources from groups outside the neighborhood. These may be governmental units, lending institutions, or community activist groups.

Realize that not all good ideas are feasible. Some projects are just too complicated given the current abilities and clout of the neighborhood.

Move from reacting and petitioning to negotiating and mutual problem solving. From time to time you will interact with local governments to head off potentially destructive actions or to secure specific benefits for the community. Your ability to act assertively as a partner rather than a supplicant is a key distinction in the maturation of your organization.

Plan for higher level results. Link activities to outcomes that change conditions (Kibel & Miner, 1996).

Develop methods and practices to handle internal disputes. Internal squabbling and unresolved conflicts drain energy and undermine resolve. Keep clear records regarding money, a common source of conflict. Focus more on action than on arguments over arcane sections of the bylaws.

Identify and develop neighborhood leaders. Like any other organization, developing leadership is a fundamental requirement. Recognize and support likely leaders and nurture new leadership. People who are visible and credible in the neighborhood, such as the rabbi or the store owner, may be able to provide leadership, particularly in the early stages. People who are known to hold professional or authority positions, such as a doctor, school teacher, architect, or police officer, are often looked to for direction. Get to know the various neighborhood networks. Each is influenced by an informal leader.

Try to identify those whose opinions carry some weight. In some neighborhoods there are no recognized opinion leaders because people simply don't know or talk much to each other. However, through your efforts to organize, you will discover potential or future opinion and task leaders. Whether it is putting together a neighborhood cleanup, preparing a newsletter, providing helpful attention to older residents, pressuring City Hall, or any other activity, neighborhood organizations are rich with opportunities for leadership. Consciously guide potential leaders into leadership roles, doing your best to match their interest and abilities with level of responsibility. Give people room to actually be leaders. Foster an atmosphere that respects individual interest and expertise. Avoid falling into the trap of relying on the same set of people to set direction and get things done. You always need to be on the lookout for this trap. It ensnares most change efforts.

Understand local government systems and forms of government. Find out which governmental jurisdiction has authority over specific matters of neighborhood concern. Typically this would be city or county government. Also, discover the formal structure of authority in the local government. For example, does your city manager or mayor hold more authority? Are your community's representatives elected by ward or by a general election of the entire community?

Discover "administrative guerrillas." These are officials in local government who believe that community involvement is desirable and act that way. They can provide valuable contributions, particularly in giving you inside information and in influencing the perceptions of other officials on neighborhood matters (Thomas, 1986).

If you are working under contract with an outside funding source, see to it that you meet contractual obligations. Make sure basic paperwork procedures, especially those having to do with finances, are demonstrably in order, particularly if you are involved in a struggle with local government or other influential community interests. Failure to comply with the terms of your contract can leave you vulnerable to those who are looking for ways to discredit the organization (Mayer, 1984).

Get the children involved. When you include children as active community members, you will find other members as well—their parents.

Get help from those who have more experience. There is no sense reinventing the wheel. Take advantage of technical assistance.

Establish mentoring relationships. Learn to benefit from the experiences of more established neighborhood organizations. Establish a mutual understanding of the mentoring relationship, otherwise the older organization may grow impatient with requests for assistance or the younger organization may feel irritated by unsolicited advice. Establish some mentoring mechanism such as once-a-month breakfasts among the leadership of both groups. You will discover that both groups benefit. Be mindful of the potential for jealousies and the mentor's need to pretend to know it all.

SOME FINAL CONSIDERATIONS

Major setbacks in life can knock us down. They can demand much of our energy as we struggle to get back on our feet. Sometimes, though, what really wears at us, tears at us, a little here, a little there, is the accumulation of all those things that tell us we just don't count. Whole groups of people are written off because of where they live. Whole groups of people, even those living in more affluent settings, can grow to accept conditions that numb the spirit. Our neighborhood, our place, is so much a part of our daily lives that we cannot escape the meaning its life holds for us.

When we act in a way that says we matter, that we are to be taken seriously, that we are no longer to be ignored, we rediscover elements of dignity. Neighborhood action is a way to reclaim and confirm our dignity. Participation in neighborhood organizations affects the feelings residents have about their own lives and their environment (Downs, 1981).

You may work in a neighborhood that has enthusiasm, confidence, and a fair amount of cold cash. You may look at such a neighborhood with eager eyes and envision conspicuous accomplishments. You may look at a different neighborhood and see the violence, the decay, the fear, the faded faces of hopelessness. You may think, "What can I possibly do? Where can I even start?" The last word of your question is your first step. Each neighborhood has something, some resource or capacity that can be a starting point. Hallman (1984) noted that all neighborhoods, both those with and those without a significant presence of social pathologies (drugs, violence, bad housing, breakdown of family life, and other problems), have personal networks, mutual support, peer groups, indigenous organizations, faith communities, social institutions, and other attributes. Your ability to look at a neighborhood not only in terms of its problems but, more important, in terms of its capacities will give you some direction and some hope, and you will learn how to pass these on.

Think about how you plan to approach the business of neighborhood change. Do you intend to develop from within, using local strengths and visions? Do you believe the most important direction and resources must come from outside the neighborhood? The way you answer these questions will direct what you do.

Similar to your work in any change effort, you will do some things very creatively and very well. You will also make mistakes. You may fear that you will not be as good as you need to be. Burghardt (1982) had a valuable commentary on this matter: "Holding onto this fear has been the undoing of many organizers, for the simple reality of organizing life is that good organizers are always making mistakes and being a little less effective than they ought to be" (p. 27).

As you recognize the value of learning by doing, you will recognize your increasing capability as you gain experience. Your experience may lead you to help transform a neighborhood and, in the process, transform the people who live there.

SOMETHING FOR THE CHILDREN

Margie Ruiz studied the door. Years ago someone cared enough to cover what had been a beige hue with a coat of something close to lime green. Not her colors, but they at least showed that someone was paying attention to the place. No one had made a recent attempt. In quite a few places, the green gave way to beige, which surrendered to the weathered wood turned gray by sun and rain. Again she rang the doorbell.

Knowing that she needed to get out of her office and into the neighborhood, she knew even more clearly that she didn't want anyone to open that door. Margie didn't like talking to complete strangers, and she liked even less that the stranger might think her a busybody. After all, what was she really doing here? Even if she could stammer out an introduction, she knew that in some ways she was saying, "You people in this neighborhood don't have your act together, and you need me to help you figure things out." There was something vaguely rude about her standing on that doorstep, and Margie Ruiz did not consider herself a rude person.

Margie jumped a little as the door opened. She hadn't heard anyone coming, and whoever it was took so long to answer that she had almost turned to go.

"I'm sorry, young lady, did I frighten you?"

Margie could see that the door was still partially secured by a chain latch. She could barely make out the face that peered out at her through the small space. Embarrassed, all she could think to say was, "I don't know, maybe," which didn't seem to be a good start to the conversation. But it was.

Mabel Hughes had lived in Sunvale Gardens for more than 40 years, and she had once liked lime green. The gangs and the arthritis had moved her from her tiny front yard to the chair on her front porch and, finally, indoors. Margie found out that they had not taken her wit nor her intelligence. They had not taken her memories of a nicer neighborhood nor her knowledge of who was doing what to whom today.

Through Mabel, Margie was introduced to Mr. Richards, who ran the small grocery store on the corner. She met Mrs. Metcalf, who lived two doors down, and Reverend Metton from the Baptist church. And from them she met others. It took her a while, almost 6 months, but Margie began to know the people who lived in Sunvale Gardens and the things that bothered them.

All this was nice, but she still had her casework duties to take care of at the agency. Yet it was those same casework duties that led her to Mrs. Hughes's door: the young, single mothers talking about their babies getting lead poisoning from the paint peeling from the walls; the young men acting so tough, so cool, and looking to belong; the children falling behind in school, unable to do their times tables but able to figure out all you could buy with a month's allotment of Food Stamps. She talked to all of them about what was going on, or what wasn't, in the gloomy area called Sunvale Gardens. And she asked them what could be done to make things better. They said, "nothing," and shook their heads and laughed at her. Except for Jerome, all of 17 and twice a father, who said, "Go talk to Mrs. Hughes."

Maybe she'd better stick with casework. Six people showed up at the meeting tonight. The first real meeting Margie had called. She had gotten the school district to give her the cafeteria for the night. Mr. Corrigan, the principal, didn't even bother to make the short presentation he'd prepared.

She knew all the things that were bothering the people in the neighborhood. A person can learn a lot in 6 months. She had told them about her plans to put together an organization that would make the changes they all wanted. She had told them about the people she knew who worked for the city, and how they said they were going to help. She had put so much into this. Now, six people. She tried not to be angry, but she had to fight the urge to yell at them all, "Okay, just sit there, be glad you're stuck in all this, don't even think things could be different!"

Margie didn't yell. Margie wasn't rude. She looked at Mabel, just an old woman whom she had talked into going to a meeting at night. She sighed to Reverend Metton, the minister, and she wished that prayers were enough. She saw Mr. Richards and wondered who was minding the store. The young college student Dwight Hoopes had shown up. So did Loretta Looth, and Margie wondered where Loretta found a babysitter for her three kids.

Margie sat down. She spread out her hands and said, "Now what do we do?" It was Mrs. Hughes who broke the silence. "I'm glad you asked us, Miss Ruiz. Maybe we could start with something for the children."

REFLECTION QUESTIONS

1. If there are no major changes in the way the change effort is being conducted, how is this story likely to end?

2. What information or assumptions led you to this conclusion?

3. If you were Margie Ruiz, what would you have done differently? What would you have done the same?

4. What can Mabel Hughes or any of the others attending the first meeting contribute?

5. What are some of the significant problems facing the neighborhood? Which seem to be the best targets for initial action?

6. What assets or resources might be available to the group?

7. What particular steps would you take at this point that would enhance the prospects for success?

GROUP ACTIVITY: THINKING ABOUT YOUR NEIGHBORHOOD

1. Answer the following questions about your neighborhood. (You decide what "your neighborhood" means.) (7 minutes)

- What are the three most significant features of your neighborhood?

- What are three neighborhood assets that as an organizer you could put to use to mobilize your neighbors to strengthen your neighborhood?

- Name at least one good experience that involved some of your neighbors.

- Name three different neighbors and mention one fact about each.

2. Divide into teams of four members and listen to each member's answers to these questions: What did you learn from your level of knowledge about your neighborhood? What did that lead you to think about? (10 minutes)

3. Discuss the information and what it might mean. For example, what were some similarities and differences; what might be some things that you hadn't thought about before; what things about the neighborhood seemed to be important? What else might you talk about? (7–10 minutes)

4. Identify three important discoveries or results of your discussion that you can offer to the larger group, and select a spokesperson for your team. (3–5 minutes)

5. Describe your three discoveries to the larger group. (2–3 minutes)

HELPFUL WEBSITES

A number of public and private organizations can direct you to information, technical assistance, or other resources you might need as you work to strengthen your neighborhood. Links to the organizations listed here are on the companion website at www.cengage.com/humansvcs/homan.

Aspen Institute

Association of Community Organizations for Reform Now (ACORN)

Asset-Based Community Development Institute (ABCD)

Affordable Housing Design Advisor

Center for Community Change

CFED

Charles Stewart Mott Foundation

Community Associations Institute

Gamaliel Foundation

Institute for Community Economics

Join Together

Knowledgeplex

Living Cities, Inc./The National Community Development Initiative

National Center for Economic and Security Alternatives

National Community Reinvestment Coalition

National Crime Prevention Council

National Low Income Housing
 Coalition
National Neighborhood Coalition
Neighborhood Funders Group
Neighborhood Networks
Neighborhood Reinvestment Corporation

NeighborWorks
Neighborhoods USA
Pro Neighborhoods
United Neighborhood Centers of America
United States Department of Housing and
 Urban Development

Chapter 14

＊

Increasing the Effectiveness of Health and Human Services Organizations

CHAPTER HIGHLIGHTS

- Organizations as creatures of human design
- Improvements in organizations increase work effectiveness
- Organizations respond to both internal and external pressures
- All organization members can initiate change
- Value and loyalty conflicts of organization members
- Seven types of agency change
- Organizations as systems
- Moving from service to development
- Organization structure, processes, and philosophy affect the change effort
- Factors that influence successful change
- Principles to increase your effectiveness

- Know your issue well
- Involve client partners
- Gain support of external advocacy groups
- Capitalize on external threats and opportunities
- Create worker support systems
- Identify stakeholders, attract investors, and secure allies
- Understand the organization's culture
- Create a receptive environment
- Expect, identify, and deal with resistance
- Reduce personal risks
- Implement and confirm the change
- Minor changes can have major benefits
- Organization improvement is an ongoing process

In this chapter the focus is on more formal, well-established organizations; among them are the health and human services agencies where you may work. These kinds of organizations have some characteristics not necessarily present in the less formal, grassroots organizations preceding chapters have described. However, they also have many similarities.

Organizations are creatures of human design, empowered by the strength of human creativity and purpose, and limited by human foibles and ignorance. Organizations can be bungling or competent. They can be shortsighted or forward-looking. They can be defensive or insightful. They can be productive or wasteful. They can neglect or take care of themselves. In short, organizations are collections of people, and they tend to act, not surprisingly, like people.

Most of the work of human services professionals is done through some organization, usually a public or private agency. The usefulness of this work is, to some extent, constrained by the imperfections of those organizations themselves. Improvements in the quality of our organizations translate into improvements in the effectiveness of our work.

Thus the organizations become arenas for change. Workers in human services aren't the only ones who have noticed the need to improve their organizations. Business corporations, large and small, have been the subject of many a writer's or consultant's attention. There is much to be learned from the examples, good and bad, that the business world provides. Yet despite their many similarities, it would be naive to think human services organizations and private, for-profit businesses should operate in the same way. Their purposes are different, and certainly the societal demands they face are not the same. As a consultant and a practitioner in both worlds, I have seen those differences.

Many of the thoughts and suggestions in this chapter have been informed by my experience. But they certainly are not my ideas alone. You will find the perspectives of a number of writers in the following pages. I have particularly relied on the observations of Belasco (1990), Bishop (2001), Brager and Holloway (1977, 1978), Brueggemann (2006), Cohen and Austin (1994), Cooperrider, Whitney, and Stavros (2008), Frey (1990), Goldberg (1980), Gottlieb (1992), Gummer (1978), Heintze and Bretschneider (2000), Holloway (1987), Hyde (1992), Kettner et al. (1985), Kirst-Ashman and Hull (2009), Lewis, Packard, and Lewis (2007), Litwak, Shiroi, Zimmerman, and Bernstein (1970), Lumsden et al. (2010), Magliocca and Christakis (2001), Martin (1980), Morgan (2007), O'Connor and Netting (2009), O'Looney (1993), Patti (1974, 1980), Patti and Resnick (1975), Resnick (1978), Resnick and Menefee (1994), Richan (2006), Roloff and Paulson (2001), Senge (2006), Senge et al. (1994), Sherman and Wenocur (1983), Weinbach (1984), and Wernet (1994).

Organizations certainly respond to outside pressure. They need to and do respond to threats, opportunities, and trends in the larger political and economic environment. In fact, if they don't respond, if they don't fit, they will cease to exist. But it is not those forces alone that shape the process of change. Members of the organization, perhaps even you, will work to ward off direct demands for change "outsiders" may make. One likely reason is that members feel threatened by the implication that if they were doing their jobs well, no pressure would need to be brought. Another related reaction is defensiveness. There is often the perception that those outside the organization "just don't understand." They don't understand the organization's mission, its funding constraints, the value of its current methods, the difficulties involved in making the change, and on and on. This increases the value of making changes from within.

All people who make up an organization are capable of initiating some change, although the discussion of organizational change issues is frequently directed to the top leadership of organizations. Executives and administrators are counseled on ways to streamline the organization, develop strategic initiatives, assess the orientation toward change of key players, or manage personnel for greater productivity. Although effective action from those in the highest positions of the organization's hierarchy can produce important changes, the responsibility and opportunity to promote change should hardly rest there. In the course of your daily activities, each of you will be able to identify barriers to effective client service or opportunities to create even more effective approaches. Regardless of your formal position in the organization, that recognition will spark an interest in organizational change. It is to you that this chapter is addressed.

It is likely that you will come face to face with some fundamental value conflicts as you work within a service agency, especially a large service agency. You may want to promote the interests of clients, whereas the organization wants to promote its status. Your values of being readily responsive to changing conditions and promoting the value and uniqueness of each individual might be at odds with an organization interested in maintenance and predictability, one that believes in objective, impersonal relationships. Organizational values of service may run counter to your beliefs about empowerment. A host of other conflicts may also be in store.

First you must recognize that these value conflicts are likely. If you expect them, you won't be thrown off stride when they show up. Second, you need to develop attitudes and skills for dealing with them constructively. Otherwise you will end up hating your work, being angry with yourself, and, if you do not leave the organization in the hope that the next place will be magically different, you will retreat into burnout.

Change efforts initiated by workers not in formal leadership positions face a number of obstacles. Although many excellent corporations in the for-profit sector have discovered the value of fostering worker initiative, human services organizations have been slow to tap the potential of this creative force. Rarely does line staff have formal authority to initiate change. Doing so requires workers to engage in activities normally seen as outside their areas of responsibility. Further, the strategies and tactics required to promote recognition and response to a given issue may conflict with organizational norms and expectations of "professional" behavior. This is further complicated by a sort of necessary role reversal. That is, low-authority people are encouraging high-authority people to take the organization in new directions. They have, in effect, become the leaders. That is not a situation many formal leaders take lightly.

The authority embodied in professional ethics may transcend certain arbitrary limits on worker authority. A belief in professional responsibility may drive workers to seek changes that will benefit the people they serve. Many human services organizations recognize and give at least lip service

respect to the value of professional ethics. You should not dismiss this practical asset. In addition, in each organization there is the likely availability of peer support as well as assistance from some who hold higher positions of authority. Together, these dedicated individuals can mobilize for change.

Still, a tension exists between the worker's responsibility to advance community and client interests and the worker's loyalty to the agency. Though I would argue that the worker's primary duty is to work on behalf of the community members, no clear agreement among professionals, either in philosophy or in practice, exists on this point. You will continue to ponder this question throughout your career and continue to answer it through your actions.

You will see the term "client" used in several parts of this chapter. I use "client" to communicate the special relationship that some members of the community have with the agency. This does not imply dependency (see Chapter 1). How you see this relationship is critical. Clients are community members whose circumstances have brought them into a relationship with agency professionals. They are partners who are bringing their abilities and resources into a relationship with you and your abilities and resources to change conditions, perhaps even distinctly personal conditions, that affect them. I use the term here because it is the one most agencies commonly use to describe this relationship.

TYPES OF CHANGES

As a worker in human services, you may seek changes in the way the organization relates to broader systems (for example, government authority or community expectations), to its immediate systems (client groups), or to its internal systems (agency procedures or agency staff). Engaging in organizational practice to help your agency function effectively is a basic professional role. O'Connor and Netting (2009) stated that "all human service practitioners engage in organization practice, regardless of their focus" (p. 3). There are a number of ways that you can strengthen your organization and what it does. Seven basic types of changes could produce valuable results.

1. *Develop agency assets to promote employee capacity and enhance the quality of life of the people who "live" there.* Sometimes people just take things for granted. This can happen in a neighborhood where residents just accept distressing conditions. This may happen elsewhere in the community where members don't even think about making things better because, after all, that's just how things are. This can happen in the places we work as well, when learning to put up with things that take away the light and life from our work becomes part of the job. If we are not intentionally engaged in improving the system in which we work, we support the maintenance of the problems we face in trying to do our jobs. The principles of appreciative inquiry (see Chapter 2) can guide your approach for making use of the many strengths available in your agency to cultivate attitudes and practices that promote quality work and respect for members. Major problems cannot persist in an environment that not only recognizes and values each member's contributions and potential for further growth but intentionally acts on this belief. Are you willing to help shape the conditions under which you work, or are you content to be shaped by them? These are not just things that happen to us; they happen with us.

   Our organizations are communities. Job stress caused by factors such as workers having little sense of control, feeling that their skills are underutilized, performing tasks that have little meaning, being left out of decision making, or not having enough time to complete tasks can lead to a variety of health-related problems (Arrington, 2008; National Institute for Occupational Safety and Health, 2009). For community members to be healthy, our communities need to be healthy. To engage in development work with communities outside of our workplace, we might need to develop the internal agency community. How would it be to work in a place that has crafted a culture to develop the capacity of each member and to assist members in sharing information, knowledge, skill, and other resources?

2. *Mobilize the organization to engage external systems for the benefit of community, clients, or workers.* Workers may attempt to involve the agency in public policy discussions relating to changes in laws or in regulations affecting public programs. The agency may assert its influence as an advocate on matters involving program design and implementation. It may address matters of funding, particularly as they may affect investment in community building efforts, the reach of program operations, benefit levels of public welfare programs, compensation for employees, or increases in the number of program staff (resulting in an improvement in the staff-to-client ratio). Moving a public social welfare agency to vigorously seek an increase in the number of Child Protective Services workers to substantially reduce caseloads would be an example of this type of activity. Agency participation in a livable wage campaign would be another example of this type of activity.

3. *Undertake a community development agenda.* In this role the organization becomes a key actor, partnering with community members to improve community conditions so that each member has increased opportunities to live full and satisfying life and to contribute to the community. That is, the agency doesn't just serve clients but convenes and organizes clients to build their own power to serve their own interests. The agency directs its resources to build community capacity. This moves the organization from the service orientation to a development orientation (see Chapters 2 and 3). An organization needs to accept that it will be learning by doing. This is made easier when all levels of staff are involved in learning basic principles and when the internal structure is aligned with its external goals (Brown, Colombo, & Hughes, 2009).

4. *Remove procedures that inhibit service.* All rules at one time made sense, or at least seemed to. Unfortunately, some rules or procedures take

on a life of their own and outlive any usefulness they may have had. Sometimes rules that made sense in one situation are applied to situations that have different demands. Or rules are created apart from the context of day-to-day reality. They are fashioned more out of concern with what might happen than with what actually does happen. The list could go on. The simple fact is that some rules serve neither clients nor the goals of the organization. Workers can gain relief from cumbersome or inappropriate rules and procedures by seeking to establish more helpful or empowering policies.

5. *Develop programs or projects.* Workers may institute entirely new programs or undertake new projects within a program to better reach an underserved population. Establishing a gang prevention program within a neighborhood might represent a new direction for an agency traditionally wed to counseling services.

6. *Modify programs or projects.* Workers may alter the design of existing activities to increase benefits to clients or to promote accessibility and utilization of services. This may involve a change in service methods (for example, from individual to group counseling or incorporation of development features). It also may deal with matters such as program relevance to client interests, program location, or community awareness of the program.

7. *Utilize clients' views when setting agency direction.* Most workers would adhere to the principle of client decision making with regard to choices related to individual matters. Yet this same ethic is conspicuously absent when it comes to the design and delivery of services and setting agency direction. Workers may redress circumstances that promote client dependence and program irrelevance by investing clients with the skills and authority to influence agency decisions. Clients are seen as resources and become partners (Bess, Prilleltensky, Perkins, & Collins, 2009). An example of this would be including a significant number of clients on agency boards of directors and other agency decision-making committees.

ELEMENTS AFFECTING THE BEHAVIOR OF ORGANIZATIONS

A brief consideration of the framework of the arena of organizational change is in order. Why do members of human services organizations or the organizations themselves act the way they do? I will not pretend to provide you with a comprehensive answer to that question, but I can offer a few insights to help you make sense of some of the things you will see.

Organizations as Systems

As you recall from the discussion of systems theory, communities function as systems. In this case, the community is your organization. Systems are set within even larger systems and are composed of a number of smaller systems. As all these systems act to meet their needs, they influence and are influenced by one another. You can see how this applies to your organization. The general rules of the organization, its resources, and even the size of the organization itself influence its component systems (or subsystems). Those subsystems (for example, administration, various operational programs, and clients) all affect each other and influence the organization as a whole. Although the various parts of the organization and the organization itself influence you, *you also influence the organization.*

Another aspect of a systems orientation that applies to your desire to make changes is the fact that your organization is constantly responding to obvious and subtle pressures from inside and outside the organization. That is, *it is constantly changing in some way.* Your awareness of the changes taking place will help you develop and direct these forces to accelerate change in a desired direction.

CAPTURING CONCEPTS
Moving the Organization from Service to Development

"Human service systems are, by design, essentially dysfunctional for today's world. They were designed in a previous time for a different set of circumstances. Today's realities call for new theory, new design, new practice, new preparation and a new quality of leadership" (Lofquist, 2008).

One of the most meaningful changes you can help an agency make is to move from a service orientation to one that emphasizes development philosophy and practice. If we are to build stronger, more capable communities, we need to build strong, capable organizations committed to and capable of engaging in that work.

This represents a shift in responsibility. Typically agencies are expected to fix problems. It is seen as their job, their responsibility. This is an impossible task. It's not their job anyway; this is a shared responsibility. Agencies committed to development philosophy and practice will no longer attempt to do the work of communities but will work with communities to improve conditions that affect lives. As this work builds momentum, agency professionals, local community members, and people currently seen as in need of services will routinely collaborate to identify possibilities to promote community health, moving beyond a belief that fixing problems is the best that we can do.

This shift in thinking and acting creates a transformative change in agency mission, values, and culture, which may take a number of years to fully root. Still, even the early changes will produce important results in the community and contribute to a redirection of the agency's understanding of its purpose and role within the community.

In my experience, to be ready to engage in a new behavior, key actors within an organization need to move through a **behavior shift**, which typically consists of five stages:

1. *Understanding*. You first have to understand what community development is before you can start to do it.
2. *Believing in its importance*. You have to have a strong enough belief in the importance of community development that you are willing to try it.
3. *Valuing*. Community development must relate to something that gives you meaning for you to continue to move forward in your learning.
4. *Initial competency*. You need some confidence that you know how to go about doing community development, or you won't really try to do it.
5. *Safety*. You have to feel that those in authority, whether formal (boss) or informal (friend or colleague), will let you undertake community development work and make some mistakes along the way.

All five of these must be sufficiently, though not totally, in place before a behavior shift can occur.

None of this will lead to change, however, unless you put your intention into action. **Behavior integration** proceeds through four steps:

6. *Initial action*. You actually start doing some community development work.
7. *Encouragement*. You start to see some progress or improvement as a result of your community development work and this is publicly acknowledged by those with sufficient authority (including community members) to support the continuation of the work.

A human services organization is influenced by an array of external forces to which it must respond to justify its very existence. The fact that these forces are often at variance with each other creates tension in the organization that can produce problems. Particularly, the contradictory values and beliefs of the general society relating to social welfare are evident in conflicting directives issued to organizations and expressed through the behavior of service organizations. Imagine the various constituencies an organization may try to please: diverse political interests, funding sources, professionals, clients, other agencies, referral sources, and the general public. When you consider the number of disparate interests to which it responds, you can begin to understand some of the reasons the organization does not operate with peak efficiency.

Here, again, you are faced with both a dilemma and an opportunity. By collaborating with interests both inside and outside the organization, you may be

8. *Reflection.* You reflect on your experience, learn from it, and refine your theories, methods, and techniques. Reflecting with agency and community partners will help you learn how to do community development better and how to apply your learning to your next action.

9. *Connection.* You begin to invite other organizational units into community development work, helping them move through the various stages until their competence becomes routine.

Most health and human services organizations have hierarchical power structures. Imagine taking a vertical slice of the organization from director, through middle management, to frontline workers. For shift and integration to occur, you will need actors at each level who are in relationship with each other to proceed through each stage. You can initiate a change in direction with a fairly small number of actors who are working together in this vertical relationship. It is wise to start with those who are *interested* in doing development work rather than starting with those who *should* do it. You will increase your chances of success if you begin with willing participants who can accept the setbacks that are part of learning. This is much like starting in one neighborhood or one part of the community and working to initiate broader community change. Further, if the work of these members can become visible and connected to other organizational units, the chances for accelerating agency change increase. If the work goes largely unnoticed or is put off to the side, it will likely remain there for quite some time.

Research by Kathy Germann and Doug Wilson (2004) uncovered four **necessary conditions** for an organization to fully embrace community development. First, there needs to be an organizational commitment to community development, which is rooted in values and beliefs. Over time this becomes an interpretive scheme that provides a lens through which the organization views the world. Leaders, particularly at the upper levels of the organization, need to understand and value development principles, articulate their understanding, and advocate their use. Next, organizational structures need to support community development processes. This includes having a clear understanding of workers' roles in development work and viewing this work as a priority. Evaluation procedures and planning efforts must recognize that the community drives the process, not the agency, with building community capacity as the primary goal, over producing a particular project outcome. Third, adequate resources of funding, time, information, and people must be invested to promote a development agenda. Time means understanding that development is not a quick fix but requires building relationships, testing ideas, and growing confidence and expertise—not just on the part of staff, but within and among community members. Finally, the organization itself needs to model development principles and practices. You have to practice what you preach and teach. It is unrealistic to think that workers will engage effectively in empowerment processes if they do not feel empowered themselves.

able to neutralize some of these forces while marshaling others. When these forces are focused on a particular aspect of the organization's functioning, you can influence both the rate and the direction of change.

The more you understand the organization's relationship to its external environment, the more you are also able to recognize opportunities to strengthen the organization. Even though your agency may be operating in the world of nonprofits, it is still operating in a competitive marketplace. Its ability to make strategic decisions to reach groups that have not been effectively served by other organizations or to better serve current "customers" can attract resources that help the organization flourish.

The Organization as a Political System. An organization is a political system. Those who have the power to set policies usually do so in a way that serves their interests, often at the expense of others. Do not make the mistake of ignoring this process or assuming that it confirms the evil lurking in the hearts of policymakers. It is a fairly normal process,

one in which you probably engage from time to time in your personal if not professional life. Whoever is involved in decision making tends to make policies reflecting their own norms, values, and beliefs. In the process of involving more people in decision making, you will influence development of new norms as you mix new values and beliefs into the policy-making process.

The Organization as an Economic System. The organization provides a type of product (a service or development activity) to the larger system or community in exchange for the resources (usually funding) it receives. It also has an internal economic system as goods and services are bartered or paid for. The ability to provide or withhold funding to various programs or to staff positions within the organization affects relationships. Certain behaviors produce rewards; some others are costly. An informal exchange system of rewards and favors is also always in operation. Both formal and informal systems have a powerful influence on the nature and direction of change within the organization. You need to take them into account.

The Organization as an Ideological System. Which fundamental beliefs drive the organization? What convictions about what it should and should not do direct its actions? How does it view its

mission? How highly does it value its very approach to the work that it does? How strong is its adherence to its history and traditions? What doctrines does it hold to be true? By understanding the organization's view of its purpose, its process, and its past, you can introduce change in a way that reduces resistance.

The Organization as a Social System. Human services organizations are different from other communities in the degree of interaction among the members and the degree of meaning members attach to their participation. In few communities do members spend a significant portion of their waking day in direct relationship with one another and with their common purpose. Neighbors may see each other from time to time, social workers meet in professional gatherings a few times a year, and cycling enthusiasts may pedal past one another on occasional Saturdays. Workers in social agencies see each other almost every day, for hours. They work side by side or together to advance the community's goals. They assist or interfere with each other's professional careers. The time they spend supporting or gossiping about each other is greater than the total time most of them spend in general conversation with members of any other community in which they participate.

Because so much of their time is given over to their involvement with this community, what goes on there becomes very important. Members' degree of satisfaction with their membership in this community is often directly affected by their social relationships within it. Many members even derive their personal identity from their participation in the community: "I am a human services worker, a program manager, a counselor." These are not trivial matters. They intensify the change experience. It is much easier to contact members, much easier to bring them together, and much easier for change to threaten.

Structural Characteristics of Organizations

The structure, processes, and philosophy of the organization as well as the perceptions of its members will have an impact on how you proceed to make changes. What is the size of the organization? Is the organization composed of many different programs and functional units or only a few? The more complex an organization, the more forces that can assist or inhibit the organization you will have to recognize. Does the organization have a centralized hierarchy of authority? Does your boss have a boss who has a boss who must get yet another boss to approve the change? Your assessment of whether the organization vests decision making in the hands of a few or invites broad participation will suggest the tactics you will use. Does your organization have an elaborate set of rules governing everything from hiring practices to bathroom usage? An abundance of policies usually inhibits change, although you may be able to find some policies that provide justification for change.

In all organizations people know incompletely; that is, each person has limited access to information. Those people who work at the direct service level are more able to comprehend problems encountered by clients. Those who struggle to balance the budget are more likely to know of the potential financial strain various programs impose. Organizations with a high degree of specialization or a rigid hierarchy of authority feel the burden of perceptual differences more severely.

With some people allowed access to information and others denied, or with some people attentive to their narrow concerns while others worry over very separate matters, it is likely that different if not contradictory perspectives will emerge. In these organizations, the ability to have and to hold particular information may define a person's domain. A desire to protect the domain may contribute to a reluctance to share information, thereby further impeding communication. As a change agent, you need to see that other people see the situation differently.

ADDITIONAL PROCESSES INFLUENCING CHANGE

See if the experiences, conditions, and possibilities described here appear in your organization. Each will affect your ability to institute change.

Overcome Success

Believe it or not, success can get an organization stuck. You only need to look at the example of many corporations in the United States to see how past successes led them to dismiss or miss new challenges and opportunities. As long as nothing changes, tried-and-true methods are functional. When conditions change, the same methods may become irrelevant or worse.

Overcome Failures

Workers may have made attempts to improve the system with little to show for their efforts but frustration. They may become jaded to new efforts (yours) and seek the protection of cynicism. Your challenge to present conditions may remind other workers of the unpleasant accommodations they have made to put up with day-to-day problems.

Feelings of powerlessness may express themselves in a variety of behaviors. Some workers may bounce from one personal crusade to another. Some may become passive and do whatever they are told. Others may find ways to sabotage the organization. Still others may reduce uncertainty through abdication, withdrawing into their own personal little niche, retreating to the safe service of regulations, or leaving the organization altogether. Of course, many will become martyrs, working hard, but unappreciated, in the selfless cause of others.

Although many, many of your colleagues may be inspired by the potential for change, you are wise to remain mindful of the reticence or the disabling coping responses past failures have wrought. Expect that people want to do a good job. But they may be afraid to get their hopes up, or they may have forgotten how to hope after so many years of trying to quiet the urge.

Recognize Potential Challenges

Throughout the preceding chapters, we have explored a number of problems associated with promoting community change. In fact, the mere thought of the potential for problems is enough to chill to inaction the enthusiasm of many a potential change agent. Although I do not want to belabor the idea of obstacles, your awareness of certain problems due to the unique nature of the organization as a community will help you keep things in perspective.

- *Procrastination.* Members of this community are engaged in other community projects, mainly their day-to-day work. There is enough for them to do to stay busy and distracted with this immediate "community work," so work on the change effort gets pushed to the side. (Of course, other factors contribute to procrastination as well.) With all the time members spend with each other, you would think that more would get done. When it doesn't, you can get overly frustrated.
  Relax. The problem is mainly a perceptual one. By using the techniques you have read about in previous chapters, you will keep moving forward. It is especially important to keep communicating the vision, keep making decisions, take concrete (even if minor) actions, and involve more people. Fear of failure and lack of clarity are twin allies of procrastination. Knocking down one will help fell the other.
- *Critics.* A few people will make light of your enthusiasm or your vision. Some will find fault with your methods, if not your intention. Some will tell you directly; most will not. Because these are people you work with, their criticisms may have more of a sting.

Anticipating the likelihood of this response will decrease the irritation you might feel. Responses to the criticism? Directly invite the critics to join with you. Ignore them. Learn from the criticism. Though the content of the criticism may provide some help in improving your effort, the fact of the criticism will be important information. As those of you involved in the undertaking provide encouragement and support to one another, you will deal with this and other obstacles constructively.

- *Unintended consequences.* Because the change you are proposing will have an impact on a highly interactive system, it may well produce significant effects you did not anticipate as well. Some of these will be good, some won't. With an eye toward evaluating actual and likely results of your actions and a willingness to make modifications, you can avoid the most detrimental repercussions.

Recognize Common Barriers

William Brueggemann (2006) identified nine barriers that work to preserve the status quo within organizations. These all relate to the nature of an environment that emphasizes routine and control. Understanding common features of an environment helps a change agent understand what is occurring or likely to occur.

Organization inertia. Organizations are geared toward predictability and maintaining a steady state. Even though innovation may be at the heart of organizational survival, those who work in organizations cling to routine methods and old habits.

Organization size. The larger the organization, the more difficult it is to shift directions because more people with possibly very different perspectives and interests need to be involved, any one of whom can cause resistance.

Organization structure. Most larger organizations have a hierarchical authority structure with unitary command, using one-way communication in which subordinates do what they are told.

CAPTURING CONCEPTS
Nasty Nine/Needed Nine

The Nasty Nine/Needed Nine is a tool for individuals and groups to use for assessing their experience in working in human services. The **Nasty Nine** are conditions that *undermine* the success of the human services enterprise and the effectiveness of each person involved. The **Needed Nine** are conditions that *promote* the success of the human services enterprise and the effectiveness of each person involved. Using the table, rank each condition as you have experienced it on a scale of 1–10, with 1 being experienced least and 10 being experienced most. By ranking each condition and then comparing your view to the views of others, you can get a good picture of which conditions need improve-

ment and which conditions might be helpful to you. This provides a starting point for action.

Don't be discouraged if you find that many conditions are ranked on the nasty side of the scale. The fact that you and others are asking these questions gives you an excellent starting point for action. Regardless of where each item is ranked, you can look at the needed nine side and, using an appreciative inquiry framework, begin to identify where apects of that condition currently exist or have existed in the organization.

SOURCE: Adapted from Bill Lofquist, personal communication, January 2007.

Nasty Nine	Needed Nine
Fragmentation	*Creative Collaboration*
• Disconnected activities	• Willingness for new ideas
• People working apart	• People working together
Reactive Mode	*Proactive Thinking and Acting*
• Acting after problems recognized	• Anticipating problems; acting ahead
• Emphasis on fixing	• Emphasis on prevention
Prescriptive Programs	*Developmental Initiatives*
• Procedures & policies dictate action	• Flexibility, ability, & local control
Superficial Networking	*Transformational Networking*
• Weak connections among people	• Connections change conditions & people
Lack of Evaluation	*Practical Evaluation*
• Evaluation not valued nor used	• Evaluation used for improvements
Lack of Strategic Planning	*System Level Planning*
• Decisions serve just the moment	• Decisions recognize interrelated parts
• Actions are isolated	• Decisions for purposeful impact
Lack of Clear Leadership	*Nurtured leadership groups*
• Influence serves self interest	• Mutual influence valued
People Viewed as Objects	*People Involved as Resources*
• Some know what's best for others	• Everyone seen as having gifts to use
Unclear Mission, Vision, and Culture	*Clear Mission, Vision, and Culture*
• Lack of purposeful focus	• Purposeful focus, inspirational intent

GLOBAL PERSPECTIVES

PERU—I consider dealing with changes in large bureaucratic organizations to be a dynamic process. The majority of changes usually come from the different decision levels. Changing the procedures and redistributing the shares of power at the interior of these institutions generate immediately major changes. The possibility of generating changes depends on the leadership, the initiative, and the particular structure of the bureaucratic organization. As the more traditional and big an institution is, it will be more difficult to generate changes. Many times changes happen because of external factors or agents that affect the institution as a whole (Mario Zolezzi, personal communication, September 16, 2002).

AUSTRALIA—Understanding issues of integrity in human services organizations requires not simply examining the vocational ethic and how staff arrive at compromises between their ideals and the realities. It involves examining the significance attached to changes and the manner of determining a moral project which can withstand the rigour of critical analysis and the rigours of changing organizational forms within which commitments are to be enacted. Constructing integrity which sustains hope, then, invokes both personal exploration and socio-political analysis—and places them as mutually reinforcing (Martyn Jones, 2000, p. 377).

SOUTH AFRICA—There are inferences in the literature that Non Governmental Organizations need to relate to their local clientele in a way that reflects local values and practices.... The humanistic view of people is in line with the stated mission of many development NGOs, although this may come into contradiction with the considerable influence of Western management approaches.... An emerging understanding and adoption of indigenous approaches may assist in organizational capacity building through the greater commitment and involvement of the community and staff (Jackson & Haines, 2007, pp. 89–90).

Chain of command. Change must proceed up and down the chain of command, with resistance possible at each level.

Bureaucratic surveillance. When subordinates are under constant surveillance from supervisors, they may give up trying to exercise initiative or imagination.

Employee dependence. Hierarchical structures promote a model of obedience and dependency. Employees who are functionaries just doing what they are told may think it inappropriate to suggest change; it's really not part of their job. Some might fear reprisals for calling attention to problems, which might imply that supervisors aren't really on top of things.

Patriarchal organization culture. Individual people are more malleable than organization culture. If the organization's culture is patriarchal, people tend to adapt to those patterns.

Disruptive nature of change. Change requires people to change their behavior, values, and view of themselves within a structure that tends to reinforce old patterns of behavior. Change and routine are apparent contradictions. Much organization behavior involves accommodation to routines, and change invites uncertainty with both procedures and outcomes. This can be stressful.

Managerial resistance. Managers may not want to hear about problems, especially to situations they may have created or at least should have recognized.

The more you are able to connect your change to the organization's ideology, goals, structure, customs, member relationships, and attitudes, the more likely you will celebrate a successful outcome.

Enlivening a State Agency with Community Development

What could changing a large organization look like? Is that even possible?

The New Mexico Department of Health, Public Health Division, has yet another change in leadership.

The new financial system not exactly glitch free. Without warning or consultation, another reorganization begun. An environment of helplessness, anger, frustration, and bitterness reigns. You might say morale is a tad low. But hope still glimmered and humor helped folks make it through the day. Three friends commiserating, feeling good about feeling so bad about things. Then the question: Why do we keep waiting for someone else to fix it? The conversation changed, and a mission to renew passion in the workplace took root. Three women, a bit up the chain of the hierarchy's command, but not removed from other workers who implemented more administrative decisions than they made. Part way up, actually, probably a pretty good place to start.

They began talking with colleagues and decided on a couple of things. They wanted to change their working conditions, that's true. They also understood that they were a community that could benefit from developing leadership, personal and agency capacity, and mutual support. One way to reclaim the passion was to learn more about community development principles and gain confidence and skills in applying them to their work and their workplace.

They quickly recognized some pretty important things. Community development means honoring not only the rights but the responsibilities of the community to make decisions on matters that affect them. So more people needed to be involved. They needed to develop a community of practice— a network of people with common interests who could come together to explore ways of working together, identify common solutions, and share good practice and ideas. They needed to get going. And they did. They invited their colleagues to come together, learn, put ideas into action, learn some more, and keep coming together to build knowledge and relationships.

The C4A's—the Cross Cutting Community Change Advocates—were born. A core group of about 50 agency staff are active participants. This includes a vertical slice of the division's hierarchy, from those with lots of formal authority to those with little, and a horizontal slice across geography and programs. The group is enriched with lots of different views and agency experiences. Directors, accounts managers, health educators, secretaries,

social workers, epidemiologists, physicians, and many other staff come together on equal footing. Names, not titles, count.

The C4A's soon realized that there were two sets of communities to consider. The first they called the *internal* community of Public Health Division staff, bureaus, regions, and offices. The second they saw as the *external* community of constituents, residents of different cities, towns, and villages throughout the state, along with partnering agencies, providers, and health councils. They established some goals for their internal community:

- Develop a sense of community within the Public Health Division; strengthen our internal community to enhance our external community change efforts
- Increase opportunities for mutual support and learning
- Enhance knowledge and skill building around community change
- Develop our own leadership

Their goals for working with their external community included the following:

- Communities will benefit from our enhanced skills and collaboration
- The Public Health Division as a whole will be a better partner for communities throughout the state
- Community leadership development will be an ongoing priority and practice
- Positive changes and improved outcomes will be community driven

The C4A's have done a number of things to implement these goals and to create shared ownership of the effort.

- They gather as a group every few months to offer each other a day-long sessions to better their understanding of community development and build relationships within the division. Each session includes history, purpose, and progress; community building; and community action and development. C4A's select the topics, and a team of members develops and leads the workshops. At the end of each session, a new team volunteers to organize and lead the next one. Each new team includes those who have led a previous workshop and those who will do so for the first time. Evaluation of each session gives direction for the next one.

- A condition for participation is that members want to be there. No one is required to be there. Further, C4A's look for members who are enthusiastic, passionate, willing to share, and work proactively with others in their bureau or region. They build on interest rather than trying to convince colleagues to become interested.

- They have created a strong identity with their name, a logo, a set of values, and an online communication system for posting C4A documents, sharing information on events and trainings, asking for or offering help, and so on. They have also gathered and preserved artifacts: a growing list of topics addressed in their sessions; a collection of quotes from members; banners and posters produced together; and other creations.

- They have implemented various forms of mutual support. When funding was cut for transportation and lodging expenses for attending the sessions, members got creative with fund-raising, organized ride-sharing, and found housing with other agency staff in the host community. They exchange information about topics of interest, pitch in to work across program lines, invite new colleagues to participate, and share learning with stories of success or setback.

- Everything happens through relationships. The C4A's have intentionally learned more about each other as individuals apart from the job, and they have learned more about each other's job and program responsibilities and activities as well. Taking part in job shadowing exchanges is one way to build these relationships.

- The C4A's are developing small teams to conduct mini–community development-related workshops throughout the division.

New challenges arrive on the doorstep or computer screen every day. So do opportunities. The Cross Cutting Community Change Advocates have developed confidence that they can rely on each other and make a difference within their agency and within communities throughout the state. They have learned that they will keep learning. They look forward to that.

PRINCIPLES FOR INCREASING YOUR EFFECTIVENESS

Kirst-Ashman and Hull (2009) developed an easy-to-remember process for initiating and implementing organizational change called IMAGINE.

I   Start with an *Idea*.

M   *Muster* support and formulate an action system.

A   Identify *Assets*.

G   Specify *Goals* and objectives.

I   *Implement* a plan.

N   *Neutralize* opposition.

E   *Evaluate* progress.

Once you have made the decision to make a change, your effort will be enhanced by paying attention to the following basic elements.

Know Your Issue Well

- Gather the necessary facts and figures regarding the change you propose.

- Find out the history of this issue. Has the change been sought in the organization before? If so, what happened? What lasting effect resulted?

- Has the change you are proposing been tried elsewhere? Has it ever worked? What can be learned from that? How can you use this information to garner support for your ideas?

Involve Client Partners

- Recognize the tendency to avoid the issue. Personally, I believe you need a better reason than "I don't know how" for excluding clients in efforts intended to benefit them.

- Appreciate the benefits of client involvement. If clients can easily see how the proposed change affects them, they can be tremendous assets to the effort. Clients can help shape the change, increasing the prospect that it is indeed helpful and relevant to their experience. Clients can make demands on the system that the worker may not be able to make, both in terms of standing and tactics. Further, it is hard for resisters to rationalize away problems or to justify inaction to clients.

- Promote client empowerment. When workers assist clients to recognize additional dimensions to their private struggles, when workers communicate their belief in clients' ability to act on their own behalf, and when workers indicate a willingness to learn from clients as partners, empowerment of clients has benefits far beyond the immediate change. If you have developed strong relationships with clients, or if clients have already been organized to assert their interests, the idea for change may have come from this group of community members to begin with.

Gain the Support of External Advocacy Groups

- Strengthen your effect. The ability to send a message from the outside that is consistent with the message you are sending from the inside increases the credibility of the message and the chances that it will be heard. Additionally, close working relationships will decrease the possibility that groups with similar interests but different information and perspectives will operate at cross purposes.

- Assess the organization's perception of external actors. The impact of external support (or opposition) depends on how widespread or strong the organization perceives it to be.

- Understand that public agencies respond to pressures in the political environment more than in the economic environment (Heintze & Bretschneider, 2000).

Capitalize on External Threats and Opportunities

- Seize the moment. Timing is critical to change efforts. Point out current conditions that will help the organization recognize how the proposed change can provide a public relations or financial benefit or ward off a potential loss.

Create Support Systems That Sustain Worker Involvement in Change

- Bolster your resolve. Workers often need each other's tactical and emotional support to become comfortable with taking and using power. An active support group can establish an empowering worker subculture within the organization that may replace a fragmented, defeatist orientation (Sherman & Wenocur, 1983).

- Understand the purpose and functions of an empowerment group. A support group of this type is *not* developed as a temporary mechanism to deal with a particular problem. Empowerment groups are *not* mechanisms for complaining and reinforcing values and beliefs of impotence. Members of an empowerment group commit themselves to meeting regularly, sharing problem-solving responsibility, recognizing the resources each member brings, and taking responsibility for their own actions within the organization. These actions provide a constructive way to deal with frustration, reduce worker burnout, and protect against divide-and-conquer tactics.

Identify Stakeholders, Attract Investors, and Secure Allies

- Realize that the most critical determinant of success or failure is involvement of a significant number of people in shaping the vision.

- Know who the significant actors are. Who is interested in promoting the change? Who will directly benefit? Who has authority to approve or deny the change? Who are the opinion leaders? All members of the organization are potential actors. Though some have more formal power than others, all who are aware of the change effort make decisions to ignore, support, or oppose the change. They all will decide to get involved or refrain from involvement.

- Discover the extent, degree, location, and temperament of support or resistance. What resources will these people use to support or resist?

- Identify the stakeholders in the current situation. Where and how can they find a stake in the new situation?

- Don't ignore the needs of the staff who have to implement the change. The final features of the change will be shaped by their hands.

- Avoid alienating potential allies who may not support you in the early going.

- Recognize the resources of low-ranking people: access to information; control of information; relationships with other actors; credibility, reputation, or standing; personal skills or expertise.

- Maintain the commitment and support of critical actors. Keep people oriented to the issue and what's going on to deal with it. Keep people up to date with what is going on in the change effort and involved in the actual work. Remind actors of the value of the roles various people can and are playing. Determine how to use various mechanisms to communicate that the vision is working.

Understand the Culture of the Organization

- The culture of the organization will be the single most powerful force affecting change. Significant change in the organization requires purposeful, above board discussion about the silent influence of organizational culture and ultimately a clear agreement to modify it. Over time a series of minor alterations will create cultural changes, particularly if these build on cultural traits that already exist. However, these must be steady and vigilantly maintained in order to ultimately transform the organization. Without intentionally changing an organization's culture, it will essentially return to its previous state no matter who is at the helm.

- Some organizations emphasize control and allegiance to authority and procedure, whereas others, on the opposite end of the spectrum, are committed to openness and outcomes. The rhetoric of an organization doesn't always describe its true character. If you can present

your change as being culturally consistent, and if you adhere to cultural norms in the way you present it, your chances for success will be higher than if you ignore cultural conditions. Here you amplify certain aspects of the culture that support the change.

- Understand alliances and antagonisms, especially among decision makers. You can gain valuable information by observing meetings, asking questions, and cataloguing complaints. Pay attention to the types of relationships that exist by noting who refers to whom, who defers to whom, and who spends time with whom.

- Determine which supporters can hold which resisters accountable.

- Understand and use informal networks of communication.

- Get to know the official documents and approved statements of the organization. Key information to collect includes policy manuals, authority/organization charts, promotional material the organization sends out, and budgets. These can help you spot entry points for introducing change to the organization. You will be able to identify formal relationships and procedures. You will be able to discern differences between rhetoric and practice, real and phony threats, and other inconsistencies. You may well discover that "policies" that influence decisions don't really exist at all.

- Recognize that written standards of behavior may have little influence over decisions and behavior (Roloff & Paulson, 2001).

- Acknowledge but do not rely too heavily on hearsay.

- Ask yourselves, "Which aspects of the current culture empower us, and which aspects don't?"

Create a Receptive Environment

- Create an awareness of the need for change. Identify and thoughtfully disseminate symptoms of problems or signs of opportunities. These may include letters from clients (with their permission), data on important outcomes, positive reports on other providers or other motivating comparisons to your "competitors," and worker observations.

- Consider having a workshop (or periodic workshops) to identify opportunities for improvement. Keep this focused on a particular area of operation. Participants should include staff of different levels of authority. Using an appreciative inquiry orientation would be helpful.

- Decide where in the organization to initiate discussion of the problem or potential.

- Develop your own personal influence with respect to the problem. Take steps to increase your credibility and standing.

- Understand the mission of the organization and relate the change to it. Help the organization acknowledge goal displacement.

- Consider proposing the change as being so linked to organizational values and other activities that it represents little real change at all.

- Commit yourself to learning, and promote the idea of a learning organization, one which purposefully uses its experiences to increase effectiveness and inform its actions. All actions of the organization become connected with discovery.

- Begin by focusing on one particular aspect or area of the organization. This is less threatening. Ideas are introduced to other parts of the organization, not forced on them. In a learning organization, changes in one area become models for another.

Expect, Identify, and Deal with Resistance

- Recognize that resistance is not necessarily a bad thing. The need to test your ideas against resistance will reduce the chances for unintended consequences, and it may lead to new discoveries. Avoid "tuning out" problems that need to be addressed.

- Understand that most people do not look positively on new ideas that they think will turn their world upside down, and adding on lots of reasons why the change must take place rarely makes things better (Denning, 2000).

- Recognize that bringing the change closer to reality can energize supporters and opponents alike.

- Determine the degree of similarity and difference in goals between supporters and resisters.

- Be cautious about expecting too much from your connections. Although your friendly relationship with a formal decision maker will be helpful, do not assume that it is sufficient to ensure approval of the change.

- Understand the sources of resistance. These could include lack of information or differences in information, apathy, fear, psychological investment in current operations, differing interests and commitments, lack of clarity in defining the proposed change, responses required from other components of the organization, or personal animosity among participants. Also, recognize the impact recent history or other current demands have on the organization. For example, an organization that has recently recovered from major turmoil will be more interested in promoting stability than change. An organization in the midst of budgetary woes will not want to take on additional financial burdens. An organization distracted with other issues will probably give little attention to less significant change requests. (Although this may prevent formal approval, it may be a good time to institute informal procedures that can be formalized at another time.)

- Consider using the least threatening tactics that will produce the desired result.

- Seek resister involvement and contributions. Learn skills of inquiry to complement your skills of advocacy (Senge, 2006).

- Avoid responding to hostility with hostility.

- Keep a formal record of events and agreements. Clarify timetables for actions. Your group should determine what consequences will follow if timetables and other agreements are or are not kept.

- Be prepared to confront likely manifestations of resistance. Some of the more likely include

DID YOU KNOW?   Ten Sources of Resistance or Support for Organizational Change

1. *Perceived advantage.* Not all proposals will benefit all groups within the organization. Not adequately assessing the perspectives of particular groups (decision makers, implementers, staff) can lead to resistance.

2. *Effort.* The heavier the investment of time and energy on the part of various organizational actors, the more difficult it is to sustain a high level of interest and commitment.

3. *Risk.* These are the costs incurred if the proposal fails to meet its objectives. There are three types of high-risk proposals: (1) proposals that, once adopted, cannot be terminated or reversed without incurring a substantial cost; (2) proposals that must be implemented in their entirety and cannot be done in stages; and (3) proposals that conflict with the dominant values of the organization.

4. *Sunken costs.* Proposals that challenge the investments the organization has made to support certain institutional practices will be resisted.

5. *Understandability.* An inability to condense complex proposals into simple language that is compatible with the values of the particular audience will interfere with acceptance.

6. *Ability.* The organization has to believe it has the capacity to carry out the proposed change. Assume that any proposal that requires additional funds is likely to be resisted.

7. *Depth and distance.* The more the proposal seeks to change basic goals and objectives, rather than just procedures, the more resistance will increase. Also, the greater the number of administrative levels it must pass through, the greater the chances of resistance.

8. *Idea and ideology.* Innovations that have been tested are less likely to be resisted. Those that fit the ideology of the organization are also more likely to receive support.

9. *Need.* This reflects the organization's sense that something ought to be done to fix a problem. The more that belief is shared, the more responsive the organization will be. However, just because people agree that "something must be done" does not mean there is agreement about just what that should be or how it should be implemented—another source of resistance.

10. *Generality.* This refers to the scope of the proposal. The more the proposal affects larger systems, the more it will be resisted. Proposals that affect only a small part of the organization are more likely to be tolerated.

Keep each of these factors in mind as you assess the feasibility of your proposed change and develop your strategies and tactics.

SOURCE: Frey (1990).

high-authority actors claiming little or no authority on the issue, vague statements of support with no concrete actions to indicate support, delays, exaggerating minor or unrelated issues, or divide-and-conquer tactics.

Reduce Personal Risks

- Ask forgiveness, not permission. While I don't encourage you to be cavalier or to blatantly break rules or ignore real consequences, do not inflate the risk of involvement. In my experience, many people involved in human services

are reluctant to step outside narrowly defined roles without first getting permission from those in authority to do so. Some individuals believe that working for change goes hand in hand with experiencing some personal loss. Their fears become magnified when conditions or colleagues challenge them to take part in change-promoting activities.

- Appreciate the benefits as well as the hazards. The discussion of risks itself may exaggerate their potential. In many cases, change agents experience not only strong personal fulfillment but significant professional recognition for their actions. Even so, our fears may lead us to pay more attention to instances when working for change leads to trouble. The fact is that there sometimes is a risk involved, and exaggerated or not, it should not be naively dismissed.

- Understand the more likely negative consequences. Rarely does advocating change result in loss of a job. A person who is "punished" for his involvement may experience interference with career advancement within the organization, denial of requests for authority support on other matters, or receive some form of social disapproval. These punishments may range from temporary and moderate to long-lasting and severe.

- Understand that the nature of the change, the breadth of support for the change, the tactics used to promote the change, and the outcome of the change effort are all factors relating to the consequences for change agents. You may have the chance to influence these elements in a way that reduces risk.

- Recognize attempts to intimidate change agents. One of the more common methods used by those in authority who are resisting the change is to encourage general discomfort and focus attention on one or two individuals as the "cause of all this trouble." They attempt to distract attention from the issue and attribute the pursuit of change to some character flaw exhibited by primary advocates of change, reducing matters to a "personality issue." This may frighten off potential allies and those who are hesitant to support, especially those who look to people in authority to tell them what to think. Anticipate the tactic. You who support the effort need to talk openly among yourselves about how you will handle the situation when it arises. Provide support to one another that is *visible* to everyone who is aware of the conflict.

- Don't have primary advocates of change become separated from other core group members. Have several people in visible roles. Develop a strong support base and demonstrate strong group backing for one another.

- Find yourself a partner who supports your potential and who strengthens you.

- Know your rights. Be prepared to clearly assert them if disciplinary action is brought against you.

- Put yourself in a position within the organization that gives you standing to promote change. This can be a formal position or a quasi-formal position, such as a member of an internal committee.

- Manage the perception of the change effort, particularly as it relates to the motivations of those most highly involved.

- Avoid making a fight without sufficient reason. Avoid making a fight without sufficient resources.

- Keep your discussion related to the beneficial impact of the change. Engage in personal attacks only as a necessary part of a planned strategy, and avoid attacking those who have more powerful support than you unless you can isolate them from their support.

- Focus on mutual benefits. Whenever appropriate, endeavor to diminish the fears and discomfort of opponents.

- Maintain an awareness of the message your personal demeanor sends. If you act outraged or outrageous, do so on purpose.

- Remember, you work there. The way you pursue change will leave an impression on the organization, your work community. In your selection of strategies, see if you can select an approach that helps you achieve your goal in a way that humanizes this community and makes it more respectful of its members.

- "Keep you nose clean." That is, make sure that you fulfill all of your job responsibilities. Your paper work is done correctly and on time, you arrive at work on time and don't leave early. Your relationships with clients are strong and appropriate. Don't give an opponent, particularly one in authority, any job-related deficiency to use against you.

- Use your head to avoid unnecessary risks. Don't give opponents added reasons to discredit you.

Implement and Confirm the Change

- Complete the job. The change agent's work is not done when the organization agrees to accept the change. Agreement signals an expansion or shift in attitude, but in practice the change has not yet occurred. Actually putting the change in place is what the whole business is all about. Those changes that alter the inner workings of the organization also need to be woven into the tapestry of its daily life to ensure their permanence.

- Attend to essential tasks. To make sure that the change becomes fixed within the organization (to the extent that anything is or should be fixed), you need to accomplish two important objectives. First, establish connections with other parts of the organization so these other parts begin to make use of and ultimately rely on the benefits of the change. Next, quickly move to establish clear, predictable, useful procedures. Although there will be an initial period of trial and error, it is important that other people, especially those within the organization, soon learn how to relate to the innovation. Confusion will create frustration and impede the desire of others to make use of the change. If other parts of the system avoid the new design, it will not receive the attention and support it needs to function within the organization. Like a plant, you want the change to quickly take hold and draw nourishment by becoming well rooted within the organization.

- Acknowledge and perform critical roles. You and the other advocates have some important roles to play during this rooting period. The change needs champions who will continue to assert its importance and benefits, interpreters who help explain what the change is and how it works, and troubleshooters who are alert to problems in implementation and can identify appropriate action (Brager & Holloway, 1978).

- Make necessary refinements. When your good ideas hit the reality of implementation, you will discover that a number of adjustments must be made. Some of your assumptions will be proven incorrect, and some things you didn't even think of will demand your attention. Expect that you will need to make modifications and be willing to do so. It may be helpful to publicly advance the idea of a "shakedown cruise," a period of time for working the bugs out. You have then created an expectation that alterations are an anticipated and reasonable part of the process.

- Move quickly to secure additional resources. Certain types of changes require specific resources, such as money, staff time, or space. If you are pursuing a change of this sort, you may find out that it requires more institutional support than you had thought. The time to seek additional resources is early in the implementation stage. At that time, there is likely to be an air of enthusiasm and a desire by most people for the project to succeed. If the project stumbles around for a while, people will lose interest and those in authority may be unwilling to commit new resources to an endeavor whose survival is questionable.

- Orient new staff to changes in practice, particularly new administrators. Understand that most new staff and administrators are likely to come from a professional culture that emphasizes a service orientation and hierarchical authority structures. People coming into the organization may not understand the development approaches that may have been instituted. Even though current workers strongly support a development philosophy and even if development activities have become routine, administrators groomed in another tradition may well undo all the good work that went into giving the agency a new direction. Do not assume that just because you and your colleagues grasp this new course of action that everyone else will as well. Take the time to help new members understand and recognize the value of what you are doing and build confidence in incorporating these methods into their own work.

- Evaluate the change to see if it is doing what it is supposed to do and not creating new problems.

SOME FINAL CONSIDERATIONS

It is unlikely that the problems plaguing your organization happened all at once. Unless the organization is faced with a major crisis, you will probably not "fix" it all at once. In the overall scheme of things, your efforts may represent only minor changes. However, each one of those changes may have major significance to the people who are immediately affected. Further, these things add up. Taken together, those minor changes you initiated will probably make a major difference.

Improving your organization is an ongoing process. In fact, don't be surprised if one change uncovers a need and interest for other changes. You will discover that many of the changes you brought about will fall short of your hopes. I hope this will not discourage you. Though imperfect, your efforts will lead to advancements, ones that would not have occurred if you remained confined within a narrow definition of what it means to be a professional in the field of human services.

BREAKFAST AT TOMMIE'S

Over the last 6 weeks, this group has been meeting at this small cafe. Perhaps "group" is a bit of an exaggerated description. Today, six people gathered for an early morning breakfast; that's two more than last week and three more than the week before. Today it could be called a group. Amid the clatter of dishes and competition from the conversations of other early morning risers crowded into Tommie's Cafe, plans continued to take shape.

"What do the administrators have to say about this, Beverly?"

"The administrators have a lot of things to worry about, Curtis. I doubt that anyone even cares that you are talking to each other."

"Not yet they don't, Ms. Assistant Director, but they will."

"Oh my, aren't we in a friendly mood this morning. Coffee bad, or do you always treat your guests so kindly at this hour?"

Almost 2 months ago a chance comment after yet another worthless staff meeting set Curtis Greene to thinking. It was his first job out of school, one he was glad to have, at least most of the time. In the months before graduation, he pictured himself in a nicely decorated office busily helping families get their lives back in order. In the months following graduation, still unemployed, he pictured himself maybe sitting on the other side of the desk. Finally, Darryl had called. Though he was a year behind Darryl in school, they had taken several classes together and become close, only to

drift apart once Darryl graduated and started working. The job at Brentwood Community Services, which Darryl had told him about, was now his. Although the office wasn't nicely decorated, it was his, and he could go there every day and sit on the "right" side of the desk.

It was Darryl's remark that started it: "I hope to God that I don't look like all these other people after I've worked here for 5 years." Curtis hadn't really noticed the look before, tired at 9 a.m. Maybe it was walking into the crowded, shabby waiting room to call your next client. Maybe it was the inane hoops that both the clients and the workers had to jump through to get any services at all. Sure, some of these regulations were imposed by the state, but some were made up by the agency itself, three directors ago.

Maybe it was just the inadequacy or the irrelevance of the services themselves. Curtis had really wanted to make a difference. He believed he could. Now, barely half a year on the job, he wasn't as enthusiastic or confident. In 5 years, 5 long years, how would he greet 9 a.m.?

So, he talked to Darryl. And he and Darryl talked to Jill. Three weeks later they were still talking to each other, every Friday morning at 7 a.m., feeling pretty sorry for themselves. Then Jill invited Aimee, who asked them how long they intended to whine. Aimee listened to the barrage of excuses intended as a counterattack. Then she repeated her question. Whether it was Jill's look, her barely stifled snicker, or the spontaneous realization of the absurdity of the past 3 weeks, they laughed so hard that the guy drinking coffee in the next booth jumped, adding a few new designs to his tie. And the "group" was born.

Everything seemed wrong at the agency, but where to start? The demeaning intake procedures, the preposterously high caseload, the indifference to problems in the surrounding neighborhoods, the low morale? Where? Maybe the outcome of next week's department directors' meeting would give them a clue. The group had a little surprise for the supervisors that would make them face up to the things that had been ignored too long. In the meantime ....

"You're right, Bev, that 'Ms. Assistant Director' stuff was unfair, but the 'they'll find out' part you're going to hear about in a minute. I think you need to listen to Randy."

"Beverly, I don't know if Curtis told you, but I'm president of the Darrien Heights Coalition. We're made up of several neighborhood groups. You can probably guess that the people here are pretty fed up with the gangs taking over our neighborhoods, but what you might not know is that they're fed up with you too. We've tried to meet with your director, but he says he's too busy to talk to us. The last guy gave us a lot of promises, and nothing ever happened.

"The governor's office announced last week that they were going to provide some money to groups dealing with gang violence. Maybe Brentwood and the Coalition could work together on this, though maybe the Coalition would rather picket you folks.

"Curtis said that he has some ideas about some changes at the agency that would help the situation, and he said that this group here would start drumming up support with some of the other workers. Anyway, I thought I should come here this morning and talk it over with you."

Beverly, who had glanced at Curtis at the mention of "changes at the agency," turned her attention first to Randy, then to the rest of the group. "Before you go making any changes, I think there are a few things you need to know first ...."

REFLECTION QUESTIONS

1. If there are no major changes in the way this change effort is being conducted, how is this story likely to end?

2. What information or assumptions led you to this conclusion?

3. Which of the organization's issues or opportunities would be the focus of your change effort? On what basis would you make your selection?

4. What is Beverly likely to recommend? What do you think the basis for her recommendations would be? How much would you trust her?

5. If you were Curtis Greene or any other member of the group, what would you have done differently? What would you have done the same?

6. What particular steps would you take at this point to enhance the prospects for success?

GROUP ACTIVITY: WORKERS LEAD AGENCY CHANGE

A few colleagues who work with young people and their families have become interested in incorporating community development approaches into the work that the agency does. The director has just given them the go-ahead to start exploring possibilities and has offered to work with them.

1. Divide the larger group into teams of four to six members and identify some steps your team thinks should be taken to introduce agency staff to a development philosophy and encourage their support. What are some things that your team would want to learn before you go much further? Discuss this

situation and develop a team approach by answering the following questions. (20 minutes)

- For each step you identify, mention one reason why that step would be important.
- What would "support" look like to you?

- If you were successful, what might be some common practices in the agency after 3 years?
- Draw a symbol that represents what support would look like or draw a symbol that represents common agency practices in 3 years.

2. Present your ideas and symbol to the larger group. (7–10 minutes)

HELPFUL WEBSITES

A number of public and private organizations can direct you to information, technical assistance, or other resources you might need as you work to strengthen your health or human service organization. Links to the organizations listed here are on the companion website at www.cengage.com/humansvcs/homan.

Appreciative Inquiry Commons

Harvard Business and Publishing

National Human Services Assembly

Organization Development Network

Society for Organizational Learning

Chapter 15

✳

Lobbying for Change

CHAPTER HIGHLIGHTS

- Policy practice, an important professional role
- Direct democracy
- Understand the meaning of lobbying
- Lobbying by nonprofits
- Know the foundation elements for lobbying
- Use various components in lobbying efforts

- Outline of the legislative process
- Understand opponents' views as well as your own
- Basic lobbying activities
- Face-to-face contact
- Letter writing
- Testifying
- Tips for credibility and effectiveness
- Your confidence and moxie will grow

Developing social welfare policies is hardly a rational process. It is influenced by the divergent values, motivations, and beliefs of all who have a role in defining and refining them. Competing viewpoints—from those held by the general public to those of elected and appointed public officials—find their way into laws and regulations that direct and govern our social welfare system and our daily lives. Political conflicts over the nature, causes, and necessary responses to social problems find momentary resolution in the decisions of public officials (DiNitto, 2000).

Policy practice is a compelling and vitally important method of professional intervention (Jansson, 2008; Segal, Gerdes, & Steiner, 2010). Your ability to shape the framework of policy within which resources are distributed and opportunities are provided or limitations enacted can meaningfully affect thousands and thousands of lives. Involvement in the legislative arena, where many policies are given birth, is a significant form of policy practice. Your ability to influence the creation of policies through active involvement in the legislative process is the focus of this chapter.

As community members ourselves and as workers in health and human services, we are affected every day in countless ways by public policies. The people we care about in our personal and professional lives have opportunities provided or denied by such policies. Our way of looking at one another and the world is profoundly influenced by these official doctrines and the information and misinformation that give them life. We can choose to leave all this up to somebody else and hope they get it right, or we can bring the power of knowledge and mobilized people into the crafting of public decisions. Maybe you agree with Mark Rosenman (2005), who said that those who are on the front line of this work "must claim their essential place in the vanguard of pushing for social justice" by building political advocacy skills (p. 13). We need to do this ourselves and with our colleagues, constituents, and supporters. Do you see that you should be in the vanguard? Or would you rather leave all this to those who have chosen to learn and practice their skills to serve other interests?

You can participate in policy development in a number of ways. Public agencies administering public programs set forth the rules and regulations that govern how those programs operate. Hoefer and Ferguson (2007) have observed that "regulations control implementation of laws. This vital fact concerning the policy process can often be overlooked" (p. 84). Your experience and training should be important contributors to this process. Are they? Do you know how rules and regulations are developed and the roles you and organized community members can play to influence their final form?

Direct democracy through the use of initiative and referenda can mobilize citizens to assert their interests. Initiatives are measures placed on the ballot by citizens who have collected enough signatures on petitions to demand voter attention; 24 states have provisions for initiatives. Through a popular referendum, citizens can collect signature petitions to accept or reject legislation enacted by the legislature; 24 states also have provisions for popular referendum. (Legislative referendum is the process for legislatures or government agencies to put measures on the ballot for voter approval or rejection.) These tools are also used at the local level in thousands of counties, cities, and towns across the country, and there has been a significant increase in their use over time. All but 3 states have provisions for some form of direct democracy in local government, with more than 90% of U.S. cities having some form of referendum (Initiative and Referendum Institute, 2006, 2009; National Conference of State Legislatures, 2009; Renner, 2009). These methods provide good opportunities for mobilizing community frustration or excitement, giving voice to concerns that may otherwise be ignored.

Involvement in the legislative arena, where many policies are given birth, is another significant form of policy practice. Your ability to influence the creation of policies through active involvement in the legislative process is the focus of this chapter.

This dynamic process is always open to revision and redirection. It is open to influence. Social workers and human services practitioners decide to participate in this process or to refrain from participation. Either way, there are consequences for the community and for the people these professionals intend to serve (Ezell, 2001). Even if you do not participate in the development of a lobbying campaign, your firsthand knowledge of the effects of proposed legislation can speed up the refinement of legislation and prevent harmful consequences. It can, that is, if you know how to communicate what you know and if you make sure that you do communicate it (Hofford, 2001).

Legislative advocacy involves both self-interest and community interest, particularly those community members who are affected by social welfare policies. Practitioners in social work and health and human services often must respond to attempts to restrict and overregulate their work. In fact, legislators' lack of knowledge is one of the greatest impediments to support for social work (Ewalt, 1994). However, too narrow a focus on self-interest legislation undermines credibility. If practitioners expect support for the profession, we must be seen to be active advocates for the causes we ourselves say we ought to support.

One of the most meaningful ways you as a citizen and as a professional can have an impact on this process is by lobbying public officials. By *lobbying* I mean purposeful communication with a public official with the intention of influencing a decision the official may make on a specific matter. Lobbying may be done on a number of different levels by communicating with elected officials, from the local city council to the president of the United States, to influence actions on public issues.

Decisions made by Congress certainly affect our lives. Though you may lobby your congressional

GLOBAL PERSPECTIVES

ASIA—To empower people through advocacy and lobbying, it is necessary to challenge existing conventional development paradigms and practices, promote development alternatives and influence development policies and systems of government.... To undertake this, the following specific steps are recommended:

- Training, research and documentation on advocacy and lobbying strategies, tools and techniques.
- Strengthening local/national advocacy and lobbying groups.
- Promoting cooperation among existing networks, initiating a meeting among the principle Asian networks to design working mechanisms for information-sharing, concerted advocacy and lobbying.

(Colombo Statement of Asian NGOs and People's Organizations on: People's Empowerment in Asia, as cited in Liamzon, 1997, p. 29).

ISRAEL—The connection between social work interventions and national politics is indirect, hidden and unspoken, and literature about the issue hardly exists. However, there are many situations

occurring around the world, where avoiding paying direct attention to national politics damages the implementation of social work activities. As an example, we can point to situations in which a country enters a state of war. Such situations affect the entire population, including social workers and their clients. They create fear and anxiety and increase the level of stress that might affect the behavioral and emotional functioning of both social workers and clients. The source of these threatening issues—that is, the national policy—is often not discussed in professional activities, since it is not related to the typical problems addressed in social work. Social workers are usually not perceived as responsible for national political decisions, nor are they perceived as having any influence on them. Therefore, the subject is barely discussed between social workers and clients, among social workers or in social work literature....

The main goal of politically oriented intervention is to open up new alternatives in situations where it seems to severely threaten the existence of specific client populations (Michel Shamai & Amnon Boehm, 2001, pp. 343–344, 355).

ARCTIC—Approximately 4 million people live in the Arctic, including members of 30 different indigenous groups.... Over the past several decades, Arctic indigenous peoples groups have become increasingly active in circumpolar and international environmental, scientific and political processes... (p. 74). The most prominent forum in which Arctic countries and indigenous peoples interact on environmental issues is the Arctic Council, which began operations in 1998. All eight Arctic countries as well as six permanent participants (organizations made up of at least 50% indigenous peoples) are members of the Arctic Council... (p. 75). Indigenous groups (have) prepared well articulated statements and policy positions, and pressured national governments to act on hazardous substances. Representatives of indigenous groups (have) also attended and advocated directly in a host of international political meetings and negotiations.... Circumpolar activism (has) also helped to build important connections and interests and to build identity among the indigenous peoples of the Arctic. (p. 82) (Henrik Selin & Noelle Eckley Selin, 2008, pp. 72–83).

delegation, playing a pivotal role in a sustained national lobbying campaign requires a degree of commitment that is normally beyond the scope of most professional practitioners. But a great many national policies started out as local ordinances (Schorf, Fischer, Pollack, Brophy, & Kulman, 1996), and our training and experience are important assets as we work in this arena. Our skills in one-on-one interaction and our knowledge of social problems, social interaction, and the social environment are useful in this work (Haynes &

Mickelson, 2006). You may provide information and insight to a government official who is writing regulations on a public program with the hope of increasing the effectiveness of that program. Although you may engage in lobbying, this may not be your primary profession. Even this can work to your advantage. You are likely to be regarded as someone who is involved because you are truly concerned and knowledgeable, not just someone paid to represent a point of view (Haynes & Mickelson, 2006).

In this chapter I focus on lobbying members of a state legislature because many decisions that affect the communities we live in and serve are made at this level. As policy issues devolve from the federal to the state level, attention to state-level policy-making processes accelerate in importance (Sherraden, Slosar, & Sherraden, 2002). Program implementation, such as the implementation of Temporary Assistance to Needy Families (TANF), is strongly affected by the political environments of the states, and responses to myriad issues dealing with basic issues such as poverty can be found at the state level (Anderson & Gryzlak, 2002). Further, it is likely that you can have a significant impact on decisions made by this body.

Decisions by county and other local levels of government also have an impact on issues of vital concern to your community. Though the specific steps in the process of establishing official policy are different for local government, the basic methods for influencing decisions described in this chapter have application to those arenas as well. It is a good idea to start by researching the design and decision-making procedures of the particular government body you hope to influence.

The prescribed nature of legislative bodies, such as a state legislature, provides for a rather unique community. Your understanding of this community requires an awareness of the way participants operate at both formal and informal levels. Certain rules of etiquette and of process should be recognized and commonly observed. The gamelike character adds yet another dimension to this environment. For all these reasons, I will describe this arena of change with a degree of detail.

In addition to the review of lobbying regulations, the suggestions presented in this chapter were drawn from my own experience as a lobbyist as well as from the work of the Center for Lobbying in the Public Interest (2006, 2009a, 2009b), Common Cause (1992), Dear and Patti (1984), Ezell (2001), Goffin and Lombardi (1988), Haynes and Mickelson (2006), Hofford (2001), Hrebenar and Scott (1982), Kirst-Ashman and Hull (2009), Lamiell (1984), Jansson, (2008), League of Women Voters (1976), McLean (1980), Pertschuk (1986),

Richan (2006), Siglin (1999), Smith (1979), Smucker (1999), and Speeter (1978a).

EXPLODING THE LOBBYING MYTH: TAKING AN ACTIVE ROLE[1]

"We're a tax-exempt organization, so we can't take an active role." Let's set the record straight. You most certainly can be actively involved in advocating for a change in public policy, and many of the things you can do are not even considered lobbying. That tax-exempt, nonprofit organizations cannot lobby or engage in advocacy is simply a myth. The only organizations that cannot undertake lobbying activities are private foundations (Phelan, 2002). Although a foundation cannot lobby itself, it certainly can support grantees who do lobby (Troyer, 2000).

Most social service agencies and many other social welfare organizations are 501(c)(3) organizations. These are tax exempt nonprofit organizations. People contributing to these organizations can use the contribution as a tax deduction. Let's take a closer look at what you *can* do. Under federal tax law, except for private foundations, 501(c)(3) organizations, commonly referred to as charitable organizations, can lobby. However, lobbying cannot be a substantial part of their activities. Just what constitutes "substantial" is confusing and open to judgment. An organization can continue to operate under this vague standard, or it can instead elect to operate within clear, specific limitations on lobbying expenditures. This election provision is covered under Section 501(h) of the Internal Revenue Code. Not only are these limitations clear, but some would say they are generous. Though most organizations are eligible, churches and private foundations cannot choose the 501(h) option. Check to see if your organization can qualify.

In 1990 the IRS published a new set of regulations dealing with lobbying activities for 501(c)(3) organizations. These regulations set forth a number of clarifications of what had been a pretty murky set of

1. I thank Abby Levine and the Alliance for Justice for their expertise and thorough review of the material in this section.

tax rules (American Bar Association, 2000; Troyer, 1991). The substantive changes made at that time still apply today. The following overview of provisions for lobbying has been drawn from the Alliance for Justice (2003, 2005, 2007; Abby Levine, personal communication, August 2009), Code of Federal Regulations (2009a, 2009b), Independent Sector (2002c, 2009b), Internal Revenue Service (2002, 2006, 2008, 2009b, 2009c, 2009d, 2009e), Phelan (2002, 2006), the United States Senate (2009), and Urban (2004). The following information is not legal advice and provides a very general overview of the rules. Electing to abide by the restrictions under 501(h) simply involves filing Form 5768, a one-page form. You only need to do this once, and you can change your mind later and revoke your election.

A charity can spend up to 20% of its first $500,000 of exempt purpose expenditures (generally this means its annual expenditures, with some adjustments) on lobbying activities. That's $100,000 for an organization that spends $500,000 a year! Even though the proportion it can spend for the second $500,000 and beyond continues to decrease, if its expenditures are large enough, an organization making an election under 501(h) can spend up to $1 million on lobbying! An organization can spend no more than 25% of its total lobbying limit on grassroots lobbying (rallying the troops), but it can spend as much of its total lobbying limit as it wants on direct lobbying. Only activities that involve an expenditure of funds fall under the lobbying limits. Organizations need to account for costs involved in any activity related to a lobbying effort, such as employee compensation for time spent researching proposals, preparing proposals, and communicating with lawmakers. Cost-free activities, such as volunteer time, don't count against the lobbying limit, however. The organization must keep a record of its direct and grassroots lobbying expenditures and report them on Form 990, which is filed with the IRS.

Now you know that you can lobby and how much you can spend, but what *is* lobbying? Or more to the point, what activities does the IRS consider as lobbying?

It is important to understand what counts as lobbying, because if the activity is not lobbying, the costs of doing it do not count against your lobbying limits. "Lobbying" and "influencing legislation" are

narrowly defined. As mentioned previously, there are two types of lobbying: direct lobbying and grassroots lobbying. Both involve expressing a view about specific legislation. In general, communicating with a legislator (or legislative staff) and expressing a view about specific legislation is direct lobbying, and communicating with the general public, expressing a view about specific legislation, and including a call to action is grassroots lobbying.

Communicating with a government official is only considered lobbying if that official is a member of a legislative body or staff involved in the formulation of legislation and if the principal purpose of your communication is to influence legislation. Communication is considered direct lobbying if two conditions are present: (1) the communication refers to specific legislation, meaning legislation that has already been introduced in a legislative body or a specific legislative proposal that the organization supports or opposes; and (2) the communication reflects a view on the legislation. However, discussion with a lawmaker would meet the test of specific legislation when the idea has enough substance that the lawmaker would recognize that you are discussing a specific proposal and would know what you want the lawmaker to do about it. Your bringing up a particular idea for legislative action becomes the proposed piece of "specific legislation." Specific legislation does *not* include rules or actions by nonlegislative bodies such as executive agencies and housing authorities.

For communication with the general public to be considered grassroots lobbying, it must refer not only to specific legislation and express a view on that legislation but also urge the recipient of the communication to take action on the legislation.

There are other ways that a nonprofit can influence the development of policy that are covered by regulations. For example, public charities can participate in initiative and referendum campaigns, and related expenditures are counted against the more liberal direct lobbying percentage.

The Lobbying Disclosure Act of 1995, as amended by the Honest Leadership and Open Government Act of 2007, adds some registration and reporting requirements for lobbying at the federal level and includes attempts to influence the executive branch as lobbying. Organizations that do a significant amount of federal lobbying will need to be mindful of somewhat different definitions under the federal Lobbying Disclosure Act. Very few community organizations engage in enough lobbying activities at the federal level to meet the registration threshold. If they do, they will need to file a quarterly report to the Clerk of the House of Representatives and the Secretary of the Senate on Form LD-2. In general, you will need to spend $11,500 in a quarter and have an employee spend at least 20% of her time on lobbying activities before you need to register. In addition, lobbyists and the organizations that employ them must also file semiannual reports (Form LD-203), disclosing certain contributions and certifying compliance with the House and Senate gift and travel rules (U.S. House of Representatives, 2009).

For provisions that apply to state registration, check with the department of your state government that regulates lobbying, generally the Secretary of State.

A number of other provisions in the tax code and the Lobbying Disclosure Act describe what you can and cannot do with respect to lobbying, including special provisions for organizations such as coalitions. In addition, lobbying restrictions often apply to government grants and contracts. It would be wise to sit down with an accountant or tax attorney to go over the applicable regulations. You will find that indeed you can do very much to advocate for a change in public policy.

If you work for a private, nonprofit organization or social service agency, one of the most significant steps you can take to move forward the process of change is to get your agency actively involved in shaping public policy. A community organization or social service agency has a base of power that it can put to use in partnership with its constituents. Public policies affect people. They affect your community, the people your agency serves, and even the agency itself. Knowing that your agency can also affect policy, perhaps you will decide that it should.

GETTING STARTED

Your decision to act as a lobbyist should be based on a strong commitment to the issue you are working on. Your belief in your purpose will help you

overcome many an obstacle, and your sincere dedication will make those you hope to influence more receptive to your message. If your interest is only halfhearted, it is unlikely that you will be very successful. The fact that your organization may not have a lot of money or may not be able to contribute to political campaigns can be significantly offset by the number of people you can mobilize. The self-interest of elected officials is, first and foremost, votes. Demonstrating your ability to move voters to awareness and action is a fundamentally important element in the lobbying process.

Know the regulations governing lobbying in your state. Each state has its own set of regulations. You can usually find out how these apply to you by contacting your Secretary of State's office.

Be aware of the impact of your activities on the tax status of the organization you represent. If you are acting on behalf of a tax-exempt organization, check with its accountant or attorney to be sure you are operating within Internal Revenue Service and other guidelines. Remember, a tax-exempt nonprofit agency can most definitely participate in lobbying activities, maybe more than most agencies realize.

Develop a legislative agenda. Do you intend to support or defeat legislation? Are you going to develop new legislation, influence proposed legislation, or modify legislation in process? Understand that some of the things you do will not have an immediate payoff but will set the stage for later dividends. It is not uncommon for passage of a significant proposal to take several years of effort. As a result, you may want to provide encouragement to your organization by including in your agenda some issues for which you can claim victory in one legislative session.

Be clear about what your legislation is intended to accomplish. Before seeking legislation, make sure that changes in law are really the best way to accomplish your purpose. Changes in administrative policy or administrative rule, which is the implementation of new statutes, may accomplish what you want. Many legislators are impatient with those who seek legislative change when simpler methods will do.

Gain an understanding of the legislature. Use local sources, particularly public interest groups such as the League of Women Voters and Common Cause, to provide direction. Many advocacy groups have written material that will help you. Check with them to see who publishes political directories. These will be a great aid in helping you understand basic elements of the legislature and identifying its members. Recognize that there is a turnover in membership after each election, often with new leadership and new alliances (Kirst-Ashman & Hull, 2009).

Accept coaching from veterans. As you become more and more involved, you will come to know a number of people who have a great deal of experience and expertise. Many of them will help you learn the ropes.

Subscribe to publications. Special publications that deal with legislative matters are commonly available. Read the sections of the daily newspapers that deal with political and legislative topics. Get on government mailing lists to receive legislative digests (brief summaries of legislation that has been introduced) and other related materials. You may also be able to track legislative information through various computer networks.

Explore your state government's Web page. All states have a website. It is likely that you can get committee agendas, committee rosters, a biography of each legislator, and a host of other valuable information. City and county governments also have websites that are similarly useful.

Find allies. Successful lobbying employs the energies of many people. Discover who shares your interests and work with them to develop a coordinated approach to the lobbying effort. Throughout the campaign, look for other individuals and groups who can provide assistance. A formal coalition of organizations can have a strong lobbying presence. Using the Internet, you can contact other activists and advocacy organizations throughout the country. They can help you with background information, including sample legislation.

Organize membership through your lobbying efforts. Undertaking lobbying activities is an excellent way to build your organization. Members can play a number of roles, and the process itself is exciting. With its connection to political power, there is a good potential for members to become empowered through their participation in events. Active involvement will increase your group's recognition and establish it as a power to be reckoned with.

BASIC COMPONENTS OF AN ORGANIZED LOBBYING EFFORT

A comprehensive approach to promoting change by influencing political decision making should mobilize and direct community support, create positive community perceptions of your issue, and provide direct contact with elected officials. In addition to some of the general aspects of an organization, the following elements will strengthen your hand as you play the lobbying game.

Legislative team. These people will work directly on the legislation itself. Most of these members will be in direct contact with the legislators, although some will be engaged in research and materials preparation. This team is composed of members of your organization and allied organizations as well as legislators and their staff members. Ideally you will create a team of bipartisan players. It may also include members of the governor's office. Their duties are further explained in the section describing the legislative process later in the chapter. Make sure you have team members on the inside gathering information and exerting influence as well as members on the outside who can mobilize the general public.

Alert networks. An alert network is designed to mobilize a large number of people in a short period of time. Alert networks can be used to turn people out for rallies and demonstrations, call members to assist in some simple but labor-intensive organizational tasks (like getting out a large mailing on short notice), or to communicate their opinions to selected targets. Your lobbying effort will mainly use the alert network for communication, and it is designed for this purpose. Alert networks are quantity contact systems. Their main purpose is to generate as much constituent contact as possible. The more common components of an alert network are a telephone alert system, an e-mail alert, and fax alerts. Using text messaging and social networking-sites like Facebook and Twitter are also effective means of mobilizing a response.

Electronic communications, such as e-mail and texting, can easily reach many people in a short period of time, but voice contact using the telephone can

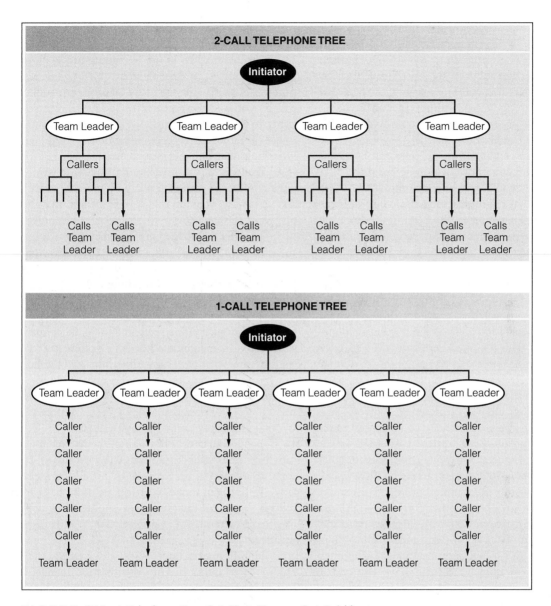

FIGURE 15.1 A Telephone Tree Gets Your Message Out Quickly

heighten the sense of urgency and increase response. A telephone alert system is an organized approach to mobilize supporters who have agreed to respond to alerts and perhaps ask others to do the same. This system generally uses a telephone tree or a variation of a boiler room operation (Figure 15.1). In a simple telephone tree, one person calls two (or more) other people, who in turn call two others, who call others, and so on. In addition to calling the other members of the tree, the person receiving the call is to call his legislator and communicate a specific message. Each recipient of a phone call is to write down the message to be delivered to the next tree member as well as to the legislator to make sure it is delivered accurately. Therefore, keep the message short and to the point. Most legislatures have a toll-free number for connecting constituents to their legislators.

A tree is usually organized into branches with each branch having its own leader. It is best to develop branches according to voting districts. You can purchase software that matches ZIP codes with legislative districts. The leader sees to it that the calls are completed without the chain being broken. The last person, on the "bottom" of the branch, is to contact the leader.

If, after a certain period of time, the leader is not called, she will initiate action up from the bottom. (There are many variations to this system. The intent is to make sure that the message doesn't get stopped or changed somewhere along the line.)

A boiler room approach is designed with the intent of increasing accuracy and making sure unanswered phones do not stop delivery of the message. Using this method, a small team of callers, usually six or seven, all call from the same location, perhaps from a social service agency or a real estate office. Each caller has a list of about 30 alert members to call. The members receiving the call only need to call their legislator. In two nights of calling, two different teams can call hundreds of members.

You can also use a Web-based calling program. This technology allows you to type in an alert message in a Web page. This message is relayed to all the participants on a call list that you have created. Using text-to-speech software, your printed message is played verbally when the call is answered.

E-mail alerts are a simple but effective way to notify your members and other potential supporters of the need for action. Chapter 10 described the use of electronic distribution lists and mailing lists. These methods can help you reach a great number of people very quickly. E-mails have the added advantage of easy response. If your message is about contacting a legislator, you can suggest some ideas that the receiver can touch on in the note to be sent to the legislator. You can put the legislator's e-mail link right into your message so that the receiver just needs to click on it to send a short note and be done. You can also organize your list by legislative district so that the recipients of your alert have their legislator's address in the message. Your subject line can say that this will take less than 2 minutes.

E-mails can also extend the number of people you contact. By asking each recipient to send the message to three other people, for example, you reach into more personal networks, which can potentially mobilize more people.

E-mail alert systems are becoming much more routine, though telephone alerts have particular potency because you are really talking with someone one on one. You are harder to ignore. With so many people receiving a flood of e-mail, it is easier to just hit the delete button if you are trying to whittle down your number of messages.

Fax alerts can be structured in the same way as a telephone tree. A fax alert can increase the clarity and reliability of your message, but there may be problems if you want to keep your communications confidential. Most professionals have access to a fax machine, so this procedure works well with them. However, many other groups don't have routine access to fax machines.

Alert networks require organization and maintenance. Members need to agree in advance to perform the actions they are requested to do. They must also receive some orientation and written instructions so they will know how to perform when called to do so. Further, the members need to be kept informed of key issues they may be requested to respond to. This is usually done by means of periodic written updates, typically through e-mail.

Finally, the alert system should be used neither too little nor too commonly. There needs to be some frequency of use, especially during the legislative session. Otherwise participants may have to relearn the system each time it is employed. Underused alert systems will fall apart due to a lack of maintenance.

Alert networks are worth the effort they require. The ability of your organization to rally a significant number of constituents can make quite an impression as phones begin to ring in legislators' offices. Legislators regularly use fax machines and e-mail, and these technologies provide members of your group with quick and easy access to lawmakers. Fax numbers and e-mail addresses are commonly printed in legislative guides. They are usually available from the legislator's office and the state's website as well.

Quality contact development. This is a system for getting specific, particularly influential community members to contact specific lawmakers. Quality contacts are those individuals who have clout in the community or who have a particular relationship with the legislator, who are willing to contact a legislator on your behalf. Those with a particular relationship would include the legislator's friends, rabbi, physician, business associates, sorority sisters, political allies, and so forth. For each lawmaker you will have a list of quality contact members you can use to convey your message. Keep accurate records regarding how often you are making requests from each person. Again, you do not want to overuse this resource. Using quality contacts is another way of enhancing your organization's stature.

Legislator dossier. You should begin collecting as much information on each legislator as possible. Good basic information includes previous relationship with your organization and its issues; key legislative interests; district interests; committee assignments; religious affiliation; professional background; other legislators who are friends, enemies, or who have influence; political allies and enemies; educational background; personal interests; social acquaintances; family information; key campaign contributors (this is easily obtainable public information); and quality contacts.

Testifier bank. From time to time you will need to present testimony before a legislative committee. It is helpful to have a team prepared in advance who can present various perspectives on the issue you are addressing. Perhaps a doctor, a single parent, an economist, an attorney, a teenager, or a priest could provide a particularly compelling point of view. These people should be purposefully recruited and prepared for their role. You don't want to scramble around at the last minute to find someone who might be able to speak to the issue. Impressions do count. Be well prepared so you can make a strong impression.

Speakers' bureau. A handful of well-versed, effective public speakers can help communicate your positions to community groups. Members of your speakers' bureau should be prepared to handle likely questions that may arise, including hostile questions. It is particularly helpful to speak to groups like the Rotary or church groups that count targeted legislators among their members.

Public affairs program. You can bring your particular message to targeted community groups through presentation of public affairs programs. These are designed to help community groups examine important community issues and governmental response to them. Such programs are effective in recruiting individual participants or coalition members.

Media relations. An organized strategy for getting your message out through the media should be developed. Stories, editorials, and letters to the editor published in local newspapers can have a strong impact on legislators. Appearing in the newspaper, particularly, or on television gives your organization and its spokespersons added credibility with legislators. Professional and trade publications are also good media resources.

External coalitions. It is unlikely that your organization alone can mount a significant legislative campaign (although you can have an impact on legislation that has a limited scope). Coordinating your efforts with other organizations will help draw attention to your efforts and provide the resources you need to accomplish the range of tasks that are necessary.

Lobbying campaigns that intend significant changes and that encounter well-organized and well-funded opposition will develop other elements to complement this basic approach. However, for most situations the approach I have described here is sufficiently comprehensive. If your lobbying aims are fairly narrow, you may not need to fully develop each of these components. However, the more attention you give to each aspect, the stronger your foundation will be.

A SKELETAL OUTLINE OF THE LEGISLATIVE PROCESS

Some variation of the elements described here will exist in your state. Except for Nebraska, all state legislatures have two houses or chambers, commonly the Senate and the House or Assembly. Some states refer to their legislature as the assembly. I will refer to the two-house model in this discussion of legislative procedures. Six states—Arkansas, Montana, Nevada, North Carolina, Oregon, and Texas—do not have regular sessions each year. Some states limit the scope of legislation that can

There are many sources of information on the Internet about government, politics, and lobbying. A number of helpful websites are listed at the end of this chapter. Check out the links to other sites as you go exploring. Remember that many other sites also deal with your particular issue, be it child welfare, hunger, a livable wage, rights of particular groups, the environment, health, or something else. It is also a good tactic to monitor your opponents'

websites. Doing so will help you understand how they are thinking and what actions they are taking or preparing to take to promote their legislative agenda. Remember that they may well be looking at your website too.

Your state legislature or assembly will have its own website, and local government sites will have links to local decision-making bodies such as city councils.

be heard during a particular session. Many have special sessions with a very narrow focus as well. Check your state legislature's website for your legislative calendar. Many states also provide a description of the basic legislative process, often called something like "how a bill becomes a law." Become familiar with your own state's process.

Legislative session. Find out when the legislature begins its session and how long it is likely to last. Many states have sessions that last just a few months. Legislative committees may be at work on issues even when the legislative session has concluded. Also, the body may be called into special session from time to time to consider a specific subject. Be aware of all legislative deadlines, such as dates for introduction of legislation and dates for completing bills in a particular chamber.

Drafting and introduction of legislation. This is the first step in the process, preparing legislation and offering it for consideration. (In some states, *bill* is a formal term designating a piece of legislation that has proceeded to a certain point in the process. I will use it here as a general term to describe a piece of legislation.) The sponsor of the legislation will work with interested parties to work out the actual language of the bill. The sponsor is the legislator who will introduce the bill and work for its passage. Under some circumstances the sponsor may have little or no interest in the legislation, but these situations are not routine, so I won't go into them here. Next, the sponsor may attempt to get other

legislators to "sign on" or cosponsor the bill. Though this indicates support on behalf of the cosponsors, simply having a large number of cosponsors does not ensure a bill's passage. The bill is then formally introduced, and usually at this time it is assigned a number. (Legislatures commonly allow bills to be filed before the legislative session actually begins, giving the legislation a kind of head start.)

First reading, assignment of bill to committee. Once the bill has been filed, it is formally read into the record and assigned to one or more committees. The committees to which the bill is assigned and the number of committees can make a crucial difference in the life of the bill. You should influence these decisions if you can. Usually the leadership of the particular chamber has some discretion in this matter. (Leadership refers to those legislators who have been elected by their peers to leadership positions; for example, Speaker of the House or Majority Leader. Leadership of the majority party is likely to exert significant control over what occurs in the legislature.)

Committee hearings. The bill is then heard in the committee. At this time, committee members may hear testimony on the bill from interested parties and make changes or amendments to it. If the bill needs substantial work, it may be referred to a subcommittee of members of the full committee. (Even though a bill has been assigned to a committee, it may not be given a hearing. You may need to work to get the bill heard in the first place.)

To continue its journey toward passage, the bill must receive the support of a majority of the sub-committee and full committee. (There are various procedural ways to keep a bill "alive" even if it is not supported by the full committee. I will touch on a few of them later in this chapter.)

Caucus action. Each political party gathers its troops for routine meetings to discuss bills and the party or caucus position on them. It is a chance to try to get party members to take a unified stand on legislation, and your inside supporters have an opportunity to affect the party's stance. These can be pretty lively meetings where positions are examined and sometimes hotly contested. Some caucus meetings are open, allowing you to get a good sense of the players and their philosophies; but often they are closed, and only members of the caucus are admitted. The party Whip generally runs the caucus discussions.

Floor action. After passing out of committee, the bill is considered by all the members of the chamber. At this time, members may debate and further amend the bill. Passage from the chamber may require two different votes, with rules for each vote being somewhat different. (Again, check the rules governing floor action in your legislature carefully.)

Action by other chamber. Once the bill has passed in the first chamber, the process is repeated once again in the next chamber.

Concurrence of amendments. Commonly, the bill will receive further amendment in the second chamber. The members of the chamber that first heard the bill must agree to, or concur with, these changes or the bill will be referred to a conference committee.

Conference committee. If a conference committee is needed, the leadership of each chamber appoints members to a special committee to resolve the differences. If the members work out an agreement, they send their report to their respective chambers for approval.

Governor's office. Once the legislature passes the bill, it is sent to the governor to sign. If the governor signs the bill, it will officially become law. The new law will probably go into effect within months of its signing. If it has been designated an emergency measure, it may go into effect immediately. (Again, the exact effective date will vary by state.)

The governor may choose to veto the bill. If this occurs, the legislature may have an opportunity to override the veto, which usually requires support of two thirds of each chamber.

Your state may have provisions for the governor to veto a bill without providing the legislature with an opportunity to override. Also, conditions for allowing the bill to become law without the governor's signature may exist.

As you can see, there are many obstacles to passing a piece of legislation. Each step provides its own little drama. That is part of the allure and the frustration of this type of change activity.

BASIC LOBBYING ACTIVITIES

If you become involved routinely in legislative action, you will soon discover that it is a year-round endeavor. Periods of intense activity may be followed by periods that are much less hurried. A good portion of the work occurs outside the legislative session. Be sure the elements of your campaign are in place and ready to go when the session begins. Those groups who wait until the legislature has begun before organizing will usually discover that they got into the game too late. Even if you are going to work on just one piece of legislation, it is important that you get an early start.

The following sequence of activities assumes that you have taken care of some of the initial tasks described earlier, such as registering as a lobbyist, developing your agenda, and gaining an understanding of the legislative process. Now you are ready to put your efforts to work lobbying on behalf of your concerns.

Gather and prepare information. Assemble data, personal stories, legislation from other states, and other information that helps you understand and communicate your issues. Prepare various background pieces and fact sheets. (A few additional tips on issue preparation are provided later in this chapter.)

Develop and prepare a legislative team. Begin developing your team a few months before you need to take action so that roles and expectations are clear. By the time the legislation has been introduced, you will have an internal team composed of key legislators and staff members and an external team composed of members of your and other organizations and perhaps some other lobbyists.

Continue to develop your internal team during the session. A solid internal team would include legislators who are interested enough in the bill to track it; a legislator who can give you the inside scoop; a legislator to whom other legislators listen; a good legislative debater; and legislators who are in influence positions (for example, leadership or committee chairs).

Not every member of the team will have equal interest. Particularly, some members of your internal team will have limited responsibility. Identify and recruit additional external team members who can help.

Target/rate legislators. To determine the degree of support or opposition you will have, it is very helpful to develop a system for ranking each legislator, particularly those who serve on committees likely to hear your bill. You can choose a simple scale of 1 to 5 to indicate how favorable each legislator is likely to be to your concerns. You can obtain this information by reading various publications, talking to other political activists, or checking voting records with interest groups (for example, Planned Parenthood, Sierra Club, or the Chamber of Commerce). You will probably revise this "score card" from time to time during the actual session.

Begin counting possible votes. Throughout the entire process, you *never stop counting votes*.

Determine your monitoring systems. Figure out how you will keep alert to rumors regarding your bills, hear about proposed action on them, and track their progress.

If you are going to introduce legislation yourself, *recruit a sponsor and cosponsors of the legislation*. Ideally, these will be individuals who have some influence within the legislature and serve on the committees likely to hear the bill. Further, the sponsor should be committed to the bill and have time to give it attention. Part of your consideration involves which chamber should initiate action on the bill.

Draft legislation. Begin working on the actual language of the bill. The sponsor should have legislative staff help you phrase your ideas in the proper language. You can start with just an outline.

Introduce legislation. The earlier your legislation is introduced, the more time you have to work it through the various hurdles.

Coordinate all steps with team members. Usually your sponsor will serve as the point person in the process. Matters such as assignment to committee, scheduling of hearing dates, and development of amendments should be coordinated for maximum advantage. You should attempt to influence these as much as possible. As feasible, you should work with legislative leadership.

Monitor the process, including rumors. Keep an ear out for amendments.

Use alert networks as appropriate throughout the session.

Use media as appropriate throughout the session.

Keep in contact with the governor's office as needed during the session. Obviously, if the governor's office is hostile to your position, or would simply hope to avoid the issue, your contact would probably only be of a general nature.

Target committee votes. Determine which members of the committee should receive most of your attention.

Lobby the committee directly. Begin to meet with members of the committee. However, do not lobby strong opponents. Also, begin to organize constituent contact and other indirect methods of influencing members.

Count votes.

Prepare testimony. Prepare testifiers and shape the message to be presented to the committee. Your message should be geared to specific legislators and to the media. (Additional points on testifying are presented later in the chapter.)

Testify. If you have a strong group of testifiers, you may decide that your personal testimony is not needed.

Lobby the chamber. Once your bill passes committee, direct your attention to other members of the chamber whom you have targeted for lobbying. Indirect methods such as demonstrations and media stories could be used at this time. (You need to determine how much and what type of attention you want to draw to this issue.) Constituent contact should swing into high gear.

Count votes. (Do you get the idea that this is important?)

CHANGE AGENT TIP

Here are 10 tips to guide you in making your argument—effectively.

1. Be able to argue the other side's point of view as well as your own. This will enable you to:

   - Identify weak points in your position you may otherwise (choose to?) ignore.

   - Better understand the opposing frame of reference so you can communicate to it.

   - Anticipate arguments so you can preempt or counter them.

   - Inoculate potential supporters by letting them know what your opposition is likely to tell them.

   - Emphasize your strengths relative to the weaknesses of the other position.

   - Demonstrate that your position is based on a strong command of the issue.

   - Discover possible areas of common ground or common interest.

2. Let the listener know your position, your professional expertise, and your experiences.

3. Focus on aspects of the issue where the listener's knowledge and values are similar to yours; relate your argument to an outcome you both desire.

4. Emphasize your areas of agreement with the listener.

5. Relate the issue to the listener's interests and personal experiences.

6. Relate the issue to consequences for constituents.

7. Use real-life examples, humor, and simple logic.

8. Elicit some emotional response (protective response, righteousness, or patriotism).

9. Avoid jargon.

10. Role-play your discussion. Have a friend play devil's advocate.

Organize and conduct floor action. Work with your internal team to identify responsibilities and communication procedures during floor action. Plan floor debate carefully. Determine who your speakers will be and how they will work together to reinforce each other's message. Anticipate and prepare for procedural maneuvers, opponents' arguments, and likely debaters. During the debate, you or other members of your external team will be sitting in the gallery. Arrange for signals so you can communicate with your legislators on the floor. Determine how you can send messages to one another if need be. You all need to pay attention and watch for weak supporters

" MAYBE WE SHOULD LISTEN TO THIS GUY ! "

Here are some tips for getting the most from face-to-face contacts with your legislator.

1. Make an appointment by phone. If you are a constituent, say so.

2. Arrive on time. Dress appropriately. Everything you do should be related to leaving a good impression on the legislator, the secretaries, and other staff. (Phoniness does not leave a good impression.)

3. Understand the time allotted for the appointment.

4. Identify yourself, including your professional position. If you are a constituent, say so. Mention any supportive connection to the legislator, particularly business, political, or social connections (for example, "Marian Turner encouraged me to meet with you").

5. Commend the legislator for current or previous actions you approve of.

6. Identify the bill you are discussing by name and number. If speaking to a particular point, refer to the page and line.

7. Provide the legislator with your one-page summary/fact sheet. It is often helpful to have an additional packet of information with a one-page "table of contents" that includes a sentence or two description of each piece in the packet. If you are suggesting new language, have that prepared to hand to the legislator. Give a copy of your fact sheet and informational packet to the legislative aide as well.

8. Present your case. (If you believe it is likely that you will be given the time to engage in actual discussion, you can save some of your points to address concerns you anticipate that the legislator will bring up. This conveys the notion that you are responsive.) Listen carefully to the legislator's concerns; don't minimize them. Be clear about your position and just what you want the legislator to do. Remain courteous. Avoid putting the legislator in a defensive position. That deepens resistance. See how you can become an information and support resource for the legislator.

9. Refer to the support of other legislators who hold similar views as the legislator to whom you are now speaking by using their comments. "Senator ____ made a good point about this. She said,...".

10. On occasion, arrange to meet with the legislator in the local district, particularly on your turf or at a site affected by the legislation. Have the legislator meet with a small group of three or four of you. Provide different "fronts" for the legislator to see (for example, client, educator, business leader, religious leader, or other person with a readily identifiable perspective). The members of the group should be carefully selected. They should clearly understand mutual roles, and each should be well prepared. You should have a lead presenter and someone prepared to manage the conversation.

11. Get a commitment if at all possible. The more publicly the commitment is made, the stronger it is likely to be. If you cannot get a commitment at this time, let the legislator know that his decision is important to you. Politely say that you will call after he has had time to give the matter more thought.

12. Thank the legislator, regardless of the outcome.

13. Notify your allies of the outcome.

14. Send a thank-you letter to the legislator. Provide answers to any questions that were raised, and tactfully reiterate one or two essential points.

Source: Some information drawn from the Center for Lobbying in the Public Interest (2007).

who may be wavering and need some additional attention.

Repeat the process in the second chamber. Essentially you must do the same things to pass your bill in the second chamber as you did in the first. If your internal team is stronger in the first chamber, see how they can assist you in your efforts to get internal support from the other chamber.

For the last time, *keep counting votes.*

Influence the composition of the conference committee. If a conference committee is needed, try to work with leadership to get members favorable to your position appointed.

Shore up support for the conference committee report. Acceptance of the conference report is normally a routine matter, but you may need to go back to certain legislators to explain the conference agreement and to confirm their support.

Lobby the governor. Members of the lobbying team and their constituents should make contact with the governor or governor's staff to urge that the bill be signed. Indirect methods and direct constituent contact could be employed as well. The type and degree of indirect methods will depend on the governor's position on the bill. Do not wait until the legislation has passed before making contact with the governor to begin conversation on the issue and determining the degree of support or opposition.

Organize an override effort if need be. This usually requires lots of direct lobbying by members of your internal and external teams, mobilization of constituent contact, and use of visible indirect methods.

Celebrate. It is important to have a victory event involving all key participants soon after the session ends.

Begin to monitor implementation. A new set of activities (outside the scope of this chapter) now needs to take place to influence the development of regulations and other procedures that will enable the new law to fulfill its promise.

Letter Writing

One of the most effective ways for you to get your voice heard is to write your legislator. Both e-mail and traditional letters will work. The more undecided a legislator is and the less controversial the issue, the greater the impact letters will have. Legislators who are more concerned about reelection are especially sensitive to letters from constituents. Post mail draws special attention from legislators because the writer of the letter has taken more effort than just making a call or sending an e-mail.

Here are a few tips that will give your words greater influence whether writing a letter or sending a message via e-mail.

- Consider having a letter writing party or potluck with members of your organization. Have people bring their own stationery. Supply some yourself. Have several different types available. Use different types of stamps. Letter writers should be instructed on how to prepare their letters, but the letters should be written in their own words. Do not use specific phrases.

- Bring letter writing materials to a meeting that has already been planned. Provide a handout describing the issue, a few points to mention in the letter, and addresses for legislators. By taking just 10 minutes or so of the meeting time, you can produce a bunch of letters, and participants will feel good about taking a concrete action to communicate with a legislator.

- Use personal letterhead or business stationery if possible.

- Because envelopes are usually thrown away, put your return address on the letter. Even your e-mailed letters should have your address and phone numbers. This is particularly important if you are a constituent.

- Letters should be timed for the greatest effect; for example, early in the session to build momentum or shortly before a vote on the bill.

- Do not send form letters. Use your own words. Avoid jargon and slogans.

- Identify the name and number of the bill, and state your reasons for writing; especially, relate issues to personal experiences. Show how the bill affects you, your family, your community, your clients, or your livelihood. Clearly identify yourself as a constituent if you are one. Mention the number of people you serve or represent.

- Open and close your letter with statements that establish rapport, such as "I know you are concerned about...."

- Ask the legislator to *do* something in the first or second paragraph. For example, ask the legislator to vote a certain way.

- Make sure your facts are accurate.

- Be reasonable. Don't ask for something that is outside the legislator's capability to provide.

- Don't use threats. Don't impugn the motives of those who oppose you.

- Thank the legislator if she has voted the "right" way on another issue.

- Focus on one issue per letter.

- Ask for a response.

- Write a thank-you letter if the legislator does what you requested.

Testifying

Your participation in legislative hearings gives legitimacy to your issue and your organization. It gets you on and in the record. It gives you access to a larger audience through media coverage of the hearing. It demonstrates visible action to your members, and it gives them an event in which they can take part. Your ability to turn out a crowd signals broad support for the measure, which will embolden those legislators thinking of supporting your position. Your testimony can provide supportive legislators with a rationale and justification for their actions. If your organization provides testimony in response to a written request from a legislative body (not from just one legislator) for technical advice, even on pending legislation, it is not considered a lobbying action that would affect your nonprofit status (Center for Lobbying in the Public Interest, 2009a).

Although testimony and demonstrations of constituent interest at public hearings may help a very few legislators make up their minds, rarely will it be effective in changing anyone's mind. Testifying, therefore, is a complement to more essential lobbying activities. It should not be the centerpiece of your efforts.

Coordinate your presentation with other members of your team and with other groups who support your position. Coordinate testimony with the committee chair if you are on friendly terms. Prime supporters on the committee with questions that will enable you to emphasize specific points.

Sponsors and some cosponsors should attend and give testimony. Often the sponsor will be the lead testifier. (The lead testifier usually summarizes the bill and its benefits.) Have a team of testifiers, each emphasizing different aspects of the bill. Each testifier represents a particular community or professional point of view: the taxpayer, the neighborhood leader, the direct beneficiary, the attorney, the economist, or whatever particular views the panel needs to hear.

To the extent possible, coordinate the order in which your testifiers will present. Consider how you want your argument to build. Understand that initial testifiers can stake out the dimensions of the debate, and they are more likely to get media coverage. Those who testify toward the end of the proceedings can counter arguments, reemphasize key points, and leave the last impressions.

Prepare two papers, one for submission for the committee's written record, and one for your presentation. Make sure that there is a one-page summary of key points for legislators.

Prepare your testimony by role-playing with friends or members of your team. Similar to preparing for an argument, someone should play the devil's advocate. Anticipate questions and prepare responses. Even plant questions with friendly legislators (Center for Lobbying in the Public Interest, 2009a). Avoid seeking last-minute suggestions; they will only confuse you.

Tailor your presentation to the legislators you most want to influence. Make distinct points using a combination of personal experiences and factual information. Things to touch on:

- Your interest in the bill, and how you arrived at your conclusions
- Who will benefit
- Who will be hurt by inaction
- Cost efficiency of the measure

Tie your message to dominant themes that are emerging in the legislative session (concern over crime, government waste, or other topics).

It is normal to be nervous. If it is troubling you, Richan (2006) suggested you say "I'm scared" to your mirror. You will find that that simple phrase releases a lot of tension. By not having to hide from your apprehension, you can more easily focus on the business at hand.

When making your presentation, begin with "Mister or Madam Chair." Then state your name, title, your agency or organization, and your position on the bill. Then state your case. Refer to the page and line numbers for specific comments. Keep your presentation to 5 or 7 minutes. Don't repeat previous testimony, or yourself. Avoid just reading your testimony; instead use more of a conversational approach.

When you have completed your presentation, ask for questions. When answering a question, first address the committee chair, then address the member asking the question.

Remain both courteous and direct. Convey the notion that committee members are reasonable individuals. Approach them in a way that emphasizes common interest. Don't argue with committee members, and don't attempt to humiliate any particular legislator. If an opponent questions your information, honestly try to answer the question and return to your main points.

If your opinion is questioned, restate the question in a manner that allows you to reiterate your basic position. If the questioner persists, it is proper to restate your basic position and state that you respect the fact that you each have different views of the matter and that you hope "we can agree to disagree."

If you do not know the answer to a question, say: "That's a good question, senator. I don't have that specific information before me. I will look into it and get you the information right away." Do not fake an answer! Be prompt in your follow-up.

Speak to the media as well as to the committee, using a few catch phrases.

After you have answered all the questions, thank the members of the committee for their interest and their attentiveness to your presentation, and ask them for their vote.

If you are clearly in a no-win situation, consider staying away from the hearing altogether to make a statement or to render the opposition's show a nonevent.

OTHER THINGS YOU SHOULD KNOW OR DO TO INCREASE YOUR EFFECTIVENESS

Your credibility is your greatest asset. Your credibility is based on three things:

- *You as a person.* Build trust. Never lie, mislead, threaten, or act in an arrogant or condescending manner. Don't promise what you cannot deliver. Keep confidential information to yourself. Don't back people into a corner. Don't ever say or write anything that you don't want attributed to you. Develop and use a sense of humor. Be courteous. Say thank you.

- *Your information.* Provide compelling specific facts and give them a face, showing how the situation affects real people. Don't exaggerate the truth or the situation. Double-check the accuracy of your information. If you don't know the answer to a question, promise to get the information. Follow up in a timely way to requests for information.

- *Your base of power.* Be able to mobilize constituents and quality contacts. Demonstrate an ability to use the media. Generate letters, e-mails, and phone calls in support of your position. Turn people out to legislative hearings. Generate workers for campaigns. If you can, generate dollars for campaigns.

Get known. Once legislators know you (or in some cases know about you), they will pay more attention to your calls, letters, and opinions. Get involved in political campaigns. Though a 501(c)(3) organization cannot be involved in political campaigns, you as a private citizen can most certainly make an impact this way. Attend legislative receptions. Send letters to newly elected officials introducing yourself and your organization and information on your issue. Attend and speak out at meetings with legislators. Invite officials to your agency or neighborhood; serve as a tour guide. Arrange to provide a briefing on issues.

Observe the body in action. Attend a few sessions or committee hearings. Keep your eyes open. Listen and learn. This will help you feel familiar with the environment before you begin taking action.

Understand the standard approach in deciding whom to lobby. Lobby supporters first, to alert them, activate them, and inoculate them from opposition arguments. *Lobby "undecideds" next,* preferably with support from their peers. *Do not lobby strong opponents.* You can use your time for more important things. You won't change their minds, and you may excite them into more vigorous opposition.

Get to know key staff people. Working with staff is not a waste of time. They may be more accessible than the elected official, and they may let you know how the official really sees things. Staff members often shape the lawmaker's perspective, and they sometimes develop a strong interest in the legislation they work on.

Acknowledge that there are few permanent friends and few permanent enemies. Don't alienate people, write them off forever, or take them for granted. Legislators are engaged in a number of battles. Past disagreements can be forgotten when building new alliances.

Understand the ways for keeping a bill alive. A bill can be resurrected as an amendment to another bill. A person who voted against the bill can ask to have it reconsidered. (You may use this as a planned tactic.) If your bill is in trouble, get it referred to a subcommittee for more work and more time to build support. Work with your supporters to get the subcommittee to convene. Recognize that the makeup of the subcommittee is important and that bills referred to subcommittee often disappear. Understand how to use the initiative and referendum procedures for your state.

Know your strengths and weaknesses. Avoid the tendency to underestimate your strengths and exaggerate your weaknesses. Be accurate in your assessment.

Don't grab personal credit. Allow legislators and, whenever possible, your organization to get the attention.

Recognize that legislators are overwhelmed with information. Don't assume or act as if your issue is the only one that matters. Assert your point while recognizing that the legislator has many other issues to think about. Determine how you will make your issue stand out.

Know your issue. For your own uses, prepare an issue brief, summarizing the history of the issue, noting the key players, organizing key facts and figures, and outlining arguments on both sides. This will empower you as you realize that you know far more about the topic than most of the people with whom you will be dealing.

Prepare fact sheets. Provide legislators, media people, and others with a one-page summary of your issue. Describe the costs and the impact of responding to or ignoring the issue, especially how this would affect the common voter. Provide opposing points of view and counter them. You may want to link your issue to the issues or themes that have come to dominate the legislative session. Include your name, your organization's name, and a phone number, fax, e-mail, and postal address where you can be reached.

Get to know other lobbyists. Particularly get to know like-minded lobbyists. Lobbyists, especially those with common interests, do meet regularly. Become part of such a group. Lobbyists help each other out in a variety of ways, not the least of which is with an exchange of information.

Get to know your opposition. Find out who is opposed to you and why. Talk to them. Generally, you will do this outside of the legislative session. You can better understand their frame of reference and information. You may even discover that their opposition is based on misperception or misunderstanding, a situation you can remedy.

Understand the legislators' screens. Legislators must contend with a huge number of decisions. In determining how to approach an issue, they see how it fits with their own philosophy and values, their constituents' or district's concerns, their party leadership or caucus positions, advocacy groups with which they identify, and fellow legislators' opinions. When you are working with legislators, see how they define the situation under discussion. On what aspects do they focus? What do they think they know about it? How does it fit with their value system?

Expect some loss of support. The more controversial your issue, the more likely a few of your supporters will get a little weak in the knees. You will lose a few votes. Be psychologically prepared for this.

Anticipate the likelihood of compromises. Rarely will you get everything you want. You may understand this as you begin the process, but when faced with the need to agree to less than you want, or to make a trade-off, you may feel real disappointment. Be clear about what you have to have—and what you cannot have. Concessions can help you in the long run or limit the possibility of future negotiation. Once the deal has been struck, are you in a better position to move forward, or will you remain mired at this point? When faced with a problem, see if you can respond by bringing new ideas to the table rather than by retreating on important concerns.

At what point is not making a deal a better choice? Remember to identify your BATNA (best alternative to negotiated agreement) before you begin negotiations. The need to make compromises

CAPTURING CONCEPTS
Ethics and Legislative Action

To lead the way toward a more open and democratic process of civic engagement, a group of public-interest advocates have proposed a set of ethical principles to guide our work.

The first principle is that public-interest lobbying must add civic value: It should involve a diverse spectrum of voices, take a broad and long-term view, and act to strengthen the public trust, not to undermine it. Alexis de Tocqueville observed in the 1830s that voluntary associations are ideally suited to bring relevant and diverse voices to the policy table.

Second, public-interest lobbying must be inclusive, engaging the community and particularly those most affected by the public policy being advocated. Government of the people, by the people, and for the people only works if the people are centrally involved....

Third, smart and ethical lobbying must be credible, trustworthy, and based on reliable facts, figures, and studies. That means obeying all laws and regulations, providing objective information without any intent to mislead, and keeping promises....

Finally, public-interest lobbying must be multifaceted and adaptive, using every available advocacy tool and taking educated risks as needed. It always must seek to serve the public good.

None of this makes us better than lobbyists serving for-profit clients, just different.

SOURCE: Cohen & Ottinger (2008, p. 32).

---

tests the relationships in an organization. Ideological purists may bang heads against dispassionate pragmatists. Deals will serve some interests better than others. Discuss how you will handle compromises before you are faced with them. Clarify who among you is empowered to make agreements with legislators.

From a strategic standpoint, try to lock your opponent into an uncompromising extreme position. Your position will look much more attractive to legislators who usually endeavor to claim the high middle ground.

Don't accept a bad bill just to get "something." Other interests may be making deals on the bill at the same time you are. Be aware of the fact that your original piece of legislation may end up with so many amendments that you hardly recognize it. If this occurs, "your" bill may no longer effectively accomplish its intended purpose. Be prepared to withdraw your support from the legislation or even act to prevent its passage in the event that changes are more harmful than helpful.

Be persistent. Know that it may take a few years before a legislative proposal becomes a law. Each session you may develop support that you can build on in subsequent sessions. Your continued attention generates greater understanding and acceptance of the idea, particularly if it is given organized support from key constituencies.

Create a responsive structure. Your organization will need to respond quickly to legislative events. Develop mechanisms for rapid decision making. Notify allies immediately of any changes, especially changes in the team's position on any point.

Monitor your messages, your relationships, and your egos. Everyone on your team should be communicating identical positions to legislators. Be very careful not to undermine yourselves by sending conflicting messages. Pay close attention to group maintenance issues, and never let disagreements among yourselves be known to anyone outside the team. Internal bickering that becomes public will seriously weaken your effort. Do not make yourself look good at the expense of any team member. This is a very serious issue. Team members should try to identify in advance how this may occur and how to guard against it.

Learn how to kill bad bills. Killing bills is easier than passing them. By reviewing the legislative process, you can see that the bill must cross many hurdles before it finally reaches the governor's desk. You can trip it up at many different points.

Use delaying tactics so there won't be enough time left in the session to pass it. Get the bill referred to a subcommittee that has difficulty meeting and agreeing. Have your legislators ask for staff to do time-consuming research on the bill. Temporarily remove the bill from the committee agenda. (These and other delaying tactics are more likely to be successful if the bill does not have a sufficient number of strong supporters.) Get the bill referred to a committee chaired by one of your supporters who can use the prerogatives of the chair to bury the bill. Amend the bill to death. Create confusion by raising doubts about its ultimate costs, its question-

able legality, its consequences for a particular group of citizens. (Legislators don't want to be seen advancing a questionable proposition, one that just might do more harm than good.) Generate adverse media attention and public displays of constituent opposition. (It is easier to mobilize people against an idea than for one.) Legislators who are in powerful positions can use their influence to make passage of the bill costly to their colleagues supporting it.

Realize, of course, that all these tactics can be used against your pet bills as well.

SOME FINAL CONSIDERATIONS

Perhaps you can understand the accuracy of public interest lobbyist Mike Pertschuk's (1986) description of members of his profession. "Public interest lobbyists," he said, "perform prodigious feats: as coalition builders—builders of mutual trust, confidence, sustained activity—as social psychologists of victory. They are strategists, parliamentary wizards, ragpickers of intelligence, networkers of knowledge, accurate head counters, deployers of experts, media mavens, modulators of intemperance.... They are the physical embodiment of watchful constituencies.... To their younger colleagues they are teachers. And

they teach not only the needs and the skills, but the joys of political engagement" (p. 24).

You will accomplish something significant in the process, improving the lives of many, many people who may have no idea of the work you have done. Your confidence and moxie will grow with your awareness of the process, your preparation, and your experience. In fact, it can grow dramatically. You will quickly pick up on the legislative culture, the game, the methods, and the key players. The activity can be pretty heady and contagious. You might get hooked.

THE HEARING

Members of the Health Committee have begun drifting into the hearing room. A few committee staff have already arrived. The small, neat stacks of papers they have built indicate that today's agenda will be full, but not frenetic. It is still fairly early in the session—before this year's promise of an expeditious and orderly completion of the legislature's work becomes the butt of yet another session's jokes. Soon they will be joined by Senator Jan Cindrich, the committee chair, and most of the other members of the committee. Today the usual number of reporters will be increased by the attendance of a few scribes from several small, rural papers. A few other rural weeklies have requested the stringers from the Capitol press corps to cover the action

on Senate Bill 1142. A photographer from Channel 7 is setting up his camera. A handful of onlookers, some intending to testify on today's items, a class of fifth-graders from a local school, and three well-heeled lobbyists complete the collection.

Over the past few weeks, Roseann Nicoletti has attended hearings to see the Health Committee in action. Those observations have helped her get a better look at how the system works. Today she fidgets in her seat. Today is for real. Looking at Dr. Jane McConnell seated to her left she feels some reassurance. Roseann is pleased that she was able to arrange for a number of people to testify on behalf of Senate Bill 1142, the Rural Prenatal Care bill. She knows that each person is well prepared to testify, and each has a specific viewpoint that the committee should hear. She hopes the work she put into developing this testimony will sway a few votes. She has heard that a number of the senators aren't much in the mood for spending money for prenatal care as the state's health care and education bills continue to mount. They are looking to cut, not add. Though she isn't quite certain who these idiots are, she is certain that if Dr. McConnell's testimony doesn't change their minds, Olivia Arvizu's story will. Olivia, a shy, attractive young woman, will tell the committee of a mother's personal anguish watching her tiny little girl struggle for life in a neonatal intensive care unit. This anguish could have been avoided if Olivia had been able to see a doctor before Raquel was born. She was lucky to have been in the city visiting her cousin when she went into labor. The hospital closest to her hometown would not have been equipped to save Raquel's life.

Roseann catches the eye of Monica Miranda, another member of The Children Need Us Now Alliance, and motions her over. Several alliance members have provided individuals for the testifying team. Though none of the members of the coalition's steering committee had ever done any lobbying, they knew enough to get an early start. Months before the session was to begin, they met with Senator Cindrich and began working on their plan to establish prenatal care centers in underserved areas. Realizing that the legislature would never fund a full network, they decided to concentrate on nonurban areas. Traditionally conservative legislators from the rural districts would probably support the idea to deliver some services to their constituents.

The comprehensive research they have done has clearly demonstrated the need for these services, and they have many supporters in key districts ready to be mobilized.

"Did you talk to Andy Wooten?" Monica whispers. "You won't believe this, Roseann, but I saw Senator Marulo this morning, and he told me that Andy wants to amend the bill to include two centers in urban areas! Do you think we can figure out just which urban areas he's talking about? Maybe ones where his agency might have an office? What a coincidence!

"This really burns me. We went through all this 2 months ago when we decided our strategy, and now Andy goes ahead and makes changes on his own. Don't worry, I told Senator Marulo that we would be satisfied with establishing centers in the rural areas this year. We'll worry about other areas at another time."

Roseann shakes her head. "To tell you the truth, Monica, I'm not all that surprised. I had a feeling he didn't really agree with this approach. Maybe we should talk to Senator Cindrich about it. We probably should be talking to her pretty soon anyway."

"Let's discuss all that later, okay? Right now I'm too preoccupied. This hearing is the main chance we have to make our point, and I want to make sure everything goes okay. I think I'll go over and talk to Randy Damon. I'm glad the Messenger sent him up here to cover the story. I see you got a few papers here too. Good work."

As Roseann walks over to talk to Randy, Monica wonders if she really has anything new to tell him or if she just needs something better to do before the hearing starts. They have given all the newspapers the same packet of information they sent to the senators. Fifteen pages of well-documented reasons this bill is needed and what it can accomplish should convince even those who never thought of this matter before.

Monica feels proud of the work they have done. Three months ago she was sitting in an office complaining. Three months ago she didn't even know the name of her state senator. Three months ago she had never written a letter to an elected official. Today she's here at the Capitol. Today she will mail more than a hundred letters that Alliance members have generated in support of S.B. 1142. Today she and Roseann will have lunch with April Jefferson and Brad Edgers, two veteran lobbyists who have offered to give the Alliance some tips. Today she is amazed at how much she has learned and the people she has met. Today, not for the first time, she noticed she's enjoying all this.

The sound of the gavel meets Senator Cindrich's voice, bringing the meeting to order.

The hearing has begun.

REFLECTION QUESTIONS

1. If there are no major changes in the way the change effort is being conducted, how is this story likely to end?

2. What information or assumptions led you to this conclusion?

3. If you were Roseann Nicoletti or Monica Miranda, what would you have done differently? What would you have done the same?

4. What particular steps would you take at this point to enhance the prospects for success?

GROUP ACTIVITY: TIME TO VISIT A LEGISLATOR

In this exercise, your Lobbying team of two members will be meeting with a Legislator, who is an influential member of a committee that will be considering a piece of legislation, and his Aide.

1. Divide into groups of four and choose two team members to be the Lobbying team and two to act as a Legislator/Aide team. (2 minutes)

2. Have the whole team decide on an issue that members of the Lobbying team know something about and can talk about with some degree of confidence. Once you have selected the issue, determine whether the Legislator is moderately interested and supportive or strongly interested and supportive. (3 minutes)

3. Both teams prepare for the Lobbying team to visit with the Legislator and his Aide to discuss the issue. The Lobbying team knows that the legislator has received a lot of pressure from those opposed to their position. The Legislator hasn't made up his mind on the issue or what he will do even if he ends up supporting the Lobbying team's position. The Legislator is willing to listen to the Lobbying team with an open mind, but he has received a lot of pressure from those opposed to the position of the Lobbying team, and this makes him kind of nervous. (7–10 minutes)

- The Lobbying team considers what information it wants to provide and what it wants the Legislator to do. Point out the support that exists for your position and what the Legislator can reasonably expect from that support. You can make some simple props that represent things like a fact sheet or a brochure.

- The Legislator/Aide team prepares for the Lobbying team's visit by anticipating questions, weighing difficulties, and considering responses. What do the opponents of the Lobbying team's position have to say about this issue? You will want to bring up some of those points during the visit.

4. The Lobbying team and the Legislator/Aide team meet for the visit and discuss their concerns. (7–10 minutes)

5. The Lobbying team and the Legislator/Aide team each holds a brief, separate discussion about how the meeting went and identifies two things the Lobbying team did well and two things they could improve upon. (3 minutes)

6. All four team members meet and discuss the experience, including what went well and what could be improved. (5 minutes)

7. The group offers one important insight from their experience to the larger group. (2 minutes)

HELPFUL WEBSITES

Links to the organizations briefly described here are on the companion website at www.cengage.com/humansvcs/homan

First Gov. Operated by the U.S. General Services Administration and describing itself as "your first click to the U.S. Government," this is the granddaddy of all federal government sites, providing a gateway to Congress and federal agencies as well as virtual warehouses of statistics and other information. You can do state searches on this site as well by starting in the Government Agencies section.

National Conference of State Legislatures. This is your door to state legislative action, providing access to information on state legislative policy issues, literally from A to Z, and a view of political developments. Here you will find a directory of all state legislatures.

Alliance for Justice. This is a national association of environmental, civil rights, mental health, women's, children's, and consumer advocacy organizations. Working to strengthen the voice of the nonprofit sector in important public policy debates, this organization provides tax-exempt organizations with a better understanding of the laws that govern their participation in the policy process. Alliance for Justice also provides one-on-one technical assistance to nonprofits via phone and e-mail. Their publications and fact sheets in both Spanish and English, found under the For Nonprofits and Foundations tab, will give you helpful guidance on advocacy and lobbying. Their Nonprofit Advocacy Project and their Nonprofit & Foundatioon Advocacy blog are particularly useful.

Independent Sector. This is a coalition of more than 600 organizations, many of whom are foundations or corporate giving programs. It promotes effective, well-informed practice and mobilizes its members to promote a vision of a just and inclusive society with effective institutions and vibrant communities. Here you will find updated information about lobbying regulations along with tips on lobbying.

Center for Lobbying in the Public Interest.
Founded in 1998 as a project of the Independent Sector, the Center for Lobbying in the Public Interest (CLPI) is now a national nonprofit

organization that helps charitable organizations increase their effectiveness and impact through advocacy. A wealth of practical information on lobbying strategies and regulations, including tutorials and "how to" resources, is available here under their Nuts and Bolts tab. They have produced some excellent publications on lobbying, and a few are available free as pdf downloads.

League of Women Voters. The grandmama of all sites for democratic action, the league provides numerous publications on political organization and advocacy. You will find valuable, nonpartisan information on issues affecting democracy, and you can connect with your local league affiliate, who will have timely and relevant information on your state and local political scene.

NPAction. This is an online resource that provides tools and information for nonprofit advocacy. It provides a constantly updated mix of information and tools, drawn from the expertise of organizations and seasoned advocates across a wide range of advocacy activities and policy disciplines, to encourage greater participation by nonprofits in the policy arena. You will find lots of good "how to" information on lobbying. It is a project of OMB Watch, a nonprofit research and advocacy organization committed to government transparency and citizen participation in democracy. You may want to visit the OMB site as well.

United States Government Office of Special Counsel. Here you will find a review of Hatch Act provisions, which affect political involvement of public employees and some employees of private organizations.

National Association of Social Workers. The advocacy section provides good information on a range of issues. There you will also find CapWiz, which will help you prepare and send e-mails or letters directly to your congressional representatives.

References

Abbe, M. A. (2000, July–August). The roots of minority giving. *Case Currents*, 36–43.

Acevdo-Garcia, D., Osypuk, T. L., McArdle, N., & Williams, D. R. (2008). *Health Affairs, 27*(2), 321–333.

Adams, D. L. (1995). *Health issues for women of color: A cultural diversity perspective.* Thousand Oaks, CA: Sage.

Adom, N., & Paniagua, T. (2009). *Bead to feed fundraising.* Retrieved from www.nafofa.org/gpage3.html

Ahern, T., & Joyaux, S. (2008). *Keep your donors: The guide to better communication and stronger relationships.* Hoboken, NJ: Wiley.

Ahlbrandt, R. S., Jr., & Cunningham, J. V. (1979). *A new public policy for neighborhood preservation.* New York: Praeger.

Alban Institute. (2007). *Appreciative inquiry helps beachside church.* Retrieved from www.alban.org/conversation.aspx?id=6058

Alesina, A., & Glaeser, E. L. (2004). *Fighting poverty in the US and Europe: A world of difference.* New York: Oxford University Press.

Alinsky, S. D. (1972). *Rules for radicals: A pragmatic primer for realistic radicals.* New York: Random House.

Alle-Corliss, L., & Alle-Corliss, R. (2009). *Group work: A practical guide to developing groups in agency settings.* Hoboken, NJ: Wiley.

Allen, C., Diaz, P. A., Duong, T., Gallo, M. M., Moreno, A., & Snee, J. (2002). *Grantmaking docket.* New York: Funding Exchange.

Allen, H., & Regional Youth Project. (1981). *The bread game.* San Francisco, CA: Glide Publications.

Allen, J. (2000). *Event planning: The ultimate guide to successful meetings, corporate events, fundraising galas, conferences, conventions, incentives and other special events.* Toronto, Canada: Wiley.

Allen, S. (1997). Benefit event fundamentals. In J. M. Greenfield (Ed.), *The nonprofit handbook: Fund raising* (2nd ed., pp. 278–298). New York: Wiley.

Allen, S. (2001a). Benefit event fundamentals. In J. M. Greenfield (Ed.), *The nonprofit handbook: Fund raising* (3rd ed., pp. 480–499). New York: Wiley.

Allen, S. (2001b). Cause-related marketing and sponsorship. In J. M. Greenfield (Ed.), *The nonprofit handbook: Fund raising* (3rd ed., pp. 648–665). New York: Wiley.

Alliance for Justice. (2003). *Worry-free lobbying for nonprofits: How to use the 501(h) election to maximize effectiveness: A handbook.* Retrieved from www.afj.org/assets/resources/resources2/Worry-Free-Lobbying-for-Nonprofits.pdf

Alliance for Justice. (2005). *When does your activity become lobbying? What your nonprofit needs to know.* Retrieved from www.spannj.org/keychanges/publicpolicy_materials09/prepworkcounts.pdf

Alliance for Justice. (2006, June 19). *Technical assistance question of the week.* Retrieved from http://allianceforjustice.org/blog/2006/06/technical-assistance-question-of-week_19.html

Alliance for Justice. (2007). *About advocacy: Lobbying.* Retrieved from www.afj.org/for-nonprofits-foundations/resources-and-publications/about-advocacy-lobbying.html

Alvarez, A. R., & Gutiérrez, L. M. (2001). Choosing to do participatory research: An example and issues of fit to consider. *Journal of Community Practice, 9*(1), 1–20.

American Bar Association. (2000, Spring). Statement by the Exempt Organization's Committee of the Section of Taxation of the American Bar Association. *American Bar Association Newsletter*, p. 32.

American Counseling Association. (2005). *ACA code of ethics.* Alexandria, VA: Author.

Amidei, N. (1987). How to be an advocate in bad times. In F. M. Cox, J. L. Erlich, J. Rothman, & J. E. Tropman (Eds.), *Strategies of community organization: Macro practice* (4th ed., pp. 106–114). Itasca, IL: Peacock.

Amiel, A. (2001). Community organizing and neighborhood planning in Jerusalem: A profile of Avner Amiel. In J. Forester, R. Fischler, & D. Shmueli (Eds.), *Israeli planners and designers: Profiles of community builders.* Albany, NY: State University of New York Press.

Amulya, J. (2004). *What is reflective practice?* Center for Reflective Community Practice: Massachusetts Institute of Technology. Retrieved from www.itslifejimbutnotasweknowit.org.uk/files/whatis reflectivepractice.pdf

Anderson, R. E., Carter, I., & Lowe, G. R. (1999). *Human behavior in the social environment: A social systems approach.* (5th ed.). Hawthorne, NY: Aldine de Gruyter.

Anderson, S. G., & Gryzlak, B. M. (2002). Social work advocacy in the post-TANF environment: Lessons from the early TANF research studies. *Social Work, 47* (3), 301–314.

Anderson, P., Homan, M., & Lawson, R. (2001). Transforming the mission of public schools. In T. McClam, & M. Woodside (Eds.), *Human service challenges in the 21st century.* (pp. 57–76). Bellingham, WA: Council for Standards in Human Service Education.

Anft, M. (2001, October 18). Raising money with sense and sensibility: Mississippi conference examines strategies for courting and keeping minority donors. *Chronicle of Philanthropy, 14,* 21–23.

Annie, E. Casey publication. (2002). *Learning from the Journey: Reflections on the Rebuilding Communities Initiative.* Baltimore, MD: Annie E. Casey.

Annie, E., & Casey Foundation. (2006). *State fact sheets on the health and well-being of America's children.* Retrieved from http://www.aecf.org/MajorInitiatives/KIDSCOUNT/ StateFactSheets.aspx

Arches, J. L. (1997). Burnout and socialization. *Journal of Progressive Human Services, 8*(2), 51–62.

Ardman, H., & Ardman, P. (1980). *The woman's day book of fund raising.* New York: St. Martin's Press.

Arizona Daily Star Editors. (1988). *Media handbook.* Tucson, AZ: Arizona Daily Star.

Arrington, P. (2008). *Stress at work: How do social workers cope?* NASW membership workforce study. Washington, DC: National Association of Social Workers.

Aspen Institute. (1999). *Introduction to CCI's.* Retrieved from www.commbuild.org/html_pages/introtoccis.htm

Associated Press. (2002a, July 16). Nigerian women, oil facility reach pact. *Arizona Daily Star,* p. A6.

Associated Press. (2002b, July 26). Protesters win jobs, loans from oil firm. *Arizona Daily Star,* p. A16.

Associated Press. (2002c, July 15). Women threaten shaming gesture. *Arizona Daily Star,* p. A7.

Associated Press (2007, February 10). Hospital van dumps paraplegic on skid row. *Arizona Daily Star,* p. A13.

Association of Fundraising Professionals. (2008). *Online fundraising in 2008: Can we blink yet?* Retrieved from www.afpnet.org/ka/ka-3.cfm?content_item_id= 24437&folder_id=893.

Attanandana, T., Yost, R., & Verapattananirund, P. (2007). Empowering farmer leaders to acquire and practice site-specific nutrient management technology. *Journal of Sustainable Agriculture, 30*(1), 87–104.

Baird, J. A. (1997, March). The three Rs of fund raising. *Fund Raising Management,* 14–17.

Baker, W., Cross, R., & Wooten, M. (2003). Positive organizational network analysis and energizing relationships. In K. S. Cameron, J. E. Dutton, & R. E. Quinn (Eds.), *Positive organizational scholarship.* (pp. 328–342). San Francisco: Barrett-Koehler.

Barker, R. L. (1999). *The social work dictionary.* (4th ed.). Washington, DC: NASW Press.

Barnes, D. (1989). Direct mail trends you need to know about. *National Fund Raiser, 15*(12).

Bartlett, H. M. (1958, April). Toward clarification and improvement of social work practice. *Social Work, 3,* 5–8.

Baso, Z. A. (2000). *Managing assets, empowering humans.* Global Network electronic conference. Retrieved from http://docs.google.com/viewer?a=v&q=cache: ZlpWB5w7rmAJ:www.ciaonet.org/wps/anz01/anz01. pdf+Managing+assets,+empowering+humans&hl=en& gl=us&pid=bl&srcid=ADGEESi3q_PxKmvz7sB4v3 Nvwzo5nLiQXEt7IlvwxoYyTBv2QTMXpbUx8 AyhcfZagAsmrgyBVWXkBl04ec4Tm1NVpvTyA4 vPIZB1s1aiRP8vX480brNMKyNiBUAdmLXZbDZ- uJ5FlTOo&sig=AHIEtbTuxwF5fXbT-B5M2X6MR skPBwCn9Q

Bearman, J. E. (2007). *More giving together: The growth and impact of giving circles and shared giving.* Washington, DC: Forum of Regional Associations of Grantmakers.

Beckwith, D. (2004). Memberships and dues. In L. Staple (Ed.), *Roots to power: A manual for grassroots organizing.* (2nd ed., pp. 331–334). Westport, CT: Praeger.

Belasco, J. A. (1990). *Teaching the elephant to dance: Empowering change in your organization.* New York: Crown.

Benne, K. D. (1985). The current state of planned changing in persons, groups, communities, and societies. In W. G. Bennis, K. D. Benne, & R. C. Chin (Eds.), *The planning of change.* (4th ed., pp. 77–81). New York: Holt, Rinehart & Winston.

Berg, L. (1999, July). *Organizing to win.* Arizona Education Association leaders' conference, Litchfield, AZ.

Berkman, C. S., & Zinberg, G. (1997). Homophobia and heterosexism in social workers. *Social Work*, 42(4), 332.

Berkowitz, W. R. (1982). *Community impact: Creating grass-roots change in hard times*. Cambridge, MA: Schenkman.

Bermant, G., & Warwick, D. P. (1985). The ethics of social intervention: Power, freedom, and accountability. In W. G. Bennis, K. D. Benne, & R. Chin (Eds.), *The planning of change*. (4th ed., pp. 449–470). New York: Holt, Rinehart & Winston.

Bernard, J. (1972). Community: Community disorganization. In D. Sills (Ed.), *International encyclopedia of the social sciences* (Vol. 3). New York: Free Press.

Bernstein, J., McNichol, E., & Lyons, K. (2006). *Pulling apart: A state-by-state analysis of income trends*. Washington, DC: Center on Budget and Policy Priorities and Economic Policy Institute.

Berry, M. L. (1999). Native-American philanthropy: Expanding social participation and self-determination in philanthropy. In Council on Foundations (Ed.), *Cultures of caring: Philanthropy in diverse American communities*. (pp. 29–106). Washington, DC: Council on Foundations.

Bess, K. D., Prilleltensky, I., Perkins, D. D., & Collins, L. V. (2009). Participatory organizational change in community-based health and human services: From tokenism to political engagement. *American Journal of Community Psychology*, 43(1/2), 134–148.

Bessette, G. (2004). *Involving the community: A guide to participatory development communication*. Ottawa, Canada: International Development Research Centre.

Bishop, A. (2002). *Becoming an ally: Breaking the cycle of oppression*. (2nd ed.). Halifax, Nova Scotia, Canada: Fernwood.

Bishop, C. H. (2001). *Making change one person at a time: Assessing change capacity within your organization*. New York: AMACOM.

Blood, S. K. (2001). *Cultural knowledge transforms community*. [White paper]. Rogers, MN: Madii Institute.

Blumenfeld, E., & Alpern, L. (1986). *The smile connection: How to use humor in dealing with people*. New York: Prentice-Hall.

Boase, J., Horrigan, J.B, Wellman, B., & Rainie, L. (2006). *The strength of Internet ties: The Internet and email aid users in maintaining their social networks and provide pathways to help when people face big decisions*. Washington, DC: Pew Internet & American Life Project.

Boney, R. (2008). Corporate donors adjust to economic slump. *Philanthropy Journal*. Retrieved from www.philanthropyjournal.org/resources/special-reports/corporate-giving/corporate-donors-adjust-economic-slump

Bonk, K., Tynes, E., Griggs, H., & Sparks, P. (2008). *Strategic communications for nonprofits: A step-by-step guide to working with the media*. (2nd ed.). San Francisco, CA: Jossey-Bass.

Booth, H., & Max, S. (1977). *Direct action organizing—Strategy planning*. Chicago: Midwest Academy.

Bourdieu, P. (1986). The forms of capital. In J. G. Richardson (Ed.), *Handbook of theory and research for the sociology of education*. (pp. 241–258). New York: Greenwood Press.

Brager, G., & Holloway, S. (1977). A process model for changing organizations from within. *Administration in Social Work*, 1(4), 349–358.

Brager, G., & Holloway, S. (1978). *Changing human service organizations: Politics and practice*. New York: Free Press.

Brakeley, G. A., Jr. (1997). Major gifts from individuals. In J. M. Greenfield (Ed.), *The nonprofit handbook: Fund raising*. (2nd ed., pp. 422–441). New York: Wiley.

Bratt, R. G. (1987). Dilemmas of community-based housing. *Policy Studies Journal*, 16(2), 324–334.

Breckenfeld, G. (1960). Chicago: Back of the yards. In M. Millspaugh, G. Breckenfeld, & M. L. Colean (Eds.), *The human side of urban renewal*. (pp. 179–219). New York: Ives Washburn.

Breiteneicher, J., & Hohler, B. (1993). *Quest for funds revisited: A fund-raising starter kit*. Washington, DC: National Trust for Historic Preservation.

Brennock, M. (2005, April 15). Taoiseach announces task force to promote citizen participation. *Irish Times*.

Brentlinger, M. E., & Weiss, J. M. (1987). *The ultimate benefit book*. Cleveland, OH: Octavia Press.

Breton, M. (1994). On the meaning of empowerment and empowerment-oriented social work practice. *Social Work with Groups*, 17(3), 23–37.

Briggs, C. L., & Mantini-Briggs, C. (2009). Confronting health disparities: Latin American social medicine in Venezuela. *American Journal of Public Health*, 99(3), 549–555.

Brill, N. (1998). *Working with people: The helping process*. (6th ed.). New York: Longman.

Brill, N., & Levine, J. (2005). *Working with people, the helping process*. (8th ed.). Boston, MA: Pearson, Allyn & Bacon.

Brookfield, S. D. (2000). Transformative learning as ideology critique. In J. Mezirow & Associates (eds.), *Learning as transformation: Critical perspectives on a theory in progress*. San Francisco, CA: Jossey-Bass.

Brown, D. R., Hernandez, A., Saint-Jean, G., Evans, S., Tafari, I., & Brewster, L. G., Celestin, M. J., et al. (2008). A participatory action research pilot study of urban health disparities using rapid assessment response and evaluation. *American Journal of Public Health*, 98(1), 28–38.

Brown, L. N. (1991). *Groups for growth and change*. New York: Longman.

Brown, P., Colombo, M., & Hughes, D. M. (2009). Foundation readiness in community transformation: Learning in real time. *The Foundation Review*, 1(1), 125–134.

Brown, S., Mason, C. A., Lombard, J. L., Martinez, F., Plater-Zyberk, E., Spokane, A. R., Newman, F., Pantin, H., & Szapocznik, J. (2009). The relationship of built environment to perceived social support and psychological distress in Hispanic elders: The role of "eyes on the street." *Journals of Gerontology Series B: Psychological Sciences & Social Services, 64B*(2), 234–246.

Browning, B. (2000). *Granturiting for dummies.* New York: Hungry Minds.

Browning, B. (2008). *Perfect phrases for writing grant proposals.* New York: McGraw-Hill.

Browning, B. (2009). *Granturiting for dummies.* (3rd ed.). Hoboken, NJ: Wiley.

Brueggemann, W. G. (2006). *The practice of macro social work.* (3rd ed.). Belmont, CA: Brooks/Cole, Cengage Learning.

Bryan, B. (2008). *Diversity in philanthropy: A comprehensive bibliography of resources related to diversity within the philanthropic and nonprofit sectors.* New York: The Foundation Center.

Bryan, T. (2005, December 1–3). *Community-based participatory research* [SWI & OCSHCN Summit]. Scottsdale, AZ: Southwest Institute for Families and Children with Special Needs.

Bryan, T., & Sullivan-Burstein, K. (1998). Teacher-selected strategies for improving homework completion. *Remedial and Special Education, 19*(5), 263–275.

Bryan, W. L. (1980). Preventing burnout in the public interest community. *The Northern Rockies Action Group Papers, 3*(3), 2.

Buchholz, D. (2005). IDA survey provides glimpse into growing field. *Assets, 1,* 1 & 11.

Buckholtz, A. (2001). *Media maps: Charting a media relations strategy.* Washington, DC: Association of Research Libraries.

Building Movement Project. (n.d.). *Features of movement capacity building for nonprofits.* New York: Author.

Burdette, H. L., Wadden, T. A., & Whitaker, R. C. (2006). Neighborhood safety, collective efficacy, and obesity in women with young children. *Obesity, 14,* 518–525.

Bureau of Labor Statistics. (2009a). *Commissioner's statement on the employment situation* [News release]. Retrieved from http://www.bls.gov/schedule/archives/jec_nr.htm.

Bureau of Labor Statistics. (2009b). *Consumer price index summary: March 2009.* Retrieved from www.bls.gov/news.release/cpi.nr0.htm

Bureau of Labor Statistics. (2009c). *Employment situation summary: March 2009.* Retrieved from www.bls.gov/news.release/empsit.nr0.htm

Bureau of Labor Statistics. (2009d). *Volunteering in the United States 2008.* [USDL 09-0078 Media Release January 23]. Retrieved from www.bls.gov/news.release/pdf/volun.pdf

Burghardt, S. (1982). *Organizing for community action.* Newbury Park, CA: Sage.

Burke, J., & Prater, C. A. (2000). *I'll grant you that: A step-by-step guide to finding funds, designing winning projects, writing powerful grant proposals.* Portsmouth, NH: Heinemann.

Burkey, S. (1993). *People first: A guide to self-reliant, participatory rural development.* London: Zed Books.

Burlingame, D. F. (2001). Corporate fund raising. In J. M. Greenfield (Ed.)? *The nonprofit handbook: Fund raising.* (3rd ed., pp. 638–647). New York: Wiley.

Burstein, K., Bryan, T., & Chao, P. (2005). Promoting self-determination skills among youth with special health needs using participatory action research. *Journal of Development and Physical Disabilities, 17*(2), 185–201.

Burt, M. R., & Pittman, K. J. (1985). *Testing the social safety net.* Washington, DC: Urban Institute Press.

Bush, N. J. (2009). Compassion fatigue: Are you at risk? *Oncology Nursing Forum, 36*(1), 24–28.

Bushe, G. R. (2001). Five theories of change embedded in appreciative inquiry. In D. L. Cooperrider, P. F. Sorensen Jr., D. Whitney, & T. F. Yager (Eds.), Appreciative inquiry: An emerging direction for organizational development. (pp. 117–127). Champaign, IL: Stipes.

Bushe, G. R. (2007). Appreciative inquiry is not (just) about the positive. *OD Practitioner, 39*(4), 30–35.

Buzan, T., & Buzan, B. (1993). *The mind map book: How to use radiant thinking to maximize your brain's untapped potential.* New York: Plume Books.

Cabral, A. (1982). Unity and struggle. In I. M. Wallerstein, & A. De Branganca (Eds.), *African liberation reader: Documents of the National Liberation Movements: The anatomy of colonialism* (Vol. 2). London: Zed Books.

Campus Compact. (2008). *2007 service statistics: Highlights and trends of Campus Compact's annual membership survey.* Providence, RI: Author.

Capek, M. E., & Mead, M. (2006). *Effective philanthropy: Organizational success through deep diversity and gender equality.* Cambridge, MA: MIT Press.

Carle, N. (2006, August). From across the pond: Continuing the conversation: Discovering the soul of our community. *Community Connecting: Valuing People with Learning Disabilities, 6.*

Case, A. C., & Katz, L. F. (1991). *The company you keep: The effects of family and neighborhood on disadvantaged youths.* Cambridge, MA: National Bureau of Economic Research.

Cavanaugh, J. (1980). Program and resource development. In R. L. Clifton, & A. M. Dahms (Eds.), *Grassroots administration: A handbook for staff and directors of small community-based social-service organizations.* (pp. 13–24). Belmont, CA: Brooks/Cole, Cengage Learning.

Cavicchio, C., & Torok, J. (2008). The 2008 Corporate Contributions Report. New York, NY: The Conference Board.

Center for Effective Collaboration and Practice. (2006). *How does cultural competency differ from cultural sensitivity/awareness?* Retrieved from http://cecp.air.org/cultural/Q_howdifferent.htm

Center for Lobbying in the Public Interest. (2006). *Make a difference for your cause: Strategies for nonprofit engagement in legislative advocacy.* Washington, DC: Author.

Center for Lobbying in the Public Interest. (2007). *Personal visits with a legislator.* Retrieved from www.clpi.org/images/pdf/07_personalvisits.pdf

Center for Lobbying in the Public Interest. (2009a). *Presenting testimony.* Retrieved from www.clpi.org/images/pdf/07_testimony.pdf

Center for Lobbying in the Public Interest. (2009b). *Public policy planning checklist.* Retrieved from http://www.clpi.org/images/pdf/Public%20Policy%20Planning%20Checklist.pdf.

Center for Women's Business Research. (2009). *Key facts about women-owned businesses.* Retrieved from www.nfwbo.org/facts/index.php

Center on Philanthropy. (2007). *Why focus on women's philanthropy?* Retrieved from www.philanthropy.iupui.edu/PhilanthropicServices/WPI/whyfocus.aspx

Center on Philanthropy. (2008a). *Key findings Center on Philanthropy Panel study: 2005 wave.* Retrieved from www.philanthropy.iupui.edu/Research/Key%20Findings%20January%202008.pdf

Center on Philanthropy. (2008b). *Weathering an uncertain economy: What effect will the U.S. economy have on charitable giving as nonprofits gear up for the year-end giving season and 2009?* Retrieved from www.philanthropy.iupui.edu/Research/docs/Weathering.pdf

Center on Philanthropy Innovative Research Group. (2007). *American Express charitable gift survey.* Indianapolis, IN: Center on Philanthropy.

Centers for Disease Control. (2007). *Heart healthy and stroke free: A social environment handbook.* Atlanta, GA: Author.

CFED. (2008a). *Assets & opportunity: Special report: Net worth, wealth inequity and homeownership during the bubble years.* Washington, DC: Author.

CFED. (2008b). *Individual development accounts: Providing opportunities to build assets.* Retrieved from www.cfed.org/imageManager/_documents/IDA_Four_Pager.pdf

CFED. (2009a). *Expanding native opportunity: Native IDA initiative.* Retrieved from www.cfed.org/focus.m?parentid=31&siteid=374&id=688

CFED. (2009b). *Individual development accounts: IDA's.* Washington, DC: Author.

Chao, J. (1999). Asian-American philanthropy: Expanding circles of participation. In Council on Foundations (Ed.), *Cultures of caring: Philanthropy in diverse American communi-*

ties. (pp. 189–254). Washington, DC: Council on Foundations.

Chaskin, R. J., Joseph, M. L., & Chipeda-Dansokho, S. (1997). Implementing comprehensive community development: Possibilities and limitations. *Social Work, 42*(5), 435–444.

Chavis, D. M. (2001). The paradoxes and promises of community coalitions. *American Journal of Community Psychology, 29*(2), 309–321.

Checkoway, B. (1987). Political strategy for social planning. In F. M. Cox, J. L. Erlich, J. Rothman, & J. E. Tropman (Eds.), *Strategies of community organization: Macro practice.* (4th ed., pp. 326–342). Itasca, IL: Peacock.

Child Welfare League of America. (2006). *CWLA 2006 children's legislative agenda: Child welfare workforce and training.* Retrieved from www.cwla.org/advocacy/2006legagenda03.htm

Children's Defense Fund. (2009a). *Each day in America.* Retrieved from www.childrensdefense.org/child-research-data-publications/each-day-in-america.html

Children's Defense Fund. (2009b). *Moments in America for children.* Retrieved from www.childrensdefense.org/child-research-data-publications/moments-in-america-for-children.html

Christ, R. (2004). Selecting the right keywords for your search engine marketing campaign: 12 tips to help create a successful campaign. *eZine 4*(23). Retrieved from www.imakenews.com/ephilanthropy/e_article000285041.cfm

Christ, R., & Fignar, H. (2005a, March 14). *Website back to basics: Core content.* Retrieved from www.afpnet.org/ka/ka-3.cfm?folder_id=893&content_item_id=20190

Christ, R., & Fignar, H. (2005b, April 11). *Website back to basics: Make your site user friendly.* Retrieved from http://www.afpnet.org/ResourceCenter/ArticleDetail.cfm?ItemNumber=3511

Christ, R., & Fignar, H. (2005c). *Website back to basics: Site search.* Retrieved June 13, 2005, from www.afpnet.org/ka/ka-3.cfm?folder_id=893&content_item_id=21069

Chuang, Y.-C. (2005). Place, identity, and social movements: Shequ and neighborhood organizing in Taipei City. *Positions, 13*(2), 379–410.

Chupp, M. (n.d.). *Appreciative inquiry broadway: Diversity in progress.* Retrieved from www.beyondintractability.org/principles_of_practice/chupp-5.pdf

Ciobanu, C. (2009). *Romania: Media spotlight on domestic violence.* Retrieved from www.ipsnews.net/news.asp?idnews=46466

City of Phoenix Neighborhood Services Department. (2009, July). *Monthly operations report.* Phoenix, AZ:

Neighborhood Notification, Education, and Training Office.

Clarke, C. A., & Fox, S. P. (2007). *Grant proposal makeover: Transform your request from no to yes.* San Francisco, CA: Jossey-Bass.

Clay, P. L. (1979). *Neighborhood renewal.* Lexington, MA: Lexington Books.

Coady International Institute. (2006). *An asset-based approach to community development: A manual for village organizers.* Antigonish, Nova Scotia, Canada: Coady International Institute.

Coady, M. (2008). *Giving in numbers, 2008 edition: Exclusive: Corporate philanthropy and the economy.* New York: Committee Encouraging Corporate Philanthropy.

Coalition of Community Development Financial Institutions. (2009a). *CDFI coalition of community development financial institutions.* Retrieved from http://cdfi.org/index.php

Coalition of Community Development Financial Institutions. (2009b). *What are CDFI's?* Retrieved from http://cdfi.org/index.php?page=info-1a

Code of Federal Regulations. (2009a). *Title 26: Internal Revenue;Part 1—Income taxes: Exempt organizations.* Retrieved from http://ecfr.gpoaccess.gov/cgi/t/text/text-idx?c=ecfr&sid=4008fde677742b369ac842993e0dc004&rgn=div8&view=text&node= 26:7.0.1.1.1.0.1.3&idno=26

Code of Federal Regulations. (2009b, April 1). *Lobbying expenditures, direct lobbying communications, and grass roots lobbying communications.* (pp. 443–457) [26CFR56.4911-2– Sec. 56.4911-2]. Washington, DC: Office of the Federal Register, National Archives and Records Administration.

Coffman, S. (2009, January 9). *Half a million nonprofits could lose their tax exemptions.* GuideStar.org. Retrieved from www2.guidestar.org/rxa/news/articles/2009/half-a-million-nonprofits-could-lose-their-tax-exemptions.aspx

Coghlan, A. T., Preskill, H., & Tzavaras Catsambas, T. (2003). An overview of appreciative inquiry in evaluation. *New Directions for Evaluation, 100* (Winter), 5–22.

Cohen, B. J., & Austin, M. J. (1994). Organizational learning and change in a public child welfare agency. *Administration in Social Work, 18*(1), 1–19.

Cohen, D., Inagami, S., & Finch, B. (2008). The built environment and collective efficacy. *Health and Place, 14*(2), 198–208.

Cohen, D., & Ottinger, L. (2008). How to guarantee respect for public-interest lobbyists. *Chronicle of Philanthropy, 20*(18), 32.

Cohen, R. (1979). Neighborhood planning and political capacity. *Urban Affairs Quarterly, 14*(3), 337–362.

Cohen, R., Kim, M., & Ohls, J. (2006). Hunger in America 2006: National report prepared for America's Second Harvest. Princeton, NJ: Mathematica Policy Research.

Coleman, J. S. (1988). Social capital and schools. *Education Digest, 53*(8), 6–9.

Coleman, J. S. (1993). The rational reconstruction of society. *American Sociological Review, 58*(1), 1–15.

Coley, S. M., & Scheinberg, C. A. (2000). *Proposal writing.* (2nd ed.). Thousand Oaks, CA: Sage.

Committee to Encourage Corporate Philanthropy. (2006). *Corporate giving standard.* New York: Author.

Common Cause. (1992). *Common cause action manual.* Washington, DC: Author.

Communications Consortium Media Center. (2009). *PSA's: Public service announcements.* Retrieved from www.ccmc.org/node/16118

Communities Scotland. (2002). Money advice for groups. *Action for Social Justice in Scotland, 9,* 2.

Community Associations Institute. (2006). *Governed by neighbors: The nature of community associations.* Alexandria, VA: Author.

Community Associations Institute. (2009). *Industry data: National statistics.* Retrieved from www.caionline.org/info/research/Pages/default.aspx

Community Empowerment Network. (2009). *CEN's achievements.* Retrieved from www.endruralpoverty.org/what-we-do/achievements

Compete.com. (2009a). *Facebook.com site profile.* Retrieve from http://siteanalytics.compete.com/facebook.com/

Compete.com. (2009b). *Twitter.com site profile.* Retrieved from http://siteanalytics.compete.com/twitter.com/

Cone. (2009). *Past. Present. Future. The 25th anniversary of cause marketing.* Boston, MA: Author.

Conference Board. (2002). *Corporate community development: Meeting the measurement challenge.* [Research Report 1310-02-RR]. New York: Author.

Conner, A. N., & de la Isla, J. (1984). Information: An effective change tool. In F. Cox, J. L. Erlich, J. Rothman, & J. E. Tropman (Eds.), *Tactics and techniques of community practice.* (2nd ed., pp. 245n). Itasca, IL: Peacock.

Coombe, C. M. (2005). Participatory evaluation: Building community while assessing change. In J. Minkler (Ed.), *Community organizing and community building for health.* (2nd ed., pp. 368–385). New Brunswick, NJ: Rutgers University Press.

Cooperrider, D. L. (1990). Positive image, positive action: The affirmative basis of organizing. In S. Srivastva, & D. L. Cooperrider (Eds.), *Appreciative management and leadership.* (pp. 91–125). San Francisco: Jossey-Bass.

Cooperrider, D. L. (2008a). *Going green maximum velocity through AI's sustainable design factory.* Retrieved from http://appreciativeinquiry.case.edu/research/bibPublishedDetail.cfm?coid=11874

Cooperrider, D. L. (2008b, November). The 3-circles of strength revolution. *AI Practitioner,* 8–11.

Cooperrider, D. L., & Srivastva, S. (1987). Appreciative inquiry in organizational life. In R. Woodman, & W. Pasmore (Eds.), *Research in organizational change and development* (Vol. 1, pp. 129–169). Greenwich, CT: JAI Press.

Cooperrider, D. L., Whitney, D., & Stavros, J. M. (2008). *Appreciative inquiry handbook: For leaders of change.* (2nd ed.). San Francisco: Berret-Koehler.

Corey, M. S., & Corey, G. (2011). *Becoming a helper.* (6th ed.). Belmont, CA: Brooks/Cole, Cengage Learning.

Cormier, S., & Hackney, H. (1993). *The professional counselor: A process guide to helping.* (2nd ed.). Boston: Allyn & Bacon.

Corporation for National and Community Service. (2007). Volunteering in America: 2007 city trends and rankings. Washington, DC: Author.

Corporation for National and Community Service. (2008a). *Community service and service-learning in America's schools* [Issue brief]. Washington, DC: Author.

Corporation for National and Community Service. (2008b). *How do volunteers find the time? Evidence from the American time use study.* Retrieved from www.volunteeringinamerica.gov/assets/resources/ATUS_Brief.pdf

Corporation for National and Community Service. (2008c, July 28). *Volunteering 61 million strong: Need and momentum grow* [News release]. Retrieved from www.nationalservice.gov/about/newsroom/releases_detail.asp?tbl_pr_id=1116

Corporation for National and Community Service. (2008d). *Volunteering in America: 2008.* Washington, DC: Author.

Coulton, C. J., Cook, T. & Irwin, M. (2004). *Aggregation issues in neighborhood research: A comparison of several levels of census geography and resident defined neighborhoods.* Association for Public Policy and Management Annual Conference, Atlanta.

Coulton, C. J. (1996). Effects of neighborhoods on families and children: Implications for services. In A. J. Kahn, & S. B. Kammerman (Eds.), *Children and their families in big cities: Strategies for service and reform.* (pp. 87–120). New York: Columbia University Press.

Coulton, C. J., Korbin, J., Chan, T., & Su, M. (2001). Mapping residents' perceptions of neighborhood boundaries: A methodological note. *American Journal of Community Psychology,* 29(2), 371–383.

Council on Rehabilitation Education. (2008, October 17). *Current CORE accreditation standards.* Schaumburg, IL: Author.

Council on Foundations. (2008). *Community foundations fact sheet.* Retrieved from www.cof.org/Members/content.cfm?ItemNumber=14341

Covey, N. (2008). *Flying fingers: Text messaging overtakes monthly phone calls.* Retrieved from http://en-us.nielsen.com/main/insights/consumer_insight/issue_ 12/flying_fingers

Cowan, G., & Egan, M. (1979). *People in systems: A model for development in the human-service professions and education.* Pacific Grove, CA: Brooks/Cole.

Cox, F. M. (1987a). Arenas of community practice: Introduction. In F. M. Cox, J. L. Erlich, J. Rothman, & J. E. Tropman (Eds.), *Strategies of community organization: Macro practice.* (4th ed., pp. 187–212). Itasca, IL: Peacock.

Cox, F. M. (1987b). Communities: Alternative conceptions of community: Implications for community organization practice. In F. M. Cox, J. L. Erlich, J. Rothman, & J. E. Tropman (Eds.), *Strategies of community organization: Macro practice* (4th ed., pp. 232–243). Itasca, IL: Peacock.

Craig, D. V. (2009). *Action research essentials.* San Francisco, CA: Jossey-Bass.

Crompton, J. L. (1985). Six steps to developing corporate support. *Parks and Recreation,* 44–65.

Cross, R. (1992). *Media data.* Tucson, AZ: Tucson Newspapers, Inc.

Cross, T. L., Bazron, B. J., Dennis, K. W., & Isaacs, M. R. (1989). *Towards a culturally competent system of care* (Vol. 1). Washington, DC: Georgetown University Child Development Center.

Crowfoot, J., Chesler, M. A., & Boulet, J. (1983). Organizing for social justice. In E. Seidman (Ed.), *Handbook of social intervention.* (pp. 253–255). Newbury Park, CA: Sage.

CTIA. (2009). *Wireless quick facts.* Retrieved from www.ctia.org/advocacy/research/index.cfm/AID/10323

Dailey, R. C. (1986). Understanding organizational commitment for volunteers: Empirical and managerial implications. *Journal of Voluntary Action Research,* 15(1), 19–31.

Dale, D. (1978). *How to make citizen involvement work: Strategies for developing clout.* Amherst, MA: University of Massachusetts, Citizen Involvement Training Project.

Dale, D., & Mitiguy, N. (1978). *Planning for a change: A citizen's guide to creative planning and program development.* Amherst, MA: University of Massachusetts, Citizen Involvement Training Project.

Daniels, S. (2002, August 29). *Understanding communities as systems.* Presentation to University of Arizona Cooperative Extension Annual Conference, Tucson, AZ.

Daun, D. (1991). Becoming a media resource. In Tucson Newspapers, Inc. (Ed.), *What's News?* (pp. 3). Tucson, AZ: Tucson Newspapers, Inc.

Davis, B. (2006). *Writing a successful grant proposal.* Minnesota Council on Foundations. Retrieved from www.mcf.org/mcf/grant/writing.htm

Davis, R. (2009). *Public service announcements.* Communication Consortium Media Center. Retrieved from www.ccmc.org/node/16118

Day, P. (2008). *61 community networks: Building and sustaining community relationships*. Public Sphere Project, Liberating Voices! A Pattern Language for Communication Revolution. Retrieved from www.publicsphereproject.org/patterns/print-pattern.php?begin=61

De Jouvenel, B. (1958). Authority: The efficient imperative. In C. J. Freidrich (Ed.), *Authority, nomos, I*. Cambridge, MA: Harvard University Press.

De Leon, C. F. M., Cagney, K. A., Bienias, J. L., Barnes, L. L., Skarupski, K. A., Scherr, P. A., & Evans, D. A. (2009). Neighborhood social cohesion and disorder in relation to walking in community-dwelling older adults: A multilevel analysis. *Journal of Aging & Health*, 21.

De Vita, C. J., Manjarrez, C., & Twombly, E. (1999). *Organizations and neighborhood networks that strengthen families in the District of Columbia*. Washington, DC: Urban Institute.

Dear, R. B., & Patti, R. J. (1984). Legislative advocacy: Seven effective tactics. In F. Cox, J. L. Erlich, J. Rothman, & J. E. Tropman (Eds.), *Tactics and techniques of community practice*. (2nd ed., pp. 185–197). Itasca, IL: Peacock.

DeFilippis, J. (2001). The myth of social capital in community development. *Housing Policy Debate*, 12(4). Washington, DC: Fannie Mae Foundation.

Delgado, M. (2000). *Community social work practice in an urban context: The potential of a capacity-enhancement perspective*. New York: Oxford University Press.

DeNavas-Walt, C., Proctor, R. D., & Smith, J. C. (2008). *Income, poverty, and health insurance coverage in the United States: 2007*. Washington, DC: U.S. Census Bureau.

Denning, S. (2000). *The springboard: How storytelling ignites action in knowledge-era organizations*. Boston: Butterworth-Heinemann.

Denning, S. (2004). *Squirrel Inc.: A fable of leadership through storytelling*. San Francisco, CA: Jossey-Bass.

DePoy, E., Hartman, A., & Haslett, D. (1999). Critical action research: A model for social work knowing. *Social Work*, 44(6), 560–569.

Deutsch, M. (2005, March). Maintaining oppression. In G. Burgess, & H. Burgess (Eds.), *Beyond intractability*. Conflict Research Consortium, University of Colorado, Boulder. Retrieved from http://beyondintractability.org/essay/maintaining_oppression/?nid=2378

Devore, W., & Schlesinger, E. (2000). *Ethnic sensitive social work practice*. (5th ed.). Boston: Allyn & Bacon.

Di Gessa, S., Poole, P., & Bending, T. (2008). *Participatory mapping as a tool for empowerment: Experiences and lessons learned from the ILC network*. Rome, Italy: International Land Coalition.

DiAngelo, R. (1997). Heterosexism: Addressing internalized dominance. *Journal of Progressive Human Services*, 8(1), 5–22.

DiNitto, D. M. (2000). *Social welfare: Politics and public policy*. (5th ed.). Boston, MA: Allyn & Bacon.

DiNitto, D. M., & Cummins, L. K. (2005). *Social welfare: Politics and public policy*. (6th ed.). Boston, MA: Pearson Allyn & Bacon.

DiNitto, D. M., & McNeece, C. A. (1989). *Social work*. Englewood Cliffs, NJ: Prentice-Hall.

Dobson, C. (2003). *The troublemaker's teaparty: A manual for effective citizen action*. Gabriola Island, BC, Canada: New Society.

Dolgoff, R., & Feldstein, D. (2007). *Understanding social welfare*. (7th ed.). Boston, MA: Pearson Allyn & Bacon.

Domhoff, G. W. (2005a). Power at the local level: Growth coalition theory. *Who rules America*. Retrieved from http://sociology.ucsc.edu/whorulesamerica/power/local.html

Domhoff, G. W. (2005b). Studying power. *Who rules America*. Retrieved from http://sociology.ucsc.edu/whorulesamerica/methods/power_structure_ research.html

Domhoff, G. W. (2005c). What social science can tell us about social change. *Who rules America*. Retrieved from http://sociology.ucsc.edu/whorulesamerica/change/science.html

Domhoff, G. W. (2008). *C. Wright Mills, Floyd Hunter, and 50 years of power structure research*. Retrieved from http://sociology.ucsc.edu/whorulesamerica/theory/mills_address.html

Doran, D. (2002, July 18). Women seize at least 4 other Nigerian oil facilities. *Arizona Daily Star*, p. A9.

Dosher, A. (1977a, February 17). *Networks: A key to person-community development*. Paper presented to Office of Youth Development, Department of Health, Education, and Welfare, Denver Hearings.

Dosher, A. (1977b, November 2). *Networking workshop outline*. Paper presented to Pima County Children Youth and Families Community Network, Tucson, AZ.

Dove, T. (1983, July/August). Business in the community: How you can make a difference. *The Journal of Insurance*, 17–22.

Downs, A. (1981). *Neighborhoods and urban development*. Washington, DC: Brookings Institution.

Downs, A. (2000). Comment on John T. Metzger's "Planned abandonment: The neighborhood life-cycle theory and urban policy." *Housing Policy Debate*, 11(1), 41–54.

Doxiadis, C. A. (1968). Foreword. In S. Keller (Ed.), *The urban neighborhood*. New York: Random House.

Dubois, B., & Krogsrud-Miley, K. (2005). *Social work: An empowering profession*. (5th ed.). Boston, MA: Pearson Allyn & Bacon.

Dugan, M. A. (2003, June). Power. In G. Burgess, & H. Burgess (Eds.), *Beyond intractability*. Conflict Research Consortium, University of Colorado, Boulder. Retrieved from www.beyondintractability.org/essay/Power/

Dupper, D. R., & Poertner, J. (1997). Public schools and the revitalization of impoverished communities: School linked, family resource centers. *Social Work, 42*(5), 415–422.

Duran, L. (2001, September–October). Caring for each other: Philanthropy in communities of color. *Grassroots Fundraising Journal, 20*(5).

Dutro, K., & Coffman, S. E. (2006). *Grant writing 102: Advice from successful grantwriters.* GuideStar.org, Retrieved March 2006 from www.guidestar.org/news/features/grantwriting102.jsp#

Early, T. J., & GlenMaye, L. F. (2000). Valuing families: Social work practice with families from a strengths perspective. *Social Work, 45*(2), 118–130.

Easton, M. (2006, May, 2). Britain's happiness in decline. *BBC News.* Retrieved from http://news.bbc.co.uk/go/pr/fr/-/1/hi/programmes/happiness_formula/4771908.stm

Edelwich, J., & Brodsky, A. (1980). *Burn-out: Stages of disillusionment in the helping professions.* New York: Human Sciences Press.

Edwards, E. D., & Edwards, M. E. (1995). Community development with Native Americans. In F. G. Rivera, & J. L. Erlich (Eds.), *Community organizing in a diverse society.* (2nd ed., pp. 25–42). Boston, MA: Allyn & Bacon.

Elliott, C. (1999). *Locating the energy for change: An introduction to appreciative inquiry.* Winnipeg, Canada: International Institute for Sustainable Development.

Ellsworth, C., Hooyman, N., Ruff, R. A., Stam, S. B., & Tucker, J. H. (1982). Toward a feminist model of planning for and with women. In A. Weicker, & S. T. Vandiver (Eds.), *Women, power, and change.* (pp. 146–156). Washington, DC: National Association of Social Workers.

Erlich, J. L., & Tropman, J. E. (1974). Overview of strategy. In F. M. Cox, J. L. Erlich, J. Rothman, & J. E. Tropman (Eds.), *Strategies of community organization: A book of readings.* (2nd ed., pp. 175). Itasca, IL: Peacock.

Erlich, J. L., & Tropman, J. E. (1987). Introduction. In F. M. Cox, J. L. Erlich, J. Rothman, & J. E. Tropman (Eds.), *Strategies of community organization: Macro practice.* (4th ed.). Itasca, IL: Peacock.

Erwin, P. C. (2008). Poverty in America: How public health practice can make a difference. *American Journal of Public Health, 98*(9), 1570–1572.

Evans, S. (2008). *How to build community on Twitter.* Retrieved from http://mashable.com/2008/11/10/twitter-community/

Ewalt, P. L. (1994). Federal legislation and the social work profession. *Social Work, 39*(4), 341–342.

Ewart, C. K., & Suchday, S. (2002). Discovering how urban poverty and violence affect health: Development and validation of a neighborhood stress index. *Heath Psychology, 21*(3), 254–262.

Ezell, M. (2001). *Advocacy in the human services.* Belmont, CA: Wadsworth, Cengage Learning.

Fabricant, M. (1985). The industrialization of social work. *Social Work, 30*(5), 389–395.

Fairbanks, A. M. (2008, April 24) Funny thing happened at the dog run. *New York Times* [Online]. Retrieved from www.nytimes.com/2008/08/24/nyregion/24meetup.html?fta=y

Fallon, D. (1993, January). Collaboration: Effective fundraising in the 90's. *Contemporary Issues in Fundraising*, 20–23.

Family Violence Prevention Fund. (2002). *Neighborhoods organizing for change.* Retrieved from http://endabuse.org/userfiles/file/ImmigrantWomen/PFV-Community%20Engagement.pdf

Fantini, M., & Gittell, M. (1973). *Decentralization: Achieving reform.* New York: Praeger.

Fawcett, S., Seekins, T., Whang, P., Muir, C., & Balcazar, Y. (1982). Involving consumers in decision making. *Social Policy, 2*, 36–41.

Federal Bureau of Investigation. (2009). *Preliminary Uniform Crime Report: January–December 2008: Table 3.* Retrieved from www.fbi.gov/ucr/2008prelim/table_3.html

Federal Financial Institutions Examination Council. (2009a). *Community reinvestment act.* Retrieved from www.ffiec.gov/CRA/default.htm

Federal Financial Institutions Examination Council. (2009b). *Home mortgage disclosure act.* Retrieved from www.ffiec.gov/hmda/history.htm

Federal Interagency Forum on Child and Family Statistics. (2002). *America's children: Key indicators of well-being.* Retrieved from http://www.childstats.gov/

Federal Interagency Forum on Child and Family Statistics. (2006). *America's children in brief: Key national indicators of well-being.* Retrieved from www.child stats.gov/americaschildren/beh4.asp

Federico, R. C. (1984). *The social welfare institution.* (4th ed.). Lexington, MA: D. C. Heath.

Fellin, P. (2001). *The community and the social worker.* (3rd ed.). Itasca, IL: Peacock.

Ferguson, D. (2009). Dayton's neighborhood school centers. *New Directions for Youth Development, 122*, 81–106.

Ferguson, J. (2006). Corporate philanthropy: Giving derives from role of business in society. *Giving Forum, Minnesota Council on Foundations, 29*(2), 1, 4.

Fessler, P. (2008). *Nonprofit groups forced to do more with less.* Retrieved from http://m.wxxi.npr.org/news.jsp?key=464047&rc=bu&p=1

Filley, A., House, R., & Kerr, S. (1976). *Managerial process and organizational behavior.* (2nd ed.). Glenview, IL: Scott, Foresman.

Fisch, J. (1989a). The eight basic truths direct mail fund raisers can't afford to forget. *Tax Exempt News, 11*(4), 5–8.

Fisch, J. (1989b). Using celebrities to raise funds: A tricky endeavor. *Tax Exempt News*, 11(4), 1–3.

Fisher, R. (1972). *International conflict and behavioral science*. New York: Basic Books.

Fisher, R. (1984, Summer). Neighborhood organizing: Lessons from the past. *Social Policy*, 9–16.

Fisher, R. (1985). Neighborhood organizing and urban revitalization: An historical perspective. *Journal of Urban Affairs*, 7(1), 74–54.

Fisher, R. (2005). Social action community organizing: Proliferation, persistence, roots, and prospects. In J. Minkler (Ed.), *Community organizing and community building for health*. (2nd ed., pp. 51–65). New Brunswick, NJ: Rutgers University Press.

Fisher, R., & Ury, W. (1991). *Getting to yes: Negotiating without giving in*. (2nd ed.). Boston, MA: Houghton Mifflin.

Flaiz, W. (2009). *Is your landing page relevant?* Retrieved from http://searchenginewatch.com/3632648

Flanagan, J. (2000). *Successful fundraising: A complete handbook for volunteers and professionals*. (2nd ed.). Chicago: Contemporary Books.

Floro, G. K. (1989). Innocence and satisfactions for a shared life voluntarism. *Wisconsin Sociologist*, 26(1), 7–14.

Fong, L. G. W., & Gibbs, J. T. (1995). Facilitating services to multicultural communities in a dominant setting: An organizational perspective. *Administration in Social Work*, 19(2), 1–24.

Foreclosures.com. (2009, August 14). *Nationwide statistics*. Unpublished manuscript.

Forrest, R., & Kearns, A. (2001). Social cohesion, social capital and the neighbourhood. *Urban Studies*, 38(12), 2125–2143.

Fosler, R. S. (2002). *Working better together*. Washington, DC: Independent Sector.

Foundation Center. (2006a). *Demystifying the 990 PF*. Retrieved from http://foundationcenter.org/getstarted/tutorials/demystify

Foundation Center. (2006b). *What are in-kind gifts and how can I find out more about them?* Retrieved from http://foundationcenter.org/getstarted/faqs/html/inkind.html

Foundation Center. (2009). *Frequently asked questions: What do nonprofit organizations need to know about the new Form 990?* Retrieved from http://foundationcenter.org/getstarted/faqs/html/990_redesign.html

Fox-McIntyre, M. (2001). Internet strategy for nonprofits. In T. D. Connors (Ed.), *The nonprofit handbook: Management*. (3rd ed., pp. 199–222). New York: Wiley.

Frechtling-Westat, J. (2002). *The 2002 user friendly handbook for project evaluation*. Arlington, VA: The National Science Foundation.

Fredrickson, B. L. (2006). The broaden-and-build theory of positive emotions. In M. Csikszentmihalyi, & I. S. Csikszentmihaliyi (Eds.), *A life worth living: Contributions to positive psychology*. (pp. 85–103). New York: Oxford University Press.

Fredrickson, B. L., & Branigan, C. (2005). Positive emotions broaden the scope of attention and thought-action repertoires. *Cognition and Emotion*, 19, 313–332.

Freedman, H. A. (1996, December). Is the party over? Charities and special events: Where are the dollars really going? *Fund Raising Management*, 26–30.

Freedman, H. A., & Feldman, K. (2007). *Black tie optional: A complete special events resource for nonprofit organizations*. (2nd ed.). Hoboken, NJ: Wiley.

Frey, G. A. (1990, March). A framework for promoting organizational change. *Journal of Contemporary Human Services*, 142–147.

Freyd, W. (2001). Telemarketing. In J. M. Greenfield (Ed.), *The nonprofit handbook: Fund raising*. (3rd ed., pp. 563–574). New York: Wiley.

Freyd, W., & Carlson, D. M. (1997). Telemarketing. In J. M. Greenfield (Ed.), *The nonprofit handbook: Fund raising*. (2nd ed., pp. 317–328). New York: Wiley.

Fridena, R. (1983, November). *When can we meet?* Paper presented to the Social Services Department, Pima Community College, AZ.

Friere, P. (1973). *Education for critical consciousness*. New York: Seabury.

Friere, P. (1995). *Pedagogy of hope: Reliving pedagogy of the oppressed* (Reprint ed.) New York: Continuum.

Friere, P. (2000). *Pedagogy of the oppressed* (30th ann. ed.) New York: Continuum. (Originally published 1970)

Gallagher, L., Truglio-Londrigan, M., & Levin, R. (2009). Partnership for healthy living: An action research project. *Nurse Researcher*, 16(2), 7–30.

Garonzik, E., & Harris, R. K. (2008). Foreword. *Grantseekers guide to winning proposals*. New York: The Foundation Center.

Garth, T. D. (1997). *1997 metro survey report*. Chicago: Metro Chicago Information Center.

Gates, B. L. (1980). *Social program administration: The implementation of social policy*. Englewood Cliffs, NJ: Prentice-Hall.

Gates, H. (2009, October 22). *Standards for culturally competent human service practice—moving forward*. Paper presented at the annual conference for the National Organization for Human Services, Portland, Oregon.

Gatewood, E. (1994). *Do it yourself: A simple approach to neighborhood improvement*. Tacoma, WA: City of Tacoma.

Geever, J. C. (2001). *The Foundation Center's guide to proposal writing*. (3rd ed.). New York: Foundation Center.

Geever, J. C. (2007). *The Foundation Center's guide to proposal writing*. (5th ed.). New York: Foundation Center.

George, S. (1986). *How the other half dies: The real reasons for world hunger* (Rev. ed.). Harmondworth, Middlesex: Penguin Books.

Germann, K., & Wilson, D. (2004). Organizational capacity for community development in regional health authorities: A conceptual model. *Health Promotion International, 19*(3), 289–298.

Giving USA Foundation. (2008a). Giving during recessions and economic slowdowns. *Giving USA Spotlight,* 3.

Giving USA Foundation. (2008b). *Giving USA.* Glenview, IL: Giving USA Foundation.

Giving USA Foundation. (2009). *U.S. charitable giving estimated to be $307.65 billion in 2008: Giving in worst economic climate since Great Depression exceeds $300 billion for second year in a row.* Retrieved from www.philanthropy.iupui.edu/News/2009/docs/GivingReaches300billion_06102009.pdf

Global Fund for Women. (2008). *Twenty years investing in women: A powerful force for change: The Global Fund for Women annual report 2007–2008.* San Francisco, CA: Author.

Goffin, S. G., & Lombardi, J. (1988). *Speaking out: Early childhood advocacy.* Washington, DC: National Association for the Education of Young Children.

Goldberg, G. S. (1980, June). New directions for the community service society of New York: A study of organizational change. *Social Service Review,* 184–219.

Golden, S. L. (2001). The grant-seeking process. In J. M. Greenfield (Ed.), *The nonprofit handbook: Fund raising.* (3rd ed., pp. 666–691). New York: Wiley.

Goldstein, J. (1993). *Countering recession with innovation.* Princeton, NJ: Davis Information Group.

Goode, T., Jones, W., & Mason, J. (2002). *A guide to planning and implementing cultural competence organization self-assessment.* Washington, DC: National Center for Cultural Competence, Georgetown University Child Development Center.

Goode, T. D., & Jones, W. (2008). *Linguistic competence.* Retrieved from www.firnonline.org/FIRNDoc/SummitSpeakerHandouts.pdf

Gordon, K. (2007). The fine line of funding in Indian Country. *Grantmakers in Arts Reader, 18*(1), 13–15.

Gordon, W. E. (1965, July). Knowledge and value: Their distinction and relationship in clarifying social work practice. *Social Work, 10,* 32.

Gottlieb, N. (1992). Empowerment, political analyses, and services for women. In Y. Hasenfeld (Ed.), *Human services as complex organizations.* (pp. 301–319). Newbury Park, CA: Sage.

Grassroots Fundraising Journal. (2006). Fundraising software comparison chart. Retrieved from www.grassrootsfundraising.org/howto/software.html

Green, M. (2001). The neighborhood becomes friendly. *NEA Today, 19*(4), 24–25.

Greenfield, J. M. (2002). *Fundraising fundamentals: A guided to annual giving for professionals and volunteers.* (2nd ed.). New York: Wiley.

Greenstein, R., & Sungu-Eryilmaz, Y. (2007, January). Community land trusts: A solution for permanently affordable housing. *Land Lines,* 8–13.

Grimm, R., Dietz, N., Spring, K., Arey, K., & Foster-Bey, J. (2005). *Youth helping America.* Washington, DC: Corporation for National and Community Service.

Grinstein-Weiss, M., Curley, J., & Charles, P. (2007). Asset building in rural communities: The experience of individual development accounts. *Rural Sociology, 72*(1), 25–46.

Grobman, G. M. (2008). *The nonprofit handbook: Everything you need to know to start and run your nonprofit organization.* Harrisburg, PA: White Hat Communications.

Grogan-Kaylor, A., Wooley, M., Mowbray, C., Reischl, T. M., Gilster, M., Karb, R., MacFarlane, P., et al. (2006). Predictors of neighborhood satisfaction. *Journal of Community Practice, 14*(4), 27–50.

Gronbjerg, K. A. (2004). Human services and philanthropy. In D. F. Burlingame (Ed.), *Philanthropy in America: A comprehensive historical encyclopedia.* (pp. 248–254). Santa Barbara, CA: ABC-CLIO.

Guerra, L. (1999). *Technical assistance and progressive organizations for social change in communities of color: A report to the Saguaro Grantmaking Board of the Funding Exchange.* New York: Funding Exchange.

GuideStar.org. (2009). *FAQs: Form 990.* Retrieved from http://preview.guidestar.org/rxg/help/faqs/form-990/index.aspx#faq1942

Gummer, B. (1978, September). A power-politics approach to social welfare organizations. *Social Service Review,* 349–361.

Gutiérrez, L. M. (1995). Working with women of color: An empowerment perspective. In J. Rothman, J. L. Erlich, & J. E. Tropman (Eds.), *Strategies of community intervention.* (5th ed., pp. 204–212). Itasca, IL: Peacock.

Gutiérrez, L. M., & Lewis, E. A. (1994). Community organizing with women of color: A feminist approach. *Journal of Community Practice, 1*(2), 23–44.

Gutiérrez, L. M., & Lewis, E. A. (1995). A feminist perspective on organizing with women of color. In F. G. Rivera, & J. L. Erlich (Eds.), *Organizing in a diverse society.* (2nd ed., pp. 95–112). Boston, MA: Allyn & Bacon.

Gutiérrez, L., Parsons, R. J., & Cox, E. O. (1998). *Empowerment in social work practice: A sourcebook.* Belmont, CA: Brooks/Cole, Cengage Learning.

Gutiérrez, L., Parsons, R. J., & Cox, E. O. (2003). A model for empowerment practice. In *Empowerment in social work practice: A sourcebook.* Belmont, CA: Wadsworth, Cengage Learning.

Hagberg, C., & Homan, M. S. (2006). *Signs of impact.* Phoenix, AZ: Arizona Department of Health Services.

Hagebak, B. R. (1982). *Getting local agencies to cooperate.* Baltimore: University Park Press.

Hagen, P. (2006). *Creating a relationship-centric organization: Nonprofit CRM—ways to acquire, retain, and enhance constituent relationships.* Retrieved from www.techsoup.org/learningcenter/techplan/page5513.cfm

Hall, H. (1996). Direct mail: Can it still deliver? *The Chronicle of Philanthropy, 8*(10).

Hall, J., & Hammond, S. (1998). What is appreciative inquiry? *Inner Edge Newsletter.*

Hallman, H. W. (1984). *Neighborhoods: Their place in urban life.* Newbury Park, CA: Sage.

Hammond, S. A. (1998). *The thin book of appreciative inquiry.* (2nd ed.). Plano, Texas: Thin Book.

Han, C.-K., Grinstein-Weiss, M., & Sherraden, M. (2009). Assets beyond savings in individual development accounts. *Social Service Review, 83*(2), 221–244.

Hancock, T., & Minkler, M. (2005). Community health assessment or healthy community assessment: Whose community? Whose health? Whose assessment? In J. Minkler (Ed.), *Community organizing and community building for health.* (2nd ed., pp. 138–157). New Brunswick, NJ: Rutgers University Press.

Hanifan, L. J. (1916). The rural school community center. *Annals of the American Academy of Political and Social Science, 67,* 130–138.

Hart, T., Greenfield, J. M., & Haji, S. D. (2007). *People to people fundraising: Social networking and Web 2.0 for charities.* Hoboken, NJ: Wiley.

Hartigan, P., & Billimoria, J. (2005). Social entrepreneurship and overview. *Alliance, 10*(1), 18–21.

Harwood Group. (1999). *Community rhythms: Five stages of community life.* Bethesda, MD: Harwood Group and Charles Stewart Mott Foundation.

Hassan, H. S. (2007). *An assessment of community participation in upgrading slum houses: A study in Addis Ababa.* Unpublished master's thesis. Graduate School of Social Work, Addis Ababa University.

Hawkins, J. D., Lonczak, H. S., Abbott, R. D., Kosterman, R., & Catalano, R. F. (2002). The effects of the Seattle social development project on sexual behavior, pregnancy, birth, and sexually transmitted disease outcomes by age twenty-one years. *Archives of Pediatric and Adolescent Medicine, 156*(5), 438–447.

Hayghe, H. V. (1997, September). Developments in women's labor force participation. *Monthly Labor Review,* 41–46.

Haynes, K. S., & Mickelson, J. S. (2006). *Affecting change: Social workers in the political arena.* Boston, MA: Pearson Allyn & Bacon.

Heintze, T., & Bretschneider, S. (2000). Information technology and restructuring in public organizations: Does adoption of information technology affect organizational structures, communications, and decision making? *Journal of Public Administration Research and Theory, 10*(4), 801–830.

Herbert, W. (1996, January 29). The revival of civic life. *U.S. News & World Report,* pp. 63–67.

Hicks, J. (1997). Grass-roots fund raising. In J. M. Greenfield (Ed.), *The nonprofit handbook: Fund raising.* (2nd ed., pp. 554–580). New York: Wiley.

Hicks, J. (2001). Grass-roots fund raising. In J. M. Greenfield (Ed.), *The nonprofit handbook: Fund raising.* (3rd ed., pp. 920–947). New York: Wiley.

Higgs, J. (2008, October 14). Organization adopts appreciative inquiry approach to Community Neighborhood Centers Inc. Engages community to learn from what's working. *Axiom News.*

Hill, C. (2009). *Don't ignore your sitemap.* Retrieved from http://searchenginewatch.com/3633562

Hodgkinson, V. A., & Weitzman, M. S. (1996). *Giving and volunteering in the United States.* Washington, DC: Independent Sector.

Hodiak, D. (2001, May 11). *Cultivating your donors on the Internet.* Retrieved from www.onphilanthropy.com/op2001-09-10h.html

Hoefer, R., & Ferguson, K. (2007). Controlling the levers of power: How advocacy organizations affect the regulation writing process. *Journal of Sociology & Social Welfare, 34*(1), 83–108.

Hoffman, S., Palladino, J. M., & Barnett, J. (2007). Compassion fatigue as a theoretical framework to help understand burnout among special education teachers. *Journal of Ethnographic & Qualitative Research, 1,* 15–22.

Hofford, R. A. (2001). Seven tips for effecting legislative change: Getting involved in state and local politics is another way you can care for your patients and community. *Family Practice Management, 8*(4), 35–37.

Holloway, S. (1987). Staff-initiated organizational change. In National Association of Social Workers (Ed.), *Encyclopedia of social work.* (18th ed., pp. 729–736). Silver Spring, MD: National Association of Social Workers.

Home, A. L. (1991). Mobilizing women's strengths for social change: The group connection. In A. Vinik, & M. Levin (Eds.), *Social action in group work.* (pp. 153–173). New York: Haworth.

Hooker, S., Cirill, L. A., & Geraghty, A. (2009). Evaluation of the walkable neighborhoods for seniors project in Sacramento County. *Health Promotion Practice, 10*(3), 402–410.

Hope, A., & Timmel, S. (1992). *Training for transformation: A handbook for community workers, Book 2.* Gweru, Zimbabwe: Mambo Press.

Horwitz, M. (1954). The recall of interrupted group tasks: An experimental study of individual motivation in relation to social groups. *Human Relations, 7*, 3–38.

Howe, F. (1985, March–April). What you need to know about fundraising. *Harvard Business Review, 24*.

Howes, M. (1997). NGOs and the institutional development of membership organizations: A Kenyan case. *The Journal of Development Studies, 33*(6), 820–848.

Hrebenar, R. J., & Scott, R. K. (1982). *Interest group politics in America.* Englewood Cliffs, NJ: Prentice-Hall.

Huang, J. (2006). *Foundation communications: The grantee perspective.* Cambridge, MA: Center on Effective Philanthropy.

Huang, Y. (2001). Women's contradictory roles in the community: A case study of the community development project in Taiwan. *International Social Work, 44* (3), 361–373.

Hunt, A. (1986, July–August). Strategic philanthropy. *Across the Board*, 23–30.

Hunt, E. (2003). *African American philanthropy: A legacy of giving.* New York: Twenty-First Century Foundation.

Hunter, L., & Homan, M. S. (2006). *Workbook for community development.* Phoenix, AZ: Arizona Department of Health Services.

Hutchinson, V. (2008). *Measuring the maybe.* Retrieved from www.scribd.com/doc/8511057/Measuring-the-Maybe-vivian-Hutchinson

Hyde, C. (1992). The ideational system of social movement agencies: An examination of feminist health centers. In Y. Hasenfeld (Ed.), *Human services as complex organizations.* (pp. 121–144). Newbury Park, CA: Sage.

Ibanez, A. (1997, October). Sustainable Tucson: A vision for the future. *Tucson Monthly*, 52–61.

IEG. (2005). '06 outlook: Sponsorship growth back to double digits. *IEG Sponsorship Report, 24*(24), 1–6.

Independent Sector. (2001). New research on the impact of information technology. *Facts and Findings, 3*(2), 6.

Independent Sector. (2002a). *Faith and philanthropy.* Washington, DC: Author.

Independent Sector. (2002b). *Giving and volunteering in the United States.* Washington, DC: Author.

Independent Sector. (2002c). *IRS letter states lobbying is legal.* Retrieved from www.clpl.org/irs_lobbying.pdf

Independent Sector. (2003). *Giving in tough times: The impact of personal economic concerns on giving and volunteering.* Washington, DC: Author.

Independent Sector. (2006). *Research: Value of volunteer time.* Retrieved from www.independentsector.org/programs/research/volunteer_time.html

Independent Sector. (2008). *The estimated dollar value of volunteer time is $19.51 per hour for 2007.* Retrieved from www.independentsector.org/programs/research/volunteer_time.html

Independent Sector. (2009a). *Public Policy—accounting and oversight: Are you ready for the New Form 990?* Retrieved from www.independentsector.org/programs/gr/Draft_Form_990.htm

Independent Sector. (2009b, February 12). *Public policy: Nonprofit advocacy and lobbying: Lobbying guidelines for public charities.* Retrieved from www.independentsector.org/programs/gr/lobby_tax_ rules.htm

Industrial Areas Foundation. (2009). *Industrial Areas Foundation: Who are we?* Retrieved from www.industrialareasfoundation.org/iafabout/about.htm

Initiative and Referendum Institute. (2006). *What is the initiative and referendum process?* Retrieved from www.iandrinstitute.org/Quick%20Fact%20-%20What %20is %20I&R.htm

Initiative and Referendum Institute. (2009). *State initiative and referendum map.* Retrieved from www.iandrinstitute.org/statewide_i&r.htm

Initiative for a Competitive Inner City. (2005). State of the inner city economies: Small business in the inner city. *Small Business Research Summary* (No. 260). Springfield, VA: Small Business Administration Office of Advocacy.

Institute for Community Economics. (2002). *The community land trust model.* Retrieved from www.iceclt.org/clt/

Institute for Community Economics. (2009a). *Community land trusts (CLTs) or sponsors of CLTs.* Retrieved from www.iceclt.org/clt/cltlist.html

Institute for Community Economics. (2009b). *The community land trust model.* Retrieved from www.iceclt.org/clt/cltmodel.html

Internal Revenue Service. (2002, November). Section 527 Political organizations revised tax filing requirements. In *Internal Revenue Service code* (FS-2002-13). Eagan, MN: West Group.

Internal Revenue Service. (2006). *Election year activities and the prohibition on political campaign intervention for section 501(c)(3) organizations.* [FS-2006-17]. Retrieved from www.irs.gov/newsroom.article/0,,id=154712,00.html

Internal Revenue Service. (2008). *Tax-exempt status for your organization.* [Publication 557]. Washington, DC: Author.

Internal Revenue Service. (2009a). *Annual electronic filing requirement for small exempt organizations—Form 990-N (e-Postcard).* Retrieved from www.irs.gov/charities/article/0,,id=169250,00.html

Internal Revenue Service. (2009b). *Exemption requirements.* Retrieved from www.irs.gov/charities/charitable/article/0,,id=96099,00.html

Internal Revenue Service. (2009c). *Measuring lobbying activity: Expenditure test.* Retrieved from www.irs.gov/charities/article/0,,id=163394,00.html

Internal Revenue Service. (2009d). *Measuring lobbying activity: Substantial part test.* Retrieved from www.irs.gov/charities/article/0,,id=163393,00.html

Internal Revenue Service. (2009e). *Social welfare organizations.* Retrieved from www.irs.gov/charities/nonprofits/article/0,,id=96178,00.html

International Federation of Social Workers. (2008, August 14). *IFSW policy statement on health.* Approved by the IFSW General Meeting in Salvador de Bahia, Brazil. Retrieved from www.ifsw.org/en/p38000081.html

International Federation of Social Workers and International Association of Schools of Social Work. (2001). *Definition of social work.* Berne, Switzerland: Author.

International Monetary Fund. (2009, April 22). World economic outlook: Global economy contracts, with slow recovery next year. *IMFSurvey Magazine: IMF Research*[Online]. Retrieved from www.imf.org/external/pubs/ft/survey/so/2009/RES042209A.htm

Isen, A. M. (2000). Positive affect and decision-making. In M. Lewis, & J. M. Haviland-Jones (Ed.), *Handbook of emotions.* (pp. 417–435). New York: Guilford Press.

Issacs, D. (2009, July 22). Squatters win high court appeal to stay. *Namibian* [Online]. Retrieved from www.namibian.com.na/index.php?id=28&tx_ttnews[tt_news]=57647&no_cache=1

Jackson, T., & Haines, R. (2007). Cross-cultural management in South African NGOs. *South African Review of Sociology, 38*(1), 85–98.

Jacobs, I. (2006, May 9). Presentation to State Steering Committee, Community Development Initiative, Arizona.

Jacobs, W. B. (2001). Beyond therapy: Bringing social work back to human services reform. *Social Work, 46*(1), 51–60.

Janis, I. L. (1982). *Groupthink: Psychological studies of policy decisions and fiascos.* (2nd ed.). Boston, MA: Houghton Mifflin.

Jansson, B. S. (1994). *Social welfare policy: From theory to practice.* (2nd ed.). Belmont, CA: Wadsworth, Cengage Learning.

Jansson, B. S. (2005). *The reluctant welfare state: American social welfare policies: Past, present, and future.* (5th ed.). Belmont, CA: Brooks/Cole, Cengage Learning.

Jansson, B. S. (2008). *Becoming an effective policy advocate: From policy practice to social justice.* (5th ed.). Belmont, CA: Brooks/Cole, Cengage Learning.

Jansson, B. S. (2009). *The reluctant welfare state: Engaging history to advance social work practice in contemporary society.* (6th ed.). Belmont, CA: Brooks/Cole, Cengage Learning.

Johnson, D. W., & Johnson, F. P. (2006). *Joining together: Group theory and practice.* (9th ed.). Boston, MA: Pearson Allyn & Bacon.

Johnson, D. W., & Johnson, F. P. (2009). *Joining together: Group theory and practice.* (10th ed.). Upper Saddle River, NJ: Pearson.

Johnson, E. M. (2007). *Regulating charitable fundraising in the 21st century.* Retrieved from www.wtplaw.com/public_document.cfm?id=74

Johnson, L. C., & Schwartz, C. L. (1997). *Social welfare: A response to human need.* (4th ed.). Boston: Allyn & Bacon.

Johnson, L. C., & Yanca, S. J. (2007). *Social work practice: A generalist approach.* (9th ed.). Boston, MA: Pearson Allyn & Bacon.

Johnson, M. (2001). Fundraising on the net. In J. M. Greenfield (Ed.), *The nonprofit handbook: Fund raising.* (3rd ed., pp. 518–536). New York: Wiley.

Johnson, N., Oliff, P., & Koulish, J. (2009). *An update on state budget cuts: At least 34 states have imposed cuts that hurt vulnerable residents, but the federal economic recovery package is reducing harm.* Center for Budget and Policy Priorities. Retrieved from www.cbpp.org/files/1-22-09bud.pdf

Johnson, R. (1991). *Press plan.* Unpublished manuscript.

Join Together Online. (2000, March 29). *Sports franchises commit to helping communities.* Retrieved from www.jointogether.org/sa/resources/fuing/reader.jtml?Object_ID=262546

Joinson, G. (1992). Coping with compassion fatigue. *Nursing, 22,* 116–122.

Jones, M. (2000). Hope and despair at the front line: Observations on integrity and change in the human services. *International Social Work, 43*(3), 365–380.

Jones, R. (2009a). *Social media marketing 101, Part 1.* Retrieved from http://searchenginewatch.com/3632809

Jones, R. (2009b). *Twitter 101, Part 1.* Retrieved from http://searchenginewatch.com/3633223

Jones, R. (2009c). *Twitter 101, Part 2.* Retrieved from http://searchenginewatch.com/3633276

Julian, J. (1973). *Social problems.* Englewood Cliffs, NJ: Prentice-Hall.

Jungk, R., & Mullert, N. (1996). *Future workshops: How to create desirable futures.* London: Institute for Social Inventions.

Jurkowski, J. (2008). Photovoice as participatory action research tool for engaging people with intellectual disabilities in research and program development. *Intellectual & Developmental Disabilities, 46*(1), 1–11.

Kagan, S. L. (1999). *Using a theory of change approach in a national evaluation of family support programs: Practitioner reflections.* Retrieved from www.aspenroundtable.org/vol2/kagan.htm

Kahn, S. (1970). *How people get power: Organizing oppressed communities for action.* New York: McGraw-Hill.

Kahn, S. (1991). *Organizing: A guide for grassroots leaders* (Rev. ed.). Silver Spring, MD: National Association of Social Workers.

Kahn, S. (1994). *How people get power* (Rev. ed.). Washington, DC: NASW Press.

Kalil, A., & Wightman, P. (2009). *Parental job loss and children's educational attainment in Black and White middle class families.* Ann Arbor, MI: National Poverty Center.

Kalil, A., & Ziol-Guest, K. (2008). Parental job loss and children's academic progress in two-parent families. *Social Science Research, 37,* 500–515.

Kaminski, A. (2001). Women as philanthropists: A new approach and a new voice in major gifts. In J. M. Greenfield (Ed.), *The nonprofit handbook: Fund raising.* (3rd ed., pp. 361–381). New York: Wiley.

Kane, M., & Trochim, W. M. K. (2007). *Concept mapping for planning and evaluation.* Thousand Oaks, CA: Sage.

Kaner, S., Lind, L., Toldi, C., Fisk, S., & Berger, D. (2007). *Facilitator's guide to participatory decision-making.* San Francisco, CA: Jossey-Bass.

Karrass, C. L. (1981). Negotiation strategies. *Business Secrets.* (pp. 44–45). New York: Boardroom Reports.

Kasper, G., Nielsen, S., & Chao, J. (2004). Democracy in action: Focus funds, the next wave of community philanthropy, are responding to the needs of both marginalized groups and new donor bases. *Foundation News and Commentary 45*(6). Retrieved from www. foundationnews.org/CME/article.cfm?ID=3064

Kassam, A. (2002). Ethnotheory, ethnopraxis: The indigenous Oromo theory of development and development practice. In P. Sillitoe, A. Bicker, & J. Potter (Eds.), *Participating in development: Approaches to indigenous knowledge.* (pp. 64–81). London: Routledge.

Kawachi, I., Kim, D., Coutts, A., & Subramanian, S. V. (2004). Commentary: Reconciling the three accounts of social capital. *International Journal of Epidemiology, 33* (4), 682–690.

Keller, G. (1983). *Academic strategy: The management revolution in American higher education.* Baltimore, MD: Johns Hopkins.

Keller, S. (1968). *The urban neighborhood.* New York: Random House.

Kennedy, D. M. (1996, August). Neighborhood revitalization: Lessons from Savannah and Baltimore. *National Institute of Justice Journal,* 13–17.

Kent, M. M., Pollard, K. M., Haaga, J., & Mather, M. (2001, June). First glimpses from the 2000 U.S. Census. *Population Bulletin, 56*(2).

Kesler, J. T. (2000). The healthy community movement: Seven counterintuitive steps. *National Civic Review, 89* (3), 271–282.

Kettner, P. M., Daley, J. M., & Nichols, A. W. (1985). *Initiating change in organizations and communities: A macro practice model.* Pacific Grove, CA: Brooks/Cole.

Kibel, B., & Miner, W. (1996). *The basics of results mapping.* Bethesda MD: Pacific Institute for Research and Evaluation.

Killion, J., & Todnem, G. (1991). A process for personal theory building. *Educational Leadership, 48*(6), 14–16.

Kimble, M. (1991). Newspapers are news.In Tucson Newspapers, Inc. (Ed.), *What's News?* (pp. 4–5). Tucson, AZ: Tucson Newspapers, Inc.

Kindervater, S. (1983). *Women working together for personal, economic, and community development.* Washington, DC: Overseas Education Fund.

King, M. A., Sims, A., & Osher, D. (2000). *How is cultural competence integrated in education?* Retrieved from http:// cecp.air.org/cultural/Q_integrated.htm

Kirst-Ashman, K. K., & Hull, G. H. (2009). *Generalist practice: With organizations and communities.* (4th ed.). Belmont, CA: Brooks/Cole, Cengage Learning.

Klayman, B. (2009, January 26). Recession slams brakes on U.S. sponsorships—IEG. *Reuters* [Online]. Retrieved from www.sponsorship.com/About-IEG/IEG-In-The-News/Recession-slams-brakes-on-U.S.-sponsorships—IEG.aspx

Klein, A. F. (1972). *Effective group work: An introduction to principle and method.* New York: Association Press.

Klein, K. (1992, December). Budgeting for fundraising. *Grassroots Fundraising Journal,* 3–5.

Klein, K. (2000). *Fundraising: For the long haul.* Berkeley, CA: Chardon Press.

Klein, K. (2002, August 23). *Dear Kim Klein: Fundraising advice.* Retrieved from www.grassrootsfundraising.org

Klein, K. (2004, January–February). The ten most important things you can know about fundraising. *Grassroots Fundraising Journal,* 11–14.

Klein, K. (2006, February). Getting over the fear of asking. *Grassroots Fundraising Journal eNewsletter.* Retrieved from www.grassrootsfundraising.org/howto/dearkim/ 2042_200602.html

Klein, K. (2009, March–April). 5 Tips for nonprofits to survive and thrive now and into the future. *Grassroots Fundraising Journal,* 13–15.

Konopka, G. (1983). *Social group work: A helping process.* (3rd ed.). Englewood Cliffs, NJ: Prentice-Hall.

Kotler, M. (1969). *Neighborhood government: The local foundations of political life.* Indianapolis. IN: Bobbs-Merrill.

Kotler, M. (2005). *Neighborhood government: The local foundations of political life.* Lanham, MD: Lexington Books.

Kornmiller, D. (2005a, November 13). Star wants your ideas for projects. *Arizona Daily Star,* p. H3.

Kornmiller, D. (2005b, September 25). Working with the newspaper. *Arizona Daily Star,* p. H3.

Kramer, R., & Specht, H. (1983). *Readings in community organization practice.* (3rd ed.). Englewood Cliffs, NJ: Prentice-Hall.

Krebs, V., & Holley, J. (2006). *Building smart communities through network weaving.* Retrieved from www.orgnet. com/BuildingNetworks.pdf

Kretzmann, J. P., & McKnight, J. L. (1993). *Building communities from the inside out.* Chicago: ACTA.

Kretzmann, J. P., & McKnight, J. L. (1997). *A guide to capacity inventories: Mobilizing the community skills of local residents.* Chicago: ACTA.

Kretzmann, J., McKnight, J., Dobrowolski, S., & Puntenney, D. (2005). *Discovering community power: A guide for mobilizing local assets and your organization's capacity.* Evanston, IL: Asset-Based Community Development Institute.

Krueger, R. A., & King, J. A. (1997). *Involving community members in focus groups.* (Focus Group Kit, Vol. 5).Thousand Oaks, CA: Sage.

Laird, W., & Hoover, K. (1993). *Evaluation of the neighborhood small grants program.* Tucson, AZ: Tucson Community Foundation.

Lakoff, G. (2004). *Don't think of an elephant! Know your values and frame the debate.* White River Junction, VA: Chelsea Green River.

Lamiell, R. (1984). The people's lobby. In L. Staples (Ed.), *Roots of power: A manual for grassroots organizing.* (pp. 188–197). New York: Praeger.

Langton, S. (1982). Networking and community education. J. M. Brandon & Associates (Eds.), *Networking: A trainers manual.* (pp. 212–213). Amherst, MA: University of Massachusetts, Community Education Resource Center, School of Education.

Latting, J. K. (1990). Motivational differences between Black and White volunteers. *Non-Profit and Voluntary Sector Quarterly, 19*(2), 121–136.

Lauffer, A., & Gorodezky, S. (1977). *Volunteers.* Newbury Park, CA: Sage.

Lautman, K. P. (1997). Direct mail. In J. M. Greenfield (Ed.), *The nonprofit handbook: Fund raising.* (2nd ed., pp. 254–277). New York: Wiley.

Lautman, K. P. (2001). Direct mail. In J. M. Greenfield (Ed.), *The nonprofit handbook: Fund raising.* (3rd ed., pp. 456–479). New York: Wiley.

Lawrence, S., & Mukai, R. (2009). *Foundation growth and giving estimates 2009 Edition: Current outlook.* New York: The Foundation Center.

League of Women Voters. (1976). *Making an issue of it: The campaign handbook.* [Publication No. 613]. Washington, DC: Author.

League of Women Voters Education Fund. (1977). How to plan an environmental conference. In F. Cox, J. L. Erlich, J. Rothman, & J. E. Tropman (Eds.), *Tactics and techniques of community practice.* (pp. 111–152). Itasca, IL: Peacock.

Lechte, R. (1983, October 27–29). *Report of the world YWCA workshop on development and social change.* Singapore.

Lefton, J. (1992). Tucson citizen supports local nonprofit organizations.In Tucson Newspapers, Inc. (Ed.), *Meet the media.* (pp. 2–3). Tucson, AZ: Tucson Newspapers, Inc.

Leher, M. (2000, April–May). Endowment building: Myth and reality checks. *Philanthropy Works AZ, 1*(2), 9.

Levine, J. R., Baroudi, C., & Young, M. L. (2007). *The Internet for dummies.* (11th ed.). Hoboken, NJ: Wiley.

Levy, C. S. (1973, Winter). The value base of social work. *Journal of Education for Social Work, 9,* 37–38.

Lewin, K. (1951). *Field theory in social science.* New York: Harper.

Lewis, J. (2002). *Welcome to the grants collection Tucson-Pima Public Library, Main Library.* Tucson, AZ: Tucson-Pima Public Library.

Lewis, J. A., Packard, T., & Lewis, M. D. (2007). *Management of human service programs.* (4th ed.). Belmont, CA: Brooks/Cole, Cengage Learning.

Lewis, M. J., West, B., Bautista, L., Greenberg, A., & Done-Perez, I. (2005). Perceptions of service providers and community members on intimate partner violence within a Latino community. *Health Education and Behavior, 32*(10), 69–83.

Liamzon, C. (1997). An overview of the concept of empowerment. In *People's Empowerment: Grassroots experiences in Africa, Asia and Latin America.* (pp. 1–32). Rome, Italy: IRED Nord.

Lindsey, K. R. (2006). *Racial, ethnic and tribal philanthropy: A scan of the landscape.* Washington, DC: Forum of Regional Associations of Grantmakers.

Lipsky, M. (1984). Bureaucratic disentitlement in social welfare programs. *Social Service Review, 58*(2), 3–27.

Litwak, E., Shiroi, E., Zimmerman, L., & Bernstein, J. (1970). Community participation in bureaucratic organizations: Principles and strategies. *Interchange, 1*(4), 44–60.

Lloyd-Jones, E. (1989). Foreword. In D. Roberts (Ed.), *Designing campus activities to foster a sense of community.* [New Direction for Student Services, 48]. San Francisco: Jossey-Bass.

Loewe, M., & Mould, D. R. (2007). *Beyond the bake sale: 100 innovative fundraising ideas for nonprofits.* Baltimore, MD: Publish America.

Lofquist, W. (2008, October 28). *A new dawn: The organization as learning laboratory.* Plenary address, National Organization for Human Services, Tucson, Arizona.

Lofquist, W. A. (1993). *The technology of prevention workbook* (Expanded ed.). Tucson, AZ: AYD Publications.

Lofquist, W. A. (1996). *The technology of development: A framework for transforming community cultures.* Tucson, AZ: Development Publications.

Lombe, M., Nebbit, V. E., & Buerlein, J. (2007). Perceived effects of participation in an asset-building program on construction of future possibilities. *Families in Society, 88*(3), 463–471.

Lombe, M., & Sherraden, M. (2008). Effects of participating in and asset-building intervention on social inclusion. *Journal of Poverty, 12*(3), 284–305.

Longres, J. (2000). *Human behavior in the social environment.* (3rd ed.). Itasca, IL: Peacock.

Lorenz, E. (2001). The butterfly effect. In R. Abraham Y. Ueda (Eds.), *The chaos avant-garde: Memories of the early days of chaos theory.* (pp. 91–94). Hackensack, NJ: World Scientific.

Lotspeich, M. L., & Kleymeyer, J. E. (1976). How to gather data about your neighborhood. *Neighborhood Technical Information Service, 1*(10) Chicago: American Society of Planning Officials.

Loughran, J. J. (2002). Effective reflective practice. *Journal of Teacher Education, 53*(1), 33–43.

Lowe, J. S. (2008). Limitations of community development partnerships: Cleveland Ohio and Neighborhood Progress, Inc. *Cities, 25*(1), 37–44.

Luke, T. W. (1989). *Screens of power: Ideology, domination, and resistance in informational society.* Urbana: University of Illinois Press.

Lum, D. (2004). *Social work practice with people of color: A process-stage approach.* (5th ed.). Belmont, CA: Brooks/Cole, Cengage Learning.

Lumsden, G., Lumsden, D., & Wiethoff, C. (2010). *Communicating in groups and teams: Sharing leadership.* (5th ed.). Belmont, CA: Wadsworth, Cengage Learning.

Lynch, D. J. (1996, September 20). Dying dreams, dead-end streets. *USA Today*, pp. B1–2.

Lynn, A. (2005). Youth using research: Learning through social practice, community building, and social change. *New Directions for Youth Development, 106*, 39–48.

Lynn, K., & Lynn, D. (1992). Common cents fund raising. *New Designs for Youth Development, 10*(2), 34–39.

Magat, R. (1998). *Unlikely partners: Philanthropic foundations and the labor movement.* New York: Cornell University Press.

Magliocca, L. A., & Christakis, A. N. (2001). Creating transforming leadership for organizational change: The CogniScope system approach. *Systems Research and Behavioral Science, 18*(3), 259–282.

Mahoney, J. (2006). *Tips for highly effective fundraising.* CompuMentor. Retrieved from www.techsoup.org/learningcenter/funding/page4306.cfm

Male, R. (1993). The politics of thriving as well as surviving. In R. L. Clifton & A. M. Davis (Eds.), *Grassroots administration: A resource book for directors, staff, and volunteers of small community-based nonprofit agencies.* (2nd ed., pp. 83–95). Pacific Heights, IL: Waveland Press.

Mamphiswana, D., & Noyoo, N. (2000). Social work education in a changing sociopolitical and economic dispensation: Perspectives from South Africa. *International Social Work, 43*(1), 21–32.

Mancoske, R. J., & Hunzeker, J. M. (1994). Advocating for community services coordination: An empowerment perspective for planning AIDS services. *Journal of Community Practice, 1*(3), 49–58.

Marais, L. (2008). Walking between worlds: Implications of indigenous practice for social justice and cultural competence. *Social and Economic Justice and Peace Section Connection, 2*(1), 3–5.

Marconi, J. (2002). *Cause marketing: How to build your image and bottom line through socially responsible partnerships, programs, and events.* Chicago: Dearborn.

Marger, M. N. (2009). *Race and ethnic relations: American and global perspectives.* (8th ed.). Belmont, CA: Wadsworth, Cengage Learning.

Margolin, J. B., & DiMaio, E. K. (2008). *The grantseekers guide to winning proposals.* New York: The Foundation Center.

Martí-Costa, S., & Serrano-García, I. (1995). Needs assessment and community development: An ideological perspective. In J. Rothman, J. L. Erlich, & J. E. Tropman (Eds.), *Strategies of community intervention.* (5th ed., pp. 257–267). Itasca, IL: Peacock.

Martin, D. (2009). *Twitter quitters post roadblock to long-term growth.* Retrieved from http://blog.nielsen.com/nielsenwire/online_mobile/twitter-quitters-post-roadblock-to-long-term-growth/

Martin, D. G. (2003). "Place framing" as place-making: Constituting a neighborhood for organizing and activism. *Annals of the American Association of Geographers, 93*(3), 730–750.

Martin, M., & Vaughn, B. (2007). Cultural competence. *Strategic Diversity & Inclusion Management*, pp. 31–36.

Martin, P. Y. (1980). Multiple constituencies, dominant societal values, and the human service administrator: Implications for service delivery. *Administration in Social Work, 4*(2), 15–27.

Martinez, A. (2005, April–May). Latinas in philanthropy. *LATINA Style Magazine.*

Martinez, B. (2002, August 23). *Donating property to charity may get easier.* Retrieved from http://homes.wsj.com/buy-sell/mortgages/20001024-martinez.html

Martinez, K., & Van Buren, E. (2008). *The cultural and linguistic competence implementation guide.* Washington, DC: Technical Assistance Partnerships for Child and Family Mental Health.

Martinez-Brawley, E. A. (2000). *Closer to home: Human services in the small community.* Washington, DC: NASW Press.

Marx, J. D. (2000). Women and human services giving. *Social Work, 45*(1), 27–38.

Mason, J. L. (1988). Investing for results: Corporate philanthropic activities. *Vital Speeches of the Day, 54*(12), 379–381.

Mason, R. O., & Mitroff, I. I. (1985). A teleological power-oriented theory of strategy. In W. G. Bennis, K. D. Benne, & R. Chin (Eds.), *The planning of change.* (4th ed., pp. 215–223). New York: Holt, Rinehart & Winston.

Max, S. (1980). *Making a first contact with a potential member.* Chicago: Midwest Academy.

Mayallah, E. (2009, April 4). Tanzania: Community development. *Arusha Times* [Online]. Retrieved from www.allafrica.com/stories/printable/200904061116.html

Mayer, N. S. (1984). *Neighborhood organizations and community development: Making revitalization work.* Washington, DC: Urban Institute Press.

Mayer, R. R. (1985). *Program planning: A developmental perspective.* Englewood Cliffs, NJ: Prentice-Hall.

McCreight, M. (2004). Using the law as leverage. In L. Staples (Ed.), *Roots to power: A manual for grassroots organizing.* (2nd ed., pp. 254–263). Westport, CT: Praeger.

McDonald, A., & Denning, P. (2008). *The capacity building challenge: A Scottish perspective.* Retrieved from www.obs-pascal.com/system/files/Capacity+Building+Challenge_0.pdf

McDonald, M., Sarche, J., & Wang, C. (2005). Using the arts in community organizing and community building. In J. Minkler (Ed.), *Community organizing and community building for health.* (2nd ed., pp. 346–364). New Brunswick, NJ: Rutgers University Press.

McDonald, M. P. (2008). The return of the voter: Voter turnout in the 2008 presidential election. *The Forum, 6*(4). Retrieved from www.bepress.com/forum/vol6/iss4/art4

McGiboney, M. (2009). *Twitter's tweet smell of success.* Retrieved from http://blog.nielsen.com/nielsenwire/online_mobile/twitters-tweet-smell-of-success

McKay, S. (1988, November). The manager: Profile artistic director. *Canadian Business,* 193–196.

McKillip, J. (1987). *Needs analysis: Tools for the human services and education.* Newbury Park, CA: Sage.

McKinnon, H. (2008). *The 11 questions every donor asks: And the answers all donors crave.* Medfield, MA: Emerson & Church.

McKnight, J. (1995). *The careless society: Community and its counterfeits.* New York: Basic Books.

McLaughlin, J. A., & Jordan, G. B. (2004). Using logic models. In J. S. Wholey, H. P. Hatry, & K. E. Newcomer (Eds.), *Handbook of practical program evaluation.* (2nd ed., pp. 7–32). San Francisco, CA: Jossey-Bass.

McLean, C. (1980). The lobbying process and the community service agency. In R. L. Clifton, & A. M. Dahms (Eds.), *Grassroots administration: A handbook for staff and directors of small community-based social service agencies.* (pp. 133–140). Pacific Grove, CA: Brooks/Cole.

McLinden, S. (2006). Worth a second look: Nonprofits reveal urban opportunities missed by the U.S. census. *Shopping Centers Today.* Retrieved from www.icsc.org/srch/sct/sct0706/worth_second_look.php

McPherson, M., Smith-Lovin, L., & Brashears, M. (2006, June). Social isolation in America: Changes in core discussion networks over two decades. *American Sociological Review,* 71, 353–375.

Media Audit. (2004). *Internet use continues growing: Most new growth driven by older age groups.* Local Market Surveys December 7.

Meenaghan, T. M., & Gibbons, W. E. (2000). *Generalist practice in larger settings: Knowledge and skill concepts.* Chicago: Lyceum.

Meenaghan, T. M., Gibbons, W. E., & McNutt, J. G. (2005). *Generalist practice in larger settings: Knowledge and skill concepts.* (2nd ed.). Chicago: Lyceum.

Meenaghan, T. M., & Washington, R. O. (1980). *Social policy and social welfare: Structure and applications.* New York: Free Press.

Melanesian Council of Churches. (1977). *Lilik Buk: A rural development for Papua New Guinea* (English ed.). Wewak, PNG: Wirui Press.

Mendes, P. (2009). Teaching community development to social work students: A critical reflection. *Community Development Journal, 44*(2), 248–262.

Metro Chicago Information Center. (2008). *Community vitality index: Methodology.* Retrieved from http://info.mcfol.org/www/datainfo/cvi/methodology.asp

Metzger, J. T. (2000). Planned abandonment: The neighborhood life-cycle theory and urban policy. *Housing Policy Debate, 11*(1), 7–40.

Meyer, A. E. (1945, June 5). *Washington Post.*

Meyerson, D. E. (1994, December). Interpretations of stress in institutions: The cultural production of ambiguity and burnout. *Administrative Science Quarterly,* 39, 628–653.

Midgely, J. O. (1995). *Social development: The developmental perspective in social welfare.* Thousand Oaks, CA: Sage.

Midgely, J. O. (2009). The definition of social policy. In J. O. Midgely, & M. M. Livermore. *The handbook of social policy.* (pp. 3–20). Thousand Oaks, CA: Sage.

Midwest Academy. (2001). *Organizing for social change: Midwest Academy manual for activists.* Santa Ana, CA: Seven Locks Press.

Minch, H. (2005, Summer). Considerations at the intersection: Community organizing and strategic communications. *Social Policy.* Retrieved from www.socialpolicy.org/index.php?id=1504

Minieri, J., & Gestos, P. (2007). *Tools for radical democracy.* San Francisco, CA: Jossey-Bass.

Minkler, M., & Wallerstein, N. (2005). Improving health through community organization and community building: A health education perspective. In J. Minkler (Ed.), *Community organizing and community building for health.* (2nd ed., pp. 26–50). New Brunswick, NJ: Rutgers University Press.

Mirazo, C., Hicks, T., Taylor, C., & Ferlazzo, T. (2001). Small is not beautiful. *Social Policy, 32*(2), 39–43.

Mirkin, H. R. (1978). *The complete fundraising guide*. New York: Public Service Materials Center.

Mitchell-Clark, K., & Autry, A. (2004). *Preventing family violence: Lessons learned from the community engagement initiative*. San Francisco, CA: Family Violence Prevention Fund.

Mizrahi, T., & Rosenthal, B. B. (2001). Complexities of coalition building: Leaders' successes: Strategies, struggles, and solutions. *Social Work, 46*(1), 63–78.

Moerschbaecher, L. S., & Dryburgh, E. D. (2001). Planned giving: Gift vehicles. In J. M. Greenfield (Ed.), *The non-profit handbook: Fund raising*. (3rd ed., pp. 788–823). New York: Wiley.

Molnar, B. E., Gortmaker, S. L., Bull, F. C., & Buka, S. L. (2004). Unsafe to play? Neighborhood disorder and lack of safety predict reduced physical activity among urban children and adolescents. *American Journal of Health Promotion, 18*(5), 378–386.

Mondross, J. B., & Berman-Rossi, T. (1992). The relevance of stages of group development theory to community organization practice. In A. Vinik, & M. Levin (Eds.), *Social action in group work*. (pp. 203–221). New York: Haworth.

Morales, A., & Sheafor, B. W. (1986). *Social work: A profession of many faces*. (4th ed.). Boston: Allyn & Bacon.

Morales, A. T., & Sheafor, B. W. (2010). *Social work: A profession of many faces*. (12th ed.). Boston, MA: Pearson Allyn & Bacon.

Morgan, G. (2007). *Images of organization* (Updated ed.). Thousand Oaks, CA: Sage.

Morley, E., Vinson, E., & Hatry, H. P. (2001). *Outcome measurement in nonprofit organizations: Current practices and recommendations*. Waldorf, MD: Independent Sector.

Moroney, R. (1991). *Social policy and social work: Critical essays on the welfare state*. New York: Aldine de Gruyter.

Morrison, J. D., Howard, J., Johnson, C., Navarro, F. J., Placheta, B., & Bell, T. (1997). Strengthening neighborhoods by developing community networks. *Social Work, 42*(5), 527–534.

Morth, M., & Collins, S. (1996). *The Foundation Center's user-friendly guide: A grantseeker's guide to resources*. (Rev. ed.) New York: Foundation Center.

Moss, J. (2002, July–August). The power of the community press. *Shelterforce Online,* 124. Retrieved from www. nhi.org/online/issues/124/press.html

Mottino, F., & Miller, E. D. (2004). *Pathways for change: Philanthropy among African American, Asian American, and Latino donors in the New York metropolitan region*. New York: Center on Philanthropy and Civil Society, City University of New York/Coalition for New Philanthropy.

Muirhead, S. A. (2006). *Philanthropy and business: The changing agenda*. New York: Conference Board.

Mupedziswa, R. (2001). The quest for relevance: Towards a model of developmental social work education and training in Africa. *International Social Work, 44*(3), 285–300.

Murray, A. (2005). *Add charity shopping to your web site: Shop online and generate profits for your nonprofit*. Retrieved from www.techsoup.org/learningcenter/funding/page2298.cfm

Mutz, J., & Murray, K. (2006). *Fundraising for dummies*. (2nd ed.). Hoboken, NJ: Wiley.

Nagy, G., & Falk, D. (2000). Dilemmas in international and cross-cultural social work education. *International Social Work, 43*(1), 49–60.

Naparstek, A. J., & Dooley, D. (1997). Countering urban disinvestment through community-building initiatives. *Social Work, 42*(5), 506–514.

Napier, R. W., & Gershenfeld, M. K. (1989). *Groups: Theory and experience*. (4th ed.). Boston, MA: Houghton Mifflin.

Napier, R. W., & Gershenfeld, M. K. (2004). *Groups: Theory and experience*. (7th ed.). Mahwah, NJ: Erlbaum.

Nation, M. (2008). Concentrated disadvantage in urban neighborhoods: Psychopolitical validity as a framework for developing psychology-related solutions. *Journal of Community psychology, 36*(2), 187–198.

National Association of Social Workers. (1973). *NASW standards for social service manpower*. New York: Author.

National Association of Social Workers. (1982). *Standards for the classification of social work practice. Policy Statement,* 4. New York: Author.

National Association of Social Workers. (1997). *The National Association of Social Workers code of ethics*. New York: Author.

National Association of Social Workers. (2001). *NASW standards for cultural competence in social work practice*. Retrieved from www.socialworkers.org/practice/standards/cultural_competence.asp

National Association of Social Workers. (2002). *Social work profession overview*. Retrieved from www. socialworkers.org/profession/factsheet.htm

National Association of Social Workers. (2008). *Code of ethics*. Washington, DC: Author.

National Association of Social Workers. (2009). *Specialty practice sections*. Washington, DC: Author. Retrieved from www.socialworkers.org/sections/default.asp

National Association of State Charity Officials. (2001). *The Charleston principles: Guidelines on charitable solicitations using the Internet*. Retrieved from www.nasconet.org/CharlestonPrinciples,Final.pdf

National Center for Economic and Security Alternatives. (2002a). *Models and innovations: Community development financial institutions*. Retrieved from www.ncesa.org/html/comdevfin.html

National Center for Economic and Security Alternatives. (2002b). *Models and innovations: Land trusts*. Retrieved from www.ncesa.org/html/landtrust.html

National Commission on Neighborhoods. (1979). *People, building neighborhoods. Final Report to the President and the Congress of the United States.* Washington, DC: U.S. Government Printing Office.

National Community Reinvestment Coalition. (2008). *CRA Toolkit: Protecting and preserving the Community Reinvestment Act.* Retrieved from www.ncrc.org/images/stories/era/cra%20toolkit_v8_remarks_joint_statement.pdf

National Conference of State Legislatures. (2009). *Initiative, referendum and recall.* Washington, DC: Author. Retrieved from www.ncsl.org/default.aspx?tabid=16600

National Foundation for Women Business Owners. (2000, November 14). *Survey finds business owners are philanthropic leaders* [News release]. Retrieved from www.womensbusinessresearch.org/Research/11-14-2000/11-14-2000.htm

National Institute for Occupational Safety and Health. (2009). *STRESS . . . at work* [Pub. no. 99-101]. Retrieved from www.cdc.gov/niosh/docs/99-101/

National Organization for Human Services. (2000). Ethical standards of human service professionals. *Human Service Education, 20*(1), 61–68.

National Organization for Human Services. (2009). *Human services.* Retrieved from www.nationalhumanservices.org/mc/page.do?sitePageId-89926 &orgId=nohs

Neighborhood Centers Inc. (2009). *Appreciative inquiry.* Retrieved from www.neighborhood-centers.org/en-us/content/page.aspx?pageid=418

Neighborhood Funders Group. (2009). *Working group on labor and community.* Retrieved from www.nfg.org/labor/index.htm

Nelson, G. M. (2000). *Self-governance in communities and families.* San Francisco, CA: Barrett-Koehler.

Nelson-Jones, R. (1992). *Group leadership: A training approach.* Pacific Grove, CA: Brooks/Cole.

Netting, F. E., Kettner, P. M., & McMurtry, S. L. (1998). *Social work macro practice.* (2nd ed.). New York: Longman.

Network for Good. (2009). *How can we help you become a fundraising superhero?.* Retrieved from www.fundraising123.org

Neuber, K. A., Atkins, W. T., Jacobson, J. A., & Reuterman, N. A. (1980). *Needs assessment: A model for community planning.* Newbury Park, CA: Sage.

New, C. (2001). Grants from the government. In J. M. Greenfield (Ed.), *The nonprofit handbook: Fund raising.* (3rd ed., pp. 692–712). New York: Wiley.

New Tithing Group. (2005). *The demographics of charitable giving.* San Francisco, CA: New Tithing Group.

Nicholas, T. (2003). Unpublished dissertation. Western Washington University.

Nichols, J. (2001). *Pinpointing affluence in the 21st century: Increasing your share of donor dollars.* Chicago: Bonus Books.

Nielsen Company. (2009). *How teens use media: A Nielsen report on the myths and realities of teen media trends.* Retrieved from http://blog.nielsen.com/nielsenwire/reports/nielsen_howteensusemedia_june09.pdf

Nielsen Online. (2009). *United States: Average web usage month of March, 2009.* Home panel. Retrieved from www.nielsen-online.com/press_fd.jsp?section=pr_netv&nav=3

Nonprofit Counsel. (1986, March). Planned giving: It's for all: The ten steps for beginning. *Nonprofit Counsel,* 4–9.

Nonprofit Pathfinder. (2002). *MOMS and COPS: Managing our maternity services and community-oriented policing services.* Retrieved from.

Nord, M., Andrews, M., & Carlson, S. (2008). Household food security in the United States, 2007. *Economic Research Report.* (No. ERR-66) Washington, DC: Economic Research Service, U.S. Department of Agriculture.

Novak, J. D., & Cañas, A. J. (2008, January 22). *The theory underlying concept maps and how to construct them* [Technical Report IHMC CmapTools 2006-01 Rev 01-2008]. Florida Institute for Human and Machine Cognition. Retrieved from http://cmap.ihmc.us/Publications/ResearchPapers/TheoryUnderlyingConceptMaps.pdf

Nutt, P. C. (1985). The study of planning process. In W. G. Bennis, K. D. Benne, & R. C. Chin (Eds.), *The planning of change.* (4th ed., pp. 198). New York: Holt, Rinehart & Winston.

O. M. Collective. (1971). *The organizers manual.* New York: Bantam Books.

O'Connor, M. K., & Netting, F. E. (2009). *Organizational practice: A guide to understanding human services.* (2nd ed.). Hoboken, NJ: Wiley.

Olasky, M. (1996). *Renewing American compassion: How compassion for the needy can turn ordinary citizens into heroes.* New York: Free Press.

Olney, P. (2001). A vital contribution to community building. *Social Policy, 31*(4), 44.

O'Looney, J. (1993, December). Beyond privatization and service integration: Organizational models for service delivery. *Social Service Review,* 501–534.

O'Neill, J. V. (2002, January). Welfare reform found to stress agencies. *NASW News,* p. 4.

Organization for Economic Co-operation and Development. (2001). *The well-being of nations: The role of human and social capital.* Paris, France: Author.

Osten, M. (2001). Technology and strategy for organizational effectiveness. In T. D. Connors (Ed.), *The nonprofit handbook: Management.* (3rd ed., pp. 319–347). New York: Wiley.

Owen, A. L., & Videras, J. (2006). *Reconsidering social capital: A latent class approach.* Retrieved from www.socialcapitalgateway.org/paper-owen.pdf

Pace, P. R. (2006, July). Child welfare staffing addressed on Hill. *NASW News*, p. 5.

Page, S. E. (2007). *The difference: How the power of diversity creates better groups, firms, schools and societies.* Princeton, NJ: Princeton University Press.

Palmer, P. (1993). *The promise of paradox.* Notre Dame, IN: Ave Maria.

Panas, J. (1989). *Research shows eight reasons why philanthropists make major gifts.* Chicago: Panas, Linzy, & Partners, Inc.

Papworth, J. (1995). *Small is powerful: The future as if people really mattered.* Westport, CN: Praeger.

PARfem. (2003). *Participatory feminism.* Retrieved from www.einaudi.cornell.edu/parfem/index.htm

Parsons, R. J. (1989). Empowerment for role alternatives for low income minority girls: A group work approach. In J. A. B. Lee (Ed.), *Group work with the poor and oppressed.* (pp. 27–42). New York: Haworth.

Patti, R. J. (1974). Limitations and prospects of internal advocacy. *Social Casework, 55*(9), 537–545.

Patti, R. J. (1980). Internal advocacy and human services practitioners: An exploratory study. In H. Resnick, & R. J. Patti. *Change from within: Humanizing social welfare organizations.* (pp. 287–301). Philadelphia: Temple University Press.

Patti, R. J., & Resnick, H. (1975). Changing the agency from within. In R. M. Kramer, & H. Specht (Eds.), *Readings in community organization practice.* (2nd ed., pp. 65–74). Englewood Cliffs, NJ: Prentice-Hall.

Patton, C. V. (1987). Citizen input and professional responsibility. In F. M. Cox, J. L. Erlich, J. Rothman, & J. E. Tropman (Eds.), *Strategies of community organization: Macro practice.* (4th ed., pp. 343–350). Itasca, IL: Peacock.

Peck, M. (1987). *The different drum: Community making and peace.* New York: Simon & Schuster.

Pendleton, N. (1981). *Fund raising.* Englewood Cliffs, NJ: Prentice-Hall.

Penna, R., & Phillips, W. (2005). Eight outcome models. *The Evaluation Exchange, Harvard Graduate School of Education, 11*(2), 4–5.

Perlman, R., & Gurin, A. (1972). *Community organization and social planning.* New York: Wiley.

Pertschuk, M. (1986). *Giant killers.* New York: Norton.

Peters, S. J., Gregoire, H., & Hittleman, M. (2004). Practicing a pedagogy of hope: Practitioner profiles as tools for grounding and guiding collective reflection in adult, community, and youth development education. In M. Reynolds, & R. Vince (Eds.), *Organizing reflection.* (pp. 194–218). Hampshire, England: Ashgate.

Petersen, S. W. (1979). *Successful fundraising.* New York: Caroline House.

Pew Internet and American Life Project. (2009). *Demographics of Internet users.* Retrieve from www.pewinternet.org/Static-Pages/Data-Tools/Download-Data/~/media/Infographics/Trend%20Data/January%202009%20updates/Demographics%20of%20Internet%20Users%201%206%2009.jpg

Pew Partnership for Civic Change. (2001). *Ready, willing, and able: Citizens working for change.* Retrieved from www.pew-partnership.org/pubs/rwa/printable/full_report.html

Pew Research Center for People and the Press. (2008, August 17). *Key news audiences now blend online and traditional sources.* Retrieved from http://people-press.org/report/?pageid=1353

Phelan, M. E. (2002, April). Nonprofit enterprises: Corporations, trusts, and associations (2002-1). In *Cumulative Supplement* (Vol. 1). Eagan, MN: West Group.

Phelan, M. E. (2006). Charitable organizations and the charitable deduction. Nonprofit enterprises: Corporations, trusts, and associations (2002-1). In *Cumulative Supplement* (Vol. 1). Eagan,, MN: Thomson West.

Philanthropy.org. (2002). *Multicultural philanthropy: Issues and trends, updates: Latino reports.* Retrieved from www.philanthropy.org/inside/multicultural_philanthropy/updates_latino_funds.htm

PhotoVoice. (2009, February 23). *Who are we?* Retrieved from www.photovoice.org/html/whoarewe/

Piccard, B. (1988). *Introduction to social work: A primer.* (4th ed.). Pacific Grove, CA: Brooks/Cole.

Picker, L. A. (1997). The corporate support marketplace. In J. M. Greenfield (Ed.), *The nonprofit handbook: Fund raising.* (2nd ed., pp. 372–395). New York: Wiley.

Picker, L. A. (2001). The corporate support marketplace. In J. M. Greenfield (Ed.), *The nonprofit handbook: Fund raising.* (3rd ed., pp. 615–637). New York: Wiley.

Pima County Public Library. (2009, February 24). *Research and resources: Search engines—databases vs. websites FAQ.* Retrieved from www.library.pima.gov/research/searchengines/webordatabase.cfm#what

Pincus, A., & Minahan, A. (1973). *Social work practice: Model and method.* Itasca, IL: Peacock.

Plested, B. A., Edwards, R., & Jumper-Thurman, P. (2006). *Community readiness: A handbook for successful change.* Ft. Collins, CO: Tri-Ethnic Center for Prevention Research.

Poderis, T. (2006). *Fund-raising with a net: The Internet.* Retrieved from www.raise-funds.com/010902forum.html

Poley, J. (2001). Management implications and opportunities of global communications: "Hawken-Kraks Howl" and Global dot com: Storm, norm, form. In T. D. Connors (Ed.), *The nonprofit handbook: Management.* (3rd ed., pp. 162–177). New York: Wiley.

PolicyLink. (2006). *Community land trusts.* Retrieved from http://policylink.org/EDTK/CLT/

Pollack, D. (2003). *Social work and the courts: A casebook.* (2nd ed.). New York: Brunner-Routledge.

Polycarpe, M. (2004, August 6). Black philanthropy: Harnessing a growing resource. *onPhilanthropy.* Retrieved from www.onphilanthropy.com/site/News2?page=NewsArticle&id=5348

Portes, A., & Landolt, P. (1996). Unsolved mysteries: The Tocqueville Files II. *The American Prospect, 7*(26).

Potts, D. (2005). *Models of cultural competence.* Unpublished manuscript.

Power, E. (2001). Coping with change: A primer for developing human resources. In T. D. Connors (Ed.), *The nonprofit handbook: Management.* (3rd ed., pp. 716–725). New York: Wiley.

Prager, D. J. (1999). *Raising the value of philanthropy: A synthesis of informal interviews with foundation executives and observers of philanthropy.* Portage, WI: Denis J. Prager Strategic Consulting Services.

Pretty, J. (2000). Towards sustainable food and farming systems in industrialized countries. *International Journal of Agricultural Resources, Governance, and Ecology, 1*(1), 77–94.

Prilleltensky, I., & Fox, D. R. (2007). Psychopolitical literacy for wellness and justice. *Journal of Community Psychology, 35,* 793–805.

Pruitt, D. (1981). *Negotiating behavior.* New York: Academic Press.

Pryor, J. H., Hurtado, S., DeAngelo, J., Sharkness, J., Romero, L. C., Korn, W. S., & Tran, S. (2009). *The American freshman: National norms for fall 2008.* Los Angeles, CA: Higher Education Research Institute.

Pryor, J. H., Hurtado, S., Saenz, V. B., Santos, J. L., & Korn, W. (2007). *The American freshman: Forty year trends 1966–2006.* Los Angeles, CA: Higher Education Research Institute.

Public Health Leadership Society. (2002). *Principles of the ethical practice of public health.* New Orleans, LA: Author.

Pumphrey, M. W. (1959). *The teaching of values and ethics in social work education.* New York: Council on Social Work Education.

Pumphrey, R. (1971). Social welfare: History. In *National Association of Social Workers, Encyclopedia of social work* (16th ed., Vol. 2, pp. 1446–1461). Silver Spring, MD: National Association of Social Workers.

Putnam, M., Sherraden, M., Lin, Z., & Morrow-Howell, N. (2008). Age differences in IDA savings outcomes: Findings from the American Dream Demonstration. *Journal of Aging and Social Policy, 20*(1), 45–63.

Putnam, R. D. (1993). The prosperous community: Social capital and economic growth. *The American Prospect,* 35–42.

Putnam, R. D. (1995, January). Bowling alone: America's declining social capital. *Journal of Democracy, 6*(1), 65–78.

Putnam, R. D. (1996). The strange disappearance of civic America. *The American Prospect, 24,* 34–49.

Putnam, R. D. (2000). *Bowling alone: The collapse and revival of American community.* New York: Simon & Shuster.

Putnam, R. D. (2004). Commentary: "Health by association": Some comments. *International Journal of Epidemiology, 33*(4), 1–4.

Putnam, R. D., Feldstein, L. M., & Cohen, D. (2003). *Building together: Restoring the American community.* New York: Simon & Schuster.

Quick, J. A., & New, C. C. (2000). *Grant winner's toolkit: Project management and evaluation.* New York: Wiley.

Quick, J. A., & New, C. C. (2001). *Grant seeker's budget toolkit.* New York: Wiley.

Quinn, L. (2005). *Selecting an online donation tool: Part 2.* Retrieved from www.techsoup.org/learningcenter/funding/page4202.cfm

Ramos, H. A. J. (1999). Latino philanthropy: Expanding U.S. models of giving and civic participation. In Council on Foundations (Ed.), *Cultures of caring: Philanthropy in diverse American communities.* (pp. 147–188). Washington, DC: Council on Foundations.

Rathbun, S. (1986, January 26). *Working with the media.* Presentation to the National Association of Social Workers, Arizona Chapter, District II.

Reed, M., & Dewees, S. (2005). *Strategic philanthropy: Assessing the needs of the Native philanthropic sector.* Fredericksburg, VA: First Nations Development Institute.

Reed, M., Nuvayestewa, M., & Dewees, S. (2006). *Power of giving: Conference report: Strengthening philanthropy in native communities.* Fredericksburg, VA: First Nations Development Institute.

Reeves, R. A., Macolini, R. M., & Martin, R. C. (1987). Legitimizing paltry contributions: On-the-spot vs. mail-in requests. *Journal of Applied Social Psychology, 17*(8), 731–738.

Regan, D. T. (1971). Effects of a favor on liking and compliance. *Journal of Experimental Social Psychology, 7,* 627–639.

Reinhart, P. C. (1990, July). Forecasting the 1990's: The art of fund raising for the next decade. *Fund Raising Management,* 42–48.

Reisch, M., & Gorin, S. H. (2001). Nature of social work and future of the profession. *Social Work, 46*(1), 9–18.

Renner, T. (2009). *Local initiative and referendum in the U.S. Initiative and Referendum Institute, University of Southern California, School of Law.* Retrieved from www.iandrinstitute.org/Local%20I&R.htm

Resnick, H. (1978). Tasks in changing the organization from within (COFW). *Administration in Social Work, 2*(1), 29–44.

Resnick, H., & Menefee, D. (1994). A comparative analysis of organization development and social work, with suggestions for what organization development can do for social work. *Journal of Applied Behavioral Science, 29* (4), 432–445.

Rich, R. C. (1979, Fall). The roles of neighborhood organizations in urban service delivery. *Urban Affairs Papers,* 1, 81–93.

Richan, W. C. (2006). *Lobbying for social change.* (3rd ed.). New York: Haworth.

Richan, W. C., & Mendelsohn, A. R. (1973). *Social work: The unloved profession.* New York: New Viewpoints.

Richardson, J. A., & London, J. K. (2007). Strategies and lessons for reducing persistent rural poverty: A social-justice approach to funding rural community transformation. *Community Development, the Journal of the Community Development Society,* 38(1), 92–107.

Riley, J. (2000, July 17). Charitable work sells at a number of firms. *Arizona Daily Star,* pp. D1–3.

Rimsza, S. (2000). *State of the neighborhoods address.* Retrieved from http://phoenix.gov/CITYGOV/statnbhd.html

Rivera, F., & Erlich, J. (1998). *Community organizing in a diverse society.* (3rd ed.). Boston, MA: Allyn & Bacon.

Roach, M. J., & O'Brien, D. J. (1982). The impact of different kinds of neighborhood involvement on residents' overall evaluations of their neighborhoods. *Sociological Focus,* 15(4), 379–391.

Robinson, A. (2002). *Selling social change: Without selling out.* San Francisco, CA: Jossey-Bass.

Robinson, A. (2004). *Grassroots grants: An activists guide to proposal writing.* (2nd ed.). San Francisco, CA: Jossey-Bass.

Robinson, B., & Hanna, M. G. (1994). Lessons for academics from grassroots community organizing: A case study—the industrial areas foundation. *Journal of Community Practice,* 1(4), 63–94.

Robinson, D., & Williams, T. (2001, December). Social capital and voluntary activity: Giving and sharing in Maori and non-Maori society. *Social Policy Journal of New Zealand,* 52–71.

Rohe, W. M. (2009). One hundred years of neighbourhood planning. *Journal of the American Planning Association,* 75(2), 209–230.

Rohrer, J. E., Arif, A., Pierce, J. R., & Blackburn, C. (2004). Unsafe neighborhoods, social group activity, and self-rated health. *Journal of Public Health and Practice,* 10(2), 124–129.

Roloff, M. E., & Paulson, G. D. (2001). Confronting organizational transgressions. In J. M. Darley, D. M. Messick, & T. R. Tyler (Eds.), *Social influences on ethical behavior in organizations.* (pp. 53–68). Mahwah, NJ: Erlbaum.

Ronnby, A. (1995). *Mobilizing local communities.* Brookfield, VT: Avebury.

Ronnby, A. (1996). Local development and new cooperatives in Sweden: A grassroots approach. In Bauhaus Dessau Foundation & European Network for Economic Self-Help and Local Development (Eds.), *People's economy, wirtschaft von unten: Approaches toward a new social economy in Europe.* (pp. 69–81). Dessau, Germany: Bauhaus Dessau Foundation.

Ronnby, A. (1998). Mobilizing the local community. In P. Saukkonen, & H. Vihinen (Eds.), *Rural and regional development.* (pp. 65–80). Helsinki, Finland: University of Helsinki, Mikkeli Institute for Rural Research and Training.

Roper Center for Public Opinion Research. (1999, February). *Ethnic patterns in attitudes to philanthropy: A special report to the W. K. Kellogg Foundation.* Storrs, CT: Roper Center for Public Opinion Research, University of Connecticut.

Rose, S. (2000). Reflections on empowerment-based practice. *Social Work,* 45(5), 403–412.

Rosell, S. A. (2000). *Changing frames: Leadership and governance in the information age. Report of the Roundtable on Renewing Governance.* Retrieved from http://viewpointlearning.org/publications/books/changing_frames.pdf

Rosenman, M. (2005). Why social service groups must mobilize. *ACOSA,* 19(2, Summer), 1, 13.

Ross, R. K. (2006). A new approach to grant making. *Chronicle of Philanthropy,* 18(15). Retrieved from http://philanthropy.com/free/articles/v18/i15/15003501.htm

Rothman, J. (1968). Three models of community organization practice. In F. Cox, J. Erlich, J. Rothman, & J. Tropman (Eds.), *Strategies of community organization: A book of readings.* (pp. 3–26). Itasca, IL: Peacock.

Rothman, J., & Tropman, J. (1987). Models of community organization and macro practice perspectives: Their mixing and phasing. In F. M. Cox, J. L. Erlich, J. Rothman, & J. E. Tropman (Eds.), *Strategies of community organization: Macro practice.* (4th ed., pp. 3–26). Itasca, IL: Peacock.

Rubin, H., & Rubin, I. (1986). *Community organizing and development.* Columbus, OH: Merrill.

Rubin, H., & Rubin, I. (2008). *Community organizing and development.* Boston, MA: Allyn & Bacon.

Rubin, H. J., & Rubin, I. S. (2001). *Community organizing and development.* (3rd ed.). Boston, MA: Allyn & Bacon.

Ruby, J. F., & O'Brien, M. A. (1978). *United Way-Tucson: Communications kit.* Tucson, AZ: United Way-Tucson.

Rushton, M., & Brooks, A. C. (2006). Government funding of nonprofit organizations. In D. R. Young (Ed.), *Financing nonprofits: Putting theory into practice.* (pp. 69–92). New York: Altamira.

Russo, J. R. (1993). *Serving and surviving as a human service worker.* Prospect Heights, IL: Waveland Press.

Sachs, J. (1991). Action and reflection in work with a group of homeless people. In A. Vinik, & M. Levin (Eds.), *Social action in group work.* (pp. 187–202). New York: Haworth.

Saegert, S. (2006). Building civic capacity in urban neighbourhoods: An empirically grounded anatomy. *Journal of Urban Affairs, 28*(93), 275–294.

Sagasti, F. (1990). Interview in *Against the odds* [Videotape]. Visions in video series. (Available from South Carolina Educational Television Network, Columbia, SC.)

Saguaro Seminar. (2001). *Social capital benchmark survey.* Boston: Harvard University.

Saguaro Seminar. (2006). *Civic engagement in America: Factoids.* Retrieved from www.ksg.harvard.edu/saguaro/factoids.htm

Salgado, D. (2006). *2005 Annual service statistics.* Providence, RI: Campus Compact. Retrieved from www.compact.org/about/statistics/2005/index

Salkowski, J. (2002, March 11). Empowered, but how? *Arizona Daily Star,* pp. B1, 3.

Sampson, R. J., & Bean, L. (2006). Cultural mechanisms and killing fields: A revised theory of community-level racial inequality. In R. Peterson, L. Krivo, & J. Hagan (Eds.), *The many colors of crime: Inequalities of race, ethnicity, and crime in America.* (pp. 8–36). New York: New York University Press.

Sampson, T. (2004). Coalitions and other relations. In L. Staples (Ed.), *Roots to power: A manual for grassroots organizing.* (2nd ed., pp. 309–315). Westport, CT: Praeger.

Sander, T. (2005a, September 4). *E-Associations? Using Internet to connect citizens: The case of Meetup.com.* Paper for American Political Science Association Conference, Washington, DC, Panel 40-3.

Sander, T. (2005b, November 14). A friend in need. *The Boston Globe.* Retrieved from www.boston.com/news/globe/editorial_opinion/oped/articles/2005/11/14/a_friend_in_need/

Sarner, A. (2008). *Generation virtual.* Retrieved from www.forbes.com/2008/04/30/genv-gartner-marketing-oped-cx_asa_0430genv.html

Schaller, L. (1972). *The change agent.* Nashville, TN: Abingdon.

Scheie, D., Williams, T., Mayer, S. E., Kroll, B. S., & Dewar, T. (1997a). *Building support for neighborhood action: Lessons from the community foundations and neighborhoods program, 1991–1995.* Minneapolis: Rainbow Research.

Scheie, D., Williams, T., Mayer, S. E., Kroll, B. S., & Dewar, T. (1997b). *Helping neighborhood groups and leaders grow stronger: Lessons from the community foundations and neighborhoods program, 1991–1995.* Minneapolis: Rainbow Research.

Schelling, T. C. (1963). *The strategy of conflict.* Cambridge, MA: Harvard University Press.

Schelling, T. C. (1980). *The strategy of conflict.* Cambridge, MA: Harvard University Press.

Scherch, J. (2000). Riverton: Envisioning a sustainable community. In D. P. Fauri, S. P. Wernet, & F. E. Netting (Eds.), *Cases in macro social work practice.* (pp. 157–171). Boston, MA: Allyn & Bacon.

Scheuring, J. (2002). *The magic of community development in action: Case from Upper Volta 1972.* Unpublished manuscript.

Schindler-Rainman, E. (1975). Community development. In K. D. Benne, L. Bradford, J. R. Gibb, & R. Lippit (Eds.), *The laboratory method of changing and learning: Theory and application.* (pp. 447–448). Palo Alto, CA: Science & Behavior Books.

Schindler-Rainman, E. (1977). Goals to action. In E. Schindler-Rainman, R. Lippitt, & J. Cole (Eds.), *Taking your meetings out of the doldrums.* La Jolla, CA: University Associates, Inc.

Schladweiler, K. (2001). *The Foundation Center's guide to grant seeking on the Web, 2001 edition.* New York: Foundation Center.

Schmolling, P., Jr., Youkeles, M., & Burger, W. R. (1997). *Human services in contemporary America.* (4th ed.). Pacific Grove, CA: Brooks/Cole.

Schneider, J. A. (2006). *Social capital and welfare reform: Organizations, congregations, and communities.* New York: Columbia University Press.

Schön, D. (1983). *The reflective practitioner.* New York: Basic Books.

Schön, D. (1987). *Educating the reflective practitioner: Toward a new design for teaching and learning in the professions.* San Francisco, CA: Jossey-Bass.

Schorf, J. M., Fischer, D., Pollack, K., Brophy, B., & Kulman, L. (1996, February 19). Speak up! You can be heard! *U.S. News & World Report, 120,* pp. 42–52.

Schreiner, M., & Sherraden, M. (2005). Drop-out from individual development accounts: Prediction and prevention. *Financial Services Review 14,* 37–54.

Schumacher, D. (1992). *Get funded: A practical guide for scholars seeking research support from business.* Newbury Park, CA: Sage.

Schwab, W., & Ringel, B. (1991). An evaluation of the utility of five models of neighborhood change: The case of Cincinnati, Ohio. *Free Inquiry in Creative Sociology, 19*(2), 125–133.

Schwirian, K. P. (1983). Models of neighborhood change. *Annual Review of Sociology, 9,* 83–103.

Sechler, C. (2000, February–March). Curled up with a good 990 lately? *Philanthropy Works AZ,* 1(1), 15.

Seel, R. (2008). *Introduction to appreciative inquiry.* Retrieved from www.new-paradigm.co.uk/introduction_to_ai.htm

Segal, E. A., Gerdes, K., & Steiner, S. (2010). *An introduction to the profession of social work: Becoming a change agent.*

(3rd ed.). Belmont, CA: Brooks/Cole, Cengage Learning.

Selin, H., & Selin, N. E. (2008). Indigenous peoples in international environmental cooperation: Arctic management of hazardous substances. *Review of European Community and International Environmental Law, 17*(1), 72–83.

Seltzer, S. (2001). *Securing your foundation's future: A complete guide to fundraising strategies.* New York: Foundation Center.

Senge, P. (2006). The leader's new work: Building learning organizations. In J. V. Gallos (Ed.), *Organization development.* (pp. 765–792). San Francisco, CA: Jossey-Bass.

Senge, P., Kleiner, A., Roberts, C., Ross, R., & Smith, B. (1994). *The fifth discipline field book.* New York: Currency Doubleday.

Seymour-Rolls, K., & Hughes, I. (2000). Participatory action research: Getting the job done. *Action Research E-Reports, 4.*

Shacat, J. (2008, October 9). World beats path to master potter's town. *Arizona Daily Star,* p. B3.

Shaffer, R. (1983). *Beyond the dispensary.* Nairobi, Kenya: African Medical and Research Foundation.

Shamai, M., & Boehm, A. (2001). Politically oriented social work intervention. *International Social Work, 44*(3), 343–360.

Sharp, G. (1973a). *The politics of nonviolent action: Part one: Power and struggle.* Boston, MA: Porter Sargent.

Sharp, G. (1973b). *The politics of nonviolent action: Part two: The methods of nonviolent action.* Boston, MA: Porter Sargent.

Sharp, G. (1973c). *The politics of nonviolent action: Part three: The dynamics of nonviolent action.* Boston, MA: Porter Sargent.

Shaw, S. C., & Taylor, M. A. (1995). *Reinventing fundraising: Realizing the potential of women's philanthropy.* San Francisco, CA: Jossey-Bass.

Sheldon, K. S. (2000). *Successful corporate fund raising: Effective strategies for today's nonprofits.* New York: Wiley.

Shepard, G. (1991). Backlash in the American Dream: Resurgence of racism and the rise of the underclass. In G. Shepard, & D. Penna, *Racism and the underclass.* (pp. 3–22). New York: Greenwood Press.

Sherif, M. (1936). *The psychology of group norms.* New York: Harper & Row.

Sherman, W. R., & Wenocur, S. (1983, September–October). Empowering the public welfare workers through mutual support. *Social Work,* 375–379.

Sherraden, M. (2000). From research to policy: Lessons from individual development accounts. *Journal of Consumer Affairs, 34*(2), 159–181.

Sherraden, M. S., Slosar, B., & Sherraden, M. (2002). Innovation in social policy: Collaborative policy advocacy. *Social Work, 47*(3), 209–221.

Shulman, L. (1991). *Interactional social work practice: Toward an empirical theory.* Itasca, IL: Peacock.

Siglin, D. (1999). How to win the advocacy game: Rarified air. In R. B. Smucker (Ed.), *The nonprofit lobbying guide.* (2nd ed., pp. 121–124). Washington, DC: Independent Sector.

Simpson, D., & Gentile, A. (1986, Spring). Effective neighborhood government. *Social Policy,* 25–30.

Singh, G. K., Kogan, M. D., & van Dyck, P. C. (2008). A multilevel analysis of state and regional disparities in childhood and adolescent obesity in the United States. *Journal of Community Health, 33*(2), 90–102.

Sinnock, B. (1995, August). Fundraising trends move towards more choice, fewer dollars. *The Nonprofit Times,* 27–30.

Smalley, R. E. (1967). *Theory for social work practice.* New York: Columbia University Press.

Smith, D. (1979). *In our own interest: A handbook for the citizen lobbyist in state legislatures.* Seattle: Madrona.

Smith, S. C. (1989). *Reflections on grantseeking.* Vancouver, WA: M. J. Murdock Charitable Trust.

Smucker, R. B. (1999). *The nonprofit lobbying guide.* (2nd ed.). Washington, DC: Independent Sector.

Speeter, G. (1978a). *Playing their game our way: Using the political process to meet community needs.* Amherst, MA: University of Massachusetts, Citizen Involvement Training Project.

Speeter, G. (1978b). *Power: A repossession manual.* Amherst, MA: University of Massachusetts, Citizen Involvement Training Project.

SPIN Project. (2002). *Media tools on the net.* Retrieved from www.spinproject.org/resources/internet_pr/tools.php3

SPIN Project. (2006). *Developing relationships with reporters.* Retrieved from http://spinproject.org/downloads/Reporters.pdf

SPIN Project. (2008). *Broadcast media and spokesperson skills.* Retrieved from www.spinproject.org/downloads/BroadcastSpokesperson.pdf

Splain, M. J. (1984). Negotiations: Using a weapon as a way out. In L. Staples (Ed.), *Roots to power: A manual for grassroots organizing.* (pp. 166–170). New York: Praeger.

Spring, K., Dietz, N., & Grimm, R. (2007). *Youth helping America: Leveling the path to participation: Volunteering and civic engagement among youth from disadvantaged circumstances.* Washington, DC: Corporation for National and Community Service.

Stannard-Friel, J. (2004, November 5). Proving the win-win strategy of cause related marketing. *onPhilanthropy.* Retrieved from www.onphilanthropy.com/site/News2?page=NewsArticle&id=5622

Staples, L. (Ed.), (1984). *Roots to power: A manual for grassroots organizing.* New York: Praeger.

Staples, L. (2004). *Roots to power: A manual for grassroots organizing.* (2nd ed.). Westport, CT: Praeger.

Staudt, A., Huddleston, N., & Kraucunas, I. (2008). *Understanding and responding to climate change: Highlights of National Academies reports, 2008 edition.* Washington, DC: National Academy of Sciences.

Stein, M. (2001). Nonprofit success on the Internet: Creating an effective online presence. In T. D. Connors (Ed.), *The nonprofit handbook: Management.* (3rd ed., pp. 223–243). New York: Wiley.

Stein, M. (2003). *What is a charity portal or a charity mall?* Retrieved from www.techsoup.org/community/qod_answer.cfm?qotdid=296

Steinman, E. W. (2005). Legitimizing American Indian sovereignty: Mobilizing constitutive power of law through institutional entrepreneurship. *Law and Society Review, 29*(4), 759–792.

Steptoe, A., & Feldman, P. J. (2001). Neighborhood problems as sources of chronic stress: Development of a measure of neighborhood problems, and associations with socioeconomic status and health. *Annals of Behavioral Medicine, 23*(3), 177–185.

Stevenson, H. (2006). *Appreciative inquiry: Tapping into the river of possibilities.* Novelty, OH: Cleveland Consulting Group. Retrieved from www.clevelandconsulting group.com/articles/appreciative-inquiry.htm

Stewart, G. (2009). *Should local marketers get twitterpated?.* Retrieved from http://searchenginewatch.com/3633609

Stoecker, R. (2005). *Research methods for community change: A project-based approach.* Thousand Oaks, CA: Sage.

Streeter, R., & Jordan, S. (2008). *Report on the state of corporate community investment.* Washington, DC: U.S. Chamber of Commerce.

Suchman, D. R. (1993). Recreating Vermont Avenue. *Urban Land, 52,* 20–24.

Suchman, D. R. (1994). *Revitalizing low-income neighborhoods: Recommendations from ULI advisory series panels.* Washington, DC: Urban Land Institute.

Suchman, D. R., & Lamb, M. I. (1991). West Dallas poised for change. *Urban Land, 50,* 10–16.

Sullivan, D. (2002, October 14). *Search engine placement tips.* Retrieved from www.searchenginewatch.com/webmatsters/tips.html

Sun, A.-P. (2001). Targeting women donors: A response to "Women and human service giving." *Social Work, 46*(1), 79–81.

Szreter, S., & Woolcock, M. (2004). Health by association? Social capital, social theory, and the political economy of public health. *International Journal of Epidemiology, 33*(4), 650–667.

Temkin, K. (2000). Comment on John T. Metzger's "Planned abandonment: The neighborhood life-cycle theory and urban policy." *Housing Policy Debate, 11*(1), 55–60.

Tenbrunsel, A. E., & Messick, D. M. (2001). Power asymmetries and the ethical atmosphere in negotiations. In J. M. Darley, D. M. Messick, & T. R. Tyler (Eds.), *Social influences on ethical behavior in organizations.* (pp. 201–216). Mahwah, NJ: Erlbaum.

Texas Department of Health, National Maternal and Child Health Resource Center on Cultural Competency. (1997). *Journey towards cultural competency: Lessons learned.* Vienna, VA: Maternal and Children's Health Bureau Clearinghouse.

Thomas, J. C. (1986). *Between citizen and city: Neighborhood organizations and urban politics in Cincinnati.* Lawrence, KS: University of Kansas Press.

Totah, P. (2008). *Parents and the high price of health care.* Arlington, VA: National Association of Child Care Resource & Referral Agencies.

Traynor, W. J., & Andors, J. (2005, March–April). Network organizing: A strategy for building community engagement. National Housing Institute. *Shelterforce Online, 140.* Retrieved from www.nhi.org/online/issues/140/LCW.html

Trevino, Y. (2008). *Appreciative inquiry: Interview for Community.* Children's Trust and Prevention Funds. Retrieved from https://www.msu.edu/user/nactpf/images/initiatives/Parentsresourcespdfs/Section4_eValuation.pdf

Trochim, W. M. K., Milstein, B., Wood, B. J., Jackson, S., & Pressler, V. (2003). Setting objectives for community and system change: An application of concept mapping for planning a statewide health improvement initiative. *Health Promotion Practice, 5*(1), 8–19.

Tropman, J. E., Johnson, H. R., & Tropman, E. J. (1979). *The essentials of committee management.* Chicago: Nelson-Hall.

Troyer, T. A. (1991, May 18). *What the non-specialist needs to know about the new lobbying rules for charities.* Paper presented to the American Bar Association Tax Section, Washington, DC.

Troyer, T. A. (2000, May). *Private foundations and influencing legislation.* Washington, DC: Caplin & Drysdale.

Tucker Rambally, R. E. (1999). Field education in a developing country: Promoting organizational change and social development. *International Social Work, 42*(4), 485–496.

Tuckman, B. W., & Jensen, M. A. C. (1977). Stages of small group development revisited. *Group and Organizational Studies, 2*(4), 419–427.

Tupper, S. L. (2007). *Electronic communications and you: How CAN-SPAM and the TCPA affect communications by nonprofit organizations. Legal Lines: Legal issues for nonprofits.* Detroit, MI: Community Legal Resources.

Tyler, K., Johnson, K, & Brownridge, D. (2008). A longitudinal study of the effects of child maltreatment on later outcomes among high-risk adolescents. *Journal of Youth and Adolescence, 37*(5), 506–521.

Ulin, S. B. (1997). Benefit event enhancements. In J. M. Greenfield (Ed.), *The nonprofit handbook: Fund raising.* (2nd ed., pp. 299–316). New York: Wiley.

Ulin, S. B. (2001). Benefit event enhancements. In J. M. Greenfield (Ed.), *The nonprofit handbook: Fund raising.* (3rd ed., pp. 500–517). New York: Wiley.

United States Senate. (2009). *Lobbying Disclosure Act guidance.* Retrieved from www.senate.gov/legislative/resources/pdf/S1guidance.pdf

United Way. (2006). *What United Ways Do.* Alexandria, VA: United Way of America.

United Way Ghana. (2005). *United Way Ghana activity report: Nov. 2003–Sept. 2005.* North Ridge Accra, Ghana: Author.

United Way of Tucson and Southern Arizona. (2006). *United Way brings our community together to achieve what matters most—results for people.* Retrieved from www.unitedwaytucson.org/index.htm

Urban, J. J. (2004, December 9). Charity law and the public interest [letter]. Washington, DC: Internal Revenue Service.

U.S. Bureau of the Census. (1991). *1990 Census Population, General Population Characteristics* (1990 CP-1) and *1990 Census of Housing, General Housing Characteristics* (1990 CH-1), report series published 1992–1993; and Summary Tape File (STF) 1A. Washington, DC: Author.

U.S. Census Bureau. (2001). *The two or more races. Population: 2000* [Census 2000 Brief C2KBR/01-6]. Washington, DC: Author.

U.S. Census Bureau. (2004). *U.S. interim projections by age, sex, race, and Hispanic origin.* Retrieved from www.census.gov/ipc/www/usinterimproj/

U.S. Census Bureau. (2005). *Statistical abstract of the United States: 2006.* (125th ed.). Washington, DC: Author.

U.S. Census Bureau. (2008a). *An older and more diverse nation by midcentury.* Retrieved from www.census.gov/Press-Release/www/releases/archives/popula tion/012496.html

U.S. Census Bureau. (2008b). *Selected economic characteristics: 2005–2007.* Data set: 2005–2007 American community survey 3-year estimates. Washington, DC: Author.

U.S. Census Bureau. (2008c). *Selected housing characteristics: 2007.* Data Set 2007 American Community Survey 1-year estimates: Selected housing characteristics. Retrieved from http://factfinder.census.gov/servlet/ADPTable?_bm=y&-geo_id=01000US&-qr_name=ACS_2007_1YR_G00_DP4&-ds_name=ACS_2007_1YR_G00_&-_lang=en&-_caller= geoselect&-redoLog=false&-format=

U.S. Census Bureau. (2009). *American Housing Survey National Tables: 2007.* American housing survey for the United States, 200: Series H-150. Retrieved from www.census.gov/hhes/www/housing/ahs/ahs07/tab2-8.pdf

U.S. Department of Commerce, Bureau of Economic Analysis. (2009a). *Bureau of Economic Analysis National Economic Accounts: Gross domestic product: First quarter 2009* (Advance). Retrieved from www.bea.gov/newsreleases/national/gdp/gdpnewsrelease.htm

U.S. Department of Commerce, Bureau of Economic Analysis. (2009b). *Personal income and its disposition.* Table 2.1 Retrieved from www.bea.gov/histdata/NIyearAPFFiles.asp?docDir=Releases/GDP_and_PI/2009/Q1/Final_June-25-2009&year=2009&quarter=Q1

U.S. Department of Health and Human Services. (2005). *The health and well-being of children: A portrait of the states and the nation 2005.* [The National Survey of Children's Health 2003]. Rockville, MD: U.S. Department of Health and Human Services, Health Resources and Services Administration, Maternal and Child Health Bureau.

U.S. Department of Housing and Urban Development. (1999). *New markets: The untapped retail buying power in America's inner cities.* Washington, DC: Author.

U.S. Department of Housing and Urban Development. (2001, May). *Our homes, our neighborhoods* [AHB/O1-2]. Washington, DC: Author.

U.S. Department of Housing and Urban Development. (2005). *Promising practices in grantee performance measurement.* Washington, DC: Author, Office of Policy Development Research.

U.S. Department of Housing and Urban Development. (2006). *Economic development webcasts.* Retrieved from www.hud.gov/offices/cpd/economicdevelopment/library/webcasts.cfm

U.S. Department of Housing and Urban Development. (2008). *Home investment partnerships program.* Retrieved from www.hud.gov/offices/cpd/affordablehousing/programs/home/

U.S. Department of Housing and Urban Development. (2009a). *About HOPE VI.* Retrieved from www.hud.gov/offices/pih/programs/ph/hope6/about/index.cfm

U.S. Department of Housing and Urban Development. (2009b). *Welcome to the Community Renewal Institute: HUD's initiative for empowerment zones and renewal communities (EZ/RC).* Retrieved from www.hud.gov/offices/cpd/economicdevelopment/programs/rc/index.cfm

U.S. Department of Labor. (2000). *Changes in women's labor force participation in the 20th century.* Retrieved from www. bls.gov/opub/ted/2000/feb/wk3/art03.htm

U.S. Department of Labor, Women's Bureau. (2009). *Quick stats on women workers, 2008.* Retrieved from www.dol.gov.wb/stats/main.htm

U.S. Department of the Treasury. (2007). *Community development financial institutions fund: About the CDFI fund.* Retrieved from www.cdfifund.gov/who_we_ are/about_us.asp

U.S. Department of the Treasury. (2008). *Community development financial institutions fund: Overview of what we do.* Retrieved from www.cdfifund.gov/what_we_do/overview.asp

U.S. House of Representatives. (2009). *Lobbying Disclosure Act guidance.* Retrieved from www.lobbyingdisclosure.house.gov/amended_lda_guide.html

U.S. Postal Service. (2006). *Postal facts 2006.* Retrieved from www.usps.com/communications/organization/postal-facts.htm

U.S. Postal Service. (2008a). *The household diary study: Mail use and attitudes in FY 2007.* Washington, DC: Author.

U.S. Postal Service. (2008b). *Postal facts.* Retrieved from www.usps.com/communications/newsroom/facts/postalfacts2008.pdf

Valente, M. (2002, March 25). *Argentina's new neighborhood assemblies: The seed of a new form of citizen participation.* Retrieved from www.commondreams.org/headlines02/0325-06.htm

Vance, N. (1985). *Stories of resurgence.* Unpublished manuscript.

Vargas, J. A. (2008). *The clickocracy: Obama raised half a billion online.* Retrieved from http://voices. washingtonpost.com/thetrail/2008/11/20/obama_raised_half_a_billion_on.html

Veneklasen, R. (2009, May). RHNA Talent Bank. *Rincon Heights Neighborhood Association Newsletter,* p. 2.

Vernon, R., & Lynch, D. (2000). *Social work and the Web.* Belmont, CA: Wadsworth, Cengage Learning.

Von Hoffman, N. (n.d.). *Finding and making leaders.* Unpublished manuscript.

Vukic, S. (2008, December 5). *Anti government protests fizzle.* Associated Press. Retrieved from www.sfgate.com/cgi-bin/article.cgi?file=/n/a/2008/12/05/international/i120343S03.DTL

W. K. Kellogg Foundation. (2000). *Emerging philanthropy in communities of color: A report on current trends.* Retrieved from www.wkkf.org/Programming/RenderRes.asp?ID=687&CID=12

W. K. Kellogg Foundation. (2004). *Logic model development guide.* Battle Creek, MI: Author.

W. K. Kellogg Foundation. (2009, May 4). *Cultures of giving profile.* Retrieved from www.wkkf.org/default.aspx?tabid=90&CID=299&ItemID= 5000632 &NID=61&LanguageID=0

Wagner, A. R. (1995, February 25). *Hope for the American neighborhood: Creating a fourth sector—the community sector.* Paper presented for the Nobel Prize Forum at Augsburg College, Minneapolis.

Wallace, N. (2006). Charities making faster connections. *Chronicle of Philanthropy, 18*(17). Retrieved from http://philanthropy.com/free/articles/v18/i17/17001901.htm

Wallace, N. (2008). After the flood. *Chronicle of Philanthropy, 20*(17). Retrieved from http://philanthropy.com/free/articles/v20/i17/17000701.htm

Wallack, L. (2005). Media advocacy: A strategy for empowering people and communities. In J. Minkler (Ed.), *Community organizing and community building for health.* (2nd ed., pp. 419–432). New Brunswick, NJ: Rutgers University Press.

Walker, A. (1987, Spring). The good that they do. The case for corporate in-kind contributions. *Public Relations Quarterly,* 222–223.

Walker, D. (2008, November 6). *Salvation Army tries text message to raise funds: Donors can give $5 by texting specified number.* Associated Press.

Wang, C. C. (2003). Using photovoice as a participatory assessment and issue selection tool: A case study with the homeless in Ann Arbor. In M. Minkler, & N. Wallerstein (Eds.), *Community based participatory research for health.* (pp. 179–196). San Francisco, CA: Jossey-Bass.

Wardip, K. E., Pelletiere, D., & Crowley, S. (2009). *Out of reach 2009.* Washington, DC: National Low Income Housing Coalition.

Warheit, G. J., Bell, R. A., & Schwab, J. J. (1984). Selecting the needs assessment approach. In F. Cox, J. L. Erlich, J. Rothman, & J. E. Tropman (Eds.), *Tactics and techniques of community practice.* (2nd ed., pp. 41–55). Itasca, IL: Peacock.

Wark, L. (2008). The advocacy project. *Human Service Education Journal, 27*(1), 69–81.

Warren, R. B., & Warren, D. I. (1977). *The neighborhood organizer's handbook.* Notre Dame, IN: University of Notre Dame Press.

Warren, R. B., & Warren, D. I. (1984). How to diagnose a neighborhood. In F. Cox, J. L. Erlich, J. Rothman, & J. E. Tropman (Eds.), *Tactics and techniques of community practice.* (2nd ed., pp. 27–40). Itasca, IL: Peacock.

Wartenberg, T. E. (1990). *The forms of power: From domination to transformation.* Philadelphia: Temple University Press.

Warwick, M. (2009). *Fundraising when money is tight: A strategic and practical guide to surviving tough times and thriving in the future.* San Francisco, CA: Jossey-Bass.

Watkins, J. (2006). *E-philanthropy: Lessons learned from TouchDC and the D.C. Strengthening Partners Initiative (SPI).* Retrieved from www.guidestar.org/news/features/touchdc_spi.jsp

Watkins, J. M., & Mohr, B. J. (2001). *Appreciative inquiry: Change at the speed of imagination.* San Francisco, CA: Jossey-Bass-Pfeiffer.

Waugh, C. E., & Fredrickson, B. L. (2006). Nice to know you: Positive emotions, self-other overlap, and complex understanding in the formation of a new relationship. *Journal of Positive Psychology, 1*(2), 93–106.

Webb, C. (1982, May). Communications in fundraising. *Fund Raising Management, 13,* 60.

Webster, H. (2000, December). From hopeless to homerun. The community land trust of Cape Ann in Glouster, Massachusetts. *Planning, 66*(12), 18.

Weinbach, R. W. (1984, May–June). Implementing change: Insights and strategies for the supervisor. *Social Work,* 282–285.

Weinbach, R. W. (1990). *The social worker as manager: Theory and practice.* New York: Longman.

Weinreich, N. K. (2003). *What is social marketing?* Retrieved from www.social-marketing.com/whatis.html

Weltman, E. (2004). Media relations. In L. Staples (Ed.), *Roots to power: A manual for grassroots organizing.* (2nd ed., pp. 264–266). Westport, CT: Praeger.

Welytok, D. S. (2008). *What do you think about the new rules under CAN-SPAM Act?* Wisconsin Technology Network. Retrieved from http://wistechnology.com/articles/4928/

Wenocur, S. (1992). Should community organization be based on a grassroots strategy? Yes. In E. Gambrill, & R. Pruger (Eds.), *Controversial issues in social work.* (pp. 289–293). Boston, MA: Allyn & Bacon.

Wernet, S. P. (1994). A case study of adaptation in a non-profit human service organization. *Journal of Community Practice, 1*(3), 93–111.

Westley, F., Zimmerman, B., & Patton, M. Q. (2007). *Getting to maybe: How the world is changed.* Toronto, Canada: Vintage Canada.

White, D. E. (2001). Why do people donate to charity? In J. M. Greenfield (Ed.), *The nonprofit handbook: Fund raising.* (3rd ed., pp. 347–360). New York: Wiley.

Wiborg, A. (1998). Changing women in rural areas in change: New challenges for rural development. In P. Saukkonen, & H. Uihinen (Eds.), *Rural and regional development.* Helsinki, Finland: University of Helsinki.

Wickramaratne-Rebera, R. (1998, September). *Organizations and structures: A case study.* Retrieved from www.worldywca.org/common_concern/sept1998/organizations and structures.html

Wilensky, H., & Lebeaux, C. (1965). *Industrial society and social welfare.* New York: Free Press.

Williams, M. R. (1985). *Neighborhood organizations: Seeds of a new life.* Westport, CT: Greenwood Press.

Williams, M. R. (1989). *Neighborhood organizing for urban school reform.* New York: Teachers College Press.

Wilson, M. (1980). Effective volunteer programs. In R. Clifton, & A. Dahms (Eds.), *Grassroots administration: A handbook for staff and directors of small community-based social service agencies.* (pp. 111–122). Pacific Grove, CA: Brooks/Cole.

Winters, M.-F. (1999). Reflections on endowment building in the African-American community. In Council on Foundations (Ed.). *Cultures of caring: Philanthropy in diverse American communities.* (pp. 107–146). Washington, DC: Council on Foundations.

Wireman, P. (1984). *Urban neighborhoods, networks, and families: New forms for old values.* Lexington, MA: Lexington Books.

Wismer, K. (2007). *Does theory really matter: The value of understanding appreciative inquiry's underlying theory of social construction.* Retrieved from www.odnetwork.org/events/conferences/conf2007/pdfs/T12B.pdf

Wolff, T. (2001). Community coalition building—contemporary practice and research: Introduction. *American Journal of Community Psychology, 29*(2), 165–173.

Wolpert, J., Mumphrey, A. J., & Seley, J. E. (1972). *Metropolitan neighborhoods: Participation and conflict over change.* [Resource Paper No. 16]. Washington, DC: Association of American Geographers.

Women at Work. (2002). *Women at work background.* Retrieved from www.womenngo.org.yu/sajt/english/sajt/women_groups_directories/women_at_work/index.htm

Women's Funding Network. (2003a). *Donor circles: Launching and leveraging shared giving.* San Francisco, CA: Author.

Women's Funding Network. (2003b). *Making a difference: New wealth women and philanthropy: Partnerships for supporting women and girls.* San Francisco, CA: Author.

Women's Funding Network. (2009). *Women's Funding Network: Powering women-led solutions; Annual report 2008.* San Francisco, CA: Author.

World Bank. (2009). *Understanding poverty.* Retrieved from http://go.worldbank.org/K7LWQUT9L0

World Health Organization. (1948, April 7). *Constitution of the World Health Organization.* New York: Author.

Wrong, D. (2004). *Power: It's forms, bases, and uses.* (3rd ed.). New Brunswick, NJ: Transaction.

York-Barr, J., Sommers, W. A., Ghere, G. S., & Montie, J. (2006). *Reflective practice to improve schools: An action guide for educators.* (2nd ed.). Thousand Oaks, CA: Corwin Press.

Zack, G. M. (1997). *Tax issues of not-for-profit organizations.* Greenbelt, MD: Nonprofit Resource Center.

Zastrow, C. (2001). *Social work with groups.* (5th ed.). Chicago: Nelson-Hall.

Zastrow, C. (2004). *Introduction to social work and social welfare: Empowering people.* (9th ed.). Belmont, CA: Brooks/Cole, Cengage Learning.

Zastrow, C. (2007). *The practice of social work: Applications of generalist and advanced content.* (8th ed.). Belmont, CA: Brooks/Cole, Cengage Learning.

Ziliak, J. P., Gunderson, C., & Haist, M. (2008). *The causes, consequences, and future of senior hunger in America.* Lexington, KY: Center for Poverty Research, University of Kentucky.

Zippay, A. (1992, May). Corporate funding of human service agencies. *Social Work,* 37, 210–214.

Zunz, S. J. (1997). School climate and community norm change. In E. Norman (Ed.), *Drug free youth: A compendium for prevention specialists.* (pp. 47–72). New York: Garland.

Index